Self-Representational Approaches to Co

Self-Representational Approaches to Consciousness

edited by Uriah Kriegel and Kenneth Williford

A Bradford Book
The MIT Press
Cambridge, Massachusetts
London, England

MIT Press books may be purchased at special quantity discounts for business or sales promotional use. For information, please email special_sales@mitpress.mit.edu or write to Special Sales Department, The MIT Press, 55 Hayward Street, Cambridge, MA 02142.

This book was set in Sabon by SNP Best-set Typesetter Ltd., Hong Kong, and was printed and bound in the United States of America.

Library of Congress Cataloging-in-Publication Data

Self-representational approaches to consciousness / edited by Uriah Kriegel and Kenneth Williford.
   p. cm.
"A Bradford book."
Includes bibliographical references and index.
ISBN 0-262-11294-9 (hc : alk. paper)—ISBN 0-262-61211-9 (pbk. : alk. paper)
1. Consciousness. 2. Mental representation. I. Kriegel, Uriah. II. Williford, Kenneth.
B808.9.S45   2006   2005056118

10   9   8   7   6   5   4   3   2   1

Contents

1　Introduction

Uriah Kriegel and Kenneth Williford

The theory of consciousness has assumed center stage in recent philosophy of mind. It features two distinct, and largely independent, debates. The first surrounds the physical reducibility of consciousness. The second concerns positive theories of consciousness.

There is a connection between these two debates inasmuch as most theories of consciousness are reductive. A reductive theory attempts to account for phenomenal consciousness in nonphenomenal terms. For a physicalist, these nonphenomenal terms are bound to be, ultimately, (micro)physical. The two debates are nonetheless logically independent, since one can offer a reductive theory of consciousness in nonphenomenal terms that does not bottom out in physical terms,[1] or one can offer an altogether nonreductive theory.[2]

Within the discourse on reductive theories of consciousness, two major competitors have emerged over the past decade or two: the representational theory of consciousness (RTC) and the higher-order monitoring (HOM) theory. According to the former, a mental state is conscious if and only if it represents in the right way. According to the latter, a mental state is conscious if and only if it is *represented* in the right way. Importantly, for RTC it does not matter how, nor whether, the state is represented; and for HOM it makes no difference how, nor whether, the state represents.[3]

The purpose of this volume is to showcase an alternative reductive theory of consciousness that has been gaining visibility of late but still remains, in the opinion of the editors, underdiscussed. This is what we call the self-representational theory of consciousness. It holds that a mental state is conscious if and only if it represents itself in the right way. On this view, it is true of conscious states both that they are conscious in virtue of representing and that they are conscious in virtue of being represented. Therefore, it also matters both that they represent and that they are represented.

Both RTC and HOM theory have their attractions. Both, however, also face what often appear to be insurmountable challenges. It is quite possible, then, that the self-representational theory, which combines elements of each in a novel fashion, may inherit their attractions without their difficulties. It is not the purpose of this introductory chapter to make the case for this with any seriousness, but let us just sketch how such a case might be made, if only by way of motivating the self-representational theory.

1 The Case for the Self-Representational Theory

The major attraction shared by RTC and HOM is that they pave the way to a reductive account of consciousness in representational terms. Assuming we have decent prospects for understanding representation in nonphenomenal terms, and probably even purely physical terms, this generates a reductive, perhaps even narrowly physicalist, account of consciousness.[4]

Both theories reveal fundamental deficiencies, however. There are, in the first instance, the myriad putative counterexamples such theories are routinely presented with.[5] But beyond those, they are also plagued by principled problems.

Consider RTC. On the assumption that any environmental feature can be represented either consciously or unconsciously, it is unclear how the mere representation of such a feature can render the representing state conscious.[6]

HOM theory overcomes this problem by introducing a higher-order representation of conscious states. What renders a given representational state conscious is precisely the fact that the representation is itself represented. It is when a mental state is thus represented by the subject that there is something it is like *for the subject* to be in that state.

But the introduction of higher-order representations carries its own price. In particular, higher-order representations, like their first-order counterparts, can misrepresent. Moreover, they may misrepresent not only the properties of their targets, but also their very existence. It follows from HOM theory that targetless higher-order representations result in a subjective impression of being in a conscious state without actually being in any conscious state: there is no conscious state the subject is in, but there is something it is like for the subject at that moment.

The self-representational theory avoids these problems. Like HOM theory, it can account rather straightforwardly for the difference between conscious and unconscious representations of the same environmental feature: the former are also self-representing, the latter are not. Thus, when one has a conscious experience as of a red tomato, one is in an internal state that represents both a red tomato and itself.

The case for the self-representational theory can thus be divided into two steps. The first step argues that conscious states are states the subject is somehow aware of being in. The second step argues that the subject's awareness of her conscious states can be accounted for best (perhaps only) by these states' self-representational profile.

The resulting two-stepped argument unfolds as follows: (1) conscious states are states one is aware of being in; (2) states one is aware of being in are represented states; therefore, (3) conscious states are represented states; (4) when a state is represented, it is represented either by itself or by a different state; but, (5) there are good reasons to think a conscious state is not represented by a different state; therefore, (6) there are good reasons to think that a conscious state is represented by itself. The first step, consisting in (1)–(3), excludes RTC and leads to the notion that conscious states involve their subject's awareness of them. The second step, consisting in (4)–(6), excludes HOM theory and leads to the self-representational theory.

The fundamental *motivation* for the theory may be purely phenomenological. Both steps of the case for the theory can be cast as phenomenological moves. First, there is a phenomenological intuition that we are aware of our conscious states, in some subtle and somewhat elusive way. But second, the phenomenology of conscious experience is one of a unity of world-awareness and self-awareness that is suggestive of the self-representational picture, in which a single mental state anchors the subject's awareness both of the external stimulus and of herself and her awareness of that stimulus.

Ultimately, it would be preferable if the explicit case for the self-representational theory did not rest purely on analysis of the phenomenology, if only because it is all but impossible to rebut objections to the effect that one has unduly inflated the phenomenology one has constructed one's theory to account for. In the large yet rarely discussed literature surrounding the self-representational theory, less phenomenologically based arguments have been proffered in furtherance of both the above steps. The chapters that make up this volume discuss the merits and demerits of the self-representational theory of consciousness from this more argumentative angle.

2   Challenges to the Self-Representational Theory

It is only very recently that analytic philosophers of mind have attended to the self-representational theory. The view, or close variations thereupon, can be discerned in Brook and Raymont (2006, ch. 5); Carruthers 1996; 2000 (ch. 9); Caston 2002; Gennaro 1996, 2002; Hossack 2002, 2003; Kobes 1995; Kriegel 2003a,b, 2005; Lehrer 1996a,b, 1997 (ch. 7); Smith 1986,

1989 (ch. 2), 2004; Van Gulick 2001, 2004; and Williford 2005, among others.

Despite this surge in publications favoring the theory, there have been few critical examinations of it. This is a testament to the lack of exposure the theory has had to-date. Some worries with the theory have nonetheless emerged in the writings of its proponents and sympathizers. Three of them stand out.

The first surrounds the very possibility of (mental) self-representation. What does it mean for a mental state to represent itself? Assuming token identity of mental and cerebral states, how is it possible for a neural state of the brain to self-represent? Assuming a causal (or causation-based) account of reference or representation, how can a mental state represent itself if it cannot cause itself (as is presumably the case)?[7]

The second worry hails from the phenomenological tradition. In reaction to Brentano's self-representational theory, some phenomenologists have argued that the theory falls into an infinite regress: the self-representation must be conscious in virtue of being itself (self-)represented, and so on.[8]

The third concerns the question whether the self-representational theory does justice to the true phenomenology of experience. The pressure here comes from both directions. From the deflationist camp, it has been argued that conscious experiences, when examined carefully, do not in fact involve the subject's awareness of them. Rather, they involve the subject's awareness *via* them. Any suggestion to the contrary is based on philosophical confusion. From inflationist quarters, it has been argued that the phenomenology of conscious experiences, when considered attentively, suggests that the subject's awareness of them is too intimate—too intrinsic or nonrelational—to be captured by something like a reflexive relation of self-representation.[9]

These worries have to be addressed by the proponents of the self-representational theory in future research. To some extent they *have* been addressed (in past research), including in some of the chapters below. But they have also inspired a number of retreats to *weakened forms* of the self-representational theory.

One weakened form is the claim that conscious states are characteristically self-representing, but not necessarily, perhaps not even universally, so. Another is the claim that although self-representation is a necessary condition for consciousness, it is not a sufficient condition. A third one is the claim that although conscious states are not quite identical to the states that represent them, they nonetheless entertain constitutive, noncontingent relations to them, so that the two are not quite logically independent either.[10] These reactions to the challenges have also been taken, including in some of the chapters below.

3 Synopsis of the Book

The book is divided into four parts. The first part contains six chapters arguing broadly in favor of the self-representational theory of consciousness. The second part contains five chapters arguing broadly against the theory. The third part contains five chapters broadly exploring connections of the theory to a number of related philosophical issues. The final part features two somewhat longer articles by major scientific figures on connections to their respective disciplines. In what follows, we offer a lightning-fast exposition of the chapters in each part.

The first part opens with a chapter by Robert Van Gulick, who offers a presentation of his higher-order global states theory of consciousness, which is effectively a version of the weakened form of the self-representational theory. The next chapter, by Terry Horgan, John Tienson, and George Graham, begins with the observation that certain forms of global skepticism about our conscious life do not have the same grip on us as do their external-world counterparts, and argues that the only plausible account of this involves the supposition that conscious experiences are self-presenting. Next, Kathleen Wider argues (i) for a self-representational theory, and (ii) that the essentially affective nature of conscious experiences is the source of their self-representational character. Andrew Brook offers a comprehensive interpretation of Kant's theory of consciousness that gives a central place to self-representing representations. In the last two chapters of this part, the editors defend the pure self-representational theory (Williford) and the weakened one (Kriegel).

The second part opens with a chapter by Joseph Levine arguing that neither pure nor weakened forms of the self-representational theory can bridge the explanatory gap, or even capture the nature or source of the gap. In the next chapter, John J. Drummond argues (i) that Brentano's self-representational theory (and any such) leads to an untoward duplication of the object of conscious experience—which appears once in the first-order, world-directed content and again in the self-representational content—and (ii) that Husserl's introduction of the notion of (an irreducible) act-awareness by way of trying to account for the phenomenology is preferable inasmuch as it avoids such duplication. Rocco J. Gennaro's chapter in fact defends a weakened version of the self-representational theory, but focuses mostly on the difficulties with the pure self-representational theory that could cause one to retreat from it. Christopher S. Hill's chapter argues for the superiority of representational theories of perceptual consciousness that do not involve any reference to a self-representing structure. The final chapter of this part, by Dan Zahavi, offers an argumentative exposition of work on the self-representational theory within the phenomenological tradition, culminating in the claim that the theory does not do justice to the phenomenology of experience, which suggests a purely intrinsic conception of consciousness.

The third part of the volume considers connections between the self-representational theory and such philosophical issues as the nature of propositional attitudes, knowledge, attention, and indexical reference. Peter Carruthers argues that conscious experiences occupy the sort of functional role that bestows on them a self-representational status, but beliefs and desires do not have that functional role, and consequently, beliefs and desires are never—and cannot be—conscious. Robert W. Lurz then argues against Carruthers, and develops a "same-order monitoring" approach to conscious beliefs and desires. The next chapter, by Jason Ford and David Woodruff Smith, explores the possibility of naturalizing and demystifying the self-representation involved in consciousness using the psychological literature on attention and its functioning. The penultimate chapter in this part, by Tomis Kapitan, argues (i) that indexical thoughts and experiences involve a form of self-awareness, and (ii) that since, as is plausible, all conscious states are indexically mediated, self-awareness is ubiquitous in conscious life. In the last chapter of this part, Keith Lehrer forays into the undercharted territory of the epistemology of consciousness, which leads him to the conclusion that the source of the problematicity of consciousness is conscious states' "lucid content"; he then argues that a satisfactory account of representational lucidity will implicate the thesis that conscious states involve (almost universally) a particular kind of self-representation.

The fourth part of the volume contains only two chapters, but they are longer than the others, exploring connections of the self-representational theory to the sciences. David Rudrauf and Antonio Damasio propose an empirically verifiable identity thesis linking consciousness *as lived* with consciousness *as described in neurobiological terms*, by arguing that subjectivity and affectivity (feeling) are essentially connected and that the phenomenology of affect can be mapped onto the dynamics of the brain-and-body structures and processes known to be associated with consciousness.[11] The book's last chapter, by Douglas R. Hofstadter, defies easy summary. At the core of consciousness, argues Hofstadter, is something quite like the "strange loop" of mathematical self-reference brought to light by Gödel's incompleteness theorems.[12]

4   Conclusion

We hope, and certainly believe, that this volume will make an important contribution to current debates on consciousness. To many who have been frustrated with the two main reductive theories of consciousness, the self-representational approach offers a new alternative to examine. We hope that the present volume will constitute a main source of discussion for the case for and against the approach, the various ways it might play out, and its possible implications for other issues in philosophy and the cognitive sciences.[13]

Notes

1. Thus, one could offer a theory of consciousness that explains phenomenal consciousness in biological terms but then argue that biological properties are irreducible to purely (micro)physical ones. This appears to be the view of Searle (1992).

2. See Chalmers 1996. In Chalmers's nonreductive theory, phenomenal consciousness is treated as a fundamental feature of the world, one that therefore cannot possibly be accounted for in nonphenomenal terms. Still it lends itself to theorization insofar as one can isolate the lawful regularities that govern the behavior of the phenomenal and its interaction with the physical.

3. Some HOM theorists (e.g., Lycan [1996]) happen to hold that conscious states are not only represented but also represent. Nonetheless even for them these states are not conscious *in virtue of* representing. Other HOM theorists (e.g., Rosenthal [1990]) maintain that some conscious states are altogether nonrepresentational.

4. This is a major attraction, because while we find the phenomenal at least initially mystifying, the nonphenomenal (and surely the physical) is unmysterious. Thus a reductive theory of consciousness holds the promise of *demystifying* consciousness.

5. For putative counterexamples to RTC, see Peacocke 1983, ch. 1, and Block 1990. For putative counterexamples to HOM, see Dretske 1993 and Block 1995.

6. See Kriegel 2002c; Chalmers 2004.

7. This worry is developed by Levine 2001a, ch. 6; Kriegel 2005; Williford 2003b, pp. 142, 208–209.

8. This worry is developed systematically by Zahavi 1998, 1999, as well as by members of the so-called Heidelberg school (see, e.g., Henrich 1966).

9. For the deflationist claim, see Dretske 1993 and Siewert 1998. For the inflationist one, see Levine 2001a, ch. 6, and Zahavi 1999.

10. Lehrer (1996a,b) provides a good example of the first sort of retreat. The third form of retreat can be found in Kriegel 2003b, 2005, and Van Gulick 2001, among others.

11. The chapter unifies the authors' long-standing concerns with affect and self-consciousness as central to all consciousness. Their framework for linking affect and subjectivity bears interesting resemblances to the one developed by Wider's chapter in this volume.

12. Those fond of Douglas Hofstadter's other writings will not be disappointed. Among other things, Hofstadter develops rich descriptions of phenomena associated with various kinds feedback loops and shows how the varieties of self-representation can be illuminated by analogy with them. It must be noted, however, that the essay "What Is It Like to Be a Strange Loop?" has been substantially reduced in size (with the author's permission, of course). This unavoidably entailed the removal of many nuanced and rich discussions of important issues related to consciousness and mind, and we offer our apologies for this. We understand that the full version of the piece is to be published soon as a separate book.

13. We would like to thank Anya Williford for her help with the bibliography, Chad Kainz for his help with the index, Greg Landini for his advice on certain technical questions, and Bill Frucht at Basic Books for arranging for us to reprint images from *Gödel, Escher, Bach*.

I | In Favor of the Self-Representational Approach to Consciousness

2 Mirror Mirror — Is That All?

Robert Van Gulick

Consciousness and self-awareness seem intuitively linked, but how they intertwine is less than clear. Must one be self-aware in order to be conscious? Indeed, is consciousness just a special type of self-awareness? Or perhaps it is the other way around: Is being self-aware a special way of being conscious?

Discerning their connections is complicated by the fact that both the main relata themselves admit of many diverse forms and levels. One might be conscious or self-aware in many different ways, and to varying degrees. Thus the real questions of linkage must be posed more specifically. We need to ask not whether the two are bound in general, but whether and how being conscious in some specific sense and degree relates to some particular sort of self-awareness. Only those more specific questions are likely to have fully determinate answers.

However, I will argue that each form of consciousness seems to involve a corresponding type and degree of self-awareness. Self-awareness may not be the whole of consciousness, but it is one of its most important aspects. Though no single perspective by itself can give us a complete understanding of consciousness, viewing it through the lens of self-awareness can help us see a lot about its nature and place in the natural world that we might otherwise miss.

In that spirit, I will offer and defend a particular model of consciousness as self-awareness, the "HOGS" or higher-order global state model. I will aim to motivate the HOGS view both in its own right as a model of consciousness and by situating it within a more general and independently plausible teleopragmatic view of mind.

I Higher-Order Theories of Consciousness

The link between consciousness and self-awareness has found prominent recent support among advocates of the so-called higher-order (HO) theory of consciousness. The theory comes in many versions, but they all agree in treating the distinction between conscious and nonconscious mental states as a relational matter of whether or not the given state is itself the object of some higher-order (or meta-intentional) state directed at it. Conscious mental states are states we are aware of being in.

According to standard HO theory, what makes a mental state M conscious is not some difference in M's intrinsic properties but the relational fact that M is accompanied by a higher-order state whose intentional content is that one is in M. For example, to have a conscious desire for a glass of champagne is to have both a desire for champagne and a higher-order awareness of having such a desire. "Higher-order" here means simply a meta-mental state, that is, an intentional state whose content itself concerns or is about a mental state: a thought about a thought, a belief about a desire, or an awareness of a mood or sensation. Unconscious desires, thoughts, or memories are simply those we are not aware of having.

Higher-order theories come in several forms, differing especially with regard to the psychological modality of the relevant conscious-making higher-order states. Higher-order thought (HOT) models treat those meta-states as thoughtlike, and higher-order perception (HOP) models regard them as at least quasi-perceptual and resulting from some form of inner monitoring or inner sense. The differences are potentially important, but for present purposes I will largely ignore them. My current concern is with the basic HO view, and with problems that affect it in both its main versions.[1]

HO models in general, whether HOT or HOP, have at least three major strengths.

Common usage HO models accord well with at least one common use of "conscious." In everyday folk-psychological practice and in the neo-Freudian view that pervades contemporary culture, the conscious–unconscious distinction divides our mental states between those of which we are aware and those of which we are not. The fact that a desire, memory, or perception is unconscious in this sense is nothing more than our being unaware of it, which HO models analyze as our lacking the relevant HOT or HOP about it. Insofar as it is this notion of conscious mental state that the models aim to capture, they seem on target.

Scientific practice HO models also conform well with empirical scientific practice in determining when a subject does or does not have a particular conscious state, especially insofar as those practices rely on a first-person report criterion. For example, the method of judging subjects to have had a conscious perception of a word just if they can report having had such a perception fits quite naturally with the HO view that what makes a perception conscious is our having a meta-awareness of it. When we are aware of it, we can report being in it, and when we are not we cannot. David Rosenthal has been explicit in claiming that the content expressed by such a first-person report is exactly the content of the HOT that would make the relevant state conscious (Rosenthal 1990, 1993b, 2002). Thus the HO theorist might plausibly claim that his analysis is not merely consistent with scientific practice but explains why those methods work.

Naturalism   HO models, if successful, would effectively reduce the problem of consciousness to that of intentionality. Since many theorists of mind regard the latter problem as more tractable, indeed as having already been at least partially resolved in a naturalistically acceptable way, it would be a significant advance if the problem of consciousness could be subsumed within it (see, e.g., works by Dretske, Millikan, Van Gulick). This, of course, assumes that the meta-intentionality of the sort HO theory requires could be explained in much the same way as other sorts of intentionality—for example, in terms of covariance relations, tracking conditions, teleological relations, or whatever else that does not seem implausible. Thus HO models promise to dispel the air of apparent mystery about how consciousness might be explained as part of the natural world.

Despite its strengths, the higher-order approach has faced a great many objections, of which six deserve particular mention.

1   "Too Fancy" Objection

The meta-intentional conditions are criticized as being too sophisticated and demanding to be met by many beings we regard as conscious: dogs, bats, and small children. A newborn baby seems to have conscious perceptions, but is it plausible to regard it as having metathoughts with contents such as [I am now having a perception]? In response:

i. Some HO theorists deny that the relevant meta-intentionality need be so sophisticated or conceptually demanding (Rosenthal 1993b).

ii. Others "bite the bullet" and deny that small children and animals have conscious mental states (Carruthers 2000).

2   Extra Conditions Problem

Higher-order theories need to include further conditions to rule out obvious counterexamples to the sufficiency of the higher-order analysis (e.g., that the meta-intentional state be simultaneous with its lower-order object and that it be arrived at noninferentially). But those conditions call into question the theory's basic idea of explaining consciousness solely in terms of meta-intentional content. The extra conditions may be required to sort the cases correctly, but it is not clear *why* they should matter, which suggests there may be some other factor (e.g., mode of representation) that makes the real difference and with which those conditions merely coincide.

3   Generality Problem

In general, having a thought or perception of some object of type T does not make it into a conscious T. My having a thought or perception of a stone or a pencil does not produce conscious stones or pencils. So why should having a thought or perception of a mental state transform it into a conscious state? (See Dretske 1995a; Byrne 1997.)

4   Phenomenal Adequacy Issue

Even if standard higher-order theory captures one sense of "conscious state" it does not so obviously capture another, namely, the phenomenal sense. Being a conscious state in this latter phenomenal sense involves the intuitive idea that there is "something that it's like to be in that state" (Nagel 1974).

5   "Stranded Qualia" Problem

The transition from states that are not conscious in the "what-it's-like" sense to states that are may seem to require the addition of qualia. But that seems to conflict with the basic higher-order claim that a state's becoming conscious involves not changes in its intrinsic properties, but only the addition of an extrinsic factor, namely a meta-state directed at it. How can the addition of a merely relational element make a state into one that there is something that it's like to be in?

Some higher-order theorists have a surprising answer. They distinguish having sensory qualities from having what-it's-likeness. They restrict the latter to states that are conscious in the higher-order sense, but they allow sensory qualities to occur as properties of unconscious states that there is nothing it's like to be in. What-it's-likeness on this view involves not merely sensory qualities but an awareness of sensory qualities. Some such theorists (Lycan 1996) apply the word "qualia" to unconscious sensory qualities and others apply it only to conscious sensory qualities, but the basic explanatory move is the same: to account for what-it's-likeness as a matter of having a higher-order awareness of sensory qualities that can and do occur as properties of unconscious states.

On this view, one can have qualitative but unconscious mental states such as unconscious color perceptions or pains, but there is nothing it is like to be in such a state. Only when one becomes aware of the state by having the requisite HOT or HOP is there something it is like to be in it. The transition from states that are unconscious in the "what-it's-like" sense to those that are conscious does not involve adding qualia or sensory qualities to the state, but rather becoming aware via a meta-state of the qualia that the lower-order state already had.

The view requires unconscious qualia, which many find incoherent or contradictory, as they do the idea of unfelt pains. Moreover, it seems to strand the notion of phenomenal or experiential feel in a "no-man's-land" unable to quite take hold at either the lower or the metalevel. According to the proposal:

• Qualia can be fully present in unconscious states that there is nothing it is like to be in.

• Conversely, and almost paradoxically, the meta-states whose addition supposedly accounts for first-person experiential feel are themselves devoid of any qualia.

Thus the proposal requires a commitment both to qualia of a sort that do not by themselves produce any "what-it's-likeness" and to states that produce what-it's-likeness but themselves lack any qualia. It is in that sense that the qualia seem "stranded." Some HO theories (Lycan 1996) deny there is anything wrong, as opposed to merely unfamiliar, about such qualia, but the sense of a problem is not easily dismissed.

6   The Error/Illusion Problem

The possibilities of metalevel error or illusion create further problems:

• Error: What if the first-level mental state has quale Qi (e.g., red) but the HO state represents it as having a different quale Qk (e.g., blue)?

• Illusion: What if the relevant HO state occurs when there is no associated Q-state at all?

In such cases, what sort of what-it's-likeness would the person experience? In the error case, would it seem red or blue? And how could it seem red (in the relevant *phenomenal* sense of "seem") in the illusion case when there is no relevant lower-order state with qualia for the person to be aware of? None of the available answers seems satisfactory:

• If one opts for the what-it's-likeness that is associated with the lower-order state, that would imply that the higher-order awareness is not really responsible for what-it's-likeness. Contrary to the HO proposal, it seems to be the quale itself, not the awareness of the quale that matters.

· If one opts for the what-it's-likeness that is associated with the higher-order state, that would imply that what-it's-likeness does not derive from awareness of a quale as the proposal claims, since in the error and illusion cases there is no state with a quale (or none of the relevant type) of which to be aware.

· If the HO theorist tries to avoid the problem by claiming that error and illusion are impossible in such cases, he or she must provide some non–ad hoc support for the claim, and none is obvious as long as one follows standard HO models in treating the meta-state and the lower-order state as distinct.

Thus, despite their obvious strengths, existing higher-order models of consciousness face substantial objections. Their supporters may in the end be able to offer adequate replies, but it may be useful to explore alternative versions of the higher-order approach that aim to preserve its essential insights while avoiding the problems that affect the current models. I have elsewhere (Van Gulick 2001, 2004) tried to provide such an alternative in terms of higher-order global states or HOGS. My goal for the remainder of this chapter is to further develop that alternative model, with special emphasis on two linked features that are of special relevance to this volume:

A. The extent to which the HOGS model *weakens the distinctness assumption* found in the standard HO models.

Most existing HOT and HOP versions of higher-order theory treat the conscious-making meta-intentional states they posit as distinct and separate from their lower-order mental objects. Let us call this the *distinctness assumption*. On such models, a conscious visual experience of a clock face involves the occurrence of a visual perception VP of the clock face, which is made conscious by the simultaneous occurrence of a separate intentional state HO whose higher-order content concerns the occurrence of VP. However, as the HOGS model shows, there may be good reasons for not regarding the two states as fully separate and distinct, but rather as two interrelated intentional aspects of one and the same state.

B. The respect in which the HOGS model implies that the relevant meta-intentionality is implicit rather than explicit and thus *rejects the explicitness assumption*.

Standard HOT and HOP models treat the required meta-intentionality as the *explicitly represented* content of a distinct higher-order state, either thoughtlike or quasi-perceptual. Let us call this the "explicitness assumption." Along with weakening the distinctness assumption, the HOGS view differs from the standard models in analyzing the relevant meta-intentionality primarily in terms of information or understanding that is *implicitly embedded* in the structure, organization, and dynamics of the relevant global states. The HOGS view thus also rejects the explicitness assumption.

To bring these two features of the HOGS model into clear focus, we need to back up a bit and see the model within a larger context, specifically that provided by the teleopragmatic view of mind (Van Gulick 1980). Understanding consciousness requires us to situate it within a general account of mind and its place in nature. Thus in section II, I will sketch the basic teleopragmatic picture with special attention to those of its features most relevant to the HOGS model. Having filled in that background, I will address its application to reflexive intentionality in section III, and then return to the HOGS model itself in section IV.

II The Teleopragmatic View of Mind

The *teleopragmatic* perspective regards mind, at least in the first instance, as a biological aspect of reality. Though we may one day be able to create minded nonbiotic systems, mind as we know it is *biological in origin and nature*. Attending seriously to its biological dimension brings into relief important aspects of mind that might otherwise be missed. Indeed it highlights features that are directly relevant to understanding the HOGS model and the reflexive meta-intentional nature of consciousness.

The teleopragmatic view might be classed as a version of *functionalism*, but that latter term has been associated with so much extra and often dubious philosophical baggage (computationalist, reductionist, or analytic) that it may be best to avoid it altogether. Insofar as we do treat it as a version of functionalism, the view is unsurprisingly closest to so-called teleofunctionalism (Van Gulick 1980; Lycan 1981; Millikan 1984). A *teleological* aspect looms large in both, insofar as mental states are described in terms of the *roles they are meant or selected to play in contributing to the successful operation of a complex goal-directed system or organism*.

The "pragmatic" in the name reflects the fact that minds and the forms of understanding associated with minds are fundamentally anchored in *practice and practical use*, and "teleo" signifies that it is in the pursuit of *goals and ends* (Greek "telos") that minds find their central application.[2] Minds, as well as their premental predecessors, evolved as means by which organisms might better adapt their action to the structure of their worlds. Organisms gather, store, integrate, transform, and act on information, but always in the end the aim of any information process is to enhance the organism's chances for success in meeting whatever goals it has for growth, food, sex, survival, reproduction, and all the other sometimes far less basic needs and ends that organisms so purposefully pursue.[3]

The two interrelated notions of *information* and *understanding* are central to the teleopragmatic view, and both get anchored in a biological framework. An organism is informed about some feature of its world insofar as its own structure and organization are specifically shaped or adapted with respect to that feature in ways that enhance the realization of its goals. The bat is informed about the location and direction of the moth of which it aims to make a meal insofar as the echo signal that it processes guides its flight and attack in just the way that enables it to catch its moving target. But the bat's wing as well carries implicit information about the bat's world insofar as its structure has been specifically and adaptively shaped to reflect the dynamic properties of the air through which it flies. Indeed, from the teleopragmatic perspective, life itself is largely an informational process, one through which lifeforms—phylogenetically and ontogenetically—come to adaptively reflect their worlds in ways that meet their needs or ends.

Understanding is similarly grounded in successful pragmatic engagement. The bee understands the correlation between the flower's fragrance and its supply of nectar insofar as its system of behavioral control guides it along the gradient of scent that maximizes its foraging success.

The idea of understanding is particularly apt in several respects for expressing the teleopragmatic view of intentionality and cognition.

• In contrast with standard notions of knowledge, the concept of understanding emphasizes the *element of practical engagement* from the outset. The domain of knowledge is all too easily imperialized by its more intellectual form of knowing-that, demoting know-how to second-class status as a lesser and marginal mode of cognition. By contrast, the notion of understanding is linked at its core with the idea of enabling successful engagement. Thus one is far less likely to lose sight of the practical dimension of cognition when one talks of understanding than when one talks in terms of knowledge.

• There is also a tendency to think of knowledge as an all-or-nothing matter, whereas understanding is naturally regarded as *admitting of many forms and degrees*. As we will see below, such variations of degree are an important and biologically salient aspect of the teleopragmatic view. From an evolutionary perspective, they are just what one would expect.

• Some understanding is *essentially mutual and reciprocal*. In such cases, the practical engagement afforded by the relevant understanding depends on the reciprocal causal interface between the understander and the aspect of the world that is being understood. A clear example is that of the mating dance of jumping spiders. Such spiders go through a complex multistage exchange of signal, response, countersignal and counterresponse with each action provoking just the response that in turn stimulates the appropriate next signal from the originator. This entire ritual *pas de deux* is choreographed on the basis of innately programmed mechanisms that are ready to run in spiders that have never before seen an opposite member of their species. What is crucial for present purposes is the respect in which the spider's biologically based understanding is embedded in those aspects of its sensorimotor interface that support its reciprocal causal engagement with its mate in what might be called a "dynamic lock-and-key" system.

• Some understanding is *constitutive*, or *self-constitutive*; the act or process of understanding in such cases at least partially underlies or helps create that which is understood. This aspect of understanding is connected with the reciprocal causal feature just discussed, but it goes beyond it insofar as it involves an ontological interdependence between understander and understood in such cases. Consider another example of social engagement, in this case human rather than arachnid. Long-married couples come to understand each other in rich and subtle ways, but more importantly each member of such a couple will often have developed into a person who plays a distinct and specific set of roles in the context of the marriage. Not only do such couples understand each other in the standard cognitive sense, but they understand each other in the more ontological sense that their respective natures and personalities are supported and maintained by their ongoing mutual engagement. In that latter respect, they "understand" each other in a way that reflects the literal etymology of the word; they "stand under" and support each others' distinctive personal nature. Some may think talk of "understanding" in this sense is just a verbal joke or a play on words, but I believe it is more than that, and as we will see below it may have relevance for explaining conscious minds as self-understanding systems.

For present purposes I need not give a comprehensive account of the teleopragmatic theory. I want to focus instead on one important aspect of the view, namely, the many variations in the type and sophistication of content that it permits, or indeed predicts. Organisms can be informed about or understand some feature of their world to many varying degrees. All such cases involve nonrandom correlation or tracking between the organism and the features about which it is informed, as well as ways in which that match enhances the organism's success in achieving its goals in ways that are specifically responsive to those features. But within that general framework there is room for a wide diversity of cases.

Two parameters are of particular importance: the range of possible applications that the relevant information or understanding affords, and the degree to which that specific information is capable of being integrated with other information in appropriate content-sensitive ways. At one extreme would be cases in which some adaptive but narrow, fixed, and inflexible response is triggered and guided by the relevant information. The organism is able to apply the information, but only in the limited way provided by that single mechanism, and it is not able to bring it into play with other things it understands or about which it is informed. The relevant information or understanding involved in such a case will be crude in content insofar as it is locked into the specific isolated behavior-controlling process. At the other pole are cases in which the organism has a capacity to bring the information to bear in a more or less open-ended range of adaptive applications, including many that depend on combining it with other information in ways sensitive and appropriate to their respective contents. The wider the range of the possible applications and the richer the field of other contents within whose context the particular item's significance is actively linked, the more the organism can be said to understand the meaning of the relevant information.

Contrast, for example, the state you or I are in when we believe that a fly is buzzing round the table with the state that a frog is in when a similar fly is stimulating its retina in ways that link with the tongue-control system in its amphibian brain. The frog's visual system processes information about the location, direction, and speed of the fly as well as detecting its likelihood of being "foodlike," with the result that it triggers and guides the frog's tongue to intercept the fly in midflight and ingest it. The information the frog acquires and what it understands about the situation are undoubtedly adaptive and put to practical use in successful pursuit of its goals. Its behavior is informationally sensitive in appropriate ways. Yet the content of its intentional state is crude. It has only a limited understanding of what it sees and the content of the information it acquires is correspondingly crude in terms of both of the key parameters. The range of possible applications that the frog can make of that information is very narrow, and the frog has little or no ability to integrate it with other contents in inferentially appropriate ways or to situate it within a larger context of meaning. However, when you or I believe *that a fly is buzzing around the table*, there are all sorts of ways we can adapt our behavior in response to that information and a nearly open-ended range of other beliefs and intentional contents with which we can connect it to better appreciate its significance.

It is important to note that the transition from states with crude content to those with more sophisticated intentionality is not a move from cases in which having information is linked with application to others that involve a purely intellectual way of being informed that is unconnected to application. Rather, the progression is from cases in which an organism has information that can be only narrowly applied in fixed ways, to cases in which the organism can apply the information in a far wider and diverse range of ways including many that require connecting it in content-sensitive ways to other information and other intentional contents. To put it in a slogan framed in terms of the hoary know-that/know-how dichotomy: knowing-that is still a form of knowing-how, just a much richer kind of know-how.

As noted above, what is true of knowledge and information is also true of understanding. With understanding, the practical dimension seems central from the start; what and how we understand some object, process, person, or other aspect of the world is inextricably bound up with the nature of our engagement with it. Moreover, understanding clearly comes in many forms, which each in its own way affords some partial mode of access for successful interaction.

Though much more would need to be said to spell out the complete teleo-pragmatic story, I hope what I have offered suffices to explain how such an account naturally generates a continuum of content and varying degrees of intentional sophistication based in part on variations along our two key parameters: range of application and richness of content-sensitive links to other contents.

III Implicit Self-Understanding and the Reflexive Loop

We are now in a position to ask how all this applies to the higher-order view of consciousness. The standard HOT and HOP models think of meta-intentional content as a highly sophisticated form of intentionality that arises only at the level of propositional states, specifically propositional meta-states. Whether thoughtlike or perception-like in mode, they are taken to have sophisticated that-clause type contents. The alternative I am proposing allows that much of the meta-intentionality that underlies and supports consciousness is much less sophisticated in content and often embedded in procedures that play important intramental roles in producing the sorts of self-modulation, self-regulation, and self-transformation that are essential to the structure and dynamics of consciousness. Insofar as those procedures are specifically adapted to the intentional nature and content of the states and processes to which they apply, they can be taken to constitute the possession of information about or understanding of those mental items and their contents. But the content of the relevant meta-understanding may fall far short of the propositional level in its limited range of application and the poverty of the field of other contents to which it is sensitive.

Consider a parallel case involving learning rather than consciousness (Van Gulick 1988). An organism's ability to learn gives it the ability to adapt its responses not only to general regularities of its environment of the sort that might be gained through natural selection, but also to idiosyncratic patterns and regularities of its local situation. This obviously has lots of biological advantage. But the capacity to learn itself presupposes the existence of underlying processes and mechanisms that make learning possible, and they in turn must have been adaptively shaped to fit the causal structure and contingencies of the organism's world if they are to do their job successfully (Lorenz 1977). Most importantly for present purposes, those learning mechanisms will be effective only insofar as they have been adapted to fit the mental and intentional properties of the processes they modify. To be successful, a learning process must at least to some degree be informed about or implicitly understand the psychological significance and intentional contents of the processes it modifies.

Consider the famous example of Garcia's rats that learned not to eat foods whose ingestion had been after several hours followed by the injection of a nausea-inducing drug (Garcia and Koelling 1967). They did not acquire similar learned aversions to foods that were followed after a similar interval by equally aversive electric shocks. The relevant learning mechanism is tuned or adapted to the fact that unwholesome foods cause nausea but may not do so until several hours have passed. The learning mechanisms that underlie learned food aversions in rats are thus adapted to the causal fact of that delay. They are also adapted to the psychological significance of the feeding control systems that they modify. The learning mechanism does not make a random change in response to the induced nausea; rather it changes the feeding mechanism in just the way that alters the organism's future response to the very food that was eaten a few hours before the onset of illness. The learning mechanism is thus "tuned" in at least two respects: to the causal structure of the external world and to the mental or intentional structure of the organism's own internal organization. Its job indeed is to better harmonize the two in the context of the individual organism's local situation.

Insofar as at least some capacity to learn goes way down the phylogenetic scale, so too does the existence of at least implicit meta-intentional understanding. Indeed, the possibility of minds of more sophisticated kinds depends on the evolution and existence of such less sophisticated forms of meta-intentional understanding to provide the system of underlying processes that make more complex types of mind possible. You cannot have beliefs without a substantial capacity to learn; indeed beliefs are partly constituted by their links to learning. But the ability to learn, as we have just seen, presupposes and depends on the existence of subpropositional procedurally embedded forms of meta-intentional understanding. So beliefs must depend on the existence of such understanding as well.

From a teleopragmatic perspective, reflexive meta-intentionality is a pervasive and major feature of the mental domain. Once one recognizes the diversity of degrees and forms in which it can occur implicitly as well as explicitly, one finds it playing a key role in all sorts of contexts and organisms that one might not ordinarily associate with meta-intentionality. Rather than coming in only at the latest and most sophisticated levels of evolution and mentation, one finds some degree of reflexive meta-intentionality playing an important role at both the lower levels of the phylogenetic scale and the lower organizational levels of complex mental systems.

Indeed, the self-reflexive loop appears to be one of the basic processes driving the evolution of mind. Organisms come to better understand their worlds by coming to better understand themselves and the ways in which their own structures engage their worlds. The organism–world interface evolves in a reflexive feedback cycle that continuously tunes their engagement, enabling the organism to more fully and completely understand the reality of its world and itself. Thus looking at consciousness from the perspective of that larger reflexive process should help us better understand both its nature and its place in the natural realm.

IV The HOGS Model

Having gotten a basic grasp on the reflexive loop, we are now ready to consider the alternative version of the HO theory promised at the outset. The aim is to show that full-blown phenomenal consciousness depends on a high degree of implicit self-understanding and meta-intentionality that is built into the processes that underlie it and generate its organization and its exquisitely content-sensitive dynamics. The central claim is that we are able to be conscious in the phenomenal sense at the personal level (or whole organism level) only because we embody such a rich store of implicit and procedural self-understanding at the subpersonal level.

The basic idea of what I have elsewhere labeled the HOGS or higher-order global state model of consciousness is that transforming a nonconscious state into a conscious one is a process of *recruiting* it into a *globally integrated complex* whose organization and intentional content embodies a heightened degree of *reflexive self-awareness*. The meta-intentional content, on the HOGS model, is realized not by a distinct and separate external meta-state but rather by the organization of the complex global state itself, and the object state is a component of the global state into which it has been recruited.

The motivation for the HOGS model derives from many sources, but two ideas are especially important.

The first is Daniel Dennett's metaphor of consciousness as a form of "cerebral celebrity." The idea is that conscious mental states (and conscious intentional contents) are more widely and powerfully influential within the minds in which they occur. They are more broadly and richly connected, and their contents are more widely accessible by other subsystems throughout their containing mind–brain. Similar ideas are found in so-called global workspace models of consciousness such as that of Bernard Baars (1988, 1997). Conscious states are thus typically able to have more effect on the overall system's evolving mental state and on the organism's behavior.

Scientific evidence about the neural correlates of consciousness provides a second motive for the HOGS model. Based on imaging studies, most current empirical models do not treat consciousness as localized in any specific module or subsystem of the brain. Though the evidence is still far from certain, there does not appear to be any privileged region in which conscious events occur. Rather, the neural substrates seem to be distributed globally across the brain, and to involve large-scale patterns of integrated and recip- rocal activation among disparate regions, whether they are entrained through synchronous oscillation or coherently bound through some other, and perhaps less direct, physical means.

The HOGS model departs from more standard HO models in just the ways proposed in section II. It weakens the distinctness assumption and explicates the meta-intentional aspect of consciousness in a more implicit way. The latter link is obvious and immediate. Insofar as the relevant meta- intentionality is located in subpersonal procedures that underlie phenomenal consciousness, it is realized implicitly by the way in which those procedures embody the relevant understanding in their organization, much as do the procedures that underlie our capacity to learn.

Divergence from the distinctness assumption similarly results from the systemic requirements for supporting consciousness and its dynamics. As noted above, standard HOT and HOP models treat the transformation of a nonconscious mental state into a conscious one as a matter of adding a distinct and separate meta-state directed at it. The object state gains no new intrinsic properties. The transformation to conscious status involves only *extrinsic relational* changes; indeed it involves only added *intentional relations* directed at it by the conscious-making meta-state.

By contrast, the HOGS model of the basic transformation does not isolate the meta-intentional element in a distinct and separate state, but rather locates it in the organization of the global state into which the formerly nonconscious state is recruited and of which it itself becomes a component. Thus the distinctness principle is weakened, but not totally abandoned. Although the object state is retained as a component of the global state, it is typically altered somewhat in the process. In that respect the transition to conscious status involves some changes in the state's intrinsic properties, as well as its gaining a new systemic significance in virtue of the larger active context into which it is recruited. It's the same state, yet importantly different. Indeed, as we will see below the question of whether it is the same state or a different state gets somewhat blurry, and the answer largely turns on how we individuate states.

To get a better grasp of the HOGS model, consider a specific case such as the transition from nonconscious visual perception to conscious visual experience. The nonconscious state may register various features of the visual scene and make that information available for guiding at least some forms of adaptive behavior. It might for example register the presence of a bluish sphere just off to the left of my line of sight, and generate behavior that is situationally apt toward an object with those features. If that visual perception then gets recruited into the global state that is the transient substrate of my conscious experience, its contents [bluish, spherical, and off to the left] will all be preserved, but they will acquire a different sort of significance as features of an object in my phenomenal, experienced, lived-in world.

This is not accomplished by re-representing the relevant information again in another module of the mind or brain, and certainly not in the infamous "Cartesian theater." Rather, it involves incorporating the original representation into a new dynamic context that integrates it with a larger, richer network of other active states that bind it together in content-linking ways that reflect the unity and continuity of both the phenomenal world of objects and of the self to whom they are present in experience, about which more will be said below in section V, which also makes clear in just what respects this model is a higher-order model and not merely a global state theory.

This larger network of connections underlies both the richer and wider web of influences that constitute its enhanced cerebral celebrity and also its role as an intentional constituent of an integrated and unified phenomenal reality.[4] The relevant network of connections is itself in turn realized or underlain by the global patterns of coherent reciprocal activation among the widely distributed regions that are constantly forming and reforming as the transient substrates of conscious experience. Or at least, that is what the HOGS model proposes.

V What's Higher Order about HOGS?

At this point, some readers may find the basic idea of the HOGS model attractive and even agree that a mental state's becoming conscious is largely a matter of its being recruited into a globally active and integrated state, yet doubt that the HOGS model is really a version of a higher-order theory. What, they might ask, is distinctly or essentially higher-order about it? Indeed why not just treat it as a global state (GS) model and drop the higher-order aspect altogether? Is the latter really needed, and does it do any real explanatory work? To speak in terms of acronyms, "Where is the HO in the HOGS? Why not just opt for a GS model of consciousness instead?"

The answer lies with the *particular nature* of the relevant global states and *how* they underlie conscious mentality. As noted above, the HOGS model treats the nonconscious–conscious transformation as a process of recruitment into a globally integrated complex *whose organization and intentional content embodies a heightened degree of reflexive self-awareness.* The requisite globally integrated states are able to serve as the substrate of consciousness only because their specific form of integration realizes and embodies the sort of reflexive intentionality and self-understanding that it does—or so the HOGS model claims in general. However, to make that claim plausible we must give some more specific and detailed account of just *how* that global organization embodies reflexive intentionality and *how* in doing so it contributes to the realization of distinctively conscious forms of mentality. Thus I will aim to do just that for the balance of this section.

The goal is to spell out some of the major explanatory links between the three main dimensions of the HOGS model: global integration, reflexive intentionality, and consciousness. In what ways must global integration involve reflexive intentionality in order to contribute to the realization of conscious mental states?

The nature of the link depends in large part on *which sort* of consciousness one is concerned to explain. If one's concern is with the commonsense notion of a conscious mental state as simply a "state one is aware of being in" then the need for reflexive mentality is immediate. The substrate for being conscious in that sense, whether globally integrated or otherwise, would of necessity have to produce reflexive intentional content directed at the state that is being made conscious. If it did not, the basic conditions for being aware of the object state would not be met, and the state could not be a conscious one in the relevant sense.

However, if one's concern is with states that are conscious in a phenomenal or "what-it's-like" sense, the need for reflexive intentionality is less evident. It is not obvious why an explanation of how global integration contributes to phenomenal consciousness should need to pass through or rely on an account of how that integration contributes to reflexive intentionality. Though they are less obvious, those latter links between phenomenal consciousness and reflexive mentality are crucial to understanding the higher-order aspect of the HOGS model.[5]

Looking at four interrelated aspects of phenomenal consciousness may help reveal the connections. Each is a salient and essential feature of our phenomenal and experiential mental life, and each can be seen on examination to involve an important reflexive meta-intentional aspect, which might in turn be realized in part through global integration. The four key phenomenal features are:

· the presentational aspect in which objects seem immediately present to us in experience;
· the unity of experience;
· the autopoietic flow and dynamics of experience; and
· the affective and pragmatic aspect of experiential content.

There are many other important features of phenomenal consciousness, but these four are all quite central, and if we can see how they involve or require reflexive meta-intentionality that should go a long way toward making the case on behalf of the higher-order aspect of the HOGS model. I will consider each of the four in turn, though as will soon become apparent they are strongly interconnected.

Experiential presence Objects, scenes, and events are not merely *represented* in experience, they are phenomenally *present* to us. They *appear* to us, and we experience them as real and present to us here and now. We experience trees and chairs themselves as well as the flow of water from the tap as the objects and events they are, that is, we experience them as real parts of the world directly there before us. Whatever one may make of direct realism as an epistemological or philosophical theory of perception, it is hard to deny that the phenomenal feel of normal experience is directly realist, and a large part of that realism consists in the way in which the objects of experience are *experienced as present* to us here and now.

However, the notions of presence and appearance require a second pole. They are coherent only insofar as objects are *present to* some conscious subject, or insofar as they *appear to* some self that experiences them in relation to itself. The notion of appearance thus implicitly supposes the existence of an experiential subject to which objects appear and to which they are present (Alston 1999; Kriegel 2003c).

It is partly in this sense that the intentional content of experience is reflexive. Insofar as that content involves objects being present or appearing to us, it essentially incorporates a reflexive aspect. The claim is not that reference to the experiencing self is an explicit element of the content of experience, and certainly not that it requires the sort of content that would be involved if one were to think to oneself, "I am having a visual experience of a cat sleeping on a carpet." It is rather a claim about the intentional framework of experience. Insofar as that framework enables us to experience objects as present and appearing to us, its very structure must implicitly incorporate at least some understanding of the self or subject to whom objects can be present and appear. The required intentional structure could not support the experience of presence without at least implicitly incorporating some grasp of there being a self or subject to whom objects appear. Thus some degree of reflexive intentionality seems inescapably required by the experiential presence of phenomenal consciousness.

Having made that claim, let me make it clear that the relevant reflexive element need not involve explicit, sophisticated, highly conceptualized understanding. The teleopragmatic view allows for many types and degrees of understanding, and the minimum grasp of the reflexive intentionality required for the experience of presence needs to be set low enough to allow for the experiential lives of young children and nonhuman animals. Obviously, two-year-old toddlers and Fido the family dog do not have articulate propositional beliefs about themselves as conscious subjects of experience. Nonetheless, experience is not blind, and their capacity to experience a world of objects immediately present to them in itself manifests at least some implicit grasp of the reflexive structure of experience.

Unity of experience   Two interdependent unities pervade the realm of phenomenal experience: the unity of the experienced world and the unity of the experiencing self.

We do not normally experience isolated sensory qualities or objects; we do not typically see mere colored regions, hear mere sounds, or feel mere shapes. Our phenomenal experience is of a world of independently existing, relatively stable objects located in a unified arena of space and time within which we ourselves are located as conscious perceivers. The objects we experience and the world within which they exist have a phenomenal and intentional "thickness," not merely in the literal three-dimensional sense but also in the richness of their properties and relations and in the diversity and density of the connections that hold among them in constituting "a world" of objects.

On the correlative side of the experiential relation is the more or less unified self that coheres as a single subject of experience both at a time and diachronically, bound by links of content, inference, access, and memory. Our experience is not a mere sequence of distinct experiential episodes; rather it is the unfolding experiential flow of an ongoing self or subject, and its being experienced as such is a key part of its phenomenal feel as well as its structure. Nor is our experience at a moment the experience of isolated sensory items. When I stop to make a cup of tea, I hear the whistle of the kettle that I see before me on the stove as I also feel my hand reach out to turn off the burner on which it sits. All those experiences cohere in the moment as experiences of mine.

The two experiential unities—that of world and that of self—are mutually interdependent. The experienced world coheres as a unity largely from the point of view of a self located in it. Objects are experienced in terms of the relations they bear to each other from the perspective of the self, itself located in space and time. I experience the trees waving in the wind as out across the yard beyond the window through which I look, the pines to the left of the spruce and much taller than they were a few years back. My experience of them as *real objects of my world* is bound up with the spatiotemporal location and ongoing unity of the selflike point of view from which they are present to me. Conversely, the experiential unity of self coheres largely in relation to the world of objects present to it. The unity of the self is the coherent ongoing unity of a perspective on that unified world, indeed of a perspective located within it.

To put the matter in loosely Kantian terms, our experience of self is very much an experience of self-in-relation-to-world, as is our experience of world essentially an experience of world-in-relation-to-self. We experience each in relation to the other; so it should come as no surprise that their respective phenomenal unities are equally interdependent.

These two unities, and the thickness and richness of connection that underlie them, are just the sorts of intentional phenomenal features that might be produced through global integration. It might occur within a sensory modality when seen colors, shapes, sheen, and use all get bound together as features of a single object. Or perhaps it may bind across sense modalities when sights and sounds are integrated as aspects of a single situation, as when the kettle on the fire sings while the toast pops up from the toaster off to the left. Or it may involve more distant forms of binding as between present experiences and past memories, or between current perceptual inputs and background information about the relevant actors or objects. Such integrative processes must be at work whenever as a matter of experience I see a small white sugar cube on a plate, reach for my ringing alarm clock, or recognize the man in the shop as the person who spoke up at last week's council meeting (Metzinger 1995; Cleermans 2003).

Given that interdependence, both unities obviously embody a substantial measure of reflexive intentionality. The unity of the self pervades both, and each requires a heightened degree of reflexive self-understanding. Given the intentional structure of phenomenal experience, one could not be able to have such experience without also having the necessary sorts of understanding that it presupposes. And much of that understanding with respect to the unity and reality of the experienced world turns out to be at least in part self-understanding and to be reflexively bound up with the phenomenal unity of the self. You can experience your eyeglasses sitting on a blank sheet of yellow paper only if you already grasp the reality of the world within which those glasses exist as objects. And understanding that reality, both of the world and of the things in it, is in part a matter of understanding them in relation to one's experience of them from one's perspective as an ongoing, continuing self within that world. Thus, given the interdependence of the two unities, there can be little doubt that both involve a substantial degree of reflexive higher-order intentionality and self-understanding. Insofar as the unity of the self requires higher-order intentionality, and the unity of the experienced world is in turn bound up with the unity of the self, it follows that the unity of the phenomenal world as well depends on reflexive higher-order intentionality.

Autopoietic dynamics and flow   Experience is ever changing, and reflexive intentionality manifests itself in the dynamics of its flow as much as it does in its synchronic unity and presence. In part this reflects the two unities we have just been discussing. Our experience is that of an ongoing self within an ongoing world. So we would expect the unities of world and self to be expressed in the order of experience, and indeed they are. But consciousness is also active and self-organizing; its state and content at one moment typically shape what happens next. To use the apt Greek-derived term that has of late found its way from embryology into the science of mind, consciousness is an "autopoietic" process, that is, one that is self-making, self-creating, and self-organizing (Lorenz 1977; Varela, Thompson, and Rosch 1991; Van Gulick 2003).

The process is self-organizing and reflexive not only in the direct sense that early stages bring about and produce later ones in an orderly content-related way, but also in the sense that the intentional structure within which those patterns and relations are produced is essentially that of a self—indeed that of an active self—one that shapes and controls its own phenomenal flow, and which experiences that control as part of the feel of its own mode of conscious awareness. My visual experience can change because the cat wakes up and moves or because the doorbell rings, but it also changes when I shift my eyes or even the focus of my visual attention, as well as when I call up an image of a meal I ate last summer with friends in Florence, or when I think my way through the argument of this paragraph. In every case, my active experiential state at one moment is a major cause of what I experience next, and that fact of control is itself a key feature of the felt quality of my own phenomenology.

The autopoietic dynamics of experience provide obvious links to the two features of mind we have been aiming to connect: global integration and reflexive meta-intentionality.

The sort of control system required for experience to modulate and transform its own ongoing state as it does would clearly require a rich network of integrating connections and content-sensitive interactions to move it from one phenomenal intentional state to its appropriate target successor. On the HOGS model, what is needed is for each episodic stage in the transient flow of globally integrated states to be capable of organizing its successor by selectively recruiting and binding together its intentional constituents, continually adding and deleting elements from its global ensemble of reciprocally activated components. In many cases, of course, outside factors and stimuli will play a big part as well—doorbells do ring unexpectedly—but even in those cases the prior phenomenal state of the system and the globally integrated base on which it depends will still be major factors in shaping its subsequent evolution.

These experiential dynamics have an important reflexive aspect as well. The intentional structure within which one stage of experience produces another does not rely merely on links between the contents of those states but also essentially on their being states of one and same conscious subject or self. I aim to call to mind the trattoria in which last summer's dinner took place, and I thereby change the flow of my own visual phenomenology. The transition is apt not only because the image of the restaurant matches the content of what was aimed at, but also because it occurs as part of *my* experiential flow. Moreover, that reflexive aspect—*my* acting to shape *my* experience—is itself a central aspect of the intentionality and felt phenomenology of the dynamics of experiential flow. I experience it not as a passive observer but as an active agent shaping my own experiential path. Nor is it likely my experience would have the autopoietic control power that it does if it lacked that reflexive meta-intentional structure.

Philosophers concerned with phenomenal consciousness sometimes focus solely on its static or synchronic features, but its dynamic diachronic flow is also a central feature of how we experience ourselves and our world.

Affective pragmatic aspect of experiential content   The role of the conscious mind as active autopoietic agent provides a transition to our fourth and final phenomenal feature, one that ties in nicely with the general teleopragmatic view of mind. From that perspective, mind is seen to have an essential pragmatic dimension, and notions such as information, understanding, and awareness are treated as having an important practical and contextual aspect. If minds evolved to enable organisms to successfully engage their worlds, then one would expect conscious minds to reflect that practical aspect in the intentional content and phenomenology of their experience. Indeed, one finds exactly that.

Although we may sometimes experience objects in ways that have little if any relation to our purposes or interests, our everyday experience is typically infused with practical significance. The intentional content of experience is shot through with modes of presenting and categorizing objects and situations in terms of their relevance to our needs or interests and the opportunities or affordances they present for interaction or engagement. This is especially true in social and culturally constructed contexts, but it applies across the board to pretty much all domains of experience. I see the jetway before me as a path to my plane, I hear the bark of the dog as a warning, and I feel the keyboard under my fingers as a means to produce the text of this sentence. Fresh coffee, angry scowls, can-openers, and even the layout of trees in a wood are typically present in experience in ways that at least partly incorporate some implicit recognition of their affective significance and their possibilities for practical engagement.

Once again, there are plausible links with the two key aspects of the HOGS model. Like our three earlier phenomenal features, the affective pragmatic aspect of experience bears interesting explanatory connections both to global integration and to reflexive intentionality.

As we noted above in section II, the teleopragmatic view regards the move toward a more objective mode of intentionality and representation not as a move away from pragmatic engagement, but rather as a matter of setting representations within a wider and richer context that in fact allows for a larger and more open-ended range of possible relevant engagement. Our conscious experience of the world presents objects to us with a wealth of open possibilities. When I see the box on my desk, there is almost no end to the understanding ways I might respond to it. I can open it, throw it away, stack books on top of it, cover a stain with it, use it as a color sample to match some paint, drum a rhythm on its lid, or take it to class as a prop for a lecture on the *Investigations*. Indeed it is this very openness to such limitless possibilities of engagement that largely constitutes or contributes to the felt reality and objectivity of the experienced world (Merleau-Ponty 1945).

Producing an understanding system with such flexibility of response and application would obviously require a sophisticated underlying system of connections to integrate all the various modules and action-guiding subsystems that would have to interface and harmonize to realize such open-ended possibilities for purposive engagement. The most plausible way of freeing up practical understanding encapsulated within specific modules is by integrating and harmonizing those modules with others to increase the sphere within which that understanding might be applied. Insofar as phenomenal experience shows a high degree of such pragmatic openness, it likely requires just the sort of global integration the HOGS model proposes.

Reflexive intentionality comes in again as well in many ways, some obvious and some less so. Insofar as we experience objects in relation to our needs and wants and to our embodied means of interacting with them, the content of such experience must obviously incorporate some measure of reflexive intentionality. Understanding objects and situations in relation to our goals requires having at least some implicit understanding of those goals and of them as one's own.

However, the need to support pragmatic engagement may involve reflexive intentionality in other ways that are more subtle but potentially deeper and more important.

The processes through which organisms successfully engage and understand the world typically loop back and forth between the organism and its context, with each side generating signals and replies that pass back and forth in resonant harmonic cycles. Insofar as phenomenal consciousness in part provides an interface for real-time causal interaction with the world, it likely generates not only efferent signals but anticipations and expectations of the reafferent response that it will receive back from the world. Successful engagement will typically require a good match between expectation and actual reafferent, or at least one good enough to establish an effective harmony between the two coupled sides of the interaction. Imagine how ineffective and clumsy one is when one's inner timing or sense of distance or direction fails to match the sensory feedback from one's actions. Try for example to cut a paper pattern with scissors using only a mirror-reflected image to guide your own action. One can learn to do it, but most of us at first can manage only some slow and awkward snipping.

Indeed, some have proposed (Gray 1995, 2004) that this system for matching predicted and actual reafferents is the core basis of conscious experience. However, even if one is not willing to go quite that far, it seems likely that such loops play at least some role in producing the felt experience of being and acting in the world. If so, then these loops present an important way in which consciousness, or at least one key aspect of consciousness, can be explained as an example of the teleopragmatic process through which organisms come to better understand objects in their worlds by coming to better understand the ways those objects affect them, as well as coming to better understand themselves by gaining a better understanding of their effects on those objects.

An even more radical option is suggested by another teleopragmatic feature of experience discussed back in section II. We noted there that understanding sometimes involves cases of reciprocal constitution, in which the understander and that which it understands mutually depend on each other and their resonant interaction for their nature and even for their existence as the sorts of things they are. Examples in the social domain seem most evident, but nonsocial cases are also surely possible. Perhaps phenomenal consciousness itself presents a crucial case of such "bootstrapping." If conscious minds are active autopoietic systems and they experience their objects in terms of their pragmatic potential for reciprocal engagement, then the existence of conscious minds as self-understanding systems may depend on a reflexive version of such mutual reciprocal constitution.

Conscious minds, on such a model, would have the properties they do in part because they understand themselves as having those very properties; they would in a more than punning sense be self-understanding systems in two connected senses: they would understand themselves in the *constitutive* sense by understanding themselves in the more ordinary *cognitive pragmatic* sense. The idea is suggestive if radical, and perhaps it could be successfully developed, though perhaps not. For now, I leave it as just a suggestion whose exploration will have to wait another day.

Let us sum up what we have learned from our four phenomenal features about how the reflexive and higher-order aspects of the HOGS model might work together to help explain consciousness, and in particular about why one needs the HO in HOGS. We found that each of the four involves explanatory links in both directions. Global integration is required in every case to provide the rich network of connections that underlies the relevant phenomenal feature, whether it be the unity of the experienced world, the self-organizing dynamics of experience, or the open-ended pragmatics associated with the phenomenal experience of an objective reality. Similarly, we found that they all involved an essential, if sometimes implicit, aspect of reflexive higher-order intentionality, whether in the phenomenal feature of presence as presence *to self*, the unity of the experienced world *in relation to self*, or the autopoietic dynamics through which consciousness understands and organizes itself as the experience of a unified ongoing self. Moreover, in every case we saw that the two aspects of the HOGS model were not only both relevant but that they reinforced each other in explanatorily important ways.

VI HOGS and the Objections to HOT and HOP

Back in section I, we listed six common objections that have been raised against the standard HOT and HOP models of consciousness. I hope in the last few sections to have given a plausible account of the HOGS model and what it involves. Thus I will close by returning to those original objections, and asking how the HOGS model might deal with those challenges and whether it can give replies that are not otherwise available to more standard defenders of the HO point of view. Indeed, I believe it can.

Recall the six objections. HOT and HOP theories were jointly faulted on the basis of six difficulties:

· the "too fancy" objection
· the extra conditions problem
· the generality problem
· the phenomenal adequacy issue
· the "stranded qualia" problem
· the error/illusion problem

I believe the HOGS model has something distinctive and useful to say in response to each. In some cases, the relevant objection does not even really apply to the HOGS model and thus can be simply dismissed. In others, the general objection is still relevant, but the HOGS model has additional resources to answer the challenge.

The generality problem and the extra conditions problem are two that fail to apply against the HOGS model. They get their bite against more standard HO models that explicate the nature of a conscious mental state as a relational matter of there being separate higher-order states directed at it. Whether the relevant HO states are thoughtlike or perception-like, it is still their distinct existence that supposedly explains the original state's transformation from nonconscious to conscious status. Thus the objections: Why doesn't the same apply to stones and pencils we perceive or think of? And why doesn't the transformation take place if the HO state is produced by inferential means?

On the HOGS model, the nonconscious–conscious transformation is a matter of its being recruited into a globally integrated state that crucially embodies a heightened degree of higher-order reflexive intentionality, and not merely a matter of having a separate HO state directed at it. Pencils and stones are never recruited into any such globally integrated states—indeed the idea of their being so does not even really make any sense. So the generality problem does not apply to the HOGS model. Similarly, there is no need to justify extra conditions such as the noninferential requirement to rule out counterexamples like those that would otherwise threaten more standard HO theories. Again the relevant cases do not involve the sort of recruitment the HOGS model requires, so they do not count as even apparent counterexamples to it, and thus there is no need to motivate extra conditions to exclude them.

The "too fancy" objection is also easily met by the HOGS model, especially if the model is placed within the larger context of the teleopragmatic view of mind, with its varying degrees of understanding and intentional content. On the HOGS model, much of the relevant reflexive higher-order intentionality is implicitly embedded in the structure and organization of the globally integrated states, and its content need not be as sophisticated as that associated with explicit higher-order propositional attitudes of the sort that seem too fancy for attributing to dogs or toddlers. No doubt the intentional contents associated with the experiences of infants and cats differ from those associated with adult human experience, and their conscious lives involve a less sophisticated understanding of themselves as mental subjects. Yet that provides no reason to doubt they could have the sort of implicit self-understanding that the HOGS model builds into the organization and structure of experience.

The phenomenal adequacy issue poses a genuine challenge to the HOGS model, as it would to any model of consciousness. No theory can be considered satisfactory as a general account of consciousness unless it successfully addresses the phenomenal and qualitative aspects of our conscious mental life, though what would count as success is itself an open question.

As noted in section I, standard HO models seem most plausible at explaining the commonsense notion of a conscious state as a "mental state of which we are aware." Their supporters believe such models can be extended or supplemented with an independent account of qualia to provide an explanation as well of states that are conscious in the phenomenal or "what-it's-like" sense. Perhaps they can indeed do so, but their attempts so far have failed to produce widespread optimism on that score. The HOGS model, though itself relatively new, may hold more promise for helping to explain states that are conscious in the problematic phenomenal sense. Indeed, as I tried to show in section V, the two key aspects of the HOGS model can be used together to build explanatory connections that help explain the nature and basis of key features of phenomenal experience such as its unity, presence, and autopoietic dynamics. I do not suppose the HOGS model will in itself explain everything we want to understand about phenomenal consciousness; given my teleopragmatic commitment to explanatory pluralism I doubt any model could suffice for complete understanding. Nor is the HOGS model intended as a reductive theory; it aims only to provide some insights into what phenomenal consciousness is and how it could be realized that might otherwise be missed. And if it does so, that might be enough to count as at least a partial explanatory success.

Whatever general success or limits it may have in explaining consciousness, the HOGS model does not have to deal with the specific problem of "stranded qualia" that gets raised against more standard HO theories. The HOGS model does not separate qualia and "what-it's-likeness" in the way that generates the objection. In particular, it does not treat qualia as *properties of mental states* at all, neither of lower-level states nor of higher-level states directed at them. Rather, the HOGS model treats qualia as *properties of experienced objects*, and thus it regards the problem of qualia as explanatorily posterior to the project of explaining how it is possible to experience a world of objects in the first place. Only when we have made progress on that prior issue is one likely to get a sense of how qualia might come in. If one gets off on the wrong foot by treating qualia as properties of our mental states rather than as properties of experienced objects, one may well fall into further confusions; indeed that may be how the "stranded qualia" problem arises. In any case, the specific problem does not apply to the HOGS model.

Finally, there is the error/illusion problem. Standard HO models seemed to have no satisfactory choice about what would determine the specific "what-it's-likeness," if any, present in such cases. Nor did they have any non–ad hoc bases for ruling out the possibility of such higher-order errors or illusions. The HOGS model by contrast has a natural way to exclude them. On standard HO models the meta-state is a separate and distinct state directed at the object state that it makes conscious. Given their separate and independent existence, there must be at least the logical possibility of a mismatch between them. Hence the problem.

However, on the HOGS model the nonconscious–conscious transformation is a matter of recruiting the original state into a globally integrated complex, which retains it, or at least some near successor state, as a component of the overall integrated state. If one thinks in terms of recruitment, the possibility of a problematic mismatch does not arise. The original state is not the mere object of a separate higher-order thought or perception, but is itself an essential component of the integrated state, whose higher-order aspect is embodied in its organization through which it unites its component states into the experience of a real and ongoing world of objects. I do not claim that the HOGS model rules out all possibility of error about what qualities one encounters in experience. There are many interpretative metaprocesses that generate a diversity of explicit beliefs and attitudes about our mental lives. Surely they can sometimes go wrong, and they can probably err even about qualitative features of experience. But they would be mistakes of a different sort than those that provoked the error/illusion objection against standard HO models. The HOGS model does not attempt to explain the specific "what-it's-likeness" of experience in terms of the contents of any such explicit meta-states, and so the possibility of error or illusion with respect to them causes it no special problems or dilemmas.

The HOGS model thus seems able to avoid or answer all six of the original objections raised against more standard HO theories. That should surely count in its favor, though of course it does not by itself establish the validity of the HOGS model nor even its overall superiority to HOT and HOP models. There could conversely be other objections that specifically tell against the HOGS model but not against the more standard HO views. Thus it is too soon to reach any conclusive judgment.

Nonetheless, I hope to have shown that the HOGS model offers new and interesting explanatory options, in particular for understanding how phenomenal consciousness might be linked to other functional and intentional processes, such as those involving global integration and reflexive intentionality. The HOGS model provides an alternative slant on higher-order theory that clearly merits further consideration.

Notes

1. Those interested in their comparative merits can see Van Gulick 2001, which offers an evaluation that finds no clear winner; Lycan 2004, which argues for the relative superiority of HOP theory over HOT; and Carruthers 2000, which defends the opposite.

2. The appeal to teleology carries no nonnaturalistic implication; the only sort of teleology required is that which can be accommodated within standard theories of evolution and adaptation. Just which explication of teleology is best for which context remains open to debate, but there seems little doubt that at least some theoretically and explanatory useful notions of teleology can be explicated in naturalistically acceptable ways.

3. Indeed with humans the range of possible ends is more or less open-ended—whether racing bicycles up mountains or writing philosophical essays.

4. This may provide a reason for doubting that Ned Block's (1995) distinction between *access consciousness* and *phenomenal consciousness* marks a division between two different processes. It may instead merely distinguish two interrelated aspects of one and the same process.

5. Of course some higher-order theorists have denied the distinction between the two sorts of consciousness, or at least denied that consciousness in the what-it's-like sense can be separated from consciousness in the higher-order sense (Rosenthal 1991a; Carruthers 2000).

3 Internal-World Skepticism and the Self-Presentational Nature of Phenomenal Consciousness

Terry Horgan, John Tienson, and George Graham

In this essay we describe a puzzling phenomenon that arises at the interface of epistemology and philosophy of mind, and we argue that this phenomenon has important consequences concerning the nature of direct, introspective access to one's own mental life. The phenomenon is this: A certain potential kind of radical skepticism about one's current mental life—*internal-world* skepticism, as we call it—gets no grip psychologically, unlike radical external-world skepticism; also, not being gripped by such skepticism seems eminently rationally appropriate.[1] The puzzle is, why is this so? What most plausibly *explains* the rational non-grippingness of internal-world skepticism? We argue that the best explanation adverts to a feature that both is essential to phenomenal consciousness and also is possessed *only* by phenomenally conscious states—specifically, a distinctive kind of self-presentational feature that precludes the possibility of being radically deceived about one's own current, phenomenally conscious mental states. Thus, internal-world skepticism gets no psychological grip—and rationally so, because all conscious states are phenomenological.

Our argument for this proposed explanation proceeds largely by elimination of potential alternatives. We canvass several initially plausible-looking attempts to explain the non-grippingness of internal-world skepticism independently of phenomenal consciousness, and we argue that none of them succeeds in providing an adequate explanation. We then consider certain nontendentiously phenomenal mental states—current, immediately accessible, sensory-experiential states. We propose an explanation of the non-grippingness of internal-world skepticism about these states that relies essentially on their phenomenal character. Finally, we argue that this same approach provides the only tenable explanation of the non-grippingness of internal-world skepticism about other kinds of current, immediately accessible mental states—for example, current thoughts, desires, wonderings, suspectings. Thus, the non-grippingness of internal-world skepticism provides additional support, complementary to other considerations that have been put forth in recent philosophy of mind, for the existence of cognitive phenomenology—a "what-it's-like" of states like occurrent beliefs, occurrent deliberations among alternatives, occurrent wishes, and so on.

1 Internal-World Skepticism and Its Non-Grippingness

The commonly discussed form of radical skepticism focuses on the external world; it is concerned with the question whether one's beliefs about the external world are radically mistaken (including one's beliefs about one's own apparent body and its apparent physical characteristics). Curiously, there is not much discussion of what we will call *internal-world* skepticism—which is concerned instead with the question whether one's immediate, noninferential, introspective beliefs about one's own current mental states are radically mistaken.

A striking fact about internal-world skepticism is that it *gets no grip* on people psychologically, whereas external-world skepticism does get a psychological grip. Getting a grip, in the relevant sense, need not be—and for most people, is not—a matter of coming to have genuine doubts about whether one's beliefs of the relevant kind are really true. It need not be—and for most people, is not—a matter of actually becoming a skeptic about knowledge and/or justified belief. Rather, it is a matter of judging that it is a *genuine epistemic possibility*—albeit perhaps a wildly unlikely, hugely implausible possibility—that one's beliefs of a certain kind are systematically and radically false. (Or at any rate, it is a matter of being *disposed* to so judge *if prompted in the right way*—e.g., in an introductory philosophy class.) Skepticism concerning external-world beliefs, for example, grips the philosophical imagination in light of the apparent conceptual and epistemic possibility that one might actually be the victim in a radical-deception scenario—for example, one might be undergoing systematically nonveridical experiences caused by Descartes's Evil Deceiver, or (the contemporary high-tech variant of this scenario) one might be an envatted brain that gets systematically deceiving sensory inputs from an attached computer that stimulates the brain's sensory cortex and monitors its motor cortex, or, more simply, that one might be dreaming nonveridically.

Internal-world skepticism, by contrast, tends not to strike people as philosophically problematic in the same way. People simply are not gripped by the idea that their introspective beliefs about what is currently going on in their own minds might be systematically false. Indeed, Descartes himself in the *First Meditation* displayed no tendency even to consider such a putative possibility, even though his avowed purpose in that text was to practice methodological doubt vis-à-vis everything doubtable, as a means toward the end of determining what cannot be doubted (and thereby, he hoped, placing human knowledge claims on a solid epistemological foundation). For instance, when he was entertaining the thought "Perhaps I am really dreaming right now," he did not consider the putative possibility that he was not presently entertaining that very thought at all; nor do other people consider this putative possibility while entertaining that thought, even when methodological doubt is the task at hand.

A further dimension of the non-grippingness of internal-world skepticism is that one's own failure to be thus gripped does not strike one, on reflection, as a lapse in rationality—as a mistake. On the contrary, it seems eminently rational. The occurrent episodes in one's current and very recent mental life strike one as directly *given* in experience—and as given in such a way that one's current beliefs that *these* episodes are occurring (or have very recently occurred) seem epistemically unassailable.[2] For instance, it seems directly given introspectively that one is now thinking about what to cook for dinner, or that one is now experiencing a toothache, or that one is now wishing one were in a swimming pool, and so on.

But the non-grippingness of internal-world skepticism—the failure to become philosophically puzzled by the putative possibility that one's own current noninferential beliefs about one's current mental states might be radically mistaken—generates a philosophical puzzle in its own right. The puzzle is this. *Why* aren't we gripped psychologically by internal-world skepticism, and why does our failure to be thus gripped strike us, on reflection, to be rationally appropriate? The phenomenon of non-grippingness calls out for explanation.

One possibility is that the right explanation is a *debunking* explanation of some sort—an explanation that treats non-grippingness as a ubiquitous error, perhaps resulting from some kind of subtle cognitive illusion to which humans are highly prone. An advocate of a debunking explanation would claim that internal-world skepticism *ought rationally* to be gripping, even though it fails to be because of this pernicious psychological blindspot. Ceteris paribus, however, a nondebunking explanation is theoretically preferable to a debunking one, especially if it can be situated within a theory that is otherwise independently plausible. We will propose such an explanation in sections 5 and 6, after first examining several (nondebunking) explanatory strategies that, despite looking promising at first sight, fail to deliver the explanatory goods.

2 "Access Consciousness"?

The kinds of beliefs we are focusing on are beliefs that (1) are directly and noninferentially generated by one's cognitive mechanisms, and (2) are about which current, occurrent mental states one is currently undergoing. We will call such beliefs *direct current-occurrent-mental-state beliefs*, hereafter abbreviated as *direct COMS beliefs*.[3] One canonical way to express such a belief to oneself in public language is via indexical constructions, as in "This mental state has this property"—where "this mental state" indexically refers to the token COMS, and "this property" indexically refers to a mental state-type of which the given token state is an instance. For example, as one introspectively attends to one's current, occurrent toothache experience, one thinks to oneself that this (i.e., this specific mental episode) has this property (i.e., this specific qualitative character). Likewise, as one introspectively attends to one's current, occurrent state of wondering whether to serve meatloaf for dinner, one thinks to oneself that this (i.e., this specific token mental state) has this property (i.e., being a wondering about whether to serve meatloaf for dinner).

We first consider a construal of direct COMS beliefs that many are apt to find attractive. It appeals to the enormously influential distinction that Ned Block (1995) makes between phenomenal consciousness and what he calls "access consciousness." Let us lay our cards on the table right away. We maintain that the Block-inspired construal of direct COMS beliefs utterly fails to provide any plausible explanation of the non-grippingness of internal-world skepticism. But it will prove to be an instructive failure.

Block explains as follows the two distinct concepts each of which he claims is sometimes expressed by the word "consciousness":

First, consider phenomenal consciousness, or P-consciousness, as I will call it. . . . P-consciousness is experience. P-conscious properties are experiential properties. P-conscious states are experiential states, that is, a state is P-conscious if it has experiential properties. The totality of the experiential properties of a state are "what it is like" to have it. . . . I now turn to the nonphenomenal notion of consciousness that is most easily and dangerously conflated with P-consciousness: access consciousness. A state is A-conscious if it is poised for direct control of thought and action. To add more detail, a representation is A-conscious if it is poised for free use in reasoning and for direct "rational" control of action and speech. (Block 1995, pp. 380–382 in the reprint in Block et al. 1997)

Suppose for the moment that Block is right in claiming that there is a notion of access consciousness that is conceptually independent of phenomenal consciousness. Also, suppose for the moment that various forms of access consciousness actually occur in humans without involving any distinctive, essential, proprietary phenomenal character. On this picture, the fact that certain COMS beliefs are directly and noninferentially accessible to the person undergoing those states is just a fact about human cognitive architecture. The key architectural feature is this: There is a *reliable noninferential belief-forming mechanism*, built into cognitive architecture, that tends reliably to directly generate within the cognitive agent accurate COMS beliefs. Or, at any rate, this mechanism tends reliably to generate such beliefs insofar as the agent actively undertakes to form COMS beliefs at all. This architectural feature is wholly a matter of access consciousness, the fan of Block's distinction will say. Whether or not a given mental state is *phenomenally* conscious is supposedly just an orthogonal matter, vis-à-vis the cognitive agent's capacity to directly, noninferentially form accurate beliefs about her or his current first-order mental states; being phenomenally conscious is not necessary for the first-order states to be access conscious, and it is not sufficient either.

But does this picture of the noninferential belief-formation of COMS beliefs allow for an explanation of the non-grippingness of internal-world skepticism? Clearly not, we submit. For, if direct access were entirely just a matter of the operation of a reliable belief-forming mechanism that leads directly from current first-order mental states to accurate COMS beliefs, then there would arise the epistemic possibility that one's own direct COMS beliefs *are never (or hardly ever) actually produced by such a belief-forming mechanism at all*, and hence there would also arise the correlative epistemic possibility that these beliefs *are systematically false*. This would be not only a conceptually coherent epistemic possibility, but also one that is epistemically roughly on a par with radical external-world skepticism. Just as external-world skepticism invokes radical-deception scenarios—Cartesian Evil Deceivers, or brain-in-vat setups—in which one's spontaneous external-world beliefs fail to be reliably caused by worldly states of affairs that render those beliefs true, likewise internal-world skepticism would invoke comparable radical deception-scenarios in which one's direct COMS beliefs (i.e., one's spontaneous *internal-world* beliefs) fail to be reliably caused by the kinds of first-order mental states that would render these beliefs true.

How might a suitable thought experiment go, to illustrate such a radical internal-world skeptical possibility? That is, what might be the appropriate internal-world analogue of the Cartesian Evil Deceiver, or the brain-in-vat setup? Well, the internal-world Evil Deceiver could be a divinely powerful creature who directly generates COMS beliefs in the experiencing agent, in ways that systematically fail to accurately reflect the actual first-order mental states that the agent is undergoing when these COMS beliefs occur. Likewise, an internal-world analogue of a deceptive brain-in-vat setup would be a situation in which a computer (perhaps a small one that is surgically implanted within a hapless person's skull) directly generates COMS beliefs in the person's brain, once again in ways that systematically misrepresent the actual first-order mental states that the person is undergoing.

The key line of thought here is just the following: (1) If the direct generation of COMS beliefs is conceived as a matter of "access consciousness" that has nothing essentially to do with phenomenal consciousness, then direct COMS beliefs are *ontologically independent* of the first-order mental states that are supposed to reliably cause these COMS beliefs. (Causes and effects are, as Hume said, "independent existences.") But (2) if the first-order mental causes are indeed ontologically independent of the COMS beliefs that they supposedly reliably cause, then the skeptical possibility that the real causes of the COMS beliefs are something other than truth-conferring first-order mental states looms very large—just as large as the skeptical possibility that the real causes of one's external-world beliefs are something other than truth-conferring states of affairs in one's external environment. Thus (3) the approach to direct COMS beliefs now under consideration provides no explanation of why radical internal-world skepticism fails to get a psychological grip, or of why it rationally ought to fail to get one. On the contrary, (4) given the putative ontological independence of the first-order mental causes from the COMS beliefs that supposedly are their effects, it seems easy enough to describe thought-experimental scenarios that are straightforward internal-world analogues of the familiar external-world skepticism—analogues of the Cartesian Evil Demon or the envatted brain. So (5) under the "access consciousness" approach to direct COMS beliefs, internal-world skepticism ought rationally to be no less an epistemological issue than—and hence no less psychologically gripping than—ordinary external-world skepticism. So much the worse for the "access consciousness" approach.

3 Ontological Constituency?

The critique in section 2 of the proposed Block-inspired account of direct COMS beliefs was premised on the supposition that the current, occurrent mental state itself and the second-order direct belief about that first-order mental state are "separate existences" in the Humean sense. But another kind of account of direct COMS beliefs that might be put forward—which once again makes no essential appeal to phenomenal consciousness, and does not require the relevant first-order states to be phenomenally conscious—would rest on two ideas: First, the first-order mental state is literally a *constituent* of the COMS belief; second, the COMS belief is intentionally directed, reflexively, on this constituent-state.[4]

For instance, when one sees an apple on a table, and believes that one is seeing an apple (or something red), the seeing of the apple is itself a constituent of the belief that one sees an apple. That constituent-state is not only intentionally directed on the apple, but is also reflexively intentionally directed on itself: it is *self*-presenting, to the agent who is undergoing it. Likewise, when one occurrently thinks that the Patriot Act is the worst piece of legislation in U.S. history, and one forms the belief that this is what one is thinking, that very thinking is a constituent of the second-order belief. This thinking-episode too is intentionally directed not only on the Patriot Act, but also—reflexively—on itself. Thus, one's belief about what one is thinking is grounded in the self-presentational nature of the thought itself.

According to the account of COMS beliefs now being described, since a direct COMS belief cannot occur unless the relevant first-order mental state simultaneously occurs as a constituent of this belief, it is impossible for a direct COMS belief to be radically nonveridical. That is, it is impossible for the belief to purport to refer to some first-order mental state when no actual mental state is an eligible referent; and it is impossible for the belief to be highly inaccurate about the nature of this referent-state. These impossibility facts, grounded in the ontological structure that the account attributes to direct COMS beliefs, could then be put forward as an explanation of both the non-grippingness of internal-world skepticism, and of the rationality of that non-grippingness.

We do not necessarily want to question the claim that first-order mental states are constituents of direct COMS beliefs, or the claim that these beliefs are reflexively intentionally directed on these constituents. These claims may well be right—a matter to which we return below. But our contention is this: insofar as one tries to harness these ideas in a way that makes no essential appeal to phenomenal character, one cannot provide an adequate explanation of the non-grippingness of internal-world skepticism. In particular, insofar as one applies this approach to beliefs about first-order mental states that one maintains do not even have any essential or proprietary phenomenal character, no adequate explanation can be given.

Suppose someone reasons as follows:

We do have direct COMS beliefs, of course. But it is impossible for direct COMS beliefs to be radically nonveridical. For, consider an introspective internal-world belief $B(M)$, to the effect that one is currently undergoing a mental state of type M. $B(M)$

is a direct COMS belief only if (i) $B(M)$ contains an occurrent mental state of type M as a constituent, and (ii) $B(M)$ is intentionally directed, reflexively, on M itself. Hence, there is no rational basis for being gripped by internal-world skepticism—which is why it is not in fact gripping.

The trouble with this reasoning is this. Given the proposed ontological-constituency account of direct COMS beliefs, a pertinent kind of radical internal-world deception scenario would put into question the contention that one possesses *genuine* direct COMS beliefs.

Here is one such scenario. Imagine an agent, I. W. McGoo (short for "Internal World McGoo"), whose spontaneous, noninferential COMS beliefs are all just like your own in terms of their "downstream" causal role within the agent's psychological economy; among other things, I. W. McGoo's internal-world beliefs have the very same tendencies to generate sincere first-person verbal descriptions about what is currently going on in his own mind. However, I. W. McGoo's first-order mental life actually differs substantially from your own. Furthermore, his spontaneous COMS beliefs do *not* contain as constituents the first-order mental states that these COMS beliefs attribute to him; thus, they are not reflexively intentionally directed on such mental states. Rather, his spontaneous COMS beliefs are directly caused in him by a Cartesian Evil Deceiver. The Deceiver cleverly and systematically produces spontaneous COMS beliefs that constitute a perversely coherent—albeit wildly inaccurate—ongoing first-person story about what's going on in I. W. McGoo's own mental life (much as the severely near-sighted cartoon character Mr. McGoo always had a wildly mistaken but perversely coherent first-person story about what was going on around him in his local external environment). These spontaneous COMS beliefs do not count as full-fledged *direct* COMS beliefs, according to the account of such beliefs now under consideration. But because they have the same downstream causal tendencies as would direct COMS beliefs with the same contents, we will call them *quasi-direct* COMS beliefs.[5]

Others who interact with I. W. McGoo find him to be a curious mix of the normal and the bizarre—similar in some ways to certain aging people who vacillate between mental lucidity and ordinary behavior on one hand, and bizarre beliefs and correlatively bizarre behavior on the other hand. Insofar as I. W. McGoo is engaging with the world, and with other people, in ways that do not require him to draw on quasi-direct COMS beliefs, he behaves quite normally, both verbally and nonverbally. When he reports on what is currently going on in his mind, however, what he says makes him seem like a bizarrely coherent lunatic. And when behavioral tasks arise that call on him to draw simultaneously both on certain current first-order mental states and certain quasi-direct beliefs about what is now going on his mind, his resulting behavior can be very peculiar indeed—especially in the mismatch between what he actually does (and why) and what he thinks he is doing (and why). For example, perhaps he votes for George Bush because he wants George Bush to be reelected, while simultaneously telling you that he is ringing his neighbor's doorbell because he wants her to offer him a piece of her fresh peach cobbler. (The systematic nonveridicality of his spontaneous COMS beliefs extends to beliefs about what he is doing, at least insofar as he conceives his behavior under action-concepts rather than as raw bodily motion.)

But although I. W. McGoo seems strange and bizarre to the rest of us, he detects nothing peculiar from his own first-person perspective. His ongoing beliefs about what is going on in his mind and about what he is doing fit together very smoothly and consistently. The mutual fit among his radically mistaken internal-world beliefs is every bit as tight as the mutual fit among the original Mr. McGoo's external-world beliefs.

With the I. W. McGoo scenario before us, let us return to the main dialectical thread in the present section. Consider again the contention that direct COMS beliefs need not involve phenomenal consciousness, and the claim that they instead involve the containment of the very first-order mental states to which they are intentionally directed. The trouble with this position is that it simply does not foreclose the possibility of one's being in a radically deceptive situation with respect to one's internal-world beliefs—a situation like that of I. W. McGoo. Hence it provides no real explanation of the non-grippingness of radical internal-world skepticism, or of the rational appropriateness of this non-grippingness. For suppose one concedes (at least for argument's sake) that direct COMS beliefs are to be characterized in the way now being considered; and suppose one also concedes (again, at least for argument's sake) that direct COMS beliefs, as so characterized, cannot be radically mistaken. This simply does not foreclose the possibility that one's own spontaneous COMS beliefs are radically mistaken. Rather, it means only that if they are radically mistaken, then they are only *quasi-direct* COMS beliefs rather than genuine *direct* COMS beliefs. So, radical internal-world skepticism still looms large, as the possibility that you yourself are constantly undergoing spontaneous COMS beliefs that are only quasi-direct and are radically in error.

At this point someone might protest, "But I have trouble even imagining what it would be like to be in I. W. McGoo's epistemic situation, let alone taking seriously the suggestion that I myself might be in such a situation. Surely what his mental life is like—with all that bizarre internal mismatch between what's going on in his mind and what he *thinks* is going on in his mind, and with the correlative mismatch between the actions he actually performs and the ones he thinks he is performing—cannot be the same as what my own mental life is like."

This reaction seems exactly right—something we readily and cheerfully acknowledge. We can readily acknowledge it because locutions such as "what it is like," "what it would be like," and the like are the quotidian ones used to pick out the *phenomenal* aspects of human mentality. The right direction to go, in seeking out a satisfactory explanation of the non-grippingness of internal-world skepticism, is toward phenomenal consciousness.

Before turning in that direction, however, let us consider an alternative tack one might try instead—a way of embellishing the ontological constituency approach while still denying that phenomenal consciousness needs to play a role, in an effort to fend off the objection we have raised in this section. It will be useful to see why this alternative does not succeed.

4 Ontological Constituency Plus Long-Armed Functional Role?

In response to the argument of section 3, a fan of the constituency approach to direct COMS beliefs might say that commonality of downstream causal role just isn't enough to make I. W. McGoo's internal-world beliefs have the same content as one's own. It might be claimed, for instance, that what's required for content identity is total commonality of "long-armed" causal-functional role, or anyway something close enough to this that the relevant requirement is not satisfied in the case of I. W. McGoo. (Long-armed causal-functional role incorporates various causal, and/or covariational, and/or historical connections between one's inner states and various circumstances in one's external environment.) If the constituency account of direct COMS beliefs is wedded to such a treatment of content-individuation, then perhaps this package-deal position can deliver an explanation of the non-grippingness of internal-world skepticism. Thought-experimental cases like that of I. W. McGoo will not count as skeptical scenarios, because content-identity of internal-world beliefs will not be preserved between oneself and the agent in such a situation.

This move complicates the dialectic somewhat, but ultimately it won't help. To see why not, let us first consider how *external*-world skepticism fares in light of strongly "externalist" treatments of mental content. Suppose one encounters a philosopher who thinks that overall long-armed causal-functional role is constitutively determinative of what makes a given state-type count as the mental state-type it is, with its specific intentional content. Such philosophers balk at standard, familiar scenarios that are typically put forward as ones in which the mental agent's *external-world* beliefs would be radically false. For example, someone who has a view like this is apt to say that an always-envatted brain would not have radically false external-world beliefs at all, because its beliefs would actually be about the computer states that generate them, and these beliefs would actually be true of those computer states.[6]

Does such an approach to mental content render external-world beliefs immune to radical skepticism? No, and it is important to see why not. When confronted with such a view, one simply needs to construct one's radical-deception scenario more carefully, so that even if the pertinent, strongly externalist account of mental content is correct, the agent in the scenario still will have beliefs that are content-identical to one's own beliefs.[7]

One good way to do that is as follows. Consider the possibility that you yourself have been leading a perfectly normal life, with internal states having perfectly normal long-armed causal-functional roles, up until last evening. Last evening, however, aliens captured you in your sleep, drugged you, then removed and envatted your brain and hooked it up to a computer in such a way that your mental life hereafter will continue much as it would have anyway, with no clue ever arising that you have become a brain in a vat. This is an epistemically possible scenario in which your *present* external-world beliefs, based on your *present* sensory experience, are radically non-veridical. These beliefs retain their ordinary content (for now, anyway) because, according to the pertinent account of content determination, that content accrues to them by virtue of the long-armed causal-functional role they had *up until last evening*. This kind of radical-skeptical scenario surely ought to get a grip psychologically, even on someone who is enamored of a strongly externalist picture of mental state individuation and mental content determination.

Return now to internal-world skepticism. We were considering a position comprising the following claims. (1) What makes a belief count as a direct COMS belief is (a) that (a token of) such a belief contains as a constituent (a token of) the relevant first-order mental state, and (b) that the belief is reflexively intentionally directed toward this constituent state. (2) In general there is nothing essentially phenomenal about such direct COMS beliefs; although *some* of them can be *about* first-order phenomenal states, others can be about first-order mental states that do not have any essential, proprietary phenomenal character at all. (The fan of the view under consideration might say, for instance, that direct COMS beliefs about one's first-order *thoughts* are like this, on the grounds that thoughts—or at least most thoughts—allegedly lack phenomenal character.) (3) Overall long-armed causal-functional role is crucially constitutive in the individuation of mental states generally (and direct COMS beliefs in particular), and likewise in determining the intentional content of mental states generally (and direct COMS beliefs in particular). Hereafter in this section, we will call this the *package-deal* view; the package comprises the claims (1)–(3).

The trouble with this view is that certain kinds of radical-deception scenarios can still be constructed, consistently with its tenets—which means that the view still does not provide adequate resources to explain the non-grippingness of radical internal-world skepticism. The pertinent kind of scenario will be constructed in a way that's relevantly analogous to the kind of radical-deception scenario lately described, only tailored to internal-world skepticism rather than the external-world variety. We will describe one such scenario, in three steps.

First step. Imagine someone who is mentally just like yourself except that she or he has never undergone states that, according to the account of direct COMS beliefs we are considering, count as *genuine* COMS beliefs. Rather, they are quasi-direct COMS beliefs. They have two key features. First, they do not actually contain as constituents the first-order mental states that they are about. (This is why they are not genuine direct COMS beliefs, according to the constituency account of such beliefs.) But second, they have the same overall long-armed causal-functional roles within this doppelgänger that the corresponding, genuinely direct COMS beliefs play in yourself. They arise spontaneously without any conscious inferential steps; they normally arise only when the relevant first-order states are in fact currently instantiated; they have the same downstream causal tendencies; and so forth.[8]

Second step. Insofar as phenomenal character of the second-order belief-state itself plays no constitutive role in what makes a given COMS belief count as the kind of belief it is, with its specific intentional content, the advocate of the package-deal view has no principled, credible basis for saying that the quasi-direct COMS beliefs in question are different in content from the corresponding direct COMS beliefs in yourself. Rather, evidently the only resources available to the fan of the view we are criticizing, for purposes of content individuation of the relevant second-order belief states, involve the respective *long-armed functional roles* of those states. But, ex hypothesi, these are just the same in the envisioned doppelgänger as they are in you—

even though in the doppelgänger, the second-order mental states in question are only quasi-direct COMS beliefs, since they don't contain the relevant first-order mental states *as constituents*.

A way to put this difference between you and the doppelgänger would be as follows. Although your direct COMS beliefs do contain the relevant first-order mental states as constituents, whereas your doppelgänger's quasi-direct COMS beliefs do not, this is really only a purely *implementational* difference between you and the doppelgänger. For it is a difference that does not affect the respective long-armed functional roles of the respective kinds of second-order beliefs in you and your doppelgänger, respectively. And yet, since phenomenal character is not being appealed to at all in characterizing what is essential to these second-order beliefs, long-armed functional role is all that is available to be appealed to, in order to mark a nonimplementational difference between such beliefs in yourself and in your doppelgänger, respectively.

Third step. Now comes the radical deception part of the story. Your doppelgänger gets operated on during the night by alien neuroscientists; they do some rearrangement of the doppelgänger's internal neural wiring, so that hereafter its spontaneous, quasi-direct COMS beliefs are systematically false vis-à-vis its own current, occurrent mental states. But these higher-order belief-states are just the kind that *up until yesterday* typically arose only when the relevant first-order states were actually present; and the higher-order belief-states still have content-appropriate downstream causal roles within the brain's cognitive economy. So these higher-order beliefs still have the same contents that such states had prior to the recent brain operation. Yet the beliefs are radically nonveridical, while still having the same content (on the first morning of postoperation awakening, at any rate) they would have had were the agent still normal, because they got this content from the long-armed functional role they played in the doppelgänger back when the doppelgänger was still normal.

The upshot is that we are left without an adequate explanation of the non-grippingness of radical internal-world skepticism, or of the apparent rationality of not being so gripped. It does not help to wed the constituency account of direct COMS beliefs to a strongly externalistic treatment of mental-state individuation and mental-content individuation. This is no help because, insofar as phenomenal character is left out of the account of the nature of direct COMS beliefs, the difference between direct and merely quasi-direct COMS beliefs turns out to be merely an implementational difference. This in turn means that (1) one cannot be sure that one is undergoing genuinely direct COMS beliefs rather than merely quasi-direct ones, and (2) radical-deception scenarios can be constructed with respect to the quasi-direct ones.

5 Phenomenal States as Self-Presenting Modes of Presentation

The various accounts of direct COMS beliefs we have so far considered seek to characterize these beliefs independently of phenomenal consciousness. The accounts do not appeal to phenomenal character as an essential feature of such beliefs, and they do not require (although they do permit) these beliefs to be about first-order mental states that are themselves phenomenal states. Therein, we suggest, lies the source of their inability to explain the non-grippingness of internal-world skepticism. An adequate explanation must appeal to phenomenology.

Phenomenal states, as is often said, are those mental states such that there is "something it is like" to undergo them. There are two key aspects here. First, there is *what* it is like—so-called phenomenal character. But of course, to experience this "what," this distinctive phenomenal character, is not something different from undergoing the relevant phenomenal state itself. Rather, experiencing the phenomenal character *just is* undergoing the phenomenal state. Thus, sensory-phenomenal states do not merely present apparent objects and properties to the experiencer—for instance, redness, as an apparent property of an apparent object in one's visual field. In addition, they present *themselves*, since a given phenomenal state-type *is* a specific type of phenomenal character.[9] There is something that *experiencing* red is like. Visual experience of red objects acquaints you not merely with those objects and *their* redness, but with the distinctive what-it's-like-to-experience-redness character of the experience itself.[10]

Second, there is something that it is like *for the experiencer*. What-it's-likeness is essentially subjective, essentially "me-involving." "For-me-ness" is an ineliminable aspect of phenomenal consciousness. There can only be something that being in a state is like insofar as the state is like something for an experiencing subject.

These two correlative features make phenomenal states *self-presenting* to the subject, in a way that nonphenomenal states are not. A phenomenal state presents itself—*what* it is like; and it presents itself to the experiencing subject—what it is like *for me*.

Many philosophers, ourselves included, maintain that there are profound philosophical puzzles associated with these features of phenomenal consciousness—what Levine (1983) calls the *explanatory gap*, and what Chalmers (1995a, 1996) calls the *hard problem*. But our present purpose is not to address those puzzles, or to discuss their level of difficulty and prospects for their resolution. Nor are we suggesting that the idea of self-presentation somehow eliminates the puzzles, or somehow provides a basis for a naturalistic account of phenomenal consciousness. On the contrary, the distinctively self-presenting nature of phenomenal states is a fundamental part of what's puzzling, because it is so intimately bound up with the two correlative aspects of what-it's-likeness, namely, phenomenal character and subjectivity.

Instead, we propose to invoke the self-presentational character of phenomenal consciousness, puzzling though it may be in itself, to explain the non-grippingness of internal-world skepticism. We will set forth our proposed explanation in two stages. The first stage, in the present section, will be confined to current, occurrent mental states (COMSs) that we take to be nontendentiously phenomenal, namely, sensory-experiential states. The second stage, in the next section, will extend the account to cover COMSs that are often thought not to have phenomenal character at all, such as occurrent thoughts about matters other than the contents of one's present sensory experience.

So, focusing for now on sensory-experiential states, let us take up four tasks in turn. The first is to set forth our own recommended account of COMS beliefs concerning such first-order mental states. The second is to argue that under this account, such COMS beliefs cannot be radically mistaken. The third is to argue that such COMS beliefs cannot be mimicked by beliefs that have the same content and yet are (according to the proposed account) mere quasi-direct COMS beliefs. The fourth is to harness the proposed account, together with these two corollaries, to explain the non-grippingness of radical internal-world skepticism concerning such COMS beliefs.

First: Suppose you have specific visual experience as of a red, round object on a surface before you—a quintessentially phenomenal state, we take it. Suppose too that you spontaneously and noninferentially form a *belief* that you are now having a visual experience of this kind—and that this is the sort of direct COMS belief about which radical internal-world skepticism gets no grip on you. What is the nature of this belief?

Our proposal goes as follows. The first-order phenomenal state, being self-presenting in the way that only phenomenal states can be, figures directly in the belief, as a *mode of presentation* of itself. In calling it a mode of presentation—using terminology inspired by Frege—we incorporate the neo-Fregean idea that a mode of presentation contributes to the intentional content of the belief in which it figures. Change the mode of presentation, and you thereby change the specific content of the belief—even if you do not change the *referent* (if any) of that mode of presentation. Thus, the first-order state is a constituent of the belief that is intentionally directed on it—an idea we take over from the two approaches to direct COMS beliefs that we discussed in sections 3 and 4. However, its role as constituent is not merely a matter of how the belief is implemented in cognitive architecture—so that another creature could have the same belief, with the same content, even if the belief is implemented in such a way that the first-order state is not a constituent of it. (The problem of constituency as merely implementational is, in effect, part of what defeated those nonphenomenal constituency-invoking approaches.) Rather, the first-order state is a *content-determining* constituent of the higher-order belief, because the first-order state constitutes a specific mode of presentation of its referent (in the neo-Fregean sense). Furthermore, the referent of this first-order state is this very state itself; this state figures, within the direct COMS belief, as a *self-presenting mode of presentation*.[11]

Second: Under this proposal, it turns out that a direct COMS belief cannot be radically mistaken.[12] The belief is bound to refer to a current, occurrent token mental state of the kind it purports to refer to, because the belief employs (a token of) this very state as the vehicle for mentally referring to that state token; this self-presenting state token is deployed, *qua* singular denoting constituent of the belief, to refer to itself. Moreover, this first-order token mental state also is bound to fall under the phenomenal state-type that the belief attributes to it, because the belief picks out that phenomenal state-type too by using this same token mental state as the vehicle for mentally referring to that state-type. That is, this first-order mental state-token is deployed, *qua* predicative constituent of the belief, to refer to a phenomenal type that the token presents itself as belonging to. (One natural way to express such a direct COMS belief to oneself linguistically would be "This is like *this*"—where the first occurrence of the indexical picks out the phenomenal token, and the second one picks out the type.)

Third: Under this proposal, it also turns out that a direct COMS belief cannot be mimicked by a belief that is merely quasi-direct but still has the same intentional content. This is because the specific content of the direct COMS belief depends essentially on this belief's deploying the relevant first-order mental state as a self-presenting, neo-Fregean mode of presentation; thus, an otherwise functionally equivalent state that lacked this mode of presentation would not have the same content.[13] For instance, suppose that there could be a pain-zombie with internal states that (1) lack any of the distinctive phenomenal character of pain, and yet (2) play a causal-functional role in relation to sensory inputs, behavioral outputs, and other mental states that is otherwise exactly similar to the causal-functional role of pain experiences in normal humans. Such a zombie would simply be incapable of forming a COMS belief whose content is the same as a normal human's direct COMS belief about now being in pain, because the zombie's internal state would entirely lack the requisite content-determining mode of presentation—the phenomenal "what-it's-like" of being in pain.

Fourth: These observations can be harnessed to explain why internal-world skepticism is not gripping with respect to direct COMS beliefs about sensory-phenomenal states. One need only suppose that people appreciate (1) that sensory-phenomenal states are self-presenting, (2) that one's immediate beliefs about which such states one is currently undergoing cannot be radically mistaken, and (3) that immediate beliefs of this kind cannot occur in the absence of the self-presenting sensory-phenomenal states themselves. Positing an appreciation of these facts also explains why it seems rationally appropriate not to be gripped by internal-world skepticism concerning direct beliefs about one's current, occurrent sensory-phenomenal states: for the very nature of these beliefs guarantees that they cannot be radically mistaken.

6 Cognitive Phenomenology and the Scope of Direct COMS Beliefs

The account just offered of the non-grippingness of skepticism concerning direct COMS beliefs about sensory-phenomenal states depends crucially on the phenomenal character of the first-order states. The phenomenal character of the first-order state plays an essential role within the direct COMS beliefs too, since it figures within the belief not only as a constituent but also as a self-presenting, content-individuating mode of presentation.

The non-grippingness of internal-world skepticism, however, extends to numerous higher-order beliefs about one's first-order mental states, including beliefs about many kinds of first-order states other than sensory-experiential states. Non-grippingness extends, for instance, to one's direct COMS beliefs about what one is now thinking, what one now occurrently believes and occurrently wants, what alternatives one is now deliberating among, what propositions one is now hypothetically entertaining, and so on.

It is widely maintained in philosophy of mind that phenomenal character is possessed only by a relatively narrow subclass of those mental states that are conscious as opposed to unconscious—for example, sensory-experiential states and perhaps other closely related states such as mental imagings. Those who advocate such views typically deny that there is such a thing as *cognitive phenomenology*—that is, a what-it's-like of states like occurrent beliefs, occurrent deliberations among alternatives, and so on. Meanwhile, however, a number of philosophers have been arguing that phenomenal character is really much more ubiquitous, extending to virtually all of human conscious (as opposed to unconscious) mental life; see, for instance, Flanagan 1992; Strawson 1994; Siewert 1998; Horgan and Tienson 2002, 2005; Pitt 2004; and Horgan, Tienson, and Graham 2004.

If the advocates of cognitive phenomenology are right, then the explanation in section 5 of the non-grippingness of internal-world skepticism is directly extendable, mutatis mutandis, from the special case of direct COMS beliefs about sensory-experiential states to direct COMS beliefs about first-order mental states of all kinds. Cognitive and conative states are self-presenting, and they too serve as their own modes of presentation.[14] However, if the advocates of cognitive phenomenology are wrong, then as things now stand, there is evidently no adequate explanation for the non-grippingness of internal-world skepticism concerning direct COMS beliefs about one's current, occurrent cognitive and conative states. This dialectical state of affairs provides yet further reason, in addition to other arguments lately on offer, to believe in the reality of cognitive phenomenology.[15]

7　Conclusion

Skeptical doubt, in order to get a psychological grip, requires that there be a contrast space between what is and what is believed about what is. In the case of phenomenally conscious current mental states, there is no such contrast space; rather, what is phenomenally accords with what is believed about what is phenomenally. The former does not just cause the latter (in some sense), but rather partially *constitutes* it: what is phenomenally serves as mode of presentation in one's belief about what is phenomenally, thereby determining the very content of this belief. Beliefs of this kind cannot be radically mistaken. People appreciate this fact, and this is why internal-world skepticism gets no psychological grip.[16]

Notes

1. Our claim will be that radical skepticism concerning *certain* beliefs about one's mental life gets no grip psychologically, not that this non-grippingness pertains to *all* such beliefs; more on this below. Also, we do not claim that the pertinent beliefs are outright infallible; see notes 12 and 15 below.

2. Hereafter, for simplicity of formulation, we will use "current" to cover what is sometimes called the "specious present"; this includes the very recent past.

3. The point of the modifier "direct" is to distinguish the COMS beliefs we are focusing on from COMS beliefs that are generated via a process like conscious inference. For instance, one might form inferential or quasi-inferential beliefs about one's own *unconscious* COMSs—say, by reliance on some theory one accepts about subconscious cognitive processing. And it might even be possible to form nondirect, inferential or quasi-inferential beliefs about certain conscious COMSs. For instance, while one is engaged in hand-to-hand knife combat with an enemy terrorist, one might be so absorbed by the task that one does not notice the pain from a knife wound recently inflicted on oneself by the terrorist; yet in the throes of the fight, one might think to oneself (perhaps as a technique for staying calm and focused), "That nasty gash must hurt, even though this is the kind of situation where one tends not to notice such pains."

4. This approach is in the spirit of Burge (1988).

5. Both direct and quasi-direct COMS beliefs are indeed beliefs about one's own current, occurrent mental states. A quasi-direct COMS belief is spontaneous and noninferential, but lacks a feature that the account under consideration says is essential to full-fledged direct beliefs—viz., containing as a constituent the first-order mental state that the COMS belief is about. It bears emphasis that such a belief counts as merely quasi-direct, rather than as genuinely direct, *according to the account of direct beliefs now under consideration*.

6. See, for instance, Putnam 1981, and Chalmers 2005. We think such a view is deeply wrongheaded; see Horgan and Tienson 2002, and Horgan, Tienson, and Graham 2004. But our point here will be that wedding it to the constituency view of direct COMS states won't help anyway.

7. Careful construction of a radical deception scenario, so that the resulting scenario comports with strongly externalist accounts of mental content, should not be taken as an endorsement of such accounts. We ourselves would maintain that the palpable conceptual coherence of the more familiar scenarios used to pose the problem of radical external-world skepticism—Descartes's Evil Deceiver, an always-envatted brain—shows that strongly externalist theories of mental content are just wrong. (See Horgan, Tienson, and Graham 2004.) But our argument in the text strives to be neutral about the matter; hence the revised radical-deception scenario.

8. *Objection*: "But the *full* long-armed functional role of a direct COMS belief includes the fact that it contains as a constituent the first-order mental state that it is about." *Reply*: There is no principled basis to include such a fact as an aspect of long-armed functional role, rather than construing it as a fact about *implementation* of functional role. What matters functionally is that one's cognitive architecture is so structured that in general, a COMS belief occurs spontaneously and noninferentially only when the cognitive agent is currently undergoing a COMS belief of the kind that the COMS belief says she or he is currently undergoing. *How* this functional-role

requirement gets met is merely a matter of implementation. See step 2, just below in the text.

9. See also Brentano 1995, especially pp. 126–129. Whether our view is exactly like Brentano's is a matter of interpretation. Alexius Meinong too uses the term "self-presentation" and claims that mental states and all their parts (including their contents) are self-presenting; see, for instance, Meinong 1910/1983, pp. 190 ff. For Meinong on self-presentation see also Marek 2003.

10. Adverbial constructions are sometimes used to pick out the relevant feature of the experience itself—as in "experiencing redly." Special-purpose adjectives and nouns are sometimes used too, such as "reddish/reddishness" (see Levine 2001a).

11. For one illuminating elaboration of this generic idea, see Chalmers 2003.

12. Whether or not it can be *somewhat* mistaken, and if so in what ways, are issues we leave open here. Subtle questions arise, inter alia, about how to distinguish direct COMS beliefs—about which radical skepticism gets no grip—from other beliefs that are closely related but are also susceptible to radical skeptical doubts. Linguistic articulations of one's beliefs can blur these differences. For instance, when I express a belief by saying or thinking to myself "I am now in pain," the belief I thereby express might—or might not—carry the presupposition that the concept I am now expressing by "pain" is the one expressed by "pain" as used by others in my linguistic community and is also the concept that I myself express by "pain" at other moments in time. If it does carry this presupposition, then there is a possibility that I am radically mistaken in classifying my present state as a pain. If my belief does not carry this presupposition, however, then it cannot be radically mistaken.

13. We say *otherwise* functionally equivalent because we are leaving open whether or not phenomenal character itself is a matter of some kind of subtle functional role. We ourselves would deny this, but our argument in the present essay is neutral on the matter.

14. The term "cognitive" is often used contrastively vis-à-vis "conative," but also is often used as a broader rubric that subsumes both conative states and cognitive states (narrowly so-called). Lately the term "cognitive phenomenology" has been gaining currency, with "cognitive" intended in the broader sense.

15. A range of subtle issues arise concerning which kinds of belief about one's current mental life are susceptible to the grip of radical skepticism and which kinds are not. Let us briefly mention two aspects of this complex matter, in a way that connects it to other work of ours on cognitive phenomenology. First, in Horgan and Tienson 2002, it is argued that the phenomenology of undergoing an occurrent cognitive state typically has two discernible phenomenal aspects: (1) the what-it's-like of a cognitive state's having intentional content p (apart from the type of attitude it is—e.g., occurrently believing that p, occurrently wondering whether p), and (2) the what-it's-like

of the attitude type (e.g., thinking, wondering, doubting). A question arises about whether one's belief about which attitude-type is tokened by a current, occurrent mental state is susceptible to the grip of radical skepticism. Can I be sure, for example, that a particular mental state I'm now in that has content p is really a state of *wondering whether p*—as opposed, say, to a state of *doubting that p*? The answer may well depend on whether or not my present use of the phrase "wonder whether," and also the specific concept I am currently deploying that I now express with these words, carries certain presuppositions that are susceptible to the grip of Cartesian skepticism. (This is closely related to the remarks in note 12 above.) Second, in Horgan, Tienson, and Graham 2004, a distinction is made between two kinds of mental intentionality: *phenomenal* intentionality, which is constituted wholly phenomenally and is "narrow," and *externalistic* intentionality, which is constituted by the interaction of phenomenal intentionality and certain externalistic factors—and is "wide." Radical Cartesian doubts certainly can arise about whether my current mental states possess externalistic content at all (which they do not if I'm in an Evil Deceiver or brain-in-a-vat situation) and about what their specific externalistic content is. The kind of content that we would claim is not susceptible to the grip of radical skepticism, on the other hand, is the *phenomenal* intentionality of one's current conscious cognitive states.

16. This paper also appears in Marek and Reicher 2005. For helpful comments and discussion, we thank Jenann Ismael, Keith Lehrer, Jerrold Levinson, Matjaz Potrc, Charles Siewert, Houston Smit, Mark Timmons, Michael Tye, Timothy Williamson, and especially Uriah Kriegel. The underlying idea for this paper owes much to Levine (2001a, especially pp. 159–174).

Kathleen Wider

There have been philosophers, perhaps as far back as Aristotle, who have believed that one cannot be conscious without being conscious of oneself. Descartes, Locke, and Kant held such a view, and more recently philosophers in both the analytic and continental traditions have defended this view. Most who hold this position, in examining the source of self-awareness, focus on the thinking and knowing activity of the mind. Kant, for example, argues that the synthesis of the sensory input in the imagination is what produces both awareness of the world and awareness of the self as the owner of experience.

I agree with these philosophers that all consciousness involves consciousness of self, but I will argue that it is not the thinking activity of the mind alone that produces the most basic level of self-awareness. It is the affective nature of consciousness, which usually includes a cognitive element, that does. Using Thomas Nagel's (1974) terminology, I will argue there is always something it is like to be a subject of consciousness, to be me at this moment, here and now, and that "something it is like" is constituted by a feeling.[1] It is the emotional tinge that all conscious states have that produces a sense of the self as the owner of one's present experience. This most basic sense of self is rarely experienced in its pure state beyond early childhood, although it may be experienced in this way by people with certain kinds of memory loss. This feeling of the self is usually in the background of experience. On most occasions conscious attention is directed outward from oneself as the subject of consciousness, and so such self-awareness is usually pre-reflective rather than reflective.[2] Although it requires thought as an element of feeling, it does not require linguistic capacity.[3] There certainly are other elements of consciousness that contribute to the sense that an experience is one's own; but without the affective nature of consciousness, there is no sense of the ownership of experience, and with it there is always at least a *minimal* sense of ownership. Higher-level cognitive activity and linguistic abilities are no doubt important for more sophisticated levels of self-awareness and for an ongoing sense of oneself as the owner of one's experiences through time. But it is the affective nature of consciousness and its contribution to a basic level of self-consciousness upon which I will focus in this essay.[4]

In section 1, I specify the meaning of two key terms in my argument. In section 2, I review evidence from phenomenology, neuropsychology, and neuroscience that suggests that all consciousness has an affective nature. I argue, in section 3, that the affective quality of consciousness is a source of self-revelation and hence makes all conscious states self-conscious on the prereflective level. Finally, in the last section, I examine some objections to my position and respond to them.[5]

1   Mapping the Conceptual Terrain

Before I begin expounding my argument, let me clarify my use of two terms that play a central role in the argument: *self* and *emotion*. I am not claiming that my use of each term is the only use possible. I am simply indicating what use I am making of each term, so the claims I make in this essay will be understood.

What I mean by *self* when I argue that the affective nature of consciousness is the basis for a minimal level of self-awareness is the self that is present even when one's capacity to weave a narrative of oneself as existing through time has not yet developed or has been diminished or lost through a neurological disease or disorder. This self is the body as a presence to the world, that is, the self as embodied consciousness.[6] Awareness of this self is awareness of what it is like to be me, this bodily subject of consciousness, at this particular time and place.[7] This self-awareness is usually experienced within the context of a narrative of the self as lasting through time, but it is present even when the possibility for such a narrative is absent.

I will position my use of the term *emotion* in terms of a central question about emotion: Can one have an emotion without feeling it, that is, without being aware of it? There are two approaches to this question, one physiological and the other conceptual. What I am calling the physiological approach (for want of a better name) is the one that asks whether a person can have bodily responses to an emotion-inducer without being aware of those responses. William James (1884) answers no. James argues emotion and feeling are inseparable because the bodily changes produced by an emotion-inducer are always accompanied by an awareness of those changes. For James, every change in one's bodily state "is *felt*, acutely or obscurely, the moment it occurs" (James 1884, p. 192). So there can be no unconscious emotion.

Two of the most famous of present day neuroscientists working on emotion, Joseph LeDoux and Antonio Damasio, reject James's identification of emotion with feeling. Although LeDoux (1996) grants that bodily states play a role in emotions, he rejects James's definition of emotion as a conscious awareness of bodily responses to emotional stimuli in the environment. LeDoux argues that there are various emotional systems within the brain—different ones for fear, for sexual feeling, and so on—and it is the activity of one or more of those systems that produces certain bodily changes, for example, the increase in heart rate when one is afraid. The same activity that produces the bodily changes can produce feelings of fear, for example; but it does not always do so. There could be bodily changes in response to an emotional stimulus without a felt awareness of those changes. For LeDoux one can indeed have an emotion without a conscious experience of it (1996, pp. 17–20).

Damasio would agree. He has written extensively on the emotions, most notably to a general audience in the three books he has published since the mid-1990s: *Descartes' Error: Emotion, Reason, and the Human Brain* (1994); *The Feeling of What Happens: Body and Emotion in the Making of Consciousness* (1999); and *Looking for Spinoza: Joy, Sorrow, and the Feeling Brain* (2003). In his first book he does not directly address the issue of whether one can have an emotion without feeling it, although scattered remarks seem to indicate he believes it is possible but rare. He does offer distinct definitions for emotion and feeling in this work. An emotion is "a collection of changes occurring in both brain and body, usually prompted by a particular mental content" and a feeling is the perception of those changes (1994, p. 270).[8] In his second and third books he is explicit in his belief that unconscious emotions are possible. In these works he maintains his original distinction between emotions and feelings and claims that an emotion can exist without a feeling. That is, a stimulus may cause a collection of bodily responses to it in a particular person without the person perceiving those bodily responses.

The conceptual approach answers the question about whether one can have an emotion without feeling it by distinguishing between emotion as a disposition and emotion as an occurrent mental state. Three philosophers who have offered recent, detailed discussions of emotion are Richard Wollheim (1999), Peter Goldie (2000), and Martha Nussbaum (2001). All three believe one can have an emotion without feeling it. For Wollheim an emotion is a mental disposition, not a mental state, although it is closely related to mental states. A disposition (to feel fear in the presence of snakes, for example) can be initiated by, terminated in, reinforced or altered by, and manifests or expresses itself as a mental state. However, for Wollheim, an emotion is only derivatively a mental state. Although both a mental disposition and a mental state have intentionality and grades of consciousness (unconscious, preconscious, and conscious), only a mental state has subjectivity; there is something it is like to be in that state. So it is only when an emotion expresses itself that feeling (of fear for example) occurs. Consequently, for Wollheim, emotion and the feeling of an emotion are distinct although closely connected. Goldie distinguishes emotions from episodes of emotions, as Wollheim does, and believes, as Wollheim does, that one can have an emotion even when one is not currently experiencing it. Nussbaum shares with Wollheim and Goldie the distinction between an emotion and episodes of an emotion, although she makes that distinction in a slightly different way.[9]

I have spent so much time on the discussion of the distinction between a conscious and an unconscious emotion and between an emotion as a disposition and as an episode in order to make clear from the beginning that the affective quality that I argue all conscious states have is constituted by a *conscious* emotion. When I speak of a conscious emotion, I am referring to what James, LeDoux, and Damasio call a feeling and what Wollheim and Goldie refer to as an episode of an emotion.[10] I leave unaddressed the question of whether one could have an emotion and not feel it. In the context of my discussion of emotion and self-consciousness, I am interested only in emotional responses one does feel.

Therefore, when I use the term *emotion*, I should be taken to be using it as shorthand for all conscious affective states, including ones we usually call *moods*. Mood is typically contrasted with emotion because it is an affective experience that is usually less intense and longer lasting than an emotion. Irritability, certain kinds of depression, boredom, and anxiety are all examples of moods. Even happiness and sadness can be moods. Unlike emotions, moods are often characterized as objectless, although the distinction between a mood and an emotion is not a clear-cut one. A mood may give way to an emotion and vice versa. In the discussion that follows, then, my use of the term *emotion* can be taken to refer to conscious emotions or moods.

2   The Affective Quality of Consciousness

In this section, I offer evidence to support the plausibility of the belief that whenever one is conscious there is always a *how* one is as well as a *what* one is conscious of. This "how one is" is not simply what it is like to be a human or have human consciousness; nor is it simply what it is like to be conscious of what I am at present conscious of (the soothing tone of my friend's voice, for example). It is, as I said above, what it is like to be me at this particular time: this person, this body, this subject of consciousness at this time and place. Many factors, both inner and outer, contribute to the production of this feeling: ones we are conscious of and ones of which we are not conscious. Of course, being human and being currently conscious of a particular object (a thought, a memory, a distant vista, for example) will affect how it feels to be me—a subject of consciousness—at any given time, but neither of those factors constitute the feeling.

What it is like to be me is not some one something; it varies from day to day, even moment to moment. We wake up in a mood: on the wrong side of the bed, unaccountably happy or sad, ready to take on the world or to shrink from it. Before we have even begun to focus on our surroundings or the tasks of the day, we are in a mood. That is not to say we can always name the mood in which we find ourselves upon awakening. I might say, "I woke up in such an odd mood today," although I cannot say what that mood was exactly nor why I awoke in that mood. Our vocabulary for moods unattended by known causes is slim. As we go through the day, if we wish, we can answer at any time the question, "How do I feel?" Do I feel calm, tense, bored, neutral, blah, angry? I am not claiming that we always have a word for how we feel or that there are not some people who are better at paying attention to their moods and emotions than others. My claim is simply that we never find ourselves without a mood or emotion, without some affective quality to our awareness, although we are frequently only prereflectively aware of this quality. To add plausibility to this claim, I will look at Heidegger's phenomenological analysis of mood as well as evidence from neuropsychology, including dream research, and from neuroscience.

2.1 Phenomenology

Since I began teaching existentialism many years ago, I have been intrigued by Heidegger's discussion of mood and self-disclosure. In *Being and Time*, Heidegger questions the meaning of Being as such by questioning a particular kind of being: human being—what he calls Dasein, literally, "being there." A phenomenological analysis of Dasein reveals that Dasein always finds itself there: in the world, in one mood or another, and never without a mood. Heidegger uses the German term *Befindlichkeit*, which is often translated as "the state of mind in which one may be found," although some scholars (Kaelin [1988] and Nicholson [1986]) prefer to translate the German as "affectivity" to avoid the connotation that a mood is a characteristic of a disembodied mind, since Heidegger rejects such a Cartesian view. For Heidegger mood is something I find myself in, not something I choose. I might try to fight it or change it or enjoy it, and I may be more or less successful. Nonetheless I *find* myself in a mood and I may have no idea of its cause. This characteristic of Dasein reveals to each person what Heidegger calls one's "thrownness" into the world. One finds oneself there in the world. Mood discloses one's being "delivered over to," abandoned if you will, to a world and a self one did not make. Mood is not a knowledge one comes to but a lived experience of being human.[11] Mood makes one present to oneself as well as to the world.[12]

2.2 Neuropsychology

William James was perhaps the first in the modern era to claim that all consciousness is affective in nature. But today there is a growing number of scientists and philosophers who argue for that claim, relying on evidence from various branches of the cognitive sciences, including the neurosciences and experimental psychology.[13] In this section I will focus on the neuropsychological evidence Damasio presents in *The Feeling of What Happens* for his position that consciousness depends on emotion. To understand this position, one must understand his distinction between core and extended consciousness. For Damasio (1999) there are different levels of self: proto-self, core self, and autobiographical self. We have no consciousness of the proto-self, which is a neural representation of the body at any given moment. It is only when the body interacts with its environment and its neural representation is thus modified that self-consciousness appears. He calls this level of consciousness *core consciousness*, and it is consciousness of both the object of consciousness and the subject of consciousness (the body) simultaneously. Core consciousness provides one with a sense of self here and now: "Core consciousness does not illuminate the future, and the only past it vaguely lets us glimpse is that which occurred in the instant just before" (1999, p. 16). Extended consciousness, on the other hand, has many levels and grades. It gives one a sense of oneself as a person situated in time with a sense of one's own personal history, an awareness of one's present position in the world, and anticipations of the future (ibid.). With extended consciousness, which relies on conventional and working memory and is enhanced by language, an autobiographical self comes into being.

Damasio claims that even if all other emotional capacities are damaged by neurological disease, what he calls "background emotions" survive (ibid., p. 53). These are emotions, as the name implies, that are in the background;

so we are not usually reflectively aware of them.[14] He distinguishes them from basic and secondary emotions. Such background emotions—for example, that a person is tense, edgy, down, or cheerful—may be detected, he says, by such things as a person's tone of voice, manner of carrying her body, and/or speed of her movements (ibid., p. 52).[15] Background emotions remain even if there is a loss of extended consciousness such that only core consciousness remains. But all emotions, including background emotions, disappear with the disappearance of consciousness. Damasio uses cases where both consciousness and emotion disappear together as evidence for his view that consciousness depends on emotion. For Damasio, emotion, as a collection of physical changes in the body and brain, can exist without consciousness; but the reverse appears not to be the case.[16] To support his view that consciousness cannot exist without emotion, he gives detailed descriptions of cases where both emotion and consciousness, including core consciousness, disappear and yet the patient remains awake.[17] I will discuss the first two kinds of cases he examines: epileptic absence seizures followed by epileptic automatism and akinetic mutism.

In epileptic absence seizures the patient freezes, but remains awake. She does not fall over or have convulsions; the eyes remain open and muscle tone is maintained. Sometimes these seizures are followed by absence automatism in which the patient begins to perform actions such as getting dressed, moving about, getting a drink, and so on. During the episode Damasio describes, and by implication all the cases he has witnessed, the patient shows no signs of emotions at all. When the episode ends and consciousness returns, the patient has no recollection of what happened during the seizure and the period of automatism (ibid., pp. 96–101).

Damasio offers a second type of case of wakefulness without consciousness: akinetic mutism. Again he gives the details of one particular case to illustrate the condition and the absence of emotion along with the absence of consciousness. Patients with this condition, although awake and capable of movement, fail to initiate movement, and they rarely if ever speak. When the patient he describes came back to life, so to speak, she reported that she remembered no experiences, emotional or otherwise, during the months she was in this condition (ibid., pp. 101–103).

I have argued elsewhere (Wider 1997, pp. 167–168) that the inability to report on one's experience after it has occurred is an insufficient criterion for establishing a lack of consciousness during such episodes. However, in the cases Damasio describes, he appeals not only to this criterion but also to his attempts at interaction with the patients *during* the episode to support his characterization of these cases as cases of unconsciousness.

Damasio (1999) also looks at cases where extended consciousness is impaired but core consciousness remains, and emotional reactions, along with a sense of self, are still present. One such example is his discussion of transient global amnesia (1999, pp. 202–209). Patients with this condition are not "zombies" in the way patients with the conditions discussed above are. Although extended consciousness and a sense of one's autobiographical self is diminished or extinguished, such patients still retain core consciousness, expressions of emotion, and a sense of the self in the here and now. He refers the reader as well to his discussions of cases of a reverse type in Damasio 1994, in which patients suffer impairment but not complete loss of their emotional capacities without suffering loss of consciousness.

In summary, Damasio reviews (1) cases where consciousness and emotion disappear together, (2) cases where consciousness is impaired but not removed and feelings remain, and (3) cases where there is partial impairment of emotional capacity without loss of consciousness. He offers both third-person evidence of behaviors during the conditions and the reports of the patients themselves either after they "come to" (in the first kind of case) or while they are in the condition (in the second and third kinds of case) to support his claim that consciousness and emotion disappear together and return together. Such evidence alone does not *prove* that emotion is necessary for consciousness, but it adds support for that claim.[18]

2.3 Dream Research

J. Allan Hobson, a dream researcher at Harvard, argues that emotions are part of all our conscious states including our dream states. They are a way of both perceiving and orienting ourselves to the world. In fact he believes emotion is "an essential building block of our conscious states" (Hobson 1999, p. 151). He and his team at Harvard have studied a large sample of individuals, having them record their dreams and then write next to each line of their descriptions of their dreams what emotions they were feeling and at what intensity. Emotion was an element in all parts of the subjects' dreams. Dreams, he believes, help us to rehearse strategies for reacting to emotional responses we may experience towards things or events in our waking environment. Whatever the function of dreams may be, his research provides support that even dreaming consciousness has an affective quality.

2.4 Neuroscience

The central claim of my essay is that it is the affective nature of consciousness that makes all conscious states self-conscious. If this thesis is true, then there must be structures in the brain that bind together consciousness, emotion, and a sense of self as the owner of one's experience. Jaak Panksepp, who has been working in the field of affective neuroscience for the past thirty years, proposes, as does Damasio, such a theory. Both acknowledge that at this stage in the investigation of the brain their respective theories can only be offered as speculative hypotheses about how the brain operates to produce consciousness, affect, and self-awareness; but they offer these hypotheses as the foundation for concrete research programs in neuroscience.[19] I will examine Panksepp's theory, which he began developing over two decades ago and has been refining ever since. Panksepp, like William James and Damasio, believes that "every moment of our conscious lives is undergirded by feelings" (1998a, p. 567). He distinguishes various levels of consciousness and examines in detail what he calls primary process consciousness, a pre-propositional form of consciousness which he believes is the foundation for all higher forms of consciousness. This primary process consciousness is linked to emotional systems in the brain and to motor areas. This allows the organism to evaluate action alternatives in terms of their efficacy in serving its survival needs. This type of consciousness generates "that ineffable feeling of experiencing oneself as an active agent in the perceived events of the world" (1998b, p. 310). This primitive affective consciousness is the foundation of our felt sense of self. At its center is what he calls the primal SELF, which stands for "simple ego-type life form" (1998b, p. 309). He describes this SELF as "the neurosymbolic representation of the primordial body" (2000, p. 36). It is this body representation that provides the neural underpinnings for a primitive level of emotional self-awareness.

Panksepp (1998b) gives the details of his theory, offering as a provisional hypothesis that "the foundation of the most basic form of conscious activity, the generation of SELF-representation along with various basic affective states, arises from the intrinsic neurodynamics of the PAG [periaqueductal gray], as well as the direct extensions of this tissue upward in the brain to intralaminar and midline thalamic areas, to widespread hypothalamic areas, to the various branches of the cerebral canopy" (1998b, p. 314). He notes that there is neuropsychological and neurobehavioral evidence consistent with this hypothesis. When the intrinsic, subcortical, emotional systems are electrically stimulated, people report experience that has a feeling of belonging to them as opposed to its feeling artificially imposed (2000, pp. 19, 23). It should also be the case, if his hypothesis is true, that if there is neurological damage to areas of the brain that generate feelings then one's sense of self should diminish. The cases of neurological damage that Damasio (1999, pp. 96–103, 202–209) and others have examined support this prediction. In addition, damage to PAG in cats and monkeys produces deficits in consciousness, including an absence of responsiveness to emotional stimuli. It is also the case that lower levels of electrical stimulation to this brain area produce a greater variety of emotional responses than stimulation to any other area of the brain (Panksepp 1998b, pp. 312–314). Panksepp does not deny that cortical activity is necessary to generate the autobiographical self, but he claims this self rests on the activity of subcortical systems, which generate primitive affective consciousness and the sense of self as the owner of one's experience that accompanies such consciousness.[20]

My intention in this section has not been to argue that this theory is correct. As I noted earlier, even its proponent acknowledges that it is much too soon to offer any such theory as definitive. But it does offer at least a plausible early attempt to create an empirically testable theory of how the brain works such that it can underpin the tightly woven interconnections between consciousness, affect, and self-awareness for which I am arguing.

3 Self-Consciousness and Emotion

As I argued in the preceding section, evidence suggests that all conscious states have an affective quality. I argue in this section that there are two reasons why the affective nature of consciousness is the source of at least a minimal sense of self-consciousness.[21] The first reason is that emotions affect how one experiences the world, and because of that consciousness of the world reveals to the subject of consciousness how it is with her now. The second reason is that emotions involve bodily feelings and so make one aware of oneself as a *bodily* subject of consciousness. Let me explain each reason in turn and then draw the two together.

It is because of the nature of emotion that its presence as a quality of consciousness affects one's consciousness of the world.[22] An emotion is an attitude or orientation of a particular person toward the world. Both Wollheim (1999) and Goldie (2000) argue for this view of emotion and against earlier belief/desire propositional attitude accounts of emotion. They argue that although having an emotion often involves beliefs and desires, they are not sufficient for an emotion since they can be explained without reference to what it is like to have an emotion from the point of view or perspective of the person whose emotion it is. But such a perspective, they believe, is of the essence of an emotion. That is why Goldie argues that feelings are a more fundamental intentional element to emotional experience than beliefs or desires because feelings embody a point of view or perspective on the object of the emotion. For Goldie, every feeling is an attitude of some sort (2000, p. 81). Wollheim takes a similar line: although desire and belief figure in the originating conditions of an emotion, and an emotion can generate desires that (combined with the right beliefs) could lead to action, the emotion itself is neither a belief nor a desire. At its core an emotion is an attitude, an orientation toward the world. For Wollheim, an emotion is the transformation of the original experience of the frustration or satisfaction of a desire into an attitude that colors the world: "If belief maps the world, and desire targets it, emotion tints and colors it" (1999, p. 15). The personal element is central to the nature of emotion for Nussbaum (2001) as well. What distinguishes the various emotions from each other is not simply the object of the emotion, but how a particular person sees the object. Emotions are always tied to a particular person's goals and ends; they embody a particular person's way of seeing.

Because an emotion is an attitude toward the world, a way of seeing the world relative to one's desires and goals, and because some affective quality characterizes all conscious states, whenever I am conscious of an object, such consciousness is never impersonal. It is always *my* consciousness of the object in question, *my* way of experiencing the object. Because of this, how I experience the objects of consciousness at a particular time is a mode of self-revelation. It reveals to me how it is with me—a subject of consciousness—at this time.

When I speak of the affective nature of consciousness being the source of a revelation of oneself at *this* time, the time referred to could be a second, a day, or even longer. In the course of a normal day, one usually undergoes a wide variety of emotional experiences. I might begin the day anxious about a paper I have to deliver later that day; but then, as I am distracted by the news on the television, my emotional state may change to one of anger. Over breakfast I may have a conversation with a colleague that sparks laughter on my part and lightens my experience of other things. Tracking the rapidity of these changes is as difficult as the task James Joyce set himself in reproducing the stream of consciousness of his characters in *Ulysses*.

Sometimes, however, a particular emotion is so intense and lasts long enough that it can affect my consciousness of almost everything I experience throughout a day or even longer. It is easier to see in a case such as this how an emotion is an attitude toward the world. If my anger, for example, is pervasive enough, it can seem that everyone and everything is working against my goals. The driver who has just moved into my lane has *purposely* cut me off. My children have the volume on the television turned up high to irritate me; even the carpet I trip over has, I feel, tripped me. Everything of which I am aware is present to me in a certain way in part because of my emotional state.[23] When one experiences the intense feeling of romantic love, everything becomes sexualized in the sense that the experience of the carnality of the world, including one's own body, is heightened. The seventeenth-century metaphysical poets are famous for showing, by the use of poetic conceit, how one's emotional state transforms the world. Consider John Donne's poem "The Sunne Rising" (1933). Because the lover in the poem wants more time for lovemaking, the sun is seen as a "busie old foole" (1933, p. 10). The lovers' bed is not only the center of the world to them, but also the whole of the world. When I am bored, everything I experience is boring: an event I am watching, a conversation I am having, even my own thoughts.

The reason these and other states of affect reveal me to myself is that I am *prereflectively* conscious of *myself* as bored or angry, for example, *in being conscious of* everything I experience as boring or as frustrating of my desires and goals. It is in virtue of the affective quality of consciousness that whenever I am conscious, I am prereflectively conscious of how it is with me now.

It is also the case that the affective nature of consciousness in making me conscious of myself as bored or angry, for example, makes me *at the same time* conscious of myself as a *bodily* subject of consciousness, since bodily feelings are necessary for the conscious emotion that constitutes the affective quality of consciousness at any given time. I am not defending James's position that all bodily responses to emotional stimuli are felt. My claim is that conscious emotions involve an awareness of at least one or more of the bodily responses that are triggered by an emotional stimulus. Both LeDoux and Damasio, reviewing evidence from affective neuroscience, hold that it is changes in the body, including or limited solely to brain activity, that may—although they do not always—cause the feeling of an emotion.[24] Damasio (1994, pp. 135–139) describes the variety of possible types of bodily responses to real or imagined emotion-inducers. Such responses may include an increase in one's heart rate, the flushing of the skin, the tightening or relaxing of various muscles in different parts of the body, and so on. For Damasio, as I noted above, a feeling is a perception of those changes.[25] For LeDoux (1996, pp. 296–299) the connection between feeling and the body's responses to emotional stimuli is more indirect. However, LeDoux does say that "the body is crucial to an emotional experience, either because it provides sensations that make an emotion feel a certain way right now or because it once provided the sensations that created memories of what specific emotions felt like in the past" (1996, p. 298). So for LeDoux, bodily sensations, present or remembered, are necessary for a conscious experience of an emotion.

Many philosophers, however, especially in the second half of the twentieth century, rejected the view that bodily feelings are necessary for a particular emotion to occur. They argued that no particular bodily responses are necessary for a particular emotion to occur,[26] but that certain propositional attitudes are necessary for the occurrence of a particular emotion. The connection between a certain response of the autonomic nervous system, for example, and emotion A is contingent. However, the connection between certain beliefs, or beliefs and desires, and emotion A is necessary. So the set of bodily responses S, although perhaps associated with A, is not part of what A is, not part of the meaning of A, since A could occur without S. Fear of a lion, for example, is simply the belief that a lion is dangerous, or, that belief combined with the desire to avoid dangerous things. Paul Griffiths (1997, ch. 2) does an excellent job of reviewing the standard objections to these propositional attitude accounts of emotion. One objection that is particularly relevant to my argument is that such accounts leave out an element essential to conscious emotion: bodily feeling. There is still strong resistance among many philosophers to the idea that bodily feelings are necessary for the occurrence of conscious emotions. There are more recent theories of emotion that, while rejecting the traditional propositional attitude accounts of emotion, share at least one belief in common with those accounts: bodily feelings are neither necessary nor sufficient for an emotional experience.

Nussbaum calls her theory of emotion a "cognitive-evaluative" view of emotions (2001, p. 23). For Nussbaum, emotions are judgments of value about things that are important to our well-being; these are usually things we do not fully control, and so emotions make apparent our neediness and our lack of self-sufficiency. Emotions are not thought plus something else (feeling, movement, etc.). They just are thoughts of a certain sort; they are constituted by our beliefs about the value of things that are important to our flourishing. Thought can be dynamic; it can move slowly or quickly, hesitantly or directly, she argues. That is at least one reason why we associate feeling with emotion; but unless the feeling is part of the movement of thought, it is not part of an emotion. Nussbaum stresses, as Wollheim and Goldie do, the intentionality of emotion; an emotion is about something. But she goes on to argue that bodily states (agitation, trembling, etc.) have no object and hence are not part of emotion and so are unnecessary for emotion.

I grant that bodily feelings alone rarely if ever constitute an emotion, but I think Nussbaum has gone too far in claiming that they are unnecessary for emotion. She acknowledges that thoughts are bodily states. She is right. A characterization of my thoughts as racing is as much a description of my bodily feelings as is a characterization of my heart as racing. I think the refusal to accept this characterization in terms of thought arises from separating the body and the brain in much too stark a fashion.[27]

Goldie (2000), as I mentioned above, rejects traditional propositional attitude accounts of emotion because they leave out feelings. However, for Goldie, the feelings that are necessary for emotional experience are not bodily feelings. He argues that although bodily feelings may frequently occur as part of an emotional experience, they are neither necessary nor sufficient for such an experience because (1) an emotional trigger can cause bodily changes in a person without that person being conscious of those changes, and (2) there are emotions that lack associated bodily feelings, "perhaps pride" (2000, p. 52), he says.

I grant that one can have a bodily response to an emotional trigger and be unaware of it. It is not my claim that one must be aware of *all* bodily responses to an emotional trigger in order to experience a conscious emotional response to that stimulus. However, if the person is aware of none of the bodily responses, I contend that no conscious emotion occurs. Unless one is aware of at least one bodily response to an emotional trigger (the tightening of the stomach or face muscles, the pounding of the heart, or the speeding-up of thought, for example), one does not have a conscious emotional experience. The body may be processing input that triggers activation in the emotional centers in the brain, but that alone is insufficient to bring about a conscious emotional experience.

Goldie offers pride as a possible example of an emotion that does not involve bodily feelings. I disagree, if we are speaking of an episode of pride rather than referring to pride as simply a disposition. We describe pride in physical terms: his chest is puffed up with pride. We use metaphors of this kind for a reason. They capture what the bodily feeling is like when one is actually experiencing pride.

Finally, Goldie is unsuccessful in distinguishing what he calls "feelings toward," which are essential to emotional experiences, from bodily feelings. On Goldie's account, bodily feelings are such things as a racing heart or sweaty palms, but having a "feeling toward" an object is thinking of it with feeling. He acknowledges one can think of pudding, for example, as disgusting without having feelings of disgust toward it. But then what are these feelings that are necessary for the experience of disgust, if not bodily feelings? His answer is that one cannot really say; it is like trying to explain what it is like to be angry or afraid or in love. If you have experienced these, then you know what they are like. Otherwise, perhaps all I can do, according to

Goldie, is direct you to literature to give you some idea of them. That is not a very satisfactory answer from a philosophical point of view.

One of the most common arguments used to support the view that bodily feelings are not an essential element of emotional experience is one that is used by traditional propositional attitude theorists as well as by Nussbaum and Goldie. It goes as follows: Emotions have intentionality. Bodily feelings do not. Therefore, bodily feelings are neither necessary nor sufficient for emotion. There have been counterexamples offered against both premises. Griffiths (1997, p. 28) gives a list of emotions that may occur without any intentional object: depression, elation, and anxiety, for example. Wollheim (1999, p. 118) offers an example of bodily feelings that do have intentionality: "when our fingers register a particular kind of silk." Even if these counterexamples fail, at most the argument proves that bodily feelings are not sufficient for emotion to occur. But my argument does not entail that they be sufficient for an emotional experience to occur.

Among recent philosophical analyses of emotion, Wollheim gives perhaps the most nuanced and careful analysis of the proper place of bodily feeling within emotion. He maintains the spirit of James in accepting bodily feelings as essential to emotion without regarding them as the whole of emotion. I am defending no particular account of the role of bodily feelings in emotion. I am simply arguing that they do have a role. Bodily feelings are essential to conscious emotions and the role such emotions play in self-awareness. Because bodily feelings are always a part of conscious emotion and because such emotions constitute the affective nature of consciousness, all conscious states make me, at least prereflectively, aware of myself as an embodied consciousness.

It is the affective nature of consciousness that makes all consciousness self-consciousness. It does so because it is at least one source of the double-directedness of consciousness.[28] Consciousness points outward to the object of awareness. However, given that its objects are always experienced in a certain way because of the affective quality of a particular person's consciousness at a particular time, it also points back to the subject of consciousness, the owner of the experience, and how it is with her now. Since how it is with the subject of consciousness now is constituted, at least in part, by bodily feelings, all consciousness points back to the self as a bodily subject of consciousness. Of course, the affective nature of consciousness contributes to more than just an awareness of a momentary self. Normally the self-revelation that is part of any state of consciousness is woven into and understood in light of a narrative of one's life.[29] But even if all the self there is, either because of infancy or a neurological disease or disorder, is a short-lived self, consciousness is still a revelation of that self. One is always, at least prereflectively, in the presence of oneself in being present to the world. The affective nature of consciousness, which ensures such presence to oneself, is what makes a conscious state mine. If it is the case, as evidence suggests, that all consciousness has an affective quality, then whenever I am conscious there is always, as I have argued above, a "how it is with me" as the subject of consciousness as well as an object of which I am conscious. It is my present emotional state as an embodied consciousness that affects how I experience the world at this time. In doing so, it makes such experience mine, and, at the same time, such experience reflects back to me how it is with me now. Consciousness always involves a two-way flow between the world and myself.

4 Objections and Replies

I can see in my mind's eye those hands up anxious to raise objections to my position. Are you really willing to accept that infants and at least some nonhuman animals are self-conscious? What about quadriplegics? They don't feel their body and yet they experience emotions and have a sense of self. I would agree that if I am right in my characterization of this basic level of self-consciousness, then infants possess such self-awareness. Animals do too if they are capable of affective experience. However, I will leave the nonhuman animals aside and focus on human infants. Nussbaum (2001) argues convincingly that although infants in the first few months of life have no definite sense of themselves or objects as substances that endure through time, they do have a definite enough awareness of themselves and objects in the world to make appraisals of things as good or bad relative to their needs for security and well-being, although such appraisals cannot, at that stage, be expressed in linguistic form. Infants have both emotions and a sense of self. These two go hand in hand, since making appraisals of what things in my environment are good or bad requires an appraisal of what is good or bad from my perspective, that is, for me. At this stage survival needs are the dominant—perhaps the only—goals directing these appraisals.[30]

Earlier I said that emotions generally involve cognition as well as feeling and so self-consciousness would as well. But can infants really make cognitive judgments? Unless the answer is yes, they cannot be said to be self-conscious. José Luis Bermúdez in *The Paradox of Self-Consciousness* (1998) argues at length that they can. In chapter 1 he offers a careful review of the literature on self-consciousness rooted in linguistic analysis and associated with many analytic philosophers of the last half-century. These are philosophers who hold that self-consciousness requires the ability to use the first-person pronoun to ascribe predicates to oneself and the ability to think "I-thoughts." Bermúdez argues that this kind of explanation is insufficient to explain the most basic level of self-consciousness. He raises what he calls the acquisition problem: How can a child come to have a form of self-consciousness that requires language mastery if she does not have self-consciousness to begin with? To explain the mastery of the first-person pronoun by reference to a capacity for "I-thoughts" and to explain the capacity for "I-thoughts" in terms of the linguistic capacity for self-ascription, as many analytic philosophers do according to Bermúdez, is explanatorily circular.

In order to overcome the acquisition problem, Bermúdez argues there must be prelinguistic forms of self-consciousness that form the basis for the mastery of the first-person pronoun in the normal course of development (Bermúdez 1998, pp. 76–77).[31] In chapter 3 of his book, he offers evidence from both infant research as well as paleoneurology and comparative primate neuroanatomy to support his contention that cognitive abilities emerge prior to language development both ontogenetically and phylogenetically. Bermúdez's arguments and the empirical evidence he reviews are given to support two important points: (1) there are multiple levels of self-consciousness, and (2) the higher levels ultimately rest on a level that involves a nonlinguistic, first-person perspective. Although Bermúdez is not arguing as I do that the most basic level of self-consciousness arises from the affective nature of consciousness, he does ground the first-person perspective in pre-linguistic, cognitive abilities.

Studies of infants' capacity to imitate the facial expressions and gestures of adults provide another source of support for the belief that even very young infants have a form of self-consciousness. Piaget argued that infants were incapable of what he called "invisible imitation" until they were at least eight to twelve months old. He contrasted this form of imitation with what he called "manual imitation." Psychologists Andrew Meltzoff and Keith Moore have studied infants' ability at invisible imitation and have shown that Piaget's position is incorrect. They describe the difference between invisible and manual imitation this way: in manual imitation a child imitates an adult action that can be seen by the infant when performed by itself as well as when performed by the adult. Imitating the hand movements of an adult would be an example of this type of imitation. The child can use visual input to guide its imitative behavior. But in invisible imitation the child is imitating behavior that it cannot see in its own case. Imitations of facial expressions and gestures are forms of invisible imitation. The child must imitate an action it can see the adult perform but which it cannot see itself perform. The infant must match a behavior of its own, which is felt kinesthetically, with a behavior of another, which it sees (Meltzoff and Moore 1995, p. 49).

As Meltzoff and Moore (1992) point out, classical psychological theories argued that this kind of imitation must come later than manual imitation because of its sophistication and because it requires learning from experience of oneself in mirrors and manual exploration of one's own and others' faces. Many earlier studies of the development of a sense of self in infants focused on the exhibition of self-recognition in the mirror test. This is a test used with chimps and modified for human infants in which a red mark is applied to the subject's forehead and ear, and self-recognition is thought to be present if the subject looks in the mirror and reaches up to touch the mark on its own head (Meltzoff 1990). Infants fail this test until they are eighteen to twenty-four months old (Butterworth 1990). Meltzoff and Moore (1977) argue that studies of imitation and related phenomena in infants indicate an earlier, more primitive notion of self than that exhibited in mirror studies. Such imitation is not a reflex action since when infants are delayed in attempting to imitate the adult, they resume their attempt after the delay (Meltzoff and Moore 1977). A 1982 study showed that newborns whose average age was thirty-six hours could discriminate and imitate three facial expressions (all of which were emotional expressions): happy, sad, and surprised (Field et al. 1982). A later study showed that infants as young as forty-two *minutes* old could imitate adult facial gestures and that they worked at the gesture until it matched the adults' (Meltzoff and Moore 1983).[32] Since such imitation requires distinguishing between as well as matching the *feel* of one's own body and the *look* of the other's body, it stands to reason that the most basic sense of self is that which is grounded in the experience of one's own body.

If I am right in my characterization of basic self-consciousness, then patients, even those with severe long-term memory deficits, should be able to experience emotions and have a sense of self, although it may be a sense of only a momentary or abbreviated self depending on how extensive the damage is to the person's long-term memory system. Most patients with such neurological damage retain memory for events before the occurrence of the injury or onset of the disease that deprived them of their ability to retain new experiences in memory. Daniel Schacter (1996, pp. 134–137), a well-known memory researcher, recounts the case of Frederick, who was in the early stages of Alzheimer's disease, but already suffering severe loss to his capacity to lay down new memories of events. Schacter invited Frederick to play golf one day to test his memory skills. Frederick could remember how to play golf and the language of golf, but in a few minutes after teeing off or putting, he would forget he had done so. When he had one particularly good shot, over water and onto the green, he expressed excitement and began to think about *his* next shot. But immediately after Schacter teed off, Frederick set up his ball in order to tee off again from the same hole. He had completely forgotten his magnificent drive of a few minutes earlier and he had forgotten his emotional reaction to it. The deterioration of episodic memory, the kind of memory deficit Frederick exhibited, increases as the disease progresses and diminishes the sense of self. However, it does not extinguish that sense altogether until a person reaches the end-stage of the disease when she enters a state similar to that of epileptic automatism. At this stage the person may be awake at times but consciousness disappears (Damasio 1999, pp. 104–105). This should be the case given my thesis. As long as there is consciousness and affect, a sense of self, at least in a minimal sense, should remain. When they disappear it should disappear as well.

Since I have argued above that a basic self-consciousness rests, at least in part, on our ability to experience our own body, it should also be the case that with a loss of the feeling of one's body, there should be a corresponding loss of the sense of self. Oliver Sacks (1985, pp. 42–52) describes such a case. Christina was a patient of Sacks who suddenly lost proprioception, our "sixth" sense, by which we monitor and adjust the position, tone, and motion of our muscles, tendons, and joints. She described her situation phenomenologically as a state of disembodiment. She said she could no longer feel her body and she experienced this loss of her connection with her body as a profound loss of self. Sacks notes that those with high transections of the spinal cord also experience this feeling of disembodiment. But neither Christina nor those with spinal cord damage completely lose their sense of self or their ability to experience emotions.

Nussbaum (2001, p. 58), among others, argues that quadriplegics offer a counterexample to the view that a feeling of one's body is an essential ingredient of emotion. Both LeDoux (1996, p. 294) and Damasio (1999, pp. 289–294) explain why these cases cannot work as counterexamples to that view. Such patients still retain the capacity for a full range of emotional experience because (1) spinal cord injury does not damage the vagus nerve through which much information between the body and the brain passes; (2) information between the body and the brain is also conveyed through the bloodstream by means of peptides and hormones; and (3) the connections between the facial nerves and the brain are direct and do not use the spinal cord. Hobson (1999, p. 155) makes a point similar to Nussbaum's, arguing

that dream emotion provides proof that bodily sensations are neither necessary nor sufficient for emotions. When we sleep, the brain is not receiving
input from the body and yet we still experience emotions. I think one could
use against this possible counterexample a modified version of the argument
that LeDoux and Damasio use in the case of quadriplegics. The possibility
of information being exchanged between the body and the brain via the
bloodstream remains present even while we sleep.

If I am correct in arguing that self-awareness at its most basic level is a
presence to oneself as a conscious, bodily orientation toward the world, then
it should follow that the more intense one's experience of an emotion is, the
more intense the experience of oneself as an embodied subject of experience.
I think this fits with the facts. When we are swept up in an intense experience of one of the basic emotions—anger, fear, love, hate, disgust—we have
a heightened sense of our own body. In fear, for example, we become hyper-
aware of our embodied, conscious existence because of the strong bodily
feelings that particular emotion involves and because we experience a threat
to ourselves and our ends and goals.[33] Even moods can heighten our sense
of our embodied self. In depression the body feels heavy and the world
dulled. The possibility of reaching one's goals appears diminished. In con-
tentment the body feels light and balanced. The world appears benevolent
and seems to bend more easily to our desires. Jean-Paul Sartre (1956) gives
a powerful phenomenological description of an experience of shame and its
relation to the shamed person's experience of his embodied self, a self with
its own ends now thwarted and transformed by another. Neuroscientist
Susan Greenfield (2000) argues the more emotional one is, the less self-
conscious. This position appears in direct opposition to my own. She
describes intense experiences of emotions as a loss of self. But her descriptions of examples such as bungee jumping make it clear that what she thinks
is temporarily lost in these cases is consciousness of the autobiographical
self, not of the self of the here and now. I am arguing that intense emotional
experiences make you more than ever present to the core self. This self is
the basis for any other sense of self.

The affective nature of consciousness, which I have argued is the root
of a basic form of self-consciousness, also contributes directly I think to an
ongoing sense of self, the autobiographical self, but in a much more complex
way. To understand how this is the case would require spelling out exactly
what is involved in this sense of oneself as enduring through time. This higher
form of self-consciousness involves of course more than just affect; it makes
use of language and other developed cognitive skills as well. In this essay, I
have confined my argument to a defense of the view that the affective nature

of consciousness generates a consciousness of the self of this moment. I leave unexplored the question of how more sophisticated forms of self-consciousness arise from this basic form and what neural mechanisms might give rise to these higher levels.[34] I also leave aside the question of whether understanding the neural substrates of this basic form of self-awareness would allow us to overcome the explanatory gap. Finally, I take no stand on whether nonhuman animals also have something akin to this basic form of self-awareness, although I am inclined to believe members of at least some species do.

I will end as I began, with Kant, who argued that we meet the human dimensions of our knowledge in our experience of the world. The ordering forms of our sensations, time and space, as well as the inborn conceptual apparatus we bring to our experiences are revealed in our consciousness of the world. My purpose in this essay has not been to defeat this Kantian claim, but to argue for a more powerful experience of the self in our experience of the world. Since all consciousness is tinged with emotion, all experience carries the affective state of the organism into the environment. In seeing the world as gray or brilliantly lit, for example, we see ourselves written into the language of the external.

Notes

1. I will argue in section 3 that this feeling involves both thought and bodily feelings. I will spell out in sections 1 and 3 exactly what I mean by "me at this moment." I am using Nagel's terminology but not for the same purpose for which he uses it. He uses it to argue that the subjective character of experience (what the experience is like for the creature whose experience it is) can never be fully captured by an objective, scientific account. I agree with Nagel that there is always "something it is like" for a creature to be a subject of consciousness; however, I am using his terminology to argue that all consciousness is self-consciousness, which is not a conclusion to which he explicitly commits himself.

2. In a prereflective conscious state, one is engaged with the world or the object of consciousness, whatever that object is. One is not focusing on oneself as the subject of consciousness or on the present state of consciousness itself. But with reflective consciousness one turns to oneself as the subject of consciousness or to a specific previous state of consciousness. For example, I may be absorbed in watching a sunset; if I then turn to examine the experience of watching the sunset or myself as the one watching the sunset, I have moved to the level of reflective consciousness. Writers often identify reflective consciousness with self-consciousness. But I am arguing that there is a kind of self-consciousness present even at the prereflective level, and that this is because of the affective nature of all consciousness.

3. It may be that to make such self-awareness available to reflective consciousness would require linguistic ability, but I won't decide that issue here.

4. There has been much study of the role of emotion in motivating action, in storing and retrieving memories, and in focusing attention. But until recently there has been almost no attention to its role in self-awareness.

5. I wish to thank Ken Williford for very helpful suggestions on an earlier draft of this essay.

6. I use *consciousness* in two senses. One sense is that of consciousness as a global state of an organism. We use it this way when we ask of an accident victim, for example, "Did he lose consciousness?" or "Has he regained consciousness yet?" I also use it to refer to specific states of consciousness, such as wondering what movie to go to or hearing the saxophone solo in that jazz piece I love.

7. When I speak of a bodily subject of consciousness, I am referring to a human person as a biological organism. It is a person, not a brain or group of neurons, that is conscious.

8. At one point in discussing feelings, Damasio (1994, p. 143) says that "all emotions generate feelings if you are awake and alert." Damasio (1999, p. 37) also says that there could be unconscious *feelings*, but he abandons that claim in his third book.

9. For Nussbaum, background emotions are beliefs that are usually not conscious and are, as the name implies, in the background, for example, one's fear of death (which is the belief that death endangers most if not all of my ends). A background emotion can become a conscious emotion (she sometimes refers to these as "situational emotions") when the background judgment is combined with an event that brings that judgment to the fore; for example, the death of a close friend might bring to consciousness my own fear of death (Nussbaum 2001, pp. 70–73).

10. I think Wollheim has put the cart before the horse in defining emotions as dispositions and taking the actual experience or episode of an emotion to be an emotion only in a derivative sense. We would not attribute to Smith a disposition to flare up in anger over small things, for example, if there hadn't been repeated occasions on which Smith had actually flared up in anger. It is also true that if there were an absence of such incidents over a course of time, we would no longer attribute this disposition to Smith. In addition, one way I check on whether I still have a certain feeling (love toward a particular person or anger toward another) is to see whether I still feel love or anger when I imagine or actually encounter that person. The emotion proper is the experience of the emotion, not the disposition to experience it as Wollheim contends. However, nothing in my argument rides on whether I or Wollheim is right about this.

11. Heidegger would not countenance the use of the term *consciousness* because of its Cartesian connotations of (a subject of) consciousness as independent of the world.

My original relation to the world is not as a mind that is distinct from the world. I find myself in the world, alongside of things, from the beginning. This is akin to Sartre's point that I cannot be a point of view on the world unless I am in the world (Sartre 1943/1976).

12. Matthew Ratcliffe (2002) does an excellent job of relating Heidegger's discussion of mood to recent work in neuropsychology. He cites that work in support of Heidegger's argument against those, like the positivists, who would argue that the objective, scientific understanding of ourselves and the world is primary and that emotions either undermine or are irrelevant to this understanding.

13. See Lakoff and Johnson 1999, Greenfield 2000, and also Ravven 2003, which draw on evidence from cognitive science and the affective neurosciences to support Spinoza's claim that all thought is affective. See also Luc Ciompi 2003 for a defense of the view that all conscious states have an affective character utilizing cognitive and social psychology, psychopathology, and evolutionary theory. He argues for this view from a functionalist-computational perspective on mind.

14. Ratcliffe notes the commonality of role played by mood for Heidegger and the role played by what Damasio calls "background feelings." They both serve "as a [pre-propositional] background that constitutes one's sense of self, world and one's place in the world" (2002, p. 299).

15. He returns to a discussion of background emotions in Damasio (1999, pp. 285–286). Background feelings are present when one is aware of these emotions.

16. Damasio (1999, p. 16) asserts that "consciousness and emotion are *not* separable" (emphasis in the original). But he offers a more tentative version of his view later in this work: "I venture that absence of emotion is a reliable correlate of defective core consciousness, perhaps as much as presence of some degree of continuous emoting is virtually always associated with the conscious state" (p. 100).

17. These cases are in contrast to cases, such as dreamless sleep and coma, in which not only consciousness but also wakefulness is lost.

18. LeDoux (1996, ch. 9) would appear to be at odds with Heidegger's and Damasio's view that all conscious states have an affective quality. But since LeDoux is examining only basic emotions, fear in particular, I think he expresses no position with regard to mood or background feelings. He is interested in the neuroscience of emotion, not the subjective experience of emotions.

19. In chapter 6, Damasio (1999) offers his speculative hypothesis about how the brain generates core consciousness and with it the core self and the primitive feeling of the self. He offers evidence for this theory in chapter 8. It shares some similarities with Panksepp's (1998b) theory.

20. See Watt 2000 for a defense of a similar theory and an examination of the connection between consciousness and emotion. See also Watt 1999 for an excellent review and critique of Panksepp 1998b.

21. The reader should keep in mind that it is conscious emotional episodes I am talking about in ascribing an affective nature to all states of consciousness.

22. I use "world" to include not only things and events, but past states of oneself, memories, the attitudes of others—anything that can be an object of consciousness.

23. This emotional state can last anywhere from a few seconds to several hours. If it lasts a long time, it may be characterized as a mood. As long as it exists as an emotion or mood of which I am, at least prereflectively, conscious, it colors my consciousness of the world. Of course, I am not arguing that my emotional state alone determines how I experience the world at any given time. My position in time and space, the knowledge base I bring to my experience, and many other factors can also affect my experience of the world. There is a two-way relation between myself and the world. That is why news of Iraq makes me angry, but does not make my neighbor angry. It is not simply the object of consciousness that creates an emotional response in the subject; it is the object in interaction with a particular person, a particular bodily subject of consciousness.

24. See Damasio 2003 (pp. 96–105) for the empirical evidence he offers to support this point. LeDoux (1996) argues brain activity causes other bodily changes and that those changes do not cause feelings; only the brain activity does. Damasio (1994, pp. 157–158) argues against this view.

25. There is debate over whether or not Damasio believes perception of those changes alone constitutes the feeling of an emotion. McGinn (2003) thinks he does and offers sharp criticism of him for this view. Nussbaum (2001, pp. 117–119) offers a for more nuanced understanding of Damasio's position and thus a more nuanced critique of it.

26. The main empirical evidence philosophers offered for this view is an experiment conducted by Schacter and Singer (1962). For criticism of both philosophers' interpretation and reliance on this experiment, see Griffiths 1997 (pp. 81–84), which notes experiments, both before and since that of Schacter and Singer, that provide empirical evidence that there are particular, individuating bodily responses associated with at least some emotions. See also Wollheim 1999 (pp. 125–128) for criticisms of the Schacter and Singer experiment itself.

27. Nussbaum (2001) is not the only one to do so. It is a common and misguided practice in much of the literature in philosophy of mind.

28. In Wider 1997, I argued that all consciousness involves at least bodily self-awareness because all consciousness of the world requires the processing of bodily input as well as input from the world. Since my consciousness of the world is the

result of the blending of self and world input, consciousness of the world is always a prereflective consciousness of the self. In this essay I am arguing once again that consciousness of the world is always a prereflective consciousness of the self. But the self I am arguing that consciousness reveals, given its affective nature, in being aware of the world, is not simply the perceiving, acting self, but the self as the *owner* of one's experience, that is, the self as a consciousness that always has an attitude or orientation toward its objects. There are ways in which these two revelations of the self intertwine; however, to discuss those here would take us too far afield.

29. Wollheim (1999), Goldie (2000), and Nussbaum (2001) all believe that emotions can be fully understood only in light of a narrative of the self.

30. Panksepp's neurobiological theory discussed in the previous section could support Nussbaum's analysis. Nussbaum (2001), in chapters 2 and 3, offers evidence from experimental psychology to support her claim that both animals and infants can make judgments and have beliefs about their world and themselves and their relation to the world in terms of their goals.

31. Bermúdez believes that conceptual abilities are linked to language mastery, and so he argues for a nonconceptual form of thought and self-consciousness. I do not think one needs to accept that having a concept is necessarily linked with a certain linguistic ability in order to accept the gist of Bermúdez's argument. The important point is that the form of self-consciousness linked with language abilities must be grounded in a nonlinguistic form of self-consciousness and cognition.

32. See Wider 1999 for an extended argument that imitation in infants involves self-consciousness.

33. This threat does not have to be physical to induce bodily feelings and so make us aware of our embodied existence.

34. See Panksepp 1998a (pp. 569, 573, 578–579) for some interesting suggestions on the neural level.

Kant: A Unified Representational Base for All
    Consciousness

Andrew Brook

Kant had the makings of an extremely rich and interesting version of the
idea that self-presenting representations are the representational base of
consciousness. Stripped down to its bare minimum, the view he held is that
common or garden variety representations present not just what they are
about, not just their object. They also present themselves and they present
oneself, their subject, that is to say, the thing that has them.

The situation with respect to the evidence that he held this view is complicated, however, more complicated than is usually the case even with Kant.
Because of the way the mind fit, or did not fit, into his overall projects, everything he had to say about the mind is sketchy and incomplete. Also, Kant's
route into his point of view is very different from any of the routes that
researchers follow now. As a result of the latter, he does not consider many
of the issues that are now at the center of discussion. So let us start with his
overall project and how the mind in general and consciousness in particular
fit into it.

1   Kant's Overall Project

Kant's most famous work is the *Critique of Pure Reason (CPR)* of 1781/1787
(two editions). For purposes of understanding his views on the mind and
consciousness, this work and a small book worked up from lecture notes
late in his life, *Anthropology from a Pragmatic Point of View* (1798), are
the two most important works.[1] Since the *Anthropology* was based on
popular lectures, it is often superficial compared to *CPR*, which therefore is
the main work for our purposes. Until middle age, Kant was a conventional
rationalist.[2] Then memories of reading David Hume "interrupted my dog-
matic slumbers," as he put it (1783, Ak. IV:260). He called the new approach
that ensued *Critical Philosophy*.

Two Main Projects

In the part of the critical philosophy of interest to us, two of Kant's main projects were to:

• Justify our conviction that physics, like mathematics, is a body of necessary and universal truth (1781/1787, B19–21).[3]
• Insulate religion and morality, including the possibility of immortality and of free will, from the corrosive effects of this very same science (Bxxx).

Kant accepted without reservation that "God, freedom and immortality" (Bxxx) exist but feared that, if science, or any evidence or argument, were relevant to demonstrating or refuting their existence, it would provide reason to doubt their existence. So Kant wanted to insulate such matters from all evidence and argument. Fortunately, as he saw it, neither scientific evidence nor philosophical argument can touch these questions. If so, God, freedom and immortality could be accepted on the basis of faith (and Kant did so accept them) without being at risk from science. "I have found it necessary to deny *knowledge*, . . . in order to make room for *faith*" (Bxxx, his italics).

The first aim occupies much of the first big part of *CPR*, which Kant called the Analytic. The work of insulation comes in the second big part of *CPR*, which Kant called the Dialectic and which consists of a series of attacks on, as he saw them, unjustifiably grand aspirations of the metaphysics of rationalism. "Dialectic" was Kant's name for a certain kind of faulty reasoning in which one's conclusions run out far beyond what one's premises can support. The specific faulty arguments that concern us here are about the nature of the mind or soul and its possible immortality.

In the course of pursuing the first aim, putting knowledge in general and physics in particular on a secure foundation, Kant asked the following question: What are the necessary conditions of experience? More specifically, what must the mind be like for our knowledge to be as it is (A96–97)? Put simply, he held that for our experience, and therefore our minds, to be as they are, our experience must be tied together in the way that physics says it is. So the status of physics is secured. But this also tells us quite a lot about what our minds must be like. In particular, it tells us about how the mind must be able to function.

Notice how the mind enters Kant's project here. It enters not as an object of interest in its own right but as a means to an end, the end being to justify our conviction that physics is a secure science. As a result, his explorations of the mind are sketchy and incomplete, carried as far as he needed to carry them for the purposes of his project and no further. As he put it, "This enquiry . . . [into] the pure understanding itself, its possibility and the cognitive faculties upon which it rests . . . is of great importance for my chief purpose, . . . [but] does not form an essential part of it" (Axvii). It is also, he tells us, "somewhat hypothetical in character" (Axvii). (Kant did not retain this passage in the second edition of *CPR* but the sentiments it expresses remain.) There is no sustained, focused discussion of the mind anywhere in Kant's work except the *Anthropology*, which, as we said, is quite superficial.

In addition, the two chapters of *CPR* in which most of Kant's remarks on the mind occur, the chapter on the Transcendental Deduction (TD) and the chapter on what he called Paralogisms of Pure Reason (faulty arguments about the mind mounted by his rationalist predecessors), were the two chapters that gave him the greatest difficulty. Indeed, they contain some of the most impenetrable prose ever written. Kant completely rewrote the main body of both chapters for the second edition (though not the introductions, interestingly).

TD is where Kant attempts to realize the first and most important part of the first project; the Paralogisms chapter is devoted to the part of the second project concerned with the mind. In the first edition, he seems to have achieved a stable position on self-consciousness only as late as this chapter, which comes well into the second half of *CPR*. Even his famous term for consciousness of self, "I think," occurs for the first time in the first edition only in the introduction to the chapter on the Paralogisms.

Model of the Mind Arising Out of the First Project

Kant's exploration of the necessary conditions of experience in the first project led him to a number of substantive claims about the mind. The most famous is his claim that representation requires *concepts* as well as *percepts*—rule-guided acts of cognition as well as deliverances of the senses. As he put it in one of his most famous sayings, "Concepts without intuitions are empty, intuitions without concepts are blind" (A51 = B75). In more contemporary terms, the functions crucial for knowledge-generating activity are processing of sensory inputs and application of concepts to sensory inputs. Cognition requires both concepts and percepts. As we might say now, to discriminate, we need information; but for information to be of any use to us, we must organize the information.

Kant also urged that the functions that organize sensory and conceptual raw materials into experiences are different abilities to synthesize. He postulated that there are three kinds of synthesis (A98–110; the three have a more diffuse presence in the second edition than in the first, though all of them are still there). Synthesis of Apprehension in Intuition locates the raw materials of experience temporally (and presumably also spatially, though Kant does not say so). Synthesis of Reproduction in the Imagination associates spatiotemporally structured items with other spatiotemporally structured items. And Synthesis of Recognition in a Concept recognizes items using concepts, the Categories in particular. This threefold doctrine of synthesis is one of the cornerstones of Kant's model of the mind.

In fact, Kant held that to organize information as we do, we require two kinds of Synthesis of Recognition in Concepts. The first ties the raw material of sensible experience together into objects (A105). This is now called binding. Put in contemporary terms, initially colors, lines, shapes, textures, and so on are represented separately. For an object to be represented, the contents of these representations have to be integrated.

The second kind of synthesis ties the contents of these individual representations and the representations themselves together so as to produce what might be called a *global representation*, a notion that will prove to be central to his story about self-presenting representations. A global representation connects individual representations and their contents to one another in such a way that to be conscious of anything thus tied together is to be conscious of other things thus tied, too, and of the group of them as a single group. Kant thought that the capacity to form global representations is essential to both the kind of cognition that we have and the kind of consciousness that we have.

Kant's model of the mind is a model of cognitive function, not underlying mechanisms. This is an effective way to approach the mind, as cognitive science has shown, but Kant had a special reason for adopting it. One of his most deeply held general convictions was that we know nothing of anything as it is. We know things only as they appear to us—including the mind, even our own mind. However, various things he said seem to imply that we *do* have knowledge of the mind—that it must apply concepts, synthesize, and so on. He never addressed the tension squarely but a natural way out for him would have been to distinguish the mind's functions from its composition, what makes it up, and then maintain that what we can know are its functions and what we lack all knowledge of are its composition and makeup. This would be merely a radical version of the functionalist idea that function does not dictate form—a given function could be implemented by systems having very different forms (multiple realizability).[4]

Claims about Consciousness Arising Out of the Second Project

The mind enters the second project somewhat indirectly, too, even though it was here that Kant made many of his most penetrating observations about consciousness, especially consciousness of self.

As we saw, Kant's second project was to insulate "God, freedom and immortality" from all argument and evidence, fearing that, if either were relevant to the question of their existence at all, it would provide reason to doubt their existence. Immortality is the topic of interest to us here. His rationalist predecessors, Descartes and Leibniz for example, thought that they could prove that the mind is substantial, is simple (without parts), and persists in a special way. These conclusions would at minimum leave immortality an open possibility. (Thomas Reid took this approach, too, even though he wasn't in other respects a rationalist.[5]) Since the conclusions would appear to many people to follow from things Kant himself had said about the unity of consciousness in the first part of CPR (specifically in TD), if his strategy for insulating the possibility of immortality was to work, he also had to show that his earlier claims contain no such implications.

Kant's official topic in the chapter is faulty rationalist arguments and conclusions claiming to yield knowledge of the nature of the mind or soul as it is in itself. However, as he saw it, introspection provides strong prima facie support for the rationalist conclusions about what we can know about the mind. In introspection, we appear to ourselves to be substantial, simple, and persisting, just as rational psychology held ("rational psychology" was Kant's name for these views). If so, he had to show that introspection reveals nothing of the sort. It was in the course of his deflationary attack on introspection that Kant made many of his most acute observations about consciousness of self.

Kant held surprisingly strong and not entirely consistent views on introspection and empirical methods generally as a basis for knowledge about the mind. Sometimes, he maintained that any empirical study of the mind is hopeless. Of course, he is notorious for harboring a similar skepticism about chemistry (in his defense, it should be said that there was nothing resembling a single unified theory of chemical reactions in his time). The empirical method most directly in his gun-sights here was introspection. The key text is in The Metaphysical Foundations of Natural Science (1786). After stating his view of chemistry, he went on, "the empirical doctrine of the soul . . . must remain even further removed than chemistry from the rank of what may be called a natural science proper" (Ak. IV:471). The contents of introspection, in his terms inner sense, cannot be studied scientifically for at least five reasons.

First, having only one universal dimension and one that they are only *represented* to have at that, namely, distribution in time, the contents of inner sense cannot be quantified; thus no mathematical model of them is possible. Second, "the manifold of internal observation is separated only by mere thought." That is to say, only the introspective observer distinguishes the items one from another; there are no real distinctions among the items themselves. Third, these items "cannot be kept separate" in a way that would allow us to connect them again "at will," by which Kant presumably means according to the dictates of our developing theory. Fourth, "another thinking subject [does not] submit to our investigations in such a way as to be conformable to our purposes"—the only thinking subject whose inner sense one can investigate is oneself. Finally and most damningly, "even the observation itself alters and distorts the state of the object observed" (1786, Ak. IV:471). Indeed, introspection can be bad for the health: it is a road to "mental illness" ("Illuminism and Terrorism," 1798, Ak. VII:133; see 161).

At other times, Kant links "self-observation" to observation of others and calls them both sources of anthropology (Ak. VII:142–143). It is not clear why he didn't respect what he called anthropology more highly as an empirical study of the mind in his critical moments, given that he himself did it.[6]

At any rate, no kind of empirical psychology could ever yield necessary truths about the mind. In light of this limitation, how *should* we study the mind? Kant's answer was: by the transcendental method using transcendental arguments. If we cannot observe the connections among the denizens of inner sense to any scientific purpose, we can study what the mind *must* be like and what capacities and structures (in Kant's jargon, faculties) it *must* have if it is to represent things as it does. With this method we can find universally true, that is to say, "transcendental" psychological propositions. We have already seen what some of them are: minds must be able to synthesize and integrate, for example.[7]

Whatever the merits of Kant's attack on the rationalist picture of the mind and its introspective running mates, in the course of mounting it he made some penetrating observations about consciousness of self and the knowledge of self that it yields or does not yield. He urged that:

1. There are two quite different kinds of self-consciousness, consciousness of one's states and consciousness of oneself as the subject of these states.
2. The cognitive and semantic machinery used to obtain consciousness of self as subject is quite unusual. In it, we "denote" but do not "represent" ourselves (A382). Put otherwise, we designate ourselves without noting "any quality whatsoever" in ourselves (A355).
3. When one is conscious of oneself as subject, one is conscious of oneself in a way that does not provide consciousness of features of oneself, a way in which "nothing manifold is given" (B135).
4. One is conscious even of oneself only as one appears to oneself, not as one is.

As he put the latter point,

inner sense . . . represents to consciousness even our own selves only as we appear to ourselves, not as we are in ourselves. For we intuit ourselves only as we are inwardly *affected* [by ourselves]. (B153)

And he underpinned all these views with an interesting view of the representational base of consciousness, which he built out of an equally interesting notion of self-presenting representations. Notice that, as with the first project, here too the mind enters Kant's analysis only indirectly, in the service of other ends. Here too the result is a sketchy, incomplete treatment of the aspects of mind thus drawn in.

2 Representational Base of Consciousness

By "the representational base of consciousness," I mean whatever it is about representation and representing that subserves consciousness. Whether consciousness simply *is* representational or not, it at least *requires* representation of some kind. Kant's view of the representational base of consciousness is mainly an offshoot of his first project, specifically, of his work on the question about what the mind must be like to have experiences. The core of it is quite straightforward: the representational base of consciousness of oneself and/or one's psychological states is not a special experience of either but any experience of anything whatsoever. Though he never developed the view in any single discussion or in any detail at all, here is what he seems to have had in mind. Consider the sentence:

I am puzzled by what Kant says about apperception in A107.

Kant's thought seems to have been that my representation of the page, the sentences, and so on, is all the representation that I need to be conscious not just of the page, the sentences, and so on, but also of the act of seeing them, and of *who* is seeing them, namely, me. A single representation can do all three jobs. Kant once put it this way: consciousness of representation and self is given "not indeed in, but with . . . intuitions" (B161). Let us call an act of representing that can make one conscious of its object, itself, and oneself as its subject the *representational base* of consciousness of these three items. Here is how Kant's story goes.

Two Kinds of Consciousness of Self
The first thing we need to see is that Kant sharply distinguished consciousness of one's own psychological states from consciousness of oneself as

subject of those states. Kant's term for the former was "empirical self-consciousness." His leading term for the latter was "transcendental apperception" (TA). (Kant used the term "TA" in two very different ways, as the name for a faculty of synthesis and as the name for what he also referred to as the "I think," namely, one's consciousness of oneself as subject. It is the latter usage that is in play here.) In a passage from the *Anthropology*, Kant distinguishes the two kinds of consciousness of self very clearly:

the *"I" of reflection* contains no manifold and is always the same in every judgment. . . . *Inner experience*, on the other hand, contains the matter of consciousness and a manifold of empirical inner intuition. . . . (1798, Ak. VII:141–142, emphases in the original)

Here is another passage from the *Anthropology*:

§24. Inner sense is not pure apperception, consciousness of what we are doing; for this belongs to the power of thinking. It is, rather, consciousness of what we undergo as we are affected by the play of our own thoughts. This consciousness rests on inner intuition, and so on the relation of ideas (as they are either simultaneous or successive). (1798, Ak. VII:161)

Kant makes the same distinction in *CPR*:

[T]he I that I think is distinct from the I that it, itself, intuits . . . ; I am given to myself beyond that which is given in intuition, and yet know myself, like other phenomena, only as I appear to myself, not as I am. . . . (B155)

This distinction is reflected in his doctrine of the representational base in the following way. The "consciousness of what we undergo as we are affected by the play of our own thoughts" (and, presumably, perceptions, emotions, memories, and so on) is the consciousness of representations that having the representations gives us. The content of this kind of consciousness varies from representation to representation. The consciousness of oneself as the subject of those thoughts (and . . . and . . .) is also given to us by having those representations, but this consciousness "contains no manifold and is always the same in every judgment."

Representational Base of Consciousness of One's Psychological States and of Oneself

The two kinds of consciousness of self may appear to have very different sources. The source of empirical self-consciousness (particular representations) is said to be what Kant called *inner sense*. He did not work out his notion of inner sense at all well but seems to have had in mind something like perception of one's own psychological states. Here are just a few of the problems. Kant insists that all representational states "belong to" (presumably he means, "are presented by") inner sense, including those representing the objects of outer sense (i.e., spatially located objects):

Whatever the origins of our representations, whether they are due to the influence of outer things, or are produced through inner causes, whether they arise *a priori*, or being appearances have an empirical origin, they must all, as modifications of the mind, belong to inner sense. (A98–89)

However, he also says that the body (including one's own) is the object of outer sense; the object of inner sense is the soul. Is outer sense part of inner sense, then? Sometimes he talks like it is, sometimes not. He comes close to denying that we can be conscious of the denizens of inner sense—they do not represent inner objects and have no manifold of their own. Yet he also says that we can be conscious of them—representations can themselves be objects of representations, indeed, representations can make us conscious of themselves. In its role as a form of or means to consciousness of self, apperception ought to be part of inner sense. Yet Kant regularly contrasted apperception, a means to consciousness of oneself and one's acts of thinking, with inner sense as a means to consciousness of—what? Presumably, particular representations: perceptions, imaginings, memories, and so on. So do we have two means to consciousness of the same, or some of the same, particular representations, or of different representations?

Whatever exactly Kant meant or should have meant by the term "inner sense," he said that one way in which we become conscious of the representational denizens of inner sense is quite different from the way in which we become conscious of the objects of those representations, and he said it a number of times. Notice the phrase in the passage quoted in the previous section from §24 of the *Anthropology*: "consciousness of what we are doing"—*doing* (1798, Ak. VII:161). The way in which one becomes conscious of an *act of representing* is not by receiving what he called intuitions, that is, sensible contents, but by doing it: "synthesis . . . , as an act, . . . is conscious to itself, even without sensibility" (B153); "this representation is an act of *spontaneity*, that is, it cannot be regarded as belonging to sensibility" (B132). "Sensibility" and "intuition" are closely related terms referring to the objects or contents of representations of the world, what can be sensed. Thus Kant is saying that we do *not* become conscious of our own representational acts in the way in which we become conscious of the objects of those acts, by receiving a raw manifold of inputs and then working them up in acts of synthesis. We become conscious of our own representational acts by *performing* them.

So what about consciousness of oneself? What is the source of consciousness of oneself as subject?

Man, . . . who knows the rest of nature solely through the senses, knows himself also through pure apperception; and this, indeed, in acts and inner determinations which he cannot regard as impressions of the senses. (A546 = B574)

More specifically:

[T]he mind could never think its identity in the manifoldness of its representations . . . if it did not have before its eyes the identity of its act, whereby it subordinates all [the manifold] . . . to a transcendental unity. . . . (A108)

The acts in question are acts of apperception. Kant is saying that performing acts of apperception is the basis of consciousness of oneself as subject. I am conscious of myself as the single common subject of a certain group of experiences by being conscious of "the identity of the consciousness in . . . conjoined . . . representations" (B133). Moreover, we can be conscious of ourselves as subject *merely* by performing acts of representing. No further representation of the act or of oneself is needed.

That the mind is active and knows itself as active was of fundamental importance to Kant. When one is conscious of oneself by doing cognitive and perceptual acts, one is conscious of oneself as spontaneous, rational, self-legislating, free—as the doer of deeds, not just as a passive receptacle for the contents of representations: "I exist as an intelligence which is conscious solely of its power of combination" (B158–159), of "the activity of the self" (B68) (see Sellars 1970–71; Pippin 1987).

From Individual Representation to Global Representation

So far we have focused on individual representations. For Kant, however, the acts of representation that serve as the representational base of consciousness of oneself as subject are usually much "bigger" than that, that is, contain multiple objects and often multiple representations tied together into what Kant called "general experience":

When we speak of different experiences, we can refer only to the various perceptions, all of which belong to one and the same general experience. This thoroughgoing synthetic unity of perceptions is the form of experience; it is nothing less than the synthetic unity of appearances in accordance with concepts. (A110)

Here are some other expressions of what appears to be the same thought. Our experience is "one experience"; "all possible appearances . . . stand alongside one another in one experience" (A108). We have "one and the same general experience" of "all . . . the various perceptions" (A110), "a connected whole of human knowledge" (A121). Kant's term "general experience" being a bit on the bland side, let us call what he is introducing here a *global representation*.

Transcendental apperception (hereafter TA) now enters. It is the ability to tie "all appearances" together into "one experience":

This transcendental unity of apperception forms out of all possible appearances, which can stand alongside one another in one experience, a connection of all these representations according to laws. (A108)

It performs a "synthesis of all appearances according to concepts," "whereby it subordinates all synthesis of apprehension . . . to a transcendental unity" (A108). This, he thought, requires unified consciousness. Unified consciousness is required for another reason, too.

The introduction of unified consciousness opens up an important new opportunity. Kant can now explore the necessary conditions of conscious content being unified in this way. To make a long story short, Kant now argues that conscious content could have the unity that it does only if the contents themselves are tied together causally. With this, his deduction of the relational categories is complete, and his first project, the defense of the necessity of physics, is well under way.

If we now make *global* representations the representational base of consciousness, the story would go this way. When I am conscious of many objects and/or representations of them as the single object of a single global representation, the latter representation is all the representation I need to be conscious not just of the global object but also of the global representation itself and of myself as the common subject of all the constituent representations. To reintroduce a relevant passage just quoted:

[T]he mind could never think its identity in the manifoldness of its representations . . . if it did not have before its eyes the identity of its act, whereby it subordinates all [the manifold] . . . to a transcendental unity. . . . (A108)

I am conscious of myself as the single common subject of a certain group of experiences by being conscious of "the identity of the consciousness in . . . conjoined . . . representations" (B133). Alas, it has to be admitted that none of this is nearly as clear in the original texts as my reconstruction would suggest.

Unity of Consciousness

At the heart of the notion of a global representation is the unity of consciousness. Though by no means everything in a global representation need be consciously accessible to us (Kant is widely misunderstood on this point), Kant thought that we have unified consciousness of a good deal of what our current global representation represents, and that having the representation is the base for being or becoming conscious of the representation itself as a single, unified representation and of oneself as its subject. Indeed, two kinds of unity are required:

1. The consciousness that this subject has of represented objects and/or representations must be unified.
2. The global representation must have a single common subject (A350).

Kant said little about what a "single common subject" is like, so we won't say anything more about it. He never said what he meant by "unified consciousness," either, but he did use the notion often enough for us to be able to see what he had in mind.

Kant refers to the unity of consciousness both as the unity of consciousness (A103) and as the unity of apperception (A105, A108). The notion plays a central role in both projects. In the first project, Kant argues that we could not have unified consciousness of a range of items unless we could tie the items themselves together causally. (This argument is not successful, though it is better than some neo-Kantian moves that have spun off from it [Brook 2004].)

Unity of consciousness is also a central topic of the second project. The first edition attack on the second paralogism (A352) focuses on the unity of consciousness at a given time (among other things) and what can (or rather, cannot) be inferred from it about the nature of the mind. The attack on the third paralogism focuses on what can(not) be inferred from unified consciousness over time. These are all from the first edition of *CPR*. In the second edition, Kant makes further remarks about it, quite unlike anything in the first edition, for example, "this unity . . . is not the category of unity" (B131).

By "unity of consciousness," Kant seems to have had something like the following in mind: I am conscious not only of single experiences of single objects but also of experiences that have many normal objects as their single, integrated object. The same is true of actions; I can do, and be conscious of doing, a number of actions at the same time. In addition to such synchronic unity or unity at a time, many global representations, as we called them, display diachronic unity or unity across time: current representation is combined with retained earlier representation. In fact, any representation that we acquire in a series of temporal steps, such as hearing a sentence, will have diachronic unity (A104; A352). Thus, diachronic unity is often part of synthesis of recognition.

Kant himself did not explicate his notion of unified consciousness but here is one plausible articulation of the notion that we find at work in his writings:

The unity of consciousness = *df*. consciousness of a number of representations and/or objects of representation in such a way that to be conscious of any of them is also to be conscious of others of them and of at least some of them as a group.

As this definition makes clear, consciousness being unified is more than just being one act of consciousness. The act of consciousness in question is not just singular, it is unified.

In Kant's view, moreover, to have unified global representations, we must unify them. We must synthesize them using unifying acts of synthesis, acts of transcendental apperception (in one of his uses of this term). It takes a unified consciousness to perform unified acts of synthesis. The unity of consciousness and Kant's views on it are complicated issues (see Brook and Raymont 2001). What matters for present purposes is that it is representations providing unified consciousness of their objects that are the representational base of consciousness of one's psychological states and of oneself as their single, unified subject. The notion of a self-presenting representation scattered through Kant's work is a rich one indeed!

If having a unified self-presenting global representation is the representational base of consciousness, is having one also sufficient for consciousness? We need to break this question down into bite-sized chunks. Is it sufficient for consciousness of the world around us? Kant never said. Nowadays we would require at least that the representation be cognitively active before we would grant that it provides consciousness of the world, but Kant did not investigate the matter, part of his general neglect of action and the body. Consciousness of the representation itself? Again, Kant said little that bites directly on the question. However, he did have something to say about the third issue, consciousness of oneself as subject. What he said is both interesting in its own right and relevant to the second question. Kant required only that we *be able* to attach "I think" to our representations (B130), not that we must always do so. That is to say, we must *be able* to become conscious of our representations, that we are having them, and so on, but we need not actually be conscious of them or of having them. Note that the passage just discussed is from the second edition, which makes more use of consciousness of self than the first edition, where he did not require even this much. So the answer would seem to be, no, Kant did not hold that unified consciousness of the world is sufficient for consciousness of oneself as subject.

If so, what else might be required? Here Kant gives almost no guidance. From the fact that he mentions it only once and in a footnote (B156fn.)—a footnote moreover irrelevant to the current issue—it would seem that direction of attention, many theorists' favorite candidate at the moment, would not have been Kant's candidate. However, he never addressed the question, so we have no way of knowing what his candidate would have been.

To close off our reconstruction of the picture of representation that seems to make up the substructure of Kant's thought, we should note that he also had the makings of a story about how global representations are implemented in a cognitive system. When the system synthesizes representations and/or represented objects with other representations and/or represented objects by bringing the various items together under concepts, specifically, under the relational categorial concepts, then a unified global representation results.

3 Putting the Self-Presenting Global Representation to Work

We now turn to the interesting question of what work Kant's notion of the self-presenting global representation and the notion of the representational base built on it can do. First, what work did he get out of them? At least this much: The job of the Paralogisms chapter is to insulate the possibility of immortality from all possible attack by argument or evidence. He does so by urging that we know nothing of our nature, therefore nothing about whether we might be immortal or not. Therefore, immortality remains a possibility.

As part of mounting this argument, Kant has to show that our consciousness of ourselves yields no knowledge of our nature. Here he has to resist arguments of two kinds. First, if consciousness is to be unified, it would appear that the separate bits cannot be anything like separate parts of a machine. Distribute the words of a verse among a number of items, defined how you like. Nothing will be aware of the whole verse (A352). It would seem to follow that the mind must be simple (i.e., not made of parts). But this would entail that it is not material. If this argument goes through, we would know a lot about the mind, including things directly relevant to the possibility of immortality. So Kant has to resist the argument. Second, we just appear to ourselves to be substantial and simple and to persist in a special way. So Kant has to explain this appearance away.

Moreover, at least by the time of the second edition of *CPR*, Kant had come to see that it would be quite implausible to maintain that when one is conscious of oneself, one is conscious only of appearances, highly doctored representations of oneself—that even when one is conscious of oneself as the subject of one's experience, agent of one's acts, by having these experiences and doing those acts, one has no consciousness of one's actual self. In the second edition, he reflects this sensitivity as early as B68; at B153, he goes so far as to say that an apparent contradiction is involved.

Kant's doctrine of global representations as the representational base of consciousness of self contains the basis for everything he had to say on both issues, though it takes some reconstructive surgery on our part to see the connections.

No Manifold in Consciousness of Self

First, Kant held that when one is conscious of oneself as subject, one is not, or need not be, conscious of any properties of oneself, certainly not any properties that are contingent or changing. One has the same consciousness of self no matter what else one is conscious of—thinking, perceiving, laughing, being miserable, or whatever. Kant expressed the thought this way: "through the 'I,' as simple representation, nothing manifold is given" (B135), and this way: "the I that I think is distinct from the I that it . . . intuits . . . ; I am given to myself beyond that which is given in intuition" (B155). This idea is similar to Shoemaker's notion of "self-reference without identification," the notion that reference to self as subject involves or need involve no identification of oneself as anything (Brook 2001). Since, on Kant's view, it is not just identifying properties but any properties of oneself whatsoever that one does not need to know in order to refer to oneself as oneself, "nonascriptive reference to self" might capture what is special about this form of consciousness of self better than Shoemaker's term.

Consciousness of Self Is not Knowledge of Self

The notion that in consciousness of self as subject, no manifold is given, is or can be interpreted as the idea that in it, no properties of the self are represented. (We will see major support for this interpretation in a moment.) It immediately gives Kant what he needs to be able to allow that when one is conscious of oneself as subject, one is conscious of oneself, not just of an appearance of oneself, while continuing to maintain that one has no knowledge of oneself as one is. If consciousness of self ascribes nothing to the self, it is or could be a "bare . . . consciousness of self [as one is]" that yields no knowledge of self, indeed, that is "very far from being a knowledge of the self" (B158).

But how is ascriptionless reference to self possible? Here Kant offered some remarkably prescient insights about reference to self, insights that next appeared only in Wittgenstein (1934/1935) or perhaps even Castañeda (1966) and Shoemaker (1968). Moreover, whereas neither Castañeda nor Shoemaker had an explanation for them, they flow directly from Kant's idea of the representational base of consciousness of self. I discuss the ideas first, then their explanation by reference to the representational base.

Referential Machinery of Consciousness of Self

Here are some of the things that Kant said about reference to self as subject. We have already seen him say that it is a consciousness of self in which "nothing manifold is given" (B135). In the kind of reference in which we gain this consciousness of self, he says that we "denote" but do not "represent" ourselves (A382). We designate ourselves "only transcendentally" without noting "any quality whatsoever" in ourselves (A355).

The idea behind these claims is a remarkably penetrating one; remember, the study of reference and semantics generally is usually thought to have begun only with Frege. Kant is anticipating two important theses about reference to self that next saw the light of day two hundred years later:

1. In certain kinds of consciousness of self, one can be conscious of something as oneself without identifying it (or anything) as oneself via properties that one has ascribed to it (Shoemaker's self-reference without identification);[8]

and,

2. in such cases, first-person indexicals (I, me, my, mine) cannot be "analyzed out" in favor of anything else, in particular anything descriptionlike (the essential indexical) (Perry 1979).

Was Kant actually aware of (1) and/or (2) or had he just stumbled across something that later philosophers recognized as significant?

One standard argument for (1) goes as follows:

My use of the word "I" as the subject of [statements such as "I feel pain" or "I see a canary"] is not due to my having identified as myself something [otherwise recognized] of which I know, or believe, or wish to say, that the predicate of my statement applies to it. (Shoemaker 1968, p. 558)

A standard argument for (2), that certain indexicals are essential, goes as follows. To know that *I* wrote a certain book a few years ago, it is not enough to know that someone over six feet tall wrote that book, or that someone who teaches philosophy at a particular university wrote that book, or . . . or . . . or . . . , for I could know all these things without knowing that it was *me* who has these properties (and I could know that it *was* me who wrote that book and not know that any of these things are properties of me). As Shoemaker puts it, "no matter how detailed a token-reflexive-free description of a person is, . . . it cannot possibly entail that I am that person" (1968, p. 560).

Kant unquestionably articulated the argument for (1):

In attaching "I" to our thoughts, we designate the subject only transcendentally . . . without noting in it any quality whatsoever—in fact, without knowing anything of it either directly or by inference. (A355)

This transcendental designation, that is, referring to oneself using "I" without "noting any quality" in oneself, has some unusual features. One can refer to oneself in a variety of ways, of course: as the person in the mirror, as the person born on such and such a date in such and such a place, as the first person to do X, and so on, but one way of referring to oneself is special: it does not require identifying or indeed any ascription to oneself. So Kant tells us.

The question is more complicated with respect to (2). We cannot go into the complexities here (see Brook 2001). We will just note three passages in which Kant may be referring to the essential indexical or something like it.

The subject of the categories cannot by thinking the categories [i.e., applying them to objects] acquire a concept of itself as an object of the categories. For in order to think them, its pure self-consciousness, which is what was to be explained, must itself be presupposed. (B422)

The phrase "its pure self-consciousness" seems to refer to consciousness of oneself as subject. If so, the passage may be saying that judgments about oneself, that is, ascriptions of properties to oneself, "presuppose . . . pure self-consciousness," that is, consciousness of oneself via an act of ascription-free transcendental designation.

Put the above beside this, "it is . . . very evident that I cannot know as an object that which I must presuppose to know any object . . ." (A402), and this:

Through this I or he or it (the thing) which thinks, nothing further is represented than a transcendental subject of the thoughts = X. It is known only through the thoughts which are its predicates, and of it, apart from them, we cannot have any concept whatsoever, but can only revolve in a perpetual circle, since any judgment upon it has always already made use of its representation. (A346 = B404)

The last clause is the key one: "any judgment upon it has always already made use of its representation." Kant seems to be saying that to know that anything is true of me, I must first know that it is me of whom it is true. This is something very like the essential indexical claim.

Now we make the connection to the consciousness without knowledge issue. If reference to self takes place without "noting any properties" of oneself, the consciousness of self that results will not provide any knowledge of self. But what right does Kant have to help himself to his notion of transcendental designation?

Transcendental Designation and the Representational Base of Consciousness
The answer is: Every right. Even though he did not explicitly make the connection himself, that reference to self as subject is "transcendental," that is, nonascriptive, flows directly from the idea that the representational base of such reference is having global representations. A global representation will have no neighbor, to use a phrase of Wittgenstein's. That is to say, while we can distinguish the subject from all objects (A342 = B400), we cannot compare it to, contrast it with, one subject *rather than another*. There will be no other simultaneous global representation of which one is conscious in the same way (namely, by having it, though Kant never says this explicitly) that presents a subject from which to distinguish the subject presented in one's current global representation.

If not, reference to self as subject will not, to use a phrase of Bennett's, be experience-dividing—"i.e. [statements expressing it have] no direct implications of the form 'I shall experience C rather than D'" (Bennett 1974, p. 80). In a statement such as

I am looking at the words on the screen in front of me

the verb expression or the object expression may divide experience but the subject expression will not. If so, awareness of self as subject can proceed and, to the extent that ascription requires dividing experience, must proceed without any ascription to self.[9] From this it follows that consciousness of self as subject will have all the special features delineated earlier: reference that does not ascribe, manifoldlessness, and a consciousness of self that yields no knowledge of self. In this account, Kant goes further than any theorist past or present.[10]

Kant's Notions and Current Issues

Can Kant's notion of the representational base or the rich notion of a self-presenting global representation that underlies it help us with any contemporary issues? Perhaps. Start with the question, in virtue of what are certain states conscious states? Kant did not address this question, but he seems to have assumed that when having a global representation is not just the base of being conscious of it but is actually providing such consciousness, then the global representation will simply *be* a conscious state—nothing else needed. (Thus, Kant would probably have been very dubious about the idea that *qualia*, felt qualities, are somehow different from and outstrip the representational properties of representations.)

What about the relationship of the various forms of consciousness? Earlier we saw that Kant allowed that one can have a global representation of, and therefore presumably be conscious of, the world without being conscious of the representation or oneself. All he demanded is, as we saw, that one be *able* to attach "I think" to each such representation. If global representations are self-presenting, he might well have insisted that they provide all the representation needed, that nothing representational could be missing. But he could happily have allowed, indeed the claim about "I think" suggests that he would have allowed, that something else needed for consciousness could still be missing.

Certainly Kant's view has implications for some contemporary doctrines about consciousness. In common with most views anchored in self-representing representations, his view entails that nothing higher-order is needed for consciousness. *Pace* Rosenthal (1990), each representation can present itself; no higher-order state taking the first representation as its object is needed.

Equally, Kant's approach puts real pressure on the so-called transparency thesis. The transparency thesis is the thesis that we are not directly, noninferentially aware of our own representations. Being aware of representing redness is no more than being aware of the redness represented (Harman 1990; Dretske 1995a). We are aware *via* representations but not *of* representations. On Kant's view, having a representation can make us just as conscious of the representation as of what it represents. If Kant is right, the transparency thesis is wrong.[11]

In short, Kant's notion of self-presenting representations, the notion that representations present not only their objects but also themselves and their subject, the thing that has them, and the attendant theory of the representational base that he sketched and hinted at in various places are unusually rich and interesting, more rich and more interesting than most contemporary discussions of these and related issues.[12]

Notes

1. He was already 57 when he wrote the first edition of the first *Critique*, yet he went on to write two further *Critiques*, the *Critique of Practical Reason* (1788) on moral reasoning and the *Critique of Judgment* (1791), a work devoted to a number of topics including reasoning about ends, the nature of judgment, and aesthetics, and books on natural science, cosmology, history, geography, logic, anthropology—the list is long.

2. To oversimplify as well as stick to the official line on the topic: rationalists hold that we can discover truths just by thinking about things, without need of observation or experience.

3. All further references to Kant will be to this work unless otherwise noted. "A" refers to passages in the first edition, "B" to passages in the second. The symbol "=" means that the passage occurs in both editions.

4. As Meerbote (1989) and many others have observed, Kant held a functionalist view of the mind almost 200 years before functionalism was officially articulated in the 1960s by Hilary Putnam and others. Kant even shared functionalists' lack of enthusiasm for introspection, as we will see, and their belief that we can model cognitive function without knowing anything very much about underlying structure. Given his personal hostility to materialism about the mind (1783, Ak. IV, end of §46), he would have found the naturalizing tendencies of much contemporary functionalism repugnant. However, because the unknowability of things as they are in themselves, one of his most deeply held views, entails that one must be utterly neutral about what the underlying composition of the mind might be like, he would have had to allow that multiple realizability and even naturalism are open *intellectual* possibilities, however repugnant they might have been to him or dangerous to issues of the deepest importance to him, namely, that we have free will and that personal immortality is possible (for a fine discussion of these issues, see Ameriks 2000, postscript).

5. The relationship of Kant to Reid is interesting. Among other things, they were near-contemporaries and some of the phrasing of views that Kant attacks is very similar to phrasing that Reid used. I explore the matter briefly in Brook 1994, pp. 191–192.

6. Indeed, what Kant called anthropology is very like what we would now call behavioral psychology. He lectured on the subject every year for decades and finally pulled his lectures together into the little *Anthropology* (1798). Yet not only does he not exempt what he called anthropology from his strictures on the empirical doctrine of the soul, he does not even mention it when he is attacking empirical methods!

7. The core of a transcendental argument is what we now call inference to the best explanation: postulate unobservable mental mechanisms to explain observed behavior. To be sure, Kant thought that he could get more out of his arguments than just "best explanations." He had a tripartite doctrine of the a priori. He held that some

features of the mind and its knowledge had a priori origins, i.e., must be in the mind prior to experience (because using them is necessary to have experience). That mind and knowledge have these features are a priori truths, i.e., "necessary" and "universal" (B3/4). And we can come to know these truths, or that they are a priori at any rate, only by using a priori methods, i.e., we cannot learn these things from experience (B3). Kant thought that transcendental arguments were a priori or yielded the a priori in all three ways (Brook 1993). Nonetheless, at the heart of this method is inference to the best explanation. The latter was just the approach taken up by researchers when introspection fell out of favor about 100 years ago. Its nonempirical roots in Kant notwithstanding, it is now the major method used by experimental cognitive scientists.

8. Thesis (2) is often taken to be closely related to another putative peculiarity of consciousness of self, what Shoemaker calls immunity to error through misidentification with respect to the first person (Shoemaker 1970; he claims to have found the core of the idea in Wittgenstein 1933/1935, pp. 66–70). We will not explore this issue here (see Brook 2001).

9. So awareness of self as subject also does not distinguish me from or identify me with anything of which I am aware as an object, anything in "the world." Something of great interest for Kant's second project follows: so far as anything my awareness of myself as subject could tell me, I could be *any object* or *any compilation of objects* or *any succession of objects* whatsoever. Not by accident are these exactly the topics of the first three Paralogisms. That is to say, Kant himself put the idea of transcendental designation to work to explain how one can appear to oneself to be substantial, simple, and persisting without these appearances reflecting how one actually is. The reason that one appears in these ways is not that the self is some strange, indefinable being. It is because of the kind of referring that we do to become conscious of oneself as subject. One of the mistakes of rational psychology was to take the simplicity (lack of manifoldness) in the unified representation of self to be a representation of simplicity and unity in the self.

10. This is a short version of a rather long story. For the full story, again see Brook 2001.

11. There is some reason to think that Kant might be right here. Being conscious of touching something rather than seeing it, being conscious of seeing it dimly rather than clearly—that we make these and a thousand other discriminations, while perhaps not conclusive, certainly suggests that we are conscious not just of what representations represent, but also of the representations themselves.

12. Brook and Raymont (2006) attempt a contemporary account that takes full account of Kant. Thanks to Uriah Kriegel, Rick DeVidi, Julian Wuerth, and especially Paul Raymont for helpful comments and discussions—in Paul Raymont's case many, many, many such discussions.

6 The Self-Representational Structure of Consciousness

Kenneth Williford

Sans doute, dira-t-on, mais il y a cercle. Car ne faut-il pas que je compte *en fait* pour que je puisse avoir conscience de compter? Il est vrai. Pourtant, il n'y a pas cercle ou, si l'on veut, c'est la nature même de la conscience d'exister "en cercle."
—Sartre, *L'être et le néant*

It seemed that in order to understand common knowledge . . . , circular propositions, various aspects of perceptual knowledge and self-awareness, we had to admit that there are situations that are not wellfounded under the "constituent of" relation.
—Jon Barwise, foreword to Peter Aczel's *Non-Well-Founded Sets*

I Introduction

I will not review the evidence for the claim that consciousness always involves some form of self-representation.[1] Following Tomis Kapitan, I call this thesis *ubiquity*.[2] Its distinguished history, prominence in careful descriptions of consciousness, and visible if disputed place in the philosophy of mind, AI, and neuroscience lend the claim substantial prima facie credibility.[3] I will *assume* that it is worth taking seriously.

Classic higher-order representation (HOR) theories do not really do justice to the phenomenology behind ubiquity, though some such theorists do admit to sharing it. David Rosenthal, for example, writes, "There is a strong intuitive sense that the consciousness of mental states is somehow reflexive or self-referential."[4] Such theorists arguably push the self-representational aspect of consciousness into the unconscious and thus betray the likely original experiential motivation for their theories. Other theorists take the data seriously but deny that primitive self-consciousness can be understood in relational terms. As Dan Zahavi writes, "[I]t is necessary to differentiate *prereflective* self-awareness, which is an immediate, implicit, irrelational, nonobjectifying, nonconceptual, and nonpropositional self-acquaintance, from *reflective* self-awareness. . . ."[5] The distinction Zahavi draws is indisputable and has been marked, variously, by almost all ubiquity theorists. But we need not accept all his negative characterizations of prereflective self-consciousness, and, in particular, we need not accept that it is irrelational.

I defend a version of ubiquity that does justice to the data but remains relationalist. Episodes of consciousness, on this view, literally bear some form of representation relation to themselves. I develop this version in the course of answering the classic objection to ubiquity, namely, that it entails an infinite regress. I show that the possible views in ubiquity's vicinity cluster around this objection in a familiar way. And I show that a relationalist version of ubiquity can escape the objection. I then give a set-theoretical characterization of the version and derive some suggestive results from it. I argue that the model, if nothing else, at least demonstrates the possibility of precisely representing some of the invariant structures of consciousness. And this, in line with the general idea of neurophenomenology, could aid the search for the neural correlates of consciousness.

Here are some preliminary caveats. I use the word "representation" and its derivatives. But I am unsatisfied with all existing theories of representation. I assume it is a relation, or, at least, *like* a relation in important respects. At points I distinguish kinds of representation in *phenomenological* terms, but this is appropriate given my largely descriptive aims.

However, the view I defend is *in principle* compatible with a naturalist program. As long as one's naturalistic theory of intentionality accommodates reflexive representation, there is no principled difficulty. Some naturalistic theories might preclude this, but others, including Ruth Millikan's theory and Peter Carruthers's theory, do not.[6] In this regard, the view is on a par with classic HOR theories. Both, otherwise plausible or not, can be formulated in terms of states and external relations—the one positing an external relation between two states and the other an external relation between a state and itself.[7] The latter, *in abstracto*, is no more mysterious than the idea that one can flagellate oneself.

It is not clear how either sort of theory could "solve the hard problem."[8] I do not think that the hard problem *can* be solved via a *straightforward* reductionist path in any case. I believe that the only sense in which consciousness *can* be explained is as follows. First, we must identify its neural correlates, which (I assume) will have a structure nontrivially isomorphic to its phenomenologically ascertainable invariant structure.[9] Once the correlates have been identified, the problem of explaining consciousness reduces to the problem of explaining, in neurobiological terms, the implementation of the relevant brain processes.

However, some of the philosophical longings behind the hard problem will be addressed if it turns out that there is a structurally characterizable property possessed by conscious brains alone that can more or less intuitively be seen to amount to subjectivity. The particular model I offer might indicate that consciousness amounts to *real*, *concrete* nonwellfoundedness. And it is not *entirely* implausible to see that as tantamount to subjectivity.[10] I discuss this speculation briefly in the conclusion. For most of my purposes, it is enough that consciousness has an experientially accessible representational structure, no matter what theory of representation turns out be correct and no matter if consciousness is exhausted by its representational features or not.

II   The Regress Arguments

According to the oldest objection, ubiquity is involved in at least one of two infinite regresses. Put as a dilemma, it is that ubiquity entails either that there are infinitely many distinct conscious mental states or that a single conscious mental state must represent infinitely many objects individually. The desire to avoid the first regress while doing justice to the phenomenology behind ubiquity has, historically, partly motivated relationalist versions according to which each state of consciousness represents itself along with its other objects.[11] But the second regress has typically been brought forward against exactly such versions and is a putative *reductio* of the claim that conscious representation admits of reflexivity.[12]

Classic HOR theorists escape both regresses by allowing for the unconscious representation of lower-order mental states, where they identify the latter with the conscious ones.[13] Most relationalist ubiquity theorists have not seen this appeal to unconscious mental states helpful, even if they thought the idea of unconscious representation intelligible.[14] Nonrelational theorists of self-representation maintain a robust version of ubiquity and reject HOR theory, but they avoid both regresses at the risk of dropping into obscurity insofar as they· treat primitive self-awareness as a *sui generis*, nonrelational feature of consciousness.[15]

But a relational version of ubiquity can escape both regresses.

II.1   The First Regress

This argument is familiar enough. If every conscious mental state is an object of another conscious mental state, and there are no representational cycles, then, if there is one, there are infinitely many. If ubiquity amounted to this antecedent, then, in affirming the existential claim, its proponents would be committed to an infinity of mental states.[16]

Let's consider the argument in a somewhat generalized setting. First, regress arguments *of this sort* will count as refutations only if the "regional ontology" in question will not countenance infinitely many entities. One possible response then is just to expand the ontology. One sees this in rejections of the cosmological argument that rest on the Hume–Edwards principle, in Peter Klein's justificatory infinitism, and in Spinoza's embrace of a KK thesis, an embrace that might suggest his general acceptance of the first regress.[17]

Second, typical regress-engendering theories begin by offering a relational analysis of some target property. Predicates denoting the property will often have grammatically monadic formulations (e.g., being epistemically justified, being causally explained, being conscious). But to be regress-engendering, the relation cannot have certain characteristics. Above all, it cannot admit of *circularity* (in the technical sense), that is, it must preclude cycles of whatever size (aRa or aRb, bRa or aRb, bRc, cRa, etc.).[18] The relation can be transitive, as it arguably is in the cases of epistemic justification and representation (*of the sort in question*), but it need not be. However, if it is transitive, it must also be irreflexive. Transitivity and irreflexivity entail asymmetry and noncircularity.[19] In the epistemic case, this precludes justificatory circles. In the causal-explanatory case, it precludes an event being in its own causal-explanatory ancestry. In the case at hand, it precludes reflexive representation and all other representational cycles.

Third, regress-engendering theories include a "generation thesis" (GT):

$$(\forall x)[(\exists y)(xRy) \supset (\exists z)(zRx)]$$

Given our restrictions on R and the existential premise $(\exists x)(\exists y)(xRy)$, this formula will be satisfiable only in an infinite domain.[20]

Given the existential premise, the options are these: (0) We could embrace the Aleph with Spinoza and Klein, a radical option. We could otherwise (1) deny the GT or (2) allow that the relation admits of circularity. There are two versions of option 1.

(1a) We might allow that the initial object in the sequence is just not such that anything else bears the relevant relation to it. In epistemology one might be some sort of contextualist.[21] In philosophical cosmology, one might allow that there was a brute, initial event in the causal-explanatory ancestry of all subsequent events. In the theory of consciousness, one might adopt a classic HOR theory.

(1b) We could hold that the initial object in the sequence is an entity enjoying a special version of the relevant property that does all the required work but is not covered by the relational analysis. In epistemology we have the noninferentially justified beliefs of the foundationalist. In the cosmological argument of Samuel Clarke, for example, we have the First Cause, which is in the causal-explanatory ancestry of all events but is itself an uncaused but logically necessary being.[22] In the context at hand, we have the view of Dan Zahavi that ubiquitous prereflective self-consciousness is an irrelational, *sui generis* feature at the foundation of all relational forms of self-consciousness.

Moves of type 1b are typically met with resistance; the properties postulated seem mysterious because of their unanalyzability or because they engender other difficulties.

Option 2 is more promising if the subject matter allows it. Of course, our response to a regress argument in one domain need not match our response in another. And the implications of an option 2 response will be more or less counterintuitive given the domain. Thus, few are willing to countenance causal-explanatory or justificatory loops, but many find acceptable Aristotle's venerable regress argument for things desired for their own sakes.[23]

In the theory of consciousness, the classic response to the first regress argument against ubiquity has been of type 2, that is, to maintain that the representation relation admits of reflexivity, and hence, circularity. Ubiquity is preserved because all episodes of consciousness represent themselves, in addition to representing other objects. An episode of consciousness is itself among its objects. And this certainly does not imply that there are infinitely many such episodes. From a purely logical point of view, there need be only one. By dropping the ban on circularity, we can model the GT in a finite domain. In terms of the *logic* of the situation, option 2 responses cannot be faulted. Given that Aristotle, Brentano, and Sartre famously and with *logically* unassailable arguments set out their ubiquitist views in *explicit* response to versions of this regress argument, it is a wonder that often the first objection one encounters after proposing a type 2 version of ubiquity is that it engenders just this regress.

II.2 The Second Regress

Versions of this argument have been put forward by HOR theorists, nonrelationalist ubiquity theorists, and others.[24] Roughly, the idea is that if an episode of consciousness represented itself, then it would have to represent all of its representational properties. Thus, it would have to represent its property of representing itself, represent its property of representing its property of representing itself . . . and so on. Hence, if it represents itself it must represent infinitely many distinct representational properties of itself; but that is absurd.

Here is a more precise formulation. Consider a nominalization operator that we will symbolize by square brackets []. If we have, for example, aRa, then [aRa] is its nominalization. We can read the latter indifferently as "the fact that aRa" or "a's representation of a" or "a's property of representing a." I prefer the last. Nominalizations of formulas with individual constants in place of variables count as individual constants and can be the values of variables; they count as terms. Quantification *into* nominalized contexts is allowed.

Let α be any term and Ξ any context in which α occurs. Let every instance of this schema be an axiom (Schema 1):

$$\alpha \neq [\Xi \; \alpha]$$

For the cases of interest, this codifies the claim that no mental state can be *identified* with its *property* of representing an object.

Next, we have the following axiom (Axiom 2R):

$$(\forall x)(xRx \supset (\forall y)(xRy \supset xR[xRy]))$$

This codifies the claim that if something represents itself, then, for everything it represents, it represents the corresponding representational property.[25] Coupled with an existential premise $((\exists x)(xRx))$, this and Schema 1 are sufficient to generate an infinite regress.

A schematic derivation is sufficient to indicate this:

1. aRa   (EI)
2. aRa $\supset$ aR[aRa]   (1, Ax. 2R, logic)
3. aR[aRa]   (1, 2, MP)
4. aR[aRa] $\supset$ aR[aR[aRa]]   (1, Ax. 2R, logic)
5. aR[aR[aRa]]   (3, 4, MP)

. . . and so on. From Schema 1, it will follow that none of the terms in the sequence a, [aRa], [aR[aRa]], [aR[aR[aRa]]] . . . are identical. Thus, Schema 1, Axiom 2R, and the existential premise can be modeled only in an infinite domain.

In response, we could (0) embrace the regress, (1) deny Schema 1, or (2) restrict Axiom 2R.

(0) To embrace this regress is to hold that every state of consciousness has an infinite representational content and infinitely many actual representational properties. It is not absurd to think that a conscious thought can have an infinite content. It is after all possible to think about the set of natural numbers and other infinite sets. But in another sense, the representational

content of such thoughts is finite. One thinks about all of these numbers not one by one, but as objects collected into *one* set. The same can be said of some thoughts involving quantification. The quantified proposition is one, even if the domain of discourse is infinite. Perhaps such thoughts have an infinite content in an innocuous way. This intuition can be buttressed by the point that considering each of the natural numbers individually would involve an infinite, sequential thought process.

Our capacity to think about the set of natural numbers—though not all infinite sets—might presuppose that we come equipped with a set of cognitive rules for generating any natural number (e.g., by counting). If so, then this option's proponents could maintain we have a similar set of cognitive rules for generating higher-order thoughts. There are limitations, but these could be regarded as merely contingent; and the possession of the capacity could be regarded as sufficient for grounding the actual representation.[26] Just as one does not think about each of the natural numbers individually when one thinks about their set, one need not think about each representational property individually. In effect, a state's self-representation could be taken as a representation of the infinite set of its representational properties. The fact that these can be regarded individually only via a sequential thought process is perhaps some evidence for this view. But this would solve only the phenomenological difficulty with the view.[27] The ontological difficulty remains; it is still hard to swallow the claim that the mind has infinitely many *actual* representational properties. But there are better responses.

(1) We could stop the regress by denying Schema 1 and maintaining that for some α and some Ξ, α = [Ξ α], or, put ontologically, by allowing that some conscious mental state just *is* the representational property in question. This allows one to identify some state a with *its representation of* another object or itself (e.g., a = [aRa] or a = [aRb]) and allows us to model Axiom 2R in a finite domain. But most find weird the idea of *identifying* a state with a property. One might also think this entails yet another infinite regress. If, say, a = [aRb], then doesn't it follow that a = [[aRb]Rb] = [[[aRb]Rb]Rb], and so on? Indeed, it does, but there is a ready response. The fact that there are infinitely many distinct terms that pick out the same state does not imply that there are infinitely many such states. Clearly a single object can be picked out by many distinct expressions. And perhaps what we have here is but a rule for generating distinct ways of picking out the same object. In fact, such rules are easy to concoct.

But is this a cheat? Isn't the idea that, say, a = [aRb] supposed to tell us *something* informative about the state and its structure? Indeed, in such cases the emergence of the relevant expression-forming rule does indicate something important about the structure of these objects. The substitution-based rule is not contrived but follows immediately from the characterization of the structure. Many such circular structures have this feature. If one tries to represent them with means more intuitively suited to the representation of noncircular structures, then the result can be what merely *appears* to be the implication of an infinite ontology. In fact, what such representation involves is but the generation of a rule for picking out the same structure in infinitely many ways. And this stems from the finitely characterizable structure itself. This will be important in the sequel.

In any case, identifying a mental state with its own representation of an object has a curious plausibility to it. If you buy the Moorean, Sartrean, representationalist line that consciousness reveals its objects but is otherwise diaphanous, you should feel the pull of this idea. But this would mean that a state of consciousness is much more *like* a monadic property of its *objects*, as Butchvarov has argued, than it is like a distinct entity that bears a relation to its objects.[28] With the Sartrean insistence on ubiquitous prereflective self-consciousness, we get something like the view that consciousness is *its* representation of its objects among which is its representation of its objects, that is, itself. In effect, we get the view that a state of consciousness is *like* a monadic property exemplified by other objects as well as itself. Phenomenologically, this view is not implausible; it highlights what we might call, with Fregean analogy, the "unsaturated" nature of consciousness as such. But the view does not, I think, have the resources to characterize what is special about the sort of self-representation involved in consciousness, and much of its plausibility can be accommodated without resorting to transcategorial identifications. But it is clear that the view can escape from the second regress. And the "third regress" it seems to engender only raises a point about circular structures to be exploited later.

(2) We can indeed maintain that the self-representation of a mental state entails its representation of the corresponding representational property, but we can argue that the representation of such properties simply terminates.[29] (That is, e.g., aRa entails aR[aRa], but there it stops.) This amounts to the acceptance of a restricted version of Axiom 2R. In effect, we deny that the variables range over nominalizations.[30] The main problem with this response is that it seems ad hoc. Why should the representation stop just where it does? Some considerations about cognitive economy could motivate this restriction. Perhaps it was adaptive for our cognitive/conscious system to involve the representation of first-level representational properties, and any-

thing beyond that was a waste of resources. And if we think, for whatever reason, that the representation should go out to a higher level, we can formulate a new, likewise restricted axiom, that codifies that, for example: $(\forall x)(x\mathrm{R}x \supset (\forall y)(x\mathrm{R}y .\supset. x\mathrm{R}[x\mathrm{R}y] \,\&\, x\mathrm{R}[x\mathrm{R}[x\mathrm{R}y]]))$.

The response, however, is not ad hoc. Axiom 2R, unrestricted, amounts to the claim that, at least with respect to its representational properties, a state of consciousness *completely* represents itself. There is no obvious reason for accepting this claim and no reason to think that every relationalist version of ubiquity is *ipso facto* committed to it. It will take some work, however, to remove the smell of arbitrariness.

First, let us say that x *completely represents* y if for every property, relational or monadic, P of y, x represents [Py].[31] With regard to *everything*, this sort of complete representation is hard to come by. Generally speaking, then, it should not be surprising if a state of consciousness does not represent itself completely. The second regress can arguably be taken as a proof that it cannot be complete even with respect to its representational properties alone. But this *does not* imply that it does not represent itself.

Some will object that this entails that consciousness has "hidden" representational properties. But so be it. This is quite in line with the very plausible idea that consciousness has various sorts of properties that are introspectively inaccessible to it. It does not at all threaten our experientially motivated ubiquity claim. And it does not collapse the view into an HOR theory. The self-representation involved is *not* to be construed as higher order; the very state represents *itself*, albeit incompletely.

Though an episode of consciousness cannot represent all of its representational properties, it can represent a good many of them. And it should be apparent why there would be a strong inclination to think that it must represent all of them. If we have introspective access to all and only the ones it does represent, then our lack of access to the ones it does not could naturally be taken to indicate that there are no such properties. In effect, even if consciousness does not represent all of its properties to itself, it will still seem to itself that it does. But which of its representational properties does an episode of consciousness *in fact* represent in representing itself? And what is the manner of that representation?

The short answer to the first question is that we need not suppose it to represent more of its representational properties than seem to be revealed in reflection. But absent a more detailed understanding of the function of consciousness in our cognitive economy and the limits imposed by its architecture and instantiating materials, we cannot give a complete answer.[32]

Presumably there are possible conscious systems that represent more of their own representational properties than we do, and likely there are some actual ones that represent fewer. But *that* there is a limit is established a priori (*modulo* the assumption that consciousness cannot have infinitely many representational properties and the rejection of transcategorial identity claims).

There are two facts about the manner in which an episode of conscious- . ness represents itself that give some intuitive sense to the notion of incomplete self-representation. Prereflective self-consciousness is both "empty" and "marginal" in senses to be defined. And there are good reasons for thinking that both forms of representation are relatively informationally poor.[33]

The two richest forms of representation at our disposal are the sensory and the propositional, the former for its "analogue" determinateness and specificity, the latter for the host of accessible (relevant) logical implications carried by every proposition entertained. Self-consciousness does not seem to involve any special sensory content, and some HOT theorists have inferred from this that its mode of representation must be propositional, must be a matter of thought. However, save in the case of explicit introspective thoughts, self-consciousness does not seem to involve the entertaining of propositions, and the very possibility of such thoughts rests on a more basic from of self-awareness. Such thoughts merely *describe* what we were *already* aware of.[34] Many assume that the sensory and the propositional are our only modes of representation. Not so. There is a ubiquitous mode of representation that is neither sensory nor a matter of entertaining propositions. But its corresponding kind of content is phenomenal in the sense that it makes a manifest difference to the ways in which objects, even objects of sensory consciousness, appear.

It was a common theme of the phenomenologists that the content of perceptual consciousness goes well beyond what one *senses* at any one time.[35] The objects of perceptual consciousness are always given via a series of profiles. For example, at any one time I see at most three sides of a book sitting on a table. But the content of the episode clearly encompasses more of the book than is currently seen. If the content of the perception were limited to its immediate sensory content then I might be surprised to find that the book had an unseen side. If I lived in a deviant world in which one could never be sure that physical objects had back sides, all such objects would appear quite differently, even if the synchronic sensory contents, narrowly construed, were very often indistinguishable from those enjoyed in the actual world. Likewise, time-consciousness involves the nonmemorial retention of the immediate past and the protention of the immediate future.

Neither mode of representation is sensory or involves the entertaining of propositions, but both make a difference to the way in which the present moment appears. For example, the very same tone heard in a simple melody will sound quite different if preceded by one sequence of tones rather than another, but one *hears* only one tone at a time.

This nonsensory and nonpropositional mode of representation, which I shall call "empty," is informationally poorer than sensory and propositional modes. For example, though I emptily represent the unseen sides of the book, I need not also emptily represent their specific color. But some specific color or colors will be in any sensory presentation of some side of the book. Though for any property of an object one cares to single out, one *could*, under suitable circumstances, emptily represent it, the general point stands. There will always be some specific information sensation affords that goes beyond anything emptily represented. In protention as well, we represent only a certain range of possible futures. If I throw an object into the air, I protend its falling and landing (again, without entertaining any propositions), but this leaves open many of the details about its exact trajectory and the definite way in which it will land. Few people, for example, protend that a fair coin will come up heads. Retention, no doubt, carries more information than protention but still less than was present in the episode of consciousness retended and much less than the occurrent one.

I am suggesting that an episode of consciousness represents itself in an analogous, nonpropositional, nonsensory, "empty" way. And like other forms of empty representation, it is informationally impoverished but has *phenomenal* consequences. In particular, I maintain, this empty self-representing constitutes the *subjectivity* of consciousness. By "subjectivity," I do not mean the qualitative, sensory dimension of experience. I mean, rather, the fact that all conscious experiences are *for* a subject.

On this view, the subject of consciousness is just the conscious episode itself.[36] Subjectivity is, informatively, identified with (incomplete) empty self-representation. We thus avoid the postulation of some sort of homunculus behind consciousness. This does justice to the Moorean intuitions about consciousness while making some sense of how we could be aware of it in spite of its *sensory* diaphaneity and nonpropositional character.

Our R in Axiom 2R should be identified with this nonsensory, nonpropositional form of representation. And on that interpretation, aRa, aR[aRa], and aR[aR[aRa]], for example, could be true while aR[aR[aR[aRa]]] is false. It might be tempting to think that something of the form [xRy] picks out what could only be *thought* or represented propositionally. But this is false. The nonpropositional or "pre-predicative" representation of properties and facts is actually quite common, something reflected in the attributive use of adjectives.

On this account empty self-representation partly grounds our capacity to form reflective *thoughts*. That capacity also demands that we have a cognitive/conceptual system capable of abstracting a good many of the properties characteristic of representations as such. Clearly we do have such a system. But, in principle, a creature could emptily self-represent without having one. And this allows us to make sense of the idea that animals and infants could be conscious (and self-representing in this way) without being able to formulate higher-order thoughts.

But note well, the view is not that empty self-representation is fully analogous to the empty representation that occurs in perception. In visual perception, for example, one typically emptily represents, among other things, the parts of the objects that are not currently present in the visual field. But one can, by, say, rotating an object, acquire a filled representation corresponding to the previously empty one; simultaneously, previously filled representations will become empty. In Husserl and others, the fact that physical objects give themselves via these profiles while consciousness does not was taken to be a clear phenomenological way of distinguishing between the two.[37] I do not wish to dispute that, though, again, it is gravely erroneous to take this to mean that consciousness reveals all of its properties to itself. In claiming that consciousness emptily represents itself, I am not claiming that it is given to itself the way physical objects are given to it. It is not a matter of consciousness intimating hidden features of itself that can then become the objects of filled representations.[38] When we reflect we do not, presumably, discover anything that was not in some way present before we reflected. The main relevant similarity is just that such intending is nonsensory, does not involve the entertaining of propositions, and is thus informationally impoverished. Perhaps then I should not call this sort of intending "empty." The original rationale for that term, after all, stems from the contrast with representations that involve sensory (or perhaps imagistic) content, the "filled" ones.

But there is an analogy strong enough to motivate this extension of the term. We can take reflections to be somewhat like filled representations in the sensory-perceptual domain. The relevant transformation is from a marginal (i.e., inattentive) and nonpropositional mode of awareness to an attentive and, in some cases, propositional one. And perhaps in all cases, reflection involves some form of categorial intuition.[39] Though reflective self-awareness remains nonsensory, it is not too far a stretch to take reflections to be *filled* by new categorial and, often, propositional content descriptive of what one was prereflectively aware of in a pre-predicative and nonpropositional way.

In any case, we can fully dispel any doubts about the informational poverty (incompleteness) of prereflective self-representation by considering its other important feature.

Aron Gurwitsch was perhaps the first to claim with sufficient explicitness that ubiquitous, prereflective self-consciousness is *marginal*.[40] The primary distinction between prereflective self-consciousness and reflective self-consciousness, on this model, is drawn in terms of attention. In reflective self-consciousness one attends to one's own episodes of consciousness. In prereflective self-consciousness, they are unattended, only marginally present. When one shifts into the reflective mode, that reflective act itself becomes its own object of empty, marginal representation. This can, in turn, ground further acts of reflection of still higher-order, out to some capacity limit.

Taking a common and generally good analogy drawn in terms of the visual field too seriously might make one think this is a faulty characterization of experience. Often one can be brought to understand the notion of marginal consciousness by noting that in vision there are always objects central to the field and objects in the periphery. Usually one is also attending to the central objects and not the peripheral ones, even though they are just as much a manifest part of the conscious visual experience.

Carrying the analogy over to consciousness itself, the claim is that what one typically attends to are the objects of the experience, not the experience of the objects, even though that experience is self-present. And this helps to explain the ease with which we can focus our attention onto the experience itself and away from the objects it presents. When we reflect, the worldly objects become marginal and the experience itself attended. This is not unlike shifting one's visual gaze from something in the center of the field to something in the periphery. If one thought that, on this account, the episode of consciousness would have to be in its own field in exactly the same way as the objects of peripheral vision are in the visual field, involving as they do some distinguishable sensory content, then one would view this as a misdescription. But in prereflective self-consciousness the episode is represented in a nonsensory way, so the worry is easily resolved.

We tend to operate with a conception of consciousness that presupposes that is both attentive and concept involving. Attentive, conceptual consciousness stands out readily. But if we identify all consciousness with such attentive, conceptual consciousness, then we will miss the general phenomenon of marginal consciousness and its important features. First, marginal consciousness is, in a certain sense, passive. Its objects are merely present and are not made the objects of conscious cognitive operations. Second, when we have marginal consciousness of something for which we do have concepts, it is as if the object is presented in a way that at least approximates the way it was presented before we had any such concepts. It is reasonable to think this because our primitive perceptual and representational capacities do not undergo absolutely radical transformations upon our conceptual development.

But one need not have any concepts for what one is marginally conscious of, and that allows us to say that at the beginning of a creature's conscious life, all self-consciousness is nonconceptual.[41] If the creature has a sufficiently powerful cognitive apparatus, it will develop conceptual modes of self-consciousness. After development, it will have the ability to cognize and describe its conscious episodes at will. In effect, as soon as it decides to attend to its own conscious episodes, those concepts will be effortlessly deployed. But this applies to marginal consciousness quite generally; a similar story could be told about one's marginal consciousness of background refrigerator hums. We can, if we like, call the marginal consciousness of objects for which we have concepts "conceptual," but it should be understood that such concepts are not deployed, save perhaps in some unconscious way, before the shifting of attention to those objects.

It is true as well that one need not have any concepts other than demonstrative ones in order to be attentively conscious of something. The attentional–marginal and conceptual–nonconceptual distinctions thus cut across one another. One can turn one's attention to something simply as a "that." Presumably, this ability is required for there to be any consciousness-mediated conceptual development. Of course, we come with a large stock of innate conceptual or pattern-recognition capacities. And an important set of similarities and differences in the world is surely reflected in the field of consciousness prior to conceptual development in a way that suits our innate cognitive capacities. If this were not the case, I don't see how there could be any consciousness-mediated conceptual development, at least not any that would have a good chance of accurately reflecting the relevant contours of the world. Rudimentary, attentive consciousness seems essential to such development. One attends to these similarities and differences and develops the corresponding concepts. But that development takes place against the backdrop of a field of which one is conscious but which includes many items for which one may not yet have any developed concepts. And no matter how conceptually developed one becomes, there is always more to articulate and categorize on the horizon.

When we want to understand something new or deepen our knowledge of something already familiar, we focus our attention in that direction and often repeatedly over a long period of time. In doing this, we are able to acquire more and more information about the object of interest. The acquisition of more information about an object guides the refinement of the system of concepts through which we understand it. Attention probably has several functions, but the important one here is that it allows one to go from a more impoverished to a richer representation of an object. It is a commonplace that the more attention one focuses on something the more information about it one is likely to absorb and the better one's subsequent spontaneous cognition of the object will become.

When an object is shifted from being marginal to being attended, the amount of detail in which it is represented increases. What was before only sketched or vaguely intimated becomes open to better view. And properties of the object that before were not represented at all can suddenly come to be represented. This is familiar. I turn on a light in the basement. I am focusing my attention on the sometimes slippery descending stairs. (I have fallen on them before.) While so engaged, there is a swift blur moving across the floor in the periphery of my visual field (and in the margin of my stairwell-attending consciousness). I turn my head to get a better look. A slightly less blurry figure is now visible in the corner. Is it a spider? I finish my descent and approach the corner slowly. Now it looks like it has too many legs to be a spider. Right, it's not spider. What is it? I get even closer. Hmm . . . some sort of weird-looking centipede. I've never seen one like that before. I had no idea centipedes could move so quickly. I should put it in a jar and have an even closer look.

While it was marginal, the representation of what turned out to be a centipede was informationally extremely thin. The focus of attention toward it yielded more information, enough to allow me to make certain reasonable guesses. More attentive investigation ruled out my first guess and eventually revealed something I had never encountered before. Now when I go into the basement I am poised to regard any flitting blurs on the floor as centipedes of this variety. That information is thus poised to configure even my marginally conscious representations, though I can still be wrong. There are also spiders in the basement, just not as many. If I want to be sure, I have to pay more attention. The initial informational poverty of marginal consciousness should be evident from such examples as should the information increase provided through attention.[42]

Applying this to the case of marginal self-consciousness, we can draw the lesson that it is, in essence, informationally much poorer than attentive self-consciousness. It is reasonable to suppose that it is informationally rich enough to allow for more or less accurate attentive-reflective judgments, and rich enough to eliminate any surprises upon reflection, but we need not suppose it to be much richer than that. This means that in prereflective self-consciousness certain representational properties of consciousness are indeed represented and represented accurately enough. But this indicates that the number of representational properties of consciousness represented pre-reflectively is limited, and it certainly means that there is no representation of an infinite hierarchy of them. These considerations should serve to rebut the claim that our response to the second regress is ad hoc.

Still, one might think that attentive self-consciousness does not reveal any information about an episode of consciousness not already prereflectively represented in it. In *one* sense I think this is correct. This is why, among other things, we are not simply taken aback upon introspection. Moreover, all of the phenomenological distinctions we make, be these the stuff of folk psychology or the results of more rigorous methods, have their basis in pre-reflective experience. I reject views according to which such distinctions are theoretical and merely *imposed on* that experience. Just as one can *learn from experience* a system of concepts that facilitates cognition in some empirical domain, so too one can *learn from our experience of our experience* the system of concepts that more or less accurately reflects its contours. In both cases, the lion's share of the learning involves attending to what was already present but hitherto unthematized.

If noticing distinctions, previously present but hitherto ignored, can be regarded as the acquisition of new information, then, in *that* sense, attentive self-consciousness can reveal more about any particular episode of experience than is (self-)represented in it prereflectively. Further, the system of phenomenological concepts develops via generalization. It is based on attention to *many* episodes of experience. Its reflective deployment, no matter how spontaneous it becomes, brings to experiences subsequently reflected-on general information that goes well beyond what is contained in any particular episode. But, in effect, this is information about the specific experience *qua* member of a genus or, in some cases, information about the relational properties of the experience that can stand out only after the consideration of numerous instances. Thus, *that* an episode of consciousness belongs to a specific experiential category need not be (self-)represented prereflectively *in* that experience, even though all of the properties *on the basis of which* it would be reflectively categorized in a particular way *are* so prereflectively represented. This makes sense of the idea that attentive self-consciousness can reveal more about an episode of experience than is prereflectively self-represented in it without simply "projecting" properties onto it.

III A Sketch of a Model

One plausible route to the construction of a scientifically respectable theory of consciousness is to proceed according to the following directives: (A) begin with the phenomenological data; (B) develop an abstract model of the invariant structures of consciousness based on that data; (C) search the model for interesting implications; and, finally, (D) articulate and experimentally verify a neurobiological interpretation of the model. This section is a *gesture* in the direction of a model that might have a hope of satisfying directive B.

The data I shall attempt to capture here in an abstract and idealized way are these: (1) the representational character of consciousness in both its hetero- and auto-representational aspects, (2) the synchronic unity of consciousness, (3) the difference between attentive and marginal consciousness, and (4) the temporality of consciousness. Other important features will be omitted. In particular, the model will be insensitive to the differences between propositional, sensory, and empty modes of representation, to the attitudinal and affective dimensions, to the qualitative and "gestalt" aspects of phenomenal fields, to the conceptual–nonconceptual distinction, and to the ontological status of the objects of representation. Perhaps some of these can be captured by suitable enrichments, but we will not pursue that here. And whether it, in some sense, captures differences in the informational richness of representations will depend on how we interpret the construal of the difference between marginal and attentive consciousness. Finally, the model abstracts from any details pertaining to the "guts" of the implementation and is in principle compatible with many different theories of representation.

(1) Hetero-representational and auto-representational character All episodes of consciousness, we assume, simultaneously exhibit hetero-directed and auto-directed intentionality. We will assume that representation is a relational matter, and even if it is not, perhaps a suitable translation of the model could be formulated. The *direct* representation relation will be taken to be the converse of the set membership relation. Thus "x represents y" will be expressed by "$y \in x$." Because the relation will admit of reflexive instances, *direct* self-representation (for x) will be expressed by "$x \in x$." Interpreted in terms of membership, this will mean that x is a member of itself and that x is thus a nonwellfounded set or "hyperset." Accordingly, the set theoretical framework we adopt is that of nonwellfoudned set theory (ZFA in particular).[43] This may seem radical, but nonwellfounded sets have already been used to model self-referential propositions and a variety of other circular phenomena.[44] I am proposing that these techniques be extended to the modeling of the circular structure of consciousness.[45] This idea is really implicit in the two quotations (from Sartre and Barwise) with which this essay begins.

It is extremely important that one not *confuse* models of circular structures with circular explanations. On the view presented here, each episode of consciousness has a circular structure in virtue of its ubiquitous (though incomplete) self-representation. The episodes are somewhat analogous to self-referential propositions.[46] But this does not mean we are attempting to *explain* consciousness in terms of itself. In fact, we are here aiming only at accurate *description*, a prerequisite for any attempt at explanation.

Note as well that the use of sets to model representational systems is prima facie attractive because there is an analogy between the individuation of sets in terms of their members and the individuation of representations in terms of their objects.[47]

All representations will be construed as sets. I will say that metarepresentations *indirectly* represent the object of the lower-order representation. Thus $\{x\}$ corresponds to a representation whose only object is x. A set $z = \{y, \{x\}\}$, for example, picks out a representation whose objects are y and $\{x\}$. I will say that y and $\{x\}$ are *directly represented* by z and that x is *indirectly represented* by z. Thus, if one wants to characterize, in a way that abstracts from order, the *full* representational content of a state as modeled by a set, one can take transitive closure of the set. That is, one can form the set that has all the members of the initial set, all the members of the members, the members of the members of the members, and so on.[48]

Finally, I shall assume that there are representations of objects that are not themselves representations. These will be "ur-elements," members of our sets that are not themselves sets. I will assume that we are in no danger of running out of them. Just what interpretation one places on them will be partly a function of one's theory of representation and partly a function of one's underlying ontology. We abstract from both of these.

(2) Synchronic unity   At any moment, there will be many objects of which one is conscious. But it is incorrect to posit separate, ongoing acts of consciousness corresponding to each one of these. Rather, each episode has a differentiated but unified intentional structure, *one* complex field. That field can be articulated in terms of many objects. But one is conscious, at once, of the entire field, and marginally conscious of that whole unified episode. This will be reflected in the model in that each set corresponding to an episode of consciousness can have as large a (finite) number of elements as one would like, and any change in elements reflects a change in episode.

(3) **Attentive vs. marginal consciousness**   This difference can be represented as a matter of ordering. And this, once one gets used to it, is an intuitive way to represent it. For example, think of those days when you have, as we say, a million things to do. One can, in a certain way, apprehend at once everything one must do. One might make a list to get clear about all the tasks. But then in carrying them out, one must attend to them serially. The present task will occupy one's attention, but the next task will often be in the immediate margin, the one after that, further in the margin, and so on. But it should be clear that this ordering of represented objects is not a temporal ordering. The objects of attention are presented at the same time as the marginal objects. The model will thus have a particular phenomenological interpretation; the claim is not that we understand the phenomenology in terms of either spatial of temporal order. The notion of order is much more general than that.

Given the set-theoretical framework, we can represent order by means of the Kuratowski definition. On this model, then, an episode of consciousness will be represented by an ordered n-tuple. Intuitively, the objects of attentive consciousness will appear first in the ordering while the objects of marginal consciousness appear later. This will allow us to represent degrees of marginality and thus perhaps to recapture Gurwitsch's distinction between merely co-present objects (marginal in his technical sense) and objects in the thematic field (those objects more closely relevant to the objects of attention).[49] And because an episode of consciousness is always its own marginal object, it itself will occur in the ordering. That is, the set that corresponds to it will be either a member of a member of itself or a member of a member of a member of itself . . . and so on, depending on where in the ordering it occurs.

It might be possible to analyze this ordering in terms of the degree of information content with which each object is represented, attended objects represented with the higher degree, and marginal objects with lesser and lesser degrees. Thus the object first in the ordering would be represented in the informationally richest way and the last object in the ordering in the informationally poorest, where this measure abstracts from readily deployable information one *brings to* an experience. We assume that there is such a correspondence but will not pursue the analysis further. But this makes clear sense of some of the intuitions behind the rather vague and strictly speaking erroneous talk of "degrees of consciousness."

(4) Temporality By "temporality" I mean the idea, classically articulated by Husserl and recently put to such interesting neurophenomenological use by Dan Lloyd, that consciousness, no matter its ever fluctuating content, has an invariant, tripartite retentive–occurrent–protentive structure.[50] Again, in hearing a simple melody, I occurrently hear only the note sounding now, but I retend the just past notes and protend the notes to come, where retention is not to be identified with memory and protention is not to be identified with an attended or thinkingly articulated anticipation. Retended and protended episodes of consciousness are also marginal data. And this complex of retentions and protentions makes a major, nonsensory contribution to the character of occurrent experience.[51] Husserl suggested, and Lloyd (following the work of Jeffrey Elman) develops into a neural network model, the idea that retention is a "recursive" process in which a given episode of consciousness retends its immediate predecessor episode, which retends its predecessor . . . and so on, back to some cut-off point.[52] This too can be easily modeled by means of sets.

Before we present a sketch of our model, we should show how the use of nonwellfounded sets does not involve us in yet another infinite regress. Consider, for example, a set x such that $x = \{o,x\}$ ($o \in x$ and $x \in x$, and x and o are the only members of x). Isn't that set identical to $\{o, \{o,x\}\}$, to $\{o, \{o, \{o,x\}\}\}$, and so on? Yes, but this does not commit us to infinitely many objects. The set x has only two elements. Moreover, x is *hereditarily finite*. It is finite, has no infinite sets in its membership chain, and has only finitely many elements in its membership chain. The transitive closure of our x is finite.[53]

What might mislead us here, once again, is the idea that a difference in representation corresponds to a difference in entity. The expressions $\{o, \{o,x\}\}$, $\{o,\{o, \{o,x\}\}\}$, and so on all pick out our x, but this implies neither that x has an actually infinite structure nor that it has infinitely many elements nor that x is not hereditarily finite. Instead, as before, this particular multiplicity of ways of representing x stems from the fact that x has a circular structure.[54] It is true that x, and sets like it, can be used to represent repetitious sequences of whatever length one wants, but they do this by finite means. This is less mysterious than it might seem.

Suppose that the *barber of* relation does not admit of circularity, and suppose a finite number of people. Pick a person at random and find the person's barber. Now find the barber of the person's barber, and continue the process. On these suppositions, we will eventually find a rather hirsute barber who has no barber—we can suppose that everyone else has one. But if we allow that the *barber of* relation admits of circularity, then we need not ever find a barber who has no barber. Moreover, we could iterate the successful search as long as we want, but this would not imply that there are infinitely many barbers; instead we would, at some point, just "loop." Similarly, we can iterate the *member of* "search" on a nonwellfounded set as long as we want, but that in no way entails that there are infinitely many sets. If we found some B who is his own barber, to take the smallest possible cycle, B would be picked out by "the barber of B," by "the barber of the barber of B," and so on. In effect, we would have a rule for generating (in principle) infinitely many expressions that pick out B. But clearly this does not involve us in postulating infinitely many barbers or a barber with an infinite structure! And something analogous can be said about the nonwell-founded sets of interest to us. These have a circular, not infinite, structure. Their structure is in itself finite and finitely describable, and this becomes clearer when one sees the directed graphs commonly used to represent them.

It is not an accident that some of those who have attempted to picture the Aristotle–Brentano relational ubiquity theory of the representational structure of consciousness have ended up producing directed graphs that look very much like the directed graphs used to represent nonwellfounded sets.[55] Consider our set $x = \{o, x\}$. Its directed graph is shown in figure 6.1. The set x, represented by the dot, is at the origin of the arrows. The arrows represent the converse membership relation. In other words, if something is a member of x, then there will be an arrow originating from x and terminating at the element (here, both x and o are elements). It is easy to see how this could be used to interpret the representation relation obtaining between a mental state and its objects, and this means that one could just as easily interpret the representation relation in terms of the converse membership relation, as we have done here. Note that if our o above had any members, we could represent that as well by drawing arrows from o to its elements.

Now let's consider an overly simplified version of our model. Let $c = \langle o, c \rangle$, where o is an ur-element. This notation is meant to indicate that c is the ordered pair consisting of o and c itself. The fact that o comes first is meant to indicate that it is the object of attention. Likewise c is in the second position to indicate that it is an object of marginal consciousness. The set c, itself, is to be thought of as representing a (very primitive) episode of consciousness. Now, using the Kuratowski definition of ordered pair, let's transform

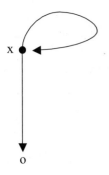

Figure 6.1

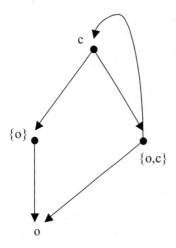

Figure 6.2

this into the notation of sets: $\langle o,c \rangle = \{\{o\}, \{o,c\}\}$. Now let's graph this simple set, as in figure 6.2. Of course, graphs of n-tuples that more closely approximate the representational content of an actual episode of consciousness would be rather unwieldy, but there is no problem in principle here.

Using the notation for ordered n-tuples, we can present the simple sketch. We can represent the "stream" of consciousness as a family of sets. The "streaming" will not simply be a matter of the external ordering of the family, but will be represented within each set via "recursive" retention. That is, except for the initial set, each set in the family has its predecessor somewhere in its ordering; and this captures the nesting of retentions. Via protention, of course, the immediate successor of a given set in the family will also occur in the ordering. But recall that we are abstracting from representational peculiarities. The relevant peculiarity in this case is just that a protended episode of consciousness is an empty, marginal projection of the representational content of the subsequent episode. It thus may be incorrect in a way that retention cannot. But, again, we are abstracting from that.[56]

Consider then a family of sets, each one modeling a distinct episode of consciousness, constructed along the following lines.

(1) $c_n = \langle o_1, \ldots o_t, c_{n+1}, c_n, c_{n-1} \rangle$

(2) $c_{n+1} = \langle o_1, \ldots o_t, c_{n+2}, c_{n+1}, c_n \rangle$

... and so on.

Take $o_1, \ldots o_t$ in this sketch to be, in effect, variables. Thus, for example, o_1 in c_n need not be identical to o_1 in c_{n+1}. If we wanted to represent some concrete episode, we could plug in some combination of sets (representations) and ur-elements (nonrepresentations) in place of the variables. Again, the position of the object in the ordering corresponds to the degree to which it is attended.

Note that this allows us to model the difference between introspective or reflective self-consciousness and prereflective (marginal) self-consciousness quite easily.[57] Again, we simply identify reflective self-consciousness with attentive self-consciousness. When one attends to a past or presently occurring episode of consciousness, one is reflecting. As one should expect, the difference will be represented as a difference of order. If one is inclined to think that reflection always involves a kind of retrospection or (very short-term) memory, then all such thoughts will have something like the following structure:

$c_n = \langle c_{n-m(n>m>0)}, o_2, \ldots o_t, c_{n+1}, c_n, c_{n-1} \rangle$

If one thinks that one can attend to one's own occurrent episode of consciousness, then one would need only place c_n first in the ordering above to model that.

IV Some Considerations

First, the sketched model is static. It seems to build in the assumption that episodes of consciousness come in discrete "packages." But it is not unreasonable to think that consciousness is dynamic to its core. However, this does not mean that the model is incompatible with a dynamic one. After all, many kinds of processes exhibit invariant patterns that emerge from the "flux." The set-theoretical model of these invariants should in principle be compatible with many theories of the underlying dynamics.

Now, consider again the very simplified model of a conscious episode ($c = \langle o,c \rangle$) represented in figure 6.2. If we take seriously the Kuratowski method of representing ordered n-tuples,[58] then we can derive the following unforeseen results about the structure of consciousness. First, it turns out that consciousness is indeed a matter of metarepresentation. But the sort of metarepresentation involved is importantly very different from the usual varieties considered. This is reflected in the fact that the elements of our simple set $c = \{\{o\}, \{o,c\}\}$ are themselves sets, $\{o\}$ and $\{o,c\}$. Second, an episode does not represent itself directly. This will be the case no matter how many objects we place in the ordering. Put in terms of the representation relation, c represents a representation, $\{o,c\}$, that in turn represents c. Thus c represents itself *indirectly*. Of course, in representing c, $\{o,c\}$ represents a representation that also represents it; so, $\{o,c\}$ indirectly represents itself as well. If we take this picture seriously, it seems to indicate that consciousness is the product of the coupling of two representational systems, and that the self-representation characteristic of consciousness is achieved indirectly via that coupling.

This is highly suggestive because it is known that indirect (and incomplete) autodescription via a sort of "mirroring" can be achieved without infinite regress.[59] Moreover, this kind of indirect autodescription can serve as a basis for replication. If it can allow for replication with input-mediated modification, then perhaps it will turn out that the same structures that account for marginal self-consciousness also account for retention. On this understanding, an episode of consciousness is the "child" of its predecessor. Its other parent is just the new information folded into the ongoing replicative process. In effect, it is the reincarnation of its parent *as modified by new input*. Perhaps the ubiquitous self-representation manifest in consciousness *just is* the autodescription required by the replicative process, which in turn undergirds retention. But I cannot pursue this hypothesis further at present.[60]

V Conclusion

Even if this model turns out to be too mathematically trivial to be of much further use, it at least indicates the practicability of the idea of capturing the invariant, accessible structures of consciousness by suitable mathematical means. The model might indicate something about the representational architecture of the brain systems that implement consciousness, or this might be a mere artifact. But such questions and the models that enable their formulation should be pursued.

Finally, the model might suggest a more radical speculation. If we interpret the nonwellfoundedness in a fully realistic way, then one might reasonably think that the sort of structure uniquely associated with consciousness is just that: real, instantiated-in-the-world nonwellfoundedness. We would then have something quite reminiscent of Hofstadter's "strange loops." If the descriptions that motivate the model are correct, then we already know that there is something that appears to exhibit this structure. Each one of us already has (or can have) a *phenomenological* model (now in both of the classical senses of "phenomenological") of a concrete, nonwellfounded entity. If we further assume that this appearance is not a mere illusion and assume that consciousness is identical to some concretely instantiated brain process, it follows that that process will have such a structure as well. If this line of reasoning is correct, then we should probably begin attempting to determine the conditions under which a physical system can instantiate nonwellfoundedness. Moreover, there is something intuitive about the association of nonwellfoundedness with subjectivity. It is not too far a stretch to think that any such system would have to be a subject. On the other hand, a lesson to be drawn from *Vicious Circles* by Barwise and Moss is that *many* concrete phenomena can be modeled by means of hypersets. Thus to defend this identification one would have to find a way to distinguish those concrete phenomena that are, so to speak, nonwellfounded *an sich* from those that are merely modelable by these means where that modeling is not to be interpreted realistically.

And this indicates another problem with our line of reasoning. Whatever one wants to model in ZFA, one can model in standard ZF.[61] Moreover, it seems that computation over nonwellfounded domains is unproblematic.[62] This might suggest that models framed in terms of nonwellfounded sets, in the end, employ a mere *façon de parler*, one that is fully translatable into models that do not involve it. Depending on one's philosophical tastes with regard to the foundations of set theory and one's attitude toward the "hard problem," this will bode either well or ill for the idea that the model presented here has explanatory implications that take us beyond the phenomenology.[63]

Notes

1. I use "consciousness," "awareness," and "experience" synonymously. I dislike the phrases "state of consciousness" and "conscious state," but use them. I sometimes use "act" and "episode" instead of "state."

2. Kapitan 1999 and this volume.

3. On the history of the thesis and connected issues see, e.g., Caston 2002; Wider 1997; Zahavi 1999; Williams 1998. For AI-connected work the *locus classicus* is Hofstadter 1979; cf. Case 1994; Perlis 1997; and Khromov 2001. For neuroscience-connected work see, e.g., Damasio 1999 and Metzinger 2003.

4. Rosenthal 1986, p. 345; cf. Gennaro this volume.

5. Zahavi 1999, p. 33.

6. See Kriegel 2002a, pp. 526–527, and Levine this volume for discussions of this worry. See Millikan 1993, p. 98 and Carruthers 2000 and this volume. See also Kampis 1995 and Hart 1987.

7. Nonclassic HOR theories include Gennaro's "WIV" view and Carruthers's theory. For quite different reasons, both theories arguably end up positing *internal* relations.

8. See Chalmers 1995a.

9. I assume a kind of identity theory. If the invariant phenomenological structure is *representational*, perhaps we will not be able to identify it in the brain absent a theory of neural representation. However, it would do us little good if there is no ascertainable transformation from the structure of the objects represented to the structure of the representation. But if there is this transformation, then a model of the representational structure of consciousness could aid us in developing a theory of neural representation. The best policy is to proceed with the modeling and see where it leads.

10. Cf. Rucker 2005, pp. 37–42. I suspect that the problem of "gappy" identities between brain (or functional) states and so-called phenomenal states that troubles Levine (2001a and this volume) and others can be *dissolved* by considerations stemming from self-representation. This has to do, I speculate, with a certain correspondence between undecidability and indefinability and with the fact that for self-representative systems of sufficient complexity there is no way to "compress" the description of them. See Gödel's remarks, quoted in von Neumann 1966, pp. 55–56, and Chaitin 1999 for the theoretical background.

11. See Aristotle, *De anima* 3.2, 425b12–17; 1981, pp. 43ff.; Brentano, *Psychology* 2.2.7–11; 1995, pp. 121–134; Sartre, *Being and Nothingness*, introduction, 3; 1956, pp. lii–liii. Though Sartre does seem to embrace a relationalist version of ubiquity in that location, elsewhere (e.g., 1940/2004, p. 14) he sounds much more like Zahavi. It should be no surprise then that there are many interpretations of the exact content of his view. See, e.g., Wider 1997; Zheng 2000; Gennaro 2002; and Zahavi this volume.

12. By locutions like "admits of reflexivity" I mean to indicate that the relation will not necessarily be reflexive on the set of all the objects in question. It is not the case that everything standing in a representation relation bears that relation to itself. But according to ubiquity, representation is reflexive on the set of conscious episodes.

13. For an excellent introduction to the varieties of HO theory, see Gennaro 2004a.

14. It is clear from Brentano's presentation of the argument (see esp. 1995, pp. 129–130) that he does *not* take as a premise the claim that there are no unconscious mental states. Rather, he argues that the regress argument does not *establish* the existence of unconscious mental states precisely because of the possibility of representational reflexivity.

15. Cf. Zahavi quoted above. One motive behind such views is the idea that there is something problematic with taking an episode of consciousness to be its own object. But it is question-begging to build into the very notion of "*x* is an object for *y*" the implication that $x \neq y$. It is difficult to understand why anyone would think this. The main problem with such views is that it is not easy to understand what they assert. They speak of "self-acquaintance," which sounds relational. But then they deny that they are positing a relation. See also Tugendhat 1986, pp. 53–54.

16. See Kriegel 2003a; Caston 2002; and Perrett 2003 (including their notes) for more on the long history of the argument.

17. The Hume–Edwards principle is, roughly, just the claim that if every member of an (infinite) collection of events has a causal explanation, then the there is no need for a causal explanation of the entire collection as such (Klein 2005; Spinoza 1994; p. 132). Fales (1996, pp. 160–165) holds a dispositionalist version of the KK thesis.

18. Cf. Barwise and Moss 1996, p. 24: "[A binary relation] R is said to be *circular* if there is a finite sequence $b_0, \ldots, b_k$ such that $b_0 = b_k$ and $b_{n+1} R b_n$ for each $n = 1, \ldots, k$. Such a sequence is called a *cycle* in R. If there are no such cycles, then R is called *noncircular*."

19. Asymmetry implies irreflexivity. Asymmetry and transitivity jointly imply noncircularity; and noncircularity implies irreflexivity as reflexivity implies circularity.

20. For explicitness, the following set of formulas is satisfiable only in an infinite domain (see Sanford 1984b, p. 109):

(1) $(\forall x)(\forall y)(\forall z)(x R y \ \& \ y R z \ . \supset . \ x R z)$ Transitivity

(2) $(\forall x) {\sim} (x R x)$ Irreflexivity

(3) $(\forall x) \ [(\exists y)(x R y) \supset (\exists z)(z R x)]$ Generation Thesis

(4) $(\exists x)(\exists y)(x R y)$ Existential Premise

21. Cf. Moser 1985, pp. 29ff.

22. See my 2003a for details.

23. Lehrer (2002, p. 430) accepts a certain sort of justificatory loop in order to stop a regress. He also accepts the loop solution to the first regress as well; see Lehrer 1991 and this volume.

24. See, e.g., Ryle 1949, pp. 162–163; Kim 1978, pp. 201ff.; Gennaro this volume. The argument has been recently discussed by Kriegel (2003a, pp. 125–126) and Caston (2002, pp. 796–798). Dan Zahavi (1999, pp. 30–31) has argued that relationalist ubiquity leads to an infinite *explanatory* regress. There are echoes of this in Rosenthal (1986, pp. 339–347). In effect, both use these considerations to rule out type 2 responses to the first regress, and then Zahavi argues for a 1b response, accepting self-consciousness as a kind intrinsic property, while Rosenthal argues for a 1a response, finding 1b responses incompatible with his reductionist motivations. As I see it, Zahavi is really presenting a version of the second regress. This is borne out by his reference to Cramer (1974, p. 581); see also Caston 2002, pp. 796–798; and Drummond this volume. Explanation, however, is not at issue. Rather, it is the proper *description* of the structure of consciousness. The argument is analogous to the regress of complete self-representation that comes up in context of the theory of self-reproducing automata. Von Neumann showed how to achieve self-replication (and a form of self-representation) while avoiding the regress, though this is left rather implicit in von Neumann 1966, pp. 118ff. But see Sipper and Reggia 2001 and Case 1994. The regress is vividly and visually illustrated in Hofstadter's presentation of self-swallowing TV screens in *Gödel, Escher, Bach* (1979, pp. 490–491) and this volume. See also Rucker (2005, pp. 38–41), who points out that Josiah Royce (1899/1959, pp. 494ff.), in effect, embraced this regress and held the mind to be infinite.

25. Cf. Caston 2002, p. 797.

26. Carruthers (2000, pp. 241ff.) argues that the mere disposition of a thought to "go higher-order" confers on it *actual* higher-order ("dual") content; this is a consequence his theory of content. He stops the regress this seems to threaten by denying that we really have third-order recognitional concepts. I find that implausible. But his general response is effective as long as there is some "order of thoughts" we do not have the capacity to form. However, it is not clear that his view can adequately distinguish between reflective and prereflective self-consciousness. And it seems to imply that a system's possession of the concept of experiential subjectivity, in effect, *generates* the very things (its conscious experiences) to which the concept applies. One then wonders how the concept of experiential subjectivity came about in the first place. It seems more plausible to hold that that concept is abstracted from preexisting experiences and that the conceptual machinery that enables that abstraction evolved precisely because there were experiences it might be good for a system to reason about. Another way to stop the regress is to hold that we merely have the disposition to think higher-order thoughts. See Kim 1978 and Perrett 2003. However, this does not do justice to the phenomenological fact of *actual* prereflective self-awareness. That actual awareness, on my view, is what, partly, grounds the disposition to reflect. And the regress seems to threaten any actualist ubiquity view.

27. The phenomenological part of this answer to the second regress cannot be faulted by proponents of higher-order thought (HOT) theory. Once we have dispensed with

considerations of phenomenological plausibility, there is no obvious reason why the "consciousness-making" thoughts cannot involve quantification over infinite domains or be about sets of infinite cardinality.

28. Butchvarov 1979, pp. 248–253 and 1998, p. 55. On Moore, Sartre, and the significance of diaphaneity, see my 2004.

29. This is, more or less, the response of Caston 2002, pp. 797–798; Kriegel 2003a, pp. 125–126; and Metzinger 2003, pp. 337–339 (which offers a rich theoretical framework to justify it). See also Kampis 1995.

30. But we allow quantification *into* nominalized contexts.

31. The sort of representation involved here should not be understood to be "by courtesy," i.e., the fact that x represents y and y has P is not, by itself, to be regarded as sufficient for x to represent $[Py]$. If I represent an anthill, it does not follow that I represent all of the properties of the anthill or all of its parts.

32. But see Rudrauf and Damasio, this volume, for some significant steps in this direction.

33. In this context I am content to leave the notion of informational poverty/richness somewhat vague. It seems intuitive to think that the more properties of an object one represents specifically in representing the object, the informationally richer the representation. And this seems to hold across all modes of representation.

34. I am here identifying the propositional "mode of representation" with the entertaining of thoughts (where these are often but need not be expressed via language). There is clearly a sense of "propositional content" in which sense perception does involve it. Sense perception inseparably (save by abstraction) presents sensory qualities as well as objects and their properties and relations. The latter are, so to say, "propositionalizable." One *can* entertain propositions about these, e.g., one can think "That snow sure is bluish," but their initial presentation need not involve such thought (or "entertaining" of the proposition).

35. See, e.g., Sartre 1940/2004, pp. 120–122 and Lloyd 2004, pp. 249–274.

36. See Kapitan this volume.

37. See, e.g., Levinas 1930/1995, pp. 26ff.

38. On the other hand, if we interpret the diaphaneity of consciousness as a matter of consciousness simply not representing a host of its properties (viz., all of its non-representational and, presumably, some of its representational ones), then perhaps we could argue that consciousness is presented to itself in a way somewhat analogous, after all, to the presentation of physical objects. The crucial difference would be that it is presented to itself in an empty way that *does not admit* of filling, as if one could only see one side of a disk, as if it seemed to vanish when one turned it over.

39. Arguably, the new content corresponds to a new categorial intuition, whether this involves the entertaining of a proposition or not. When I see a white tree, for example, I can also note the *fact* that the tree is white, though I need not. It is not implausible to think that there is a kind of nonsensory intuition involved in this. I can confront the *fact* even though there is no new sensory content involved. Note also that the fact that the tree is white is involved in the experience of the white tree even if one does not have the conceptual capacities necessary for representing this. On categorial intuition see, e.g., Zahavi 2003d, pp. 35ff.

40. This can be taken as a clearer statement of Aristotle's notion of self-representation "en parergo" ("on the side" or "by the way"), Brentano's claim that an act of consciousness is its own *secondary* object, and Sartre's notions of "non-positional" and "non-thetic" self-consciousness. Gurwitsch (1985, pp. 4–5, 107) indicates as much with regard to Brentano and Aristotle. See also Kriegel 2004 on "transitive" and "intransitive" self-consciousness and peripheral and focal awareness. My only problem with the transitive vs. intransitive grammatical analogy is that unlike an intransitive verb, marginal self-consciousness, on my view, does "take an object."

41. See Bermúdez 2001 for a relevant recent discussion of nonconceptual self-consciousness.

42. See Gurwitsch 1985, p. 43 and Brentano 1995, p. 277. In Petitot 1999, p. 352, there is an interesting discussion of Husserl on the differences in resolution between the foveal and peripheral zones of the visual field. I think here the analogy between the structure of the visual field and the structure of the entire field of consciousness is quite strong. In effect, part of the field of consciousness (the visual field) has the same structure as the whole field.

43. That is, Zermelo-Fraenkel set theory with the anti-foundation axiom (instead of the foundation axiom). See Barwise and Moss 1996. See also Aczel 1988; Devlin 1993, ch. 7; and Moschovakis 1994, appendix B. For our purposes, the important fact about ZFA is that it allows for self-membered sets, sets that are members of their members, and so on.

44. See Barwise and Etchemendy 1987 and Barwise and Moss 1996.

45. Cf. Arzi-Gonczarowski 2001, pp. 11–12 and Rucker 2005, pp. 40–41. Something like this idea is considered rather unfavorably by Walicki (1987) who comes to conclusions somewhat similar to Zahavi's.

46. Compare the construal of episodes of consciousness presented below with the construal of self-referential propositions in Barwise and Etchemendy 1987 (see, e.g., pp. 42–44). Cf. Rieger 2000, pp. 250–252.

47. It should be noted that the axiom of extensionality alone does not allow one to distinguish between, e.g., $x = \{x,o\}$ and $y = \{y,o\}$ where these are the only members of x and y. The anti-foundation axiom takes care of this problem; according to it x

and y will be identical. See, e.g., Devlin 1993, pp. 151–155. But this presents no difficulties for our application.

48. On the "transitive closure operation" see, e.g., Barwise and Moss 1996, p. 14.

49. See Gurwitsch 1964, p. 4.

50. See Lloyd 2004, pp. 260–274.

51. Marginal self-consciousness bears an essential connection to temporality. Embedded in each episode of consciousness is a representation of a tripartite order— *upcoming, now-this, just past*. Marginal self-consciousness grounds the representation of the present, and this suggests a path for grounding other kinds of indexical content. Cf. Ford and Smith this volume and Zahavi this volume.

52. Husserl 1991; Elman 1990; Lloyd 2004, pp. 272–332. Cf. Mensch 2001, pp. 98–111.

53. See Moschovakis 1994, p. 175; Aczel 1988, p. 7; Barwise and Etchemendy 1987, pp. 53–55; and Devlin 1993, pp. 160–163. There are three different ways of defining hereditary finitude discussed in Barwise and Moss 1996, pp. 268–274. One definition is suitable only in the universe of wellfounded sets. The other two capture all the wellfounded hereditarily finite sets as well as the nonwellfounded ones. On one of the definitions, $HF^{1/2}$, a set is hereditarily finite if its transitive closure is finite. This applies to all the nonwellfounded sets we consider in this paper. Schweizer (1994) employs nonwellfounded sets in representing his solution to the "Third Man" regress. He too points out the hereditary finitude of the sets he employs (1994, p. 38).

54. Similarly, there are many directed graphs one could use to represent the set. See Aczel 1988, pp. 6–9, and Barwise and Etchemendy 1987, pp. 39–42.

55. See, e.g., Grossmann 1984, p. 52; Caston 2002, p. 778; and Gennaro this volume.

56. This representation of retention and protention has the unintuitive consequence that the transitive closure of each set in our family is identical. This will mean that what I called the *full* representational content of each episode so modeled will be the same. But this is a technical problem that can be remedied by well-motivated technical modifications. As noted, in protention we *project* the representational content of the subsequent episode of consciousness. And our projection can be wrong. In terms of the model, this will mean that the elements of the "protended" set need not match the elements of the actual successor. Retention also exhibits gradual "trailing off" or informational decay in the sense that the more deeply nested a retention, the less its content is preserved until, finally, the only difference it could make to present consciousness is via memory. This too could be remedied by suitable technical stipulations. If we are worried about the very first episode of consciousness in a stream, we can simply stipulate that the null set occurs in its retention position.

57. This seems to indicate that the difference can be captured in a functional frame-work. See Levine's related remarks in this volume.

58. In principle any other definition will have analogous implications, as long as it is not "flat" (see Forster 1994), but we can work from the assumption that we implement the representation of order in the most elegant, nonflat way. There are many possible set-theoretic definitions of order of this sort, but Kuratowski's seems preferable because of its elegance. See Mendelson 1997, pp. 229–230, and esp. Oberschelp 1991; Oberschelp argues that the Kuratowski definition is, in effect, the best possible.

59. See Case 1994. Case speaks of "complete low-level" self-models. This does not conflict with our claims about incomplete self-representation, which, in his terms, amounts to the claim that nothing finite could manage a complete *high-level* self-model. Cf. the end of note 21 above.

60. Perhaps the model suggests that there are *two* coupled, replicative systems.

61. See Forster 1994. This is related to the fact that there is a relative consistency proof for ZFA (i.e., if ZF is consistent then so is ZFA). See Devlin 1993, pp. 155, 173ff.

62. See Cotogno 2003, pp. 195–197.

63. This essay is a refinement and extension of some of the work carried out in my Ph.D. dissertation, "The Structure of Self-Consciousness" (2003, University of Iowa). I would like to thank (in no particular order) my advisors, Panayot Butchvarov, Evan Fales, and Gregory Landini, and the other committee members, Antonio Damasio, Laird Addis, and Richard Fumerton, for the years of discussion, argument, and encouragement. Greg Landini must be singled out for special mention. Over the last year or so he painstakingly discussed every aspect of this paper with me and practically every word. And, more generally, his friendship and intellectual companionship have been hugely important to me. I dedicate this paper to him. I must also thank Jean Petitot, Alexei Grinbaum, Bernard Pachoud, David Chavalarias, and others at CREA for very stimulating and incisive discussions of an earlier version of this paper. In fact, a question raised by Petitot led me to reorganize the paper into its present form. I must thank four mathematicians: Mike Simpson who introduced me to *Gödel, Escher, Bach* so long ago; Oleg Svidersky who first suggested to me the idea that nonwellfounded sets could be used to model certain aspects of consciousness; my colleague at St. Cloud State, Steve Walk, who gave me some crucial feedback on an earlier draft of this paper; and Lawrence Moss for patiently answering some questions about ZFA. Finally, let me thank my friend and collaborator, Uriah Kriegel, as well as David Rudrauf, Douglas Hofstadter (thanks for A5!), Tomis Kapitan, Bill Heald, Pete LeGrant, David Taylor, Greg Jesson, Matthias Steup, Denny Bradshaw, Yiwei Zheng, Thomas Metzinger, and, above all, Anya!

7 | The Same-Order Monitoring Theory of Consciousness

Uriah Kriegel

1 Introduction

One of the promising approaches to the problem of consciousness has been the higher-order monitoring theory of consciousness. According to the higher-order monitoring theory, what it is like to be in a conscious state, and there being anything it is like to be in it, is determined by the way the state is represented to the subject. More precisely, a mental state M of a subject S is conscious iff S has another mental state, M^*, such that M^* is an appropriate representation of M (Armstrong 1968, 1981; Lycan 1996, 2001; Mellor 1978; Rosenthal 1986, 1990, 2002, 2005).

Typically, the conscious state and its representation are construed as logically independent of each other: M could occur in the absence of M^*, and vice versa. Recently, however, several philosophers have developed a higher-order monitoring theory with a twist. The twist is that M and M^* entertain some kind of *constitutive relation*, or *internal relation*, or some other *non-contingent* relation, so that they are *not* logically independent of each other. For want of a better term, I will call this the *same-order monitoring theory of consciousness*.[1] For the sake of clarity, I will reserve the name "higher-order monitoring" for the standard version that insists on the logical independence of M and M^*.

Versions of the same-order monitoring theory can be found in recent writings by Brook and Raymont (2006, ch. 5); Carruthers (2000, ch. 9); Caston (2002); Gennaro (1996, ch. 2, 2002, 2004b); Hossack (2002, 2003); Kobes (1995); Kriegel (2002a, 2003a,b, 2005); Lehrer (1996a,b, 1997, ch. 7, 2002, 2004); Lurz (2003a,b, 2004); Natsoulas (1993a, 1996a,b, 1999, 2004); Sanford (1984a); Smith (1986, 1989, ch. 2, 2004); Thomasson (2000); Van Gulick (2001, 2004); and Williford (2003b, 2005). Despite this surprising number of proponents, there has not been among philosophers of mind an explicit awareness of the emerging appeal of this new and distinctive approach to consciousness—at least not *as such*, that is, *as* a new and distinctive approach.

In this paper, I will first expound and then propound the same-order monitoring theory (SOMT). The paper accordingly divides in two. Sections 2 and 3 attempt primarily to articulate the basic idea behind SOMT and to offer an exposition of several accounts of consciousness from the recent philosophical literature that are effectively versions of SOMT, as well as assess the relative plausibility of these different versions. Sections 4 and 5 argue the superiority of SOMT over the higher-order monitoring theory (HOMT), by developing two major difficulties for HOMT that do not apply to SOMT.[2]

Naturally, the concerns of the present essay will be of interest primarily to those who have at least *some* trust in the monitoring approach to consciousness and who find at least *some* merit in standard HOMT. But I hope that the discussion of the subtler developments of the approach will interest also those with no sympathy for it, if only because doing away with the monitoring approach to consciousness would presumably require squaring off with its best version. It is therefore worthwhile to consider what the best version is.

2   The Same-Order Monitoring Theory

HOMT and SOMT agree that the presence of a higher-order representation of M is a *necessary* condition for M's being conscious. The standard argument for this goes something like this (see Lycan 2001):[3]

1. Mental states the subject is completely unaware of are unconscious states; so,
2. If mental state M of a subject S is conscious, then S must be aware of M; but,
3. Awareness of something involves a representation of it; therefore,
4. If M is conscious, then S must have a representation of M.

It is clear, however, that the presence of a higher-order representation is not a *sufficient* condition for M's being conscious.[4] This is why the monitoring approach appeals to the notion of an "appropriate" or "suitable" higher-order representation: even though the presence of a higher-order representation is not a sufficient condition for M's being conscious, the presence of an *appropriate* higher-order representation is. The question is what makes a given higher-order representation "appropriate" in the relevant sense.

This is where versions of the monitoring approach differ. There are several dimensions along which these various versions contrast with each other. Perhaps the most widely acknowledged distinction is between versions that construe the higher-order representation as perception-like and versions that construe it as thoughtlike. Thus, according to Rosenthal, a higher-order representation is appropriate only if it is a thought, whereas according to Armstrong and Lycan, it must be a quasi-perceptual state. This distinction leads to a contrast between higher-order thought (HOT) theory and higher-order perception (HOP) theory.

The contrast that concerns us here is between HOMT and SOMT. According to SOMT, one of the requirements on an "appropriate" higher-order representation is that it bear some constitutive relation, some logical connection, to M; HOMT rejects this requirement.[5] By way of introducing such a requirement, Kobes (1995, p. 294) writes:

[Let us introduce] a token constituency requirement: the first-order mental state or event must, at the time that it is conscious, be a constituent part of the HOT [higher-order thought] event token.

In similar vein, Van Gulick (2001, p. 295) writes:

Although both HOP and HOT theorists assume distinctness or nonidentity [of the monitored state and the monitoring state] . . . one could try to develop the higher-order view in a way that rejected or at least weakened that assumption . . .

Let us make this contrast explicit by formulating the two competing accounts as follows:

(HOMT) A mental state M of a subject S is conscious iff S has a mental state M^*, such that (i) M^* is an appropriate representation of M, and (ii) there is *no* constitutive relation between M and M^*.

(SOMT) A mental state M of a subject S is conscious iff S has a mental state M^*, such that (i) M^* is an appropriate representation of M, and (ii) there *is* a constitutive relation between M and M^*.

That is, SOMT postulates an internal, noncontingent relation between S's conscious state and her awareness of her conscious state. HOMT construes these two as completely logically independent.

Different constitutive relations define different versions of SOMT.[6] The strongest constitutive relation is of course *identity*. Accordingly, the strongest version of SOMT holds that M is identical with its higher-order representation. This means, in effect, that M represents *itself*.[7] The view can be formulated as follows:

(SOMT₁) A mental state *M* of a subject *S* is conscious iff *S* has a mental state *M**, such that (i) *M** is an appropriate representation of *M*, and (ii) *M* = *M**.

This is equivalent to:

(SOMT₁′) A mental state *M* of a subject *S* is conscious iff *M* is a representation of itself.[8]

This sort of view has been recently defended by Smith (1986, 1989, ch. 2, 2004),[9] Thomasson (2000); Caston (2002); Kriegel (2003b); Hossack (2002, 2003); Williford (2003b); Brook (ms.); Raymont (ms.); and Brook and Raymont (2006).[10]

Another version of SOMT appeals to the *part–whole* relation, also a constitutive relation. (That it is a constitutive relation can be seen from the fact that some philosophers—e.g., Armstrong [1978], Lewis [1991]—conceive of the part–whole relation as *partial identity*.) On this view, for a mental state to be conscious, it is not sufficient that the subject be aware of it; the subject's awareness of it must be *part of* that very same mental state. A view of this sort is defended by Gennaro (1996, ch. 2, 2002, 2004b); Van Gulick (2001, 2004); and Kriegel (2002a, 2003b, 2005). It may be formulated as follows:

(SOMT₂) A mental state *M* of a subject *S* is conscious iff *S* has a mental state *M**, such that (i) *M** is an appropriate representation of *M*, and (ii) *M** is a (proper) *part of M*.

The relevant notion of parthood here is not spatial or temporal, but *logical*.[11] There are complicated questions surrounding the explication of the notion of logical parthood, questions to which justice cannot be done here.[12] But an example may suffice to illustrate the nature of the logical part–whole relation. When I am *glad* that the weather is nice, I necessarily also *believe* that the weather is nice; it is impossible to be glad that the weather is nice without believing that this is so. But my belief that the weather is nice is not an extra mental act, which occurs *in addition to* my gladness. Rather, the belief is somehow *inherent in*, or *built into*, the gladness. In other words, my belief is *part of* my gladness, in a logical sense of "part of." So my believing that the weather is nice is a *logical part* of my being glad that the weather is nice.[13] Likewise, according to SOMT₂, our awareness of our conscious states is a *logical part* of those conscious states. When I have a conscious experience of blue, I am aware of my conscious experience. But the awareness is not an extra mental act, which occurs *in addition to* the experience. Rather, the awareness is *inherent in*—it is *built into*—the experience. It is in this sense, then, that *M** is claimed in SOMT₂ to be a logical (proper) part of *M*.

In the above formulation of SOMT$_2$, it is explicitly required that M^* be a *proper* part of M. This is intended to ensure that SOMT$_2$ be exclusive of SOMT$_1$.[14] But it is significant that a version of SOMT can be formulated that will remain silent on whether M^* is a proper or improper part of M, thus covering both SOMT$_1$ and SOMT$_2$. This version would be formulated as follows:

(SOMT$_3$)   A mental state M of a subject S is conscious iff S has a mental state M^*, such that (i) M^* is an appropriate representation of M, and (ii) M^* is a (proper *or improper*) part of M.

When M^* is a *proper* part of M, SOMT$_3$ accords with SOMT$_2$; when it is an *improper* part, SOMT$_3$ accords with SOMT$_1$. But SOMT$_3$ allows both structures to be involved in conscious states.

A close neighbor of SOMT$_2$ is the idea that for M to be conscious is for it to have *two* parts, such that one represents the other. The view may be formulated as follows:

(SOMT$_4$)   A mental state M of a subject S is conscious iff (i) M^* is a (proper) part of M, (ii) $M^\diamond$ is a (proper) part of M, and (iii) M^* is an appropriate representation of $M^\diamond$.

The idea here is, in a way, that the conscious state involves a "mereological sum" of the monitoring state and the monitored state. (Again, the relevant notion of mereology is that of *logical* mereology, not spatial or temporal mereology.[15]) This is to be distinguished from HOMT, in which the conscious state is identified with the monitored state solely.[16]

Again, SOMT$_4$ is formulated in terms of proper parthood in order to make it exclude the previous versions of SOMT, but more general versions can be formulated. We could remain silent on whether $M^\diamond$ is a proper or improper part of M, thus formulating a position that covers both SOMT$_2$ and SOMT$_4$:

(SOMT$_5$)   A mental state M of a subject S is conscious iff (i) M^* is a (proper) part of M, (ii) $M^\diamond$ is a (proper or improper) part of M, and (iii) M^* is a representation of $M^\diamond$.

When $M^\diamond$ is a *proper* part of M, SOMT$_5$ accords with SOMT$_4$; when it is an *improper* part, SOMT$_5$ accords with SOMT$_2$. But SOMT$_5$ itself allows for both structures to be involved in conscious states.

Another possible view in the same ballpark is that the conscious state is a part of the awareness of it, rather than the other way round. This view may be formulated as follows:

(SOMT$_6$)   A mental state M of a subject S is conscious iff S has a mental state M^*, such that (i) M^* is a representation of M, and (ii) M is a (proper part) of M^*.

SOMT$_6$ appears to be defended by Kobes (1995) and Fumerton (in conversation).[17]

It is possible to define an umbrella view that would cover all the previous ones as specific versions. This would be done by liberally allowing both M^* and $M^\diamond$ to be either a proper or an improper part of M:

(SOMT$_7$)   A mental state M of a subject S is conscious iff (i) M^* is a (proper or improper) part of M, (ii) $M^\diamond$ is a (proper or improper) part of M, and (iii) M^* is a representation of $M^\diamond$.

SOMT$_7$ allows four different structures to qualify as conscious states: where both M^* and $M^\diamond$ are proper parts of M (as in SOMT$_4$); where both are improper parts of M (as in SOMT$_1$); where M^* is a proper part and $M^\diamond$ an improper part of M (as in SOMT$_2$); and where M^* is an improper and $M^\diamond$ a proper part of M (as in SOMT$_6$).

Because SOMT$_7$ covers all the other versions as special cases, we may refer to it as *generic SOMT*. Its advantage is that it is less likely to turn out to be false than any other version of SOMT, since it is, in a manner, a disjunction of all these versions. Its disadvantage, however, is in its logical weakness or permissiveness: it allows many very different structures to qualify as conscious states.

3   Comparing the Plausibility of SOMT's Different Versions

In the previous section, we were concerned primarily with articulating the different versions of SOMT, not with their plausibility. In the present section, I want to make some inconclusive remarks on plausibility.

Let us distinguish between disjunctive and nondisjunctive versions of SOMT. SOMT$_3$, SOMT$_5$, and SOMT$_7$ are disjunctive versions, in that they consist in fact in disjunctions of the other versions. SOMT$_1$, SOMT$_2$, SOMT$_4$, and SOMT$_6$ are nondisjunctive versions.[18]

I have already remarked that the disjunctive versions are more plausible than the nondisjunctive ones, in that their truth requires the truth of only one of the disjuncts, but that they are correspondingly weaker, in that they claim less.

There may, however, be a significant problem with the disjunctive versions of SOMT. The term "consciousness" appears to denote a natural kind. This suggests that there is an underlying unity in the phenomenon—something that ensures that the class of conscious states exhibits a strong homogeneity. The disjunctive versions of SOMT, in their lax construal of what makes a mental state conscious, may well miss out on this homogeneity.

As for the nondisjunctive versions, each has a stain on its plausibility. The problem facing $SOMT_1$ is how to account for the alleged ability of conscious states to represent themselves. Claiming that they just do is not enough. We must understand *how* this is possible. Moreover, there may be a principled problem with reconciling self-representation with naturalist accounts of mental representation.[19]

The main difficulty with $SOMT_2$ concerns the explication of the notion of logical parthood and how it might apply to *states*. Although the notion of spatial parthood, and its application to three-dimensional objects, is quite straightforward, this is not the case with logical parthood and its application to states and events.[20]

The problem with $SOMT_4$ is that it appears to be only superficially, indeed *verbally*, different from HOMT. All it requires for consciousness is the compresence of a monitored state and a monitoring state. The only difference is that it calls "conscious state" not just the monitored state but the compound of both states.

$SOMT_6$ is implausible in a more plain and prima facie way. It simply appears to be unmotivated. The phenomenological facts about conscious experience do not suggest that the experience is normally part of the awareness of it, but the other way round.[21] Moreover, if it were correct, our whole conscious life would be conducted in the second-order, as it were, since the overall conscious state would be a second-order state.

It is perhaps worth noting that one way $SOMT_4$ (and hence $SOMT_5$) could play out is as follows: the subject is (indirectly) aware of her whole conscious state *by* (or *in virtue of*) being aware (directly) of a part of it. Just as a perception (or for that matter a painting) can represent a cabinet *by* (or *in virtue of*) representing the cabinet's front door, so a higher-order representation can represent a mental state *by* representing a part of it. In this way, M^* may represent the whole of M by representing the "other" part of M. This may be formulated as a specific version of $SOMT_4$:[22]

($SOMT_8$) A mental state M of a subject S is conscious iff (i) M^* is a (proper) part of M, (ii) $M^\diamond$ is a (proper) part of M, and (iii) M^* represents M by representing $M^\diamond$.

$SOMT_8$ may be used to relieve some of the implausibility attached to $SOMT_4$, in that it is different from HOMT in a more substantial way.

This version does accrue a new set of problems, however. First, there is the explication of the distinction between direct and indirect representation. Second, it is not clear in what way the notion of indirect representation is supposed to apply to states and events (as opposed, again, to three-dimensional objects).[23] Third, what is the fact of the matter that distinguishes a direct representation of $M^\diamond$ that serves as the basis for indirect representation of M from direct representation of $M^\diamond$ that does not so serve? Fourth, one may worry that what is indirectly represented is not strictly given in consciousness, and so the indirect content (if you will) of M^* is irrelevant to the structure of a conscious experience *as such*.[24]

Another, perhaps better way to deal with the main problem facing SOMT$_4$ may be the following. There are two different ways M^* and $M^\diamond$ may be conjoined to make up a single mental state, rather than two numerically distinct states. According to Gennaro's (1996, ch. 2; 2002) "wide intrinsicality view," what makes them two parts of a single mental state is simply our decision to treat them as such. There is no psychologically real relation between them that unites them into a single, cohesive mental state. By contrast, according to Van Gulick's (2001, 2004) "higher-order global states" account and my "cross-order information integration" model (see Kriegel 2002a, 2003b, 2005), what makes M^* and $M^\diamond$ two parts of a single state is the fact that they are integrated and unified through a psychologically real cognitive process of information integration.[25] So a conscious state arises, on this view, when a mental event ($M^\diamond$) and the subject's awareness of it are integrated into a single unity through the relevant sort of cognitive process.

One way to capture the ontological difference between these two versions of SOMT$_4$ is through the mereological distinction between *sums* and *complexes* (Simons 1987, ch. 9). A complex is a sum whose parts are essentially interconnected, or bound, in a certain way. The interconnection between these parts is an existence condition of a complex, but not of a sum.[26] Thus, a molecule is a complex of atoms rather than a sum of atoms, since for the atoms to constitute a molecule they *must* be interconnected in a certain way. So whereas for a sum to go out of existence, it is necessary that one of its parts go out of existence, this is not the case with a complex. A complex can go out of existence even when its parts persist, provided that the relationship or connection among them is destroyed.[27] More generally, suppose W is a whole comprising components $C_1, \ldots, C_n$; then W is a sum iff W's failure to persist entails a C_i's failure to persist and is a complex iff its failure to persist does *not* entail a C_i's failure to persist.

Gennaro's view seems to construe M as a mere *sum* of M^* and $M^\diamond$, whereas Van Gulick's and mine appear to construe it as a *complex* whose parts are M^* and $M^\diamond$.[28] This is because the latter view requires that there be a specific relationship between M^* and $M^\diamond$ for them to constitute a conscious state, namely, the relation effected by their cognitive integration. M^* and $M^\diamond$ would fail to constitute a conscious state if this relationship failed to hold (or to be instantiated). There is no such provision in Gennaro's view: all it takes for M to exist is for M^* and $M^\diamond$ to be compresent. This contrast can be captured through the following pair of theses:

(SOMT$_9$) A mental state M of a subject S is conscious iff (i) M^* is a (proper) part of M, (ii) $M^\diamond$ is a (proper) part of M, (iii) M^* is a representation of $M^\diamond$, and (iv) M is a *sum* of M^* and $M^\diamond$.

(SOMT$_{10}$) A mental state M of a subject S is conscious iff (i) M^* is a (proper) part of M, (ii) $M^\diamond$ is a (proper) part of M, (iii) M^* is a representation of $M^\diamond$, and (iv) M is a *complex* of M^* and $M^\diamond$.

These are ontologically distinct versions of SOMT$_4$ (and hence of SOMT$_5$). The point I wish to press here is that SOMT$_{10}$ is substantially, not merely verbally, different from HOMT. This can be seen clearly by noting that if the monitored and monitoring states are unified through a *psychologically real* process, that process would presumably make a difference to the causal powers of the complex of the two—something that would not happen if the monitored and monitoring states are simply "summed up."[29]

I belabor this distinction because, unlike SOMT$_9$, SOMT$_{10}$ clearly presents a genuine—that is, substantive rather than verbal—alternative to HOMT, one that at the same time does not appeal to the problematic notion of self-representation. The problem with SOMT$_9$ is that there is a sense in which it retains the logical independence (postulated in HOMT) between the monitoring state and the monitored state, since it construes M^* and $M^\diamond$ as completely independent of each other. This is the problem overcome through SOMT$_{10}$, since the latter posits an essential connection between them. In a way, SOMT$_{10}$ goes a step beyond generic SOMT, in that it construes as constitutive not only the relation between M^* and M but also between M^* and $M^\diamond$.[30,31]

SOMT$_{10}$ does still appeal to the problematic notion of logical part. But although the notion is difficult to analyze, it is not so difficult to illustrate, as we have seen in the case of believing and being glad. That illustration suggests that there is a viable notion of logical parthood that does apply to mental states; it is just that explicating this notion is not easy. I suggest that we consider this a matter for further investigation, proceeding now on the assumption that the notion of logical parthood is sound.

Elsewhere, I have argued in greater detail for a view of consciousness that can be ontologically cast as a version of SOMT$_{10}$ (see Kriegel 2002a, 2003b, 2005). One thing that makes SOMT$_{10}$ preferable to SOMT$_9$ (beyond the fact that it is more clearly *substantially* different from HOMT), is that some possible cases of unconscious states appear to satisfy the condition laid out in SOMT$_9$. Consider, for instance, Siewert's (1998, ch. 3) *spontaneous reflective blindsighter*, who can prompt herself to form judgments about what she "blindsees", as well as reflective, second-order judgments about those judgments.[32] Such a person may have an unconscious perceptual state accompanied by a second-order judgment about it. We can ascribe to such a person a state that is the sum of a first-order perceptual state and a second-order judgment about it, in accordance with SOMT$_9$, even though we cannot ascribe to her a conscious perceptual state. What we also cannot ascribe to her, however, is a *complex* made of the perceptual state and the second-order judgement.[33] The perceptual state and the second-order representation of it are not integrated through a cognitive process in such a way as to make the person's awareness of her perceptual state internal to that perceptual state.[34]

It may be objected that SOMT$_9$ is not really a coherent position, since despite characterizing M as a mere sum of M^* and $M^\diamond$, it does postulate an essential relationship between them, namely, the relation of representation that M^* bears to $M^\diamond$. The objection is that a view such as Gennaro's in fact construes M as a complex, not a mere sum. However, the representational relation M^* bears to $M^\diamond$ is essential to the identity of M^*: M^* would not be the state that it is if it did not represent $M^\diamond$. So if M^* did not bear the representational relation to $M^\diamond$, it would go out of existence. It would then fail to be the case that M's two parts continue to exist while M itself ceases to exist–as is required for M to qualify as a complex and not a mere sum.[35]

This brings into sharper focus the relationship R that has to hold among the parts of a whole in order to make the whole a complex rather than a mere sum. For R to be a complex-making relation, R must be (i) an existence (and identity) condition of the whole, but (ii) neither an existence condition nor an identity condition of any of the parts.[36] The relation between M^* and $M^\diamond$ postulated in Van Gulick's account is of this sort; the one postulated in Gennaro's is not.

Before closing, let me note that SOMT$_8$ and SOMT$_{10}$ are perfectly compatible, and therefore can be conjoined to generate an even more specific version of SOMT$_4$:

(SOMT$_{11}$)   A mental state M of a subject S is conscious iff (i) M^* is a (proper) part of M, (ii) $M^\diamond$ is a (proper) part of M, (iii) M^* represents M by representing $M^\diamond$, and (iv) M is a complex of M^* and $M^\diamond$.

Given the plausibility of SOMT$_{10}$, it appears that if the special problems attending SOMT$_8$ could somehow be neutralized, SOMT$_{11}$ would be a promising account of the ontology of conscious experience.

There are other versions of SOMT that I have not discussed at all and that do not fit comfortably into the framework I have presented in the last two sections (hence into any of SOMT$_1$—SOMT$_{11}$). In particular, Carruthers (2000, ch. 9) and Lurz (2003a,b) have developed versions of SOMT that offer genuine and credible alternatives to the versions discussed above.[37] But I will not discuss their views here. My hope is that the above discussion is sufficient to bring out the special character of the kind of account envisioned by a same-order monitoring approach to consciousness. I now turn to the task of arguing that SOMT has resources to deal with problems that are fatal, or at least critical, to the viability of the more traditional HOMT.

4   The Problem of Immediacy

In section 2, I noted that a higher-order representation of M is a *necessary* condition for M's being conscious, because conscious states are states the subject is aware of, and awareness of something involves representation of it. I also noted that a higher-order representation of M is not a *sufficient* condition for M's being conscious, because some mental states the subject is aware of (and hence represents) are not conscious. This is why we must appeal to an "appropriate" higher-order representation of M.

From what has already been said, it is clear that some mental states the subject is aware of are conscious and some are unconscious. The question is what makes the difference between an awareness of M that guarantees M's being conscious and an awareness that does *not*. One intuitively plausible suggestion would be that awareness of M makes M conscious if it is *immediate* awareness, and that it fails to make M conscious if it is not immediate. Thus, if S is of reflective disposition, she may infer that she must be distressed or anxious about something, on the basis of how unfocused and unproductive she has been, or how lightly she has been sleeping recently. But even if S really is distressed or anxious about something (e.g., a looming banquet with the in-laws), S's newfound awareness of it would not make the distress or anxiety conscious in the relevant sense. The reason is that the awareness lacks the requisite immediacy, being as it is mediated by reflection and inference.

So one requirement on an "appropriate" higher-order representation of M is that it make S not just aware of M, but aware of M with the requisite immediacy. The problem is that HOMT appears to fail this requirement (see Goldman 1993a; Natsoulas 1993b; Kobes 1995; Moran 2001).

Suppose S has a conscious perception of a tree. According to HOMT, the perception, M, is conscious because S has another mental state, M^*, which is an appropriate higher-order representation of M. Now, surely M normally has a role in the causal process leading up to the formation of M^*. Just as the tree normally has a central role in the causal process leading up to the perception of it, so the perception itself normally has a central role in the causal process leading up to the higher-order representation of it. This means that the formation of M^* is not exactly simultaneous with the formation of M. Rather, there is some sort of (temporally extended) causal process starting with M and ending in the formation of M^*.[38] This process *mediates*, in effect, the formation of M^*. This, it might be argued, poses a problem for HOMT, for it appears to imply that S's awareness of her perception of the tree is mediated by the causal process in question and is therefore *not* immediate.

David Rosenthal (1993a) addresses this problem. But before I examine Rosenthal's treatment, let me note his admission that the problem does not even arise for a view such as SOMT. Rosenthal writes (1993a, p. 157; italics mine):

One way to answer the question about immediacy is just to stipulate that one's being [aware] of a conscious mental state is *internal to* that state itself. Immediacy is thus guaranteed. Our being [aware] of the state would be a *part or aspect of* the state itself, so nothing could mediate between the state and one's being [aware] of it.

The phrases "internal to" and "part or aspect of" can be understood along the lines of $SOMT_1$ and/or $SOMT_2$. They are certainly consistent with the generic $SOMT_7$. Since on all these versions of SOMT what makes S aware of M is M itself or a (logical) part of M, there is no causal process that mediates the formation of S's awareness of M: M *comes with* the awareness of it, if you will. The problem evaporates.

Thus, generic $SOMT_7$ handles the problem in a relatively straightforward way. $M^\diamond$ would normally have a causal role in the process leading up to the formation of M^*. But until M^* is formed, the conscious state M does not yet exist. M comes into existence only upon the completion of the causal process leading up to the formation of M^*. Once M comes into existence, it already envelopes within it $M^\diamond$ and M^*; no further causal process is required. So M itself does not play a causal role in the process leading up to the formation M^*, for M does not exist before M^* does. Thus once S enters the conscious state M, S's awareness of $M^\diamond$ is not mediated in any way. In other words, once M comes into existence, no further process is needed that would mediate the formation of M^*. The awareness constituted by M^* is therefore immediate.

It appears, then, that SOMT faces no serious difficulty regarding the immediacy of our awareness of our conscious states. But Rosenthal claims that HOMT can account for this immediacy as well. According to Rosenthal, what is required for S's awareness of M to be immediate is not that the formation of M^* *be* unmediated, but rather that it *seem* unmediated *to S*. Or perhaps even more minimally, the formation of M^* must not seem mediated to S. As long as it does not seem to S that the formation M^* is mediated, her awareness of M will be immediate. (Note that the way I am using the terms "immediate" and "unmediated," the two are *not* synonymous, at least as applied to awareness. An awareness that is immediate may not be unmediated, as when an awareness is mediated by processes of which the subject is unaware, as we will presently see.)

There are two ways the formation of M^* may not seem mediated to S. One is when the formation of M^* *really is* unmediated. Another is when the formation of M^* is mediated, but the processes by which it is mediated are processes S is completely unaware of. If S is completely unaware of the processes that mediate the formation of M^*, M^*'s formation will seem unmediated to her, or at least it will not seem mediated to her. This latter way in which the formation of M^* may not seem mediated to S is the one appealed to by Rosenthal. Rosenthal's claim is that while it is true that the formation of M^* is mediated by a causal process starting with M and ending in the formation of M^*, the subject is completely unaware of this process, and therefore her awareness of M is immediate, in that it does not seem mediated to her.

To meet the requirement of immediacy, Rosenthal therefore claims that an "appropriate" higher-order representation must be *noninferential*, where this means that the higher-order representation is not formed though a conscious inference. For such a *conscious* inference would be a mediating process of which the subject *would be* aware (since it is conscious).[39] In other words, where P is the process leading from M to the formation of M^*, M is conscious just in case P is unconscious; when P is conscious, M is unconscious.

(Note that the way Rosenthal uses the terms, inference is by definition conscious. To be sure, we could call certain unconscious cognitive processes "inferences," and so allow for unconscious inference. But this is not how Rosenthal uses the term. He allows that there may be unconscious processes resembling inference in every other respect, but reserves the term "inference" to those that are conscious. For the sake of clarity, I will align my usage with Rosenthal's. To refer to the unconscious cognitive processes that are otherwise just like inference, I will use the phrase "unconscious inferential processes."[40])

Rosenthal's treatment of the problem of immediacy may initially appear satisfactory, but it does not withstand scrutiny. The problem is to account for the difference between S's awareness of her conscious states, which is immediate, and S's (occasional) awareness of her unconscious states, which lacks the requisite immediacy. Rosenthal's suggestion is that the *conscious* states are those the awareness of which is formed through unconscious inferential processes, whereas the *unconscious* states are those the awareness of which is formed through conscious inferences.[41] This suggestion, I will now argue, is unlikely to work.

Let us start by adopting a certain principle regarding inferential processes. The principle is that a conscious inference can only start from conscious "premises." More precisely, for any process P leading from mental state M_1 to the formation of mental state M_2, P is conscious only if M_1 is conscious. If M_1 is unconscious, then P is necessarily unconscious.[42]

The problem with Rosenthal's suggestion is that M is *always* unconscious before the formation of M^*, since M^* is what bestows consciousness on M. So *every* process leading *from* M to the formation of M^* would have to start from an unconscious state, and therefore itself be an unconscious process. This ensures that *every* higher-order representation formed though a process leading from its object (the first-order state) would be noninferential and therefore would bestow consciousness on the first-order state.[43]

My claim is not that there can be no awareness of M formed by conscious inference. There surely can. My claim is rather that there can be no awareness of M formed by conscious inference from M *before* M is conscious. More generally, there can be no conscious states formed by conscious inference *from these states* (before they are already conscious). A subject can certainly become aware that she harbors an unconscious anger at her mother on the strength of her therapist's testimony, in which case her awareness of her unconscious anger is consciously inferred from the evidence presented to her by the therapist. But in such a case, the subject's awareness of M is not formed by conscious inference *from M* (or *on the basis of M*). Rather, it is formed by conscious inference from (or on the basis of) the therapist's testimony. Rosenthal's account is incompatible with this, however, for the reason provided in the previous paragraph.

Rosenthal might modify his account of immediacy accordingly. Instead of claiming that the difference between S's awareness of her conscious states and her awareness of her unconscious states is that the first is formed through unconscious inferential processes whereas the second is formed through conscious inferential processes, he might suggest that the first is formed through processes that do not emanate from the relevant conscious states whereas the second is formed through processes that do.

This modified account is, however, extremely implausible, indeed somewhat absurd. On the suggestion under consideration, what makes S's awareness of M immediate is precisely that it is formed not responsively to M, but as an upshot of some other process. Whenever M happens to lead to an awareness of it, M is bound to remain unconscious. This appears to get things exactly backward.

On the other hand, the proponent of HOMT cannot opt for the opposite modification, according to which the difference between S's awareness of her conscious states and her awareness of her unconscious states is that the former is formed through processes that *do* emanate from the relevant conscious states, whereas the latter is formed through processes that do *not*. This is because awareness of some conscious states may emanate from these states through conscious inferential processes. Such inferential processes would be causal processes of which S is aware, and would therefore *seem mediated* to S.

Finally, a proponent of HOMT could retreat to the view that immediacy is *not* what distinguishes the awareness we have of our conscious states from that of our unconscious states. But this, besides being quite ad hoc and prima facie implausible, would leave HOMT without an account of the difference between conscious and unconscious states of which are aware. Furthermore, the immediacy that characterizes our awareness of our conscious states is a phenomenon that calls for explanation regardless of its theoretical role within an account of consciousness.

In conclusion, HOMT faces a serious difficulty in its attempt to account for the immediacy that characterizes the awareness we have of our conscious states (and does not characterize the awareness we have of some of our unconscious states).[44] SOMT, by contrast, faces no serious difficulty from that quarter. In essence, SOMT's position is that the awareness we have of our conscious states is immediate simply because it *really is* unmediated.

5 The Problem(s) of Relationality

An important aspect of HOMT is that it construes consciousness as a relational property: mental states are conscious in virtue of standing in a certain relation to other mental states. Many philosophers find this counterintuitive. What it is like to be in a given conscious state seems to be an intrinsic property of that state. For some philosophers, this alone is a ground for rejecting HOMT (see, e.g., Smith 1989; Gennaro 1996; Natsoulas 1999). In this section, I will argue that construing consciousness as relational is not only counterintuitive, but also raises the specter of two serious problems for HOMT. This would constitute a third advantage of SOMT, since these difficulties do not even arise for SOMT, given that it construes consciousness as an intrinsic property of the conscious state, as we will see toward the end of the section.

A decade or two ago, the most widely discussed problem in the philosophy of mind concerned the causal efficacy of mental content. After externalist accounts of content (which construe it as a relational property of mental states) became popular,[45] it was noted that such accounts appear to render mental content causally inert.[46] The reasoning was this: only intrinsic properties of a mental state contribute to its fund of causal powers, because causation is a local affair; so if content is an extrinsic, relational property, it makes no contribution to the state's causal powers, and is therefore causally inert, or *epiphenomenal*.

That problem was never resolved to everyone's satisfaction. Different solutions, of various merits, have been offered, but no agreement is in sight.[47] One thing almost everybody accepted, though, was the thesis that the causal powers of a mental state reside fully in its intrinsic properties.[48,49]

This thesis threatens to undermine HOMT, since HOMT construes consciousness as relational. If consciousness were indeed a relational property, M's being conscious would fail to contribute anything to M's fund of causal powers. And this would make the property of being conscious epiphenomenal (see Dretske 1995a, p. 117 for an argument along these lines).

The causal efficacy issue is, by all appearances, a serious problem for HOMT. Why have philosophers failed to press this problem more consistently? My guess is that we are tempted to slide into a causal reading of HOMT, according to which M^* *produces* the consciousness of M, by impressing upon it a certain *modification*. Such a reading does make sense of the causal efficacy of consciousness: after M^* modifies M, this intrinsic modification alters M's causal powers. But of course, this is a *misreading* of HOMT. It is important to keep in mind that HOMT is a *conceptual*, not *causal*, thesis.[50] Its claim is *not* that the presence of an appropriate higher-order representation *yields*, or *gives rise to*, or *produces* M's being conscious. Rather, the claim is that the presence of an appropriate higher-order representation *constitutes* M's being conscious. It is not that by representing M, M* *modifies* M in such a way as to make M conscious; rather, M's being conscious simply *consists in* its being represented by M*.

A person could, of course, propound HOMT as a causal thesis. But such a person would not take HOMT to be an account of consciousness itself; she would take it to be merely an account of the *causal origin* of consciousness. To the extent that HOMT is meant as an account of consciousness itself, then, it puts in jeopardy the causal efficacy of consciousness.

When proponents of HOMT have taken this problem into account, they have responded by downplaying the causal efficacy of consciousness.[51] But if the intention is to bite the bullet, *downplaying* the causal efficacy is insufficient; what is needed is *nullifying* the efficacy.[52] The charge at hand is not that HOMT may turn out to assign consciousness too paltry a fund of causal powers, but that it may deny it *any* causal powers. To bite the bullet, proponents of HOMT must embrace epiphenomenalism. Such epiphenomenalism can be rejected, however, both on commonsense grounds and on the ground that it violates what has come to be called *Alexander's dictum*: to be is to be causally effective.[53,54] Surely HOMT would be better off if it could legitimately assign some causal powers to consciousness. But its construal of consciousness as a relational property makes it unclear how it might do so.

Another consequence of the alleged relationality of consciousness would be the following. According to HOMT, M's property of being conscious is just the property of being appropriately represented by another internal state. Some critics have charged that the property of being appropriately represented by another internal state is a property that internal states of inanimate objects can also instantiate (see again Dretske 1995a, p. 97).[55] If so, they argue, HOMT is committed to attributing conscious states to inanimate objects. Thus, when a person harbors an appropriate representation of the internal physical state of a stone, the internal state of the stone is appropriately represented by another internal state, and so there would be no non-arbitrary way to deny consciousness to the stone's internal state.[56]

Proponents of HOMT may respond that internal states can be conscious only when appropriately represented by a separate state *of the same organism* (or object). But this reply would not do. There are states of our skin of which we have appropriate representations, and yet these states are not conscious, even though they are states of the same organism that has the appropriate higher-order representations.

A more sophisticated rejoinder is that it need not be part of HOMT that *any* internal state can become conscious upon being appropriately represented by another internal state. In particular, it is often suggested that only *mental* states (perhaps only mental states of a certain *kind*) are such as to become conscious upon being suitably represented by another internal state.[57] This reply has less merit to it than may initially appear. Again, the problem is that we are tempted to read HOMT causally instead of conceptually. If *M** *gave rise* to consciousness by modifying *M*, then it would make a difference what characteristics *M* has (e.g., being mental). Thus, it could be claimed that only states with such characteristics can be so modified by being appropriately represented as to become conscious. But recall that according to HOMT, conscious states do not undergo any (intrinsic) change in response to the fact that they are appropriately represented. It is not so clear, then, what difference it makes whether an internal state has certain characteristics or not. To claim that only a certain kind of internal state is "the right kind" of state for becoming conscious upon being appropriately represented, even though nothing has to happen with those states when they are thus appropriately represented, is to introduce a completely artificial, ad hoc condition to the account.[58]

In summary, the relational construal of consciousness lands its proponents in significant trouble. It appears to cast consciousness as causally inert and moreover suggests that consciousness may be a ubiquitous property of nature, including inanimate nature. No doubt the proponents of HOMT may devise ways of dealing with these problems. Any such "ways of dealing with these problems" are likely, however, to complicate the theory considerably. And in any case, it is clearly preferable to avoid these problems altogether. An account that construes consciousness as an intrinsic property of conscious states would therefore be preferable, inasmuch as it would not raise these problems in the first place.[59] SOMT seems to be such an account. At least the versions of it we have considered in section 2 construe consciousness as intrinsic in the relevant sense.

According to SOMT$_1$, for instance, *M* is conscious in virtue of representing itself. This means that *M* need not stand in a relation to any *numerically distinct* state (or entity). There is a sense, of course, in which the property of being self-representing is relational, in that it is a matter of its bearer standing in a certain relation to itself. But in *that* sense, the property of being self-identical is also relational. This is clearly not the relevant sense of relationality: it is not the sense in which relationality may put in question the causal efficacy of a state, for instance. In the sense in which we are interested, a property is relational only when its bearer stands in some relation to *something other than itself.* Thus, a mental state's property F is relational when the mental state in question instantiates F in virtue of standing in a certain relation to a numerically distinct state (or, more generally, to another entity). In *this* sense, the property of being self-representing, like the property of being self-identical, is a nonrelational property.

In this regard, the part–whole relation is similar to the self-identity relation: it does not require that its bearer stand in any relation to a numerically distinct entity. My body's property of having my left arm as a part is a nonrelational property of my body, in that it does not require that my body stand in any relation to something other than itself (requiring instead that my body stand in relation to a part of itself). Likewise, if M^* is a part of M, then M's property of standing in a certain relation to M^* (namely, the relation of being represented by M^*) is a nonrelational property in the relevant sense. This ensures that in $SOMT_7$, the generic version of SOMT, consciousness is construed as a nonrelational property in the relevant sense.

The fact that SOMT construes consciousness as an intrinsic property of conscious states, whereas HOMT construes it as a relational property of them, means that certain difficulties that arise for HOMT but not for SOMT. This, too, is an advantage of SOMT over HOMT.[60]

6 Conclusion

For almost two decades now, the higher-order monitoring theory has been at the forefront of attempts to make intelligible the place of consciousness in nature. However, the theory faces a number of serious difficulties, some technical, and some fundamental. Moreover, many philosophers share the sentiment that it fails to what is capture special about consciousness. At the same time, it is built on the sound notion that conscious states are states we are somehow *aware* of being in. It is perhaps for this reason that, in recent work on consciousness, one detects an interesting, and significant, development of the monitoring approach to consciousness. A surprising number of accounts that are happy to construe consciousness in terms of monitoring attempt to bring closer together the monitoring state and the monitored state, in such a way that the two are not "independent existences," but are somehow constitutively, or "internally," or otherwise noncontingently connected to each other.

My goal in this essay has been twofold: first, to identify this trend and lay out its conceptual foundations; and second, to suggest that the trend is indeed a positive development, in that the emerging account of consciousness can overcome a number of fundamental difficulties that have seemed to bedevil the project of the more traditional higher-order monitoring theory.[61]

Notes

1. This label was devised, independently, by Brook (ms.), Kriegel (2002a), and Lurz (2003b). It no doubt fits some of the accounts of consciousness I have in mind better than others, but it is the best generic label I could find.

2. In the literature on consciousness one can find a great number of arguments directed against HOMT: Aquila 1990; Byrne 1997; Caston 2002; Dretske 1993, 1995a; Goldman 1993a; Guzeldere 1995; Kriegel 2003a; Levine 2001a; Lurz 2003a,b; Moran 2001; Natsoulas 2001, 1993b; Neander 1998; Rey 1988; and Seager 1999 develop some of them. Some of these arguments may apply with equal force to SOMT, though some of them clearly do not.

3. Both premises 1 and 3 can certainly be denied. In particular, Dretske (1993) argues that a mental state's status as conscious does not require that its subject be aware of it. I will not discuss this issue here, as it is tangential to the main concern of the essay. For a defense of the notion that the subject necessarily has an awareness of her conscious states, see Lycan 1996 and Kriegel 2004.

4. The standard example of a mental state that is higher-order represented but is still nonconscious involves a person who learns of a repressed emotion or belief through therapy and comes to represent to herself that she has the repressed emotion or belief in question, without the repressed state thereby becoming conscious. So the repressed state can remain unconscious despite being (higher-order) represented. This issue will be discussed more fully in section 4.

5. The way I frame the distinction between SOMT and HOMT, the "constitutive relation requirement" is not suggested to be the *only* requirement on an appropriate higher-order representation. That is, an "appropriate" higher-order representation may be required to exhibit other features, beyond the requirement of being constitutively related to the conscious state. However, most versions of SOMT would probably see this as the key requirement for an appropriate higher-order representation.

6. In the remainder of this section, I articulate several specific versions of SOMT. The main purpose is not to evaluate these versions, but to try to articulate the conceptual foundations of this still underdiscussed approach to consciousness. The hope is that this will give the reader a clearer sense of the sort of account of consciousness offered by SOMT.

7. There is one sense in which, once M is a representation of itself, it is not really a *higher*-order representation, since it is a first-order state. But in another sense, it still is a higher-order representation, since what it represents is a representation. This is, I take it, but a verbal difference, with no metaphysical significance. I will continue to

use the term "higher-order representation" in this sort of context, but everything I will have to say can be said without this term.

8. We must keep in mind, however, that M's representation of itself has to be appropriate in other ways as well, in case the constitutive relation requirement is not the only requirement on appropriate higher-order representations. A similar point applies to the formulation of SOMT$_2$ and SOMT$_3$ later in the text.

9. Smith was the first to argue for this sort of view in Anglo-American philosophy. He writes (1986, pp. 149–150): "A mental state is *conscious* if and only if it includes a certain awareness of itself, that is, in having the experience, the subject is aware of having it." And further along: "That inner awareness, I should like to propose, lies (to begin with) in a certain *reflexive* character in experience. That character is ascribed in the following phenomenological description, for the case of seeing a frog: . . . 'In this very experience I see this frog.'. . . Thus, the reflexive structure 'in this very experience' qualifies the presentational structure 'I see this frog': indeed, the former would seem already implicit in the latter" (ibid., p. 150).

10. More traditionally, this view was developed and defended by Brentano (1874/1924) and probably also by Aristotle (see Caston 2002).

11. It is clear that the part–whole relation between M and M^* is not (or at least not primarily) a spatial or temporal part–whole relation. Moreover, it is not clear how such a relation would apply to states, as opposed to individual objects.

12. For discussion of the logical part–whole relation, see Lewis 1991; Paul 2002; Simons 1987; Smith and Mulligan 1983; and Mulligan and Smith 1985. A full discussion of it would take us too far afield, but it may be worthwhile to at least state the logical properties of the relation of proper parthood: it is antireflexive (x cannot be a part of itself), antisymmetrical (if x is a proper part of y, then y is not a proper part of x), and transitive (if x is a proper part of y and y is a proper part of z, then x is a proper part of z). The relation of parthood (construed as covering improper parthood as well), by contrast, is areflexive, asymmetrical, and transitive.

13. Examples of this sort are provided by Smith (1994, ch. 3).

14. I am working here with the traditional notion of parthood, where x can be said to be a part of y even if there is no part of y that is not a part of x. In that case, x is an improper part of y, where this is more or less the same as x's being identical with y.

15. Mereology is the theory of parts and wholes, or the part–whole relation. If the notion of a logical part–whole relation is accepted, so should the notion of logical mereology. For the legitimacy of the notion of logical mereology, see especially Paul 2002.

16. Perhaps the clearest proponent of this sort of view is Gennaro (1996, 2002). He writes (1996, p. 23): "We can understand consciousness as involving the property of

'accompanied by a MET [metapsychological thought].' . . . But we might individuate conscious states 'widely,' i.e., in a way that treats consciousness as an intrinsic property of those states. On this account, the MET is part of the conscious state. I will call it the 'wide intrinsicality view,' or WIV."

17. Thanks to Paul Raymont for pointing out to me that Kobes's account is really a version of $SOMT_6$, and to Richard Fumerton for making the case that this is a plausible view worth pausing to articulate. François Recanati (in conversation) also expressed sympathy for this sort of view.

18. To repeat, $SOMT_3$ is a disjunction of $SOMT_1$ and $SOMT_2$; $SOMT_5$ is a disjunction of $SOMT_2$ and $SOMT_4$; and $SOMT_7$ is a disjunction of all four nondisjunctive versions of SOMT. Note also that $SOMT_3$ through $SOMT_5$ are all themselves versions of $SOMT_2$.

19. For development of this specific line of thought, see Levine 2001a, ch. 6, and Kriegel 2003b, 2005. I will not discuss these arguments here.

20. Perhaps some help can be found in work on the part–whole relation in mathematics, which is clearly not a spatial relation, but rather a logical or "formal" one. For a recent treatment of the mathematical part–whole relation, see Bell 2004.

21. At least this is the case with normal conscious experiences, where the focal center of attention is an external object, not an internal state of the subject. When one has an introspective, focal awareness of one's internal state, the phenomenology might be captured fairly in terms of the structure suggested in $SOMT_6$. But this is not the case with regular, nonintrospective conscious experience.

22. Note that it is also a version of $SOMT_2$.

23. I would like to thank Dan Zahavi for pressing me on this latter issue.

24. I would like to thank Paul Raymont for pointing this out to me.

25. Cognitive processes of integration are not unfamiliar. At the personal level, there is the conscious inference in accordance with "conjunction introduction," as when one consciously infers that the wall is white and rectangular from one's beliefs that the wall is white and that the wall is rectangular. At the subpersonal level, there is the widely discussed process of *binding*, as when the brain binds information from the auditory cortex and from the visual cortex to form a single, unified audiovisual representation of the sound and color of the same distal stimulus, say, a car. On Van Gulick's and on my view, what makes M^* and $M^\diamond$ parts of a single mental state is the fact that they are integrated into a single mental state through a cognitive process of this type. The process in question is probably different from either feature binding or conscious inference in accordance with conjunction introduction. But there is no reason to think that these are the only processes of integration employed by our cognitive system. Any process in which two separate mental states or contents are unified

in such a way that they are superseded by a single mental state or content that encompasses both will qualify as a process of cognitive integration. (For a specific discussion of how such information integration may work out at the implementational level, see Kriegel 2003b.)

26. An example of a complex is the state of Hawaii (to be distinguished from the geographical location Hawaii). The state is not merely a sum of the seven islands making up Hawaii. It is also a matter of their political interconnection as answering to the same state government. If that government dissolved permanently, the state of Hawaii would go out of existence, even though all its parts would persist.

27. The notion of a complex-making relation, as opposed to a mere sum, is similar to Levey's (1997) notion of *principles of composition*. According to Levey, objects are not just sums of disparate parts, but the parts put together in accordance with a principle of composition.

28. At least this is how I understand Gennaro's and Van Gulick's views as they appear in print. It is quite possible that I am misinterpreting one or both of them. My primary interest, however, is in the views themselves, not so much in an exegesis of Gennaro's and Van Gulick's work. In particular, some passages in Gennaro's work may suggest that he is more of a complex theorist than a sum theorist (see especially Gennaro 1996, pp. 29–30). More explicitly, in response to the present essay, Gennaro (this volume) argues that his is a complex rather than sum view.

29. I am indebted to Paul Raymont for the crucial point concerning the difference in causal powers (or functional role).

30. The result, then, is a web of constitutive interrelations among M, M^*, and $M^\diamond$.

31. Moreover, $SOMT_{10}$ may help provide a fact of the matter to distinguish direct representation of a part that serves as a basis for indirect representation of the whole from one that does not. When the whole in question is a mere sum, (direct) representation of its part does not constitute (indirect) representation of it. When the whole is a complex, (direct) representation of its part does constitute (indirect) representation of it. If a cabinet could be a mere sum of its door and its frame, without the two being necessarily connected in a certain way, then representation of the door could not constitute also a representation of the whole cabinet. But since the door and the frame must be connected in a specific way in order for their whole to function as a cabinet, representation of the door can double as representation of the larger unit of which the door is a part. (This may at least provide a necessary condition on doubling as indirect representation of the whole.)

32. My thanks to Terry Horgan for pointing me to this example.

33. As Siewert notes—though not in so many words—we *can* ascribe to her a complex of the first-order judgment and the second-order judgment; but we still

cannot ascribe to her a complex of the first-order perceptual state and the second-order judgment.

34. Gennaro's particular version of $SOMT_9$ is a bit more complicated and compounds other implausibilities. Thus, according to Gennaro, M^* is an *unconscious part* of the conscious state that M is. This is doubly implausible. First, although mental states are bearers of the property of being conscious, it is not clear in what sense state-parts can be said to be conscious or unconscious; and second, even if there is a sense in which state-parts can be said to be conscious, presumably what makes a state-part conscious is that it is part of a conscious state—making the notion of an unconscious part of a conscious state contradictory.

35. A similar objection may be that Gennaro's view, in order to be at all plausible, must require that M^* and $M^\diamond$ be roughly simultaneous and occur in the same subject's head, but such relations would make his view a complex view rather than a sum view. In response, it may be claimed that temporal and spatial relations are not substantive enough to be complex-making.

36. If we take into account the point raised in the previous note, we must also require (iii) that R not be a merely spatial or temporal relation.

37. According to Carruthers, M^* is somehow inherent in M in virtue of the fact that it is part of M's inferential role in S's cognitive system that it is disposed to bring about the occurrence of an M^*-type state. This inferential role determines the content of M; therefore M^* is a determinant of M's content. According to Lurz, M^* represents not M itself, but rather M's content. It is the fact that M not only represents what it does, but is also accompanied by a representation of what it represents, that makes M conscious. Lurz explicitly calls his view "same-order monitoring."

38. There are places where Rosenthal claims explicitly that there is normally *no* causal connection between M and M^* (e.g., Rosenthal 1990, p. 744). These comments are sporadic and unmotivated, however. The resulting HOMT is, if anything, less plausible than it should be (see Kobes 1995).

39. The reason the subject would necessarily be aware of this process is that it is conscious, and conscious states and processes are states and processes the subject is aware of having or undergoing.

40. It is important to stress that no substantive issue is at stake here. If we insist that there are unconscious inferences, Rosenthal need only rephrase his thesis. Instead of claiming that M^* is an appropriate representation of M only if it is noninferential, he could claim that M^* is an appropriate representation of M only if it is nonschminferential, where "schminference" is a conscious inference.

41. One might interpret the view otherwise, though. The suggestion might be thought to be that M^* is not formed through any process, but rather "forms" some-

what spontaneously—or that it is formed either through an unconscious inferential process or through no process whatsoever. However, the notion of a mental state that is unformed, or forms spontaneously through no process, is not obviously intelligible.

42. It is important to distinguish here between a process being conscious and its product being conscious. There are certainly inferential processes whose product is conscious even though the "premises" are not. But that is not the same as the inferential processes themselves being conscious.

43. Consider a normal case in which a higher-order representation M^* is formed. Before M^* is formed, M is not conscious (since it is not represented). There then takes place a process leading from M to the formation of M^*, at the end of which M becomes conscious (due to its representation by M^*). What Rosenthal must do is distinguish between processes that would make M^* an immediate awareness of M and processes that would make M^* an awareness lacking the requisite immediacy. His suggestion is that the former are unconscious inferential processes, whereas the latter are processes of conscious inference. However, at the beginning of all these processes, M is supposed to be unconscious. So if we accept the principle that conscious inference can start only from conscious "premises," the fact that at the outset of the process M is unconscious means that the process cannot possibly be a conscious inference. So in fact no awareness of M can be formed through a conscious inference from M (before M is already conscious). (It is, of course, possible to make a conscious inference from one of one's conscious states to an awareness of that state. But the awareness formed through such inference is not the kind that initially bestows on the state its consciousness, since the state must already be conscious for the awareness of it to arise in this way.) Therefore, there is no explanatory force in the distinction between awareness of M formed by conscious inference from M and awareness of M formed by unconscious inferential processes emanating from M. It is not this distinction that marks the difference between immediate awareness of M and awareness of M that lacks immediacy.

44. Another, related problem with Rosenthal's original suggestion for distinguishing immediate awareness from awareness lacking immediacy—which I do not discuss in the main text—is brought up by Kobes (1995, p. 293): "suppose that, by feedback training or neurosurgery, I become [aware] of the . . . inference that yields the HOT [higher-order thought M^*]. Then it follows on Rosenthal's view that [M] is no longer conscious. But it is not credible that the addition of [awareness] of processes whereby the HOT is derived should cause loss of consciousness of the first-order state." That is, it is absurd to think that a conscious mental state would suddenly become unconscious when the subject becomes aware of the process that mediated the formation of the higher-order representation.

45. See Putnam 1975 and Burge 1979.

46. Perhaps the most poignant presentation of the problem is in Stich 1979.

47. Perhaps the most common approach was to claim that even if mental content lacks causal powers, it is nonetheless *explanatorily* relevant in psychology (see Burge 1989). Another popular strategy, identified with the internalist camp, was to construct a notion of *narrow content*—that is, content that is fully determined by the intrinsic properties of the state whose content it is (see Fodor 1987)—and to claim that this narrow content is the causally efficacious content.

48. For a defense of this thesis in this context, see Kim 1982.

49. Sometimes, it has been claimed not that causal efficacy resides solely in intrinsic properties, but that it resides solely in properties that *supervene* on intrinsic properties ("locally supervenient" properties). This does not make a difference to the present argument, though. The present argument is based on the fact that HOMT construes consciousness as an extrinsic relational property. But HOMT *also* construes consciousness as not locally supervenient. Thus, according to HOMT, two mental states that are intrinsically indistinguishable can differ in consciousness: one can be conscious and the other not—because one is appropriately represented and one is not. If so, the property of being conscious is not locally supervenient.

50. By calling the thesis "conceptual," I do not mean to suggest that it is merely a piece of conceptual analysis of the *concept* of consciousness. Rather, I mean to say that the thesis in question is not a thesis about what causes or brings about consciousness, but about what consciousness *is*. Also, by saying that the thesis is not causal, I don't mean to suggest that causality has no place in the HOMT view. Rather, I want to emphasize that the view is not that suitable higher-order monitoring *causes* consciousness, but rather that it *constitutes* consciousness.

51. Thus Rosenthal (2002, p. 416; italics mine): "It's easy to *overestimate* the degree to which a state's being conscious does actually play any [causal] role. . . . [In fact,] whether or not a state is conscious will not affect the state's [causal] role in planning and reasoning."

52. Epiphenomenalism about consciousness has been explicitly propounded by some (Velmans 1992, and to a significant extent, Chalmers 1996). But I take it that it is still a virtue of an account of consciousness that it does not render consciousness epiphenomenal. Epiphenomenalism is a liability, not an attractive feature.

53. Kim (1998) is responsible for reintroducing this dictum into philosophical discourse. In fact, what HOMT violates is an even weaker principle: to be is *at least* to be causally efficacious.

54. There may also be an epistemological problem involved in epiphenomenalism: if genuine knowledge requires causal interaction, as some philosophers have maintained

(e.g., Goldman 1967), there can be no knowledge of epiphenomenal entities or phenomena. This would make HOMT entail the absurdity that we cannot, in principle, have any knowledge of the existence of consciousness.

55. Dretske (1995, p. 97) writes: "Some people have cancer and they are conscious of having it. Others have it, but are not conscious of having it. Are there, then, two forms of cancer: conscious and unconscious cancer? . . . Experiences are, in this respect, like cancers. Some of them we are conscious of having. Others we are not. But the difference is not a difference in the experience. It is a difference in the experiencer—a difference in what the person knows about the experience he or she is having." See also Van Gulick 2001.

56. Since this reasoning applies to just about everything in nature, some have framed the problem in terms of panpsychism: HOMT appears to lead to the claim that everything in nature is capable of consciousness. Although some philosophers have flirted with panpsychism (e.g., Chalmers 1996), such panpsychism would not sit well with the reductive and demystifying ambitions of HOMT.

57. Thus Lycan (1990a, pp. 758–759; I am quoting from the reprint in Block, Flanagan, and Güzeldere 1997): "What is it that is so special about physical states of that certain sort, that consciousness of them makes them 'conscious'? That they are themselves mental. . . . It seems psychological states are called 'conscious' states when we are conscious of them, but nonpsychological things are not." Lycan's view is particularly implausible, as he seems to hold that there is nothing substantially different about mental states that makes them conscious upon being suitably represented—it is simply that we are unwilling to *call* internal states of inanimate objects conscious when they are suitably represented.

58. After all, as we can see with Lycan's view (see the previous note), there is nothing theoretically (or explanatorily) relevant in the fact that these states are mental. The upshot must be that there is an arbitrary fact that makes suitably represented mental states, but not other suitably represented internal states, conscious. In Lycan's case the arbitrary fact in question is that we are willing to *call* the former, but not the latter, "conscious." This line of rejoinder, if seriously pursued, would be at odds with the fact that conscious states most probably constitute a *natural kind* and in any event seem to share something objective that is common and peculiar to them.

59. Or if it would, this would have to be for some other reason.

60. This is also connected to one of HOMT's best-known difficulties, namely, the problem it faces with second-order misrepresentations of the very existence of a first-order mental state (see Byrne 1997; Neander 1998; Seager 1999, ch. 3; Levine 2001a, ch. 4). As several authors have noted, this problem does not present itself for a view like $SOMT_1$: a mental state may misrepresent its own *properties*, but it is impossible that it should misrepresent its own *existence* (see Caston 2002; Kriegel 2003a;

Raymont ms.). Whether this solution extends to other versions of SOMT is something we will not have occasion to consider here.

61. For comments on earlier drafts of this essay, I would like to thank Rocco Gennaro, Terry Horgan, Joe Levine, Robert Lurz, Barry Smith, Cybele Tom, Dan Zahavi, and especially Paul Raymont. I have also benefited from presenting this essay, or parts of it, to audiences at Cambridge University, Dartmouth College, Institut Jean Nicod, North Carolina State University, and the State University of New York at Buffalo. I would like to thank the audiences there as well.

II | Against the Self-Representational Approach to Consciousness

8 Conscious Awareness and (Self-)Representation

Joseph Levine

1 Consciousness certainly is connected with awareness. In fact, some people would say the two terms are synonymous. To be conscious of something is to be aware of it. Conscious mental states are those we are aware of. From these simple platitudes comes the motivation, or intuitive support for theories of consciousness built on the notion of representation, whether it be representation of the conscious states themselves or of their objects. Of course a crucial element linking the platitudes about awareness with representationalist theories is the thought that awareness can be captured or understood in terms of representation. I don't deny that awareness—conscious awareness, that is—entails representation; how could it not? What would it mean to be aware of something without somehow representing it? What I am suspicious of, however, is the idea that awareness is exhausted by representation. It seems to me that there is something going on with awareness that takes us beyond mere representation—or maybe it's a matter of a special kind of representation—that leaves every version of representationalist theory I know of inadequate as a theory of consciousness.

The plan for the essay is as follows. In sections 2 and 3 I will characterize how the notion of representation has been employed in theories of consciousness, identifying two sources of motivation for appealing to a notion of self-representation in the process. In section 4 I will describe three levels at which conscious awareness operates, and speculate on ways of formulating an integrated account of all three involving the notion of self-representation. In sections 5 and 6, I'll try to vindicate the suspicion mentioned in the paragraph above.

2 The simplest way of reducing awareness to representation is by what can be called "externalist representationalism." Consider a paradigm conscious mental state, such as seeing a ripe tomato sitting on the kitchen counter. One natural way to characterize the state is this: one is (visually) conscious of the tomato. What this amounts to on the representationalist theory is that one's

visual system is representing (something to the effect) that there is a red figure of a certain shape and texture in one's visual field.

Now there are two features of conscious sensory states that require theoretical elucidation: *qualitative character* and *subjectivity*. The former is implicated in the distinction between sensory states and nonsensory cognitive states like thoughts and beliefs, while the latter is implicated in the distinction between conscious and unconscious mental states. In the case at hand, seeing a ripe tomato, there is both a distinctive qualitative character to be reckoned with and also the fact that the state is conscious—"for the subject"—in a way that unconscious states are not.

Representationalism tries to solve the problem of qualitative character by putting the qualia out in the world, so to speak. For one's experience to have a reddish qualitative character is just for one's experience to be representing red (or some specific shade of red). To distinguish seeing red from thinking about it, which also involves representing it, certain further constraints on the format and content of sensory representations are imposed. A popular move is to claim that sensory representations involve so-called nonconceptual content, and this is what distinguishes them from thoughts, which have conceptual contents. Sometimes this idea is joined with the idea that sensory representations employ a more "pictorial" format than the more "symbolic" format of higher-level cognitive capacities (Dretske 1995a; Tye 1995—for criticism of their externalist representationalism, see Levine 2003).

On the question of subjectivity, what distinguishes conscious from unconscious states, externalist representationalists differ. Those who eschew any type of second-order representationalism opt for some condition on the relative availability of the sensory representations to higher-level cognitive processes, particularly those involving planning, action, and speech (e.g., Tye 1995). So, for instance, what makes the visual experience of the tomato conscious, and, say, the apprehension of an X in the blind visual field of a blindsight patient unconscious, is the fact that one can spontaneously report on the tomato, use the information in the visual sensation to plan one's lunch, and the like. In this sense the information about the tomato is there for the subject in a way that the information about the X is not in the blindsight case.

Many philosophers feel that the mere availability to higher cognitive processes cannot properly capture the sense in which a visual experience such as seeing the tomato on the counter is a conscious state. They feel that aside from the dispositional property of being, as it were, ready to hand for planning and the like, there is a more active, or categorical sense in which the state is a part of one's current awareness. Conscious states, on this view, are states one is conscious of, not merely states through which one is conscious of objects and events like the tomato on the counter.

There are many versions of higher-order views, but one significant division is between those that posit a distinct second-order state that represents the first-order state and those that maintain that the conscious state somehow represents itself. On both views, the consciousness, or awareness, is constituted by the representation of the target state. To be conscious of seeing the tomato is to represent that one is seeing it. The difference, again, has to do with whether this representation of the fact that one is seeing it takes place in a separate state or is a feature of the visual state itself.

Two-state higher-order views have been subjected to extensive critique in the literature. One reason for exploring the viability of a one-state, self-representational higher-order view is that it may seem to overcome some of the problems attending the two-state view (see Kriegel 2003b and this volume). One advantage in particular is that it seems to better capture the phenomenological situation.

Consider again the simple example above. I consciously see a ripe tomato on the kitchen counter. Clearly the primary object of my conscious state is what I'm seeing, the scene on the counter. But it also seems to be the case that my very awareness of the tomato on the counter includes within it somehow an apprehension that I am seeing what I'm seeing. That certainly seems to be part of what it means to say this visual state is conscious. Granted, both objects of awareness, the external situation and the visual state itself, are made objects of awareness by the two-state view. However, what isn't captured by that view is the way these two acts of apprehension seem intimately connected within a single state of mind. Only the one-state, self-representational view seems to capture this.

3   So far we've been discussing the relation between awareness and representation in the context of attempts to provide a theory of consciousness itself—of what makes a mental state a conscious state. But there is another dialectical route by which one can arrive at the idea that self-representation is involved in our awareness of our conscious states. It's worthwhile to incorporate this other route into our discussion, since in the literature on consciousness these two sources of motivation for appealing to self-representation have been important. It would be interesting to see how the two concerns relate to each other.

The other route has to do with what are called "phenomenal concepts." We begin with the problem of the explanatory gap, or, what for our purposes amounts to the same thing, the "intuition of distinctness" (see Levine 1983; Papineau 2002). When we consider the qualitative character of a visual color sensation, such as seeing that ripe tomato on the kitchen counter, and compare that property of our experience with a third-person characterization of what is going on in the relevant part of our brain's visual system at the time, the two seem utterly disparate. The idea that we are talking about the same state, or property, or that one can explain the reddish qualitative character by appeal to what is going on in the brain, just seems bizarre. Since materialists are committed to the claim that these are the same state or property, or that the qualitative property is realized in the brain property (and so therefore should be explicable in terms of it), they need to explain away this strong reaction against the relevant identity or explanatory claims.

In developing this critique of materialism it is common to contrast the qualia–brain state case with other instances of theoretical identifications. There doesn't seem to be any special problem swallowing the idea that water just is H_2O, or in explaining any of the superficial properties of water in terms of its molecular structure (together with other chemical facts and laws). So, the argument goes, what accounts for this special intuitive resistance when it comes to this theoretical identification/reduction? Dualists have a ready response: it's because qualitative mental properties really are distinct and irreducible to physical or functional properties, connected to them only by brute, fundamental laws, that the former cannot be explained in terms of the latter. The burden is then on the materialist to come up with another explanation.

This is where the appeal to phenomenal concepts comes in (Loar 1990; Tye 2000). Qualia, it is argued, are nothing over and above physical (or functional) states of the brain. However, there is something special about them; it's a matter of our cognitive access to them. Unlike other objects and properties, we have special first-person access to qualia, which means that the concepts we form of them through this route—phenomenal concepts (which means here concepts of phenomenal properties, not concepts that are themselves phenomenal—though wait a minute)—are different in important ways from other concepts. This difference in kind is then used to explain our cognitive inability to appreciate the relevant psycho-physical identity/ reduction.

Earlier I said that there were two aspects to the problem of consciousness: qualitative character and subjectivity. Insofar as versions of representationalism have been employed to address both aspects, we see a close connection between them. But now we see another close connection. The problem of qualia immediately leads to the problem of subjectivity, in that we find ourselves in need of an account of the latter to explain away certain problems with the former. Higher-order theories, in attempting to provide an account of the distinction between conscious and unconscious mental states, addressed subjectivity directly through the device of representation. But even those theorists who eschew the higher-order account of what makes a state conscious find themselves in need of a theory of higher-order representation to overcome the intuition of distinctness and the explanatory gap. In fact, both higher-order theories of consciousness and theories of phenomenal concepts face the same issue: how to understand the special cognitive relation that attends the first–person point of view.

One aspect of this special, first-person relation that seems crucial is something we might call, for lack of a better term, "cognitive immediacy." There seems to be a more intimate cognitive connection between the subject and what she is conscious of, or the consciousness itself, than is present in other circumstances. Of course "immediacy" and "intimacy" are both metaphors, and it is notoriously difficult to characterize this feature in an illuminating way. Yet it does seem to be the core feature that distinguishes first-person access from other forms of cognitive access.

In the case of higher-order theories of consciousness, one way the issue of immediacy arises is this: it's clear that not just any representation of a mental state makes it conscious. The standard example is one's coming to believe that one has repressed desires in therapy, even though the desires themselves are still unconscious. The kind of representation of a mental state that constitutes being consciously aware of it has a special immediacy about it. It is thus a burden of the higher-order theory to provide an illuminating account of what this cognitive immediacy comes to.

In the case of phenomenal concepts there is also a need for an account of the special first-person cognitive immediacy. The problem is that merely appealing to a difference in the concepts by which one apprehends a phenomenon like one's occupying a certain sensory state is not sufficient to explain the particular cognitive resistance we feel to reduction and identity claims in the psycho-physical case. After all, the way we access the substance we call both "water" and "H_2O" also involves two very different concepts. Why should it be so hard to see how a phenomenal property is identical or explanatorily reducible to a physical property yet not at all hard to see how water could be H_2O? The answer purportedly lies somewhere in the idea that first-person access, by way of phenomenal concepts, provides an especially immediate form of access to sensory states that thereby makes them seem so different in kind from the sorts of states we conceptualize in third-person theoretical terms. (Whether or not this really answers the question is a topic to which I will return in section 5.)

Bringing these two concerns together—the need for an account of immediacy both for higher-order theories of consciousness itself and for phenomenal concepts—we converge on the idea of self-representation. Perhaps what is special about the kind of representation involved in being aware of one's sensory states is that it is that very state that is representing itself, not a distinct state as in standard versions of higher-order theory. Similarly, the sort of first-person access involved in apprehension of a qualitative state by way of a phenomenal concept might involve using that very qualitative state to represent itself. Certainly it's hard to see how one can get more "immediate" a form of cognitive access than having a state represent itself. Perhaps then the grand unifying theory of consciousness and the explanatory gap can be built around the notion of self-representation. Well, let's see.

4   Before embarking on an evaluation of self-representation theory, I want to address another question. We identified two points at which cognitive immediacy becomes an issue: at the awareness of one's experience that makes it conscious in the first place and at the awareness that is constitutive of possessing a phenomenal concept. How do these two forms of self-representation relate to each other? Are they the same thing?

On the face of it, one would think not. On one theory, self-representation is what distinguishes conscious states from nonconscious states. Having a conscious experience is itself a matter of occupying a state that reflexively represents itself. On the other theory, self-representation is used to distinguish phenomenal concepts from other ways of representing conscious experiences. On this view, there isn't anything particularly reflexive about a conscious experience per se. Rather, it's when we adopt an explicitly introspective attitude toward the experience that self-representation comes into play.

These two theories answer to different concerns as well. The first type of self-representational theory is attempting to analyze what it is to be conscious. It is motivated by the relational approach of higher-order theory, but departs from the standard version in locating the representation relation that is constitutive of conscious awareness inside a single state. The theory of phenomenal concepts proposes no analysis of conscious awareness itself. Conscious awareness is taken to be identical with some physical or functional property, whatever that may turn out to be. The entire appeal to self-representation has to do with explaining why there is cognitive resistance to accepting the identity of conscious awareness with whatever it turns out to be, described in whatever theoretical vocabulary turns out to be appropriate to it. So why would one expect a single account to satisfy both of these quite different motivations? Again, on the surface it doesn't seem likely.

Yet, despite these differences, it seems to me that there ought to be a way to integrate them. As I pointed out above, both seem to appeal to self-representation as a way to realize a kind of cognitive immediacy that is supposedly distinctive of the first-person point of view. It would be extremely odd if these two domains in which this distinctive cognitive immediacy were present weren't intimately connected. In fact, whether or not one accepts self-representation as an account of first-person cognitive immediacy, the two phenomena to which the two self-representation theories are addressed ought to be capable of integration. The fact that our access to our conscious experiences is special when we introspectively reflect on them must have something to do with the fact that consciousness involves a kind of self-awareness in the first place.

Just to complicate the story a bit more, let me add a third kind of cognitive immediacy that seems involved in conscious experience. Consider again our example of a typical conscious experience, my seeing a ripe tomato on the kitchen counter. We have focused so far on the fact that there is a qualitative character to that experience, and that this character seems to be something of which I'm aware. But another feature of the experience is the way that the ripe tomato seems immediately present to me in the experience. I am not in any way aware of any cognitive distance between me and the scene in front of me; the fact that what I'm doing is representing the world is clearly not itself part of the experience. The world is just there.

This sense of the immediacy afforded by sensory experience is part of what fuels the transparency argument employed by externalist representationalists about qualia. Look, they say, the redness isn't experienced as a feature of your visual state, but rather as a feature of the tomato. It's all out there. Isn't that what you find when you reflect on your experience? they argue—persuasively, to my mind. I don't intend to engage externalist representationalism here (see Levine 2003); I just wanted to note that transparency and the immediacy of the objects of conscious awareness seem to be part of the same phenomenon. When we encounter the world in perception, it doesn't seem to be merely represented by us, but *presented* to us.

So we've got three levels of representation in play; let's just call them levels one, two, and three. Level one is the representation of the world outside by a visual experience; the spatial layout, textures, and colors constitutive of the scene involving the ripe tomato on the counter—call it "spatial layout L." Level two is that awareness of the experience that seems inseparable from any experience, whether made the focus of attention or not. Level three is the representation of the experience when it is made the object of explicit introspective attention, as in the sorts of judgments concerning identity and reduction for which appeal to phenomenal concepts is made. Can we integrate them all into an account of conscious cognitive immediacy that is based on self-representation?

Here's my quite tentative proposal. To begin with, it's important to remember that any claim to immediacy in the level-one content has got to be tempered by the recognition that perception cannot really afford immediate, or unmediated access to the world. After all, there are hallucinations and illusions. It can look to me for all the world as if there is a ripe tomato on the counter in front of me even when there isn't—even when I'm sitting in a completely dark room, so long as my brain occupies the relevant state. No doubt perceptual experience *seems* to deliver the world directly to me in this very hard-to-characterize way, but it can't be just as it seems, or hallucinations and illusions wouldn't be possible.

The point is that it isn't immediacy itself, perhaps, that requires explanation, but the *appearance* of it. So how does this help? How does the fact that the explanandum is now the appearance of immediacy at level one make it easier to see how appeal to the self-representational content alongside the externally directed content serves to explain it? Well, it might be that this appearance of immediacy between subject and external object is a kind of cognitive illusion engendered by the *actual* immediacy possessed by the self-representational content itself.

To see what I mean, let's turn now to level two. As I look at the ripe tomato on the counter—the whole scene, spatial layout L, being the level-one content of my experience—I am simultaneously aware, alongside the primary awareness of L, of the fact that I am now having a visual experience as of L. Consider just this secondary self-awareness for a moment. This level-two representation doesn't seem to involve making the visual experience a full-fledged object of awareness in its own right, the way that the experience does with the spatial layout L or the level-three introspective state does with the level-one state. Yet, it does seem to involve mentally registering, in some way, that one is having the experience.

One feature that seems to go along with this intermediate character—that is, that it involves a kind of registering yet without focal attention—is the idea that the awareness of the experience is somehow intrinsic to the experience itself. Here we have the most intimate form of cognitive immediacy in the entire three-level structure. Conscious visual experience seems to be just the type of state that must, by its very nature, be also apprehended as it affords apprehension of the external scene. The idea that this secondary, level-two kind of representation should be self-representation—the experience representing itself—certainly seems inviting.

But of course appeal to self-representation here still only serves to explain, if anything, the immediacy and intrinsicality of the level-two form of awareness itself. How would this help with level one, the awareness of the tomato on the counter? Consider what it is we are aware of at level two. We said that the representational content at issue is something to the effect that I am having (or it is now occurring—whether explicit reference to a subject is included is not clear) a visual experience as of spatial layout L. But this means that it's the content of the level-one representation that is the object of the self-representation. This fact might be the key to the apparent immediacy of level one itself.

Perhaps what is going on here is a kind of transparency phenomenon, a connection already noted above. That is, the self-awareness of level two involves "seeing through" its object, the level-one content, to what that content is about—but only apparently, of course. In our apprehension of the visual experience, a relation that itself has genuine cognitive immediacy, we somehow transfer that sense of immediacy to the external scene, the spatial layout L represented by the level-one content of the experience. One way to put it is this: what is genuinely immediately "open" to us, in the context of a visual experience, is the intentional object corresponding to layout L. We interpret this, in the experience, to mean that L itself is immediately open to us. But this, it turns out, is only apparent, a kind of cognitive illusion.

The foregoing account is wildly speculative of course. My goal here is to explore how far we can go in explaining the peculiar nature and structure of a conscious experience by appeal to the notion of self-representation. Since something we've been calling, for lack of a better name, "cognitive immediacy," seems to be one of the crucial features at each of the three levels of representation associated with a conscious experience, it would make sense that whatever form of self-representation posited as essential to consciousness should somehow unify these phenomena. The story above is an attempt to show how this might be done at least for the first two levels.

Let's turn now to the connection between levels two and three. We're assuming, at least for the sake of argument, that some appeal to the immediacy of the relation between phenomenal concept and phenomenal state would explain the cognitive resistance that is naturally felt when considering certain psycho-physical identity statements or explanatory reductions. Some philosophers then go on to appeal to the idea of self-representation to explain the relevant sense of cognitive immediacy (Block 2002; Papineau 2002). The question I want to consider now is whether or not the self-representation at issue here is plausibly identified with the self-representation involved with the first two levels.

Here's roughly what they have in mind. In contexts where I find myself puzzling over how this qualitative state could be a neurophysiological state (or something along these lines), I am actually using a token of the very qualitative state type at issue to represent that type (or the relevant property). Papineau (2002) compares what's going on here to quotation, where a token of the type is used to refer to the type itself. So the question is what relation this form of self-representation—involved in the exercise of a phenomenal concept—bears to the self-representation involved in the mere having of a conscious experience.

Before we address that question, we need to be somewhat clearer about how to understand the self-representation theory of phenomenal concepts. When I entertain the thought that reddish experiences might be identical to (or realized by) neural states, do I literally have to be having those very experiences? Right now I am perfectly capable of wondering about this question with respect to the look of ripe tomatoes, but I'm not in fact now looking at a ripe tomato. But if I were employing a token of that experience type to represent it in thought, wouldn't I have to be right now having the experience?

Of course sometimes I am having the experience when I think about it. Often it is the case that it's as I'm staring at that ripe tomato that I find myself puzzling about the experience's alleged physical nature. So perhaps in those cases the theory makes sense. But what about the other times, like now, when I can find myself having gappy worries about visual experiences of tomatoes without actually looking at one? Well, it's plausible that even now—and in my own case I find it borne out—when not actually visually experiencing the ripe tomato, what's going on is that I'm calling up an image of a ripe tomato and focusing on that. If this phenomenon is general, if in order to get into the relevant puzzling state of mind, to have gappy worries, it's necessary that one at least imagine the relevant experience, then perhaps that will do. We can say that the image token is representing a certain type that is shared by the full-fledged experience. There may be problems with this move, but let's accept it for the moment.

The question before us now is how to understand the relation between the self-representational nature of conscious states themselves and that of phenomenal concepts. One possibility is that the very same representation that captures the awareness inherent in a conscious state—qua being conscious—is itself the form of representation employed when thinking about a conscious state through a phenomenal concept: that is, perhaps levels two and three collapse. If one could make a case for this proposal, it would certainly unify the various phenomena at issue and to that extent provide a more satisfying theory.

Offhand this proposal doesn't seem promising though. What is supposedly special about level two is that it doesn't involve the kind of focused attention that is clearly involved when expressing gappy worries. How could that, as it were, off-to-the-side, by-the-way kind of awareness that seems to attend every conscious experience be the very same form of representation that is involved when I think hard and explicitly about an experience? The two kinds of awareness seem so different in character that it's hard to see how the very same representational means could underlie their exercise.

Yet, it really would be odd if these two kinds of awareness, both possessing that kind of immediacy that suggests self-representation, weren't at root the same. I am tempted again to speculate, as follows. The basic phenomenon here is the awareness/self-representation of level two. This is where whatever is peculiar to conscious experience seems to reside. This is the level where subjectivity, the experience being "for me," has its home. Somehow, when I focus on my experience in an explicitly introspective way, that very awareness which is only of the inattentive sort when my attention is directed outward, is built into a full-fledged explicit awareness on that occasion.

What I imagine, and again this is quite speculative, is something like the following. We begin with a state that has two contents, the external content and the reflexive content (corresponding to awareness levels one and two). Given the nonfocal nature of level-two awareness, it makes sense to characterize the reflexive content as a secondary content, with the primary content being the external one. What "primary" and "secondary" amounts to would have to be spelled out in functional terms. That is, it would be a matter of the role the state played that determines which of its two contents is primary. In the case of normal perceptual experience, the relevant state is primarily being used for the information it's conveying concerning matters external.

However, on occasion, one is concerned mostly about the state itself. I'm having an experience and it's telling me about the external world, but my interest is in the experience, not in the situation it's telling me about. Suppose this functional shift involved treating the reflexive content as primary and the external content as secondary. Level-three awareness, then, need not involve the introduction of a new representational vehicle, but rather a change in the functional role of the vehicle that is already there. This would be as tight a connection between levels two and three as you could get, and therefore an especially appealing way of integrating the concerns that motivate positing these two levels in the first place.

Let me summarize. Conscious experience seems to involve a special, immediate cognitive relation on three levels. First, there is a relation between the subject and the primary object of her conscious state, whatever state of the external world is presented to her in the experience. Second, in the very act of being conscious of some state of her external environment, she is simultaneously aware of her conscious experience itself. Third and finally, when explicitly contemplating her conscious experience, her cognitive relation to the experience seems to partake of the very same sort of immediacy as manifested at the other two levels.

I have speculated that the fundamental form of immediate awareness is that of the second sort, level two. The immediacy that apparently attaches to the first level is really a kind of mistaken projection from the second level. We are immediately aware of our own experience, but since what this experience consists in is a representation of the world around us, that content is presented as if it too were immediately present. That this is only apparent is demonstrated by the possibility of hallucination and illusion.

On the other side, the idea is that explicit second-order forms of awareness (which we've called level-three representation), the kind involved in full-fledged introspection of a conscious experience, is somehow constructed out of the awareness already present at level two. This would explain why level-three awareness would also possess the immediacy needed to distinguish it from other forms of cognitive access. The fundamental principle then is that the awareness that makes a state conscious, a state for the subject, is what gives it its presentational character vis-à-vis the external world and also its puzzling character vis-à-vis physicalist theories. What endows a conscious state with this fundamental sort of awareness, its subjectivity? The hypothesis on the floor is that what makes it conscious, subjective, in this way is that the state in question, in addition to representing whatever external content it represents, also represents itself.

5   According to the account above, phenomenal concepts achieve their special cognitive immediacy through the mechanism of self-representation. It's worth asking, however, just what work cognitive immediacy, implemented through self-representation, is supposed to do here. Sometimes it's said that qualia serve as their own modes of presentation (Loar 1990). Others emphasize how getting oneself into the gappy state of mind, and thus employing phenomenal concepts, usually involves either currently having the relevant experience, or conjuring up an image that shares certain qualitative features with the original experience (Papineau 1995), so that one is in effect saying, "but how could *that* be a physical/functional state/property?" as one contemplates the experience (or the image) itself.

But how is this connection with the conscious state itself supposed to explain why conceiving of it through this means produces cognitive resistance to the idea that it is identical to, or explicable by reference to, a physical state? After all, suppose I look at a glass of water and consider the claim that it is identical to H_2O. It doesn't seem as if the fact that I'm currently encountering it through one of its superficial properties, its appearance, makes it especially difficult to accept the idea that it is composed of invisible molecules two parts hydrogen and one part oxygen. Why is the special connection between a phenomenal concept and an instance of the experience itself, or an image qualitatively similar to it, of particular significance in explaining cognitive resistance to both explanatory and identity claims?

Of course, one explanation for the significance of immediacy in accounting for the relevant cognitive resistance is not friendly to materialists. One is tempted to say, as we reflect both on an experience we're having and its neurological or functional description, that the first-person way of conceiving it provides us a glimpse of something left out of the third-person theoretical description. We see it as it really is—capture its essence, as it were—in a way that can't be accomplished otherwise. But this account implies that some feature of the experience really is left out of the theoretical description and can be cognized only through the conscious experience itself. This can't be what the materialist has in mind.

Some philosophers (Perry 2001a) have compared the way we conceive of our conscious states in the first-person mode to indexical representations. This of course would fit the self-representation model very well, since *self-representation* is a kind of indexical representation. But, as I've argued elsewhere (most recently, Levine forthcoming), this doesn't help much either. For one thing, we have all sorts of informative identity claims involving indexicals that do not cause the kind of cognitive resistance we seem to face with psycho-physical identity/explanatory reduction claims. "Where are we?" the lost driver asks, of course knowing that she's "here." She is then informed by the passenger that they've just crossed a certain intersection, say Main Street and 9th Avenue. There isn't any problem identifying "here" with the nonindexical description in terms of street names. Imagine the puzzled reaction she'd get if she complained, "but how could Main and 9th be *here*?" (unless, of course, she had some reason to think she was quite some distance from that intersection, which is a different kind of puzzlement entirely).

There is another problem with the appeal to indexicals, which relates to a matter that will come up again later.[1] Indexicals and demonstratives are inherently subject to ambiguity. When you point at an object and say "this," what is picked out is not a function only of the demonstrative and the pointing, but also of the intention behind the utterance. With reference to individuals, the ambiguity can probably be resolved by the addition of a sortal, such as in "this coffee mug." But when dealing with what Loar calls a "type demonstrative," where you are picking out a kind, or type, by virtue of demonstrating an exemplar, or token, the problem of ambiguity becomes much more intractable. Each token is a token of an indefinite number of types. Which one are you demonstrating? Even if you add an experience type, that won't pin it down sufficiently since each token experience is a token of many different experience types. The more constraining information you load into the intention with which the demonstrative is employed to cut down on the possible ambiguity, the less work is done by the demonstrative itself. My bet is there's no way to successfully refer to the type intended by "this (type of) experience" without already having the type in mind. But then the demonstrative does no work at all.

Somehow, the very fact that entertaining a phenomenal concept involves occupying the phenomenal state itself is supposed to engender a special cognitive relation, one that prevents establishing the kind of conceptual link that comes with identity and explanatory reduction claims. Why should that be, if it isn't, as the dualist claims, that first-person modes of presentation actually present something we can't get any other way? I don't pretend to have a good answer to this question. But having pressed it so far, let me take the following account as at least a first step toward an answer. What I will argue is that even if we find this account satisfactory, any form of self-representation that is plausibly naturalizable won't really fill the requisite role.

What we want to avoid clearly is the dualist challenge that first-person access puts us in touch with a feature of our mental state that cannot be accessed in any other way. We don't want anything genuinely new to pop up there. So if what's represented isn't new, the phenomenon causing the relevant cognitive resistance must reside in the mode of access itself. Perhaps there is some unique cognitive relation that is created when a state is used to represent itself. Let's call this relation, for lack of a better word, and for obvious historical reasons, "acquaintance." The claim then is that we have two modes of access to phenomena: acquaintance and (well, why not?) description. It is simply a fact about ourselves that we cannot conceptually link what we are acquainted with to what we describe even if the two are really the same thing.

As I said, I don't pretend to know quite how this story is supposed to go. But however it goes, I don't see how any standardly naturalizable account of self-representation could implement it. There are three ways to naturalize representation that I know of: causal history, nomic dependence (with perhaps some historical-teleological elements added), and functional role. The first two are nonstarters for self-representation (but see below). Causal history is a mechanism that works most naturally for singular terms. Current uses of "Joe Levine" refer to me because they have a causal ancestry leading back to an original baptism, or something like that. Nomic dependence grounds information that, when appropriate bells and whistles are added, yields representation of properties. One type of bell or whistle is to throw in some causal history via evolution. So a current state's representational content is that property that nomically covaried with states of its type in ancestors of this organism and because of which those states contributed to the organism's survival. It seems pretty clear that since everything covaries with itself, and states don't cause themselves, that neither nomic dependence nor causal history can serve as the mechanism of self-representation.

What's left, then, is functional role. Again, I won't pretend to know just how a state's functional role determines its content, but for our purposes the case of indexicals serves as a model. It has long been thought that what makes a term an indexical must be something special about its particular role in reasoning and planning action. So, for instance, one crucial difference between conceiving of myself in the first person, as "I" or "me," and conceiving of myself via a description that picks me out, or even my name, is that only the first-person way hooks directly into my action planning. If I think I'm about to be hit by a car, that will immediately cause me to (attempt to) get out of the way; whereas thinking that that guy is about to be hit, while pointing at what is (unbeknownst to me) my reflection in the mirror, will cause me to shout "get out of the way." Let's assume then, for the sake of argument, that there is some functional role such that playing it is sufficient for having a reflexive content of the sort claimed to be involved in phenomenal concepts.

But now here's the problem. Normally the way a functional state is physically implemented is irrelevant to the role, except that the implementer must meet the role's description. But other than that, we don't pay attention to the way the role is implemented: what's of psychological significance is the role itself. That's what functionalism is all about. That's why it's not supposed to matter whether a subject is made out of brain cells, computer chips, or Swiss cheese. Nothing changes when the functional roles involve representation. Which physical tokens are used doesn't matter, so long as the appropriate pattern of interactions among the tokens is maintained.

Of course one could grant this general point about functional roles and yet still maintain that in this case the nature of the role-implementer relation is of psychological significance. Why? Since the role in this case is self-representation, then the identity of the implementer provides the identity of what's represented. I grant this, but now it seems as if all we have is indexicals again. The place picked out by "here," or its mental representation equivalent, and the time picked out by "now," are whatever place and time happen to be where and when the relevant tokens occur.[2] But again, this fact about indexicals leads to no general cognitive mystery about the nature of the present moment or location.

Why should the fact that we use a token of that very type to represent it make any difference? Why should it cause us to be unable to understand how an identity could be true when one side of the identity is represented in that way and the other side by symbols not of that type? I think the reason this sort of account has any intuitive appeal is that we aren't thinking of it in this way really; that is, we aren't thinking of a functional system that uses a reflexive device to refer to a type that that very token instantiates. Rather we're thinking of the fact that on one side of the identity is a representation that somehow involves a full-fledged conscious experience whereas the other side does not. Yes, if we're pointing at an experience—a cognitively rich and special phenomenon—and saying that *that* is identical to what is picked out by this other description, one can see perhaps why that would be hard to accept, why it would meet the sort of cognitive resistance we're trying to explain. But merely to point out that a physical state type is represented reflexively by a token of that type doesn't seem to really explain that cognitive resistance. The latter explanation, as far as I can see, borrows all its intuitive plausibility from the former. However, once we're already appealing to what is distinctive about experience in the explanation, we're taking what most needs to be explained for granted.

Let me put this another way. Here I am contemplating this visual experience of the red tomato. I'm told that having the experience is the same thing as (or to be explained by appeal to) my brain's being in a certain neural state. I find this unintelligible, mysterious. Along comes the materialist and explains my reaction this way. "You see," she says, "you are representing this state in two very different ways. On the one hand, you are describing it in terms of its physical properties. On the other hand, you are representing it by experiencing it. Your being in the state is itself your way of representing it. Therefore, since one side of the proposed identity involves your actually being in the state and the other doesn't, you can't find the idea that it's really the same thing intelligible."

But your being in the state as your way of representing it seems to make a difference precisely because being in the state is a matter of having an *experience.* However, if all being an experience amounts to—all that distinguishes it for these purposes from nonexperiential mental states—is being a state that is used to represent itself, then we can't appeal to our intuitive notion of experiential character to explain the cognitive resistance to the identity claim; we can only appeal to the self-representational character. If that's all that's involved, though, it's hard to see why it gives rise to any mystery. Why should it matter whether an indexical picks out itself or something else? Why is that of such psychological moment?

6 The argument of the last section was aimed at the self-representation associated with level three. When we explicitly reflect on our conscious experience, we encounter cognitive resistance to proposed explanatory reductions and identity claims couched in physical or functional terms. It was supposed to be the self-representational character of phenomenal concepts, the form of representation employed when we introspect on our experience, that accounted for this cognitive resistance. If what I've argued above (and in Levine forthcoming) is right, then this account is inadequate. But how does this affect the claim that self-representation provides a decent account of level-two conscious awareness?

In one sense it affects it only indirectly. What I mean is this. One problem faced by the self-representation theory that is shared by every broadly functionalist theory of conscious experience is the explanatory gap/intuition of distinctness. I'm looking again at that ripe tomato on the counter (it's *very* ripe by now). I reflect on this visual experience, and consider the proposition that what it is is a brain state that is representing itself. Really? Well it certainly seems as if I can coherently conceive of a device that is occupying a state that meets whatever are the appropriate functional conditions for self-representation and yet isn't having a conscious experience at all. It really doesn't seem at all like that is an explanation of what is going on with me now. Is that a problem?

Well, if one were looking to the self-representation theory itself to solve the problem of the explanatory gap, then it would be. But even if that isn't the goal, one still has to deal with it, and, if the argument of section 5 is right, one can't appeal to the special (perhaps self-representational) character of phenomenal concepts to do the job. So in this sense, the fact that self-representation theory doesn't succeed as a theory of what is special about phenomenal concepts is a problem for self-representationalism about conscious experience itself. But this problem isn't specific to self-representationalism; it affects any broadly functionalist theory, as I said.

As mentioned above, the problem just presented only indirectly affects the account of level-two awareness. Is there something in the very considerations

I used to undermine the self-representational account of phenomenal concepts that would affect the account of level-two awareness as well? I think there is, and what unites these two objections is that they both stem from the inadequacy of the self-representational account as an explanation of cognitive immediacy. Before I go into this, however, I want to consider another question, one that will help clarify some aspects of the self-representational account. The question is whether the self-representational view really does overcome some of the standard objections that have been pushed against the two-state higher-order theory.

Two objections in particular seem relevant (and are explicitly discussed in Kriegel 2003a). The first was briefly mentioned above. On the standard two-state view, conscious awareness is a relation between two states, the higher-order state that, as it were, is the consciousness of a particular mental state and the target state of which one is conscious. On this theory the higher-order state is not itself conscious.[3] But this seems phenomenologically bizarre. The consciousness of the experience of seeing the ripe tomato seems as much a matter of which we are conscious as the ripe tomato itself. How can we say that the consciousness itself is not something we are aware of from within the first-person point of view?

The second objection has to do with the possibility that one might have the higher-order state in the absence of the first-order state. After all, we have hallucinations, which are representations of scenes outside us that don't really obtain. Why couldn't our internal monitoring system suffer a similar hallucination? If it did, would we be having a conscious experience? It seems that the higher-order theorist would have to say we were having a conscious experience, or at least it would be for us just as if we were. But if it is just as if we were having a conscious experience, what more do you need to call it an actual conscious experience? If one grants that this would count as an experience, however, it seems to totally undermine the relational character of the higher-order theory. All that seems to matter resides now in one state, the higher-order state.

It should be clear how adopting the one-state view at least appears to overcome these objections. With regard to the first objection, since this one state that is representing both the ripe tomato on the counter and itself is conscious, we aren't leaving a crucial piece of consciousness outside itself, as it were. All is enclosed in one state and part of our phenomenology. With regard to the second objection, the imagined kind of internal hallucination isn't possible. Since it's one state that is representing itself, if the representer is there, so is the represented.

Before we accept this appearance of overcoming the objections, however, we need to get clearer about how to understand the one-state view. There are of course a number of different ways of distinguishing versions of the view (see Kriegel this volume), but I'm interested in one way in particular. Let's call them the one-vehicle model and the two-vehicle model. On the one-vehicle model, what we have is one representational vehicle with two contents, one content directed outward and the other reflexively directed on itself. On the two-vehicle model, the one state contains two representational vehicles, one directed outward, and the other directed at the first. On the latter model, the two vehicles constitute distinct parts of a single state.

When talking about individuating vehicles (as Kriegel 2003b does), it's crucial to be clear about the level at which the individuation is taking place. If we're individuating by physical types, then probably any state that is suitable for realizing a psychological state will be one that could be broken down into parts in some way. But this fact, that the physical state in question can be seen as having parts, is not relevant to our purposes. The relevant question for distinguishing between the two models just described is this: are the two representational contents that both models posit (the outwardly directed one and the reflexive one) attributed to two separate physical states/mechanisms that constitute distinct parts of a larger physical state, or does the very same physical state/mechanism express both representational contents? So long as there isn't any principled way of associating one of the contents with one of the physical state's parts and the other with a different part, even if at the physical level the state clearly has parts, this will still count as a "seamless" one-state vehicle. So the question is, which of these two models does the advocate of self-representationalism have in mind? (Note that both one-vehicle and two-vehicle models are models of the one-state view, as the two vehicles in the latter model are characterized as parts of a single state.)

Kriegel (2003b) argues for the second model, on the grounds that it can utilize a causal theory of content. One part of a state can have a causal impact on the other, though a single state can't cause itself. In section 5 I was assuming the one-vehicle model when I argued that both nomic dependence and causal history were nonstarters for implementing self-representation. I allowed that perhaps there was going to be a functional-role account, but admittedly it's not easy to see what that would be.

Despite the fact that the two-vehicle model will have an easier time with finding ways to implement the relevant representation relation, I think the one-vehicle model better captures the spirit of self-representationalism, and better overcomes the objections that attend the two-state higher-order theory.

Take the second objection, for instance: the problem was that it seemed possible to have the higher-order state without its target state. But why can't that occur on the two-vehicle one-state model? Just because the two parts of the state count, for certain taxonomic purposes, as one state, that doesn't mean that one part of the state can't occur without the other.

Consider now the first objection to the two-state view, that the awareness itself is left out of consciousness. Well, if one part of a state is representing the other, then it doesn't really capture the way in which consciousness of the experience is inherently part of the experience itself. If A and B are distinct, B with its outward content and A referring to B, then even though we're calling the joint state A-B a single state, it still seems as if A isn't itself something of which we're consciously aware, which seems to conflict with the intuitive advantage the one-state view was supposed to have over the two-state view.

As mentioned above, state individuation is very sensitive to considerations of level of analysis. What may be one item from one perspective, is more than one from another. In his attempt to show that there can be sound empirical reasons for individuating the relevant states one way or another, Kriegel (2003b) points to the synchronization phenomena discussed by Crick and Koch (1990). He imagines two events, N1, representing the sound of a bagpipe, and N2, representing N1. So far we have a standard two-state, higher-order theory. But now suppose that the firing rates involved in the two events are appropriately synchronized, so they are "bound" to each other. Now, we have a principled basis for calling the joint state, N1-N2, a single state, and empirical vindication of the one-state (two-vehicle) view.

But what matters is not merely whether N1 and N2 are physically bound through their synchronized firing rates, but whether they are psychologically bound.[4] That is, does the synchronization of their firing rates effect a psychological integration of the two states? In particular, does it bind them in the sense that together they express the content or contents attributable to them? The point is, so long as we think of the two representational contents as still belonging to N1 and N2, with N2 having N1 as its content, and N1 having the sound of the bagpipe as its content, I don't see a principled difference between this position and the standard two-state higher-order theory, despite the synchronization of their realizers. On the other hand, if their synchronization yields a joint state possessing two contents that are, as it were, diffused throughout N1-N2, representing both the sound of the bagpipe and the representational state itself, with neither physical part bearing one of these two contents on its own, then it does make a difference. But then we have the one-vehicle model.

Let's assume then that we are dealing with one integrated representational vehicle that possesses two contents. One problem is of course the one mentioned above, that it's not easy to see how this state that represents some outward scene comes to also possess its reflexive content. Carruthers (2000) has an account, but I have argued that it doesn't really motivate the assignment of the secondary, reflexive content (Levine 2001b). I don't want to repeat that argument here, and of course he has a reply (Carruthers 2001). Let's just leave it that finding a basis for attributing the reflexive content is an issue this theory must face.

However, lest one wonder why in section 5 I was quite content to assume some functional account or other would suffice and here I am questioning the basis for the self-representational content, let me point out that there is an important difference between level-two and level-three self-representation. At level three, the level at which phenomenal concepts operate, we are imagining a mechanism that takes a state and uses it to refer to itself. In the context of that employment of the state, it isn't being used to represent what it normally represents. Rather, we're imagining some indexical-style device that picks out that state itself. On level two, however, we're imagining that the target state retains its primary representational function of providing information concerning the immediately surrounding environment. Level-two awareness is a secondary, added-on representational content. In that situation it's harder to see what the requisite grounds for attributing the reflexive content might be.

But let's suppose that there is some functional role played by the state such that it grounds this secondary, reflexive content. I grant that the one-vehicle one-state view does overcome the two objections cited earlier to the standard two-state higher-order view, so it certainly passes that test. So why is there still an explanatory gap here? I think that though self-representation is probably part of what it is for a mental state to be conscious, the problem is that the notion of representation employed by the theory, the kind that could plausibly be implemented through some sort of functional role, isn't adequate to capture the kind of representation involved in conscious awareness. The problem, in other words, is that conscious awareness seems to be a sui generis form of representation, and not merely because it's reflexive. Something about the representation relation itself—that it affords acquaintance, and not just representation—is such as to yield a mystery concerning its possible physical realization. In the remainder of this section I'll try to elaborate on this idea.

I think there are two ways in which the immediacy of conscious awareness seems to elude explanation by appeal to standard, "functionalizable" representation (by which I mean any notion of representation that is broadly functionalist, including nomic/causal relations under that rubric). The first has to do with the subjectivity of conscious experience. Subjectivity, as I described it earlier, is that feature of a mental state by virtue of which it is of significance for the subject; not merely something happening within her, but "for her." The self-representation thesis aims to explicate that sense of significance for the subject through the fact that the state is being represented.

But now, what makes that representation itself of significance for the subject, and thus conscious? Remember, it was the felt need to endow the awareness of the visual state with consciousness itself that motivated the move from the two-state higher-order view to the one-state (and one-vehicle) view in the first place. So how is this done?

Well, it's supposed to be taken care of by the fact that the very state that bears this content is also its representational object. But that isn't sufficient, since we want to know how it's being the object of its own content is itself a matter of significance for the subject. In the end, the answer for the (reductive) representationalist has to be that it's a matter of the state's functional role (either that or yet another representation, which of course leads to regress). That is, the content counts as something of which the subject is consciously aware because it maintains a set of access relations to other states, playing the requisite roles in planning behavior, available for verbal report, and the like. But if this is what it comes to, then couldn't we have been satisfied with the first-order representationalist's accessibility account of conscious awareness to begin with? That is, if a higher-order representation's being conscious is a matter of its functional role, then why couldn't that be the case for a first-order representation?

What distinguishes a subject for whom there is something it is like to occupy her states from one for whom there is nothing it is like is not the presence or absence of representational states; it is how those states constitute representations *for* the subjects in question. First-order representationalist theories of consciousness, as described earlier, try to make that significance for the subject out of availability to other processes. Standard two-state higher-order theories are motivated by the insight that that is inadequate, so instead seek to capture the in-the-moment significance through representation by another state. The one-state higher-order view is motivated by the insight that that too is inadequate, since the representing that constitutes the conscious awareness is left outside the conscious state. But now I'm claiming that even the one-state view is inadequate on this score. It isn't enough to stick the higher-order representation into the state it's a representation of.

We need for that higher-order representation itself to be of the right sort of significance *for* the subject, and merely being a representation playing its requisite functional role doesn't seem to cut it.

I think the moral of the story is that we can't pin the kind of significance for the subject that distinguishes a moment of conscious awareness from a mere representation by just piling on more representations, for it doesn't yield genuine explanatory payoff. Somehow, what we have in conscious states are representations that are intrinsically of subjective significance, "animated" as it were, and I maintain that we really don't understand how that is possible. It doesn't seem to be a matter of more of the same—more representation of the same kind—but rather representation of a different kind altogether.[5]

I said there were two ways that conscious awareness seems to outstrip mere representation. The first had to do with significance for the subject. The second is closely linked to that. It's a matter of subjective significance as well, though not of the awareness itself, but of what one is aware of. In a way, this is just the problem I pointed out for level-three awareness concerning the immediacy of qualitative character reappearing at level two. The way in which we are aware of what is going on with ourselves when having a visual experience, say, seems to bring us into immediate cognitive contact with it. One-state higher-order theory, the self-representation theory, supposedly accounts for that by having the representer be identical with the represented, a pretty immediate relation one has to admit. But as I mentioned in section 5, it isn't clear why this physical immediacy should have anything to do with the kind of cognitive immediacy we're trying to explain.

Again, consider our typical conscious experience, my seeing the ripe tomato on the counter. The way the tomato appears with respect to color is part of what it is like for me to have that visual experience. What's supposed to capture that, there being a way it's like for me, on the self-representational theory is the secondary reflexive content possessed by the relevant perceptual state. But how does this make the color appearance available to me? It does so either by re-representing the color within the secondary content or by demonstrating it.

On the first model, the secondary content is of the form ⟨I am now representing that there is a red tomato in front of me⟩ (or ⟨there is now occurring a representing of a red tomato at such-and-such location⟩). On the second model, it is more like ⟨I am now representing this⟩, pointing at itself, as it were. Neither model seems to get at the way it is like something for me to have this experience. On the first model, it really does seem irrelevant that the secondary content is attached to the very same state as the first. We get no more cognitive immediacy than we would get from a two-state theory. True, the secondary content is realized by the same state as the first, but again this is an implementation matter, not a psychological matter.

The second model might seem to do better. But on this model, on which it does seem to at least make a representational difference which vehicle is carrying the content, the secondary content doesn't contain a representation of the quale in question, the reddish appearance—it just points to it. In a sense, from the point of view of the secondary representation, it doesn't matter what's on the other end of the pointer. Note again the relevance of the consideration mentioned above concerning the inherent ambiguity of demonstration. To pick out the relevant phenomenal type, one must be capable of genuinely thinking about it, not merely pointing at it. We can put it this way: the relevant phenomenal type must be "in mind" in a contentful way, not merely "in the mind" to exemplify what's being demonstrated.

7 Several decades ago, when the computational model of mind was the fresh new idea, some philosophers objected on the grounds that if one posited representations in the brain, then one had to posit little men (in those days no one posited little women) for whom they were representations. Representations, so the argument went, required subjects that understood them, or they weren't really representations after all. But of course this way lies infinite regress, since understanding, being a mental process itself, must then be a computational process involving the manipulation of representations as well: little people inside little people.

The computationalist's response was to note the power of functional role to implement understanding without requiring a separate process of understanding. In this sense computational devices were provided with what were sometimes called "self-understanding" representations—representations that meant what they did by virtue of their causal role within the system, together with their causal connection to the world around them.

In a way, my complaint about the attempt to construct conscious awareness out of a functionally characterizable self-representation is similar in spirit to that original objection to computational representationalism way back when. True, the computationalist response did dispense with that objection by grounding—or, better, providing the conceptual space for eventually grounding—intentionality, or representational content, in the causal network that constituted the machine. But although this method of implementing representation seems sufficient to make the representation count as a representation for the machine, it doesn't seem up to the task of making a representation "for" a conscious subject. So we still need to know, whether it's plain representation or the fancier self-representation: what makes it for me?

What makes it the case that I am consciously aware? How, with the causal materials at hand, do we turn the light on?[6]

Notes

1. I'm indebted here to an argument of Jerry Fodor's conveyed to me informally. That argument had nothing to do with this issue, and I make no claim to be presenting his argument accurately.

2. I don't mention "I" in this connection because it's plausible that its referent is the subject of conscious experience, and so this case is infected with the question at issue.

3. Of course it would be conscious if it were the target of yet another state that represents it, but this isn't the typical case; and besides, this process of having representations of representations couldn't go on forever.

4. Of course the original "binding problem" for which this synchronization phenomenon was proposed as a solution is a matter of psychology. But it isn't clear how that notion of binding is supposed to apply to this case.

5. In conversation, Uriah Kriegel brought up the following response. Suppose the self-representation included explicit reference to the subject, so that it had the form "I am now experiencing such-and-such." Wouldn't the presence of "I" secure that sense of being "for the subject" that we're looking for? But given what we've said already about what makes a representation an "I" representation in the first place—not merely its reference to the subject, but its role in initiating action (and the like)—it's not clear how this helps. We still have no sense of a representation being intrinsically for the subject. The "animation" is what we need to explain, and having a functionally specified "I" doesn't do it.

6. I'd like to thank audiences at New York University, the University of Arizona, and the University of Massachusetts at Amherst for helpful discussion on the topic of this essay. I'm also especially indebted to Uriah Kriegel for extensive comments on an earlier draft.

John J. Drummond

I

The view that self-awareness is intrinsic to object-awareness traces its lineage to Aristotle. This essay shall explore that lineage as it runs from Aristotle to Brentano and to Husserl. My main purpose is to outline a phenomenologically grounded descriptive account—influenced, most significantly, by Husserl—of the phenomenon of self-awareness rather than to navigate the arguments and counterarguments offered for or against some of the many theoretical approaches that have been forwarded in recent debates about the nature of consciousness and self-awareness. My account will, of course, have implications for some of those theories; I shall mention some of them in order to locate the present account within their landscape.

Let us consider a relatively simple, although typical, example. While taking a picture of my wife standing against the backdrop of a lake in the Rocky Mountains, I am suddenly saddened by the bad news I recall we received yesterday and the necessity of our impending departure; I imagine (or wish) returning for another visit with my wife to enjoy again the beauty of the mountains; and then I hear the call of a bird that interrupts my reveries. To be self-aware in this situation is to be aware of my seeing my wife, to be aware of my recalling the receipt of bad news (even as I hold on to the perception of my wife but shift my primary attention to the news we received), to be aware of my being saddened by this recollection, to be aware of my imagining (or wishing) our return, and then to be aware of my hearing the birdcall. I am aware, in other words, of separable—albeit related—experiences each having their own temporal duration, and I am aware of each of these relatively distinct experiences as belonging to a temporally organized stream of experience that is mine. It is worth emphasizing here that self-awareness so described has two aspects: I am aware of the particular experience I now undergo, and I am aware of this experience as belonging to a self whose experience extends beyond this particular experience (or set of experiences) and to which this experience (or set) belongs. It is just this first-personal character of my experience that is central to that self-awareness that is both prior to and a condition for any explicit reflection on these experiences.

In considering this example, I suggest—to use a grammatical metaphor—that the intentional experience of an object (object-awareness, for short) with its occurrent self-awareness has a case-structure.[1] For example, I perceive my wife facing me against the backdrop of the lake and mountains; I perceive S as p. The object S is the *accusative* of the perceiving, what the perceiving is directed to or aimed at. S's appearing, on the other hand, is an appearing *to* the perceiver, that is, S appears as p to me. It is part of the sense of appearing that appearing is always an appearing-*to*. The subject is the *dative* of the object's appearing. Hence, in perceiving an object, one is aware *of* the object as appearing in a determinate manner *to* oneself. In perceiving an object, the subject is therefore at the same time self-aware. I am aware of *my* perceiving the object in just that determinate manner in which the object appears, or conversely, I am aware of the object as appearing to *me*.

This structure is generalizable to other kinds of experience. In judging, for example, one is aware of a state of affairs, say, that S is p. The judging subject articulates a situation involving a determinate relation between S and p such that it becomes aware not simply of the object in its determination but of the structured state of affairs. The articulating judging is directed *to* the articulated state of affairs (the accusative), which, in the same experience, manifests itself *to* the articulating subject (the dative) in a determinate manner. I am aware of *myself* experiencing the situation in just that determinate manner that is the articulated state of affairs; I am aware of the situation as articulated by *me*. Similarly, emotional experiences intend objects, situations, agents, or actions as having affective properties or value attributes (Goldie 2000, 2002; Drummond 2002a,b, 2004, 2006). Fear, for example, discloses an object or situation as dangerous for the one experiencing fear. In such experiences the same structure of double awareness is at work, and can be noticed perhaps even more vividly. The subject's experience is directed to the object or situation as affecting the subject in a particular way. The affectively or evaluatively charged object or situation is the accusative of the experience, and the subject for whom the object or situation is affectively or evaluatively charged is the dative of the experience. In the awareness of the object or situation as affectively or evaluatively charged, I am necessarily self-aware: the situation manifests itself as fearful for *me*. And this self-awareness carries over into the volitions that are rooted in the emotions and desires. In acting, I am aware of a state of affairs that can be realized through action as valuable (in some way) to myself as agent of the action (and perhaps valuable, in a different way, to others as well).

Even feelings that are not involved in the presentations of objects can have an accusative insofar as they are capable of presenting states of the body. In experiencing pain, for example, the subject encounters an arm as injured (see Husserl 1984b, p. 406; 1970b, p. 572; Tye 1995, pp. 111–116). The arm-as-injured is the accusative of the pain; the pain is directed to the arm and the injury is experienced as displeasing. Pains, however, might not explicitly present the body. One might be only implicitly aware of the body when, for example, feeling tense. This implicit awareness of the body is an important aspect of the prereflective self-awareness that accompanies one's perceptual and emotional experiences, for these experiences necessarily have physiological aspects (sensations and feelings) that are encompassed by our self-awareness. By extension, this implicit bodily awareness accompanies all those experiences, including higher-level experiences such as judgments, in which the affective dimension of experience remains in force for us.[2]

The case-structure I have suggested, however, unpacks only what is involved in our object-awareness. The object is the accusative of consciousness, and the subject is the dative of the object's appearing. How are we to characterize the case-structure belonging to self-awareness, that is, to the subject's awareness of itself as a subject? I have already hinted in stating my example that the case properly characterizing self-awareness is the genitive. In what follows I attempt to give flesh to this hint.

II

A problem that immediately arises when we examine the language of self-awareness or consciousness is that it too easily borrows the case-structure of object-awareness. Insofar as one claims that in being aware of an object one is also aware *of* oneself, it suggests that the self too is an accusative of consciousness. On this view the intentional directedness of consciousness is bent back on itself so that one encounters one's own experiences as inner objects. This view is stated classically by Locke in his distinction between simple ideas of sense, which are object-directed, and simple ideas of reflection, which are self-directed: "The mind receiving the ideas [of sense] from without, when it turns its view inward upon itself, and observes its own actions about those ideas it has, takes from thence other ideas, which are as capable to be *objects* of its contemplation as any of those it received from foreign things" (Locke 1688/1959, I, p. 59, my emphasis). Moreover, on

Locke's formulation, the reflecting experience$_2$ is extrinsic to the experiences$_1$ of which the subject is aware in its self-awareness.

On the model of this Lockean view, I define as a "reflection theory" one that takes (i) the self to be the accusative of consciousness and (ii) self-awareness to be extrinsic to object-awareness. There are two ways to understand the extrinsic character of the self-awareness, and the difference is marked by the temporal relations between the reflecting awareness and the self on which that awareness reflects. In the first case (which I shall call S-reflection), of which Locke's formulation is an example, one turns one's attention in a *subsequent* experience to one's *past* experiences, and, in so doing, grasps a determinate "I" that can be characterized in definite ways as having had a certain kind of life. In the second case (which I shall call O-reflection), one, in presently experiencing an object, is *occurrently* turned back on itself such that it is aware in a second, roughly contemporaneous, higher-order aware- ness of its own awareness of the object and, indeed, aware of this experience as directed to that object. Contemporary theories such as higher-order per- ception theory (e.g., Armstrong 1968) and higher-order thought theory (e.g., Rosenthal 1986) are thus instances of a reflection theory of self-awareness in that (i) the self is the accusative of an occurrent higher-order perception or thought and (ii) this higher-order perception or thought is extrinsic to the experience of which it is aware.

All reflection theories, however, suffer from the same fundamental problem, a problem that can be stated in the form of a dilemma. Given that experi- ence$_1$—the experience of the object—is the accusative of the reflecting experi- ence$_2$, and that the reflecting experience$_2$ is extrinsic to experience$_1$ of which the subject is self-aware, the subject is either aware of the reflecting experi- ence$_2$ itself or she is not. If, on the one horn, the subject is aware of the reflecting experience$_2$, then the subject is aware of it only in another reflecting experience$_3$ extrinsic to the reflecting experience$_2$ that is its accusative and whose accusative in turn is experience$_1$, and so on ad infinitum. If, on the other horn, the subject is unaware of the reflecting experience$_2$ (or some other reflecting experience in the chain), the reflecting experience is itself unconscious (Rosenthal 1986, p. 336).

The first horn with its commitment to an infinite regress of reflecting experiences is counterintuitive. In self-awarely perceiving$_1$ my wife, I am simply unaware of any reflecting experience$_2$, much less an infinite number of them. Nor is it conceivable that nondivine conscious subjects would be capable of an infinite number of S-reflecting or O-reflecting experiences.

Aristotle was the first to argue against the possibility of the duplication of experiences and the infinite regress of experiences entailed by this horn of the dilemma. He argues that, on pain of a duplication of experiences and of an infinite regress, self-awareness must be intrinsic to object-awareness:

Since it is through sense [sensing] that we are aware that we are seeing or hearing, it must be either by sight [seeing] that we are aware of seeing, or by some sense [i.e., some sensing] other than sight [seeing]. But the sense [sensing] that gives us this new sensation must perceive both sight [seeing] and its object, viz. colour: so that either there will be two senses [sensings] both percipient of the same sensible object, or the sense [sensing] must be percipient of itself. Further, even if the sense [sensing] which perceives sight [seeing] were different from sight [i.e., the seeing of color], we must either fall into an infinite regress, or we must assume a sense [sensing] which is aware of itself. If so, we ought to do this in the first case. (*De anima* 425ᵇ12–18)

Caston's (2002) illuminating article, noting that terms such as "perceive" and "sense" can refer both to the capacity for perception and sensation or to the exercise of those capacities (2002, p. 762), argues—correctly, I believe—against a "capacity-reading" and for an "activity-reading" of this passage (ibid., pp. 763–775), a reading I have interpolated into the passage quoted above. Hence, Aristotle avoids the fundamental problem of reflection theories by denying "in the first case" that there are two occurrent or consecutive experiences, the first-order seeing and an extrinsic second-order experience (a perceiving, believing, or reflective experience) having as its object the first-order seeing (and, by extension, the external object as well). Instead, the perceiving of one's own perceiving (an object) is intrinsic to the perceiving (of the object). And it is just this intrinsic character of self-awareness that forecloses the possibility of an infinite regress of perceivings, at least as long as one holds what we might call the "self-awareness principle," the view, namely, that *every* object-awareness involves an occurrent, intrinsic self-awareness.

It is clear that Aristotle himself held such a principle. In arguing against the Empedoclean and Platonic view that the eye is composed of fire, he first identifies the evidence offered in support of this view, namely, that when the closed eye is pressed or rubbed and then opened in a darkened space, we see "fiery" spots. However, he says, this phenomenon should also occur when the eye is not pressed, "for, unless a man can perceive and see without being aware of it, the eye must see itself" (*Sense and Sensibilia* 437ᵃ27–28). But, of course, we do not see these fiery spots when the eye is not pressed; hence, the eye is not composed of elemental fire. As Caston points out (2002, pp. 757–759), the argument depends crucially on the self-awareness principle, for the fact that the eye does not always see fiery spots (that is, the eye itself) does not rule out the eye's being composed of fire if it is possible to perceive without self-awareness (that is, without seeing the eye). Since Aristotle takes it to be the case that the eye not seeing fire when not pressed rules out the view that the eye is composed of fire, he must take the self-awareness principle to be true. This is clearly suggested by the conditional proposition inserted into his argument as well as by assertions elsewhere in the corpus that all perception is accompanied by the awareness of oneself as existing and perceiving (cf. *Sense and Sensibilia* 448^{a}26–30 and *Nicomachean Ethics* 1170^{a}29–^{b}1).

Although Aristotle's position avoids the first horn of the dilemma facing reflection theories, the self-awareness principle on which it relies is challenged by the second horn, that is, the claim that the reflecting experience$_2$ in which we are conscious of our experience$_1$ of an object is (or can be) itself unconscious. Aristotle has offered no argument against this possibility. It is unclear, however, what sense one can give to the idea that the reflecting experience$_2$ is itself unconscious.

An S-reflection theory, such as Locke's, involves the explicit turning of attention to one's own past experiences. But it is impossible to conceive how one could be explicitly aware of past experiences as one's *own* without being aware in some way of these experiences as belonging to the *same* self directing its attention to them, that is, without being aware of the reflecting experience as belonging to the same self that the past experiences do. This is impossible if the reflecting experience is not self-aware. Although an O-reflection theory, such as Armstrong's or Rosenthal's, does not involve this explicit turning of one's regard to past experiences, the same problem arises in a slightly different form. If the awareness$_2$ is not conscious, it is impossible to understand how it can recognize the awareness$_1$ as belonging to the same self as that to which awareness$_2$ belongs (cf. Henrich 1971, p. 11; Cramer 1974, p. 563 as quoted in Zahavi 1999, p. 18). Moreover, if we accept the reflection theory in any of its forms, it is impossible to think that reflective awareness$_2$ is unconscious, for if the subject is unconsciously aware, say, of its perceiving an object, it cannot be consciously aware of the object as perceived. The second horn of the dilemma, in other words, is equally counterintuitive.

Moreover, the claim that there can be an unconscious awareness, including an unconscious self-awareness, reflects an inadequate understanding of the unconscious (Zahavi 1999, pp. 203–220). The unconscious, on this understanding, simply becomes a reduced form of conscious awareness; it is intentional consciousness stripped of self-awareness. The unconscious, however, is better understood as the passive *background* to conscious awareness. As such, it can be brought to conscious awareness in reflection and reappropriation, although in certain limit cases unconscious experiences might lie beyond our ability to reawaken and reappropriate them. The unconscious, then, affects our present consciousness without rendering the affected consciousness unconscious.

Given that the reflection theory cannot on its own terms escape the dilemma it presents, and given that the reflection theory is characterized by the notion that the reflecting experience$_2$ is extrinsic to the experience$_1$ reflectively grasped and that the experience$_1$ reflectively grasped is the accusative of the reflecting experience$_2$, the correction required for a more adequate account of self-awareness is either (i) to deny the extrinsic, reflective character of self-awareness (versus the infinite regress) and to affirm the intrinsic, prereflective character of self-awareness (versus the possibility of an unconscious consciousness), or (ii) to deny the accusative character of the experience of which I am self-aware, or (iii) both. Aristotle's account has explicitly taken path (i), but I shall take path (iii). I shall claim, in other words, that it is insufficient to characterize self-awareness as intrinsic to object-awareness without also insisting that the experiences of which I am self-aware are *not* accusatives of consciousness.

III

Caston, we have seen, argues that Aristotle's account avoids the pitfalls of higher-order theories (2002, p. 776) as well as their counterintuitive claim that self-awareness is extrinsic to object-awareness (ibid., pp. 779–780).[3] He also argues that Aristotle's account preserves the chief advantage of higher-order theories, namely, the view that self-awareness is not an unanalyzable attribute of consciousness (Rosenthal 1986, pp. 340–341) but is rather a matter of intentionality that can be analyzed and articulated (Caston 2002, p. 780). Object-awareness, for Caston, can be self-aware because an aspect of the object-awareness itself is the intrinsic, *reflexive* grasp (as opposed to an extrinsic, *reflective* grasp) of the object-awareness itself.

Caston here again develops Aristotle. In yet another affirmation of the views that object-awareness is always self-aware and that self-awareness is intrinsic to object-awareness, Aristotle says, "But evidently knowledge and perception and opinion and understanding have always something else as their object, and themselves only by the way" (or "on the side," as Caston translates it) (*Metaphysics* 1074^{b}35–36). The question, then, is to determine the nature of this intentionality "by the way" or "on the side."

A number of thinkers in, related to, or influenced by the phenomenological tradition have explored the themes of both intentionality and self-awareness

(Brentano 1874/1995; Brough 1972, 1989, 1991; Gurwitsch 1964, 1985; Henrich 1971; Husserl 1966b, 1991; Kriegel 2003d; Sartre 1936/1957, 1943/1956, 1948/1967; Smith 1986, 1989, 2004; Sokolowski 1974; Zahavi 1998, 1999). These thinkers adopt accounts of intrinsic self-awareness reminiscent of Aristotle's view. This is unsurprising since Brentano, a grandfather of the phenomenological tradition, was also a careful student of Aristotle's works who, as Caston notes (2002, p. 768), adopted an activity-reading of Aristotle's argument in *De anima*.[4] What is left ambiguous—but, I think, implied—in Caston's reading of Aristotle becomes explicit in Brentano, namely, the view that the experience of which I am reflexively self-aware is an accusative of consciousness. The Brentanian claim, in other words, is not that there are two *experiences* each with its own object but that there are two *objects* of a unified, but complex, intrinsically self-aware experience. The unified awareness is directed both to the object and to the experiencing of the object. My claim is that the view that there are two objects of experience—in other words, that the self (or momentary experience) is also an accusative of consciousness—cannot be sustained.

Brentano (1995, p. 127) states the position as follows:

Thus certainly we would in our case [of the presentation of a tone] have to decide the question about the number of presentations affirmatively if we determined them according to the number of objects; just as certainly we must answer it negatively if we determine them according to the number of mental acts in which something is presented. The presentation of the tone and the presentation of the presentation of the tone form no more than a single mental phenomenon, which we—while we considered it in its relation to two different objects, of which one is a physical and the other a mental phenomenon—divided it *conceptually* into two presentations. In the same mental phenomenon in which the tone is presented we simultaneously apprehend the mental phenomenon itself. . . .

Brentano's claim, then, is that every experience directed to an object is a real unity that has two inseparable but distinguishable parts, one directed to the intentional object of the experience and the other directed to the experience itself (cf. Mulligan and Smith 1985, p. 633). The experience, as Caston claims is the case for Aristotle, is complex, comprising two distinguishable but unified awarenesses. Moreover, the self-awareness concomitant with the object-awareness is a matter of intentionality and can be analyzed and articulated. That self-awareness is a matter of intentionality is a crucial point to which I shall return.

Brentano's position, however, raises an immediate problem, for it is clear that the two objects—the external object and the experience itself—cannot be objects in the same way. In perceiving a tree, the subject is not aware of itself as an object as it is in an explicit act of reflection; the subject is aware of itself *as a subject*, as experiencing and not as experienced. Hence, the intentional direction to the self cannot simply be of the same sort as the intentional direction toward the object. Brentano, again following the Aristotelian hint, says, "we can call the tone the primary object of the hearing and the hearing itself the secondary object" (1995, p. 128). But just as it is a problem to know what Aristotle means by "having an object by the way (or on the side)," it is a problem to know what Brentano means by "secondary object."

Brentano's attempt to unpack the intentional relations underlying this view raises significant issues:

The consciousness that accompanies the presentation of the tone is a consciousness not so much of this presentation but of the whole mental act in which the tone is presented and in which it is itself also given. Apart from the fact that it presents the mental phenomenon of the tone, the mental act of hearing becomes at the same time in its totality its own object and content. (Ibid., p. 129)

But if we take Brentano at his word, then my perceiving is directed both to the tree and to itself (the perceiving) in its totality. But since the perceiving both includes the content "tree" and is self-aware, the self-awareness that occurs is directed to the "self-aware perceiving of the tree." The self-aware perceiving, in other words, is directed to an object-awareness that is already self-aware (Zahavi 1998, p. 139; 1999, pp. 30–31). This explanation of the self-awareness at work in object-awareness explains too much: it accounts for our awareness of ourselves as self-aware, an awareness that is one step beyond what we are trying to explain. When I am aware of myself perceiving an object, I am not aware of my awareness of myself perceiving an object. This kind of self-aware experience of my self-awareness is available only in reflection. Brentano's view, then, either introduces a redundancy for which there is no phenomenal evidence or it blurs the distinction between a reflexive but nonreflective self-awareness and a reflective self-awareness. In either case, we must reject his account of self-awareness, and consider how to differentiate more clearly the intentionalities at work in self-aware experiences.

There are contemporary accounts that attempt to develop the Aristotelian-Brentanian account of self-awareness. I shall consider two of them. The first (Kriegel 2003d) seeks to emphasize the notion that the self of which one is self-aware is experienced as subject rather than as object. Insisting that self-awareness is a matter of intentionality, however, this view falls back into an

Aristotelian ambiguity because a univocal notion of intentionality forces us to consider the self as an object rather than as a subject. The second account (Smith 1986, 1989, 2004) insists that the self of which one is self-aware is not an object, not part of the intentional content of the self-aware experience. It locates the distinction between object-awareness and self-awareness not in the object but in the awareness itself.

Kriegel (2003d, p. 13), following Aristotle and Brentano, claims that object-awareness is explicit whereas self-awareness is implicit. Kriegel does not attempt to work out the details of this implicit awareness, but he does offer suggestions about how we think about it. These suggestions, however, immediately introduce an ambiguity into his account. On the one hand, he recognizes that self-awareness differs from object-awareness in that in self-awareness one is aware not of an object but of "oneself as the *thought owner*, that is, as the thinking subject" (ibid.). And he stresses the difference between explicit self-reflection and implicit self-awareness in the following manner: "In explicit awareness of self, the self is represented as the *object* of reflection. By contrast, in implicit awareness of self, the self is represented qua *subject* of thought" (ibid., p. 14). This manner of drawing the contrast contains, I believe, the seeds of the problem. The language of "is represented" suggests a view of intentionality that is more appropriate, I believe, for object-awareness and unsuited for self-awareness.

Indeed, Lycan takes the fact that intentionality is representational to be a crucial piece of the argument for a higher-order reflection theory (Lycan 2001, p. 4). For Lycan, a conscious state—one in which the subject is aware of being in it—is characterized by the *of* of intentionality. Moreover, he argues, intentionality is the representing of an intentional object. Just this fact is what necessitates postulating a higher-order state that is aware of the first-order state. I think Lycan is correct that if we characterize intentionality as representational, then to say that a state is intentional is to say that it represents an *object*. I also think, however, that it is incorrect to characterize intentionality simply as representational. Indeed, I believe that anyone holding that self-awareness is intrinsic to experience cannot hold a representationalist account of intentionality without falling into the insuperable difficulties associated with either the reflection theory or a double-object theory. Brentano himself—at least in the *Psychologie von empirischen Standpunkt*—adopts a representationalist approach, and this is why, I suggest, he is clear that the presentation itself is a second *object* of the presentation of the tone. Husserl, on the other hand, rejects such a representationalist understanding of intentionality (Drummond 1990, 1992, 1997, 1998, 2003), adopting instead an account that distinguishes different kinds of intentionality, a point to which I shall return below.

What Lycan's argument suggests to us in the present context is that in Kriegel's differentiation of explicit self-reflection and implicit self-awareness, the latter, by virtue of its representational character, must still be understood along the lines of object-awareness. In perceiving the tone, I am aware of the objective content "tone," but I am also aware of "self-as-subject." To represent self-as-subject, however, is to introduce a second objective content as the object of the implicit representing. It is thereby an attempt to distinguish two aspects of a unified, self-aware perceiving by distinguishing their objects.

Further evidence for the view that Kriegel turns self-as-subject into an objective content is his development of Brentano's view that the self-directed intentionality is secondary, which, as we have seen, Brentano understood to mean that there was a secondary object—the presentation of the object—belonging to the presentation of the object. Kriegel suggests that we might understand this secondary intentionality in terms of a "distribution of the subject's attention resources" (Kriegel 2003d, p. 17). But the example he provides to help us understand what this might mean—visually attending (primarily) to the color and shape of a car while only indistinctly (secondarily) hearing the engine's noise—is a straightforward case of object-awareness in which we distinguish between what is the thematic center of our attention and what is marginally or peripherally present to consciousness.

The theme–margin distinction, however, cannot serve to underlie an account of self-awareness. Both the margin and the periphery belong to the objective content of experience. But what characterizes self-awareness and differentiates it from object-awareness is precisely that the self is given as subject and not as something that belongs to the objective field. Kriegel's account here is reminiscent not only of Brentano's but of Aron Gurwitsch's (Gurwitsch 1964, pp. 343–344; 1985, p. 4). The view that self-awareness is a form of marginal awareness transforms self-awareness into object-awareness since it continues to analyze all awareness in terms of a subject-object correlation (Zahavi 1999, p. 61). In so doing, however, it loses the distinctive character of self-awareness, namely, that I am implicitly aware of myself as subject without any objectifying of the subject as occurs in reflection.

It is clear—and here the ambiguity repeats itself once again—that Kriegel wants to insist that the subject is given as a subject rather than as an object, but he also insists that the self of which one is aware is part of the intentional content of the experience. He tries to resolve this by suggesting that in the case of self-awareness, "the gap between subject and object collapses, such that the self is represented both as subject and as object" (Kriegel 2003d, p. 19). It is hard to know what to make of this suggestion, and Kriegel is aware that it is problematic: "An objector may protest that this would make implicit self-awareness quite mysterious, and will attribute to it a unique intentional structure. But then self-awareness *is* quite mysterious, isn't it, and its intentional structure is indeed unique" (ibid.). This suggestion seems more an abandonment of the attempt to work out the intentional structure of self-awareness than an attempt to elucidate it. It is no doubt true that self-awareness is mysterious, but it is not incoherent, which is what the idea of an intentional content that is both subject and object appears to be, at least unless and until we distinguish a kind of intentionality different from that belonging to object-awareness. It is no doubt true that self-awareness has a unique intentional structure, but we have yet to identify what it is.

David Woodruff Smith (1986, 1989, 2004) offers an imaginative neo-Brentanian account of self-awareness that avoids the problem of turning the self of which one is self-aware into an intentional or representational content and thereby turning the subject into an object. Smith (1986, pp. 150, 152) claims, as do I, that any account that makes the self the intentional content of self-awareness, that is, the accusative of consciousness, loses the distinctive feature of self-awareness's presentation of the self as subject. Instead of affirming that there are two objects of a self-aware experience, Smith introduces a new distinction into the experience itself. In this manner, Smith locates the distinctive features of self-awareness in the intending rather than the intended, and on this point I believe he is correct.

Smith's earlier works (1986, 1989) identified what Smith calls "inner awareness" as that which makes a mental state conscious, but Smith's reprise and development of that position (2004) revises his view somewhat. He begins with the example used in the earlier work, namely, consciously seeing a frog. Smith begins his analysis of this example with the following "phenomenological description": *consciously* I now see this frog. His claim is that the character "consciously" is not part of the intentional content—or *mode of presentation*—of the object, but part of what he calls the "modality" of the presentation, that is, the intending of the object (Smith 2004, pp. 84, 99). This distinction between the modality and mode of an experience recalls Husserl's distinction between the mode or manner (*Weise*) of presentation and the how of presentation (*Wie*):

Over against the identical "appearing tree as such" with its identical "objective" how (*Wie*) of appearing remain the differences in the mode of givenness (*Gegebenheitsweise*), which change from one kind of intuition to another. . . . That identical [appearing tree as such] is at one time known "originally," at another time known "memorially," then again "imaginatively," etc. (Husserl 1976, p. 233; 1983, p. 244, translation modified)

Unfortunately for our exposition, Smith uses "modality" for Husserl's "mode of givenness" and "mode" for Husserl's "how of appearing." For Smith the mode characterizes the intentional content of the experience; for Husserl, on the other hand, the mode (*Weise*) characterizes the intending itself: the tree is given as an oak (*Wie*) and as perceived (*Weise*). Nevertheless, Husserl's distinction points, as does Smith's, toward a feature of the experience that Husserl in the *Logical Investigations* calls the "quality" of the experience (Husserl 1984b, pp. 586–588; 1970b, pp. 425–428) and in *Ideas I* calls the noesis or noetic component of an experience of an object (Husserl 1976, pp. 191–194; 1983, pp. 203–205). The quality of an experience determines the experience as perceptual, memorial, imaginative, judgmental, emotional, and so forth. It is this notion of "quality" that is the forerunner of Smith's notion of "modality." Smith's point, therefore, is a relatively straightforward one. The modality of an experience has to do with its *kind* or *type*; it has to do with whether it is perceptual, memorial, imaginative, emotive, judgmental, and so forth. But these are not the only characters that can typify experiences. I can, for example, see clearly or obscurely. All such adverbial modifiers are modal characters, and included among them are "consciously" and "unconsciously" (Smith 2004, p. 99).[5]

Smith resolves the modal character "consciously" into two aspects: a phenomenal aspect and a reflexive aspect. Together, these two characters make up the character "consciously" (Smith 2004, pp. 84–85). More specifically, the description "*consciously* I now see this frog" thus can be translated as "*phenomenally in this very experience* I now see this frog." The modal character "phenomenally" embodies the " 'raw feel' of an experience, its subjective quality, what it is like to have the experience, the way it is experienced or lived through" (ibid., p. 99), and phenomenality modifies the entire experience. Within the scope of phenomenality the character of reflexivity intimates the experience itself that it characterizes. Reflexivity as a modality, however, is neither a separate, higher-order experience nor a component experience making up the full, conscious perceiving of the frog. Since the character of reflexivity falls within the scope of phenomenality, the reflexive conscious experience is self-aware without recourse to any further experience. Inner awareness, in other words, is neither a separate experience nor unconscious (ibid., p. 100).

Kriegel (2003d, p. 19) criticizes Smith's approach on the ground that it is empirically implausible. In particular, according to Kriegel, it would double the number of modalities now known. So, for example, a conscious perceiving would have the modality not only of perception but of self-aware perception, since our awareness is directed to the entire experience to which it is intrinsically related. Moreover, it would be impossible for any state, a perceiving, say, to occur both nonconsciously and consciously, since the conscious state must include the modality of self-awareness that no nonconscious state can have.

Kriegel's criticisms, however, depend on the assumption—shared by Smith—that not every object-awareness is self-aware; for if every object-awareness is intrinsically self-aware, then the number of modalities and mental states would not in fact be doubled. If every object-awareness is self-aware, then it would be impossible for the nonconscious states to exist, and no perceiving, say, would exist in both conscious and unconscious modalities. Kriegel's criticism is a fair one, however, since Smith does allow for the possibility of both unconscious experiences and experiences that are conscious but without inner awareness.

Smith's view is an interesting and promising one. However, I think his account is both too strong and too weak. Like Brentano's, Smith's account explains too much. I would not call "in this very experience I see this frog" a phenomenological description of an experience as much as a report thereof (cf. Drummond 1990, pp. 128–129). Whether a description or a report, however, it is already too reflective. Although Smith is attempting to get at the structure of a prereflective, intrinsic self-awareness occurrent with object-awareness, he fails to do so precisely because he transforms that self-awareness into a reflective one. What he calls the "egocentric" character of the intentional experience is already the "I" (Smith 2004, p. 85). The use of the nominative "I" is revealing, for names signify the objects of our experience. The "I" names the self upon which I explicitly reflect. The experience to be explained, however, is not the experience of an "I." As I suggested at the outset, I am not prereflectively aware that *I* am perceiving an object; I am aware of *my perceiving an object*. The case-structure is properly genitive, not nominative.

At the same time, however, Smith's position is too weak. As Caston has urged in his reading of Aristotle, self-awareness is a matter of intentionality (albeit, I am suggesting, not a matter of object-intentionality); something is disclosed or made manifest to us. Although Smith's position makes inner awareness a modal character of intentionality, such characters modify not only the experience itself but also the disclosure of the *object* of experience.

I am aware of the object as distinctly perceived or as vaguely remembered. But these characters do not disclose the experience itself. By comparison, we should say that I am aware of the object as consciously perceived. Here, however, the modal character does not seem to contribute to the disclosure of the object as other modal characters do. So, we are faced with a unique modal character that modifies only the experience without having an effect on how the intentional object is disclosed. However, if "conscious" is a modal character that modifies only the experience itself, it is not clear from that fact how it is that it discloses the experience itself. Its disclosive role has yet to be clarified, and it remains unclear how this modality brings about a self-manifestation.

IV

Our task, then, is to describe the intentional structure of a self-aware object-awareness. For this we turn to Husserl's account of our awareness of the temporality of an experience, an account that is at the same time an account of self-awareness.[6] To frame my discussion, I shall outline an interpretational dispute regarding Husserl's analysis of the "absolute consciousness"[7] that underlies the consciousness of the temporality of experience.

Brough's classic account (1972; cf. also 1989, 1991) of Husserl's phenomenology of the consciousness of inner time explores Husserl's description of the intentionality at work in our experience of temporally extended objects and events. More importantly, Husserl also describes the intentionalities involved in our experience of the temporally extended experiences themselves, experiences that intend and through which appear the intended temporal objects and events in the world. In the course of these analyses Husserl recognizes that there must be a nontemporal consciousness that is the universal condition for the experience of both objective and subjective time. Husserl characterizes this consciousness as a flow that constitutes itself, that is, that brings itself to appearance (Brough 1991, p. xix). It is here that we find an intrinsic self-awareness that is a matter of intentionality.

In hearing, say, a song, I am aware not only of the presently sounding note or notes, I am aware of the song as a whole. It is only in this way that I can, upon hearing the opening bars of a song, immediately identify the song as a whole and expect what is to come as the song unfolds (and, indeed, recognize when a note is wrongly sung). This indicates both that the object of which I am aware has a temporal extent and that my experience too has a certain "stretch" to it such that I am aware in the present of notes of the song as presently sounding, as having elapsed, and as yet to come. I am also aware, however, of a beginning and an end to my hearing the song. The song, say, intruded on my thinking about what to write, and when the song ends or I "put it out of mind" and return to my writing, I am aware of a new experience. In hearing the song, I am aware, in other words, of my hearing as forming a temporally extended unity with its own position in the course of my experience—the two aspects of self-awareness identified in our opening example. When Husserl speaks of the consciousness of inner time, it is this awareness of my experiences as temporally qualified and as having a temporal position of which he speaks.

On pain of infinite regress, the awareness of a temporally extended and unified experience cannot itself be temporally qualified; otherwise we need to account for our experience of this awareness as temporal. Hence, Husserl posits an experiencing consciousness that is not itself in time but which makes possible the awareness of both objective and subjective time. This consciousness, however, cannot simply be the awareness of the now, for temporality would then simply be the accumulation of successive appearings of the now. That would account only for the succession of consciousness and not our awareness of that succession. The occurrent phase of absolute consciousness must be structured such that there is an intertwining of the consciousness of what has elapsed, of what is now, and of what is yet to come, without this momentary phase of the absolute consciousness being itself in time. The momentary phase of absolute consciousness, in other words, must be a nontemporal temporalizing of experience.

Husserl accounts for this unique feature of consciousness by identifying what he calls the "double intentionality" (1966b, pp. 80–83, 379–380; 1991, pp. 84–88, 390–392; cf. Brough 1991, pp. li–liv) of the momentary phase of absolute consciousness. Each momentary phase has a tripartite form, comprising the "primal impression" directed to the now of the experience, "retention" directed to the elapsed phases of experience, and "protention" directed to yet-to-come phases. This form of consciousness is filled by a material, that is, by experiences of a particular type (having what Smith calls the modality "act-type") having a particular intentional object. However, by virtue of retention, which holds on to (retains) elapsed phases of consciousness and protention which anticipates yet-to-come phases, the perceiving that occurs now appears as having a temporal extent that emerges out of prior appearances of the same object and runs off into yet-to-come appearances of that object. This intentionality that runs through retention and protention along the flow of momentary phases of absolute consciousness itself Husserl calls *Längsintentionalität* (1966b, pp. 81, 379—Brough translates this as "horizontal intentionality" since it runs along the flow; cf.

Husserl 1991, p. 85, n. 9), and the complex intentionality aimed at the object and comprising all the phases intended through primal impression, retention, and protention Husserl calls *Querintentionalität* (1966b, pp. 82, 380—Brough translates this as "transverse intentionality" since in its direction to the object it cuts across the flow of experience as if it were a cross section of consciousness; cf. Husserl 1991, p. 86, n. 11). The complex transverse intentionality that intends an object as enduring through phases of its appearing is possible only by virtue of the horizontal intentionality belonging to the form of consciousness itself. It is just this form that makes possible both the appearing of temporally enduring and unified experiences and the appearing of objects with temporal determinations.

Husserl's account of the consciousness of inner time, therefore, commits him to a threefold distinction regarding time. He distinguishes (Husserl 1966b, p. 371; 1991, p. 382):

1. objects with their objective, worldly time;
2. the stream of immanent experiences with their phenomenal time; and
3. the absolute time-constituting flow.

If this were all there is to say on the matter, then it would be clear that Husserl would, in articulating his notion of self-awareness, immediately encounter the problems we find in reflection theories, including those that affirm a higher-order monitoring (cf. Zahavi 1999, p. 70). Husserl runs the risk of distinguishing two different flows—the immanent flow of temporally organized experiences and the flow of time-constituting consciousness—and of characterizing their relationship as an instance of object-intentionality. Hence, we find the language of "immanent objects," but I think this an unfortunate hangover from the psychological language with which he was trained by Brentano.

There are countervailing indications that we should not understand the immanent experience as the *object* of a more fundamental object-intentionality. First, although there are three levels, Husserl denies that there is a real separation between the second and third levels. He insists that (2) and (3), although distinguishable, are inseparable such that there is only one flow of consciousness with its objects (cf. Husserl 1966b, p. 80; 1991, p. 84). Zahavi (1999), in his remarkable discussion of Husserl's view of self-awareness, stresses this unity. He stresses the fact that self-awareness involves consciousness's appearing to itself, its self-manifestation, and not the appearance of one level of consciousness to another (Zahavi 1999, pp. 70–71).

In particular,[8] Zahavi argues (i) that Brough's interpretation takes over the model of object-intentionality to account for the absolute time-constituting flow's constitution of the stream of immanent experiences and (ii) that this entails two different notions of prereflective self-awareness. That is, the absolute time-constituting flow would have to be (a) prereflectively and objectively aware of immanent experiences as immanent temporal objects and (b) prereflectively and nonobjectively aware of the absolute flow itself. Since Zahavi rejects the notion that there are two different prereflective self-awarenesses, he rejects Brough's claim that there are two levels of consciousness. To the extent that the language of levels involves the view that prereflective self-awareness has two different objects—immanent experiences and the absolute time-constituting flow—there are reasons to support Zahavi's objection to Brough's interpretation.

Brough responds, however, that Zahavi, in collapsing levels (2) and (3) in order to secure his commitment to a single self-awareness, must attribute features of the absolute flow to the experienced flow of conscious experiences. Most important, since the absolute flow is not itself in time, experiences could not be given as temporal unities, that is, as discrete experiences, except through reflection. There are texts in Zahavi that support Brough's charge (see Zahavi 1999, pp. 76–77). Brough claims that not only are there numerous texts in Husserl that point to a prereflective awareness of experiences as temporal unities (as well as numerous texts that point to a prereflective awareness of consciousness as a unity of distinct experiences) but also that to insist on such prereflective awareness of experiences is more in tune with the phenomena themselves.

Any resolution of the dispute between Brough and Zahavi would have to account for how we might have two "dimensions" or a differentiation within consciousness while preserving a single, albeit perhaps complex, notion of self-awareness. I believe such a resolution is possible. The differentiation between the time-constituting flow and the immanent flow of experiences is best considered a form–matter distinction rather than a distinction between a constituting level and a constituted level. Although the latter is true in a sense—the time-constituting absolute consciousness makes possible the disclosure of temporally qualified experience—it invites the misunderstanding of self-awareness as an instance of object-intentionality, whereas the form–matter distinction does not do so.

There is ample justification for identifying the distinction between the immanent and absolute flows of consciousness as a form–matter distinction. The text of most interest for present purposes is: "The fundamental form of this universal synthesis, which makes all other syntheses of consciousness possible, is the all-encompassing consciousness of inner time" (Husserl 1963, p. 81). What is striking about this text is its identification of the form of the universal synthesis, which is the whole of conscious life with the consciousness of inner time itself. This raises the possibility, first, of preserving the distinction between the absolute time-constituting *form* of consciousness and the *concrete* flow of subjective life itself. This preserves Brough's distinction of levels without the language of levels; it instead uses the language of form and of the concrete whole which is the form filled with its material. More important, it allows us to recognize in a new way—what both Brough and Zahavi admit—the unity of the absolute and phenomenal flows. It raises the possibility, in other words, of dispensing with the model of object-intentionality and the model of correlation in accounting for the relation between the absolute and subjective flows in favor of the language of form and the concrete composite of form and its materials.

My suggestion is this: the momentary phase of absolute consciousness—the retention–primal impression–protention form—is something like Aristotelian *noûs*.[9] *Noûs* is, first of all, a form that is itself conscious. As such, in receiving content, it makes itself, in a sense, all things through being aware of them. Similarly, the absolute form of inner-time consciousness is simply a sheer intentional form comprising two different kinds of intentionality. One kind of intentionality, Husserl's *Querintentionalität*, is more narrowly defined as "directed to *an object*" (intentional$_o$); the other, Husserl's *Längsintentionalität*, is more broadly defined simply as "tending toward" or "directed to" (intentional$_d$). Intentionality$_d$, then, is present in nonthematized and nonobjectifying awarenesses. In particular, intentionality$_d$ in the form of primal impression and retention makes possible the nonthematic, intrinsic awareness of self. Because intentionality$_d$ is inseparable from—and the condition for—intentionality$_o$, self-awareness is inseparable from object-awareness.

The sheer intentionality that is the momentary phase of absolute consciousness is, then, simply an openness to the world and itself. It is affected in various ways and in turning its attention to these affections, takes materials into itself and thereby becomes a concrete subjective life intending objects. In becoming concrete in this way, the absolute *form* of inner-time consciousness, itself nontemporal, temporalizes the *concrete* flow of subjective life such that its taking up different materials is recognized in prereflective self-awareness as a differentiation among temporal unities or experiences. But the flow as a whole is a unity by virtue of its synthesizing form and we are prereflectively aware not only of each experience as mine but of the unity of the experiences, that is, of the unified multiplicity of experiences as mine. We are aware, in other words, of a single life in multiple experiences.

The fact that the form is itself consciousness allows for the awareness both of materially determinate temporal unities as individual experiences and of the self as "transcendent to" or the "unity of" the individuated experiences. If this is correct, there are not two prereflective self-awarenesses but two aspects of a single self-awareness. As Husserl put it, we are aware (i) of the "inner temporality of the appearing (e.g., that of the perceiving of the die)" as a temporal unity, as one experience, and (ii) that "the whole of conscious life is unified synthetically" (Husserl 1963, pp. 79–80; 1970a, pp. 41–42).

Neither aspect of this self-awareness is reducible to the other. There is, to borrow a medieval expression, an "essential equivocation" in our notion of prereflective self-awareness. I am prereflectively aware of individual experiences of objects as mine, and I am prereflectively aware of myself as the synthetic unity of various such experiences. I am, as Brough would insist, prereflectively aware of (my) immanent temporal unities or experiences, and I am, as both Brough and Zahavi would have it, aware of my*self* as a flowing unity of experiences. In our opening example, I am prereflectively aware of a change in my experience as, say, my perception of my wife gives way to the recollection of bad news. I am prereflectively aware of different experiences as having a temporal position of their own. But I am also prereflectively aware that my present recollection forms a unity with my former experiences. To the extent that the self is a flowing unity in a multiplicity of experiences with differentiated contents, I am prereflectively, "simultaneously" or "at once," and inseparably aware both of the multiplicity of experiences with their temporal determinations and distinctions and of the unity of these experiences.

Precisely because the intentionality$_d$ that is the ground for our self-awareness is inseparable from and the condition for intentionality$_o$, we can say that intentionality$_o$ is inseparable from the intentionality$_d$ that is self-awareness. We can say, in other words, (i) that self-awareness is intrinsic to the experience of an object (as the form of that experience), (ii) that self-awareness is a matter of intentionality (intentionality$_d$), and (iii) that the case-structure of self-awareness is genitive. The form of time-constituting consciousness "possesses" those materials that fill it and make it a concrete consciousness aware of objects. Hence, it is possible to affirm the self-awareness principle, that any object-awareness (intentionality$_o$) necessarily involves intentionality$_d$ and to insist, in agreement with Caston's interpretation of Aristotle, that self-awareness is intrinsic and a matter of intentionality—while also insisting that the self of which I am aware in the experience of an object is not an accusative of consciousness but its genitive.

Notes

1. I discuss more fully the structures of intentionality, and especially the difficult Husserlian notion of the *noema*, in Drummond 1990, 1992, 1997, 1998, 2003.

2. The experience of objects seems invariably characterized by some measure of self-awareness, and I shall later consider this claim further. Even such apparently anomalous phenomena as blindsighted and absentminded perception are conscious phenomena, that is, experiences in which the subject is self-aware—aware of its own experiencing—although, perhaps, not directly aware of the object "blindly" or "absent-mindedly" experienced. What is "blindly" perceived takes its place inside the whole of the conscious experience that the subject undergoes, and what is absent-mindedly perceived in the horizons of the subject's focused perception is similarly an aspect of the perceptual field of the absentminded perceiver. If it were not, there would be no basis to say that there is a blindsighted or absentminded perception at all. The perceiver, while not thematically aware of what is absentmindedly perceived, is nevertheless thematically aware of another related aspect of the perceptual field and is, in this total perception, self-aware.

Husserl's discussion of horizons provides a descriptive account of how experience grasps a thematically focused objectivity against various sorts of backgrounds (spatial, temporal, historical, theoretical, and so forth); see, e.g., Husserl 1962a, pp. 160–161, 165–166, 238–239; 1963, pp. 81–83, 111–114; 1970a, pp. 44–46, 78–81; 1970c, pp. 158, 162–163, 237–238; 1976, pp. 56–60, 91–92, 145, 184–185; 1983, pp. 51–55, 94–95, 157, 195–196. This account is developed in Aron Gurwitsch's distinction between the theme, margin, and field of consciousness (Gurwitsch 1964, esp. pp. 309–375, 1985).

3. Caston (2002, pp. 780–781) also identifies other problems in the higher-order theories concerning consciousness and self-awareness that this Aristotelian approach avoids. These other problems are consequences of the view that self-awareness is extrinsic to object-awareness, and I shall not discuss them here.

4. The view summarized herein is developed in Brentano 1995, pp. 101–154. This is the second edition of Brentano's work; the first was published in 1874. In the course of developing his own position, Brentano frequently refers to the Aristotelian texts Caston discusses, and develops the activity-reading Caston endorses; see Brentano 1995, pp. 126–133. The translations of Brentano herein are my own, but I also provide references to the English translation by Rancurello, Terrell, and McAlister.

5. It is an implication of Smith's position that experiences can be unconscious (2004, pp. 108 ff.), thereby effectively denying the self-awareness principle. I shall below discuss the conditions necessary for experiencing objects with temporal determinations, the account of which is at the same time an account of self-awareness.

This discussion, therefore, will provide a justification for the self-awareness principle.

6. On this point I differ with Smith (2004, pp. 104–106) who argues that inner awareness supervenes on the awareness of time. The description that follows will provide the justification both for asserting the self-awareness principle and for denying the supervenient character of self-awareness.

7. "Absolute consciousness" in this context means (i) a consciousness that is the ultimate condition of all (temporal) awareness, and (ii) a consciousness that is complete insofar as it is the ultimate subject of all our intendings of our own experiences and of objects.

8. The exchange recounted in this and the following two paragraphs occurred in a discussion of Zahavi's (1999) book at the 2001 meeting of the Husserl Circle held at Indiana University on February 24, 2001. The members of the panel were Brough, Zahavi, and Richard Cobb-Stevens.

9. I here take up Cobb-Stevens's mention of the special kind of Aristotelian form that is soul and "is somehow all things" as providing an insight into the nature of absolute consciousness.

Between Pure Self-Referentialism and the Extrinsic HOT Theory of Consciousness

Rocco J. Gennaro

1 Introduction: Three Views of State Consciousness

The notion that there is a self-referential aspect to conscious mental states has a long tradition, going back as far as Aristotle (Caston 2002) and, more recently, Franz Brentano (1995 p. 153) who famously held that "every mental act . . . includes within it a consciousness of itself. Therefore, every mental act, no matter how simple, has a double object, a primary and secondary object."[1] For those of us who wish to offer a reductive representational account of consciousness in mentalistic terms, this idea may hold the key to a successful explanation of state consciousness.[2] In the context of arguing for the thesis that consciousness entails self-consciousness (Gennaro 1996), I introduced the *wide-intrinsicality view* (WIV) whereby conscious mental states do indeed contain a crucial self-referential element. On the WIV, first-order or world-directed conscious mental states are complex (or global) states such that one part of the state is directed at another part. Thus, conscious states are to be individuated widely and consciousness is intrinsic to them. Although similar in many ways to David Rosenthal's *"extrinsic" higher-order thought* (EHOT) theory, there are some key differences, as will become clear in the next section.[3] In section 3, I criticize what we might call Brentano's *pure self-referentialism* (PSR); namely, that a conscious mental state is literally directed back at itself. I argue against PSR and show that the WIV is indeed a more plausible theory of state consciousness. As we shall see, the WIV is located significantly between PSR and EHOT theory, and something at least similar to it can be found in the more recent literature.[4] Finally, in section 4, I further clarify the WIV by responding to a number of important objections.[5]

We thus have three positions with respect to first-order world-directed conscious states:

EHOT A mental state *M* of a subject *S* is conscious if and only if *S* has a *distinct* (unconscious) mental state *M** (= HOT) that is an appropriate representation of *M*.

WIV A mental state *M* of a subject *S* is conscious if and only if *S* has a suitable (unconscious) metapsychological thought *M** (= MET), directed at *M*, such that both *M* and *M** (= MET) are *proper parts of* a complex, conscious mental state CMS.[6]

PSR A mental state *M* of a subject *S* is conscious if and only if *S* has a mental state *M** that is an appropriate representation of *M*, and *M* = *M**.[7]

All three views take very seriously the intuitive notion that a conscious mental state *M* is a state that subject *S* is (noninferentially) aware that *S* is in (Rosenthal 1986; Lycan 2001). By contrast, one is obviously not (immediately) aware of one's unconscious mental states. The difference lies mainly in how to cash out the expression "aware that one is in." EHOT theory says that such an awareness of *M* is a distinct (unconscious) state *M** (or HOT) directed at M. PSR says that *M** = *M*; that is, *M* is literally directed back at itself. The WIV says that *M** (i.e., the MET) is an unconscious part of a complex conscious mental state (CMS) directed at *M* (which is also part of the CMS). In each case, some notion of self-reference is involved. This is perhaps more clear for PSR and WIV, but even EHOT theory says that what makes *M* conscious is a kind of self-referential (unconscious) thought; namely, "that I am in *M*" (see fig. 10.1).

2 The Wide Intrinsicality View versus Extrinsic HOT Theory

The main goals of this chapter are to defend the WIV and to argue against PSR. However, it is first very important to mention a few reasons to favor the WIV over EHOT theory. I had originally offered five such reasons (in Gennaro 1996; pp. 26–30), but will not rehearse them all here.

The first, and perhaps most relevant, reason is simply that consciousness seems to be an intrinsic property of conscious states. As even Rosenthal has acknowledged (1986, pp. 331, 345), it is preferable to have a theory that can account for this intuitive fact if it is at all possible. When we are in a conscious state, consciousness does not seem to be analogous to "being the cousin of" or "being to the left of," but instead seems to be part of the state itself. Of course, most would agree that the reality of conscious states need not match the first-person appearance, and so Rosenthal explains that EHOT

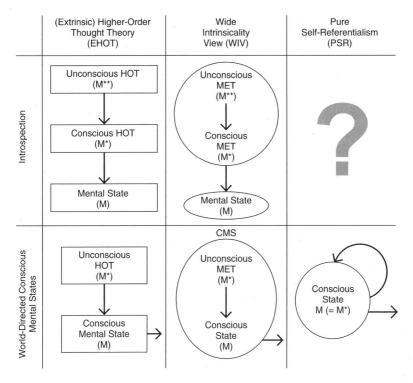

Figure 10.1

theory can still accommodate the phenomenological facts by noting that we are rarely conscious of the HOT itself that renders M conscious. Thus, Rosenthal (2004, p. 31) has recently said that we should not assume "consciousness reveals everything about our mental functioning, or at least everything relevant to the issue at hand. . . . But to save these phenomena, we need only explain why things appear to consciousness as they do; we need not also suppose that these appearances are always accurate." Fair enough, but the real problem is that Rosenthal never presents a compelling case to reject the intrinsicality of consciousness in the first place. For example, he mistakenly argues that if we treat consciousness as an intrinsic property of mental states, then conscious mental states will be simple and unanalyzable (Gennaro 1996, pp. 21–24). Rosenthal defines an "intrinsic" (as opposed to "extrinsic") property as follows: "A property is intrinsic if something's having it does not consist, even in part, in that thing's bearing some relation to something else" (Rosenthal 1990, p. 736). But even if consciousness is an intrinsic property of some or all mental states, it surely does not follow that those states are simple or unanalyzable. Conscious mental states can, for example, have the kind of complex structure described by the WIV. Rosenthal sets up a false dilemma: *either* accept the Cartesian view that mental states are essentially and intrinsically conscious (and so unanalyzable) *or* accept his version of the HOT theory whereby consciousness, or the so-called conscious-making property (i.e., being the object of a HOT), is an extrinsic property of mental states. But there is clearly an informative third alternative whereby the MET is part of the overall structure of a conscious mental state. On the WIV, then, consciousness is intrinsic to conscious states, but there is also a kind of inner self-referential and relational element *within* the structure of such states.[8]

Furthermore, it is not even clear that an intrinsic theorist must rely on any such phenomenological or intuitive evidence to make the point. Examining the issue from a third-person, neurophysiological perspective, there is still something odd in holding that what makes a mental state M conscious is *something else*. For example, if and when the neural correlates of consciousness (NCCs) are discovered, it seems to me far more likely that such NCCs will be counted as part of the (global) conscious brain state. That is, what makes a mental state conscious will be some distributed property of the state itself. There can still of course be a self-referential structure to that conscious state (as the WIV predicts), but both M and MET will be parts of the overall state.

Rosenthal (2004, p. 33) also rightly demands that an "intrinsic theory must explain what happens when a state goes from being nonintrospectively conscious to being introspectively conscious." But I have already presented and motivated the WIV version of introspection in both Gennaro 1996 and 2002. Let us first recall that the WIV says that *first-order* conscious mental states are *complex* states containing both a world-directed mental-state-part M and an unconscious metapsychological thought (MET). This alternative holds that consciousness is an intrinsic property of conscious states and also provides an *analysis* of state consciousness. My conscious perception of the tree is accompanied by a MET *within* the very same complex conscious state. Now when I *introspect* my perception, there is a first-order mental state that is rendered conscious by a complex higher-order state. Thus, *introspection* involves two states: a lower-order noncomplex mental state that is the object of a higher-order conscious complex state (see figure 10.1 again). I am consciously aware of my mental state. In this case, much like on EHOT theory, the MET itself becomes conscious and is directed at a lower-level mental state.

A second reason to favor the WIV over EHOT theory is that a number of authors have recognized that intrinsic theory seems better suited to avoid several standard problems facing EHOT theory. For example, EHOT theory arguably has a serious problem dealing with the possibility of *misrepresentation* between the HOT and its target state M (Byrne 1997; Neander 1998; Levine 2001a). If we are dealing with a representational relation between two distinct states, it is possible for misrepresentation to occur. If it does occur, then what explanation can be offered by the EHOT theorist (or HOP—higher-order perception—theorist for that matter)? If my HOT registers a thought about something green, but M registers a red percept, then what happens? What kind of experience do I have: a reddish or greenish one (or neither)? On either form of intrinsic theory (i.e., PSR or WIV), it seems more difficult to make sense of the possibility of misrepresentation, since either M is directed back at itself (Caston 2002; Kriegel 2003a) or M^* is part of the same state as M (Gennaro 2004b).

Another well-known difficulty for EHOT theory has been called "the problem of the rock" (Stubenberg 1998) and "the generality problem" (Van Gulick 2001, 2004), but is perhaps originally due to Alvin Goldman (1993a). When I have a thought about a rock, it does not thereby make the rock conscious. So why should we suppose, that when one thinks about a mental state M, it becomes conscious? This problem is again based on the notion that there is a complete separation of M^* and M. Alternatively, if this aspect of higher-order (HO) theory is rejected and M^* is therefore intrinsic to the conscious state in question, then its target must be a mental state "in the head" in the first place, and so such objects as stones cannot be potentially conscious, as the objection suggests (Van Gulick 2001, 2004; Gennaro 2005).[9]

Having said all this, it is necessary to digress for a moment to be very clear about the relative logical space that the WIV occupies, especially given the potential for terminological confusion. First, it will be noticed that the WIV is similar in structure to Rosenthal's EHOT theory. I do indeed think that there is something importantly correct about HOT theory, and my view admittedly owes much to Rosenthal's HOT theory. It may even seem that there is no real ontological difference between the two views, but this is not correct for reasons that will be made clearer in section 4. Second, some of the same objections to EHOT theory might also be raised against the WIV, so I have responded to them in print. For example, I have argued at length against the view that HOT theory entails a lack of animal consciousness (Gennaro 1993, 1996, 2004b) and against other weak attempts to criticize EHOT theory (Gennaro 2003). Thus, in these cases, I have no problem associating myself with some form of HOT theory and sometimes willingly bring such a characterization upon myself. Of course, if one *defines* HOT theory as maintaining that the HOT is a *distinct* state from its target *M*, then it would *not* be correct to say that I hold a HOT theory. I do *not* wish to define HOT theory as such in this way, but others clearly do. In my view, this is more of a terminological dispute, though some seem to have very strong views on the matter.[10] On the other hand, I have also been urged by some to reject HO theory altogether and endorse a first-order (FO) theory, perhaps more along the lines of Dretske (1995a) or Tye (1995, 2000).[11] However, for reasons that go well beyond the scope of this essay, I am not inclined to do so and, in fact, reject FO theory.[12] In any case, I take such accusations from both sides as evidence for the fact that the WIV is a truly viable "middle" position between PSR (and any FO theory) and EHOT theory. Indeed, that is precisely why I originally chose to introduce an entirely new theory name into the literature. It is also why I often use the more neutral expression "metapsychological thought" instead of "higher-order thought": there is still a metapsychological thought about *M* on the WIV.[13,14]

3 Against Pure Self-Referentialism

Let us recall pure self-referentialism:

PSR A mental state *M* of a subject *S* is conscious if and only if *S* has a mental state M^* that is an appropriate representation of *M*, and $M = M^*$.

There are a number of somewhat interrelated reasons to reject PSR, which, in turn, will also serve as evidence for the superiority of the WIV.

3.1 What Makes a Mental State a Conscious Mental State?

It is fair to say that all three views *do* try to answer the question: what is the *structure* of a conscious mental state? However, a real deficiency for PSR is that it does not even attempt to answer the crucial question: what *makes* a mental state a conscious mental state? Both the WIV and EHOT theory are, in part, trying to *explain* how an unconscious mental state becomes a conscious one. Of course, many are not satisfied by the explanation offered, but my point here is that PSR does not even *attempt* to offer any explanation at all. Two reasons for this may be that defenders of PSR are often inclined to reject reductive explanations of consciousness (e.g., Smith 2004; cf. Thomasson 2000, p. 206) and even to reject the existence of unconscious mental states (Brentano).[15] In this chapter, I will neither argue for the existence of unconscious mental states nor for the view that reductive explanations are desirable. But to the extent that one agrees with one or both of these assumptions, it seems to me that PSR has a serious problem compared to its rivals. Although both the WIV and EHOT theory answer the above question with something like "M becomes conscious when an appropriate HOT (or MET) is directed at M," PSR can offer no such explanation. PSR does provide a description of the structure of conscious states, but we must distinguish that from the kind of explanation we are seeking. If we ask "What *makes* M conscious?" for PSR, the response cannot be that M^* is directed at M because M is supposed to be *identical with* M^*. How can M^* *make* M conscious or *explain* M's being conscious if $M^* = M$? Moreover, either M^* is itself conscious or it is not, and then the familiar threat of regress (and even circularity) rears its ugly head. If M^* is itself conscious, then what makes *it* conscious, and so on? Is the consciousness of M being explained in terms of a conscious M^*? Also, if M^* is conscious, then a reductionist account of state consciousness seems out of the question. Alternatively, if M^* is not conscious, then the PSR defender would, first, have to acknowledge the existence of unconscious mental states, but, even worse, how could M be conscious and M^* be unconscious if $M = M^*$?

As I will argue in section 3.5, some supporters of PSR may really hold something more like the WIV. Thus, if we also reject EHOT theory, then the WIV represents a superior middle position. It seems necessary to bring in the notion of *parts* of conscious mental states in order to give an adequate account of state consciousness. In any case, a fundamental question that should be answered by any viable theory of consciousness goes unanswered or is ignored by PSR advocates. To the extent that M^* is introduced merely to articulate the structure of a conscious state, PSR may offer a plausible alternative (though obviously I think it is the wrong structure). But, to the extent that we want M^* to play some role in explaining how an otherwise unconscious M becomes conscious, PSR is entirely unhelpful. There is a difference between simply stating that "all (conscious) mental states have a primary and secondary object" and giving an explanation for what makes that mental state conscious.[16]

It might be replied by the PSR theorist that there is a perfectly good explanation for what makes a mental state M conscious; namely, that M becomes conscious when it acquires a particular sort of self-referential content. That is, M $(= M^*)$ has the property of being conscious in virtue of M $(= M^*)$ having the property of being self-referential. However, there are at least two problems with this response, relative to WIV and EHOT theory. First, the reply still does not help to provide a reductive explanation of state consciousness (which I am assuming is desirable) because PSR typically holds that one is conscious (in some sense) of the self-referential content itself, as we shall see more clearly below. Recall that I began this chapter by pointing out that all three positions under consideration try to understand state consciousness in terms of some kind of self-referential intentional content. Of these three theories, then, it is clear that only PSR cannot offer a reductive explanation in mentalistic terms. Second, I would again insist that the above explanation is not really *explanatory*, but rather *descriptive*. According to PSR, the self-referential content in question is a property of M itself. PSR *describes* the difference between unconscious and conscious states, but M's being conscious is not explained by appealing to M^* because M^* is identical with M. Perhaps there is some other way for PSR to provide a plausible reductive or, at least, naturalistic explanation of state consciousness, but I remain skeptical based on Kriegel's (2003b, pp. 483, 493–496) "argument from physical implausibilty." For example, suppose we understand a naturalistic explanation to include some kind of *causal* explanation. As Kriegel rightly points out, the causal relation is antireflexive and so we can, at most, make sense of such a relation by invoking talk of a part of a complex state that is directed at another part. The WIV can clearly accommodate the notion of a causal relation between M and M^* (in either direction) combining to produce CMS. Notice, however, that there is still no *pure* self-reference; that is, no conscious (brain) state (or state part) is literally causally related to itself. PSR is indeed physically implausible; it is ruled out if we take the requisite self-reflexiveness literally.

3.2 Conscious Attention Cannot Be Focused Both Outward and Inward at the Same Time

Another serious problem with PSR is the failure to recognize the implications of the fact that our conscious attention is either world-directed or inner directed (but never both at the same time), as even Brentano acknowledged (1995, pp. 128–129). When I am assembling a bookcase or working on this essay, my conscious attention is focused outside of me, for example, at the bookcase or at my computer screen. Of course, if either the WIV or EHOT theory is correct, what makes that state conscious is an unconscious HOT (or MET) directed at M. If, however, I reflect or introspect on my experience, then my conscious attention is focused inward at the mental state itself. But PSR cannot provide such a neat explanation of the difference between outer- and inner-directed consciousness. Leaving aside regress worries, if M^* is supposed to be conscious *and* directed back at the *entire* conscious mental state M, then it would seem that M^* is *both* directed at the world *and* at one's own mental state M at the same time because, after all, M is supposed to be identical with M^*. This doesn't seem possible, if it is even at all coherent. I certainly may frequently shift my attention between, say, the bookcase and my experience of working on it, but I never consciously focus on both at the same time. It therefore also seems that proponents of PSR often slide back and forth between outer-directed consciousness and introspective consciousness without even realizing it.[17]

But if PSR is to give an account of a world-directed conscious state, M, then it seems committed to the absurdity that M is both directed at the world and at itself at the same time. Of course, if M^* is not itself conscious (as the WIV and EHOT views have it), then PSR either has the problem mentioned in section 3.1 (i.e., how can $M = M^*$ if M is conscious and M^* is unconscious?), or we end up with something closer to the other theories. In any case, PSR supporters do believe that M^* is itself conscious in some sense, as we shall see. Unlike the WIV, there is no explicit belief in (unconscious) "parts" of conscious mental states. But the WIV has the advantage of holding that M is an outer-directed conscious part of a complex conscious state (CMS) within which an (unconscious) M^* is directed at M. Bringing in parts of conscious states seems unavoidable if one wants to preserve some kind of self-reference in state consciousness.

Somewhat related objections to PSR are raised by Perrett (2003) and Zahavi (1998). For example, Perrett argues that "... there is an inconsistency in Brentano's account. On the one hand, he holds that the content of an awareness is always a proper part of that awareness, where a *proper part* is a part that is not identical with the whole of which it is a part. On the other hand, the secondary awareness is also supposed to possess a content which is identical with itself, since it is its own object. Thus the content of such an awareness cannot be a proper part of itself" (Perrett 2003, p. 231). As I argued above, then, if $M = M^*$, then M^* would have to be directed back at M *in its entirety*; that is, directed back at M and M^*. But if M^* is itself conscious, then M^* is directed both at the world and at one's own mental state M at the same time. Similarly, Zahavi (1998, p. 139) notices a "disastrous problem" using Brentano's example of hearing a sound or tone: "A [conscious] act which has a tone as its primary object is to be conscious by having itself as its secondary object. But if the latter is really to result in self-awareness, it has to comprise the entire act, and not only the part of it which is conscious of the tone. That is, the secondary object of the perception should not merely be the perception of the tone, but the perception which is aware of both the tone and itself." The WIV has no such problems. An unconscious MET is directed at only *part* of the entire CMS; that is, the M that is consciously directed at the world. Moreover, the MET is therefore not consciously directed at M, avoiding the conflation with introspection.

It might be objected at this point that I have ignored a crucial distinction, frequently made by PSR advocates, between *attentive* (or "focal") consciousness and *inattentive* (or "marginal" or "peripheral") consciousness. Not all conscious "directedness" is attentive, and so perhaps I have mistakenly restricted conscious directedness to that which we are consciously focused on. The idea is that, in figure 10.1, the "back-turning" arrow for PSR represents inattentive (inner-directed) consciousness whereas the other arrow represents focused (outer-directed) awareness. If this is right, then my objection has an easy reply; namely, that first-order conscious state M is both attentively outer-directed and inattentively inner-directed. M^* is thus conscious in this inattentive sense. I have three replies to this for now. First, although it is probably true that there are degrees of conscious attention, it seems to me that the clearest examples of "inattentive" consciousness are still outer-directed; for example, perhaps some of the awareness in one's peripheral visual field while watching a concert or reading a book. But this obviously does not show that any such inattentional consciousness is *self-directed* at the same time when there is outer-directed attentional consciousness. Second, what is the evidence for such self-directed inattentional consciousness? It is based on phenomenological considerations. I will tackle the phenomenological argument more directly and thoroughly in section 3.4, but to anticipate, it suffices to say for now that I do not find such inattentive consciousness in my own experience, which should presumably show up in the Nagelian sense if it is based on phenomenological observation. Conscious experience is often so clearly and completely outer-directed that I deny we have such marginal self-directed conscious experience when in first-order conscious states. It does not seem to me that I am consciously aware (in any sense) of my own experience when I am, say, consciously attending to a movie or the task of building a bookcase. As we shall see, this point has greater force when we consider the conscious experience of animals or infants; it seems even more unlikely that they are capable of having such peripheral self-directed consciousness. Third, when PSR theorists claim to find such inattentive consciousness in their experience, a case can be made that they are philosophically "reflecting" on their experience, but then they are *consciously attending* to their experiences, which is really introspective consciousness (as we have already seen). Thus, we no longer have a phenomenological analysis of *first-order* conscious states.

3.3 PSR Offers No Plausible Account of Introspection

It is also curious that no clear account of introspection has been presented by supporters of PSR. Perhaps this is simply due to the fact that they are mainly concerned with first-order conscious states. However, the problem goes much deeper than this for several reasons. First, as we saw above, PSR theorists often conflate introspective consciousness with an explanation of first-order conscious states. If M^* is itself conscious, then that seems to indicate the presence of an introspective state, not merely a first-order conscious state. Second, some theorists who otherwise oppose any form of HOT theory are sympathetic to it as an account of introspection; that is, when one is *consciously aware* of a mental state (Block 1995). Rosenthal then reasons as follows: "if a state isn't conscious [at all], there is no HOT. That suggests that a state's being conscious in the . . . [world-directed] nonintrospective way results from something in between these two [i.e., a nonconscious HOT or MET]" (2004, p. 24). Both EHOT theory and the WIV can accommodate this important aspect of a theory of consciousness. On the other hand, PSR offers no explanation of just how such a transition from first-order conscious states to introspective states might occur. Third, if I am right thus far, it is simply difficult to understand what the structure of introspective consciousness would be according to PSR. If no unconscious thought becomes conscious during such a transition, then does an entirely new state, M^{**}, emerge as directed at M (and therefore also at M^*)? Is M^{**} itself also conscious (on pain of regress)? Would M^{**} also be "directed back at itself" so we would then also have an M^{***} directed at M^{**}?[18]

3.4 The Phenomenological Argument

Perhaps most importantly, PSR supporters argue that M^* is conscious (in some sense) based on phenomenological considerations (Kriegel 2003a; Smith 1986). Of course, in Brentano's case, M^* would have to be conscious because he did not believe in unconscious mental states. There are, as we have already seen, significant problems with holding that M^* is conscious, but I now wish to challenge this view more directly as it is likely to be at the root of the above difficulties.

Focusing on Kriegel's 2003a essay (cf. 2003b, p. 485), we find a distinction between "intransitive self-consciousness (or self-awareness)" and "transitive self-consciousness." He first rightly explains the latter in much the same way that EHOT theory and the WIV speak of introspection: "a transitively self-conscious state is *introspective*, in that the object is always one of the subject's own mental states . . ." (2003a, p. 105). On the other hand, "an intransitively self-conscious state is ordinarily not introspective, in that usually its object is an external state of affairs." So far so good. Like the WIV, each first-order conscious state contains a metapsychological component (which is indeed a form of self-consciousness or self-awareness on my view), but the conscious state is outer-directed. Moreover, when the shift to introspection occurs, then there is a *conscious* metapsychological thought directed at one's own mental state. As Kriegel also makes clear (ibid.), in such transitively self-conscious cases, there is a *further* intransitive self-consciousness accompanying *that* conscious state.

The key point here lies in the fact that Kriegel takes intransitive self-consciousness (i.e., M^*) itself to be conscious, based on phenomenological observation. As mentioned in section 3.2 in addressing inattentional consciousness, I strongly disagree with Kriegel and so am much closer to EHOT theory, at least in this respect. M^* is not conscious in any meaningful sense of the term, including the Nagelian sense. For one thing, Kriegel uses a number of vague, but typical, characterizations of M^*, for example, "subtle awareness of having M," "implicit awareness of M," "dim self-awareness . . . humming in the background of our stream of consciousness," and "minimal self-awareness" (Kriegel 2003a, pp. 104–105). Now I have no objection to these expressions as such, but it is still not at all clear to me that M^* is conscious in any phenomenological sense. Rather, I think it is far better to construe M^* as unconscious, and so I often speak of unconscious "metapsychological thought awareness" and "nonreflective self-consciousness" in Gennaro 1996 and 2002. Much like we normally understand, say, at least some peripheral vision to be unconscious, the same should go for the "subtle awareness" in question. It also does not help to speak of M^* as "experienced" or as an "experiential state" (Kriegel 2003a, pp. 121ff.) for this begs the question as to whether or not this awareness is phenomonologically consciously experienced; nor does it help to appeal to inattentional consciousness.

Three more specific problems come to mind. First, the examples used by Kriegel to illustrate the consciousness of M^* cause us to shift (phenomenologically) to transitive consciousness (i.e., introspection). We are asked, for example, to "suppose . . . that you suddenly hear a distant bagpipe. In your auditory experience of the bagpipe you are aware primarily, or *explicitly*, of the bagpipe sound; but you are also *implicitly* aware that this auditory experience of the bagpipe is *your* experience . . ." (Kriegel 2003a, p. 104). But it seems to me that the very act of performing this mental exercise results in an act of introspection or reflection. That is, Kriegel is asking us, via our imagination, to focus *consciously* on M (e.g., the experience of hearing a distant bagpipe) in considering his examples. We are really asked *to reflect on* the hypothetical case in question. How can we pretend to "consider" such a state of mind without shifting our phenomenological attention onto the mental state or experience itself? To the extent that we really can do so, for what it's worth, I think that our consciousness is completely outer directed, for example, when I am absorbed in a taxing chore or taken with a beautiful painting. Such conscious states can still have the structure of the WIV, but there is no conscious notice at all of M^* (= MET). In a sense, then, although Kriegel is not fallaciously conflating the distinction between introspection and first-order conscious states, he is, I believe, relying on one's reflective response to his examples to make the case that M^* is conscious. It is crucial to remember that the WIV also holds there is an implicit self-referential MET as part of the overall conscious state, but this is not to say that the MET is itself conscious. Indeed, if it were, then we would have a case of introspection, not a world-directed conscious state.

Second, if Kriegel's (or any) phenomenological argument is meant to support PSR, then it also fails due to the lessons learned from sections 3.1 and 3.2. If we cannot simultaneously *consciously* attend to both outer objects and inner mental states *and* $M = M^*$, then how could M^* be conscious? The very same state (without any parts) would then be both outer-directed and inner-directed, which is impossible. Moreover, if $M = M^*$ and M^* is itself conscious, it is difficult to understand how the presence of M^* can help to explain why M is conscious in the first place, especially in any reductivist sense.

Kriegel is right that "there is something artificial in calling a mental state conscious when the subject is *wholly* unaware of its occurrence" (2003a, p. 106, emphasis added). But this leaves open whether such awareness is conscious or not. Kriegel's use of the expression "wholly unaware" suggests both consciously and unconsciously unaware, but we might instead hold that a state is conscious when the subject is *unconsciously* aware of its occurrence. Kriegel's argument can only justify the weaker claim that "there is something artificial in calling a mental state conscious when the subject is *not at least unconsciously aware* of its occurrence." But this is precisely one key issue at hand between PSR and the WIV.[19]

Third, the above is particularly important to the extent that we want a *general* theory of state consciousness. That is, although it is certainly true that there are degrees of conscious attention and degrees of self-consciousness, it is desirable to offer an explanation of what *all* first-order conscious states have in common. On the WIV, this is the fact that there is an unconscious MET directed at M, both of which are parts of a complex CMS. I suggest that such a general account can be offered only if the MET (or M^*) is itself unconscious because we are so often entirely consciously focused on outer things. Moreover, if we are to allow for, say, animal and infant consciousness, the notion that M^* is itself conscious seems very unlikely. Indeed, believing otherwise could lead to the problematic conclusion that such creatures are incapable of having conscious states at all. Instead, contra Kriegel, it seems better to hold that any genuine case of a conscious M^* is really an instance of introspection, and thus any first-order conscious state is only accompanied by an unconscious M^*. In short, the problem of animal and infant consciousness applies with even greater force to PSR than to either WIV or EHOT theory.

The importance of all this can also be seen in Smith's (2004) most recent account where he retreats from what appeared to be a previous adherence to PSR (in his 1986, 1989). Smith continues to insist that "...the formal analysis of inner awareness $[M^*]$...is a task for phenomenology" (2004, p. 80). However, this leads him to abandon his earlier view that all first-order conscious states have such inner awareness (Smith 2004, pp. 109–116). Smith now allows for basic levels of outer-directed consciousness that lack such self-consciousness or inner awareness; for example, when "I am unselfconsciously hammering a nail, or driving down the highway, or choosing to hit the tennis ball crosscourt rather than down the line..." (ibid., 109). Thus, "[o]n the view now emerging, inner awareness is an integral part of higher levels of consciousness, realized in humans and perhaps other animals, but it is not present in lower levels of consciousness in humans and other animals" (ibid., 110). To the extent that Smith no longer advocates PSR, then I agree. However, I suggest that what he should really give up is the view that such "inner awareness" (= M^*) is phenomenologically revealed. If he had done so, then he would have recognized that *all* outer-directed conscious mental states can still have a WIV-like structure without giving up the belief that inner awareness or self-consciousness (of some kind) is indeed built into the structure of those states. Smith is correct, however, in recognizing the existence of conscious mental states not accompanied by a *conscious* M^*. But this should lead one to embrace something more like the WIV instead of the belief that there can be levels of consciousness without any inner awareness whatsoever, especially if one is sympathetic to any of the three positions under consideration.

Thus, I disagree with Kriegel that the only reason to posit "such [intransitive] self-awareness...is on first-personal experiential grounds" (2003a, p. 121) and disagree also that "those who insist that they do not find in their experience anything like an awareness of their conscious perceptions and thoughts probably deny the very existence of intransitive self-consciousness" (ibid.). In the absence of such alleged phenomonological evidence, it is quite appropriate to demand (as Kriegel does) other theoretical and explanatory advantages to positing such self-awareness. Although by no means conclusive, it seems to me that there is ample reason to posit such unconscious METs.[20]

In some ways, then, the phenomenological argument is at the root of the problems raised for PSR in sections 3.1–3.3. If one believes that M^* is conscious, then (a) it is difficult to offer any reductionist explanation of state consciousness, (b) one is more likely to conflate introspection with first-order conscious states, and (c) one is unable to offer an account of introspection.

3.5 Many PSR Views Are the WIV in Disguise

Finally, it seems to me that, to the extent that PSR is plausible at all, it is better construed as the WIV anyway. A close reading of the literature reveals at least some evidence for this claim. Talk of "parts" and "wholes" of conscious states abound even when characterizing Brentano's views, not to mention Kriegel's own very useful analysis (in this volume). It is doubtful that all such references can easily be explained away as merely metaphorical.

For example, consider the following sampling of quotations (emphases added). "The presentation which accompanies a mental act and refers to it is *part of* the object on which it is directed" (Brentano 1995, p. 128). This suggests that, even for Brentano, M^* (i.e., "the presentation . . .") is really only part of the "entire" conscious state. In describing Brentano's view, Natsoulas similarly explains: "Not only is a conscious mental-occurrence instance presented and directly apprehended . . . , but also there is, *as part of its occurrence*, awareness of it as this (a mental-occurrence instance) . . ." (Natsoulas 1993a, p. 117). And Smith once said that inner awareness "must be an occurrent *part of* the given mental event itself" (1989, p. 81). It is difficult to see how M could be *identical with* M^* when reading such passages. We are also told by Smith that Brentano's secondary inner consciousness is "a dependent, inseparable *part of* the given act [of consciousness]" (Smith 2004, pp. 78–79, cf. 93; see also Thomasson 2000, pp. 192, 196).

Caston (2002, pp. 792–793) also discusses the importance of the part–whole relationship in his analysis of Brentano and Aristotle. Perhaps most interesting is Caston's diagram (2002, p. 778) presumably representing PSR. But much like the WIV for outer-directed conscious states, we have an arrow going from one part of a complex conscious state (the perceiving) to another part (the seeing) divided by a broken line, in addition to the arrow representing the outer-directedness of the entire conscious state. Caston then speaks of both aspects as essential to any token perception.[21]

There has also been a noticeable emphasis on parts and wholes in the more recent writings of Kriegel, who, as we have seen, did argue for PSR in his

2003a.[22] In addition to Kriegel's chapter in this volume, he had previously said that "a brain state can be said to represent itself if *one part* of it represents *another* part of it" (2003b, p. 493, italics in original). This comes in the context of preserving some kind of self-representational view within a naturalistic framework (as was noted in section 3.1), but it also sounds much more like the WIV than PSR. Moving more clearly away from PSR, Kriegel also says that "the mental state in question does not actually represent *itself*. At most, we can say that one part of it represents another part" (2005).

The case against PSR is very strong. If we are to preserve any useful notion of self-reference at all, something more like the WIV is necessary.

4 Objections and Replies

For the sake of further defending and clarifying the WIV, let us now consider a number of objections.

4.1 The Unconscious Parts Objection

It might first be objected that the notion of an unconscious part of a complex conscious state is difficult to understand. What does it even mean to say that state parts can be conscious or unconscious? The WIV is an implausible view perhaps because the notion of an unconscious part of a conscious state sounds contradictory.[23]

There are at least two replies to this. First, the objection could be taken as committing the well-known fallacy of division; namely, that what is true of the whole must be true of each part of the whole. Water extinguishes fire, but oxygen does not. If this is the motivation behind the objection, then it clearly fails. Indeed, if we think of it in a physicalistic way, then such logic would seem to lead automatically to panpsychism. Why should we suppose that each part of a complex conscious state is itself conscious? I see no reason at all to assume that one will be consciously aware of each intrinsic part of a conscious state. Are we consciously aware of everything involved in a conscious state?—I suggest not, and this is particularly clear if we think about conscious states as globally represented brain states. All kinds of nonconscious mental activity are involved in a conscious state. Although I disagree with Colin McGinn's "mysterian" views on consciousness, he is right when he speaks of there being a "hidden structure of consciousness" such that there are "surface properties, which are accessible to the subject introspectively; and deep properties, which are not so accessible" (McGinn 1991, p. 111). Indeed, on the WIV, the MET is precisely such a deep property, but can surely still be part of (i.e., intrinsic to) the entire complex conscious state.

As McGinn puts it: "the subject is not conscious *of* the deeper layer . . . but it does not follow that this layer does not belong intrinsically to the conscious state itself. Just as F can be an intrinsic property of a perceptible object x without being a perceptible property of x, so conscious states can have intrinsic properties that they do not have consciously" (ibid., p. 98).[24]

Second, we must distinguish between the first-person and third-person perspectives on conscious states. From the first-person point of view, we cannot expect to be consciously aware of all that is "presupposed," to use a Kantian term, in a conscious state. As I have argued at greater length (in Gennaro 1996, chap. 3), we can understand the situation as follows: we passively receive information via our senses in what Kant calls our "faculty of sensibility," some of which rises to the level of unconscious mental states. But such mental states do not become conscious until the more cognitive "faculty of understanding" operates on them via the application of higher-order concepts in the METs. Thus, I consciously experience the brown tree *as a brown tree* partly because I have the MET "I am seeing a brown tree now." Once again, however, the MET itself is not conscious; thus, METs and their concepts are "presupposed" in conscious experience. The understanding unconsciously "synthesizes" the raw data of experience to produce the resulting conscious state. As Kant understood very well, there must be significant unconscious (synthesizing) activity implicit in each conscious state, and we are not conscious of that activity itself despite the fact that it is intrinsic and essential to the resulting conscious state. Indeed, it is the MET that makes the state conscious because of the conceptual activity directed at the lower-order mental state. As most would also agree, concepts are constituents of thoughts, which I construe as momentary episodic mental events unlike dispositional states (such as beliefs).

There is nothing at all implausible about the existence of unconscious parts of conscious states. On the contrary, such a view is crucial to appreciating the subtlety of the WIV.[25]

4.2 Rosenthal's Objection

David Rosenthal (1993b) objects that HOTs (or METs) cannot be intrinsic to conscious states because it would be contradictory for a single state to be, for example, a conscious doubt that it is raining and an affirmative (i.e., assertoric) thought that I am in that state. That is, we normally individuate states in terms of mental attitude.

In order to reply, let us make an important threefold distinction. First, we have the conscious *state*, that is, the *vehicle* that is identical with a mental representation and is presumably a brain state of some kind. Second, there is the representational *content* of the state in question; that is, what the state is about or directed at. Third, there is the mental *attitude* (or mode) of the state; that is, what type of mental state it is, for example, a doubt, a thought, a perception, and so on. This threefold distinction is particularly crucial when teasing apart the sometimes subtle differences between the three views under consideration (see also Hossack 2003, pp. 192, 200; Kriegel 2003b, 2005; Smith 2004). Unlike EHOT theory, virtually any form of intrinsic theory will hold that a single vehicle or state can have dual representational *content*. More specifically, the WIV (and PSR for that matter) says that the higher-order content is represented in the same state as the first-order content. This view seems perfectly defensible, though I will not argue for it here.[26] More to the point raised by Rosenthal, it also seems possible to have a single conscious state involving two *attitudes* because one will be directed at its first-order content and the other will be directed toward its higher-order content. Thus, on the WIV, a complex conscious state, CMS, can have one attitude (e.g., a doubt) directed at the weather and another (an assertoric thought) directed at the doubt. M and MET can be instances of two different attitudes and yet nonetheless be parts of a single vehicle or brain state. As Kriegel (2003b, pp. 486–488) persuasively argues, a subject's conscious state containing two attitudes would still be related differently to its two contents; a case has already been made for this view in some areas of moral psychology. There is nothing contradictory here.

Unlike PSR, however, on the WIV M* (i.e., MET) is not directed back at the *entire* CMS, as we saw in section 3.2. To reinforce the point, then, we can now symbolize WIV as follows:

S [A1 (C1) & A2 (C2)],

where S stands for a (conscious) state that includes everything in the square brackets, that is, two attitudes (A1 and A2) along with their respective contents (C1 and C2). But what is crucial is that A1 is part of C2, that is, the second inner-directed attitude (A2) is directed at A1. On the other hand, even if PSR has the same formal structure, a problem results from the notion that somehow C2 = S. This is an untenable view, as was argued in section 3. In contrast to both PSR and the WIV, EHOT theory says: S1 [A1 (C1)] and S2 [A2 (C2)], where S1 and S2 are distinct states.

4.3   A Sum or Complex Account?

This leads to another closely related question: what exactly is the real *ontological* difference between the WIV and EHOT theory? Some have claimed that the difference is merely terminological or verbal.[27] Indeed, Rosenthal himself once said that there is no nonarbitrary way of choosing between these two ways of describing higher-order theory (Rosenthal 1986, p. 345).

There really are two issues here. First, Kriegel has convincingly argued that whether there are two states or one state is not at all arbitrary and can even be understood as an empirical neurophysiological matter (Kriegel 2003b, pp. 488–494). Citing the familiar "binding problem," he explains how the difference may simply depend on whether or not two neural events, N1 and N2, taking place in different parts of the brain "are synchronized or not. If they are, then N1 and N2 are bound into a single brain state; if they are not, N1 and N2 constitute two separate brain states . . ." (ibid., p. 493). I see no reason why a proponent of the WIV cannot also agree with this statement, at least as a partial explanation of the real ontological difference between the WIV and EHOT theory.[28]

Second, there is the issue of just what the nature of such "compound" states are. Kriegel (this volume) usefully distinguishes between what he calls "sum" and "complex" theories. This division aligns with his earlier (2005) distinction between the mere *compresence* of two mental states and the *integration* of mental states.[29] The basic difference is that a mere *sum* theory says that what makes two states part of a single mental state is merely our decision to treat them as such. Once again, it is a purely verbal or stipulative difference that Kriegel (2005) calls the "conceptual-relation strategy." In contrast, a *complex* is a sum whose parts are essentially connected, or bound, in a certain way. There is a psychologically real relation or integration between the parts; hence, Kriegel (2005) calls it the "real-relation strategy."

Kriegel (2005; this volume) construes the WIV as a sum account whereas he understands his own "cross-order information integration" (or "same-order monitoring") model and Van Gulick's higher-order global states (HOGS) model as complex accounts. I strongly disagree with this characterization of the WIV, though it is perhaps understandable how one might take it that way, given the admittedly embryonic form the theory took in my 1996 book. However, I do think there is strong evidence to indicate that the WIV is also a complex account, even from Gennaro 1996. First, in rejecting Rosenthal's EHOT theory, I spoke of how the "very *nature* of conscious states is colored by the concepts [in the METs that are] brought to bear on them" (Gennaro 1996, p. 29). I urged that the MET changes the nature of the conscious state, so that, unlike EHOT theory, the object of a MET is not merely passively there unaltered by the MET.[30] Second, I criticized Rosenthal's belief in unconscious qualitative states because the conceptual activity in the

MET is essential to the very *identity* of the overall conscious state it is part of. So "a nonconscious qualitative state, *contra* Rosenthal, could not be the *very same state* as the conscious one because of the lack of conceptualization" (Gennaro 1996, p. 30). That is, when M becomes conscious as part of a CMS, it is not just the same state with consciousness added to it. Third, as was mentioned in section 4.1, I elaborated on and emphasized (even in neurophysiological terms) the Kantian-style thesis that it takes appropriate interaction and cooperation between "sensibility" and "understanding" (i.e., M and MET) to produce the resulting conscious state (ibid., chap. 3).[31] More recently, I have briefly discussed the importance of "feedback loops" in the brain to illustrate the essential mutual interaction between the parts of a conscious state (Gennaro 2004b, pp. 62–63). The WIV, thus, embodies a real-relation strategy and is a complex, not sum, account of state consciousness.

In light of this and section 4.2, it is worth noting that, in a very striking passage, Rosenthal (2002, p. 416, emphasis added) himself says that "On the HOT hypothesis, *a conscious state is a compound state*, consisting of the state one is conscious of [i.e., M] together with a HOT. So the causal role a conscious state plays is actually the interaction of the two causal roles. . . . This explains how a state's being conscious may to some extent matter to its causal role." This comes in response to Dretske's (1995a, p. 117) charge that HOT theory is unable to explain how a mental state's being conscious could have any function; that is, it would seem that the state's being conscious would make no difference to its causal role.

HOT theory thus threatens to make consciousness merely epiphenomenal. Although Rosenthal is somewhat reluctant to concede the point, he does, in the end, seem to agree that there is at least one important difference between WIV and EHOT theory; namely, that only the former can explain how the causal-functional role of a conscious state can be significantly different from the relevant target state stripped of its HOT. It seems to me he rightly suggests that (at least sometimes) M and M*, when combined, can form a uniquely new state, at least in terms of its functional role, which is therefore not a mere "sum" of M and M*. This sounds more like the WIV than EHOT theory, particularly given Rosenthal's note that the "interaction of the two roles may not be [merely] additive . . ." (Rosenthal 2002, p. 421, n. 48).

4.4 Droege's Objection

We are now in a much better position to respond to Paula Droege's (2003) complaint that "on Gennaro's theory, it is unclear whether the whole complex state is conscious and there is something it is like to be in only part of it, or whether there is something it is like to be in the whole complex state. . . . If the whole, then the theory is circular. . . . If part, then either [M] is what is conscious and we are back to [EHOT theory], or the [MET] is conscious and the theory is again circular" (Droege 2003, pp. 40–41).

This is certainly an important request for clarification. The first part of the answer is that, on my view, it would be most precise to say that "the whole complex *state* [= CMS] is conscious and there is something it is like to be in only part of it [= M]," but there are important ambiguities here. It is crucial to recall the distinctions between the first-person and third-person perspectives (section 4.1) and between a conscious state (or vehicle) and its content (section 4.2). Looking at it from a more *third-person point of view*, we can then see that the entire complex (brain) *state* should be understood as conscious. Of course, there is still something it is like to be in the whole state (CMS) if that merely means that when a subject S is in CMS, S is having a subjective phenomenal experience. However, there is something it is like to be in only part of CMS in the sense that S is only consciously aware of the *content* of M from the *first-person point of view*. We can and should deny Droege's conclusion that we are then back to EHOT theory because of what we have seen in the previous sections (4.2 and 4.3). Since the WIV is a "complex" account, the very conscious content of M is essentially interwoven with the MET. That is, M would not have the content it has without its relation to the MET or if the MET were a completely distinct state from M. The MET is presupposed in the very nature of M's conscious content and is thus part of the same state as M. Moreover, we have seen many other reasons to distinguish between the WIV and EHOT theory. The WIV is also not circular because it still attempts to reduce state consciousness to the interaction between two *unconscious* mental states, which are fused together to bring about a unique complex conscious state. This is not a claim that can be made by PSR, as we saw in section 3.[32]

4.5   Schröder's Objection

Let us also consider the remark by Jürgen Schröder (2001) that it is "doubtful whether [the WIV] does really account for our intuition that consciousness is an intrinsic property of our mental states" mainly because "although consciousness is now intrinsic to the *whole* state [= CMS], it is not intrinsic to the mental state which is a part of the whole [= M]. This is so because the conscious-making thought [= MET] is not a *property* of [M], but a mental state of its own" (2001, p. 35, n. 8). That is, since I have just acknowledged that there is only something it is like to be aware of M's content, then doesn't this undermine the initial motivation to make consciousness intrinsic to state consciousness (e.g., early in section 2)?

The answer is no, but we must again be precise. First, since the WIV is a "complex" account, it is not quite right to say that "the conscious-making thought [= MET] . . . is a *state* of its own." Once again, the MET is part of (i.e., one attitude within) the very same state that M is also part of. Second, being represented by the MET *is* a property of M, at least in the sense that the MET contributes essentially to M's conscious content. Third, Schröder seems mistakenly to equate "consciousness" with "the conscious-making thought [= MET]." As we have seen, the MET is itself not conscious at all. Finally, then, the first-person intuition that "consciousness seems intrinsic to conscious states" should be understood as a combination of two claims; namely, that consciousness seems intrinsic to M's *content* from the subject's first-person point of view, and that consciousness is intrinsic to the *state* that M is part of. When it seems to me from the first-person point of view that consciousness is not extrinsic to, say, my conscious perception of a house, I am reflecting on the commonsense "intuition" that consciousness seems intrinsic to my first-person conscious awareness *of the house* and also to the perceptual *state* that includes that conscious awareness. The WIV does accommodate this intuition.[33]

4.6 The Infallibility Objection

One final objection to the WIV is the charge it entails that knowledge of one's conscious states is infallible, especially in light of the reply to the problem of misrepresentation noted in section 2. If M and M* cannot come apart, then doesn't that imply some sort of objectionable infallibility?[34]

This objection once again conflates outer-directed conscious states with allegedly infallible *introspective* knowledge. On the WIV, it *is* possible to separate the higher-order (complex) conscious state from its target mental state in cases of introspection (see figure 10.1 again). This is as it should be and does indeed allow for the possibility of error and misrepresentation. Thus, for example, I may mistakenly consciously think that I am angry when I am "really" jealous. The WIV properly accommodates the anti-Cartesian view that one can be mistaken about what mental state one is in, at least in the sense that when one introspects a mental state, one may be mistaken about what state one is really in. However, this is very different from holding that the relationship between M and M* *within* an outer-directed CMS is similarly fallible. There is indeed a kind of infallibility between M and M* on the WIV, but this is not a problem. The impossibility of error in this case is merely within the complex CMS, and not some kind of certainty that holds between one's CMS and the outer object. When I have a conscious perception of a brown tree, I am indeed certain that I am having that perception, that is, I am in that state of mind. But this is much less controversial and certainly does not imply the problematic claim that I am certain that there really is a brown tree outside of me, as standard cases of hallucination and illusion are meant to show. If the normal causal sequence to having such a mental state is altered or disturbed, then misrepresentation and error can certainly creep in between my mind and outer reality. However, even in such cases, it is usually not doubted that I am in that conscious state at all.

5 Conclusion

The WIV is a more plausible account of state consciousness than either PSR or EHOT theory. It is importantly located between its rivals in such a way as to avoid the problems of each while retaining their virtues. We can and should acknowledge that some form of self-reference is involved in any conscious mental state. However, conscious mental states are not literally directed back at themselves; nor are they made conscious by entirely distinct HOTs. Conscious mental states (CMS) are complex states with parts such that an unconscious MET is directed at a world-directed M. Any trend in this direction in the recent consciousness literature should be looked upon as a positive one.[35]

Notes

1. Brentano's own view is actually much more elaborate than this. For example, Brentano (1874/1924, bk. 2, chap. 3) actually holds that there are *four* different aspects included in every mental act, including a feeling toward itself. However, for my purposes, these very problematic details are irrelevant and can be safely ignored.

2. Following Rosenthal (e.g., 1990), I use the expression "state consciousness" since I am mainly concerned with consciousness as a property of mental states (as opposed to "creature consciousness"). By "conscious" or "conscious state" I normally have in mind Nagel's (1974) "what it is like" sense.

3. See, for example, Rosenthal 1986, 1990, 1993a,b, 2002, and 2004. I call his HOT theory "extrinsic" in this chapter only to emphasize the fact that his theory regards the HOT *as a distinct state* from its target. Rosenthal (2004, pp. 30–35) himself has spoken of "intrinsic higher-order thoughts" in contrast to his view. I will also not

explicitly address the so-called higher-order perception (HOP) model (see e.g. Lycan 1996), though it is also an extrinsic account and much of what I say in contrast to EHOT theory also applies to HOP theory.

4. I have in mind Uriah Kriegel's cross-order information integration model (2005, and this volume; see also his 2002 and 2003b) and Robert Van Gulick's (2001, 2004) higher-order global states (HOGS) model, though I hasten to add that I owe a great intellectual debt to them for helping me to think more clearly and deeply about my own view.

5. It should be noted that Jean-Paul Sartre is also often cited as holding PSR. In Gennaro 2002, I argue that he held something closer to the WIV, though I did not explicitly address PSR in that paper. I will not address Sartre's view here.

6. This is therefore similar to Kriegel's $SOMT_2$ (this volume), but, as we shall see, I actually hold a view closest to his $SOMT_{10}$. When I say that M and M^* are proper parts of CMS, I mean that they are parts that are not identical with the whole of which they are parts. Thus, for example, M^* cannot be part of itself; nor can the CMS be part of M^*. It might be objected that my definition is circular, or at least nonreductionist, since the term "conscious" appears on each side of the biconditional. However, I do not think that this is case, as I hope will become clear by the end of the essay (especially in section 4). As we shall see, the WIV is still reductionistic because an unconscious M^* (= MET) is what makes an otherwise unconscious M conscious. The definition is also not circular because there is a crucial ambiguity in how the term "conscious" is used. The "conscious M" is meant to refer to the first-person subjective point of view whereas speaking of the whole CMS is based more on third-person considerations. I chose to put M, instead of CMS, on the left side of the biconditional in order to more clearly express the differences among the three definitions (unlike Kriegel's $SOMT_{10}$, which begins with the whole on the left side of the biconditional).

7. This is virtually the same as Kriegel's $SOMT_1$ (this volume).

8. And, unlike Descartes and Brentano, we certainly need not suppose that all mental states are conscious. I also show that Rosenthal mistakenly argues that intrinsicality entails essentiality and that extrinsicality entails contingency (in Gennaro 1996, pp. 21–24).

9. There are, I believe, many other significant advantages to something closer to the WIV. See Kriegel's discussion of the problems of immediacy and relationality (this volume, sections 4 and 5) and Van Gulick's (2004) criticism of standard HO theory's problematic handling of qualia (cf. Gennaro 1996, pp. 29–30, 74–75; 2004b). See also Natsoulas 1992.

10. Kriegel agrees that this is largely a terminological matter, but then still opts to restrict use of "higher order" to those theories that treat the HOT as a distinct state.

Hence, he calls his view "same-order monitoring" (in this volume). However, during a session at the 2004 Toward a Science of Consciousness Conference in Tucson, it also became clear that there are stronger views on this matter. Andrew Brook urged me to jettison all use of "higher order" in my theory whereas Peter Carruthers thought that Kriegel had misnamed his theory. I agree more with Carruthers here, and Van Gulick also clearly has this preference; but, again, I take this mainly to be a terminological dispute. One problem, though, is that the converging similarities between all of these positions might be lost.

11. I have been urged to do so by Andrew Brook and Robert Lurz, in conversations.

12. For example, Dretske's theory seems incapable of providing a principled distinction between unconscious and conscious mental states (see, e.g., Thomasson 2000, pp. 200–202 for some discussion). See also Carruthers 2000, chap. 6 and Lurz 2004 for additional reasons to reject standard FO theory.

13. In retrospect, perhaps I should have chosen a more catchy name for my theory, but, at this point, I am hesitant to add to the abundance of acronyms and theory names already in the literature. Even just "WIT" (wide intrinsicality theory) would at least have been easier to say. Other sexier possibilities are "intrinsic HOT theory" (IHOT) and the more provocative "one-and-a-half-order theory of consciousness" or "split-level theory of consciousness."

14. For what appears to be an intrinsic version of HOP theory, see Lormand (unpublished).

15. For some discussion of Sartre on this matter, see Gennaro 2002, pp. 299–308.

16. David Woodruff Smith (e.g., 2004) is also a good example of someone concerned solely with the structure (or "form") of conscious states at the expense of offering any kind of explanation as such. Of course, I do not claim to have solved any kind of "hard problem" in this chapter, but see Gennaro 2005 for one attempt.

17. It may be useful to distinguish between "momentary focused introspection" and "deliberate introspection" (see Gennaro 1996, pp. 19–21). The former is less sophisticated and only involves a brief conscious MET whereas the latter involves the use of reason and a more sustained inner-directed conscious thinking over time. I mainly have the former in mind throughout this chapter.

18. I should note here that Kriegel (2002a, p. 525) does briefly mention a possible Brentanian account of introspection. However, numerous questions remain regarding how faithful such an account is to Brentano and how it would help to save PSR (hence I leave the question mark in figure 10.1).

Moreover, this and the previous objection to PSR are vividly illustrated in the writings of Hossack (2002, 2003). As an apparent supporter of PSR, Hossack frequently conflates first-order consciousness with introspection. He argues for an "identity thesis," defined as "each state of which one can be conscious is numerically identical with one's *introspective knowledge* of the occurrence of that very state" (2002, p. 163, emphasis added). The problem is that Hossack often seems to have in mind inner-directed conscious focus when speaking of "introspective awareness" and "self-knowledge" (cf. Hossack 2003, pp. 196ff.). Indeed, Hossack (2002, p. 174) goes so far as to hold that the "Identity Thesis says that every experience and every action is a conscious state, identical with knowledge of its own occurrence." Thus, Hossack faces the following dilemma: either such "self-knowledge" of a conscious state is outer-directed or it is inner directed. If the former, then he is not providing an analysis of M as part of an attempt to defend PSR; that is, M^* would not be directed at M anyway. If the latter (as it appears), then he is not only conflating M^* with introspective awareness, but he also clearly cannot justify identifying M^* with conscious state M because M is an outer-directed state.

19. Moreover, Kriegel's subsequent discussion of "three positions" (2003a, pp. 116ff.) does not exhaust the possibilities. As he knows (Kriegel, this volume), a fourth option is to treat M and M^* as proper parts of a complex conscious state, even if we differ about whether or not M^* is itself conscious.

20. One such reason, mentioned in section 3.3, is to explain the transition from first-order conscious states to introspective states. There are also numerous Kantian reasons to hold such a view ranging from the way that concepts are presupposed in experience to the role of episodic memory in consciousness (see Gennaro 1996, especially chaps. 3 and 9).

21. Brook and Raymont (2006) also seem to have something related to the WIV in mind, especially in speaking of the global "representational base" of conscious states. I am also very sympathetic to their Kantian approach. However, it is unclear to me at this time just how similar or different our theories are.

22. To be fair, Kriegel has confirmed for me (in email correspondence) that he does not currently hold PSR as he did at the time of writing his 2003a. However, he does still seem to hold that M^* is itself conscious, which was my main target in the previous section.

23. See, for example, Kriegel this volume (n. 34) and 2005 (n. 24).

24. For more discussion on this point, see Gennaro 1996 (sec. 6.6).

25. It seems to me that, for example, Van Gulick's (2001, 2004) HOGS model is also arguably committed to an unconscious part of a global conscious state. The basic idea behind his "higher-order global states" theory is that "lower-order object states become conscious by being incorporated as components into the higher-order global states (HOGS). . . . The transformation from unconscious to conscious state is not a matter of merely directing a separate and distinct meta-state onto the lower-order state but of 'recruiting' it into the globally integrated state" (2004, pp. 74–75). It is

difficult to understand Van Gulick's frequent use of the expression "implicit meta-intentionality" of HOGS unless we (at least, often) think of it as an unconscious part of a conscious whole. Much like my METs that are implicitly (i.e., unconsciously) intrinsic to the structure of complex conscious states, such metaintentional parts of HOGS would presumably also not be conscious; hence, they are "implicit" and not "explicitly" contained in the structure of conscious experience. Van Gulick normally speaks somewhat neutrally about whether or not the metaintentional parts of his HOGS are conscious or unconscious, such as when he frequently says they are "built into" or "embedded in" the HOGS. This leads me to construe his HOGS as similarly containing an unconscious metapsychological aspect. However, if Van Gulick means to suggest that such metaintentionality is *consciously* part of one's outer-directed phenomenal experience, then I disagree for the same reasons given in the previous section against PSR, and especially against the phenomenological argument (section 3.4). A few passages *might* suggest such an interpretation; for example, "Experience is always the experience *of a self* and *of a world of objects*" (Van Gulick 2004, p. 81). This carries various Kantian considerations, to which I am very sympathetic, a bit too far in my opinion. It is one thing to say that M^* is "built into" or "presupposed in" the structure of conscious experience, but quite another to hold that M^* is itself a conscious part of a conscious state.

26. But see Kriegel 2003b and Carruthers 2000.

27. I am referring to Kriegel (2005), Caston (2002, p. 777, n. 54), and Ken Williford (personal communication, 2003b), but recall also, on the other hand, that some accuse me of really holding some form of FO theory.

28. Thomas Metzinger (1995, p. 454) also alludes to the view that consciousness "is something that unifies or *synthesizes* experience." He calls this process "higher-order binding" (HOB).

29. This distinction also appears similar to Natsoulas's (1996b, 1998) "concomitant" versus "interwoven" terminology in discussing the work of Gurwitsch. Natsoulas (1992, 1993b) calls EHOT theory the "appendage" theory.

30. This point is echoed in Van Gulick's (2001, 2004) discussion of Chris Hill's volume-control hypothesis, whereby introspection is an active process in the sense that it often alters its lower-order mental object. I agree with Van Gulick and Hill here; however, they are clearly discussing introspection only. What is really needed, however, is also the view that unconscious METs (or HOTs) affect the nature of their target states in those cases of first-order conscious states.

31. Also, see section 6.3 in Gennaro 1996 where I discuss Daniel Dennett's case of Chase and Sanborn in light of the WIV.

32. I lack the space here to address Droege's more positive account, which she calls "second sense theory."

33. Recall also (from section 2) that intrinsic theory need not rely solely on such phenomenological evidence to support the notion that consciousness is an intrinsic part of conscious states.

34. See Thomasson 2000, pp. 205–206 for some discussion of this objection.

35. Many thanks to Uriah Kriegel, Robert Lurz, and Kenneth Williford for very helpful comments on an earlier draft of this chapter.

11 | Perceptual Consciousness: How It Opens Directly Onto the World, Preferring the World to the Mind

Christopher S. Hill

I

In this essay I discuss a family of theories of visual experience that can naturally be called *internalist* theories. Very roughly speaking, an internalist theory maintains that the properties we are immediately aware of in visual experience have a significant internal or psychological dimension. Some internalist theories claim that the properties we are immediately aware of are properties of psychological particulars—that is, of the private mental entities that have traditionally been called *sense data*. Others allow that the properties that we are immediately aware of are possessed by external particulars, but they claim that the properties in question nonetheless carry entailments concerning psychological states. (A typical theory of this second kind claims that the properties in question have the form *being an external cause of an occurrence in the visual system with intrinsic property P*.) The central claim of the essay is that internalist theories are wrong. I will present objections to such theories and will also criticize the arguments that have been thought to provide motivation for them.

I will frequently speak in these pages of *visual appearances*. By this I will mean those aspects of visual experience that can be put into words by sentences of the form "*x* looks *F* to *y*." But this explanation is not quite sufficient, for there is reason to think that sentences of this form are ambiguous. Because of this, I need to make a few remarks about how I will understand "looks."

There is a sense of the expression "looks small" that permits it to be applied correctly both to a toy car that is held in the palm of one's hand and to a real SUV that is seen in the distance. One could also apply the expression, in exactly the same sense, to a range of cars of intermediate sizes, provided they were placed at appropriately chosen intermediate distances. I will say that "looks" is being used in its *phenomenological* sense when it is used in a way that enables applications of this sort. It is this phenomenological sense with which I will be primarily concerned.

We also find the phenomenological sense in claims about apparent shape and apparent color. Without changing the sense of "looks trapezoidal," you can apply the expression to a real trapezoid that is perpendicular to your line of sight and also to a rectangular table that you view from one end. Equally, you can apply "looks dark brown" to a piece of chocolate and to a portion of a tan wall that is cloaked in shadow.

It is important to distinguish the phenomenological sense of "looks" from a second sense. Suppose that you are watching an SUV travel along the highway at a distance of a half mile. It is true that the SUV looks small to you, in the phenomenological sense of "looks," but there is also a sense of "looks" in which it is true to say that it does not look small, but rather that it looks SUV-size, or perhaps middle-size. It is true to say that it looks SUV-size because it is true that the SUV looks to you the way SUVs normally look, in respect of size, when they are seen from a distance of half a mile. Equally, when you see a rectangular table from a perspective that makes it appropriate to say that the table looks trapezoidal, in the phenomenological sense, it is also appropriate for you to say, in another sense of "looks," that the table looks rectangular. This is appropriate because the table looks to you the way that rectangular objects normally look, in respect of shape, when they are seen from the perspective in question. Finally, when you see a tan wall that is darkened by shadow, it is appropriate to say that the wall looks dark brown, but it is no less appropriate to say that it looks tan, for it looks the way tan objects normally look when they are poorly illuminated. It is natural to call this second sense of "looks" the *objective* sense because when we say that a particular looks F, in the second sense of "looks," our claim generally carries a commitment to the proposition that if we are not subject to an illusion of some kind, then the particular really is F, or is objectively F.

I can now be more precise about the issues I will be addressing. I will be concerned primarily with internalist theories of visual appearances—that is, with internalist theories of facts that can be described by sentences of the form "x looks F to y," where "looks" is used in the phenomenological sense.

Theories of this sort fall into two main categories. Some of them make a claim about what y is *aware of* when it is true that x looks F to y in the phenomenological sense. Specifically, they claim that in such circumstances y is aware of a property that is at least partially internal in character, in the sense that its instantiation entails the instantiation of one or more purely internal properties. Other theories of the sort in question make a claim about what y's experience *represents* when it is true that x looks F to y in the phenomenological sense. Specifically, they claim that y's experience represents a property that is at least partly internal.

Is there a significant difference between these two types of internalism? From my perspective the answer is "no," for I believe that visual awareness necessarily involves visual representation. Thus, as I see it, theories of the two sorts are largely intertranslatable. There are authors who would challenge this view, but I will proceed in these pages on the assumption that it is correct. (As the reader will I think appreciate, the assumption serves largely to simplify the discussion. Much that I will have to say is independent of it in spirit if not in letter.)

The main body of this essay is organized as follows. Section II is a brief critique of the sense datum theory. Section III presents an objection to what I will call the *causal property theory*—that is, to the theory that x's looking F to y is largely constituted by a property of the form *being an external cause of an occurrence in the visual system with intrinsic property P*. Sections IV, V, and VI are concerned with three lines of thought that are important components of the traditional case for internalist theories of experience. These lines of thought are the argument from illusion, the argument that there is no external property that is present in all cases in which an object looks F to an observer, and therefore no external property that observers could be said to be aware of (or to represent) in such cases, and the inverted spectrum argument. I provide detailed expositions of the arguments and construct what I believe to be decisive objections to them. Finally, section VII spells out the implications of earlier sections for larger issues.

I conclude this introductory section with some remarks about the relevance of the themes of the essay to the main topic of this volume—the question of whether consciousness involves some sort of self-directedness or reflexivity. I will not engage this question directly, but my remarks will nonetheless have a bearing upon it, or, to be precise, a bearing upon one of its dimensions. Thus, there is an internalist theory that implies that perceptual consciousness is characterized by a weak form of reflexivity. The theory I have in mind makes the following claim: Where $R_1, R_2, \ldots, R_n$ are the representations that are constitutively involved in facts of the form x *looks F to y*, each R_i represents the property *being an external cause of an occurrence in the visual system that is a token of the representation R_i*. (As the reader will recognize, this theory is currently enjoying a vogue, largely as a result of the work of Sydney Shoemaker.[1]) Now to say that R_i represents the given causal property does not imply that R_i represents R_i. Accordingly, the present theory does not imply that episodes of perceptual consciousness are reflexive in the sense of implying that an episode of perceptual consciousness involves explicit awareness of a property of that very episode. But it does posit a weaker form of reflexivity. Thus, where e is an episode of perceptual consciousness, it implies that e involves awareness of a property P such that the instantiation of P entails the instantiation of an intrinsic property Q by e. Because of this implication, it seems appropriate to say that the theory maintains that episodes of perceptual consciousness involve an *implicit* awareness of certain of their own properties. My general objection to internalist theories will apply to this theory as a special case, but I will also state an independent objection that applies exclusively to it.

II

According to the sense-datum theory of visual experience, when an external object x looks F to y, y is directly aware of a private mental object that possesses the property F. Awareness of x is indirect: y is aware of x only in virtue of being aware of the mental object. Generally speaking, y's awareness of x is said to be inferential, and more particularly, to be grounded in a tacit ampliative inference from the fact that the given internal object has the property F. (In standard expositions of the theory, it is assumed that the properties answering to "F" are restricted to *sensible characteristics*—that is, to characteristics that can be grasped directly, like color and shape.)

The sense-datum theory is often challenged on general metaphysical grounds. Thus, it is sometimes maintained that it presupposes a form of awareness that cannot be made sense of in physicalist terms, or that sense data themselves are somehow metaphysically problematic. These objections can be avoided, however. Physicalists generally assume that it is possible to explain what is involved in being aware of an external object in physicalistically acceptable terms (and in particular, in terms of representation of the object or causal interaction with the object or both). There is no obvious reason why a similar explanation should not work for awareness of internal objects. Equally, there is no obvious reason why sense data should not be identified with physical phenomena that are products of high level visual processing, and their properties with various intrinsic or informational properties of such phenomena.

The main challenge to the sense-datum theory is not posed by physicalism, but rather by the *transparency* of visual experience. When we examine visual experience introspectively, we do not encounter images of any kind, nor do we encounter anything that could be described as a sensation. In general, nothing presents itself to introspection as an internal, private object or occurrence. It appears to us that we "see through" the experience, or in other words, that the experience provides us with direct access to external objects and their properties. I will refer to this doctrine as the *transparency principle* and will assume that it is correct.[2]

As I see it, the transparency principle leaves advocates of sense data with just one plausible option. They might maintain that the representational contents of visual experiences are concerned with internal objects and their properties, but that we fail to notice this because (a) our conceptual responses to visual experiences employ only concepts that stand for external objects and external properties, and (b) introspection does not provide us with access to the contents of visual experiences, but only with access to the contents of the accompanying conceptual responses. Suppose, for example, that I perceive that the square object in front of me is yellow. It is plausible that my total perceptual state has two components—a visual experience and a belief to the effect that the square object is yellow. An advocate of the sense-datum theory might wish to characterize this case by saying, first, that my visual experience represents an occurrence in my visual system that is downstream from the experience; second, that introspection fails to reveal this representational fact about the experience; and third, that it succeeds in revealing the content of the belief, the proposition that the square object is yellow. In defense of these claims, our advocate might go on to claim that introspection can only provide us with access to the contents of propositional attitudes, perhaps because in generating representations of internal states, it must make use of the contents of the very states that the representations represent. (Suppose introspection produces a belief to the effect that I am in a state with content p. It might be claimed that the content of this belief must include the content of the state to which it refers—namely, the content p. If this claim is correct, then the content p must be conceptually structured, for the contents of beliefs are conceptually structured.)

Now it may well be true that visual experiences have one or more types of content that are not accessible to introspection, but the thesis under consideration at present is much stronger than this claim. The thesis we are considering implies that perceptual experience does not even represent properties like square and yellow. (The thesis maintains that external objects and their properties, such as squareness and yellow, are represented by the beliefs that accompany perceptual experiences, and not by the experiences themselves.) I don't see how this very radical thesis can be correct. In effect, it denies that concepts like the concept of a square and the concept of yellow can inherit their contents from visual experiences. This denial is a serious liability, for there is no other way in which the concepts in question could acquire their contents. Could it be true that they acquire their contents by being equated with descriptions of the form "the property that causes visual experiences of type T"? No. This idea presupposes that our conceptual grasp of visual experiences is prior to our conceptual grasp of external phenomena, and also that we have some way of conceptualizing visual experiences that is independent of their contents. Both of these presuppositions seem false. But more: there is good reason to doubt that we ever go through a stage in which we frame definitions of the given sort for sensory concepts. Certainly we do not do this consciously. And to say that we do so unconsciously is to complicate our picture of the developmental process significantly. In the absence of supporting evidence, such complications are to be avoided.

It appears, then, that the transparency principle poses an insurmountable challenge to the sense-datum theory.

III

I turn now to an internalist doctrine that I call the *causal property theory*. This theory seeks to explain facts of the form x *looks F to y* in terms of facts involving representations of causal properties. More particularly, it claims that if x looks F to y, then y is representing x, at the level of conscious awareness, as causing an occurrence in the visual system that is characterized by the internal or psychological property P, and that x's looking F to y is partially constituted by y's so representing x. In other words, the theory can be understood as claiming that, necessarily, when x looks F to y, y is deploying a person-level representation R such that R has the property *being an external cause of an occurrence in the visual system with intrinsic property P* as its representational content. Advocates of this theory have put forward some very persuasive arguments for it—arguments that we will consider at length in later sections of this essay. I will maintain, however, that the theory is vulnerable to an objection that is quite serious—indeed, serious enough to count as a sufficient reason for setting the theory aside.

I begin with the observation that the property *being an external cause of an occurrence in the visual system with intrinsic property P* (hereafter, *being a cause of an occurrence with P*) can be instantiated in a wide range of contexts—contexts that differ from one another substantially in physical properties and in the laws that govern physical interactions. This is because occurrences in the visual system with P can have an immense variety of causes. Thus, in the situation in which human beings currently find themselves in the actual world, it is the case (we can suppose) that the normal causes of occurrences with P are objects with the color of newly minted stop signs. But it is easy to imagine situations in which the normal causes of occurrences with P are altogether different. It is, for example, easy to imagine a situation in which it is the norm for human brains to be located in vats, and in which the normal causes of occurrences in the visual system are computer states of a certain sort. It is also easy to imagine a situation in which it is the norm for human beings to wear virtual reality glasses all the time, and a situation in which it is the norm for human beings to interact with holographic images rather than real objects. We can summarize these facts by saying that the range of properties that *realize* the property *being a cause of an occurrence with P* is highly heterogeneous.

I will assume that the representational contents of the representations that are involved constitutively in facts of the form *x looks F to y* are determined by biology. More specifically, I will assume that if R is a representation of the sort in question, and X is the property that serves as the content of R, then (i) R indicated X during the period during when the human visual system was being shaped by evolution, and (ii) R was selected to play an enduring role in visual processing *because* it indicated X. The general idea that mental representations can acquire their contents in the way I have specified is familiar, and has been defended at length by Dretske.[3] The more specific claim that the contents of the representations that are involved in facts of the form *x looks F to y* are determined by natural selection is made plausible by several considerations, among which are the fact that the processes that cause the representations in question to be tokened appear to be cognitively impenetrable, and the fact that the representations in question appear to be largely independent of individual learning histories.

I will also assume that if a representation R represents a property X that is not itself a kind, but is rather a property that is multiply and diversely realizable, then it must be the case that the processes that were responsible for the selection of R were shaped by a broadly representative range of the physical properties that are capable of realizing X. That is to say, it must be the case that a broad range of the potentially realizing properties had a causal impact on the visual system during the period when R was selected. The rationale for the principle is just this: if the range of realizing properties that were operative during the period of selection was narrow, then it failed to reflect the full range of X's potential realizers, and there is therefore no reason to say that R was selected because it indicated X. It is more plausible to say that R was selected because it indicated a more narrowly individuated property—a property that corresponds more closely to the realizing properties that were operative. (It might be that the only available property of this sort is the *disjunction* of the physical properties that were actually operative during the period when R was selected. If it be so, then so be it. I will argue later on that it is acceptable to think of visual states as representing disjunctive properties.)

Now as we observed a bit earlier, the property *being a cause of an occurrence with P* is multiply and diversely realizable. Because of this, the principle implies that if R represents this property, then it must be the case that a broadly representative sample of the potential realizers of the property contributed causally to the process that was responsible for the selection of R. We know, however, that there are many potential realizers of *being a cause of an occurrence with P* that made no contribution to that process. Moreover, many of these realizers are altogether foreign, in physical nature, to the realizers that did make a contribution. Thus, for example, in contexts described by the brain-in-a-vat scenarios that are familiar from skeptical arguments, *being a cause of an occurrence with P* is realized by certain computer states. We can be quite confident that no computer states, and no properties that are remotely similar to computer states, contributed causally to the selection of R.

Perhaps it will be useful to restate this argument in somewhat different terms. If a representation was selected by evolutionary processes because it indicated a property X, then it must be true that X's played a causal role in the process. Moreover, it must be true that they played this role *in virtue of being X's*. It follows from this, I claim, that if a representation was selected by evolutionary processes because it indicated a property X, then, unless X is a natural kind, it must be true that a broadly representative sample of the realizers of X played a role in the selection process. (Suppose that X is not a kind, and that its realizers are therefore diverse in intrinsic nature. Then, I claim, it cannot be true that X's contributed to the selection process in virtue of being X's unless it is true that the diversity of X's realizers was reflected in the process.) Now the range of properties that realize *being a cause of an occurrence with P* is highly heterogeneous. Indeed, this is true even of the less inclusive range that contains only the realizers of the property that are nomologically possible, for this range includes, among other things, properties of virtual reality images and properties of holograms. It is clear that many of these realizing properties played absolutely no role in the processes that were responsible for the selection of R, our example of a high-level visual representation. In view of these considerations, it is implausible that R was selected *because* it indicated *being a cause of an occurrence with P* during the relevant period of evolutionary development. Instead of saying that R was selected because it indicated the causal property, we should say that it was selected because it indicated Q—the physical property, or disjunction of physical properties, that realized the causal property during the period in question. But then it must be a mistake to say that R *represents* the causal property. Contrary to what the causal property theory maintains, we should say instead that it represents Q.[4]

It appears, then, that the causal property theory faces a serious difficulty. Before going on to consider other matters, I would like to point out that there is an independent objection to the specific version of the theory that we considered briefly in section I. According to that version, which has been defended persuasively by Sydney Shoemaker, perceptual consciousness involves a kind of implicit awareness of the very representations that serve as its constituents. To be more specific, where $R_1, R_2, \ldots, R_n$ are the representations that are constitutively involved in facts of the form *x looks F to y*, each R_i represents the property *being an external cause of an occurrence in the visual system that is a token of the representation R_i* (hereafter *being a cause of a token of the representation R_i*). It is worth considering this version of the causal property theory separately because of its special relevance to the themes of the present volume, and because the motivation for it is in some ways stronger than the motivation for other versions. (It is this version that receives the strongest support from inverted spectrum arguments.)

My objection to Shoemaker's theory has the following two premises: first, if a representation R represents a property X, then it must be true that R carried information about X during the period when selective forces were endowing R with its representational role; and second, if a representation R carries information about a property X during a period P, then it must be the case that tokens of R are typically caused by instances of X during P, and moreover, it must be the case that instances of X play this causal role in virtue of being instances of X. When these premises are applied to Shoemaker's theory, we obtain the following result: During the period when the representations $R_1, R_2, \ldots, R_n$ were acquiring their representational roles, tokens of each representation R_i were caused by tokens of the corresponding property *being a cause of a token of the representation R_i*, and moreover, were caused by instances of this property in virtue of being instances of the property. We are obliged, I think, to reject this consequence of Shoemaker's theory, and with it, the theory itself. It cannot be right that tokens of R_i were caused by instances of the property *being a cause of a token of the representation R_i* in virtue of the fact that the latter were instances of that property. To say that would be to say, in effect, that tokens of R_i were caused by instances of *being a cause of a token of the* representation R_i in virtue of the fact that the latter were causes of those tokens. Instances of *being a cause of a token of the representation R_i* might have caused tokens of R_i in virtue of having some other property, such as the property of reflecting light of a certain wavelength, but how could they have caused tokens of R_i in virtue of having that very property? Things can't cause things of kind K in virtue of being causes of things of kind K.

This completes my case against the causal property theory.

IV

I turn now to consider positive arguments that have been put forward in defense of internalist theories of visual experience. I cannot hope to examine all arguments of this sort, for there are a great many of them, and the differences among them are in many cases of real theoretical significance. Instead of attempting to canvass the field, I will focus here on three lines of thought that seem to me to form a representative sample.

First up is the argument from illusion. I am going to borrow the version of the argument that A. D. Smith presents in his splendid book, *The Problem of Perception.*[5] Here it is:

Step one "There is no type of physical feature that may not appear differently from the way it really is to any sense that could possibly perceive it" (2002, p. 25).

Step two "[W]henever something perceptually appears to have a feature when it actually does not, we are aware of something that does actually possess that feature" (ibid.).

Step three "[S]ince the appearing physical object does not possess that feature which, according to the previous step, we are immediately aware of the ordinary situation, it is not the physical object of which we are aware in such a situation; or at least, we are not aware of it in the direct way in which we are aware of whatever it is that possesses the appearing feature . . ." (ibid.).

Step four Veridical perceptual situations are subjectively indiscernible from possible illusory situations; "being aware of a sense-datum is *exactly like* perceiving a normal object." Because of this, if it is true that we are aware of sense-data in cases of illusory perception, it must also be true that we are aware of sense-data in cases of veridical perception. In other words, "we are immediately aware of sense-data, and only at best indirectly aware of normal physical objects, in all perceptual situations, veridical as well as illusory" (ibid., p. 26).

Conclusion "[W]e are not directly aware of normal physical objects at all in perception" (ibid., p. 34).

The key step here is the second step. As I understand him, Smith thinks that the step is supported by a best explanation argument. Suppose you are experiencing an illusion to the effect that the wall in front of you is yellow. Here we must ask: *In virtue of what* does the wall appear to you to be yellow? What makes it true that the wall appears to you to be *yellow* rather than green or red? "How does yellow get into the picture?" (ibid., p. 37). We can answer these questions by saying that the wall appears yellow to you because you are aware of something that really is yellow. This explains why something appears yellow to you. Moreover, it explains this fact in an extremely natural way.

Before proceeding to an assessment of Smith's argument, I should note that there is an important difference between the argument and the other arguments for internalism that I will consider in later sections. The present argument is concerned with illusions involving properties like *yellow* and *round*. It endeavors to show that, contrary to common sense, such properties are actually properties of internal, psychological objects. It has implications for questions about visual appearances—that is, for questions about the facts that can be expressed by sentences of the form "*x* looks *F* to *y*," where "looks" is used in the phenomenological sense. It is not, however, concerned with such questions in any direct or explicit way. (It is directly concerned with what it is for an object to be yellow, not with what it is for an object to look yellow.) As we will see, it is quite otherwise with the other two arguments. They are directly concerned with the nature of visual appearances, maintaining that it is necessary to appeal to internal properties in order to analyze appearances successfully.

Smith considers a number of objections to the foregoing argument. One of these, which I will call the *representationalist reply*, begins by denying the second premise. It is simply not true, according the reply, that you are aware of something yellow when you have an illusion to the effect that the wall in front of you is yellow. Nor, in fact, are you aware of *any* actual characteristic of a particular. You are not aware of a characteristic of the wall, and you are not aware of a characteristic of an internal particular of some kind. Rather, what is true is that you *represent* the wall as yellow. To be sure, you are very strongly inclined to think, and to say, that you are aware of yellow in this case, but this inclination is due to the fact that you are deploying exactly the same representation that you deploy in normal cases—that is, in cases in which you are veridically representing an object as yellow. That is to say, it seems to you that you are aware of yellow because you are representing the world in exactly the same way as you do in cases in which you *are* aware of yellow.

Here is Smith's formulation of the representationalist reply: "Can we not account for the sensory character of illusory perceptual consciousness in terms of the 'intentional' presence of sensible qualities to consciousness, as it is sometimes put? The idea is that, when a white wall looks yellow to you, the wall is represented by you, or by your visual experience, as being yellow. So perhaps all we need to say here is that yellow is simply present *as represented*" (ibid., p. 42).

In my view, the representationalist reply is by far the strongest objection to the argument from illusion. Indeed, I see it as unanswerable. Smith does not share this opinion, but he takes the reply seriously, responding to it at some length. The central thesis of his response is that the representationalist reply is unable to account for the sensuous, qualitative nature of visual experience. He writes: "*No* sensory consciousness is explicitly recognized on this approach, and hence is effectively denied. 'Inside' all is 'darkness.' Indeed, most writers in this tradition wind up with the view that there is nothing qualitative in the world at all" (ibid., p. 46). A bit later he repeats this charge, maintaining that representationalism "denies that perception is *ever* sensuous" (ibid., p. 53). Because of this feature of the reply, its explanation of illusions suffers badly in comparison to the explanation based on sense data. The latter explanation "recognizes that illusory and veridical perceptions are sensuous in exactly the same way—a way that involves the *actual* presence of sensuous qualities in experience" (ibid.).

It is Smith's contention, then, that it is impossible for a representationalist account of visual experience to do justice to its qualitative dimension. This is a very strong claim, and, I think, a very implausible one. Perhaps it seems plausible to Smith because he thinks of qualia as internal properties, that is, as intrinsic features of states of perceptual awareness. When qualia are thought of in this way, they are seen as ontologically independent of the contents of perceptual representations, and therefore, as beyond the reach of representationalist theories. In my view, however, this is a very implausible picture of perceptual qualia. Consider what it is like to experience yellow, for example. As far as I can determine, what is qualitative about this experience is experienced as external to the mind. Indeed, the primary qualitative component of the experience is the property yellow, and yellow is experienced as a determination of the surfaces of external objects. Taking this aspect of experience at face value, we are obliged to set aside the view that perceptual qualia are always internal properties. When we do this, it is no longer obvious, or even plausible, that representational theories are unable to explain the distinctive features of qualia.

Let us take a closer look at the doctrine that qualia can be external characteristics. As we have seen, this doctrine has a strong intuitive appeal. In particular, it is quite plausible that yellow is a qualitative characteristic, and it appears quite correct to say that yellow is experienced as fully external. But can we make sense of the idea that yellow is qualitative if we recognize that it is fully external? It seems prima facie that the answer should be "yes." Thus, it seems that what we have in mind when we cite yellow as a qualitative characteristic is just that it is different in kind from quantitative characteristics like length, and also from structural properties like shape. (When people say that yellow is simple and unanalyzable, what they have in mind, it appears, is this apparent difference between yellow and structural characteristics.) And it seems to make sense to contrast yellow with quantitative and structural characteristics while proclaiming its full externality.

Alas, there is a problem with this quick answer: reflection shows that if qualitative characteristics are explained as characteristics that are neither quantitative nor structural, we may be obliged to deny that yellow is qualitative, and more generally, to deny that external characteristics are ever qualitative. Thus, for example, there is reason to believe that it is possible to reduce yellow to a disjunctive external property—specifically, the property of being able to reflect, produce, or transmit light whose spectral composition falls within a certain range. As is easily seen, this view implies that yellow is both quantitative and structural in character. Since similar reductions are in the offing for other alleged examples of the qualitative, the foregoing account of qualitative characteristics has the effect of calling the qualia realism of common sense into question.

To summarize: It is intuitively plausible that insofar as perceptual qualia are characteristics like yellow, they are external to the mind. It is desirable, however, to buttress this view by giving an explanation of what it is about characteristics like yellow that makes them qualitative. At first it seems that it is possible to do this by saying that yellow is neither quantitative nor structural. But science seems to imply that all external characteristics, including yellow, have significant quantitative and structural dimensions.

Fortunately, representationalist theories of color experience liberate us from this dialectic. Thus, any plausible representationalist theory will claim that the representations that are involved in color vision are quite limited in resolution, and are therefore unable to reveal the microstructures of yellow and the other colors. Now it is only at the microstructural level that the quantitative and structural aspects of yellow are in evidence. Accordingly, assuming that we are prepared to embrace representationalism, we can explain what is special about yellow and other qualitative characteristics by saying that they are characteristics whose quantitative and structural dimensions are not registered at the level of perceptual representation. This explanation allows us to continue to distinguish sharply between yellow, on the one hand, and length and shape on the other, while also acknowledging the ultimate metaphysical affinity between yellow and these other characteristics.

It turns out, then, that so far from denying that experience has a qualitative dimension, representational accounts of experience actually help us to understand that dimension and to preserve our realistic intuitions about it. By the same token, we may conclude that the representational reply to the argument from illusion is satisfactory.[6]

V

The second member of my sample of arguments for internalist theories of visual experience is a line of thought that I call the *heterogeneity argument.*

There is no external, physical property, the argument begins, that is common to all cases in which an object looks F to a subject. Nor is there a common "egocentric" relation that objects bear to subjects, such as slant relative to the observer or distance from the observer. Thus, for example, there are a number of quite different conditions under which objects can look small to observers: a toy car that is close at hand can look small, but so can a real car that is located far away. Equally, a piece of chocolate can look dark brown to an observer, but so can a tan wall that is poorly illuminated. In general, the external stimuli answering to facts of the form *x looks F to y* are quite heterogeneous, differing from one another both in intrinsic and in relational properties. It might seem possible to get around this heterogeneity and to identify underlying uniformities by considering more subtle, theoretically motivated properties such as visual angle. But this strategy turns out to be unsuccessful. For instance, it just isn't true that all cases in which an object looks to a subject to have a certain size are cases in which the object subtends a particular visual angle. There are several ways of seeing this, but the simplest is to recall such illusions of size as the moon illusion, the Ponzo illusion, and the corridor illusion. The moon looks much larger when it is close to the horizon than it does when it is directly overhead, but of course it subtends the same visual angle in both cases. In the Ponzo illusion two lines seem to be of different lengths even though they subtend the same visual angle, and so on. Other attempts to specify underlying uniformities in mathematical or scientific terminology are equally unsuccessful (or so the argument claims).

In view of these considerations, the heterogeneity argument continues, we must conclude that there are two and only two properties that are shared by the whole array of objects that look F to a subject. One is a causal property—specifically, our old friend, the property *causing an occurrence with property P*. The other is a disjunctive property—specifically, the disjunctive property D such that (a) each disjunct of D is a conjunction of external, physical properties and relations, and (b) each disjunct of D is one of the nomologically possible conditions that has a strong tendency to produce occurrences in the visual system that have property P. Clearly, the causal property and this disjunctive property are closely related. One similarity is that they are virtually coextensive in the actual world. Another is that they are both intimately related to the internal, psychological property P. (The relationship between the causal property and P is logical: the instantiation of the causal property logically guarantees that P will be instantiated. The relationship between the disjunctive property and P is causal: the instantiation of the disjunctive property contributes causally to the instantiation of P.)

Because the causal property and the disjunctive property are the only properties that are shared universally by objects that look F to subjects, it is necessary, in constructing a representationalist theory of visual appearances, to claim either that the representation R that figures constitutively in x's looking F to y has the casual property as its content, or that R has the disjunctive property as its content. The heterogeneity argument maintains that the former option is vastly preferable to the latter. There are two reasons for this assessment. One is that representation presupposes the existence of laws of nature linking representations to the properties they represent. Disjunctive properties are not the kind of properties that can figure in laws. The other is that all cases in which an object looks F to y are similar to one another, and moreover, similar in respects that are immediately manifest to y. That is to say, what y is aware of when x looks F to y is similar to what y is aware of when some other object z looks F to y. In order to capture this similarity, a theory that seeks to explain visual appearances in terms of the content of representations must, it seems, maintain that the property that serves as the content of the representation that underlies F-appearances is a *natural property* or a *kind*, that is, a property that meets the condition that all of its instances are similar in some respect. Now the property *causing an occurrence with P* seems to meet this condition, for it entails P, and P is assumed to be a natural property, albeit a natural property of occurrences in the visual system. On the other hand, the condition is not satisfied by the foregoing disjunctive property D, for the conjunctions that serve as the individual disjuncts of D have been assumed to be quite different in their intrinsic natures. All that unites the disjuncts of D is their ability to cause an internal occurrence that exemplifies P.

This completes the heterogeneity argument. To summarize, the argument maintains that when we take account of the heterogeneity of the external physical properties that occasion F-appearances, and also of the inability of disjunctive properties to provide the basis for a satisfactory theory of F-appearances, we find that we are obliged to embrace the causal property theory (or a theory that is similar to it in spirit).[7]

Whatever its other merits, I believe that the heterogeneity argument falls down badly in its treatment of the idea that disjunctive properties like D can provide the foundation for a satisfactory theory of visual appearances. I will try to show that its objections to this idea are misguided.

The heterogeneity argument makes two complaints about disjunctive properties. The first of them has two parts: the claim that representation presupposes laws, and the claim that laws are not concerned with disjunctive properties. Both of these doctrines are initially plausible, but when we reflect, we can see, I think, that the first doctrine is too strong. Thus, it is plausible that laws of nature are generalizations that satisfy two conditions: they are nomologically necessary, and they are concerned exclusively with natural properties. Now it is plausible that representation requires connections that are nomologically necessary, for it is plausible that representation requires reliable indication, and reliability seems to require levels of permanence and resistance to disruptive influences that are foreign to accidental connections. But while we are obliged by considerations having to do with reliability to say that the relationship between a representation and the property it represents is nomologically necessary, there appears to be no reason grounded in reliability to require that the latter property be a natural property. By the same token, it seems entirely permissible to take represented properties to disjunctive.

In addition to maintaining that disjunctive properties fail to satisfy a theoretical requirement concerning laws of nature, the heterogeneity argument maintains that disjunctive properties fail to provide a foundation for explaining why all objects that look F to y are experienced by y as similar. If we are to explain why all such objects are experienced as similar, the argument contends, we must suppose that the representation that is constitutively involved in F-appearances stands for a natural property, or in other words, for a kind.

Again we have a claim that is initially plausible, but here too, I think, we can see on reflection that this first impression is wrong. It seems quite possible, after all, for instances of a disjunctive property to be experienced as similar even though they have quite different intrinsic natures. To see why I say this, recall that R is the representation that is constitutively involved in F-appearances, that the property *causing an occurrence with P* is the property that the causal property theory assigns to R as its content, and that D is the disjunctive property that meets the conditions that its individual disjuncts are conjunctions of external, physical properties, and that each disjunct has a strong tendency to produce P. Further, suppose that, contrary to what the casual theory claims, R actually represents D. Finally, suppose (a) that R is tokened on two occasions when D is instantiated, (b) that on the first of these occasions D is instantiated because a certain one of its disjuncts, D^*, is instantiated, and (c) that on the second occasion D is instantiated because a certain different one of its disjuncts, D^{**}, is instantiated. Here it seems natural to say that the observer y experiences the instance of D^* and the instance of D^{**} as similar. After all, y is in exactly the same representational state when y is confronted by the instance of D^* as when y is confronted by the instance of D^{**}. It follows from this that y will be unable to discriminate between them. Surely if y is unable to discriminate between an instance of D^* and an instance of D^{**}, it is true to say that y experiences them as similar.

Here is a slightly different way of putting the point: Suppose that w and z both look F to y, and that it is therefore true that the representation y deploys in representing w has the same form and the same content as the representation that y deploys in representing z. It follows from this assumption that from y's perspective, w and z are classified perceptually in exactly the same way, at least in the respect of comparison that is invoked by the expression "looks F." But if w and z are classified perceptually in exactly the same way, then it must be the case that y experiences them as similar.

As I see it, the plausibility of the heterogeneity argument is due mainly to a tendency to confuse being aware of two items as similar with experiencing two items as similar. Since awareness is factive, it is impossible to be aware of two items as similar unless they really are similar. Further, it is impossible for two items to count as similar unless they share a natural property. It follows that being aware of two items as similar entails that there is a natural property that they share. On the other hand, as I see it anyway, it is possible to experience two items as similar even if they are not objectively similar, and therefore, even if there is no natural property that they have in common. To experience items as similar it is sufficient that they *seem* similar, and for them to seem similar it is sufficient that one's experience fails to provide one with grounds for distinguishing between them. It follows that two items will seem similar when the representation that enables experience of one is the same in form and content as the representation that enables experience of the other.

Let us agree to say that the *disjunctive property theory* of visual appearances is the view that the content of the representation R that is constitutively involved in x's looking F to y is the disjunctive property D, and that the contents of other representations of the same sort as R are disjunctive properties like D. Then it is possible to summarize our recent reflections by saying that the heterogeneity argument fails to establish that the casual property theory is superior to the disjunctive property theory.

VI

The third argument for internalism that I will consider is a version of the inverted spectrum argument—more specifically, a version that is borrowed, with modifications, from Ned Block's wonderful paper "Inverted Earth."[8] Block invites us to conceive of a planet that is similar to Earth in many respects, but on which all objective colors are inverted with respect to colors on Earth. Thus, on this imaginary planet, Inverted Earth, fire engines are green, grass is red, lemons are blue, and the sky is yellow. Suppose that Inverted Earth is inhabited by creatures who are much like ourselves, but who have evolved in such a way that the lenses of their eyes invert the wavelengths of the light waves that pass through them, converting red light into green light, green light into red light, and so on. Because of this assumption about the lenses of our imaginary creatures, it is natural to suppose that red objects look green to them, that green objects look red, and in general, that objects that are C look C^* to them, where C^* is the color that is complementary to C. After all, when an inhabitant of Inverted Earth perceives a green object, the most proximal stimulus, the light arriving at the inhabitant's retinas, is the same as the most proximal stimulus associated with perceiving red objects on Earth. Moreover, as a result of this identity of proximal stimuli, the brain processes involved in seeing a green object on Inverted Earth is the same as the brain process associated with seeing a red object on Earth. Now let us ask: What are the objective physical colors that color experiences on Inverted Earth represent objects as possessing? When an inhabitant of Inverted Earth sees a green object, the object looks red to him. But does the inhabitant's color experience represent the object as red? No. It is meant to be part of our general picture of life on Inverted Earth that the color experiences that inhabitants enjoy when they see green objects are of a type T such that T was selected by evolutionary forces because it covaries with green. Accordingly, it is natural to suppose that experiences of type T represent green on Inverted Earth. To summarize, when an inhabitant of Inverted Earth sees a green object, the object looks red to him, but his experience represents the object as being objectively green, and therefore, as having the objective color that the object really does have.

We have assumed, in effect, that if E is an Earthling and IE is the counterpart of E on Inverted Earth, then the brain process that occurs in E when E looks at a red object is the same as the brain process that occurs in IE when IE looks at a green object. Let us now make the further assumption that R is the representation that is constitutively involved in facts of the form x *looks red to* y on Inverted Earth. Finally, let us assume that R is also the representation that is constitutively involved in facts of the form x *looks red to* y on Earth. (This last assumption is really forced upon us by the first two, given the plausible principle that visual representations, considered as formal, syntactic objects, supervene on brain processes.)

Now let us ask: What is the content of R? Our assumptions commit us to saying that R has the same content on Earth and Inverted Earth, for R is constitutively involved in facts of the form x *looks red to* y in both places, and it is one of our general background assumptions that how things look to observers depends on the contents of the relevant representations. Can we take the content to be an external physical property? No. By assumption, there is no external physical property that is instantiated when something looks red to E and also when something looks red to IE. Can we say that the content of R is a disjunction of external physical properties? What disjunction would that be? Surely not the disjunction of red and green. If the content of R was the disjunction of red and green, then both red objects and green objects would look red to E, and both red objects and green objects would look green to IE. In fact, however, only red objects look red to E, and only green objects look red to IE. It seems, then, that we must suppose that the content of R is at least partially internal in character. No doubt it is the causal property *causing an occurrence with P*.

This argument stands or falls with the intuition that the way green objects look to observers on Inverted Earth is the same as the way red objects look to observers on Earth. Call this the *uniformity intuition*. I acknowledge the force of this intuition, but at the same time, I think that we cannot allow it to influence the shape of theories of visual appearances. I say this because the intuition clearly belongs to the same family as the intuition that a computer state might look red to a brain in a vat, provided that the brain was designed to respond to the computer state by deploying the same representation R that we deploy when we see a red object. It also belongs to the same family as the intuition that a being of the sort described by Prospero, a being whose whole life was but a dream, could have color experiences of the same sort as the ones that we enjoy, provided only that it was equipped with R and other representations of the same sort. These intuitions all seem to have the same source, namely, the perception that color appearances are determined exhaustively by the *form* of color representations, or, in other words, by the perception that color appearances are the same whenever the relevant portions of the brain are in the same state. Call this the *supervenience perception*. I do not think that we can trust the uniformity intuition because I do not think that we can trust the supervenience perception.

If we were to seek a theory that honors the supervenience perception in its full generality, we would not wind up with the causal property theory, but rather with the theory that representations like R stand for purely internal properties of occurrences in the visual system. It is just a small step from this theory to the sense datum theory. Indeed, reflection shows that they are the same theory. But the sense datum theory is refuted by the transparency principle.

It is uncomfortable, however, to reject a perception without having an explanation of it that in some sense deflates it or undercuts its claim on our acceptance. Is there an explanation of this sort in the present case?

Reflection suggests that the supervenience perception has two main sources, and that neither source is such as to inspire confidence in its product.

First, it seems likely that color appearances, and appearances generally, strike us as determined by internal factors because we can learn about them by introspection, and because our introspective access to them seems to provide us with authoritative beliefs about them, beliefs that cannot easily be challenged by appealing to facts about external states of affairs. If our cognitive access to an item is internal, and that access is of very high quality, then there is reason to suppose that the item has an internal nature. (If I am inclined to judge that there is something that looks F to me, you can challenge this judgment by maintaining that it is hallucinatory, but this challenge will not call into question the corresponding judgment that I am "being appeared F to.")

Although this line of thought has considerable prima facie appeal, it is undercut by the contemporary literature on self-knowledge. Beginning with a paper by Tyler Burge in 1988, there have been many contributions to this literature that present models of how it might be possible to gain knowledge of externally individuated states by introspection.[9] It seems reasonable to say that these books and papers have converged on the view that introspective reports of externally individuated states can do full justice to the nature of those states, and can be fully confirmed by them, as long as they are themselves externally individuated—or, to be precise, as long as they have contents that partially or wholly coincide with the contents of the states that they report. In particular, it seems to be widely accepted that an introspective belief can capture the essence of a visual experience with the content p provided that the belief has the content: I am having a perceptual experience as of p.

It seems likely that the supervenience perception is also due, in part, to certain intuitions concerning possible contexts of color appearances. I am now having a visual experience as of red. Focusing on the experience, it seems that I can coherently insert it, or at least insert experiences that are of exactly the same type, into imaginary contexts that are quite different from the actual context. Thus, I can coherently imagine an experience of the same sort occurring in a context in which I am looking at a green object rather than a red one. Further, I can imagine a situation in which such experiences normally occur when observers are looking at green objects, and in which they are selected by evolutionary processes because they covary with the presence of green objects in this way. Still further, I can imagine a situation in which such experiences occur only when a brain in a vat is stimulated by a certain type of computer state. Or so it seems. Moreover, here as elsewhere, it is tempting to suppose that what I can coherently imagine is genuinely possible. But to say that the scenarios are genuinely possible is just another way of giving expression to the supervenience principle.

As I see it, the right way to respond to this line of thought is to remind oneself of Thomas Nagel's distinction between the sympathetic imagination and the perceptual imagination.[10] According to Nagel, we use the former to imagine experiences and the latter to imagine external, physical circumstances. When I use the sympathetic imagination to imagine an experience, I do so by putting myself in an experiential state of roughly the same sort as the state that I am imagining. (Perhaps the state I put myself into could be called a "faint version" of the state I am imagining.) And when I use the perceptual imagination to imagine a physical circumstance of type P, I do so by putting myself in a state of roughly the same sort as the state I would be in if I was perceiving a circumstance of type P. Since these two types of imagination are independent of one another, it is possible to combine their deliverances ad libitum without creating any incoherence. But for just this reason, complex states of imagination that combine deliverances of the sympathetic and the perceptual imagination are untrustworthy guides to possibility. After all, we know that many combinations of experiences with physical circumstances are impossible. For example, it is impossible to consciously entertain the proposition that Nixon was a scoundrel unless one stands in an appropriate causal/informational relationship to Nixon. (Nagel originally developed his distinction between the sympathetic and the perceptual imagination with a view to refuting Cartesian modal arguments for property dualism. I am maintaining now that it applies with equal force to lines of thought that seek to sever the metaphysical bonds between various types of appearance and their normal environmental correlates.)

VII

Advocates of indirect realism have traditionally relied quite heavily on considerations having to do with visual appearances in articulating and defending their position. I have tried to show that these efforts have been unsuccessful. Indirect realism is committed to internalism, and internalism is called into question by powerful objections. I have also maintained that the arguments that have been thought to motivate indirect realism are misguided.

To restate these points in positive terms, the forgoing reflections make a case for the superiority of direct realism over indirect realism. I hasten to emphasize, however, that they fall far short of making a positive case for direct realism. In order to make a positive case, it would be necessary, among other things, to provide a systematic externalist account of the contents of the representations that are involved in facts of the form x *looks F to y*. In my judgment, an account of this sort lies beyond our reach at present, and will remain beyond our reach until vision science has achieved progress along several fronts. Instead of arguing constructively for direct realism by presenting a developed version of the doctrine, I have argued for it nonconstructively, by urging that alternative positions do not work.

In addition to providing support for direct realism, the foregoing reflections also have some tendency to undercut those positions in the philosophy of mind that assert that we have direct access to an internal realm of perceptual qualia. The qualia in question are generally taken to be constitutively involved in facts of the form x *looks F to y*. As against this view, I have maintained that it is possible to understand the internal, psychological components of such facts as representational states that have external properties as their contents. Further, although I have not made any specific claims about what exactly those external properties might be, I have urged that if it should prove impossible to identify them with physical kinds, or with conjunctions of physical kinds, we can avail ourselves of the option of viewing them as disjunctive physical properties. Still further, I have maintained that to a large extent, our sense that perception involves qualia is due to the fact that certain of the external characteristics that we encounter in perception seem to have a qualitative nature. Colors are prime examples of characteristics of this kind. Thus, for example, yellow seems to be qualitative because it contrasts both with quantitative characteristics like mass and length and with structural characteristics like shape and material composition. Finally, I have tried to explain the metaphysical basis of such contrasts by locating it in the fact that perceptual representations of yellow do not put us in touch with its quantitative and structural dimensions.

Expressed in positive terms, the moral of the story is that there is reason to be optimistic about the prospects of theories of perceptual qualia that combine representationalist and externalist elements.[11]

Notes

1. See Sydney Shoemaker 1996 ch. 12 and Shoemaker 2000.

2. This principle derives ultimately from G. E. Moore, but it was brought to the forefront of contemporary discussions of perceptual consciousness by Gilbert Harman's brilliant (1990) essay.

3. See, for example, Dretske 1995a. There are of course alternatives to Dretske's theory of mental representation. (See, for example, Millikan 1989.) I will make no attempt in the present essay to show that Dretske's theory is preferable to its competitors. There is no need to do so, for the objection I will present is independent of the details of Dretske's theory. All I need, strictly speaking, is a theoretical framework in terms of which there is a plausible development of the idea that the contents of appearance-level visual representations are determined by natural selection.

4. Notice that it would not help to say that what is represented by R is the property *being a normal external cause of an occurrence with P*. As it stands, this suggestion is not coherent: since "normal" is an indexical expression, the expression "being a normal cause of an occurrence with P" cannot be said to have a property as its semantic value. Rather it determines a character, in Kaplan's sense. Thus, we must understand the suggestion to mean that R represents the property that is *in fact* the normal external cause of occurrences with P. But that property will be the possibly disjunctive property that realizes the property *being an external cause of an occurrence with P* in the situations in which human beings most frequently find themselves in the actual world. That is, it will be a physical property or a disjunction of physical properties, not a causal property.

Would it help to say that what is represented by R is the property *being an external cause of an occurrence with P that produces the occurrence via a causal chain of such and such a nature*? (Here "such and such a nature" abbreviates a detailed specification, in physical vocabulary, of the causal chain that mediates between the external cause and the occurrence with P.) No. This proposal has the bizarre consequence that R represents the specific physical factors that are involved in the transmission of information about external objects, but does not represent any physical circumstance involving external objects themselves. If visual representations have the ability to represent physical properties of mediating causal chains, why don't they have the ability to represent physical properties of the initial links of those chains? Anyway, the proposal conflicts with what vision science tells us about higher-level visual representation. The visual system has the job of providing us with information about the world, not the job of providing us with information about the processes by which information about the world is transmitted.

5. Smith 2002.

6. Smith appears to have a reservation about the representationalist reply to the argument from illusion that is not addressed in the text. Thus, he seems to hold that a representationalist theory of vision must maintain that the representational system that is used by the visual faculty is entirely conceptual in character (see p. 46). This view seems quite false to me. Indeed, there are good reasons to suppose that the visual faculty employs a system of representation that is completely different from the system of conceptual representation. Several of these reasons are presented in Hill 2004.

7. I do not know of any arguments in the literature that correspond exactly in structure and generality to the heterogeneity argument as I have presented it here. It is, however, closely related to the many arguments that purport to establish that there are no objective similarities corresponding the similarities we experience when we perceive colors. Thus, for example, it is frequently maintained that, due to metamerism and other factors, there is no objective property that is shared by all objects that look red to us.

8. Block 1990.

9. Burge 1988.

10. Nagel 1974. The distinction is presented in note 11 of that paper. Nagel's ideas are developed at greater length in Hill 1997.

11. I thank the people who attended my seminars at Brown and MIT in the fall of 2003, and also Susanna Siegel, for invaluable discussions of the themes of the present essay. In addition, I thank Uriah Kriegel and Sydney Shoemaker for their outstandingly helpful comments on earlier drafts.

Thinking about (Self-)Consciousness: Phenomenological
Perspectives

Dan Zahavi

In the following contribution, I will outline and discuss some central elements in the phenomenological account of consciousness. Generally, one should not overestimate the homogeneity of the phenomenological tradition—a tradition inaugurated by Husserl (1859–1938), and comprising among its most well-known champions philosophers like Scheler, Heidegger, Schutz, Gurwitsch, Fink, Merleau-Ponty, Sartre, Levinas, Ricoeur, and Henry. Like any other tradition, it spans many differences. When it comes to the question concerning the relation between consciousness and self-consciousness, however, one will find a case of widespread agreement. Literally all of the major figures defend the view that the experiential dimension of consciousness is as such characterized by a tacit self-consciousness.

1 Consciousness and Prereflective Self-Consciousness

In *Erste Philosophie II* Husserl writes that the experiential stream is characterized by a "Für-sich-selbst-erscheinens," that is, by a self-appearance or self-manifestation (Husserl 1959, pp. 189, 412), and throughout his writings he explicitly argues that self-consciousness, rather than being something that only occurs during exceptional circumstances, namely whenever we pay attention to our conscious life, is a feature characterizing subjectivity as such, no matter what worldly entities the subject might otherwise be conscious of and occupied with. As he for instance puts it in *Zur Phänomenologie der Intersubjektivität II*, "To be a subject is to be in the mode of being aware of oneself" (Husserl 1973a, p. 151).

We find very similar ideas in Heidegger. Heidegger argues that the self is present and implicated in all its intentional comportments. Thus, the intentional directedness toward . . . is not to be understood as an intentional experience that only gains a reference to the self afterwards, as if the self would have to turn its attention back upon the first experience with the help of a subsequent second (reflective) experience. Rather, the codisclosure of the self belongs to intentionality as such (Heidegger 1989, p. 225; 2001, p. 208). As Heidegger writes, every worldly experiencing involves a certain component of self-acquaintance and self-familiarity, every experiencing is characterized by the fact that "I am always somehow acquainted with myself" (Heidegger 1993a, p. 251), or as he puts it in the lecture course *Einleitung in die Philosophie* from 1928–1929—this time adopting a more traditional terminology—"Every consciousness is also self-consciousness" (Heidegger 2001, p. 135).

As for Sartre, who is probably the best-known representative of a phenomenological approach to self-consciousness, he takes consciousness to be essentially characterized by intentionality. He also claims, however, that each and every intentional experience is characterized by self-consciousness. Thus, Sartre takes self-consciousness to constitute a necessary condition for being conscious of something. To consciously perceive a signpost, an ice cream, or a comfortable chair without being aware of it, that is, without having access to or being acquainted with the experience in question is for Sartre a manifest absurdity (Sartre 1943/1976, pp. 18, 20, 28; 1948, p. 62). This line of thought is elaborated in the important introduction to *L'être et le néant*, where Sartre claims that an ontological analysis of intentionality leads to self-consciousness since the *mode of being* of intentional consciousness is to be *for-itself* (*pour-soi*), that is, self-conscious. An experience does not simply exist, it exists for itself, that is, it is given for itself, and this self-givenness is not simply a quality added to the experience, a mere varnish, but on the contrary constitutes the very mode of being of the experience. As Sartre writes: "This self-consciousness we ought to consider not as a new consciousness, but as *the only mode of existence which is possible for a consciousness of something*" (Sartre 1943/1976, p. 20 [1956, p. liv]).

These claims should not be misunderstood. None of the phenomenologists are advocating strong theses concerning total and infallible self-knowledge; rather they are simply calling attention to the intimate link between experiential phenomena and first-personal givenness in much the same way as Nagel and Searle have later done.

Using present-day terminology, the phenomenological line of thought can be construed as follows: Self-consciousness is not merely something that comes about the moment one scrutinizes one's experiences attentively (let alone something that only comes about the moment one recognizes one's own mirror image, or becomes an object to oneself by virtue of one's social relations to others, or refers to oneself using the first-person pronoun, or constructs a theory about the cause of one's own behavior, a theory that postulates the existence of mental states). Rather, self-consciousness comes in many forms and degrees. It makes perfect sense to speak of self-consciousness as soon as I am not simply conscious of an external object—a chair, a chestnut tree, or a rising sun—but acquainted with the experience of the object as well, for in such a case my consciousness reveals itself to me. Thus, the basic distinction to be made is the distinction between the case where an object is given (object-consciousness) and the case where consciousness itself is given (self-consciousness). In its most primitive (and fundamental) form, self-consciousness is taken to be a question of having first-personal access to one's own consciousness; it is a question of the first-personal givenness or manifestation of experiential life. Most people are prepared to concede that there is necessarily something "it is like" for a subject to undergo a conscious experience (to taste ice cream, to feel joy, to remember a walk in the Alps). But insofar as there is something it is like for the subject to have the experience, the subject must in some way have access to and be acquainted with the experience. Moreover, although conscious experiences differ from one another—what it is like to smell crushed mint leaves is different from what it is like to see a sunset or to hear Lalo's *Symphonie Espagnole*—they also share certain features. One commonality is the quality of *mineness*, the fact that the experiences are characterized by first-personal givenness. That is, the experience is given (at least tacitly) as *my* experience, as an experience *I* am undergoing or living through. All of this suggests that first-personal experience presents me with an immediate access to myself, and that (phenomenal) consciousness entails a (minimal) form of self-consciousness. To put it differently, self-consciousness might be seen as a necessary condition for phenomenal consciousness. Unless a mental process is self-conscious there will be nothing it is like to undergo the process, and it therefore cannot be a phenomenally conscious process.

In analytical philosophy of mind, a similar view has recently been defended by Flanagan, who not only argues that consciousness involves self-consciousness in the weak sense that there is something it is like for the subject to have the experience, but who also speaks of the low-level self-consciousness involved in experiencing my experiences as mine (Flanagan 1992, p. 194).[1] As Flanagan quite correctly points out, this innate type of self-consciousness should not be confused with the much stronger notion of self-consciousness that is in play when we are thinking about our own narrative identity. This type of self-consciousness requires maturation and socialization, and the ability to access and issue reports about the states, traits, and dispositions that make one the person one is.

On closer inspection, the claim that there is a close link between consciousness and self-consciousness turns out to be considerably less exceptional than
might at first be expected. In fact, it might be argued that such a claim is
part of current orthodoxy since higher-order theories of consciousness typically take the difference between conscious and nonconscious mental states
to rest upon the presence or absence of a relevant meta-mental state (see
Armstrong 1968; Lycan 1987; Carruthers 1996). To put it differently (intransitive) consciousness has frequently been taken to be a question of the mind
directing its intentional aim at its own states and operations. As Carruthers
puts it, the subjective feel of experience presupposes a capacity for higher-
order awareness, and as he then continues, "such self-awareness is a conceptually necessary condition for an organism to be a subject of phenomenal
feelings, or for there to be anything that its experiences are like" (Carruthers
1996, p. 152).

But one might share the view that there is a close link between consciousness and self-consciousness and still disagree about the nature of the link. And
although the phenomenological take might superficially resemble the view of
the higher-order theories, we are ultimately confronted with two radically
divergent accounts. In contrast to the higher-order theories, the phenomenologists explicitly deny that the self-consciousness that is present the moment I
consciously experience something is to be understood in terms of some kind
of reflection, or introspection, or higher-order monitoring. It does not involve
an additional mental state, but is rather to be understood as an intrinsic
feature of the primary experience. That is, in contrast to the higher-order
account of consciousness that claims that consciousness is an extrinsic property of those mental states that have it, a property bestowed upon them from
without by some further states, the phenomenologists would typically argue
that the feature in virtue of which a mental state is conscious is located within
the state itself; it is an intrinsic property of those mental states that have it.
Moreover, the phenomenologists also reject the attempt to construe intransitive consciousness in terms of transitive consciousness, that is, they reject the
view that a conscious state is a state we are conscious *of*. To put it differently,
not only do they reject the view that a mental state becomes conscious by
being taken as an object by a higher-order state, they also reject the view—
generally associated with Brentano[2]—according to which a mental state
becomes conscious by taking itself as an object.[3]

Let us take a closer look at some of the textual evidence in support of this
interpretation, and this time start with Sartre. In the central quote from *L'être
et le néant* given above, Sartre emphasizes quite explicitly that the self-
consciousness in question is *not* a new consciousness (Sartre 1943/1976,

p. 20). It is not something added to the experience, it is not an additional mental state, but rather an intrinsic feature of the experience. Thus, when he speaks of self-consciousness as a permanent feature of consciousness, Sartre is not referring to what he calls reflective self-consciousness. Reflection (or to use the more current name "higher-order representation") is the process whereby consciousness directs its intentional aim at itself, thereby taking itself as its own object. But according to Sartre, this type of self-consciousness is derived. It involves a subject-object split, and the attempt to account for *self*-consciousness in such terms is for Sartre bound to fail. It either generates an infinite regress or accepts a nonconscious starting point, and he considers both of these options to be unacceptable (Sartre 1943/1976, p. 19).

Sartre readily admits the existence of reflective self-consciousness. We can for instance reflect upon—and thereby become thematically conscious of—an occurrent perception of a Swiss Army knife. In reflection we can distinguish the reflecting experience and the experience reflected-on. The first takes the latter as its object. But for Sartre the experience reflected-on was already self-conscious prior to reflection, and the self-consciousness in question is of a nonreflective and nonpositional kind, that is, it does not have a reflective structure, and it does not posit that which it is aware of as an object (Sartre 1936, pp. 28–29).[4] As Sartre writes: "[T]here is no infinite regress here, since a consciousness has no need at all of a reflecting consciousness in order to be conscious of itself. It simply does not posit itself as an object" (Sartre 1936, p. 29 [1957, p. 45]). Thus, Sartre speaks of prereflective self-consciousness as an immediate and noncognitive "relation" of the self to itself. If I am engaged in some conscious activity, such as the reading of a story, my attention is neither on myself nor on my activity of reading, but on the story. But if my reading is interrupted by someone asking me what I am doing, I reply immediately that I am (and have for some time been) reading; and the self-consciousness on the basis of which I answer the question is not something acquired at just that moment but a consciousness of myself that has been present to me all along.

Thus reflection has no kind of primacy over the consciousness reflected-on. It is not reflection which reveals the consciousness reflected-on to itself. Quite the contrary, it is the non-reflective consciousness which renders the reflection possible; there is a pre-reflective cogito which is the condition of the Cartesian cogito. (Sartre 1943/1976, pp. 19–20 [1956, p. liii])

To put it differently, self-consciousness has two different modes of existence, a prereflective and a reflective. The first has priority since it can obtain independently of the latter, whereas reflective self-consciousness always pre-supposes prereflective self-consciousness. So to repeat, for Sartre prereflective self-consciousness is not an addendum to, but a constitutive moment of the original intentional experience. The experience is conscious of itself at the time of its occurrence. If I consciously see, remember, know, think, hope, feel, or will something I am *eo ipso* aware of it.

When Sartre says that every positional consciousness of an object is simul-taneously a nonpositional consciousness of itself, it is essential to emphasize that this prereflective self-consciousness is not to be understood as an inten-tional, objectifying, or epistemic stance, and consequently neither to be interpreted as some kind of inner perception, nor more generally as a type of knowledge (Sartre 1936, pp. 23–24, 66; 1943, p. 19). This implies that the self-consciousness in question might very well be accompanied by a fundamental *lack of knowledge*. Although I cannot be unconscious of my present experience, I might very well ignore it in favor of its object, and this is of course the natural attitude. In my daily life I am absorbed by and pre-occupied with projects and objects in the world. Thus, pervasive prereflective self-consciousness is definitely not identical with total self-comprehension, but can rather be likened to a precomprehension that allows for a subsequent reflection and thematization.

Siewert has recently criticized Sartre's account and has argued that since Sartre is on the one hand claiming that all consciousness is consciousness of itself and on the other hand denying that this ubiquitous self-consciousness is reflective, thetic, positional, epistemic, and objectifying, his account is inconsistent, confused, extremely misleading, and totally unclear (Siewert 1998, p. 360). Is this rather harsh judgment justified? I think not. As Sartre himself points out, it is only the necessity of syntax that has compelled him to write that we are prereflectively aware *of* our experiences and that there is a prereflective consciousness *of* self. (In French, the term for self-consciousness—*conscience de soi*—literally means consciousness of self). Sartre readily admits that the use of the "of" (or "de") is unfortunate since it suggests that self-consciousness is simply a subtype of object-consciousness, as if the manner in which we are aware *of* ourselves is struc-turally comparable with the manner in which we are aware *of* apples and clouds. We cannot avoid the "of," but in order to show that it is merely there in order to satisfy a grammatical requirement, Sartre places it inside parentheses, and frequently speaks of a "conscience (de) soi" and of a "con-science (de) plaisir," and so forth (Sartre 1943/1976, p. 22; 1948, p. 62). Thus, Sartre is quite keen to avoid any phrasing that might misleadingly suggest that in order to have conscious mental states we must be aware of them as objects.[5]

As already indicated this view is shared by most of the other phenomenologists. In the beginning of the first edition of *Logische Untersuchungen* (1900–1901) we find Husserl arguing that our sensations are originally simply lived through as moments of the experience, they are according to him not objectified and taken as objects. That only happens in a subsequent psychological reflection (Husserl 1984b, p. 80). This assertion is then followed up in the Second Investigation, where we find the following very significant remark: "That an appropriate train of sensations or images is *experienced*, and is in this sense conscious, does not and cannot mean that this is the *object* of an act of consciousness, in the sense that a perception, a presentation or a judgment is directed upon it" (Husserl 1984b, p. 165).

Obviously, the central term is "conscious." Husserl is denying that our sensations are a phenomenological naught. On the contrary, they are conscious, that is, experientially given, when they are lived through, and as he points out this givenness does not come about as the result of an objectification, it does not come about because the sensations are taken as objects by an (internal) perception. The sensations are given, not as objects, but precisely as subjective experiences. The very same line of thought can be found in the Fifth Investigation. There Husserl writes that the intentional experiences themselves are lived through and experienced (*erlebt*), but he denies that they appear in an objectified manner, they are neither seen nor heard. They are conscious without being intentional objects (Husserl 1984b, p. 399). This is not to deny that we can in fact direct our attention toward our experiences, and thereby take them as objects of an inner perception. But that only occurs the moment we reflect (Husserl 1984b, p. 424).

Husserl's stance is consequently unequivocal. He does not believe that our experiences are conscious by being taken as *objects*. As he explicitly states in the Sixth Investigation: "To be experienced is not to be made objective [Erlebtsein ist nicht Gegenständlichsein]" (Husserl 1984b, p. 669). Elsewhere, Husserl operates with a distinction between perceiving (*Wahrnehmen*) and experiencing (*Erleben*): prior to reflection one perceives the perceptual object, but one experiences (*erlebt*) the perception. Although I am not intentionally directed toward the perception (this only happens in the subsequent reflection, where the perception is thematized), the perception is not nonconscious but conscious, that is, prereflectively given.[6]

If we finally turn to Heidegger, we will, in the early lecture course *Grundprobleme der Phänomenologie* from 1919–1920, find him arguing that one of the tasks of phenomenology is to disclose the nonobjectifying and nontheoretical self-understanding that belongs to experience as such (Heidegger 1993a, pp. 155–157). Thus, Heidegger clearly acknowledges the existence of a prereflective self-acquaintance that is part and parcel of experience. And as he repeatedly emphasizes, this basic familiarity with oneself does not take the form of a reflective self-perception or a thematic self-observation, nor does it involve any kind of self-objectification. On the contrary, we are confronted with a process of lived self-acquaintance whose distinctive feature is its nonreflective character, and which must be understood as an immediate expression of life itself (Heidegger 1993a, pp. 159, 165, 257–258). In a lecture course given seven years later, Heidegger pursues the same line of thought and writes:

Dasein,[7] as existing, is there for itself, even when the ego does not expressly direct itself to itself in the manner of its own peculiar turning around and turning back, which in phenomenology is called inner perception as contrasted with outer. The self is there for the Dasein itself without reflection and without inner perception, *before* all reflection. Reflection, in the sense of a turning back, is only a mode of self-*apprehension*, but not the mode of primary self-disclosure. (Heidegger 1989, p. 226 [1982, p. 159])[8]

To summarize, Husserl, Heidegger, and Sartre all defend what might be called a one-level account of consciousness. That is, not only do they argue that consciousness and self-consciousness are closely linked, but they also categorically reject the idea that (intransitive) consciousness should be accounted for by means of a process of reflection or higher-order representation. Moreover—and this might be of surprise to those who thought that one of the central doctrines in phenomenology is the doctrine of intentionality, that is, the claim that all consciousness is intentional, that all consciousness is object-consciousness—they also explicitly deny that the weak self-consciousness entailed by phenomenal consciousness is intentionally structured, is a question of a subject–object relation. In their view, when one is prereflectively self-conscious one is not aware of oneself as an object that happens to be oneself, nor is one aware of oneself as one specific object rather than another. Rather, my prereflective access to myself in first-personal experience is immediate and nonobservational and nonobjectifying. It involves what has more recently been called either "self-reference without identification" (Shoemaker 1968) or "non-ascriptive reference to self" (Brook 1994).

What is the actual argument for these claims however? The phenomenologists would probably insist that their accounts are based on a correct phenomenological description and that this is the best argument to be found.

Personally, I have much sympathy with such an answer, but if one were to look for an additional, more theoretical, argument, what would one then find? One line of reasoning found in virtually all of the phenomenologists is the view that the attempt to let (intransitive) consciousness be a result of a reflection (or higher-order monitoring) will generate an infinite regress. This is on the face of it a rather old idea. Typically, the regress argument has been understood in the following manner. If all occurrent mental states are conscious in the sense of being taken as objects by occurrent second-order mental states, then these second-order mental states must themselves be taken as objects by occurrent third-order mental states, and so forth ad infinitum. However, the standard reply to this argument has been that the premise is false and question begging. To put it differently, the easy way to halt the regress is by accepting the existence of nonconscious mental states. This is precisely the position adopted by the defenders of a higher-order theory. For them the second-order perception or thought does not have to be conscious. This will only be the case, if it is accompanied by a (nonconscious) third-order thought or perception (see Rosenthal 1990, p. 745). However, the phenomenological reply to this "solution" is rather straightforward. The phenomenologists would concede that it is possible to halt the regress by postulating the existence of nonconscious mental states, but they would maintain that such an appeal to the nonconscious leaves us with a case of explanatory vacuity. That is, they would find it quite unclear why the relation between two otherwise nonconscious processes should make one of them conscious. Or to put it differently, they would be quite unconvinced by the claim that a state without subjective or phenomenal qualities can be transformed into one with such qualities, that is, into an experience with first-personal givenness or mineness, by the mere relational addition of a meta-state having the first state as its intentional object.[9]

2 Intentionality, Temporality, Reflection, and Embodiment

The position outlined above is one shared by most phenomenologists. Important as it is, it would, however, be a mistake to think that the defense of prereflective self-consciousness constitutes the entirety of the phenomenological investigation of consciousness and self-consciousness. The phenomenological account of self-consciousness is far more complex and wide ranging than suggested so far. The shared position outlined above is only the starting point, and some might even argue that the really interesting parts are first to be found in the subsequent details and analyses. The phenomenological investigation of the relation between consciousness and self-consciousness is characterized by the fact that it is integrated into and can be found in the context of a simultaneous examination of a number of related issues, such as the nature of intentionality, embodiment, selfhood, temporality, attention, sociality, and so on. Thus, as part of their analysis of the structure of consciousness the phenomenologists also discuss—to mention just a few of the topics—(1) whether one should opt for an egological or nonegological account of consciousness, that is, whether or not every episode of experiencing always involves a distinct subject of experience; (2) how to understand the temporality of the stream of consciousness; (3) whether prereflective self-consciousness is characterized by any internal differentiation or infrastructure; (4) to what extent self-consciousness is always embodied and embedded; (5) how social interaction might change the structure of self-consciousness; (6) whether reflection is able to disclose the structure of prereflective consciousness or whether it necessarily distorts its subject matter; and (7) to what extent self-consciousness, although not being itself a form of object-consciousness, nevertheless presupposes the intentional encounter with the world.

It would lead us too far afield to treat all of these topics in detail, but in order to acquaint the reader with some of the resources to be found in the phenomenological tradition—a tradition that in its treatment of self-consciousness has often raised questions and tackled problems not found in mainstream analytical philosophy of mind—the rest of the chapter will be subdivided into short sections that briefly outline some of the phenomenological findings.[10]

A Self-Consciousness and Intentionality

Although prereflective self-consciousness might not itself be intentionally structured, there is still a close link between self-consciousness and intentionality. The first cannot be understood in isolation from the latter. As Merleau-Ponty has repeatedly insisted, self-consciousness should not be understood as a preoccupation with self that excludes or impedes the contact with transcendent being. On the contrary, consciousness is essentially oriented and open toward that which it is not, be it the world or other subjects, and it is precisely in this openness that it reveals itself to itself. What is disclosed in the cogito is consequently not an enclosed immanence, a pure interior self-presence, but an openness toward otherness, a movement of perpetual self-transcendence. It is because we are present to the world that we are present to ourselves. It is in our confrontation with that which we are not, that we are self-conscious (Merleau-Ponty 1945, pp. 431–432, 485, 487, 492; cf. Heidegger 2001, p. 328).

Similar lines of thought can be found in most of the other phenomenologists as well. As we have already seen, Sartre claims that intentionality entails self-consciousness, but he also argues for the reverse implication: consciousness can only be nonpositionally conscious of itself if it is positionally conscious *of* something; it acquires self-consciousness precisely insofar as it is intentionally conscious of a transcendent object (Sartre 1943/1976, p. 212; 1936, pp. 23–24).[11] The trivial way to make this claim reasonable would be by arguing that if I were not conscious *of* something, I would be lacking that which is self-conscious, namely the intentional experience. But Sartre is also renowned for his radical externalist interpretation of consciousness. To affirm the intentionality of consciousness is, according to Sartre, to deny the existence of any kind of mental content—including any kind of sense data or qualia—(Sartre 1943/1976, pp. 26, 363). There is nothing in consciousness, neither objects nor mental representations. It is completely empty. Thus, for Sartre, the being of intentional consciousness consists in its revelation of transcendent being, it exhausts itself in its (re)presentation of external reality (Sartre 1943/1976, p. 28). It is precisely in this strong sense that consciousness needs intentionality, needs the confrontation with something different from itself in order to *be self-conscious*; otherwise, it would lose every determination and dissipate as pure nothingness (Sartre 1943/1976, pp. 27, 214–215). To use a striking formulation by Rosenberg, one might even say that consciousness, according to Sartre, gives itself to itself only through a sort of *via negativa* (Rosenberg 1981, p. 257). Original self-consciousness is a prereflective consciousness of not being the object of which one is at the same time intentionally conscious (Sartre 1943/1976, pp. 178–179).

As for Heidegger, he persistently argues that experiential life is as such world-related, it is literally speaking "worldly tuned" (Heidegger 1993a, p. 250). To accentuate the close connection between self and world, Heidegger even introduces the notion of self-worldly (*selbstweltliche*) experiences (Heidegger 1994, p. 95). If we want to study the self, we should consequently not look inside consciousness in the hope of finding some elusive I, rather we should look at our worldly experience, and right there, we will find the situated self (Heidegger 1993a, p. 258). To put it differently, my self is present when I am worldly engaged; it is precisely to be found "out there." Just as the self is what it is in its worldly relations, self-acquaintance is not something that takes place or occurs in separation from our living in a world. Fundamentally speaking, self-experience is a question of neither an "inner perception," an introspection, or a self-reflection (Heidegger 1994, p. 95). In everyday life, I neither experience myself as a bundle of experiences and processes nor as a detached I-object, rather I experience myself in what I do and suffer, in what confronts me and in what I accomplish, in my concerns and disregards. I am acquainted with myself when I am captured and captivated by the world. Self-acquaintance is indeed only to be found in our immersion in the world, that is, self-acquaintance is always the self-acquaintance of a world-immersed self.

B Self-Consciousness and Temporality

A convincing theory of self-consciousness should not only be able to account for the prereflective self-consciousness of an occurrent experience, but should also be able to explain how I can have self-consciousness across temporal distance, that is, how I can remember a past experience as *mine*. To illuminate this issue, however, an analysis of the temporal character of consciousness is required. In fact, given the temporality of the stream of consciousness, even something as apparently synchronic as the conscious givenness of my present experience—and of course, the notion of presence has itself temporal connotations—might not be comprehensible without taking temporality, or as Husserl calls it, *inner time-consciousness*, into consideration.

In his *Vorlesungen zur Phänomenologie des inneren Zeitbewußtseins*, Husserl asks how it is possible for us to be conscious of temporal objects, objects with a temporal extension. How is it possible to be conscious of objects such as melodies, which cannot appear all at once, but only unfold themselves over time? Husserl's well-known thesis is that a perception of a temporal object (as well as the perception of succession and change) would be impossible if consciousness merely provided us with the givenness of the pure now-phase of the object, and if the stream of consciousness were a series of unconnected points of experiencing, like a string of pearls. If our perception had been restricted to being conscious of that which exists right now, it would have been impossible to perceive anything with a temporal extension and duration, for a succession of isolated, punctual, conscious states does not as such enable us to be conscious of succession and duration. This consequence is absurd, however. Thus, consciousness must in some way or another transcend the punctual now, and be conscious of that which has just been and is just about to occur.

But how is this possible? How can consciousness be conscious of that which is no longer or not yet present? According to Husserl's investigation, the basic unit of temporality is not a "knife-edge" present, but a "duration-block," that is, a temporal field that comprises all three temporal modes of present, past, and future. Three technical terms describe this temporal form of consciousness. There is (i) a "primal impression" narrowly directed toward the now-phase of the object. The primal impression never appears in isolation and is an abstract component that by itself cannot provide us with a perception of a temporal object. The primal impression is accompanied by (ii) a "retention," which provides us with a consciousness of the just-elapsed phase of the object, that is, which allows us to be aware of the phase as it sinks into the past, and by (iii) a "protention," which in a more-or-less indefinite way anticipates the phase of the object about to occur. The role of the protention is evident in our implicit and unreflective anticipation of what is about to happen as experience progresses. The concrete and full structure of all lived experience is consequently *protention–primal impression–retention*. Although the specific experiential contents of this structure from moment to moment progressively change, at any given moment this threefold structure is present (synchronically) as a unified whole (Husserl 1962b, p. 202).

To illustrate, let us take the case where we are hearing the beginning of a spoken sentence, say, "Joe, come home now! Or I will take. . . ." When hearing the last word "take," I am no longer hearing the previous words, but I must retain their sense if the sentence is to be meaningful to me. Correspondingly, when hearing the last word, I will have some anticipatory sense of where the sentence is heading. This is why I would be surprised if the sentence just ended with the word "take," or if it was continued with the words, "the blue raincoat is in the closet." But what is the dynamic structure of this temporal process? If we, for reasons of simplicity, focus on the role of retention, and if we take as our example Husserl's own preferred case of a melody or string of tones such as C–D–E, the orthodox Husserlian account is as follows. When the tone C is first heard, it is intended by the primal impression.[12] When it is succeeded by the tone D, the tone D is given in the primal impression, whereas the tone C is now retained by the retention, and when the E sounds, it replaces the tone D in the primal impression, whereas the tone D is now retained by the retention, and so on. The retention, however, is not simply a consciousness of the tone that has just passed. Every time a new tone is intended in a primal impression, the entire retentional sequence is modified. When the tone C is succeeded by the tone D, our impressional consciousness of the tone D will be accompanied by a retention of the tone C (D(c)). When the tone D is replaced by the tone E, our impressional consciousness of the tone E will be accompanied not only by a retention of the tone D, but also by a retention of the tone retained in the tone D $(E(D_{(c)}))$ and so forth (Husserl 1966b, pp. 81, 100).[13]

What does all of this have to do with self-consciousness? Husserl's analysis of the structure of inner time-consciousness serves a double purpose. It is not only meant to explain how we can be aware of objects with temporal extension, but also how we can be aware of our own fluctuating stream of experiences. According to Husserl, the retention does not merely retain the elapsed tone, but also the preceding primal impression. If $P(t)$ is the designation for the primal impression of a tone, then $P(t)$ is retained in the retention $Rp_{(t)}$ when a new primal impression occurs. As the notation makes clear, it is not only the tone that is retained, but also our consciousness of the tone. In other words, the actual phase of the flow is not only retaining the tone that has just been, but also the elapsing phase of the flow. Thus, the retentional modification does not only permit us to experience an enduring temporal object, it also provides us with temporal self-consciousness. The enduring object and the streaming consciousness are given together, and can only appear in this interdependent fashion. I can only be prereflectively aware of my stream of consciousness when I am conscious of the duration of my object, and vice versa (Husserl 1966b, pp. 80–81, 83).

More generally, for me to *remember* an episode, that is, for me to have episodic memory, is not simply for me to think of something, nor simply for me to think of something that happened in the past. It is to re-present something that happened in my own past and which I experienced when it occurred. To remember is to remember something past that has been present to me. As Brough puts it, "What is remembered was once present in the same unity of time in which the memory is now actual. To cast the matter in egological form, what is remembered is an elapsed position of my own life, recaptured through its actually present portion" (Brough 1975, p. 42). I can remember the past episode only if I implicitly remember my past experience of the episode, and I can do that only if the experience were self-conscious when it originally occurred. Had it not been, I would be unable to return to it and recall it as *mine*.[14]

Temporal objects are presented to consciousness in a continuum of phases, but what about our very perceptions of these objects? Are they also subjugated to the strict laws of temporal constitution? Are they also temporal unities that arise, endure, and perish? Husserl often speaks of the experiences themselves as being constituted in the structure protention–primal impression–retention. They are only given, only self-conscious, within this framework (Husserl 1966a, pp. 233, 293). But how is this self-consciousness to be understood? When Husserl argues that an intentional experience is constituted in inner time-consciousness, he is arguing that the experience is brought to givenness thanks to itself. It is called *inner* time-consciousness because we are dealing with a dimension that belongs *intrinsically* to the *innermost* structure of the experience itself. In other words, inner time-consciousness is not a particular intentional experience, rather it is a pervasive dimension of prereflective self-consciousness, and Husserl's account of the structure of inner time-consciousness (protention–primal impression–retention) is precisely to be understood as an analysis of the (micro)structure of the prereflective self-givenness of our experiences (Husserl 1974, pp. 279–280; 1952, p. 118).

Husserl's rather formal investigation of time-consciousness was subsequently taken up and transformed by many of the later phenomenologists. Some of these went on to stress the fundamental historicity of human self-understanding, thereby emphasizing the relation between self-consciousness and temporality in yet another way.[15]

C Self-Consciousness and Reflection

As we have seen, phenomenologists typically insist upon the difference between prereflective and reflective self-consciousness. They argue that whereas reflection is a complex form of self-consciousness that operates with a duality of moments and which involves a kind of self-fission, prereflective self-consciousness is an intrinsic and irrelational dimension of the experience. However, this preliminary differentiation is not sufficient. A more detailed examination of the precise relation between reflective and prereflective self-consciousness is called for. Two issues in particular stand out. First, if prereflective and reflective self-consciousness are so very different, how is prereflective self-consciousness then supposed to give rise to reflective self-consciousness? Second, phenomenological investigations are supposedly reflective in nature. But to what extent will reflection at all enable us to disclose the structures of lived experience?

I. Let us start with the first issue. Even if it has been granted, that reflection cannot be the primary kind of self-consciousness, it remains necessary to explain how it can rise out of prereflective self-consciousness, for as Sartre poignantly reminds us, the problem is not to find examples of the prereflective self-consciousness—they are everywhere—but to understand how one can pass from this self-consciousness that constitutes the being of consciousness, to the reflective knowledge of self, which is founded upon it (Sartre 1948, p. 63). Thus, it will not do to conceive of prereflective self-consciousness in such a manner that the transition to reflective self-consciousness becomes incomprehensible.

Sartre is by no means trying to deny the difference between a reflective and a prereflective self-consciousness, but he nevertheless insists that the two modes of self-consciousness must share a certain affinity, a certain structural similarity. Otherwise, it would be impossible to explain how the prereflective cogito could ever give rise to reflection. It is a significant feature of the lived experience that it allows for reflective appropriation, and a theory of self-consciousness that can *only* account for prereflective self-consciousness is not much better than a theory that only accounts for reflective self-consciousness. To phrase it differently, it is no coincidence that we do precisely speak of a pre*reflective* self-consciousness. The choice of words indicates that there remains a connection. The reason why reflection remains a permanent possibility is precisely that prereflective self-consciousness already involves a structural self-differentiation (Sartre 1943/1976, pp. 113, 194). In other words, reflection merely articulates the unity of unification and differentiation inherent in the prereflective lived presence: its ecstatic-centered structure of protending, presencing, retaining. Thus, most phenomenologists (Michel Henry is a notable exception) would argue that prereflective self-consciousness must be conceived not as a static self-identity, but as a dynamic and temporal self-differentiation.

II. As Husserl points out, our experiences are tacitly self-conscious, but they are also accessible for reflection. They can be reflected upon and thereby brought to our attention (Husserl 1952, p. 248). An examination of the particular intentional structure of this process can substantiate the thesis concerning the founded status of reflection. Reflective self-consciousness is often taken to be a thematic, articulated, and intensified self-consciousness, and it is normally initiated in order to bring the primary intentional experience into focus. But as Husserl also points out, it is in the nature of reflection to grasp something, which was already given prior to the grasping. Reflection is characterized by disclosing, and not by producing its theme:

When I say "I," I grasp myself in a simple reflection. But this self-experience [*Selbsterfahrung*] is like every experience [*Erfahrung*], and in particular every perception, a mere directing myself towards something that was already there for me, that was already conscious, but not thematically experienced, not noticed. (Husserl 1973b, pp. 492–493)

Whenever I reflect, I find myself "in relation" to something, as affected or active. That which I am related to is experientially conscious—it is already there for me as a "lived-experience" in order for me to be able to relate myself to it. (Husserl 1931, unpublished ms. C 10, p. 13a)[16]

In short, reflection is not an experience *sui generis*; it does not appear out of nowhere, but presupposes, like all intentional activity, a *motivation*. According to Husserl, to be motivated is to be *affected* by something, and then to respond to it (Husserl 1952, p. 217). When I start reflecting, that which motivates the reflection and which is then grasped has already been going on for a while. The reflected-on experience did not commence the moment I started paying attention to it, and it is not only given as still existing, but also and mainly as having already been. It is the *same* experience, which is now given reflectively, and it is given to me as enduring in time, that is, as a temporal experience (Husserl 1976, pp. 95, 162–164). When reflection sets in, it initially grasps something that has just elapsed, namely the motivating phase of the experience reflected-on. The reason why this phase can still be thematized by the subsequent reflection is that it does not disappear, but is retained in the *retention*, wherefore Husserl can claim that retention is a condition of possibility for reflection. It is due to the retention that consciousness can be made into an object (Husserl 1966b, p. 119); or to rephrase, reflection can take place only if a *temporal horizon* has been established.

In a passage from *Zur Phänomenologie des inneren Zeitbewußtseins* Husserl writes that the experience to which we turn attentively in reflection acquires a new mode of being. It becomes accentuated (*herausgehoben*), and he claims that this accentuation is nothing other than its being-grasped (Husserl 1966b, p. 129). Thus, rather than being a reification, a reflection might be nothing but an intensification or accentuation of the primary experience. Husserl also speaks of reflection as a process that discloses, disentangles, explicates, and articulates all those components and structures that were contained implicitly in the lived experience (Husserl 1966b, p. 128; 1966a, pp. 205, 236; 1984a, p. 244). Thus, one should not confuse the fluctuating unity of our lived experiences with a formlessness or lack of structure. On the contrary, our lived experiences possess a morphological structure and internal differentiation, and this is what makes them accessible to reflection and conceptual articulation. Moreover, this articulation is not necessarily imposed from without, is not necessarily foreign to the experience in question. In fact, rather than representing a distortion, the conceptual articulation might constitute a consummation of the experience (Merleau-Ponty 1945, p. 207). As Husserl puts it, in the beginning we are confronted with a dumb experience, which must then—through reflection—be made to articulate its *own* sense (Husserl 1950, p. 77).

A comparable view can be found in Heidegger. Heidegger resolutely rejects the idea that experiential life should be mute and chaotic (Heidegger 1993a, p. 148). Rather, our lived experience is imbued with meaning; it is intentionally structured. It has an inner articulation and rationality, and last but not least, it is in possession of a spontaneous and immediate self-understanding, which is why it can ultimately be interpreted from itself and in terms of itself. Experiential life is comprehensible because its spontaneous self-experience is itself a preliminary form of understanding, is itself what might be called a pre-understanding (Heidegger 1993b, p. 166). It is in this context that Heidegger quotes Dilthey—"Thinking is bound to life through an inner necessity; it is itself a form of life"[17]—and speaks of philosophy as a continuation of the *reflexivity* found in life (Heidegger 1993b, p. 156). In other words, the phenomenological investigation must build on the familiarity that the experiential dimension already has with itself; it must draw on the self-referential dimension, the persistent care of self that is built into the very stream of consciousness.

Just like Husserl, Heidegger can consequently claim that the phenomenological articulation and conceptualization of the lived experiences is something that belongs to the experiences themselves; it is not something that is imposed on them arbitrarily from without, as if the conceptualization were driven merely by certain epistemological or scientific concerns. A true phenomenological description does not constitute a violation; it is not an attempt to impose a foreign systematicity on the experiential dimension, rather it is something that is rooted in and motivated by experiential life itself (Heidegger 1993a, p. 59; 1994, p. 87).

D Self-Consciousness and Embodiment

So far, my presentation of the phenomenological analyses of self-consciousness has not included any explicit reference to the body. In fact, however, most of the phenomenologists (Heidegger is an important exception) consider the investigation of body awareness or bodily self-appearance to constitute an integral part of the elucidation of the structure and nature of self-consciousness. As the phenomenologists are quick to point out, the distinction between self-consciousness and object-consciousness does not coincide with the traditional distinction between mind and body. On the contrary, our body can appear in quite different ways, from a first-person perspective as well as from a third-person perspective, and an analysis of these forms of bodily appearance will not only corroborate the previous analysis of the relation between prereflective and reflective self-consciousness. It will also allow for a further elucidation of this relationship and present us with insights that are indispensable if we are to understand the link between one's awareness of oneself as an elusive subjective dimension, and one's awareness of oneself as an intersubjectively accessible entity in the world.

As Michel Henry once pointed out, a phenomenological clarification of the body must take its departure in the original givenness of the body (Henry

1965, p. 79). But how is the body originally given? When I am watching a football match, I am normally not paying attention to the turn of my head when I follow the motions of the players, nor to the narrowing of my eyes when I attempt to discern the features of the goalkeeper. When I give up and reach for my binoculars, the movements of my hand remain outside the focus of my consciousness. When I am occupied with objects and directed at goals, my perceptual experiences and their bodily roots are generally passed over in favor of the perceived, that is, my body tends to efface itself on its way to its intentional goal. Fortunately so, for had we been aware of our bodily movements in the same way in which we are aware of objects, our body would have made such high demands on our attention that it would have interfered with our daily life. However, when I execute movements without thinking about them, this is not necessarily because the movements are mechanical or involuntary or nonconscious, rather they might simply be part of my functioning intentionality, they might simply be immediately and pre-reflectively felt, as both Henry and Merleau-Ponty have argued (Henry 1965, p. 128, Merleau-Ponty 1945, p. 168). Thus, even if my movements might be absent as thematic intentional objects, this does not have to entail that they are experientially absent in any absolute sense.

Under normal circumstances, I do not need to perceive my arm visually in order to know where it is. If I wish to grasp the fork, I do not first have to search for the hand, since it is always with me. Whereas I can approach or move away from any object in the world, the body itself is always present as my very perspective on the world. That is, rather than being simply yet another perspectivally given object, the body itself is, as Sartre points out, precisely that which allows me to perceive objects perspectivally (Sartre 1943/1976, p. 378; Merleau-Ponty 1945, p. 107). The body is present, not as a permanent perceptual object, but as myself. Originally, I do not have any consciousness *of* my body as an intentional object. I do not perceive it; *I am it*. Sartre even writes that the lived body is invisibly present, precisely because it is existentially lived rather than known (Sartre 1943/1976, p. 372). This is also why Husserl repeatedly emphasized how important it is to distinguish between *Leib* and *Körper*, that is, between the prereflectively lived body, that is, the body as an embodied first-person perspective, and the subsequent thematic experience *of* the body as an object (Husserl 1973a, p. 57).

In short, phenomenologists take prereflective body-awareness to be a question of how (embodied) consciousness is given to itself not as an *object*, but as a *subject*. Whereas José Luis Bermúdez has recently claimed that "somatic proprioception is a form of perception" that takes "the embodied self as its object" (Bermúdez 1998, p. 132), the phenomenologists would argue that *primary* body-awareness is not a type of object-consciousness, is *not* a perception of the body as an object at all, but on the contrary a genuine form of self-experience.[18]

Merleau-Ponty is a thinker who has been very explicit in linking the issue of self-experience to those of embodiment and intersubjectivity. In his view, subjectivity is essentially embodied. To exist embodied is, however, neither to exist as pure subject nor as pure object, but to exist in a way that transcends both possibilities. It does not entail a loss of self-consciousness; on the contrary, self-consciousness is intrinsically embodied self-consciousness, but it does entail a loss or perhaps rather a release from transparency and purity, thereby permitting intersubjectivity. As Merleau-Ponty writes: "The other can be evident to me because I am not transparent for myself, and because my subjectivity draws its body in its wake" (Merleau-Ponty 1945, p. 405). To put it differently, since intersubjectivity is a fact, there must exist a bridge between my self-acquaintance and my acquaintance with others; my self-experience must contain an anticipation of the other, must contain the seeds of otherness (Merleau-Ponty 1945, pp. 400–401, 405, 511). If I am to recognize other bodies as embodied foreign subjects, I have to be in possession of something that will allow me to do so. But as Merleau-Ponty points out, when I experience an other and when I experience myself, there is in fact a common denominator. In both cases, I am dealing with *embodiment*, and one of the features of my embodied subjectivity is that it per definition comprises an *exteriority*. When I go for a walk, or write a letter, or play ball—to use Strawson's examples (Strawson 1959, p. 111)—I am experiencing myself, but in a way that anticipates the manner in which I would experience an other, and an other would experience me. This is not to say that a focus on embodiment and action eradicates the difference between self-ascription and other-ascription, between a first-person perspective and a second-person perspective, but it conceives of the difference in such a manner that their relationship becomes more intelligible. In short, it is because I am not a pure interiority, but an embodied being that lives outside itself, that transcends itself, that I am capable of encountering and understanding others who exist in the same way (Merleau-Ponty 1960, pp. 213, 215, 221; 1964, p. 74).

Ultimately, a focus on embodied self-experience inevitably leads to a decisive widening of the discussion. Embodiment brings intersubjectivity and sociality into the picture, and draws attention to the question as to whether certain forms of self-consciousness might be intersubjectively mediated, might depend on one's social relations to others. This is not the right place to discuss this rich and complex question, but it is important to realize that self-consciousness is an equivocal concept. It is not something that can be exhaustively analyzed simply by examining the inner workings of the mind. Rather the recognition of the existence of a primitive form of prereflective self-consciousness should not make us blind to the fact that there are more elaborate forms of self-consciousness that are theory- and language-dependent and intersubjectively constituted. But this is something all the phenomenologists are thoroughly aware of.

3 Conclusion

The presentation given so far is by no means exhaustive. Not only are there many central figures in the phenomenological tradition—figures such as Scheler, Gurwitsch, Henry, Levinas, and Ricoeur—whose contribution to an elucidation of self-consciousness I have been unable to include in my brief overview, but I have also had to skip many details in Husserl's, Sartre's, and Heidegger's accounts. Nevertheless, I hope the presentation has succeeded in conveying some of the core features of the phenomenological treatment of self-consciousness—a treatment that shares obvious concerns with the accounts found in mainstream analytical philosophy of mind and cognitive science, but which also raises questions and tackles problems not ordinarily dealt with in these accounts.

In my view, the phenomenologists have much to offer the contemporary discussion of self-consciousness. This is perhaps especially so given the current situation. Although higher-order theories of consciousness have enjoyed great popularity for a couple of decades, they have recently been met with growing dissatisfaction, and many have started to search for viable alternatives.[19] But if one is on the lookout for promising and sophisticated alternatives to the higher-order accounts, one should take a closer look at phenomenology. Given the resources of the latter, the customary stance of analytical philosophy toward it—which has ranged from complete disregard to outright hostility—can only be characterized as counterproductive.[20]

Notes

1. See Zahavi 1999, 2002a; Kriegel 2003a.

2. Brentano defends this view in his *Psychologie vom empirischen Standpunkt* from 1874. For an outline of his position, see Zahavi 1998.

3. This is not a completely uncontroversial claim, however. Both Tugendhat and Gloy have, for instance, claimed that Husserl conceived of self-consciousness in terms of a relation between two different experiences, one taking the other as its object in an

inner perception (Tugendhat 1979, pp. 52–53, Gloy 1998, pp. 296–300). They have consequently argued that Husserl due to his preoccupation with *intentionality* took object-consciousness as the paradigm of every kind of awareness and that he therefore never discovered the existence of prereflective self-consciousness. A somewhat similar criticism has also been directed against Heidegger whose lecture course *Grundprobleme der Phänomenologie*, according to Frank, offers us "a classical formulation of the reflection model of self-awareness" (Frank 1991, p. 518). As for Sartre, Gennaro has recently argued that Sartre's theory of consciousness should be interpreted as a somewhat modified version of the HOT theory (Gennaro 2002, pp. 294, 330). More specifically, Gennaro defends what he calls the "wide intrinsicality view" according to which first-order mental states are complex states containing both a world-directed mental state and a nonconscious metapsychological thought (Gennaro 2002, p. 302), and he takes Sartre to be advocating a comparable view. Thus, Gennaro claims that Sartre's reference to "non-positional self-awareness" is in fact a rather idiosyncratic way of referring to such nonconscious metapsychological thoughts (Gennaro 2002, p. 307). In my view, all of the above interpretations constitute fundamental misinterpretations of the positions in question.

4. Whereas the early Sartre speaks of an irreflective or nonreflective self-consciousness, he later increasingly opts for the term "pre-reflective self-consciousness."

5. For a more extensive discussion of Sartre's account of self-consciousness, see Zahavi 1999.

6. For a more extensive discussion of Husserl's account of self-consciousness, see Zahavi 1999, 2002b, 2003c.

7. This is Heidegger's *terminus technicus* for subject or self.

8. For a more extensive discussion of Heidegger's account of self-consciousness, see Zahavi 2003b.

9. It is, however, possible to reconstruct the regress argument in such a fashion that an appeal to the nonconscious will be unable to halt the infinite regress, but this reconstruction is not one that has been explicitly worked out by the phenomenologists themselves. For a presentation and discussion of the argument, see Zahavi 1999, 2003a, 2004.

10. For reasons of space, my presentation will in the following focus on the *results* of the phenomenological analyses. For a more extensive presentation and discussion of the analyses themselves, see Zahavi 1999.

11. As for alleged nonintentional experiences such as moods like anxiety or nervousness, Sartre would argue that although it is true that such affective states lack a specific intentional object, and although they must be distinguished from intentional feelings like the desire for an apple, or the admiration for a particular person, they neverthe-

less do retain a reference to the world. They do not enclose us within ourselves, but are lived through as pervasive affective atmospheres that influence the way we encounter entities in the world. Just think, for example, of moods like curiosity, nervousness, or happiness. Moreover, Sartre would deny that moods are mere attendant phenomena and would instead follow Heidegger in taking them to be fundamental forms of disclosure. We are always in some kind of mood. Even a neutral and distanced observation has its own tone, and as Heidegger puts it, "Mood has always already disclosed being-in-the-world as a whole and first makes possible directing oneself toward something" (Heidegger 1986, p. 137; See Sartre 1943/1976, p. 387).

12. "Intended" understood in the sense of being that which the primal impression is directed at.

13. Husserl's model is supposed to account for the fact that we are aware of the continuity of experience. But it might be objected that his theory furnishes each occurrent episode of consciousness with an exceedingly complex structure since it will supposedly contain retentional traces of every conscious state preceding it. But as Husserl also points out, as time passes the past tones (and experiences) will gradually lose their differentiation and distinctive qualities, they will recede into the background, they will become vague and will finally be lost in the night of the unconscious (Husserl 1966a, pp. 169–171).

14. Obviously, this is not to say that episodic memory is infallible. I might have false beliefs about myself, I might confuse different past experiences, and I might take something I read, heard, or dreamed about to be something that truly happened (see Husserl 1966b, p. 34).

15. See Heidegger 1927/1986, Gadamer 1986.

16. I am grateful to the director of the Husserl-Archives in Leuven, Prof. Rudolf Bernet, for permitting me to consult and quote from Husserl's unpublished manuscripts. Following the standard practice, I will append the original German text (the translation is my own): "Wenn immer ich reflektiere, finde ich mich 'in bezug auf' ein Etwas, als affiziertes bzw. aktives. Das, worauf ich bezogen bin, ist erlebnismäßig bewußt—es ist für mich etwas schon als 'Erlebnis,' damit ich mich darauf beziehen kann."

17. See Dilthey 1905, p. 326.

18. For a more extensive overview of different phenomenological investigations of the body, see Zaner 1964; Leder 1990; Waldenfels 2000.

19. For a discussion of some recent neo-Brentanian alternatives, see Zahavi 2004.

20. This study has been funded by the Danish National Research Foundation.

III | Connections: Cognition, Attention, and Knowledge

13 | Conscious Experience versus Conscious Thought

Peter Carruthers

Are there different constraints on theories of conscious experience as against theories of conscious propositional thought? Is what is problematic or puzzling about each of these phenomena of the same, or of different, types? And to what extent is it plausible to think that either or both conscious experience and conscious thought involve some sort of self-reference? In pursuing these questions I shall also explore the prospects for a defensible form of eliminativism concerning conscious thinking, one that would leave the reality of conscious experience untouched. In the end, I shall argue that while there might be no such thing as conscious judging or conscious wanting, there *is* (or may well be) such a thing as conscious generic thinking.

1   The Demands on Theories of Conscious Experience

What needs to be explained about conscious experience is its *what it is likeness*, together with a number of surrounding puzzles. The primary demand on a theory of conscious experience is that it should explain how conscious experiences come to possess their distinctive subjective dimension, and hence explain why there should be something that it is *like* for subjects to undergo them. Arguably, a good theory should also explain the distinction between conscious and *un*conscious perceptual states, accounting for the fact that the latter *aren't* conscious.[1] It should explain how we can come to form purely recognitional concepts for our conscious experiences.[2] And a successful theory ought also to explain why our conscious experiences should seem especially *ineffable* and private, why they should seem to possess intrinsic (nonrelational and nonintentional) properties, and so on.

Is it also a *desideratum* of a successful theory that conscious experiences should be shown to be somehow self-referential in character? While not in the usual catalog of things to be explained, it is arguable that the answer to this question is yes, in each of two distinct senses. First, it is plausible that the contents of perceptual experience contain an implicit reference to the self (Bermúdez 1998). Objects are seen as being closer or further away, for example, or as being above or below. Closer to or further from what? Above or below what? The only available answer is: oneself. Equally, when one moves through the world there is a distinctive sort of "visual flow" as objects approach, loom larger, and then disappear out of the periphery of the visual field. This experience of visual flow is normally apprehended as—that is, has as part of its intentional content—motion through a stationary (or independently moving) environment. Motion of what? Again the only available answer is: oneself.

There is also quite a different sense in which it can be argued that conscious experiences involve a sort of self-reference, however. This is not reference to the self (in the manner sketched above), but rather reference to the very same experience itself. For it seems that conscious experiences, in their distinctive subjectivity, somehow present *themselves* to us, as well as presenting whatever it is that they are experiences *of*. So conscious experiences, besides presenting or referring to items in and properties of the world (or of our own bodies), also present or make reference to themselves. On this sort of view, then, an experience of red, besides having the world-presenting content, *red over there*, will also have the self-referential content, *this is an experience of red over there*.

How can these varying demands on a theory of conscious experience best be met? My own view is a version of higher-order representational account. This is developed and defended at length elsewhere (Carruthers 2000; 2004a,b); here there is space for just the barest sketch. What constitutes an experience as phenomenally conscious, in my view, is that it possesses a dual representational content: both world (or body) representing and experience representing. And experiences come to possess such a dual content by virtue of their availability to a higher-order thought faculty (which is capable of entertaining higher-order thoughts about those very experiences), and by virtue of the truth of some or other form of "consumer semantic" account of intentional content.

There are a number of components that need to be set in place in order for this account to work. First, we need to accept that the intentional content of all perceptual states (whether conscious or unconscious) is nonconceptual, or at least *analog* or fine-grained, in character. Many in recent years have defended the reality of nonconceptual intentional content (Bermúdez 1995; Tye 1995, 2000; Kelly 2001; Luntley 2003). Even if one feels that these claims may go too far, and that the contents of perception are always to one degree or another *imbued with* concepts, still it needs to be recognized that perceptual experience is always *analog* in relation to any concepts that we can possess (Carruthers 2000; Kelly 2001). Our color experiences, for example, have a fineness of grain that far outstrips our capacity to conceptualize, recognize, and remember them. The same holds for movement and shape; and similar things are true in all other sense modalities.

The second necessary ingredient is acceptance of some or other form of consumer semantics. What all kinds of consumer semantics have in common is a commitment to the idea that the intentional content of a state depends in part on what the "downstream" consumer systems for that state are apt to do with it or infer from it.[3] (Teleosemantics is one form of consumer semantics; see Millikan 1984, 1989; Papineau 1987, 1993. Functional or inferential role semantics is another; see Loar 1981; Block 1986; McGinn 1989; Peacocke 1992.) In fact the only kind of semantic theory that *isn't* a form of consumer semantics is pure input-side, causal co-variance, or "informational" semantics (Fodor 1990).

These two main ingredients then need to be put together with what many consider to be a plausible architecture for human cognition, in which perceptual contents are widely "broadcast" and made available to a variety of downstream consumer systems for conceptualizing and drawing inferences from those contents (Baars 1988, 1997). Included amongst the latter will be a higher-order thought faculty capable of deploying concepts of experience, then what we get is the account sketched above. Each perceptual representation with the analog content red_a,[4] for example, acquires the higher-order analog content $seems$-red_a or $experience$-of-red_a, by virtue of its availability to a higher-order thought system capable of judging immediately and non-inferentially that one is experiencing red.[5]

Such an account can meet all of the main demands made on a theory of conscious experience. First, it can explain how conscious experiences have a subjective dimension of *what it is likeness*. This is their higher-order analog content, in virtue of which they themselves (and not just the objects and properties that their first-order contents are *of*) are presented to us nonconceptually or in analog fashion. Second, the account can explain the distinction between experiences that are phenomenally conscious and those that aren't. This will be the distinction between perceptual states that are, and those that aren't, made available to our higher-order thought faculty, thereby acquiring a higher-order analog content. Third, the account can explain how we can have purely recognitional concepts of our experiences. These will be recognitional concepts whose application conditions are grounded in the higher-order analog content that attaches to those experiences (Carruthers 2004a). Fourth, the account can explain why our conscious experiences should seem especially ineffable. This is because the fine-grained character of our awareness of those experiences, mediated by their higher-order analog contents, will seem to "slip through the gaps" of any of our attempts to describe them in conceptual terms. And so on. (For more extensive discussion, see Carruthers 2000.)

Notice that on this account there is an important respect in which conscious experiences turn out to be self-referential, in addition to the reference to the self that is implicit in their first-order intentional contents. This flows from the dual content that attaches to them. Conscious experiences of red, for example, aren't just targeted on the worldly property (redness) that is represented in analog fashion by their first-order contents. They are also targeted *on themselves*, via their higher-order analog contents of the form, *experience-of-red$_a$*. So we have a vindication of the intuition that conscious experiences don't just present the world (or our own bodies) to us, but also somehow present themselves to us. This "presenting" is done via their higher-order analog contents, which represent, and replicate in "seeming fashion," their first-order contents.

2 The Demands on Theories of Conscious Thought

If the *desiderata* for theories of conscious experience and conscious thought were the same, then one would expect that people would need to converge on theories of the same general type in respect of each. But this isn't so. While I myself endorse higher-order theories of both conscious experience and conscious thought, for example, such a combination of views is by no means mandatory. In particular, someone might sensibly combine some kind of first-order account of phenomenally conscious experience, with a higher-order account of the conscious status of thought (e.g., Kirk 1994). This suggests that the demands on explanation here are distinct.[6]

If the *desiderata* for theories of conscious experience and theories of conscious thought were the same, indeed, then one would expect that those who endorse first-order representational theories of the former (Kirk 1994; Dretske 1995a; Tye 1995, 2000) should also endorse a purely first-order account of the latter. Not only isn't this the case (Dretske and Tye are silent on the nature of conscious thinking; Kirk endorses a higher-order account), but I suspect, moreover, that first-order accounts of conscious thinking aren't even defensible. This can be brought out by considering what first-order theorists might say in response to the widespread evidence of *un*conscious perception and *un*conscious thought (Baars 1988, 1997; Milner and Goodale 1995).

In the case of conscious experience the main *desideratum*, as we noted, is to explain the properties involved in *phenomenal* consciousness. And it is always then open to a first-order theorist to respond to alleged evidence of nonconscious experience (blindsight, dual-systems theories of vision, and so forth) by insisting that the experiential states in question are actually phenomenally conscious ones, despite not being *access*-conscious. (That is, despite not being available for the subject to know of or report on directly. Tye [1995] seems to endorse a view of this sort.) There is nothing incoherent in the idea of phenomenally conscious experiences that subjects aren't aware of themselves possessing (even if such a thing is rather hard to believe).

In the case of conscious thinking, however, there would seem to be no independent target of explanation. For in this case there doesn't seem to be any scope for someone to claim that the "unconscious" thoughts investigated by psychologists are, really, conscious ones, despite being thoughts of which the subjects lack awareness. In the case of conscious thinking *the* phenomenon to be explained is the way that we (seem to have) immediate and noninferential awareness of (some of) our own thought processes. This is because thoughts aren't phenomenally conscious per se. Our thoughts aren't *like* anything, in the relevant sense, except to the extent that they might be associated with visual or other images or emotional feelings, which will be phenomenally conscious by virtue of their quasi-sensory status.[7]

There is, of course, *a* sense in which it is *like* something to entertain a conscious thought. This is that, depending on what one is thinking about, different aspects of the world thought about will loom into focus. As one's thoughts shift from one topic to another, so one's attention shifts from one aspect of the world to another. Siewert (1998) believes that this supports the view that nonimagistic thought is phenomenally conscious. But this is to conflate *worldly* subjectivity with *mental-state* subjectivity (Carruthers 1998a). Of course *the world* is *like* something to any perceiver and to any thinker, whether their states are phenomenally conscious or not. For any experience and any thought will involve a partial and partially subjective "take" on the objects of experience/thought. What is crucial for phenomenal consciousness, however, is that there should be something that the subject's *own mental states* are *like*, for them. It is the mental states themselves that are subjective in character, that possess properties that are available to introspective recognition, and so on. With this distinction in place, there is no reason to believe that nonimagistic thoughts will be *like* anything.

The only remaining puzzle about conscious thinking, in fact (given that such thinkings aren't necessarily and intrinsically phenomenally conscious) is that we seem to have immediate and noninferential awareness that we are doing it. So we might as well say that conscious thoughts *are*, then, the thoughts that we can be immediately aware of possessing. Or so, at any rate, I propose to assume in what follows. Our question will be: how is such noninferential awareness of our own thought processes even so much as *possible*?[8] We will begin with this question in section 3.

Before we get to that, however, recall the familiar distinction between thoughts as standing states and thoughts as occurrent events (acts of thinking). What is it for beliefs and desires (*qua* standing states) to be conscious? One proposal, which might seem to flow directly from the assumption we have just made, would be as follows. We might say that standing states are conscious provided that the subject has immediate non-inferential awareness of them. This won't do, however, for a variety of reasons. One (the only one I shall discuss) is that there exist a range of convincing counterexamples, drawn from both Freudian-style psychology and common sense. These are cases where a standing-state belief or desire is the target of seemingly noninferential higher-order awareness, but without thereby being conscious.

Suppose, for instance, that in a discussion of the merits and demerits of utilitarianism, someone points out to me that I have not only been putting forward utilitarian views, but that I have been speaking of utilitarians as "we," and have felt threatened and become angry when utilitarian views as such are maligned. This might strike me with the force of self-discovery. Had I been asked whether I was a utilitarian previously, I would have denied it. I did not *consciously* believe in the truth of utilitarianism. Yet my behavior suggests both that I *believe* utilitarianism to be the correct moral theory, and that I have second-order awareness of this belief (hence the fact that I feel threatened when utilitarian views are attacked).

A better answer to the question of what renders standing-state beliefs and desires conscious would be this: they are conscious just in case they are apt to emerge as conscious occurrent thinkings with the very same first-order content. This is why I didn't consciously believe in utilitarianism, in the example above: I wasn't disposed to think consciously and spontaneously, "Utilitarianism is true," or something to that effect. This answer also fits neatly with what Gordon (1996) has defended as the "question/check procedure" for self-ascribing beliefs.[9] If someone asks you whether or not you believe something, what do you do? You surely ask yourself, "Is it true that *P*?," and you ascribe the belief to yourself just in case you find yourself inclined to answer, "Yes, it is the case that *P*." In effect, you use your conscious occurrent judgment with the first-order content *P* as the basis on which to ascribe to yourself the standing-state belief that *P*.

It is plausible that the conscious status of standing-state thoughts should be explained in terms of that of their occurrent counterparts, then. At any rate (again), this is what I propose to assume in what follows. So we will need to focus on what it is for an occurrent act of thinking to be conscious. Here is a very natural proposal: a conscious act of thinking is one whose occurrence and content the subject has immediate and noninferential awareness of (Rosenthal 1993b; Carruthers 1996).[10] The awareness in question surely has to be noninferential, since otherwise judgments that I attribute to myself as a result of self-interpretation would count as conscious ones. While there is no doubt much that could be said in support of (or against) such a proposal, for present purposes I shall simply assume its correctness, and see what then follows concerning the likely reality of, and the self-referential status of, conscious thinking.

3 How Is Conscious Thinking Possible?

Can we describe a possible functional architecture that might serve to realize conscious occurrent judgment, in the sense explained above? What we need is that whenever a judgment of a certain type is being made (e.g., occurring at a particular stage in the stream of processing within the mind's executive or decision-making systems, say), then that judgment is disposed to cause or give rise to the higher-order judgment that just such a judgment is occurring. And such causation needs to be direct, in a way that doesn't count as inferential or self-interpretive.

How might such an architecture be possible? And how might it be realized? Suppose that there is a language of thought, or "Mentalese." Then when a sentence in this language, |P|,[11] is entertained at a particular point in processing, we can suppose that the system has been built in such a way that the subject is automatically disposed (if relevant, i.e., depending on what else is going on in the subject's mind) to token the sentence |I am thinking that P|. And provided that the different causal roles distinctive of belief, desire, and so forth are signaled explicitly by operators in the language of thought, then the very same sort of mechanism will also yield noninferential awareness that I am judging (factively) that P, or that I have an activated desire for P, and so on.

In functional accounts of cognition, beliefs and desires are generally represented by distinct *boxes*. But even if something like this were literally true, it would still have to be the case that token activated beliefs and token activated desires can interact with one another within other systems, such as in practical reasoning. So they would have to be tagged somehow to indicate which "box" they derive from. What we might have, then, is the belief that

P realized by a Mentalese representation |BEL- P| and the desire for P realized by |DES- P|, where the tags |BEL-| and |DES-| determine their causal roles as beliefs and desires respectively.[12] And then a mechanism can easily be imagined that would go immediately from the former to |BEL- I am entertaining the belief that P| and that would go immediately from the latter to |BEL- I am entertaining the desire that P|—where these would of course mean that I am aware that I am *judging* that P, and that I am aware that I am occurrently *wanting* that P, respectively.

Notice, too, that such an architecture (together with the truth of some version of consumer semantics of the sort appealed to in the explanation of phenomenal consciousness in section 1) might entail that conscious judgments, as well as conscious experiences, are events with a dual intentional content. For the availability of the judgment P to a consumer system apt to judge, immediately and noninferentially, *I am judging that P*, might be sufficient for the initial first-order judgment to acquire a higher-order content. And then one and the same token act of thinking would possess the dual contents P and *I am judging that P*.

4 Is Conscious Thinking Actual?

I have outlined an architecture that would vindicate the reality of conscious thinking, while at the same time entailing (given consumer semantics) that conscious thinkings are self-referential. The evidence suggests, however, that the human mind may contain no such architecture as the one just sketched above. For there is now widespread evidence that humans routinely *confabulate* explanations of their own behavior, as has emerged again and again over the last quarter century of social-psychological and neuropsychological research. (For recent reviews, see Gazzaniga 1998; Wilson 2002.) Such data are in tension with the existence of the sort of noninferential thinking-attribution mechanism envisaged above. (Some attempts to render them consistent will be considered in a moment.)

Let me quickly sketch a couple of highlights from this body of research. In one of the classic experiments of Nisbett and Wilson (1977), subjects in a shopping mall were presented with an array of four sets of items (e.g., pairs of socks or pantyhose), and were asked to choose one of them as a free sample. (All four sets of items were actually identical.) Subjects displayed a marked tendency to select the item from the right-hand end of the display. Yet no one mentioned this when they were asked to explain why they had chosen as they did. Rather, subjects produced plainly confabulated explanations, such as that the item they had chosen was softer, that it appeared to have been better made, or that it had a more attractive color.

As Nisbett and Wilson (1977) point out, what seems to happen in such cases is this. Subjects have a right-hand bias, leading them to spend a longer time attending to the right-most item. Their higher-order thought faculty, noticing and seeking to explain this behavior, proposes an explanation. For example: I am attending more to that item because I believe it to be the softest. And this explanatory higher-order belief is then the source of the subject's verbal report, as well as the subject's choice. But the subject has no access to the process of interpretative thinking that generated their higher-order belief; and that belief itself is without any foundation in the first-order facts—it certainly isn't produced by the sort of noninferential ascent-mechanism envisaged in section 3.

The second example is reported in Gazzaniga (1998), concerning one of his "split brain" patients. When the instruction "Walk!" was flashed up in the patient's left visual field (accessible to his right hemisphere, which had some capacity to comprehend simple forms of language, but no productive abilities), the patient got up and started to walk across the room. When asked what he was doing, he (his left hemisphere, which controls speech) replied, "I want to get a Coke from the fridge." This answer was plainly confabulated, generated by his higher-order thought faculty (which independent evidence suggests is located largely in the left hemisphere) in order to explain his own behavior. But the answer came to him with all of the obviousness and apparent indubitability that attaches to any of our ascriptions of occurrent thoughts to ourselves.

The thoughts that actually produced the subject's behavior, in this example, were presumably |DES- I comply with the experimenter's instruction| and |BEL- To comply with the instruction to walk, I must walk|. Whereas the higher-order thought faculty, being aware of the subject's own behavior and seeking to explain it, came up with the explanation |BEL- I am walking because I want to get a Coke from the fridge| (perhaps noticing that the fridge lay in the direction that he was walking). And the higher-order attribution of desire, here, was plainly an inference-produced product of self-interpretation, not resulting from the operations of some sort of ascent-mechanism.

This and similar data lead Gazzaniga (1998) to propose that the left hemisphere of the brain houses an "interpreter" (a higher-order thought faculty), which has access to perceptual input, but not to the occurrent conceptual thoughts and decision-making processes occurring elsewhere in the brain. The interpreter is continually weaving an explanatory story for the agent's own actions. These stories may often be true ones, in familiar-enough cases and in cases where the interpreter does its job well. But they are still a product of interpretation, and not the result of any sort of noninferential access to the subject's own thought processes. And in unusual or unexpected circumstances the subject may end up with stories that are confabulated (i.e., false).

If any such account is true, then a plausible abductive inference—in this case an application of Occam's razor—suggests that the human mind does *not* have the sort of noninferential semantic-ascent architecture that we sketched in section 3. It appears to follow, too (if these cases can be taken as representative), that there is no such thing as conscious thinking.

Can such a conclusion be ruled out of court immediately, rejected on the grounds that we can be *certain* that there is such a thing as conscious thinking? No, it can't. For we are assuming that conscious thinking requires noninferential awareness of our own thought processes. But all we can be certain of—the most that introspection can deliver—is that we are sometimes aware of our own thought processes without engaging in any *conscious* inference. We can't be certain that our awareness of our own thought processes isn't grounded in an *un*conscious inference. And if Gazzaniga is right, it always is.

It is worth noting that Gazzaniga's proposal is consistent with, and to some degree receives independent support from, an overall architecture for cognition that has been receiving increasing support in recent decades (Baars 1997; Carruthers 2000 [ch. 11]; 2002). On this account the various sensory systems produce integrated analog representations of the environment (and body), which are then widely broadcast and made available to a range of downstream conceptual systems (for higher-order thought, for folk mechanics, for folk biology, and so on). These latter systems have quite limited access to one another, however. (They are to some degree "encapsulated.") And neither do they have access to what takes place even further downstream, within practical reasoning. So on this model, although the higher-order thought faculty would have access to perceptual and proprioceptive input (and hence to whatever the agent is physically doing), it won't have any direct access to the thought processes that cause our actions. I shall return to discuss this model at greater length in section 5.

One way in which it might be argued that the confabulation data are consistent with an architecture of the kind sketched in section 3, however, would be this. Perhaps the confabulated judgments are made too long after the event to be reliable, or for the semantic-ascent architecture envisaged in section 3 to operate. It is plausible enough that the decay-time for any given occurrent thought should be pretty brief. So if the token Mentalese sentence |P| doesn't give rise to |I am thinking that P| almost immediately, the subject will have no option but to self-interpret; which might lead, in the right circumstances, to confabulation. This reply, however, doesn't really work. For a subject can be asked for an explanation immediately after she makes a choice (in the Nisbett and Wilson example), or while he is getting up out of his chair (in the Gazzaniga example). And the window for unrehearsed items to remain in working memory isn't generally reckoned to be *this* brief.

A related objection would be this. There are a range of experimental demonstrations that so-called "think aloud protocols"—in which subjects verbalize their thinking out loud *while* reasoning to the solution of some problem—are really quite reliable in providing us with a window on the underlying sequences of thought in question (Ericsson and Simon 1993). How can this be possible unless those subjects have reliable (nonconfabulated) awareness of the thoughts that they verbalize? But in fact, linguistic *expression* of a thought need not imply that the subject has higher-order awareness that they are entertaining that thought. And indeed, one of the central findings in this area is that subjects need to be induced *not* to report *on* their thoughts when they have them, since this is demonstrably *un*reliable (Ericsson and Simon 1993).

Notice that the production subsystem of the language faculty will need to be situated downstream of the various belief-forming and decision-making reasoning processes that figure in cognition, so that the results of those processes should be expressible in speech (Carruthers 2002). And although one of these systems that feeds input to the language faculty will be the higher-order thought faculty, there is no reason to assume that the language faculty can *only* receive higher-order thoughts as input. On the contrary, many of our first-order thoughts should be *directly* expressible in speech. This is sufficient to explain the Ericsson and Simon data. But then unless the linguistic expressions of thought are somehow constitutive of the thoughts being articulated, our awareness of what we are thinking will be derivative from our awareness of the sentences in which those thoughts are expressed—and it looks as if this won't, then, have the kind of immediacy required for those thoughts to count as conscious ones. (We return to some of these points in section 6.)

Another way in which someone might try to argue that the confabulation data are consistent with the required sort of semantic-ascent architecture would be this. Perhaps in the confabulation cases the thoughts in question don't occur in the right subsystem. Perhaps there are two distinct subsystems in the mind in which thinking occurs, and which can generate behavior. But perhaps only one of these has the kind of direct access to the higher-order thought faculty that we envisaged earlier. So the thoughts in this subsystem would be conscious, whereas the confabulation behaviors are produced by the other subsystem, whose contents *aren't* conscious. However, it is hard to see any plausible way of drawing the subdivisions here, that wouldn't simply be ad hoc.[13] For the confabulation examples seem pretty much like paradigmatic cases of (non-natural-language-based) judgment.

It would appear, then (if the problem of subdivisions can't be overcome), that the confabulation evidence will show that we don't have the kind of noninferential access to our own acts of thinking for those acts to count as conscious ones. Neither will our acts of thinking have the right sort of self-referential content. For if the thought P isn't available to a higher-order thought faculty that is disposed to judge immediately that I am thinking that P, then the thought P won't at the same time bear the higher-order self-referential content *I am thinking that P*.

5 An Alternative Model of the Higher-Order Thought Faculty

Let us assume that the problem of subdivisions can be overcome, however. Assume that there is some nonarbitrary way of distinguishing between those reasoning systems whose processes are directly available to higher-order thought, and those that aren't. Then what we have on the table is an alternative model of the way in which a higher-order thought faculty could be embedded into the overall architecture of the mind, to be contrasted with the model deriving from Baars (1997) sketched above. According to the latter, the higher-order thought faculty has direct access *only* to those of our occurrent states that are perceptual, necessary to construct explanations and predictions of people's behavior.[14] Call this the "mind-reading model." According to the alternative now being suggested, the higher-order thought faculty *also* has direct access to some of the other reasoning processes taking place downstream of perception, especially some of the processes that occur within *practical* reasoning. Call this the "self-monitoring model."

These two models correspond to two different accounts of what higher-order thought is *for*. According to the mind-reading model, higher-order thoughts are for interpreting and predicting behavior. The mind-reading faculty evolved in highly social creatures (such as our great-ape ancestors manifestly were) for purposes of manipulation, cooperation, and communication. This is the standard explanation that cognitive scientists offer of the evolution of our capacity for higher-order thought (e.g., Byrne and Whiten 1988). And on this account, the application of higher-order thoughts to ourselves, and the dual-analog-content that consequently comes to attach to our perceptual states, is an evolutionary spin-off.

The self-monitoring model, in contrast, will claim that higher-order thought is *also* for monitoring our own processes of thinking and reasoning—enabling us to troubleshoot in cases of difficulty or breakdown, and enabling us to reflect on and improve those processes themselves. (It could be claimed *either* that this is the *basic* function of our higher-order thought faculty, and that a capacity to predict and explain behavior came later; *or* that the mind-reading and self-monitoring functions of the faculty co-evolved.) Some cognitive scientists have begun to explore just such an hypothesis (e.g., Smith, Shields, and Washburn 2003).

There are some strong prima facie reasons for preferring the mind-reading model to the self-monitoring model, however. The most important is that the former appeals to what is, uncontroversially, a highly developed cognitive competence, whereas the latter doesn't. Everyone agrees that human beings are quite remarkably good at predicting and explaining the behavior of themselves and others through the attribution of mental states. And everyone agrees that this capacity forms part of our natural endowment, emerging in any normally developing member of the species. In contrast, it is *very* controversial to claim that humans have any natural competence in correcting and improving processes of reasoning. On the contrary, both common sense and cognitive science are agreed that naive subjects are extremely *poor* at spotting errors in reasoning, and at seeing how to improve their own reasoning.[15]

These issues are too large to pursue in any detail here. To the extent that they remain unresolved, the self-monitoring model (combined with the semantic-ascent architecture envisaged in section 3) holds out the hope that we may yet be shown to engage in conscious thinking independently of the use of sensory images. In what follows, however, I shall assume that the mind-reading model of our higher-order thought abilities is the correct one. This is partly because interesting questions then arise, concerning the extent to which sensory images could nevertheless underpin a kind of conscious propositional thinking. It is partly because it is worth exploring what would follow if the self-monitoring model turns out to be false, since it may well turn out to *be* false. And in philosophy, of course, the conditional questions are often the most interesting and important ones.[16]

6 Does Inner Speech Make Thinking Conscious?

So far, then, the evidence looks as if it might point to the conclusion that there is strictly speaking no such thing as conscious thinking (at least, to the extent that thinking isn't expressed in natural language or other imagery).

Some cognitive scientists have concluded just this (even if not in exactly these words; see Gopnik 1993). But what of "inner speech," however? Might this give us the kind of immediate awareness of our own thought processes to constitute some of the latter as conscious?

Our discussion of these questions now needs to proceed in two parts, corresponding to the contrast that I have drawn elsewhere between "communicative" and "cognitive" conceptions of the role of natural language in cognition (Carruthers 1996, 2002). According to the communicative conception of language, the only real function of language is communication (whether with another or with oneself). Natural language sentences *express* thought, but aren't *constitutive of* thought. According to the cognitive conception of language, on the other hand, at least some of our thinking takes place in natural language. So on this view, natural language sentences are at least sometimes (partly) constitutive of acts of thinking. Let us take these possibilities in turn, the former in section 6.1 and the latter in section 6.2.

6.1 Inner Speech as Expressive of Thought

Consider first, then, the traditional view that inner speech is *expressive of* thought, rather than directly (and partly) *constitutive of* it. On this account, thinking itself might be conducted in some sort of Mentalese. (Let us assume so.) But some of these Mentalese representations can be used to generate a representation of a natural language sentence in auditory imagination, creating the phenomenon of inner speech. Might this be sufficient to give us the sort of noninferential awareness of the underlying thoughts that is required for the latter to count as conscious ones?

Suppose that the contents of the Mentalese acts of thinking and the contents of the natural language sentences generated from them line up neatly one-for-one. Then thinking something carried by the Mentalese representation |BEL- P| will cause a suitable (indicative-mood) natural language sentence "P" to be imaged, where the contents of |P| and "P" are the same. But we might suppose that the imaged sentence "P" comes with its semantic properties somehow attached—for, after all, when we form an image of a sentence, we don't just hear imaginary *sounds*, we also (as it were) hear *the meaning*, just as we do in normal speech comprehension.

Then suppose that I am disposed to move from the imaged sentence "P" to the higher-order representation |I am thinking that P|, in which the content of the representation "P" is extracted and reused within the content of the that-clause. It will then turn out that it is pretty much guaranteed that such self-attributions will be reliable. Moreover, the immediacy of the causal pathway involved could be sufficient for the higher-order item of awareness in question to count as noninferentially produced, in which case the first-order thought that *P* could count as conscious. By the same token, too, that thought might qualify as having a dual content, making conscious thinking self-referential in something like the way that conscious experiences are (on my account).

There are two significant problems with this neat picture, however. The first is that even if self-attributions of thought *contents* resulting from the use of inner speech are immediate (non-self-interpretative and noninferential), self-attributions of thought *modes* (such as judging and wanting) surely aren't. This is because natural language sentences don't wear their modes on their face.

An utterance of the indicative sentence, "The door is open," can in suitable circumstances express the *belief* that the door is open, or ask a *question* as to whether or not the door is open, or issue a *command* to close the door, or merely express the *supposition* that the door is open for purposes of further inference, and so on. So whether or not an indicative-mood sentence in inner speech, "*P*," is expressive of the subject's *judgment* (i.e., occurrent belief) that *P*, simply cannot be recovered from the sentence alone. It is always going to be a matter of self-interpretation to attribute to oneself a given judgment, on this sort of account. And that seems sufficient to disqualify such judgments from counting as conscious ones.

It might be replied that in spoken language, *mode* is often indicated by tone of voice, and this can be among the contents of the auditory images that figure in inner speech. So the basis for my knowledge that I am *judging* that *P* when I token the natural language sentence "*P*" in auditory imagination is the imagined tone of voice in which that sentence is "heard." This reply won't wash, however, for two distinct reasons. The first is that although the mode in which a sentence is meant *can* be marked by intonation, in needn't be—someone's delivery can be entirely neutral, or "flat." So this couldn't be a quite general solution to our problem. But the second, and more fundamental, reason is that tone of voice must in any case be *interpreted* to yield the intended mode. If someone says, "The door is open," in a sharp, angry-sounding voice, for example, it requires interpretation to tell whether they are expressing a *belief* about something that they disapprove of, or are issuing a *command* to close the door. Telling which it is might require knowledge of our respective power/authority relations, among other things.

The second problem for the simple account sketched above is that natural-language sentence-contents and the contents of the Mentalese sentences used to generate them will rarely line up one-for-one. Language routinely makes use of contextual factors in expressing meaning. The sentence, "The door is open," leaves it to the context to determine which door is *the* door; it also leaves it to the context to determine the appropriate standard of openness (unlocked? open just a crack? wide open?), and so on. In contrast, the corresponding sentence of Mentalese must render such facts determinate. So again, one can't recover the underlying Mentalese thought from the natural language sentence alone.

It might be argued that these problems can be overcome, however, if self-generated sentences (in inner speech) can somehow carry with them the elements necessary for their interpretation. For then provided that those same meaning-determining connections are also inherited by the higher-order Mentalese sentence that replicates the content of the first-order one within a that-clause, we may still have the sort of immediacy needed for conscious thinking.

Perhaps it works like this. The underlying assertoric thought with the content P is carried by the Mentalese expression |BEL- P|. This is then used to generate a natural language sentence "Q" in auditory imagination. But that sentence comes with the connections to |BEL- P| already attached. The imaged sentence "Q," by virtue of being "experienced," is a state of the right sort to be received as input by the mind-reading faculty, which can deploy the concept of occurrent belief. The mind-reading faculty detaches the Mentalese sentence |BEL- P| from the natural language sentence received as input, and forms from it the Mentalese belief |BEL- I am thinking that P|, in which the Mentalese sentence |P| is reused with the same content as the original. The result might then count as noninferential awareness of my own act of thinking.

I suspect that there may be a good many problems with this attempted vindication of the reality of conscious thinking. Let me focus on one. It is quite widely accepted that the language faculty is divided into two distinct subsystems, one for production and one for comprehension (with perhaps each of these drawing off a single language-specific database; Chomsky 1995). It will be the work of the production subsystem to create the natural language sentence "Q" from the Mentalese representation |BEL- P|. But in order for that sentence to be displayed in auditory imagination and received by the mind-reading faculty, it needs to be passed across to be received by the *comprehension* subsystem. And there is good reason to think that the connections with the underlying thought, expressed by |BEL- P|, will thereby be severed.

One reason for this is that the comprehension subsystem simply isn't *built* to receive Mentalese representations as input. Its job is rather to receive natural language sentences as input and to construct interpretations of them, perhaps in cooperation with other systems. Another reason is that "inner speech" may well exploit the feedback loops within the overall language faculty that are used during normal speech production for phonological and semantic monitoring and repair (Levelt 1989). In normal speech production, the sentence "Q," generated from the Mentalese message-to-be-communicated |BEL- P|, is passed to the consumer subsystem to check that the intended utterance will indeed convey the intended message. This can work only if the consumer system doesn't *already* have access to the message |BEL- P|.

6.2 Inner Speech as (Partly) Constitutive of Thought

It appears, then, that if language is but a means of *expressing* thought, then there may be no such thing as conscious thinking. For although we come to be aware of our thoughts by consuming their internal expressions, in inner speech, the route from thought, to speech, to awareness of thought is too indirect and interpretative to constitute the thoughts in question as conscious ones. Everything may look a bit different if we switch to a version of the cognitive conception of language, however (Carruthers 1996, 2002), according to which inner speech *is*, or is somehow constitutive of, thinking. To be plausible, such a view should only claim that representations of natural language sentences in inner speech are *partly* constitutive of thinking. (This is because of the problems of indeterminacy attaching to natural language sentences, *inter alia*, discussed in section 6.1.)

Within the framework provided by a cognitive conception of language, an account can be given of how we have noninferential knowledge of the *contents* of our (conscious) thoughts. The sentence "Q," generated by the production subsystem, is tokened in inner speech and consumed by the comprehension subsystem. The result will be a representation of an interpreted sentence, carrying with it the connections to the Mentalese expressions, underlying data structures, perceptual experiences, or whatever else is necessary to make the meaning of "Q" determinate. In the simplest case, if the interpretation process is a reliable one, then the meaning that gets attached to "Q" might be the same as the content of the Mentalese sentence |P| that initiated the production of "Q." But this doesn't really matter in the present context, and it might not always happen. So let us work with an example in which it doesn't: let us imagine that the process of interpreting "Q" attaches to it the Mentalese sentence |R|.

Now by hypothesis (if some version of the cognitive conception of language is correct) the pairing of $\langle$"Q," |R|$\rangle$ has further consequences in cognition; and not just *any* consequences, but those that are distinctive of thinking. One way in which this might be the case is if the representation |R| is one that can *only* be formed via the construction of an appropriate natural language sentence, as "module-integration" accounts of the role of natural language in cognition suggest (Hermer-Vazquez, Spelke, and Katsnelson 1999; Carruthers 2002). Another way in which it might be true is if it is only by virtue of articulating the sentence "Q" in auditory imagination, and hence making its content available to the various inference-systems that exist downstream of perception and consume its products, that the subject comes to believe |R| for the first time. The process of articulating "Q" leads to |R| being evaluated and accepted, in a way that would not have happened otherwise.[17]

Now among the consumer-systems to which ⟨"Q," |R|⟩ is made available by the language comprehension subsystem will be the mind-reading faculty. Suppose that the latter is immediately disposed, whenever it receives such a pairing, to form the belief |I am thinking that R|. Then the result will be noninferential awareness of what I am thinking. We can regard the immediacy and reliability of the connection between the higher-order thought and the thought thereby attributed as being sufficient both to render the act of thinking that R conscious, and to mean that the sentence "Q" has both the first-order content *that R* and the higher-order content *I am thinking that R*. So now we have a single event (a token representation of the natural language sentence "Q" in inner speech) that has both a first-order and a higher-order content, similar to the case of experience.

Note that this "immediacy" needn't be at all undermined by the fact that the comprehension process that generates an interpretation for "Q" is an inferential and interpretative one. For it is the product, rather than the initial cause, of the interpretative process that gets self-attributed. And this can be attributed to oneself *without* further interpretation or inference. According to the hypothesis that we are considering (the cognitive conception of language), the sentence "Q" displayed (and interpreted) in inner speech is *itself* a thought, or is rather partly *constitutive of* a thought, given its causal role in the overall architecture of cognition. And it is *this* thought (the thought expressed by |R|) that gets reliably and noninferentially attributed.

It would appear, therefore, that if the cognitive conception of language is correct, then we have a vindication of the reality of conscious thinking. For we can have immediate and noninferential awareness of the contents of those acts of thinking that occur in inner speech, on this account. However, the point that awareness of attitude (as opposed to awareness of content) must always be inferential/interpretative remains in force. Even if the tokening of some natural language sentence "Q" in auditory imagination is sometimes constitutive of thinking, still the fact that the entertaining of that sentence is an assertoric judgment, or a wondering-whether, or an act of supposition, or whatever, will be a matter of its larger causal role *beyond* the point at which interpretation occurs. (It will be a matter of the further causal role of |R|, indeed.) And that role just can't be read off from the sentence itself. It will have to be a matter of further self-interpretation.

The upshot is that, while there might be such a thing as conscious (and self-referring) *thinking*, there might be no such thing as conscious assertoric *judging*, conscious (propositional) *wanting*, conscious *supposing*, and so forth. Put differently: although there are conscious episodic propositional *contents*, there might be no conscious episodic propositional *attitudes*.

What of the self-referential character of conscious thinking, on this conception? In what sense is it vindicated? As I presented the view above, I tacitly assumed that the higher-order thought generated from the sentence/thought pair ⟨"Q," |R|⟩ would be |BEL- I am thinking that R|. That is, I assumed that the sort of self-reference here would be a reference *to the self*. But perhaps this was unwarranted. One can just as well move directly from ⟨"Q," |R|⟩ to |BEL- *That* is an act of thinking that R|. This suggests that (assuming the truth of some form of consumer semantics) the sentence "Q" might have the dual contents R and *that is a thinking that R*, where the pronoun refers to the sentence "Q" in question. In that case, conscious thoughts may be self-referential in exactly the same sort of way that conscious experiences are (as discussed in section 1).

7 Conclusion

I have sketched an account of phenomenally conscious experience according to which such experiences always have dual (and self-referential) analog contents. I have argued that the constraints placed on a theory of conscious thinking are different from those placed on a theory of conscious experience, since conscious thoughts aren't necessarily and intrinsically *phenomenal* in character. I have sketched some reasons for thinking that there might be no such thing as conscious thinking, if natural language plays no direct role in our thoughts, since all self-attributions might then be inferential/self-interpretative ones. And I have argued that, if language *does* play such a role, then the *contents* of our thoughts might be conscious (and self-referential) even if the *attitudes* that we take to them are not.[18]

Notes

1. Consider, for example, the kinds of visual percepts that one finds in blindsight (Weiskrantz 1997), or in the online guidance of movement, if a "two systems" account of vision is correct (Milner and Goodale 1995; Jacob and Jeannerod 2003).

2. Such concepts are arguably at the bottom of inverted-qualia and zombie-style thought experiments. Possessing such concepts, there will be no incoherence in thinking, "Someone might possess states with such-and-such functional role/intentional content while lacking *this* type of state"—where the indexical *this* expresses a concept that is purely recognitional, with no conceptual connections to causal-role concepts or intentional concepts. See Carruthers 2004a.

3. The metaphor comes from conceiving of cognition as a *stream* flowing from input (sensory stimulation) to output (action). Our perceptual systems are "upstream," constructing representations as output that are taken as input by (that are consumed by) a variety of "downstream" inferential systems, belief-forming systems, planning systems, and so forth. The latter in turn produce representations that are eventually consumed by the motor-control systems.

4. Here and throughout I shall use a subscripted "a" when referring to perceptual contents, to emphasize their fine-grained analog character.

5. Note that not *any* form of consumer semantics can be endorsed, if this account is to be plausible. Rather, we need claim that it is only the *immediate* further effects of a state that are determinants of its content. Otherwise, if distant inferences were determinants of content, we would face the implausible consequence that our perceptual experiences can have the contents, $ripens\text{-}in\text{-}July_a$, $is\text{-}Aunt\text{-}Anne's\text{-}favorite_a$, and so forth. It is fortunate, then, that consumer semantics is especially plausible in respect of the *immediate* inferences that consumer systems are apt to derive from a given state. For example, it seems that part of what fixes the content of "&" as *and*, is a disposition to move from "P & Q" to "P" and to "Q"—but not necessarily any more elaborate disposition to derive "$\sim(P \supset \sim Q)$." Thus someone could surely mean P *and* Q by "P & Q," even though they lacked the inferential capacity to deduce from it "$\sim(P \supset \sim Q)$."

6. Is it any argument against imposing different *desiderata* on theories of conscious experience and thought, that "conscious" appears to be univocal when applied to experiences and thoughts? Not at all. For theories of consciousness aren't theories of the *concept* "conscious." The concept can very well be univocal while the phenomena picked out by that concept give rise to different explanatory problems.

7. Admittedly, if "inner speech" can be a kind of thought, as I am inclined to believe, and as we shall discuss briefly in section 6.2, then some thinking *will* have phenomenal properties. These will be the properties, namely, associated with the auditory images

that constitute the stream of inner speech. But even in this case it won't be *qua* thoughts that the events in the stream are phenomenally conscious. Phenomenal consciousness will attach to the imaged *sounds* of the sentences in inner speech, not to the contents of those sentences, i.e., not to the thoughts that are thereby entertained.

8. See Carruthers 1998b for discussion of the sense in which knowledge of our own thoughts has to be noninferential and immediate, in order for those thoughts to qualify as conscious ones. I certainly don't mean to rule out *all* processes that one might describe as "inferential" (cf. the processing that takes place within the visual system). But certainly *conscious* inferences are ruled out. And so, too, are the sorts of unconscious inferences that one might engage in when interpreting another person, drawing on knowledge of the circumstances, behavior, and other mental states of that person. For it is surely part of our commonsense notion of conscious thought that there is an important asymmetry between our knowledge of our own thoughts and our knowledge of other people's.

9. Note that endorsing this thesis needn't involve any commitment to Gordon's "simulation theory" of the basis on which we ascribe mental states generally. Endorsing the "question/check procedure" as the basis on which we have self-awareness of standing-state beliefs is perfectly consistent with some or other version of "theory-theory" of the overall basis of mental-state ascription.

10. Note that a major difference between the two authors cited concerns the question whether the higher-order awareness has to be actual, or whether it can be merely dispositional. (There is a perfectly respectable sense in which I can be said to be aware that zebras in the wild don't wear overcoats, of course, or to be aware that ten million and one is larger than ten million, even if I have never explicitly considered and endorsed these propositions. I may be said to be aware of these things because I *would* immediately assent to them if I *were to* consider them.) I shall be assuming the latter in what follows.

11. I shall use line-brackets when referring to sentences in the language of thought/ Mentalese, using quotation marks when referring to natural language sentences, and italics when referring to sentence contents.

12. Note that the representation |BEL- P| isn't yet a higher-order one. It isn't a representation *that* the subject believes that P. Rather, it is *constitutive of* the subject believing that P. The tag |BEL-| *causes* other systems to *treat* the representation in the manner constitutive of belief (e.g., by feeding it to inferential systems, or by feeding it to the practical reasoning system to guide action). It doesn't *represent that* the representation in question is a belief.

13. One suggestion—which definitely isn't ad hoc, since it is supported by multiple lines of evidence—would be to claim that there are dual systems for thinking and reasoning, one of which is fast, implicit, and unconscious, and the other of which is

slow, explicit, and conscious (Evans and Over 1996; Stanovich 1999). However, if, as some have argued, the explicit system implicates natural language sentences (Evans and Over 1996; Frankish 2004), then it won't exemplify the sort of Mentalese-based semantic-ascent architecture that is under discussion here. This point will be further explored in section 6.

14. The higher-order thought faculty would also need access to (activations of) standing-state beliefs, of course, such as beliefs about the target-subject's long-term goals or idiosyncratic beliefs. But this wouldn't require it to have access to the processes within the agent that generate beliefs and decisions.

15. People *can* monitor their own reasoning, of course, even if they aren't very good at improving it (although they can get better)—especially when their reasoning is verbally expressed. But this lends no support to the version of self-monitoring model under discussion here. For the best account of this capacity is that it is *realized in* cycles of operation of other systems (including language and mind-reading), and that it is—like Dennett's (1991) *Joycean machine*—heavily influenced by cultural learning (Carruthers 2002; Frankish 2004). By learning to verbalize our own thoughts we can learn to monitor and improve upon our own patterns of reasoning. But only if our verbalizations are constitutive of (a kind of) thinking will our access to our own thoughts count as immediate and noninferential. (See the discussion in section 6.)

16. As one of the characters in the Walt Disney movie *Hercules* remarks to another, "*If* is good!"

17. This might happen if the subject *avows* "*Q*," for example—where this means that they *commit themselves* to thinking and reasoning in the future as if "*Q*" were true (Frankish 2004). If the subject thereafter remembers and executes this commitment, the effect will be that the underlying representation |R| will become the functional equivalent of |BEL- R|.

18. I am grateful to Georges Rey for a series of conversations that prompted me to begin writing about the main topic of this essay. And I am grateful to Keith Frankish, Uriah Kriegel, and Georges Rey for insightful sets of comments on earlier drafts.

Robert W. Lurz

1 Introduction

Our beliefs and desires are sometimes said to be conscious in the sense of being "before our mind" (Armstrong 1973, p. 21). But what do we take ourselves to be saying when we describe a belief or desire of ours as being conscious in this sense? And given what we ordinarily take ourselves to mean, do conscious beliefs and desires, so understood, exist?

A number of philosophers, in the eliminativist tradition, have argued that conscious beliefs and desires, as the folk understand them to be, simply do not exist (Churchland 1981; Rey 1982). Following in this tradition, Carruthers (this volume) has put forward a provocative line of reasoning for the tentative eliminativist conclusion that there might be no such thing as conscious beliefs or conscious desires. His argument, roughly, is that, on our ordinary folk understanding of conscious belief and desire, to have a conscious belief or desire involves being (or being apt to be) immediately aware of our own occurrent acts of thinking and judging, and that there is no credible model within the representational theory of mind that explains how such immediate awareness is possible, and that there is some empirical evidence from studies in social- and neuropsychology that suggests such awareness does not exist.

There are a number of ways one might respond to such an argument, and Carruthers considers and responds to some. But one response that Carruthers does not consider, and one that I shall pursue in this essay, is that his argument rests upon a mistaken analysis of our folk concepts of conscious belief and conscious desire. There is, I shall argue, a rather natural way to understand these concepts such that, on this understanding, our having conscious beliefs and conscious desires can be explained within the framework of a representational theory of mind, and is in no way undermined by the empirical data that Carruthers cites in his article.

To reach this conclusion, however, we first need to get clear on what we take ourselves to be saying when we describe our beliefs and desires as conscious in the "before the mind" sense. I shall address this issue in the next two sections. I shall first examine two contemporary approaches on this issue, the first-order (FO) approach and the higher-order (HO) approach, and will show that each approach falls short of capturing our folk notions of conscious belief and conscious desire. I shall then propose my own approach, the same-order (SO) approach, and demonstrate how it succeeds where the others fail.[1] In section 5, I shall show how, on the SO approach, conscious beliefs and desires can be explained within the framework of a representational theory of mind and how their existence is in no way threatened by the empirical data cited by Carruthers. In section 6, I shall consider and reply to some challenges that the SO approach may be thought to face.

2 Paradigm Cases of Conscious Belief and Conscious Desire

Before examining the different approaches to explaining our folk concepts of conscious belief and conscious desire, I would like to describe two cases— one of conscious belief and the other of conscious desire—that I take to be representative of the phenomena that these approaches aim to explain.

Case 1 The other day a colleague informed me that someone had stolen my book bag from my office. Initially, I was not very upset, for the bag was of no great value. But not long after my colleague had informed me of the theft, it occurred to me *that my keys are in my bag!*—at which point, I immediately dialed security to see whether the thief had been apprehended and, more important, whether my bag had been recovered. At the moment when it occurred to me that my keys were in my bag, call it time *t*, something became conscious. What became conscious at time *t* was my belief that my keys were in my bag. Of course, I had this belief long before time *t*; in fact, I had it since the morning when I placed my keys in my bag. But it was not until time *t* that it became conscious—it was not until time *t*, to use the words of David Armstrong, that it came "before my mind."

Case 2 My office the other day was particularly hot, and, as a result, I was becoming rather thirsty while typing at my computer. At one point, it occurred to me *to get a drink of water*. At which point, I put aside my work and walked to the water cooler in the department office. At the moment when it occurred to me to get a drink of water, call it time t, something became conscious. What became conscious was my desire to get a drink of water. Unlike my belief in case 1, however, my desire in this case was something that I apparently did not have long before time t. Rather, I came to have the desire, it would appear, right around the time that it became conscious—right around the time, to use Armstrong's words again, that it came "before my mind."

Taking the above two cases as representative of our folk notions of conscious belief and conscious desire—at least, in the "before the mind" sense of "conscious"[2]—let us return to the issue of this section: what do we have in mind when we say that at time t, a person has the *conscious* belief that p or the *conscious* desire that q? What, in other words, are the individually necessary and jointly sufficient conditions for sentences of the form, "at time t, S has the conscious belief that p" and "at time t, S has the conscious desire that q"? Well, one obvious necessary condition is that at time t S *has* the belief that p or *has* the desire that q.[3] For if at time t, S does not have the belief that p or the desire that q, then, a fortiori, at time t, S does not have the *conscious* belief that p or the *conscious* desire that q. However, having at time t the belief that p or the desire that q is not sufficient for having at time t the conscious belief that p or the conscious desire that q, for if it were, all of the beliefs and desires that we have would be conscious, which they are not. So, what we are looking for is something in addition to S's having the belief that p or desire that q at a particular time that would make the following bi-conditional true:

At time t, *S has the conscious belief that* p *(or the conscious desire that* q)
iff

(i) At time t, S has the belief that p (or the desire that q).
(ii) ?

2.1 The FO Approach to Conscious Belief and Desire
The first approach toward filling in the missing condition that I shall examine is Fred Dretske's first-order (FO) account. According to Dretske, "a certain belief is conscious not because the believer is conscious of it (or conscious of having it), but because it is a representation that makes one conscious of the fact (that P) that it is a belief about" (1993, p. 281).[4] On this approach, to say that at time t S has the conscious belief that p is to say, roughly, that at time t S is aware of the fact that p, and is so aware because he has the belief that p.[5] A bit more formally:

At time t, *S has the conscious belief that* p *iff*

(i) At time *t*, S has the belief that *p*.
(ii) At time *t*, S is aware of the fact that *p*.
(iii) (ii) obtains in part because (i) obtains.

How does this account square with case 1 above? At first blush, it seems to give a rather straightforward explanation of what is going on there. For at time *t*, I do seem to become aware of the fact that my keys are in my bag, and it certainly seems plausible to say that I was made aware of this fact in part because at time *t* I had the belief that my keys were in my bag.

There is a problem, however. For on Dretske's FO account, a subject's awareness of some fact, which is a relational state of affairs between a subject and a fact, is constituted in part by an internal, nonrelational state of the subject (presumably a brain state) that is itself *conscious* (Dretske 1993, p. 271). On Dretske's account, then, in order for me at time *t* to have the conscious belief that my keys are in my bag, there must exist at time *t* some internal, nonrelational state of me that is itself conscious and partly constitutive of my awareness of the fact that my keys are in my bag.

But why believe that I am in such a state at time *t*? No doubt, I am at time *t* in some internal, nonrelational state or other (presumably a brain state) that is partly responsible for my being aware of the fact that my keys are in my bag. But why believe that this state of me is itself *conscious*? After all, at time *t* I do not seem to be aware of suddenly being in any such internal, nonrelational conscious state. Rather, what I seem to become aware of at time *t* is simply *that my keys are in my bag*, and this, whatever it is, is not an internal, nonrelational conscious state of me. Furthermore, whenever an internal, nonrelational state of me suddenly becomes conscious, I typically become aware of it: if I suddenly come to have a conscious pain in the side, a tickle in the back of the throat, a feeling of guilt or excitement, I typically become aware of being in such a conscious state. So the fact that at time *t* I do not seem to be aware of being in an internal, nonrelational conscious state is at least a defeasible reason for holding that at time *t* I am not in any such state—or if I am, that the state itself is not a *conscious* internal, nonrelational state. Therefore, there appears to be a defeasible reason for denying that condition (ii) on Dretske's FO account is individually necessary for having a conscious belief.

There is, however, a more serious problem for Dretske's approach. The problem is that the approach cannot be extended to explain our folk concept of conscious desire. By extending it to cover conscious desires, the approach would look something like the following:

At time t, *S has the conscious desire that* q *iff*

(i) At time t, S has the desire that q.
(ii) At time t, S is aware of the fact that q.
(iii) (ii) obtains in part because (i) obtains.

The problem is that nothing like condition (ii) is individually necessary for having a conscious desire. One can, and often does, have conscious desires without ever being made aware of any facts that one's desires could be said to be about. In case 2, for instance, I came to have, at time t, the conscious desire to get a drink of water, but at that time I need not have been aware of any fact about my getting a drink of water. For one, it may not have been a fact that at time t I was going to get a drink of water—perhaps, unknown to me there was no water in the water cooler or anywhere at that time. And two, even if it were a fact that at time t I was going to get a drink of water, I need not have been aware of it at time t. For at time t, I may have mistakenly believed that there was no water in the cooler or anywhere and, hence, that I was *not* going to get a drink of water. None of this, of course, would have prevented my coming to have at time t the conscious desire to get a drink of water.

Dretske (1997, n. 10) acknowledges that his account has this shortcoming and suggests that a radically different explanation—a higher-order explanation (see below)—should be given for our folk concept of conscious desire. But such a maneuver is, on the face of it, ad hoc. For it is rather clear, as case 1 and case 2 illustrate, that what we have in mind when we say of a desire of ours that it is conscious is something strikingly similar to what we have in mind when we say of a belief of ours that it is conscious: in both cases we are saying that the belief or desire is "before our mind." And there is nothing in the way we use "before our mind" in such contexts that would suggest that we mean something different when we use it to describe our beliefs from what we mean when we use it to describe our desires. As a result, it is surely preferable to have a unified account of our folk notions of conscious beliefs and conscious desires.

2.2 The Actualist HO Approach to Conscious Belief and Desire

One approach that offers a unified account of our folk notions of conscious belief and conscious desire is the actualist higher-order (HO) approach—championed by, among others, Armstrong (1981), Rosenthal (1990), Lycan (1996), Gennaro (1996), and Mellor (1978).[6] On this approach, to say that one has, at a particular time t, the conscious belief that p or the conscious desire that q is to say, roughly, that one is, at time t, *actually immediately aware* of having the belief that p or the desire that q. To be *actually* immediately aware of having a belief or desire is to be distinguished from being merely *disposed* to be immediately aware of having a belief or desire. It is the former type of awareness that the actualist HO theorist claims is constitutive of having conscious beliefs and conscious desires. In the next section, we shall examine a HO approach that takes that latter type of awareness as constitutive of having conscious beliefs and desires.

For a definition of "immediacy," I defer to one of the best-known exponents of the actualist HO approach, David Rosenthal. Rosenthal states that for us to be actually immediately aware that we are in a particular state of mind is for us to become aware of our being in this state of mind "without relying on any inference or observation of which we are transitively conscious [i.e., of which we are aware]" (1990, p. 738). "Our consciousness of our conscious states," Rosenthal writes elsewhere, "need not actually be unmediated and spontaneous; it need only seem that way, from a first-person point of view" (2000, p. 270).[7] So, for instance, if I were to become aware of having the desire for something in the refrigerator by way of observing my standing in front of the refrigerator and by reasoning that the best explanation for why I am now standing in front of the refrigerator is that I desire something in the refrigerator, my awareness would not be immediate—it would be mediated by an observation and an inference of which I was aware. For my awareness to be immediate, it would have to come about either without any observation or inference on my part, or without it appearing to me as if it did.

Bringing these points together, then, we can express the traditional actualist HO approach to conscious belief and desire a bit more formally as follows:

At time t, *S has the conscious belief that* p *(or the conscious desire that* q*)* *iff*

(i) At time t, S has the belief that p (or the desire that q).
(ii) At time t, S is actually immediately aware of having the belief that p (or the desire that q).[8]

How does the HO approach square with cases 1 and 2? Not very well, I think. For if the approach is accepted, then in case 1, for example, I not only have at time t the belief that my keys are in my bag, I also, at that time, come to be actually immediately aware of *having this belief*. But is there any reason to think that at time t I come to be actually immediately aware of having this belief, or actually immediately aware of any internal state of mind at all? Prima facie, it does not. After all, what occurs to me at time t, and what at that time I seem to become actually immediately aware of, is *that my keys are in my bag*, not that I *believe* that my keys are in my bag, or that I am in an *internal mental state* of some kind. Of course, at time t it could have occurred to me that I have this belief (or that I'm in a state of mind of some type), but the fact is it did not. And the fact that this did *not* occur to me at time t is at least a defeasible reason to believe that at that time I was not actually immediately aware of my having this belief (or mental state). After all, what would it mean to say that at time t it did not occur to me that I have this belief, but all the same I was immediately aware of having it?

Of course, if soon after time t I was asked whether I remember having at time t the belief that my keys were in my bag, I most likely would say that I do remember. But such a response in no way suggests that at time t I was actually immediately aware of having this belief. For after all, I can also come to remember seeing at time $t' > t$ the tiles on the floor of my office as I rushed to my desk to call security, even though it is quite clear that at that time I was not in any way actually immediately aware *of seeing* the tiles on my office floor.[9] There are, in fact, many things that we can come to remember seeing, hearing, saying, and even believing and desiring which, at the time, we were not at all actually immediately aware of ourselves seeing, hearing, saying, believing, or desiring.

Now, what *would* indicate that, in case 1 for example, I was, at time t, actually immediately aware of having the belief that my keys were in my bag would be if I could remember being at time t *actually immediately aware* of having this belief. But, if someone asked me at some time soon after time t whether I remember being at time t actually immediately aware of having the belief that my keys are in my bag, I would answer that I do not. What I remember being actually immediately aware of at time t is what actually occurred to me at time t—namely, *that my keys are in my bag*—and this, whatever it is, is not my having the belief that my keys are in my bag (or any state of my mind). And the fact that I am unable to remember being at time t actually immediately aware of having the belief that my keys are in my bag (or of any state of my mind) is at least a defeasible reason for holding that at time t I was not in fact actually immediately aware of having this belief (or of any state of my mind).[10]

A similar concern, of course, can be raised for case 2. In that case, at time t it occurs to me *to get a drink of water*, not that I *desire* to get a drink of water, or that I am in a mental state of some kind. Again, at time t it could have occurred to me that I have this desire (or mental state), but it did not.

And the fact that this did not occur to me at time t, and the fact that I cannot remember being at time t immediately aware of having this desire (or mental state), is at least a defeasible reason to believe that at that time I was not actually immediately aware of having this desire (or mental state). What in case 1 and case 2 I seem to be actually immediately aware of, and what in these cases I do not seem to be actually immediately aware of, provide at least defeasible grounds for doubting that condition (ii) on the actualist HO approach is a necessary condition for having conscious beliefs and conscious desires.[11]

2.3   Carruthers's Dispositional HO Approach to Conscious Belief and Desire

An alternative HO approach to conscious belief and desire, one which has been designed explicitly to avoid the sort of problem outlined above, is the dispositional HO approach. And perhaps the best-known proponent and defender of this alternative HO approach is Peter Carruthers. Carruthers (this volume) expresses the dispositional HO approach to conscious belief and desire as follows: "A better answer to the question of what renders standing state-beliefs and desires conscious would be this: they are conscious just in case they are apt to emerge as conscious occurrent thinkings with the very same content" (this volume). Now, it needs to be mentioned that Carruthers makes a distinction between a belief or desire being conscious in the "before the mind" sense—that is, the sense of being conscious that is exhibited in case 1 and case 2—and a belief or desire being conscious in the sense of being *disposed* to be conscious in the "before one's mind" sense. On this second sense of conscious belief and desire, it is true to say of me in case 1, for example, that all morning long I had the conscious belief that my keys are in my bag. On the "before the mind" sense of conscious belief and desire, however, I did not have the conscious belief that my keys are in my bag until time t. The quotation above is a description of Carruthers's account of conscious belief and desire in this second sense. However, Carruthers also takes his HO approach to give an account of conscious belief and desire in the "before the mind" sense. According to Carruthers's approach, a subject's belief or desire is conscious in this sense just in case it *actually emerges* as a conscious occurrent thinking with the very same content. What this amounts to I hope to make clear below.

The term "conscious occurrent thinking," for Carruthers, is a general term that covers "conscious acts of wondering-whether, judging-that, supposing-that, and the like" (1996, p. 194). On Carruthers's account, a conscious occurrent thinking is an occurrent mental event of "whose occurrence and content the subject [is disposed to have] immediate and noninferential knowledge" (this volume)—that is, it is an occurrent mental event of whose existence and content the subject is disposed to be *immediately aware.*

The kind of conscious occurrent thinking that is relevant for having conscious beliefs, according to Carruthers, is conscious occurrent judging: "On this alternative account, what constitutes the conscious status of the standing-state belief that P, is that it is apt to emerge [or actually emerges] in a conscious assertoric judgment that P" (1996, p. 175). In personal communication, Carruthers has informed me that he also takes the relevant occurrent conscious thinking for conscious desires to be, in most cases, a conscious assertoric judging and, in some cases, the mental analogue of speech acts in the optative mode, such as the act of thinking to oneself, "would that I had another beer." On Carruthers's account, then, what constitutes the conscious status of a conscious desire that q is that the desire emerges (or is apt to emerge) in a conscious assertoric judging that q, or, in some cases, in an act of thinking to oneself, "would that it were that q."[12] (Unless otherwise stated, I shall, from here on, use the expression, "thinking that p," to cover both conscious occurrent assertoric judgings that p as well as conscious occurrent thinkings that p in the optative mode.)

One way to understand Carruthers's idea of a subject's belief that p (or desire that q) *emerging* as a conscious occurrent thinking that p (or that q) is that it is the idea of the subject coming to think to himself that p (or that q) in part *because* he has the belief that p (or the desire that q). That is, what makes a subject's act of thinking that p (or that q) an *emergence* of his belief that p (or desire that q) is that it came to be, in some relevant sense, *because* the subject has the belief that p (or the desire that q).[13] If this interpretation of "emerging as a conscious occurrent thinking" is correct, then Carruthers's dispositional HO account of conscious belief and desire—in the "before one's mind" sense of "conscious"—can be expressed a bit more formally as follows:

At time t, *S has the conscious belief that* p *(or the conscious desire that* q*) iff*

(i) At time t, S has the belief that p (or the desire that q).

(ii) At time t, S thinks to himself that p (or that q).

(iii) (ii) obtains in part because (i) obtains. (This is what makes S's act of thinking to himself that p (or that q) an *emergence* of his belief that p [or desire that q]).

(iv) At time t, S is disposed to be immediately aware of his thinking to himself that p (or that q). (This is what makes S's act of thinking to himself that p [or that q] conscious.)

How, then, does Carruthers's dispositinal HO approach square with what seems to be going on in cases 1 and 2? Admittedly, Carruthers's approach fairs better than the traditional actualist HO approach. For Carruthers's approach does not require that I actually be immediately aware of having any belief or desire (or mental state of some type) at time t. Yet despite its avoidance of the problem that the traditional actualist HO approach has with cases 1 and 2, Carruthers's approach does not seem to give an accurate analysis of what is going on in either of these two cases. First, it needs to be pointed out that there is no reason to think that in either case 1 or case 2, I am, at time t, engaged in some mental act of judging or thinking to myself—at least, not on a standard way of understanding these occurrent mental events. For on a standard understanding, to judge that p, or to think to oneself that q, is to *do* something: it is to perform an intentional mental *act* (Geach 1957). But in neither case 1 nor case 2, do I *do* anything; rather, something *happens* to me. In fact, we describe the cases as ones in which something "occurs" to me or comes "before the mind"—words that suggest something much more passive than judging or thinking to oneself that such-and-such is the case—at least, on a standard understanding of such occurrent mental events. Hence, on a standard reading of "judging that p" or "thinking to oneself that q," condition (ii) in Carruthers's account does not appear to be individually necessary for having conscious beliefs or desires in the "before the mind" sense.

Of course, an occurrent mental event does take place at time t in case 1 and another at time t in case 2. In case 1, it is the event of it occurring to me that my keys are in my bag; and in case 2, it is the event of it occurring to me to get a drink of water. And perhaps all that Carruthers takes his occurrent judgings and thinkings to amount to is what I describe here as the passive event of it occurring to me that such-and-such. Fair enough. But now the question is whether, in order to explain what it means to say that at time t I have, in case 1 for example, the conscious belief that my keys are in my bag, it must be supposed that at time t I am disposed to be immediately aware of it occurring to me that my keys are in my bag. Why, in other words, is it not enough simply to say that what it means to say that at time t I have the conscious belief that my keys are in my bag is that (i) at time t, I have the belief that my keys are in my bag, (ii) at time t, it occurs to me that my keys are in my bag, and (iii) the mental event described in (ii) happens at time t in part because at time t I have the belief described in (ii)?[14] Prima facie, it seems as if conditions (i)–(iii) provide all that we need in order to analyze what we have in mind in describing me in case 1 as having at time t the conscious belief that my keys are in my bag.[15] Why suppose, as

Carruthers does, that we also must add that at time t I am disposed to be immediately aware of it occurring to me that my keys are in my bag?

My guess is that Carruthers's makes this additional requirement for the following sort of reason. Carruthers assumes that the event that occurs in case 1 at time t and the event that occurs in case 2 at time t are conscious mental events, and that the best account of what it is for a mental event to be conscious is, according to his dispositional HO approach, that the subject is disposed to be immediately aware of it and its content. Therefore, we must add to our analysis of what is going on in case 1 at time t and in case 2 at time t the condition that in each case, I am, at time t, disposed to be immediately aware of an occurrent mental event. But why believe that the event that occurs at time t in case 1 or the event that occurs at time t in case 2 is *conscious*? After all, in neither of these cases am I actually immediately aware of undergoing any mental event at time t. Again, in each of these cases what I am actually immediately aware of at time t is what actually occurs to me at that time—namely, in case 1, *that my keys are in my bag*, and in case 2 *that I'm to get a drink of water*—and neither of these things is an occurrent mental event.[16]

I do not see, then, that Carruthers has given us any reason to go beyond the minimal analysis outlined above; and, therefore, I don't see any reason for saying that condition (iv) in Carruthers's dispositional HO approach is a necessary condition for having conscious beliefs or desires. But, one might ask, is there a good reason for *denying* that condition (iv) is a necessary condition? I believe so. For if condition (iv) really were part of our folk concepts of conscious belief and conscious desire, then we should find it inappropriate to say of any creature that fails to satisfy condition (iv)—even if it satisfied conditions (i)–(iii) in the minimal analysis above—that it has conscious beliefs and desires. And this just does not appear to be how our folk concepts of conscious belief and conscious desire work. To illustrate, suppose that normal two-year-olds are not yet capable of being immediately aware of their own occurrent mental events. Suppose that this capacity does not start to develop in children until the age of three.[17] This is not too difficult to suppose, since the behaviors of normal two-year-olds provide little or no evidence that they have any such capacity.[18] Even if normal two-year-olds are not yet capable of being immediately aware of their own occurrent mental events, it certainly seems conceptually possible that they have conscious beliefs and desires in the same sense in which I have them in case 1 and case 2 respectively.

For example, it seems quite conceivable that, while playing with his blocks, two-year-old William becomes thirsty and, as a result, comes to have a desire for a drink of water. It is also conceivable that at some moment during his playing, call this moment time t, it suddenly occurs to William to get a drink of water, and it does so in part because he has the desire for a drink of water. Finally, it is conceivable that, given what occurs to William at time t, plus certain background beliefs that he has at that time, he puts aside his blocks and goes and asks his father for a drink of water. If such a thing did occur, I think we would find it quite natural to say that at time t, William comes to have a conscious desire for a drink of water, despite the fact that William, we are supposing, is not at time t disposed to be immediately aware of the fact that it occurs to him to get a drink of water.[19] I think that cases like this strongly suggest that our folk concepts of conscious desire and conscious belief do not apply *only* to creatures capable of being immediately aware of their own occurrent mental events; and, hence, I think that cases like this strongly suggest that condition (iv) in Carruthers's analysis of our folk concepts of conscious desire and conscious belief is not individually necessary.

3   The SO Approach to Conscious Belief and Desire

If what we have in mind when we say that someone has, at a particular time, the conscious belief that p or the conscious desire that q is not properly explained by either the FO or the HO approaches discussed above, then what is it that we have in mind when we say such things? To answer this question, let us return to case 1 and case 2. In each of these cases, what seems to be going on is that at time t I suddenly come to be actually immediately aware *of* something, and this something seems to be *what* I believe or *what* I desire—not, that I *believe* or *desire* something. In case 1, for example, I seem to become at time t actually immediately aware *of what* I believe with respect to the whereabouts of my keys, for at time t, what I believe with respect to the whereabouts of my keys—namely, *that my keys are in my bag*—suddenly occurs to me in a way which, from my point of view, did not involve any inference or observation on my part. In case 2, I seem to become at time t actually immediately aware *of what* I desire with respect to getting a drink of water, for at time t, what I desire with respect to getting a drink of water—namely, *that I'm to get a drink of water*—suddenly occurs to me in a way which, from my point of view, did not involve any inference or observation on my part. Now, if what one believes when one believes that p (or desires when one desires that q) is the proposition that p (or the proposition that q), then what, in case 1 and case 2, I seem to become actually immediately aware of is a proposition. In case 1, it is the proposition *that my keys are in my bag*, and in case 2, it is the proposition *that I'm to get a drink of water*.[20]

My initial suggestion, then, is that what we appear to be saying when we say that at time *t*, S has the conscious belief that *p* (or the conscious desire that *q*) is that at time *t*, S is (or becomes) actually immediately aware of the proposition that is the content of his attitude of believing that *p* (or desiring that *q*).

This first pass at a description of my account, however, is not quite right. For suppose that I have an unconscious belief that *p*. And suppose that someone says to me "*p*," and I understand what this person says—even though at the moment of comprehension, I am not aware, immediately or otherwise, of having the belief that *p*. In such a case, it seems plausible to say that, in coming to comprehend the proposition expressed by this person's utterance, I come to be immediately aware of the proposition that *p*. And so, it seems plausible to say that, at the moment of comprehension, I am immediately aware of the proposition that is the content of my attitude of believing that *p*. But, surely this is not sufficient to make my unconscious belief that *p* conscious.[21]

I agree. But the difference between this case and cases 1 and 2 is that in this case, I do not become immediately aware of the proposition that *p* *because* I believe that *p*. Rather, I come to be immediately aware of the proposition because someone said "*p*" to me and I understood the proposition expressed. I would have come to be immediately aware of the proposition that *p* in this case, all other things being equal, even if I did not believe that *p*. But in case 1, it seems rather clear that at time *t* I come to be immediately aware of the proposition that my keys are in my bag, in part, *because* I had at that time the belief that they were in my bag. If I did not have this belief at time *t*, then, all other things being equal, it would not have occurred to me *that my keys were in my bag*. And in case 2, if I did not have at time *t* the desire to get a drink of water, then, all other things being equal, it would not have occurred to me *to get a drink of water*. So, what needs to be added to the initial description of my account is a "because" clause along the following lines:

At time t, *S has the conscious belief that* p *(or the conscious desire that* q*) iff*

(i) At time *t*, S has the belief that *p* (or the desire that *q*).

(ii) At time *t*, S becomes actually immediately aware of the proposition that *p* (or that *q*).

(iii) (ii) obtains in part because (i) obtains.

On this account, since the object of the subject's immediate awareness is *the same as* the proposition that is the content of his attitude of believing or desiring, we can call it the *same-order* (SO) *account*. This, then, in rough outline, is the SO account of our folk concepts of conscious belief and conscious desire.[22]

One might initially think that the SO account is just a warmed-over version of Dretske's FO approach, since to be immediately aware of *what* one believes (or desires), when one believes that *p* (or desires that *q*), is just to be immediately aware of the fact that *p* (or the fact that *q*). But this initial assumption is mistaken. For what one believes (or desires), when one believes that *p* (or desires that *q*), is always the proposition that *p* (or the proposition that *q*), not the fact that *p* (or the fact that *q*)—for the proposition that *p* (or that *q*) may not be true and, hence, there may be no fact that *p* (or that *q*). And so, what one is immediately aware *of* when one is immediately aware of *what* one believes or desires is always a proposition, not a fact. And on the SO account, it is one's immediate awareness of a proposition that is required for having a conscious belief or desire, not one's immediate awareness of a fact. Also, unlike Dretske's FO account, the SO account does not require that a subject be in an internal, nonrelational conscious state in order for him to have a conscious belief or desire. What the SO account requires is that the subject be immediately aware of a proposition, which, on the SO account, does not require the subject to be in an internal, nonrelational conscious state.

It should also be noted that the SO account is not a version of either of the HO approaches described above. For unlike either HO approach, the SO account does not require a subject to be (or to be disposed to be) immediately aware of bearing an (occurrent or non-occurrent) attitude toward a proposition, or even to be (or to be disposed to be) immediately aware of any state of mind at all, in order to have a conscious belief or desire.[23] What the SO account requires is that the subject be immediately aware of something—namely, a particular proposition—that is neither an attitude nor a state of mind.[24]

Finally, I would like to mention some advantages that the SO account has over the FO and HO approaches that were discussed in the last section. First, unlike the FO approach, the SO account offers a unified account of our folk concepts of conscious belief and conscious desire. What we mean by describing our beliefs as conscious, on the SO account, is exactly what we mean by describing our desires as conscious. In each case, we have in mind the idea that the proposition that is the content of our attitude of believing or desiring is immediately before our mind. Second, unlike either HO approach described above, the SO account gives an accurate description of what appears to be going on in cases 1 and 2. And finally, unlike either HO approach, the SO account is consistent with our intuitions that creatures that do not have the relevant psychological concepts of believing, desiring, judging, and so on can, nevertheless, have conscious beliefs and desires.[25] For, as noted above, being immediately aware of the proposition that is the content of one's attitude of believing or desiring does not logically entail being immediately aware of oneself as bearing such an attitude (or any attitude) toward the proposition, or being immediately aware of any state of mind that one might be in at the time. Therefore, being immediately aware of the proposition that is the content of one's attitude of believing or desiring does not logically require that one have or employ any psychological concepts at all. Hence, it is quite possible, on the SO account, for young children who do not yet have such concepts to have conscious beliefs and desires. All that they would need to be able to do is to become immediately aware of *what* they believe and desire—not, that they *believe* or *desire* something. And normal two-year-olds certainly appear to be immediately aware of *what* they believe and desire, for they tell us *what* they believe and desire on a regular basis, and they appear to do this in an immediate way—that is, without engaging in any inference or observation of which they appear to be aware.

This, then, in crude form, is the SO account of conscious belief and desire, and some of the motivation for it. The account, of course, needs to be fleshed out. For one would like to know what is involved in a subject coming to be immediately aware of a proposition that is the content of one of his attitudes of believing or desiring, how the fact that the subject has the belief that p (or the desire that q) is related to his coming to be immediately aware of the proposition that p (or that q), and whether such a relation can be explained within the framework of a representational theory of mind. To these questions I now turn.

4 Immediate Awareness: Form and Content

One can become aware of something by seeing it, hearing it, or, more generally, by sensing it; or one can become aware of something by coming to have a thought about it. Whether one's awareness takes the form of sensing or acquiring a thought depends, in large part, on the object of one's awareness. If x is a concrete object in one's environment whose presence stimulates one's sensory organs, then one's awareness of x can take the form of sensing it. But, if x is an abstract entity (e.g., a number, universal, or proposition), then one's awareness of x must take the form of acquiring a thought about it.

Given that the thing that we become aware of, when we become immediately aware of what we believe or desire, is a proposition, an abstract entity par excellence, it follows that the form our awareness must take is that of acquiring a thought. To become aware of what one believes (or desires), when one believes that p (or desires that q), is to acquire a thought about the proposition that p (or that q). Therefore, to become *immediately* aware of what one believes (or desires), when one believes that p (or desires that q), is to acquire a thought about the proposition that p (or that q) "without relying on any inference or observation of which [one is] transitively conscious" (Rosenthal 1990, p. 738).

What, though, is the propositional content of such a thought? What kind of thought must one come to have when one comes to be immediately aware of a proposition that is the content of one of one's attitudes of believing or desiring? The answer, I submit, is that it is a deictic demonstrative belief of the form: *it's that p* (for some value of p). This answer is supported by two important facts about our being immediately aware of what we believe or desire. First, when we become immediately aware of what we believe or desire, that which we are immediately aware of is always presented to us as having a propositional form—as having the form of a "that"-clause. If, for instance, it suddenly occurs to me *that my keys are in my bag*, or *that I'm to get a drink of water*, what I become immediately aware of is something that has the form of a "that"-clause. To respect this fact about what seems to be involved in our being immediately aware of what we believe or desire, the thought that we acquire in such cases must be a thought that identifies the thing that one is immediately aware of as being *that p*, for some value of p.

Second, when we become immediately aware of what we believe or desire, the proposition that we become immediately aware of seems to present itself to us in a way that is analogous to the way perceptual objects present themselves to us when they are said to be in our field of perception. In fact, we sometimes say that, when it occurs to us that p, the proposition that p comes "before our mind's eye." One obvious way to make sense of this analogy, without saying that we literally perceive propositions, is to say that the thoughts that we acquire in such cases have something in common with the thoughts that we acquire in sense perception when an object is said to be in our field of view. And what is distinctive about such perceptual thoughts is that they are *beliefs* that contain *deictic demonstrative* concepts, concepts such as *this*, *it*, and *that*.[26] Upon smelling the odor coming from the house next door, for example, I come to have the belief that *that* stinks, and when I do, the smell I demonstratively identify in my belief is the object that is said to be in my olfactory field. Or, upon seeing a friend's new car, I come to have the belief that *it* is very red, and when I do, the car I demonstratively identify in my belief is the object that is said to be in my visual field. In each of these cases, the demonstrative in my perceptual belief is used deictically to pick out the thing that I perceive. So, if one acquires a deictic demonstrative belief, of some proposition *p*, that *it* is that *p*, then the thought that one acquires in such cases bears an important resemblance to those perceptual thoughts that one acquires when an object is said to be in one's field of perception; and this resemblance, I believe, allows us to make good sense of the expression that propositions are sometimes said to be "before our mind's eye" in the way that perceptual objects are sometimes said to be in our field of perception.

One might object that there is an important disanalogy between perceptual beliefs and those demonstrative beliefs that constitute our immediate awareness of propositions—namely, the referents of deictic demonstratives in perceptual beliefs are fixed by what one perceives; whereas, the referents of the deictic demonstratives in one's belief that it is that *p* cannot be fixed by what one perceives, for one does not perceive propositions. This is true. The analogy was not meant to be perfect. But, it should be noted that perception is not the only way for the referents of deictic demonstratives to be fixed. The referents of such demonstratives are also sometimes fixed by features of the context in which they occur. The referent of the demonstrative "it" in "it's time for lunch," for example, is fixed by the time of the utterance of the sentence; and the referent of the demonstrative "I" in "I'm hungry" is fixed by the speaker of the utterance. But, time and speaker are not the only relevant features of a context that determine the referent of a deictic demonstrative: causal features of the context can also be relevant. The referent of the demonstrative "it" in "it hurts," for example, is fixed by whatever it is that is causing the pain. If it is a needle, "it" refers to the needle; if it is a wound, "it" refers to the wound.

Along similar lines, then, one can take the "it" in one's deictic demonstrative belief that it is that *p* to be fixed by the proposition (that *p*) that is the content of the propositional attitude that caused one to have the demonstrative belief. If, for instance, my having the desire that I get a drink of water causes me to acquire the deictic demonstrative belief that it is that I get a drink of water, then the "it" in my demonstrative belief can be taken to refer to the proposition that is the content of my attitude of desiring that caused it. And if my having the belief that my keys are in my bag causes me to acquire the deictic demonstrative belief that it is that my keys are in my bag, then the "it" in my demonstrative belief can be taken to refer to the proposition that is the content of my attitude of believing that caused it. And since causes of the sort being considered here (i.e., structuring causes [see Dretske 1995b]) precede their effects in time, one's having the belief that p (or the desire that q) must exist at some time prior to one's coming to have the deictic demonstrative belief that it's that p (or that it's that q).

Drawing all these points together, a more developed version of the SO approach—one that offers an account of what is involved in being actually immediately aware of what one believe or desires—can be presented in the following more formal way:

At time t, *S has the conscious belief that* p *(or the conscious desire that* q*) iff*

(i) At time t, S has the belief that p (or the desire that q).
(ii) At time $t' < t$, S has the belief that p (or the desire that q).
(iii) At time t, S acquires, in an immediate way, the deictic demonstrative belief that it is that p (or that it is that q).
(iv) (iii) obtains in part because (ii) obtains.[27]

If these conditions are individually necessary and jointly sufficient for a subject to have the conscious belief that p or the conscious desire that q, and neither condition by itself presupposes that the belief or desire it attributes to the subject is conscious, then the above conditions provide a successful analysis of our folk concepts of conscious belief and conscious desire. I submit that the conditions above are individually necessary and jointly sufficient, but it needs to be pointed out that neither condition presupposes that the belief or desire it attributes to the subject is conscious. This is not difficult to show, however. For having the belief that p or the desire that q does not appear to entail that one has the conscious belief that p or the conscious desire that q. We have many beliefs and desires that never come "before our mind." So, neither condition (i) nor (ii) seems to presuppose that S has at time t the conscious belief that p or the conscious desire that q. Furthermore, the fact that one acquires a deictic demonstrative belief does not presuppose that the belief in question is conscious. As I drive home, for example, I acquire and lose many deictic demonstrative beliefs about items in my perceptual field. I acquire and then quickly lose the belief that *it* (the stoplight) is green, that *that* (the car in front of me) is turning left, and so on. But, none of these beliefs need come "before my mind." Therefore, there is no reason to think that condition (iii) presupposes that S has at time t the conscious deictic demonstrative belief that it is that p (or that it is that q). Finally, there is no reason to think that the fact that one acquires a belief as a result of having other beliefs or desires presupposes that the belief that one acquires is conscious. We often come to acquire new beliefs as a result of our possessing other beliefs and desires without the new beliefs themselves coming "before our mind." Upon finding out that Smith voted for Bush, for example, one might come to acquire numerous beliefs about him—that he is a Republican, that he is old enough to vote, that he is a U.S. citizen, that you should speak with him, and so on—as a result of certain background beliefs and desires that one has; and yet none of these numerous new beliefs need come "before one's mind" at the time of its acquisition. Therefore, there is no reason to think that condition (iv) need presuppose that S has at time t the conscious belief that it's that p (or that it's that q).

5 Immediate Awareness: Mechanism

Finally, we need to address the question of whether conscious beliefs and desires on the SO account can be explained within the framework of the representational theory of mind that is assumed by much of contemporary cognitive science. I believe that it can. What is needed to show this is a description of a possible functional architecture—an underlying mechanism—that would realize conditions (i)–(iv) in the SO account. Such a description, I believe, can be provided by making a rather simple extension to the basic representational architecture of the mind that is assumed in much of contemporary cognitive science. The basic architectural assumption in cognitive science is that to have the belief that p (or the desire that q) is to stand in a particular relation to a token representation in one's brain that is type individuated by its functional role and propositional content (Fodor 1998, pp. 1–22; Nichols and Stich 2003, pp. 1–15). Furthermore, since the structural features of these token representations appear to be analogous to the syntactical features of sentences in natural language, it makes sense to speak of them as sentences in a language of thought. According to this model, a subject's believing that p (or desiring that q) consists in his brain realizing a token sentential representation [P] (or [Q]) that functions in a characteristic way and expresses the proposition that p (or that q).

As a heuristic device, we can imagine the mind as a collection of interconnected input–output boxes, each of which holds and generates a class of sentential representations of a distinctive functional type. There will be, for example, a percept box that generates representations of the subject's current perceptual environment as a result of the stimulation of the subject's sensory organs and outputs those representations to the subject's belief box; a subject's belief box that holds those representations generated by the subject's percept box (and other boxes) and outputs those representations to the

Appendix

Diagram 1:

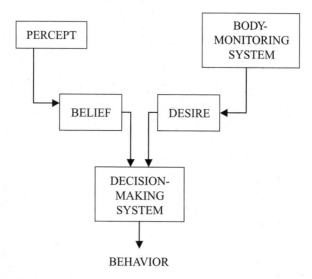

Figure 14.1

subject's decision-making system—a system that, in conjunction with the outputs from the subject's desire box, causes the subject to behave in certain ways; and finally, a subject's desire box that holds those representations generated by the subject's body-monitoring systems and outputs those representations to the subject's decision-making system. Figure 14.1 gives a "boxological" rendition of this basic cognitive architecture. All that is needed to realize conditions (i)–(iv) in the SO account within this standard architectural model is one minor addition. A mechanism needs to be introduced that takes as its input representations from the subject's belief and desire boxes and outputs a deictic demonstrative representation of a distinct type into the subject's belief box. We can call this mechanism the *content identifying mechanism* (CIM). Its function—at least, one of them—is to identify the proposition that is the content of the representation that is inputted. So, for example, if the representation [Q] in a subject's desire box is inputted into the subject's CIM, the CIM will output the deictic demonstrative representation [It's that Q] into the subject's belief box. To produce the outputted representation [It's that Q], all that the CIM need do is copy the inputted representation [Q], embed it into the representational schema [It's that__], and then place the completed representation [It's that Q] in the subject's

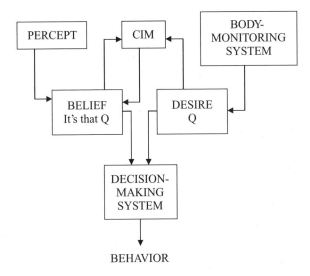

Figure 14.2

belief box. Figure 14.2 gives a "boxological" rendition of this procedure. The transformation of input to output by the CIM would be simple, mechanical, and direct—no "self-interpretation" or "inference," in Carruthers's (this volume) sense of these words, is involved. The SO account, therefore, need not posit a mysterious mechanism to realize the conditions that are necessary and sufficient for conscious beliefs and desires, and the CIM mechanism that is posited is perfectly in line with the basic representational architecture of the mind assumed by much of cognitive science.

But what about the empirical data that Carruthers cites against the existence of conscious beliefs and desires? Do they suggest that the human mind may not contain any such mechanism as a CIM? Not in the least. For the data that Carruthers cites—data from studies by Nisbett and Wilson (1977) on right-hand biases and Gazzaniga (1998) on split-brain subjects—merely suggest that the human mind may not contain a mechanism that enables us to have immediate awareness of our own propositional *attitudes*. The data in no way suggests that the human mind may not contain a mechanism that enables us to have immediate awareness of *the contents* of our propositional attitudes. In Gazzaniga's experiment, for instance, the split-brain subject incorrectly believes that he has a desire for something in the refrigerator, and he comes to have this belief (presumably) by means of an unconscious inference to an explanation of his behavior. The subject's coming to have this belief is, as Carruthers (this volume) writes, "an inference-produced product of self-interpretation." And it may be, as Carruthers suggests, that whenever *anyone* comes to have the (higher-order) belief *that he believes or desires* something, he comes to have this (higher-order) belief as the result of an inferential or self-interpretive process.

It does not follow from this, however, that whenever anyone comes to have a belief about *what* he believes or desires—comes to have a belief about the proposition that is the content of his attitude of believing or desiring—he comes to have this belief as the result of an inferential or self-interpretive process. Put otherwise: the data Carruthers cites may suggest that our awareness *that we believe or desire* something is always mediated, but they in no way suggest that our awareness *of what* we believe or desire is always mediated.[28] So, the data that Carruthers cites against the existence of conscious beliefs and desires in no way suggests that the human mind is without a mechanism like CIM.

If the representational theory of mind that is assumed by much of cognitive science is the best-going theory of mind, and if the SO account is the best-going account of our folk concepts of conscious belief and desire, then, I submit, there is no reason to join Carruthers in his tentative eliminativist position that there may be no such things as conscious beliefs or conscious desires. In fact, if the existence of a CIM is at all plausible, then there would appear to be rather good reasons to be a realist with respect to the existence of conscious beliefs and desires.

6 Objections and Replies

In conclusion, I would like to address two possible problems facing the SO account. The problems here are complex and difficult, and it is not my intention to give a definitive solution to them but merely to sketch a plausible line of response.

The problem of phenomenal character for conscious beliefs Consider the following intuitively plausible facts. First, there is something that it is like to have a conscious belief. In case 1, for instance, there is something it is like for me at time t to have the conscious belief that my keys are in my bag: had I not come to have any conscious belief at all, or had I come to have a different conscious belief (e.g., the conscious belief that my wallet was in my book bag!), what it would have been like for me at that time would have been different.[29] Second, upon reflecting on Putnamian Twin Earth scenarios, it seems correct to say that what an earthling believes when he has the conscious belief that he expresses by saying "water is wet" is not what his twin on Twin Earth believes when he has the conscious belief that he expresses by saying "water is wet." The earthling believes that water (H_2O) is wet, whereas his twin believes that twater (XYZ) is wet. Third, given that an earthling and his twin are microphysical duplicates, it seems plausible that what it is like for the earthling to have the conscious belief that he expresses by saying "water is wet" is what it is like for his twin to have his conscious belief that he expresses by saying "water is wet." And it is this third intuitively plausible fact that the SO account would appear to have a difficult time explaining. For on the SO account, the earthling and his twin, in virtue of having their respective conscious beliefs, are actually immediately aware of different propositions. The earthling is immediately aware of the proposition that water (H_2O) is wet, whereas his twin is immediately aware of the proposition that twater (XYZ) is wet. But, if they are immediately aware of different things, then how can it be the same with respect to what it is like for them?

Reply It is, of course, open to the defender of the SO account to reject one or both of the first two intuitively plausible facts listed above and thereby reject the third as well. But, I shall not offer such a line of response, since I find the intuitively plausible facts listed above to be intuitively plausible. But, contrary to what is suggested in the above objection, I do not believe that the SO account faces any insurmountable obstacle in explaining why what it is like for the earthling is what it is like for his twin. For although the propositions of which the earthling and his twin are immediately aware are different—the former contains water (H_2O) but not twater (XYZ), whereas the latter contains twater (XYZ) but not water (H_2O)—they are similar in certain respects. They have, for example, the same form—they are both cases of singular predication—and they both involve the predication of the very same property—the property of being wet. I see no reason why it can't be said that the respects in which these propositions are similar are those that are relevant in determining what it is like for the earthling and his twin. I have mentioned only two such features here—the form of, and the properties contained within, the proposition—but there very well may be others.[30]

The problem of the different phenomenal character of conscious beliefs and desires Consider the following two intuitively plausible facts. First, attitudes of believing and desiring can have the very same proposition as their contents. For example, if I believe that there is world peace and you desire that there be world peace, we have different propositional attitudes that have one and the same proposition as their content. Second, what it is like to have a conscious belief is (often) different from what it is like to have a conscious desire.[31] Surely, the way it feels to have the conscious belief that there is world peace is (at least sometimes) different from the way it feels to have the conscious desire that there be world peace. It would seem, however, that the SO account is unable to explain this last sort of fact. For on the SO account, you and I, in virtue of having our respective conscious belief and desire, are actually immediately aware of the very same proposition. And it is difficult to understand how there can be a difference in what it is like for two individuals if the individuals are actually immediately aware of one and the same thing.

Reply First, it should be noted that we often have accompanying feelings whenever we have conscious beliefs or conscious desires. Often when we have a conscious belief, for instance, we have a feeling of conviction or certitude, as when you have the conscious belief that you would never take a bribe; and in the case of having conscious desires, we often have feelings of longing or craving, as when we have the conscious desire to see an old friend or to have a cold glass of water on a hot summer's day. And it very well may be that the kinds of feelings that typically accompany conscious beliefs are different from those that typically accompany conscious desires, and that it is in virtue of this difference that what it is like to have a conscious belief is different from what it is like to have a conscious desire. So, even if you and I, in virtue of our having our respective conscious belief and desire, are immediately aware of one and the same proposition, there may very well be other distinct things that we are immediately aware of—certain distinct feelings—that account for the difference in what it is like for us. Such an explanation for the difference in what it is like for us is quite consistent with the truth of the SO approach.

Second, it may be orthodoxy that attitudes of believing and desiring can have the very same proposition as their contents, but I do not think that this orthodoxy is beyond challenge.[32] On the face of it, it seems false. For the "that"-clauses that are often used to pick out the propositions that are the contents of attitudes of believing are grammatically different from those that are used to pick out the propositions that are the contents of attitudes of desiring. The sentences that follow the "that" in the former are often in the indicative mood, whereas the sentences that follow the "that" in the latter are often in the imperative or subjunctive mood. This suggests that such clauses may be referring to different kinds of propositions. For example, if I believe that there is world peace, the proposition that is the content of my attitude is, presumably, the proposition that there *is* world peace (or the proposition that *it is the case* that there is world peace). Likewise, if you desire that there *be* world peace, the proposition that is the content of your attitude is, presumably, the proposition that there *be* world peace (or the proposition that *it is to be the case* that there is world peace). Is the proposition that there *is* world peace the very same proposition as the proposition that there *be* world peace? On the face of it, they look quite different. If it is true, for example, that I believe that there *is* world peace, and the proposition that there *is* world peace is the proposition that there *be* world peace, then it ought to be true that I believe that there *be* world peace, which it isn't. The proposition that there *is* world peace and the proposition that there *be* world peace do not appear to be substitutable *salva veritate* in contexts of belief ascriptions, which is a reason to think that they are distinct.

It may very well be, then, that the orthodox view is false, and that the attitudes of believing and desiring actually take different kinds of propositions as their contents. It may be, as Hare (1972) and Grice (2001) have argued in their marker accounts of practical reasoning, that attitudes of believing take propositions that are in the indicative mood (or propositions that are formed by an indicative mood operator or marker on a proposition), and that attitudes of desiring take propositions in the imperative or subjunctive mood (or propositions that are formed by an imperative or subjunctive mood operator or marker on a proposition).[33,34] If so, then it is open to a defender of the SO account to explain the phenomenological difference between having conscious beliefs and having conscious desires in terms of one being immediately aware of different kinds of propositions.

7 Conclusion

I have sketched an account—the SO account—of our folk concepts of conscious belief and conscious desire. I have argued that this account offers a better analysis than either of the two dominant approaches to explaining these concepts. And I have argued that, on the SO account of these concepts, Carruthers's eliminativist argument fails to show that conscious beliefs and desires—at least, as the folk understand them to be—do not exist.[35]

Notes

1. I have argued for the SO approach to conscious belief and desire—or a version of it—in Lurz 2003a,b, 2004.

2. From here on, I shall use "conscious" only in the "before the mind" sense unless otherwise indicated.

3. In what follows, I assume that to *have* the belief that *p* (or to *have* the desire that *q*) it is to *believe* that *p* (or to *desire* that *q*), and that to *believe* that *p* (or to *desire* that *q*) is to bear a particular relation—the attitude of believing (or the attitude of desiring)—toward the proposition that *p* (or that *q*). I shall take propositions to be those abstract, mind-independent entities that are the purported referents of "that"-clauses, fine-grained in nature, truth-apt, and distinct from the facts that make them true (for such a view of propositions, see Bealer 1998). Also, I shall assume that attitudes of believing and desiring are non-occurrent attitudes that a subject can possess while nothing mental or conscious is happening in his mind—say, when the subject is in a deep, dreamless sleep.

4. Dretske's account is often called a first-order (or horizontal) account because, unlike higher-order accounts (see below), it does not require a subject who has a conscious belief or desire to be aware of some mental fact—the fact, for example, that the subject himself has such-and-such belief or desire. Rather, Dretske's account requires only that the subject be in a state of mind that makes the subject aware of the fact that his conscious belief or desire is supposedly about, and this fact may be a nonmental fact about the subject's physical environment.

5. Following Dretske (1993, p. 264), I shall take "aware of" and "conscious of" to be interchangeable in these contexts.

6. There are two versions of the actualist HO approach in the literature: the higher-order thought (HOT) version and the higher-order perception (HOP) version. According to HOT, what it is for a subject to be immediately aware of having a mental state or attitude is for the subject to have an appropriately formed higher-order belief or judgment about the state or attitude in question. According to HOP, what it is for a subject to be immediately aware of having a mental state or attitude is for the subject to have a higher-order perception of the state or attitude in question. The differences between the HOT and HOP versions of the actualist HO approach are largely ignored in what follows.

7. Rosenthal appears to offer two different definitions of "immediacy," as a result of a shift in the scope of the negation used in the definition. On the first definition, one is said to be immediately aware of *x* iff one is *not* aware of coming to be aware of *x* by means of an observation or inference. On the second definition, one is said to be immediately aware of *x* iff one is aware of oneself *not* coming to be aware of *x* by means of an observation or inference. From what Rosenthal writes elsewhere, it is clear that he endorses only the first definition. I shall, then, be appealing to this definition of "immediacy" throughout the essay.

8. On this rendition of the actualist HO approach, the state that S is in at time *t* when he is said to have the belief that *p* (or the desire that *q*)—call this *M*—and the state that S is in at time *t* when he is said to be actually immediately aware of having the belief that *p* (or the desire that *q*)—call this *M**—are distinct states that are related

by co-occurrence only. Rosenthal (1990, p. 744) maintains that the co-occurrence of M and M^* is sufficient for S's belief or desire to be conscious. Let us call such HO approaches that merely require co-occurrence weak HO approaches. Not all HO approaches are weak: some require that M and M^* be identical or that M^* be a proper part of M (see Kriegel, this volume). These strong HO approaches are often called *self-referential theories of consciousness*. I would like to make one comment here about such HO theories that is relevant to my argument in this section. HO approaches—whether weak or self-referential—require a subject to be immediately aware of having the belief that p or the desire that q if the subject is to have the conscious belief that p or the conscious desire that q; and since I shall argue that this is *not* a requirement for a subject to have a conscious belief or desire, my argument, if successful, shows that self-referential approaches fair no better than weak HO approaches in providing individually necessary conditions for having conscious beliefs and desires.

9. This is not to say that at time t' I was not *seeing* the tiles on the floor, for I most certainly was. Rather, it is to say that at time t' I was not actually immediately aware *of seeing* (or aware of the fact *that I was seeing*) the tiles.

10. The argument here is not the same as the one given in section 2.1 against Dretske's account, which assumes that in order for a subject to be aware of some fact, the subject must be in an internal, nonrelational conscious state. It was this assumption that was challenged in 2.1. HO theorists make it very clear that they do not hold this assumption (Rosenthal 1990, p. 737). However, they do assume that if a subject has a conscious belief or desire, the subject must be actually immediately aware of having this belief or desire (either as a *belief* or *desire* or as a *mental state* or *attitude* of some type). It is this assumption that is being challenged here.

11. HO theorists might respond to the above objection by appealing to a distinction that they typically draw between "reflexive awareness" and "introspection" (Armstrong 1981, p. 725, in reprint in Block, Flanagan, and Güzeldere 1997; Rosenthal 1990, p. 745). Reflexive awareness is simply a subject's actual immediate awareness of something other than his immediate awareness; whereas, introspection is a subject's actual immediate awareness of his own immediate awareness. The actualist HO theorist's notion of introspection is what we might call higher-order immediate awareness. Now, the actualist HO theorist will rightly point out that it is reflexive awareness, not introspection, that figures in his account of conscious belief and desire. Armed with this distinction, the actualist HO theorist can then accuse me of confusing reflexive awareness with introspection. With respect to case 1, for example, the actualist HO theorist will maintain that although I am not at time t introspectively aware (i.e., immediately aware of being immediately aware) of having the belief that my keys are in my bag, I am reflexively aware (i.e., simply immediately aware) of having this belief. My response to this objection is that there is no such confusion being made in my argument. I had all along the notion of reflexive awareness in mind. In case 1,

for instance, I am, at time *t*, not only not reflexively aware (i.e., simply immediately aware) of having the belief that my keys are in my bag, I am also not introspectively aware (i.e., immediately aware of being immediately aware) of having such a belief. Again, at time *t*, what I seem to be reflexively immediately aware of is simply what actually occurs to me at that time—namely, *that my keys are in my bag*—and this, whatever it is, is *not* my having the belief that my keys are in my bag. Furthermore, it is simply a fact about case 1 that at time *t* it does *not* occur to me that I have the belief that my keys are in my bag. And it is part of our ordinary understanding of "immediate awareness," it seems, that if at time *t* it does not occur to one that one has such-and-such belief or desire, then at time *t* one is not actually immediately aware of having it. Again, what would it mean to say that at time *t* it did not occur to me that I have this belief, but I was nevertheless actually immediately aware of having it at that time? Finally, the fact that I do not remember being at time *t* either introspectively *or* reflexively immediately aware of having the belief that my keys are in my bag is a pretty good, although defeasible, reason for holding that at time *t* I was neither introspectively nor reflexively aware of having this belief.

12. Throughout the remainder of this section, I shall assume that the attitudes of judging and desiring can have the same propositions as their contents. In section 6, I shall suggest a challenge to this assumption.

13. I suspect that the relevant sense of "because" here is causal, but such a reading of "because" is not essential to understanding Carruthers's account or my criticism of it.

14. Or to put it in Carruthers's words, why is it not enough to say that what it means to say that at time *t* I have the conscious belief that my keys are in my bag is that at time *t* my belief emerges as the event of it occurring to me that my keys are in my bag?

15. The approach to conscious belief and desire that I outline in section 3 is a version of this minimal analysis given here.

16. Carruthers might respond that the mental event that occurs at time *t* in case 1 and the mental event that occurs at time *t* in case 2 *must* be conscious since the former is one and the same as the event of my coming to have the *conscious* belief that my keys are in my bag, and the latter is one and the same as the event of my coming to have the *conscious* desire to get a drink of water, and these events, by hypothesis, are *conscious*. But, this just begs the question of why we should think that the event of my coming to have the conscious belief that my keys are in my bag and the event of my coming to have the conscious desire to get a drink of water are conscious. The mere fact that each event involves my having something (a belief in case 1 and a desire in case 2) that is conscious is not a reason to maintain that the event itself is conscious—that would be like inferring that the event of my winning $100 is itself money because what I come to have in undergoing this event is money. Moreover, it needs

to be pointed out that it is not the *event* of my coming to have the conscious belief that my keys are in my bag, or the *event* of my coming to have the conscious desire to get a drink of water, that we describe, in case 1 and case 2 respectively, as being conscious. Rather, it is my *belief* and *desire* that I have in undergoing these events that we describe as being conscious.

17. There is, in fact, some empirical evidence in support of this supposition. The results of a series of studies by Flavell, Green, and Flavell (1993, 1995) suggest that preschoolers have a very difficult time recalling their own fairly recent acts of thinking and judging. In one study, for example, sixteen five-year-olds, while sitting in a particular location, were presented with a problem that required them to think of or make a judgment about a target object. Immediately after making their judgment, the children were asked to change locations. While sitting in their new location, they were asked by the experimenter whether they had been thinking about anything (and if so, what) while they were sitting in the first location. Forty-four percent of the children, when asked the open-ended question, said that they did not think about anything; 38 percent of the children, when asked about the particular object of which they were thinking, claimed to have been thinking about a "decoy" object which, from the setup of the experiment, it was clear that they were not in fact thinking about at the time; and only 19 percent of the children, when asked this question, said they had been thinking about the target object. Similar results were achieved in the follow-up studies that were designed to eliminate confounding variables. From the results of their studies, Flavell, Green, and Flavell (1995, p. 76) concluded that "preschoolers have very limited introspective skills." If Flavel et al. are correct in what their studies show about normal five-year-olds, then there would appear to be some reason to think that it is rather unlikely that normal two-year-olds have anything like a developed capacity to be immediately aware of their own occurrent mental events of thinking or judging.

18. Children, for instance, do not start to talk about their own mental events until their third year (Shatz, Wellman, and Silber 1983); and the nonlinguistic behaviors of two-year-olds are typically directed at manipulating objects in the physical environment, behaviors that would not, on the face of it, require an explanation in terms of these children being capable of being immediately aware of their own occurrent mental events.

19. A similar story can be told for conscious beliefs. It seems quite conceivable, for example, that upon hearing the front door open, it suddenly occurs to two-year-old Suzy that her daddy is home, and it does so in part because she comes to have the belief that her daddy is home. This seems conceivable despite the fact that Suzy, we are supposing, is not yet capable of being immediately aware of the fact that it occurs to her that her daddy is home. Notwithstanding Suzy's incapability here, I think we would find it quite natural to say that, upon hearing the front door open, Suzy comes to have the conscious belief that her daddy is home.

20. See note 3 for further specifications of what I take propositions to be.

21. I am grateful to Gene Witmer for bringing this objection to my attention.

22. One might initially object that the SO account is not an account of conscious belief or desire at all, since beliefs and desires are propositional *attitudes*. The SO account, the objection continues, gives, at most, an account of our folk notion of conscious *contents*—of what we mean when we say that *what* we believe or desire is "before our mind"—but it does not give an account of our folk notion of our conscious attitudes of believing or desiring. Reply: it is well known that "belief" and "desire" are ambiguous, that they admit of (what is sometimes called) an act-object ambiguity. We sometimes use them to refer to the contents of our attitudes of believing and desiring, and we sometimes use them to refer to our attitudes of believing and desiring. The real issue here is to determine which of these two senses of "belief" and "desire" we are using when we describe my belief in case 1 and my desire in case 2 as being conscious in the "before the mind" sense. And it seems plain that it is the sense of these terms that refers to the contents of our attitudes, not the attitudes themselves. For what becomes conscious (in the relevant sense) at time *t* in case 1, for example, is what comes "before my mind" at time *t*; and what comes "before my mind" at time *t* is *that my keys are in my bag*, which is the *content* of my attitude of believing, not my *attitude* of believing. Hence, in case 1, it seems rather clear that what we are describing as being conscious in the "before the mind" sense is not my "belief" in the attitude sense of this term but my "belief" in the content sense of this term. Similar reasoning can be given for case 2.

23. For the same reason, the SO approach is not a version of any self-referentialist HO approach. See note 8.

24. Although the SO account is not identical with either of the two dominant contemporary approaches to conscious belief and desire, it is not entirely unprecedented in the literature. Something very much like it is to be found in the traditional occurrence analysis of belief given by Price (1969) and Braithwaite (1967).

25. Does the HOP approach to conscious belief and desire escape this criticism? I think not. For as Shoemaker (1996, pp. 212–214, 224–245) has shown, the most plausible sense in which we can be said to "perceive" our own beliefs and desires is that we are disposed, in certain circumstances, to have higher-order beliefs about them. But having such a disposition would require the possession of certain psychological concepts—namely, those that figure in the higher-order beliefs. Therefore, on its most plausible interpretation, the HOP approach requires creatures that have conscious beliefs and desires to possess certain relevant psychological concepts, such as the concepts of believing and desiring.

26. Deictic demonstratives are demonstratives that are used "out of the blue" to point to something that is directly present (or recently so) to a subject. Deictic demonstratives are contrasted with anaphoric demonstratives, which are used to "cross-

refer" to something mentioned previously in thought or discourse (see Devitt and Sterelny 1987, p. 83).

27. I do not take the obtaining of (ii) to be the complete or triggering cause of (iii). Rather, I take it to be something more like a structuring cause of (iii) (see Dretske 1995b).

28. See Dretske 2004 for a similar line of argument. "Introspection," Dretske (2004, p. 10) writes, "tells me what is in my mind, what it is I am thinking, wanting, hoping and expecting. It doesn't tell me I really have a mind, mental states with such content. If I know that at all, I know it in some way other than by introspection."

29. See Horgan and Tienson 2002, Strawson 1994, and Peacocke 1998 for more developed arguments for the thesis that conscious beliefs have phenomenal character.

30. One might, for instance, include modes of presentation as another feature of propositions that is relevant to determining the phenomenal character involved in our having conscious beliefs.

31. Although as Hume (1978, p. 417) points out, some conscious desires—the "calm" ones—may be phenomenally indistinguishable from conscious beliefs. See Hume 1978 (pp. 96, 438), Russell 1948 (pp. 106, 146) and Goldman 1993b (pp. 23–24) for an endorsement of the view that conscious beliefs and desires are often phenomenally distinct.

32. Marks (1986, p. 13), for instance, considers just such a challenge.

33. For an illuminating description of the marker account of rationality, see Broome 2004.

34. Grice (1989, pp. 117–137) also employs mood operators on propositions in his account of speaker meaning in order to distinguish various kinds of propositions that a speaker might mean by an utterance.

35. I wish to thank Uriah Kriegel, Peter Carruthers, Rocco Gennaro, and Abe Witonsky for their extremely helpful comments on earlier drafts of this essay, and to Jonathan Adler, Joel Marks, and Walter Edelberg for their illuminating discussions on beliefs and desires. This work was supported in part by a grant from The City University of New York PSC-CUNY Research Award Program.

Consciousness, Self, and Attention

Jason Ford and David Woodruff Smith

1 Consciousness and Self in the Structure of Attention

Our task is to address the structure of consciousness, specifically awareness of self, by studying the role of attention in normal conscious experience. By "self-consciousness" we mean either awareness of one's passing experience or awareness of oneself in a passing experience, or both: that is, in the first person, my awareness of this state of consciousness "itself" or my awareness of "myself" as subject of that state, both achieved as integral parts of that experience. These phenomena are distinct but naturally bound together.

Thus, in early modern philosophy, Descartes focused on the self or "I" as a being that thinks (a substantial center of consciousness—*conscience*—as "I think"). Then Locke introduced self-consciousness as the distinguishing feature of consciousness (when we perceive, we perceive that we perceive). Hume then dissolved the self into a subjectless flow of perceptions, what James would call the stream of consciousness itself. Kant retained the self merely as a formal structure of cognition or consciousness (the "I think" that can accompany any representation). Amid these debates it was thus assumed that a certain awareness of one's having an experience is characteristic of consciousness.

In the first part of the twentieth-century phenomenology revived the theory of self and self-consciousness. Extending (and revising) Brentano's analysis, Husserl held that consciousness is characteristically intentional, where every act of consciousness is directed from a subject or ego toward an object (via a noema), and the act includes a certain awareness of the act itself through internal time-consciousness. For Husserl, an act of consciousness may also include certain forms of consciousness of the self, open to phenomenological analysis. Thus, Husserl characterized a pure or transcendental subject (myself *qua* subject) and also an embodied self (myself *qua* agent with kinesthetic awareness of my bodily movement, what psychologists call proprioception).

Merleau-Ponty then characterized the embodied subject, amplifying Husserl's account of kinesthetic bodily awareness in perception. The discipline of phenomenology thus described the self as subject of thought, embodied subject of perception, and embodied volitional agent of action. Especially striking is the phenomenology of one's awareness of oneself as embodied subject in seeing an object before one.

More recently, philosophy of mind, in the analytic tradition, has rediscovered these traditional issues of consciousness and self-consciousness. A vibrant literature has developed the model of higher-order monitoring, wherein each conscious experience (sensing, thinking, etc.) is accompanied by a second-order monitoring of it. The higher-order act of monitoring purportedly renders the first-order mental act conscious (see, e.g., Rosenthal 2002; Lycan 2001). An alternative model, however, defines a one-level or same-order structure, wherein consciousness involves a self-monitoring awareness that does not reside in a second higher-order act of consciousness-of-consciousness. (The same-order model is central to the present volume: see Kriegel this volume.)

Here we follow a specific model that falls within the same-order approach to consciousness (as elaborated in D. W. Smith 1986, 1989, 2004, 2005a). On the model we assume, an act of consciousness involves, as an intrinsic structural feature, an *inner awareness* of the experience. This awareness is a *reflexive* awareness of the subject's performing or experiencing the act. This reflexive awareness, we assume, renders the act conscious.[1]

On this model, inner awareness is *eo ipso* an awareness of the experience and also of the subject. Phenomenologically, inner awareness guarantees that each normal conscious state is experienced as belonging to someone, mine to me and yours to you. Our aim here is to analyze the structure of consciousness whereby one is aware of one's experience and therewith of oneself. We focus on normal adult human conscious experience, which typically has a complex structure (including, for instance, proprioception). Our tactic is to look at the structure of *attention*, a familiar but frequently neglected feature of consciousness. While the structure of attention has not been studied in the recent literature on higher-order and same-order monitoring theories of consciousness, we can look to earlier results in phenomenology.

As we shall see, the theory of attention helps clarify a number of issues that have arisen in the traditional theory of consciousness, self-awareness, and indeed the ontology of the self. As we proceed, we shall distinguish inner awareness of self from *peripheral awareness* of self. With this distinction, we hope to put in sharper relief two importantly different but interconnected forms of awareness of self.

In the course of our investigation we shall integrate two types of theorizing about attention. On the one hand, we pursue a phenomenological analysis of the structure of attention in the intentionality of consciousness (D. W. Smith 2004), an analysis that extends results of Husserl, Gurwitsch, and Merleau-Ponty. On the other hand, we pursue a model of attention that draws on results in cognitive neuroscience (Ford 2005, drawing on LaBerge 1995, 1997, 1998). As we integrate these results from phenomenology and neuroscience, we seek a reflective equilibrium between first-person phenomenological analysis and third-person experimental analysis.[2]

What we hope to show, through a detailed analysis of attention in consciousness (and its neural substrate), is how an inner awareness of oneself as subject is grounded in a peripheral awareness of one's relationship to the object of attention in familiar activities of thought, perception, and action.

2 The Structure of Inner Awareness of Conscious Experience

Consciousness is typically *intentional*, a consciousness of or about something. We assume a broadly Husserlian theory of intentionality (Smith and McIntyre 1982). On this analysis, an experience or act of consciousness is intentionally directed from a subject through a content or meaning toward an object (given appropriate background conditions). The structure of this intentional relationship is captured in a simple diagram:

background |— subject—act—content → object.

The subject is the person ("I") who performs the act (or has the experience). The content is an ideal or abstract meaning entity (Husserl's "noema") that semantically prescribes the object of consciousness. This content characterizes the object in a certain way, as seen from a given angle and distance, in a particular environment, with some features more salient than others. The background includes features of context on which the intentional relation of act to object depends.[3]

The "monitoring" models of consciousness modify and add a layer of complexity to the basic structure of intentionality. On the *higher-order model*, what we call a single experience of perception, imagination, or cogitation is really a complex of two intentional acts: a primary act accompanied by a secondary act directed toward the first act. When I see a dog running across my path, for instance, my experience would thus consist in a coupling of two mental acts: my seeing the dog and simultaneously monitoring my visual experience. There are, however, serious problems with the higher-order model, not least the fact that we do not experience ourselves performing two mental acts at once. (See the summary of issues in Kriegel, this volume.) Enter the *same-order monitoring model of consciousness*. On this model, a conscious experience includes as an *intrinsic feature or part* an awareness of the experience, a self-monitoring feature that is essential to the experience and somehow built into the experience.

What is the *form* of this awareness-of-experience? The experience has an intentional relation—a "ray" of intentionality mediated by content—extending from the experience to its object (if such exists). We hold, contrary to the higher-order model, that we should not say there is a second, higher-order act directed to the first. Instead, we might say the experience also has a secondary intentional relation or "ray" reaching reflexively back to itself. These opposing models are depicted in figure 15.1.

For the higher-order monitoring theory, the awareness-of-experience consists in a second intentional relation that is external to and independent of the experience and its intentional relation to its object. For the same-order monitoring theory, by contrast, the awareness-of-experience consists in a secondary intentional relation that is *internal* to the experience: on the best proposal, it is a *dependent part* of the experience, where the awareness could not occur without being a part of the experience. And by hypothesis the experience could not occur without the awareness that makes it conscious. Here we draw on Husserl's contrast between dependent and independent parts (in the third of the *Logical Investigations* 1900–1901/2001): in the case of a blue pen with removable cap, the cap is an independent part of the pen while the blueness in the pen is a dependent part of the pen (what Aristotle called an "accident," Husserl called a "moment," and some today call a "trope"). Inner awareness of experience consists then in an intrinsic aspect of the experience, analyzed as a "moment" or dependent part of the experience, or (better) of its intentionality. But what exactly is the form of that aspect? Is awareness-of-experience a "looping" intentional relation as depicted in figure 15.1?

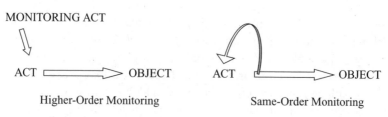

Higher-Order Monitoring   Same-Order Monitoring

Figure 15.1
Two models of monitoring.

We shall assume a *modal* theory of awareness-of-experience (Smith 1986, 1989, 2004, 2005a). On this model, what makes an experience conscious is an *inner awareness* of the experience. This inner awareness—a special form of same-order monitoring—consists in a *structural phenomenological feature* internal to the experience. The structure of a conscious experience, say, my seeing a dog, may be articulated in a phenomenological description of the form:

Phenomenally in this very experience I now see that dog.

This description of the experience, we assume, unfolds the content or meaning of the experience. The *mode of presentation* of the object of consciousness is carried in the content "that dog," which semantically prescribes a canine entity visually before the subject on the occasion of perception. This content represents the object in a certain way, but it does not represent the experience or its subject: the experience is not directed toward itself or its subject. However, there is more to the intentional structure or content of the experience: the act is directed not only *toward* its object, but also *from* its subject, *in* a primary modality (perceptual, volitional, etc.), and indeed consciously *through* itself. Accordingly, the *modality of presentation* of the object defines the way the experience is executed (and so directed toward the object). Thus, the experience is visual: "... [I] see. ...." Also, it is subjective or subject-centered: "... I [see]. ...." And it is conscious: "... in this very experience [I see]. ...." The overall modality of the experience is carried by the content articulated by the italicized phrasing, and the form of inner awareness is articulated by the adverbial modifier phrase "phenomenally in this very experience." Note the reflexive phrase "in this very experience." ("Very" emphasizes that the awareness is internal to the experience, and not as it were pointing to "this" experience from a second experience. See Perry 2001a,b and Smith 1989 and 2005a on reflexive contents.)

On this modal theory of inner awareness, there is only one experience, one intentional act. The inner awareness consists in an *aspect* of the act: part of the *modality* of presentation, an intrinsic part of the *way* the act is experienced or executed. This aspect is a dependent part of the experience, or of its phenomenological structure. But how, more precisely, should we think of this aspect? Is it a reflexive form of *intentional relation*, a reflexive ray of intentionality that is ontologically dependent on and so bound to the primary ray of intentionality? Let us provisionally depict the form of inner awareness as in figure 15.2. The reflexive character "in this very experience ..." defines a reflexive form of intentional relation that is however an intrinsic and dependent part of the primary intentional relation—as it

SUBJECT — ACT — < CONTENT>   OBJECT

Figure 15.2
Reflexive modal inner awareness.

were, a secondary reflexive ray that branches off from the primary ray of intentionality.

Within the modality of presentation we find two features of "self-consciousness": the way the *act* is experienced, "in this very experience [I see . . .]"; and the way the *subject* is experienced, "I [see . . .]." In this form of experience (a typical normal adult human form of consciousness, we assume), the modality then involves as a matter of course an *inner awareness* of the passing experience and also of the subject. We shall focus later on the problem of awareness of self.

In the type of case we have been considering, the subject and experience are not part of the object or situation toward which consciousness is directed. However, it is possible to focus one's *attention* on one's passing experience or on oneself. It is also possible to focus one's attention on some object or event in such a way that one is *peripherally* aware of one's experience or of oneself. We turn now to these structures of consciousness.

3   The Structure of Attention in Conscious Experience

Discussions of intentionality often gloss over the structure of attention. But early accounts of consciousness gave attention a natural role. William James appraised attention as part of normal consciousness, observing that when I focus attention on an object there is a "fringe" of adjacent objects of which I am to a lesser extent aware (James 1890). Similarly, Edmund Husserl held that consciousness is directed toward an object with a "horizon" of indeterminately given objects in the surrounding world. Aron Gurwitsch added to Husserl's model the structure championed by Gestalt psychology: an object of consciousness is presented against a background of other objects, so the form of what is presented is always "figure/ground." Maurice Merleau-Ponty elaborated on the Husserl-Gurwitsch-Gestalt model, finding that the phenomenal field in vision is structured in relation to the subject's living body.

We adapt this line of analysis as we proceed: consciousness takes the form, then, of a structured *field* of experience with varied intentional forms. (See Gurwitsch 1964, 1985; Merleau-Ponty 1945; Smith 2005b; Yoshimi 2001, 2005; Williford 2005 and this volume.)

On the model emerging from Gurwitsch, Merleau-Ponty, et al., the *field* of consciousness is structured by *attention* in quite specific ways. Consider an everyday experience, characterized in the first person (singular). When I see a dog running before me, my phenomenal field includes much more than the dog. Within my visual field a white standard poodle, running briskly across the path, is presented *focally*, or at the focus of attention. But a variety of other things are presented *peripherally*, or in the periphery of attention. At the left of my visual field is a fleeting black form I take for a cat. I am also visually aware of my hands on the handlebars of my bicycle at the bottom of my visual field. I am also kinesthetically aware of my pedaling the bicycle—the dog is running across the bike path in front of me, catching my attention, drawing my attention away from the bumpy dirt path my eyes were following. In my phenomenal field there is also a sharp barking sound coming from the darting canine visual form. There is also the feel of cool air upon my face as I ride. There is also my fleeting thought that poodles chase birds more often than cats. Indeed, there is a sense of my fleeting stream of consciousness of various things, framed by my recollections of things just past (the crow cawing as the dog appeared) and my expectations of things about to transpire (will the dog jump over that log?). Within my current conscious experience, my attention is focused on the barking, darting white poodle visually before me. All these other things of which I am conscious are presented peripherally, outside the focus of attention. And yet, in a peripheral way, I am indeed aware of the fleeting cat, my hands, my pedaling action, the cawing sound, my passing thoughts about dogs, and even my mood as I pedal down the serene forest path. What, more precisely, is the structure of the field of my consciousness?

When we appraise a simple act of consciousness, analyzing the act-object structure of intentionality, we indulge a tremendous simplification. A normal state of consciousness, over a brief stretch of time, typically includes all of my transpiring perceptions, thoughts, emotions, volitions, and so on. And all these component partial states or processes of consciousness are unified in appropriate ways within the structured field of my consciousness. Within that field my consciousness presents me with a rich manifold of phenomena: all I am perceptually aware of in seeing, hearing, touching, smelling, tasting, thinking; all I am kinesthetically aware of in my bodily movement and action; all I am engaged in doing in performing actions (such as bicycling as above); all my varying emotions involved in what I am doing, seeing, thinking; and so on; all of these elements structured by attention into a single experience with a focus and a periphery. So while it is proper to say that we are aware of everything within a given conscious state, we should not think that we are equally aware of all that transpires within that conscious state.

Notice that within my peripheral awareness there are presentations of my body (of my hands on the handlebars, of my pedaling bodily action): here lies part of my proprioceptive body-image, in the *periphery* of my current field of consciousness. Within my peripheral awareness there are also—less palpable, as it were—presentations of my own experience, of my passing stream of thought and perception and emotion. These *peripheral* forms of awareness of my experience and of myself are to be distinguished from the forms of *inner* awareness of experience and self that we noted earlier. Indeed, the contrast between these forms of awareness will prove instructive as we proceed.

Observing these distinctions of focal and peripheral structure in the field of consciousness, we should like to develop a systematic analysis of the types and organization of these forms of consciousness. Uncovering the structure of attention can be difficult. Whenever we attempt to catch an aspect of the periphery of a given experience, we do so by focusing attention on it. That changes the structure of the experience itself, making it nearly impossible to reflect on the experience of the periphery as peripheral. Imperfect though our reflection on direct experience may be, we do have other ways of establishing some structural features of attention (including those most relevant to this volume, pertaining to self-reference). One way to argue for these distinctions of phenomenological structure is to study cases in which something normal is missing. We then realize what is, and must be, present in the normal case. In this pursuit we integrate phenomenology with cognitive neuroscience. In developing our account of attention, we turn to a model of attention that has been developed by the psychologist David LaBerge.

4 A Triangular Circuit Model of Attention

In order to argue for our sort of same-order monitoring model (which might be called *same-act monitoring*, to distinguish it from the same-order models that involve one part of a given mental act monitoring another part, the *part-whole monitoring* models), we must address the biggest hurdle to inner-awareness models, namely, understanding just how a *single* whole conscious state could possibly represent itself (see Kriegel this volume). In this section we will address that challenge by presenting a conception of attention where all of the following are incorporated into a single act: an object in the focus, the self in the periphery, and the relations between the self and the rest of the objects in the field of attention (both in the focus and in the periphery), where the peripheral awareness of the self grounds the inner awareness of the self as subject. This model of attention will also relate the conscious act itself to the peripheral self-image, and thence to the subject of inner awareness. By turning to cognitive science and neuroscience to show how attention can implement this structure in the brain, we hope to defuse the prima facie difficulty in imagining just how a single mental act might manage all of this.

To investigate the structure of attention, we must address three features of attention. First, we need some account of how it is that objects appear to us at all, how some objects appear in the focus of attention while others appear in the periphery, and thus what feature explains the difference in salience or emphasis that gives us the distinction between focus and periphery of experience. Second, we know that our attention shifts from one thing to another, where some of these shifts of attention are under our conscious control and some are not. How then does attention change its objects?[4] Third, we need to know the mechanism that produces the first feature (the "how" behind the "what" of the focus of attention). These are features that any adequate account of attention must explain, and we will turn to David LaBerge's *triangular circuit model of attention* for an explanation of the neural mechanisms that underlie each of the three features we've found to be central to the experience of attention. First, the objects in the focus and periphery must appear to us; call that feature the *expression* of attention. Next, the focus of attention shifts from one object to others, so we must examine how the focus of attention is *controlled*. Finally, we will see how the focus is *enhanced* above the periphery and maintained over time. (We draw on LaBerge 1995, 1997, 1998.) This explanatory account will give us the foundation to show how same-act inner awareness can be an essential feature of every normal contemporary human conscious mental state.

To begin with the expression of attention, we have to make some assumptions about how brain events are related to conscious experiences in general. For some, these assumptions may be contentious (and the account we present here is necessarily simplified), but if one wishes to give a naturalistic account of consciousness at all, something like the following must hold:

The "object" of attention, whether an object of sense or an object of thought, is generally believed to be coded in some form within specific areas or modules of the cerebral cortex. Visual shapes are coded in clusters of neurons within the inferotemporal cortex (IT), and visual locations are coded in clusters of neurons within the posterior parietal cortex (PPC), while plans of action and semantic attributes of objects involve codes that appear to be distributed across specific modules of the frontal cortex. When one of these cortical codes becomes the object of attention, we presume that the corresponding module increases its activity relative to its surrounding sites. The resulting profile of activity across the target object and its immediately surrounding sites may be called the *expression* aspect of attention. (LaBerge 1997, p. 150; italics in original)

LaBerge's model is a study in cognitive psychology looking to neuroscience (through simulation models of actual brain activity). Our model will develop a phenomenological analysis of the features of conscious experience that are grounded in such neural activities according to the LaBergean model.

Though LaBerge speaks of a cortical code becoming the object of attention, we must be careful of this turn of phrase. Certainly, the object of attention is not a cortical code presented *as such*. We never experience any aspect of our experience as being the experience of increased activity in parts of our cortex, since we don't experience the cortex (as such) at all. We experience the world, via a rich stream of consciousness. What LaBerge means here is that the cortical site that represents the object in the focus of attention serves as the object-specifying component of the brain's attentive process. LaBerge continues:

Given the foregoing description of cortical column activity as the brain correlate of a component of a cognitive event, the expression aspect of attention can be defined relatively clearly. Viewed cognitively, the expression of attention is the *emphasis* of a particular component of a cognitive event, and viewed cortically, the expression of attention corresponds to a difference in activity levels between the columnar clusters corresponding to the attended (target) component and its neighboring (distractor) components (or the surround, if the attended component is presented in isolation). (LaBerge 1997, p. 153; italics in original)

We will consider a simple attentional task, to see how this works in practice. Let us suppose, in the poodle scenario above, that the subject is cycling along, attending primarily to the road. In the first person: when the poodle enters the scene, I shift the focus of my attention to the poodle. What goes on at the neurological level that produces this focusing of attention? According to LaBerge, the sites in the visual cortex that represent the poodle start out firing at roughly the same rates and levels of activation as the rest of the elements of the scene that are not focused on (that is, everything but the road). As the subject concentrates on the poodle, the cortical site that codes for the poodle becomes more active relative to the sites that code for the rest of his visual experience at that time.[5]

The cortical column that corresponds to the presentation of the "object" in the focus of attention does so because that cortical column is firing at a higher rate than the cortical columns that correspond to presentations of items in the periphery of that experience, and this relative difference in activity is caused by an increase in activity in the focal site, possibly enhanced by a suppression of activity in the peripheral sites. Let us follow LaBerge's terminology and call this aspect of cognition the *expression* of attention. If LaBerge is correct, levels of cortical activation underlie the distinction between focus and periphery. This provides us with a broad-brush answer to the question, "What is it for an object to appear in the focus of attention?"[6] Next, we will examine the *control* of the focus of attention.

There are two ways for the focus of attention to be directed toward a particular object. For some objects, our habits, interests, and perceptual mechanisms cause the corresponding objects or features to appear as more salient than the surrounding ones, and thus our attention is drawn to them (in many cases without our conscious direction). Examples of the bottom-up direction of the focus of attention are our own names, loud noises, quickly moving objects, strong smells, and the like. This also includes the mechanism of "preattentive pop-out," where some perceptual feature of the object makes it stand out for us (a square among a bunch of circles, a red flower among a bunch of yellow flowers, and so on). We can also direct our attention by an act of conscious will, often overriding the bottom-up processing that would otherwise result in our attention shifting to focus on the objects that our bottom-up mechanisms find so attractive. The consciously directed, top-down channel is also necessary to maintain a focus on the objects that have drawn our attention via the bottom-up mechanisms (even objects that do "pop-out" require maintenance if they are to remain in the focus of attention, and that maintenance is a top-down function).

Evidence for the location of a center of attention control comes from studies of the effects of localized cortical lesions on features of attentional behavior. To wit: "It is known that lesions of varying sizes and locations in the frontal cortex ... commonly report heightened distractibility in the delayed response task and a general inability to shift responses appropriately to meet changing demands of a task, both indicators implying some degree of deficit in attentional control" (LaBerge 1997, pp. 163–164). The prefrontal areas of the cortex are generally recognized as the areas where planning, organizing, and judgment occur, or are produced. These areas are certainly central in the planning and executions of *actions*. And the directing of attention should itself count as an *action* (LaBerge 1997, p. 158). As with other, more muscular actions, the top-down direction (and maintenance) of attention requires a conscious effort, takes practice, and can be done well or poorly.[7] The prefrontal cortex gives us the mechanism for the *control* of attention. That leaves the *enhancement* of the firing rates localized at the two cortical sites that we've just described, expression (cortical columns that code for objects of perception or thought) and control (the prefrontal cortex).

As LaBerge explains, a separate mechanism for the enhancement of the firing rates in the sites of expression would make the process of attention much more efficient, and we have independent evidence to believe that such a mechanism exists:

To keep separate the informational and modulatory properties of prefrontal control, a supplemental route from the prefrontal (and/or parietal) areas is needed to carry the modulatory signals that are needed to intensify the activity levels in the target columns.

The principle pathways of fibers connecting the control areas of the prefrontal cortex to cortical columns where attention is expressed are prefrontal to IT [the inferotemporal cortex] . . . for shape, and prefrontal to PPC [the posterior parietal cortex] . . . for location, but another pathway of fibers connects these prefrontal areas with their posterior cortical columns. This other pathway passes through the thalamus, and that thalamic circuitry has the modulatory ability to enhance the rate of neural signals passing through it, according to a simulation analysis (LaBerge et al. 1992). Thus, the two pathways by which a prefrontal area connects to another cortical area form a triangle, in which the direct link is mainly concerned with choosing precisely which columns shall be activated and the indirect link (which passes through the thalamus) is mainly concerned with how much the chosen column shall be intensified. (LaBerge 1997, p. 159)

This triangular connection between the pathways that carry information and the pathways that modulate and intensify the activity at the sites of expression is the basic neural unit of attention in LaBerge's theory. Fortunately, there is quite a lot of independent evidence that the thalamus plays an active and essential role in attention (summarized in LaBerge 1997, pp. 162–163).[8]

Taken together, we now have a plausible explanation of how the brain effects the enhancement of the focus of attention and the maintenance of focus over time:

1. The cortical areas that code for sense perceptions, objects, and actions provide the *expression* of attention, which presents the "object" in the focus of attention.

2. The prefrontal cortex serves to direct and *control* the focus of attention.

3. The thalamus serves to *enhance* the activations at the sites of expression and to enhance the feedback and feedforward connections between the sites of expression and control.

This model of neurocognitive activity, we note, corroborates our developing analysis of the phenomenological structure of attention in everyday conscious experience. Here we see a reflective equilibrium between phenomenology and cognitive neuroscience.

5 Divided Attention

The LaBerge model, we contend, offers a viable explanation of how the main arrow of intentionality (directed toward the object via the content) could be implemented in the brain. With that explanation in place, we can use it as a foundation to build up a more detailed account of the feature of conscious experience that concerns us here, inner awareness. For the next step in the argument, we must consider a conscious state where attention is divided between the self and another object. Once we've secured our account of divided attention, we will extend the model to cover all normal conscious states and explain the role that the self-reflexive arrow of inner awareness plays therein.

Sometimes (though perhaps not all that often) we are consciously aware of ourselves as actors in our current experience. This occurs when the focus of our attention is *divided* between our self-image and the main object of our experience. Since we find two things presented within the focus of attention, we should expect to find two triangular attentional circuits. Furthermore, since they are part of the same conscious experience, the two circuits must be connected in some way.

LaBerge explains how his model can accommodate this sort of divided attention, where the self and another object are jointly attended to. This sort of cognizance of oneself he calls "awareness." (We are not adopting that use of the term, only noting its technical meaning in the quotation that follows.) Thus LaBerge writes:

Being "aware" of something is a predicate that appears to call for a subject, and the subject is supplied by activation of the cortical areas in which the concept of selfhood is represented, presumably frontal cortical areas. . . . The role of references to the self in states of awareness has been treated elsewhere. . . . When objects give rise to perceptions, or sensations, these events may be followed by statements such as "I am perceiving X," or "I am sensing X," or "My experience is X" . . . which reflect the additional processing of some representation of the self. Thus, it is assumed here that the event of awareness requires that attention be directed to the regions where the subject is expressed at the same time that attention is directed to the cortical regions where the object is expressed. . . . Simultaneous activation of the two triangular circuits is assured if they were both activated from a common brain area in the frontal cortex, that is, the two triangular circuits would be joined at their common control center. To distinguish between the two kinds of triangular attention circuits, they will be labeled object-attended and self-attended circuits.

The action of activating both the object-attended and self-attended triangular circuits produces much more than the simultaneous (or near-simultaneous) increase in activity at the object- and self-attended cortical sites of attentional expression. Within each triangular circuit the feedback from the expression site to the prefrontal area of control is synchronized with the activations flowing from the common control site to the expression site. As a result of the temporal coincidence between the two triangular circuits, not only is attention being directed to the self along with attention to an object, but attention is being directed to "the self doing the control" of attention to the object. (LaBerge 1997, p. 173)

If LaBerge is correct about how we focus attention on one object, then this account of conjoined attentional circuits will explain how we focus on more than one object in cases of divided attention.[9] Since the point applies generally, it will necessarily cover the cases where one of the objects in the focus of attention is the self, that is, in the self-image of the person having the experience.

In this account of divided attention, we have shown how it is possible for the brain to implement a complex intentional state: one that is directed toward both an object and the self in a single conscious state. Building on that, we will now show how LaBerge's account of the self-image in divided attention can be extended to cover the more limited self-awareness present in all normal conscious states.

6 Deficits and Normal Images of Self

To change the LaBerge model into one that can cover all conscious states, we need only make one additional supposition: that what holds of divided attention also holds true of the periphery of attention. We all know that we do not only experience things in the focus of attention; our conscious experience also includes much that is peripherally given. The cortical correlates of those aspects of our experience also fire at the activation level required to allow them to appear (but at a lower level than at the focus of attention). The peripheral correlates, to the extent that they are stable, must also be receiving some degree of thalamic enhancement. This may be direct, as with the focus of attention, or it may be a result of bleed-over from the focus of attention. The mechanism isn't of central importance here (though, of course, we'd love to know more); the fact of peripheral experience is all we need. Finally, the mechanism responsible for unifying divided attention is probably the same mechanism that always operates to unify the focus with the periphery in our conscious experience.

If this hypothesis is acceptable, then we will attempt to show that the self is always presented in the periphery of every normal adult human conscious experience, though it may well go unnoticed. In order to approach these often-unnoticed features that (we will argue) must be present in normal consciousness, we will carefully consider certain forms of abnormal consciousness.

As a way of evaluating cases where we have unnoticed peripheral contribution to consciousness and those where we don't, it will help to keep two cases in mind. First, imagine a person who is lost in thought and not paying a bit of attention to what she is looking at. If that person were suddenly struck blind, she would notice the change. From this, we may conclude that visual experience was a part of the person's conscious state, even though it was not what she was attending to. Second, imagine a person lost in a pitch-dark coal mine. If that person were struck blind, she would not notice. Visual perception was not a part of that person's conscious state in the mine. On analogy with these hypothetical cases, we will examine several actual cases of altered consciousness (altered by brain lesion or pathology). If we find that the impairment or removal of some part of the self-image has an impact on that person's experience, then we may conclude that it must have been present in that person's consciousness, even if the person was not explicitly aware of it, and even if we normally do not attend to such a self-image. The cases we will examine here are *loss of proprioception*, *amnesia*, and *depersonalization*. Each of these three cases will reveal a different feature of the self-image to be necessarily present and active in every normal conscious state.

First, let us consider the body-image.[10] One aspect of the body-image, the image of the current state of the body's muscular and skeletal structures, is created and maintained by three distinct systems: proprioception, balance, and visual tracking. We will focus on proprioception here, though similar points could be made regarding the other aspects of the body-image. Proprioception is our internal sense of our muscles and joints and their relative positions. If this fails, the body becomes blind to itself, as described by Oliver Sacks in the case of "The Disembodied Lady." This unfortunate woman was struck by a polyneuritis that only affected her proprioceptive nerve fibers, removing her body's automatic sense of her own muscular activity and tone. Sacks relates her condition when it first struck:

Standing was impossible—unless she looked down at her feet. She could hold nothing in her hands, and they "wandered"—unless she kept an eye on them. When she reached out for something, or tried to feed herself, her hands would miss, or overshoot wildly, as if some essential control or coordination was gone.

She could scarcely even sit up—her body "gave way." Her face was oddly expressionless and slack, her jaw fell open, even her vocal posture was gone.

"Something awful's happened," she mouthed, in a ghostly flat voice. "I can't feel my body. I feel weird—disembodied." (Sacks 1985, p. 44)

With time and much hard work, this woman was able to partially compensate for the loss of her proprioception by developing her visual body image (which is usually rather weak). Sadly, the feeling of being disembodied never eased. The point that is relevant for our discussion is that this account vividly demonstrates that proprioception (as an aspect of the self-image) is *always active and contributing to every normal conscious experience*. Since it is omnipresent, we tend not to notice it. Although we rarely focus our attention on our sense of our bodies' position, this case demonstrates that this sense is normally always in the periphery of consciousness. If it were ever to vanish, we would notice its absence immediately.

Next, let us turn to the other side of the self-representation and consider what can happen if aspects of the conceptual or semantic self-image are lost. The semantic self-image is that part of our self-image that contains our knowledge about ourselves: autobiographical memories, the things we find most important in life, our goals and projects, and our beliefs about ourselves as persons. At least some of the semantic self-image depends on memory, so we will examine a case of amnesia.

In Korsakov's syndrome, the brain loses the ability to store new memories, creating a state of constant amnesia. People who suffer from Korsakov's syndrome lose all memory of what they've done or what has happened to them after only a few minutes. Often, long-term memories beyond a certain point will be retained. Most relevant for us, the constant updating of the semantic self is lost, so that these people become locked into a groundless present, with a past that may be decades out of date. Here is an example from Dr. Sacks's first interview with the patient known as Jimmy G.:

"I was just going to ask you—where do you think you are?"

"I see these beds, and these patients everywhere. Looks like a sort of hospital to me. But hell, what would I be doing in a hospital—and with all these old people, years older than me. I feel good, I'm strong as a bull. Maybe I *work* here ... Do I work? What's my job? . . . No, you're shaking your head, I see in your eyes I don't work here. If I don't work here, I've been *put* here. Am I a patient, am I sick and don't know it, Doc? It's crazy, it's scary . . . Is it some sort of joke?"

"You don't know what the matter is? You really don't know? You remember telling me about your childhood, growing up in Connecticut, working as a radio operator on submarines? And how your brother is engaged to a girl from Oregon?"

"Hey, you're right. But I didn't tell you that, I never met you before in my life. You must have read all about me in my chart." (Sacks 1985, pp. 24–25)

Jimmy's condition shows just what a contribution the constant updating of the semantic self-image makes to every conscious experience. Our recent past informs our present, making it possible for us to connect what we are doing now with what we did this morning (and more importantly, with who we were this morning). Of course, Jimmy G. still has a semantic self (that of a nineteen-year-old living in 1945) and a sort of continuity (he has been where he is, and is engaged in whatever he has been doing—but only for the last five minutes). His semantic self is fundamentally static—Jimmy is frozen as the person he was in 1945. This colors his experience in ways that he does not notice (just as we don't often notice this aspect of our own conscious experience), but his case illustrates these features in a very pointed and direct way. Since the early 1970s (in Sacks's report), he has operated with a 1945 mindset.

Jimmy's case shows that the semantic sense of self is part of our normal experience. If it is part of normal experience, then it must be registering in attention. Further, the most natural way to account for the updating of the semantic sense of self (through memory, what Jimmy is unable to do) is by updating the self-image, which appears in attention (either focally or periph-erally). Jimmy's case is different from that of the disembodied lady and of depersonalization (our next case) in that Jimmy is not aware of his problem. This may look like a counterexample to our strategy of checking what aspects of consciousness the subject would notice if they were removed. However, Jimmy seems like a counterexample not because we have any reason to think that the predamage and postdamage mental states are sub-jectively indistinguishable, but only because his condition prevents him from making the relevant before-and-after comparisons. We have no doubt that if Jimmy's amnesia were to suddenly evaporate, and he could recall his life as an amnesiac, he would indeed notice the profound differences of life with normal memory and life without.

Finally, we will consider depersonalization disorder. In this condition, the individual's semantic self-image becomes divorced from the body-image, perceptions, and the actions that the body is performing:

In the pathological condition of depersonalization, the self-representation is dissoci-
ated from the perceptions of the body, so that perceptions and actions of the
body are believed to be happening to someone other than the self (e.g., . . . Simeon
and Hollander 1993). In the present context, the system dysfunction could occur
in the prefrontal areas where the controls of attention to the self-representations
and to the object representations (and action representations) are closely related.
The prefrontal area is believed to have a crucial role in the temporal integration
of operations that control the actions of monkeys and humans. . . . If defects
occur in the temporal coordination of the actions controlling activities in the self-
attended and object-attended triangular circuits, then the person's experience of
self as an agency of control could be compromised, resulting in the observed disorder
of depersonalization, which disrupts the sense of awareness. (LaBerge 1997,
p. 174)

Here we see that two aspects of the self have come apart (since the perceptions and actions of the body must include the perceptions of the body image,
and that is separated from the self that gives us reports on what the person's
experience is like). Depersonalization is a failure of *integration* of different
aspects or *representations* of the self. The body image is still working, for
the person suffering from depersonalization does not tip over, lose muscle
tone, or collapse. The semantic self-image is also still working, along with
awareness of what the body is doing and experiencing, but the body is not
seen as *belonging to the person* (and it may also be felt as *unreal*). It's as if
"I" am aware of "this body" but do not take it as "my body." The profound
impact of this dissociation demonstrates that the connection between these
very elements *must be present during normal conscious awareness.* Hence,
the unified self-image must be presented and operating in the field of
attention.[11]

These three cases demonstrate that at least three features of the self-image
must be active parts of each conscious experience: proprioception, the
semantic self-image, and their unified integration. However, there is a more
general lesson to be learned from these features. We see that the complete
self-image (which is almost certainly more complex than the three features
we've discussed here) must appear as part of each normal conscious experience. It can appear in the focus (with the self as either the primary object of
attention or sharing the focus with another object), or it can appear so far
into the periphery that we fail to notice it—but it *must* appear. Indeed, the
relationship of the object to the self is a normal part of the experience of
any object. If the self-image did not appear, there would be no way for us
to track the relationships between the objects of our experience and ourselves, as we normally do.

7   Inner Awareness and Peripheral Awareness of Self

Let us take stock of what we have accomplished through our foray into cognitive neuroscience. The LaBerge model of attention, extended to include the self-image in the periphery, gives us an account of *how it is possible* for the self-image to be present in every normal conscious state. As we construe that model, the complex phenomenological structure of attention—variously observed by James, Husserl, Gurwitsch, and Merleau-Ponty—is implemented in, dependent on, or grounded in, a certain complex structure of neural activity. Assuming that neurophenomenological model of attention, we considered cases where neurological dysfunction produces psychological dysfunction: cases where something is amiss in the phenomenological structure of attention—thereby bringing to the fore the normal self-image. In this way our examination of three abnormal conscious states gave us reason to believe that the self-image is genuinely present in every normal conscious state. And since we are not usually focally aware of the self, the self-image must then be present in the periphery of attention. One step remains: to determine how peripheral awareness of self is related to inner awareness. We want to show that the peripheral self-image grounds inner awareness of self ("in this very experience I see such-and-such"), and so is responsible for the phenomenological observation that conscious experience is normally experienced as belonging to "me," even in those experiences where one is not explicitly aware of oneself as a participant in the experience. Reflective equilibrium will be achieved thus.

Notice how contingent are these structures of awareness, contingent on how the mind works in a context of dependency on neural organization (the triangular circuits) and on historical, cultural, and personal background (shaping what achieves saliency in a given experience). These contingencies of ordinary experience belie some of the rhetoric of classical transcendental phenomenology, which may suggest, in a Kantian tone, that basic forms of experience are necessary or synthetic a priori structures in any possible consciousness. Our considerations here do not join in such universalizing aspirations. We haven't shown that there is nothing common to all consciousness (which would disprove the transcendental a priori claim), but we see no reason to make the more ambitious claim.

In every instance of normal contemporary adult human conscious experience, then, we have established the presence of a self-image, usually in the periphery. How should we try to figure out exactly what is the relationship between the peripheral self-image and inner awareness? We return to phenomenology for that appraisal. From James and Husserl to Gurwitsch and

Merleau-Ponty it has been observed that in the periphery of experience there appear not only the objects peripherally presented, but also their relationships to each other (see especially Gurwitsch 1964, 1985). So, let us treat the peripherally presented self as one object among other peripheral objects, and see how it is related to the other things presented in the focus and periphery of attention.

Let us consider a familiar type of experience, characterized in the first person. As I type at the computer, I am drinking a cold can of V-8. There it sits, off to the left of my laptop screen. How is it related to my peripheral self-image? It is about a yard away from me, within easy reach. And how is it related to the self of inner awareness? *I* see it about a yard away from *me*, easily within *my* reach. In the next moment, I reach for it. Here is a hand, reaching for the can. How is the hand related to my peripheral self-image? It is *my* hand. The hand is part of my body, I get sensory (including proprioceptive) input from the hand, the hand is under my control (with my kinesthetic awareness of its movement), and part of my self-image includes this hand (my self-hand-image, if you like). And how is the hand related to the self of inner awareness? It is *my* hand, a part of *me*, part of *I* who see these things around me. As we say in phenomenological description: "In this very experience I see this V-8 can that I am grasping with my left hand." Clearly, there is a logical connection between the two "I"-awarenesses in this phenomenological structure, where the second "I" is tied back to the first (anaphorically, if you will). (For the details, see Smith 2005b.)

Thus, if we treat the peripheral self as just another peripheral object, and use the other objects that appear in consciousness to track relationships between those objects and the peripheral self, we are led to the self of inner awareness. For, every object in the field of attention appears as related (usually peripherally) to the self-image in the field, and that self-image is an image of "me," "I," the self that is the subject of consciousness, the self of which (on our assumed model) I am reflexively aware in inner awareness. I cannot have a normally structured field of consciousness, then, unless the self-image in the field designates the right self, namely me, the subject of consciousness.

But how is it possible that the experience includes a reflexive inner awareness of the self? Given the complexity of the field of consciousness, structured by a distribution of attention over a variety of things in relation to the self and experience, we contend that the *inner awareness* of self is dependent on or grounded in the presence of the self-image in the field of consciousness. In the normal range of experience, we find our various acts of consciousness both directed from a self and organized about a self and its role in the larger world in which objects including the self are presented focally or peripherally in various ways. In this context of experience, we could not have an inner awareness of consciousness and of self ("in this very experience I see such-and-such") unless the field of attention is distributed over objects including the self and its experience—that's just how things work, normally.

In different ways, then, inner awareness and the spread of attention are mutually dependent. In the context of our ordinary forms of consciousness, inner awareness could not occur without a distribution of attention including peripheral awareness of self and experience, and the familiar distribution of attention could not occur in an act of consciousness without inner awareness.

Should we then consider these two self-formations—peripheral awareness of self and inner awareness of self—to be one and the same thing, approached via two different methods? Despite the close connection, we don't think so: they are distinct but interdependent. After all, each of the people we considered in the previous section had some aspect of his or her peripheral self-image drastically altered, yet each still had intentional experiences, directed from subject to object. In that respect, they all still experience inner awareness of self. Altering the self-image may change what one is aware of, and perhaps even "who" it is that is aware of it, but the basic intentional structure is still very much present. Rather than identifying peripheral with inner awareness of self, we contend, as argued, that inner awareness of self *depends on* a functioning (though not necessarily optimally functioning) peripheral self-image. The presence of the self-image in consciousness makes it possible to have the *structure* of experience that we characterized as involving inner awareness. As we've seen, a variety of impaired self-images can still ground that structural phenomenological feature, wherein a mental act is directed *from* a subject *to* the objects in the field of consciousness.

Another way to put the difference between peripheral and inner awareness of self relies on the distinction between the mode and the modality in the form of conscious experience (Smith 1986, 1989, 2004). Since the peripheral self is presented as an object in the field of attention, it belongs to the mode of presentation in the experience, that is, it is part of the milieu of things experienced. By contrast, the inner awareness of self is part of the modality of presentation, that is, it is part of the way things are experienced, namely, by a subject.

Both experience and self are given reflexively in inner awareness and also, in distinct ways, in peripheral awareness. So our model of conscious experience is now as depicted in figure 15.3. Now we have an answer to the question, "How is it possible for a conscious state to represent itself and its object

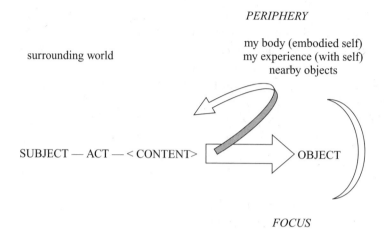

PERIPHERY

my body (embodied self)
my experience (with self)
nearby objects

surrounding world

SUBJECT — ACT — < CONTENT>   OBJECT

FOCUS

Figure 15.3
Inner awareness and peripheral awareness of self and experience.

at the same time?" A conscious state can represent itself to the person who is having it by representing the relations between the objects experienced (both focally and peripherally) and the self (whether presented focally or peripherally) in the field of attention. In order to see how this is possible, we had to investigate the nature of attention itself, looking to both cognitive neuroscience and phenomenology. In the process, we may also have uncovered the reason why the self is often missed (à la Hume) and why the higher-order models and part-whole versions of the same-order models are attractive: there is more phenomenological structure at work than meets the eye. Our goal here, looking to the complexities of attention, was to show how it is possible for a same-order, same-act theory of inner awareness to work. That we have done, even if future investigations require the modification or rejection of LaBerge's triangular-circuit theory of how attention is implemented in the brain. The structure of attention and the aspects of the self revealed in our pathological cases will remain, as part of the phenomena that any adequate theory of the mind must do justice to.

The analysis above forces us to consider the whole field of attention of a person's experience at a given time, instead of addressing only the object in the focus of attention, as many theorists tend to do. This means that the appropriate boundary for *a conscious state or act* is that of a momentary time-slice of the stream of consciousness. Within such a slice, we find the structure of attention including the self-image, usually in the periphery. Nonetheless, when we consider a time-slice of experience, we abstract the momentary phase of experience from the ongoing stream of experience, which itself is part of the periphery of attention (as Gurwitsch 1985 observed, reflecting Husserl's analysis of time-consciousness).

As we noted, peripheral contributions to consciousness can be very difficult to capture directly. However, only at this level of detail can we discern the operation of the self-image that grounds inner awareness. So we cannot simply talk, as is common, about a propositional attitude of thinking thus-and-such. If we consider only the structure "I think that p," we abstract away from the attentional self-image that is part of a normal moment of experience—the structure our analysis reveals. Of course, once we realize what we are doing, we can easily regain the positive aspects of self, like the cogito, and also the more abstract structure of propositional attitudes developed in analytic philosophy of mind and language. All of these are useful tools for legitimate purposes, but they are abstractions, and we should not forget the aspects and details of experience that have been abstracted away from.

8 Conclusion

We have analyzed different forms of awareness of the self, but the self is itself the object of those awarenesses. Thus: I am aware of myself in different ways, in inner awareness of my experiences and therewith of myself as subject of those experiences, and in peripheral awareness of myself as subject of those experiences and in peripheral awareness of my own body in my actions. The object of those awarenesses is I myself, a being that is embodied, enminded, and encultured. Once we distinguish the various roles of the self and its forms of self-awareness, there remains no problem of a substantial self: it is but I.

Notes

1. We must be careful, however, to distinguish this form of inner awareness from what might be called "self-awareness" in more everyday contexts. In the ordinary sense "self-awareness" can mean the sort of intense self-awareness that accompanies embarrassment ("Everyone is looking at me!"). It can also mean introspective reflection, focusing my attention on my current mental states ("What am I feeling now?"). Or it can involve dividing my attention between the object of my experience and my reactions to that experience ("How do I feel about that?"). These clearly do not accompany every conscious experience, and so are not what we have in mind by inner awareness.

2. The term "reflective equilibrium" is drawn from Rawls, adapted by Dagfinn Føllesdal for this back-and-forth between phenomenology and neuroscience.

3. Philosophers of language may look to a similar structure in Frege's theory of reference via sense. Analytic philosophers of mind may also look to Searle's analysis of intentionality, which marks most of the same distinctions as the Husserlian model (see Føllesdal 1969, and for an alternative interpretation, see Drummond 1990).

4. For convenience, we may refer to the object of attention, even though that locution is often ambiguous between the object in the world we are focusing on and the representation *in* attention via which we attend to the thing in the world. The tendency to speak of the objects of attention is too strong for us to try to contest it here. We hope that the context will be clear enough to avoid the confusion that often attends discussions of intentional objects. We also note that the focus of attention may rest on conventional objects, specific details or aspects of objects, or events or other entities that are not strictly physical *objects*—such as thoughts, emotions, plans, goals, events, numbers, fantasies, relations, properties, complex states of affairs, hallucinations, etc.

5. The evidence from single-neuron probes of cortical sites during attention tasks tends to indicate that this relative difference is primarily produced by increasing the activity at the focal site, rather than by suppressing the activity at the sites that correspond to the distractors, and to the surrounding perceptual periphery. Semantic priming is found in stem-completion tasks, while negative priming is revealed in the time it takes to assess a target that has just been a distractor, ignored and unseen (Mack and Rock 1998, ch. 8). Given the current evidence, we should allow that both enhancement and suppression have important roles in generating the focus of attention.

6. We will extend this account to cover the periphery of attention in section 6.

7. The connection between attention and action is suggestive, but exploring this issue fully must be deferred to another occasion.

8. The thalamus is connected to the brain stem, serves as a gatekeeper or way station for all the sensory information we receive (except smell), is connected to the hypothalamus and the limbic system (which produces and regulates our emotional responses), and is richly connected to most of the rest of the cortex. There are relevant studies from single-cell recordings in animals; lesion studies of the posterior thalamus on the visual field (Rafal and Posner 1987); studies of the chemical deactivation of the pulvinar (a thalamic structure) that impaired the disengagement of visual attention (Petersen, Robinson, and Morris 1987) and interfered with selection of a target from among distractors (though not selection in the absence of distractors) (Desimone et al. 1990); several different experiments involving PET scans show activity in the pulvinar during visual attention (LaBerge and Buschbaum 1990; Liotti, Fox, and LaBerge 1994).

9. This passage seems to indicate that temporal coincidence is enough to secure the unity of conscious experience in cases of divided attention. In fact, LaBerge provides examples (one that we will consider in detail), which indicate that some additional mechanism is needed to synchronize and unify co-occurring attentional events. We read this passage as laying out two necessary conditions: temporal coincidence and unity. This unifying mechanism is not well understood yet, but its failure in cases of depersonalization and the alien limb phenomenon show that it must be operating in all our normal conscious states.

10. The *body-image* is the composite representation of the body's current position and condition. We consider it as one component of the larger composite, the *self-image*. For the purposes of this essay, we will be primarily interested in the systems that track and represent the position and motion of the body, but to get a sense of just how much goes into the body-image, see Damasio 1999. There, we see that the body's internal regulatory mechanisms produce a large number of aspects of the body-image. The body-image contains at least these aspects, and probably more: feelings and emotions, the position and current state of the muscles, bones, and joints, the sense of touch, and our sense of our current position in our environment.

11. Dissociation disorder also shows that LaBerge's contention that simultaneous activations among the neural correlates of various object-presentations were sufficient to produce a unified stream of consciousness to be premature. Increased activation levels is necessary, but some additional mechanism must also be operating to unify the multifarious aspects of the object-presentations and the multiple object-presentations themselves into a single unified stream of consciousness.

Tomis Kapitan

1 Introduction

Self-awareness is commonly expressed by means of indexical expressions, primarily, first-person pronouns like "I," "me," "we," "my," "myself," "mine," and so forth. While all indexical contents are first-personal, indexical usage suggests a kind of reflexive awareness since its terms always convey information about the speaker. For example, hearing someone say: "You'd better be prepared; it's hot here today," I conclude that the referent of "you" is being addressed by the speaker, hence, believed by the speaker to be subject to influence through communication. Moreover, for normal usage, I assume that the day in question is the very day during which the speaker made that utterance. Again, positional expressions like "next to," "left of," "beyond," "later," and so forth, typically convey the orientation of objects and events vis-à-vis the speaker's position in time and space. Indexicals are always biographical, and therefore, from the speaker's standpoint, autobiographical. If so, self-awareness is manifested or realized by the producer of any indexical utterance or any indexical thought. If indexicality graces every conscious state, in turn, then self-awareness is ubiquitous.[1]

Does self-awareness accompany all indexically mediated states of consciousness? Answering this question—the main concern of this essay— requires close attention to the pragmatics of indexical usage and to distinctions among various notions of "awareness" and "self." Among the important contrasts to be observed is between a *direct* awareness of, say, a certain bell-like sound, and an indirect or *mediated* awareness of the bell that one thinks caused the sound. Again, I have never directly perceived George W. Bush, but I have seen images of him on TV and in newspapers, I have heard his voice, and I have winced at some of the statements he has made. I am thereby led to have thoughts about him and, in so doing, am aware *of* him in an indirect sense mediated by visual images and sounds.

A second contrast is between *conceptual* and *nonconceptual* awareness of something with respect to a particular concept, property, or classification it falls under. For example, an infant might be aware of a pain, a round object, or its mother without having a concept of *pain*, *roundness*, or *mother*, and perhaps a dog can be aware of its owner or the sun without concepts of *ownership* or *the sun*. I have a conceptual awareness of this pen as a pen, though not, say, as something manufactured in Ohio, but insofar as I am aware of it then I am aware of something manufactured in Ohio. No doubt some sentient beings are aware of things they never conceptualize in any manner, for example, their own heartbeat, the force of gravity, or life. Conceptualization typically follows upon felt contrasts and absences, and often, we fail to rise to the level of abstraction required for contrasting pervasive elements of experience.

We may also distinguish a *global* awareness of something X in its entirety from a *partial* awareness of X, namely, of a part of X. We have partial awareness of ourselves, say, of a bodily part like one's arm, a bodily event such as one's current indigestion, or one's observing Lake Michigan from atop the John Hancock Building in Chicago. A partial awareness of X might be nonconceptual if one does not realize that it is X's part that one is aware of, or, alternatively, there can be a partial conceptual awareness of X, for example, of my house while gazing at the roof. Every awareness is global in that one is aware of an individuated content, be this a physical object, a quality, a mental event, a proposition, and so forth, yet, partial insofar as that content is a part or an aspect of something else. For example, I can be globally aware of my right index finger, or, of a segment of its surface, and, at the same time, partially aware of my whole body.

There are also different degrees or levels of awareness. Perhaps the sharpest or most focused awareness of anything involves attending to it as an item of which we predicate something, an awareness that underlies reference, as when I refer to a person in saying "that man is coming over here." It is marked by representability of an item by a singular term, identification of it through a mode of presentation, and predication of some property to it. Not all awareness is referential. Suppose I point to a dot on a map and think, *that's Berlin*; while I refer to the city, the dot is also salient in my awareness even though I do not refer to it in that thought. Again, watching a television interview with the current president of France, Jacques Chirac, I notice that his tie is blue and think that he is French. I am aware of the color property *being blue* and of the sortal concept *being French* even though I do not attend to these properties as subjects of predication. They are *salient* within my conscious experience, but I am not referring to them via singular terms or thinking anything *about* them.

Something might be present in experience but not salient. As I read this essay, for instance, I am conscious of the individual words and, perhaps, the individual letters that make up those words. I am also aware of the shapes of the upper halves of each of the letters composing those words, though these shapes are not salient. I hear background noises as I compose this paper on my computer, say, the sound of a fan, or, I am aware of the chair I sit on, but, prior to thinking about that noise and that chair, I was not noticing them. I was *marginally* or *implicitly* aware of such items without focusing upon them. They were not salient. Within such marginal awareness we can distinguish *constitutive* awareness of those factors within the contents we are attentively aware of (e.g., the shapes of letters as I read this paper, the individual lights as I gaze at a distant city from a hill at night), from *extraneous* awareness of factors that merely accompany a certain attentive awareness (thus, the perception of background noise or the feel of the chair as I concentrate on my computer monitor).

I use "conscious" and "consciousness" to indicate a property of certain psychological states whereby selected contents are highlighted, emphasized, or attended to—a property that admits of degrees. Since attention always requires contrast, we cannot be conscious of anything unless we have learned to oppose it to something even if one cannot distinguish it from everything else. Because we can be aware of distinct factors that lack salience and we are not attentive to, then "aware" and "awareness" designate a broader category of which consciousness is a species. Awareness is, thereby, stratified with respect to degrees of attentiveness. At one extreme is referential consciousness, while at the other is marginal awareness folding into undifferentiated perception, for example, auditory reception of the sounds made by individual wavelets in listening to an ocean wave. The terms "experiencing," "perceiving," and their cognates designate an even broader category of feeling, taking in, or prehending stimuli, whether from within the body or from without, a process that need not be accompanied by awareness at all.[2] All awareness involves a unification of several stimuli into an awareness of one unitary content. For example, in hearing the word "aluminum," the perceptions of individual phonemes are united into one auditory awareness of a word. The visual and tactile experiences of an aluminum pot blend together the activation of vast numbers of exteroceptors and the information they deliver. The single thought that *aluminum is a metal* results from a combination of conceptualizations.

Finally, there is an ambiguity in talking about self-consciousness due to the different meanings of "self." While all self-awareness is reflexive in that it involves a cognitive relation between an agent and itself, or some part or aspect of itself, the term "self" is typically used to express that intimate self-awareness manifested by consciousness of oneself as *I*, *me*, or, *mine*, as when one says "I can do that," "she loves me," or "this book is mine." However, derivatives of "self" can be used to report a purely reflexive relationship as when we say "the injury was self-inflicted," "the horse hurt itself while galloping," or "John locked himself in the room by accident." Here there is no implication of first-person awareness, not even when "himself" or "herself" are used to report what someone observes. A familiar story of Ernst Mach entering a bus in Vienna illustrates this: "he saw a man enter at the same time on the other side and was suddenly struck by the thought, 'Look at that shabby pedagogue coming on board!'—not realizing that he was referring to himself, because he had not noticed that opposite him hung a large mirror." The pronoun "himself" is used to report Mach's reflexive awareness, but the narrative makes clear that Mach is not thinking of himself in first-person terms.[3]

Let us label this merely reflexive type of self-awareness *external*, for it is no different from the way in which we are aware of others, for example, through sensory observation or second- and third-person thinking. By contrast, self-awareness mediated by first-person pronouns or concepts is a type of *internal* self-awareness, inasmuch as it occurs through introspection, proprioception, interoception, or other forms of inner awareness. First-person awareness is internal awareness marked by the identificatory use of what I will call *executive* first-person concepts (sections 4–5), but since internal self-awareness can be nonconceptual, then it is not necessarily first-personal (section 6). The internal/external contrast can be drawn whether we are speaking of self-awareness in global or partial terms; while observing my arm as *mine* or as *me* is a matter of first-person self-awareness, I might also notice that very same arm without realizing that it is mine or me, say, when I see it reflected in a mirror.[4]

With these distinctions, an account of how indexicals both reflect and shape our thinking is set forth in sections 2–4. In its terms, our capacity for first-person identification is explained in section 5. Finally, as a consequence of this account, section 6 defends the notion that self-awareness of a marginal, constitutive, nonconceptual, and non-first-personal sort is a feature of all indexically mediated consciousness.

2   Identifying with Indexicals

Language is as much a means of thinking as it is communicating about the world. Our use of singular terms, in particular, reflects our *identification* of various items, namely, our picking out or distinguishing certain objects, events, properties, facts, and so forth, for the purposes of thinking and, perhaps, saying something about them. When we identify something we do so in terms of what is unique to it, by means of a distinguishing feature that serves as our mode of presentation. It need not be a permanent property; *being the tallest woman in this room* might serve to distinguish, but it is a transitory relational property, lost as easily as it is gained. Identifying need not require an ability to *re*identify in the same terms.

Indexicals are the preeminent instruments of identification, for purely qualitative discriminations are usually cumbersome or unavailable. We continually single out items as *this, that, these*, locate objects and events by means of *here, there, then, beyond*, direct our thoughts upon people through the mechanisms of *you, he, she, them*, and so on. We also identify in terms of complex demonstratives, for example, *those apples, that book, his hideous war*, and so on.[5] Indexical modes of presentation cannot be generic indexical concepts, say, being *you*, since many items can fall under them relative to a given utterance, for example, *You go there, but you come here!*

It is commonly held that indexical tokens *refer* only through an interplay of their meanings with the contexts of utterance within which they occur. For example, given the meanings of the indexical type "you" and "now," the referent of a "you" token designates the one addressed through its utterance, while with a "now" token we refer to an interval that includes the time of the utterance. As John Perry puts it, "a defining feature of indexicals is that the meanings of these words fix the designation of specific utterances of them in terms of facts about these specific utterances" (1997, p. 594). So viewed, the context-sensitivity of indexicals is explainable in terms of what Perry calls *utterance-reflexivity* (1997, p. 597), a semantic dependency of indexical tokens upon context because values are determined given the meaning of the words uttered, in contrast to the presemantic use of context in deciding what words and meanings are employed (Perry 2001b, pp. 40–44).[6]

Utterance-reflexivity extends beyond pure truth-conditional semantics. It also characterizes the ways in which indexicals are *used* to identify items and to communicate about them. For example, if you tell me

(1) I'll bring you a glass if you remain sitting there

it is not enough that I grasp the meanings of the component expressions to understand what you are saying. I can interpret your utterance only because I know that you uttered the sentence, when and where you uttered it, and, perhaps, something about your gestures and bodily orientation. I work *from* my grasp of the meanings of your "I," "you," and "there," and my perception of relevant contextual parameters *to* the determination of your referents using, for example, a rule that this approach identifies as the meaning of "I," namely, any token of "I" refers to the producer of that token (Searle 1983, p. 223; Kaplan 1989a, p. 520; Perry 2000, p. 338; Ezcurdia 2001, p. 203). You realize, in turn, that I am guided by the meanings of your indexicals in exploiting context and identifying your referents through modes such as, *being addressed through the utterance of "you" in* (1) and *being the speaker of* (1) (Perry 2000, p. 338).[7] The modes of presentation are themselves utterance-reflexive, since to identify through them we must grasp facts about particular utterances, and because indexical identification requires such modes then we may also speak of the identificatory procedure as being utterance-reflexive.[8]

Some qualifications are needed. If a caller hears the words "I am not here now" on an answering machine, presumably the recorder of the message intended the caller to interpret "now" as the time during which the message is heard—the decoding time, rather than the encoding time—"here" as the locale that the caller thinks he has connected with, and "I" as the person the caller hopes to speak with. The caller does not rely on contextual cues picked up from the context in which the utterance was recorded—*when* or *where* it was recorded, or, for that matter, *who* uttered the recorded words—but from the context in which the utterance is decoded. The appropriate contextual parameters here are things like the number dialed, the name the caller associates with that number, additional recorded information (if any), and so on, the identity of the speaker's voice, social conventions associated with recorded messages, and so forth. Though the simple linkage of "I," "now," and "here" with the speaker, time, and place of utterance-production is broken, the decoding context is still appropriately labeled a "context of utterance," for the one who set up the recording on that machine assumes that the caller will rely on the said information, gathered from perceiving the utterance, in order to interpret the indexical tokens.[9] Accordingly, one interprets indexicals through roughly the following procedure: (i) one perceives an utterance that mobilizes the meanings of the perceived indexical tokens; (ii) these meanings guide one's determination of relevant contextual information; and thereby, (iii) one accesses relevant modes by which one identifies the referents.

3   Contrasting Interpretive and Executive Identification

Does this utterance-reflexive view of indexicals support the idea that indexical usage is always accompanied by self-awareness? Although a first-person identification is not featured in the content of every indexical thought, since identification requires awareness of the utterance in its context, and since the speaker himself or herself is part of that context, a speaker is unable to use indexicals without self-awareness. One need not conceptualize oneself *qua* speaker; perhaps one is proprioceptively aware of oneself as utterer, for example, through "awareness of one's chest moving, the tingling of one's throat, the touch of the tongue on palate, one's mouth filled with air, the resonance in one's head" (de Gaynesford 2006, section 84). Consequently, indexical usage apparently implies that the speaker has at least an implicit internal self-awareness.

Unfortunately, the ubiquity thesis cannot be defended in this manner. One can *think* in indexical terms without uttering anything at all, in which case, indexicality cannot be explained in terms of the properties of utterances. The standard utterance-reflexivity view is suitable only as a picture of what happens while *interpreting* an indexical utterance. Obviously, utterances must be produced before they can be interpreted, and linguistic production is no more blind to semantics than is interpretation. For instance, as a speaker hoping to communicate with

(1)   I'll bring you a glass if you remain sitting there,

you know what you are talking about prior to my interpretive machinations. Do your terms reveal specifically indexical identifications guided by indexical meanings? It would seem so; the senses of "I," "you," and "there" in (1) might have been as instrumental in your picking out particular persons and a place as it was in mine. Sometimes a speaker has no means of identification other than what an indexical provides, for instance, when a demonstrative like *that* represents the only way of picking out what suddenly looms into visual or auditory awareness: *What is that?* or, when a kidnapped heiress locked in the trunk of a car thinks, *It is quiet here now*, without any other means of locating herself.[10]

Indexical meanings are instrumental in guiding thought even when no tokens are uttered. Indexical thinking is prior to linguistic processing. We can think in terms of *this* and *that*, *it* and *there*, have *now or never* sentiments, without saying anything at all. Even if we subsequently utter indexicals to convey our thoughts, the identificatory procedures we use *qua* producer differ from those employed by an interpreter. You did not arrive at the identifications you express with (1) by doing what I, the interpreter, had to do. You did not have to first perceive your own tokens and then interpret them by recourse to the context of their utterance in accordance with the familiar utterance-reflexive rules. The tokens were *inputs* of my interpretive process, but *outputs* of the executive process whereby you identified something indexically and then attempted to communicate about it. I could not interpret unless I first perceived your tokens, but you did not identify these tokens or their utterances before producing them. Nor did you begin with a thought that I am likely to have ended up with, for example,

(2) He'll bring me a glass if I remain sitting here.

So, my identifying something by *interpreting* your utterance differs—in terms of cognitive procedure—from your identifying it in the course of producing or *executing* that utterance. In particular, although utterance-reflexivity was a feature of my interpretation, of my consumption of your utterance, it was *not* a property of your own indexically mediated identifications.

Three differences between executing and interpreting indexical identifications have been noted. First, while interpretation is utterance-reflexive, execution is not. Second, tokens are causal inputs to interpretive identification but outputs of executive identification. Third, while interpretation is subsequent to the interpreter's perception of an utterance, execution is not. Even if indexical tokens are conceived as mental representations, the thinker who initiates an identification does not first become aware of these tokens and then interpret them by recourse to some sort of context in which they occur. At best, such mental tokens occur simultaneously with the producer's identifications, not antecedently as causal inputs.

A fourth difference is this. One who executes an indexical reference has room for a creative employment that an interpreter lacks. Interpreting someone's "This book has been invaluable!" requires exploiting the meaning conventionally associated with "this." Yet, within certain limits, the speaker has an option about which meaning to use, for example, "That book has been invaluable," to make the same point. Again, noticing a person approaching in the distance I think: *That person is running*, but I might have thought instead, *That man is running*, or, *He is running*. Or, a modest person might prefer self-congratulations in the second-person, *You did wonderfully!* rather than *I did wonderfully!* It is a fact about communication in general that a speaker has a choice that is not there for the interpreter, and for this reason the speaker's identification is *executive*.[11]

A fifth difference is that a speaker might have no means of identification other than what an indexical provides, for instance, when a demonstrative like *that* or a demonstrative phrase, *that over there*, represents the only way of picking out what suddenly looms into visual or auditory awareness. Consider the kidnapped heiress; her indexical representations are *autonomous* inasmuch as their having the content they do does not depend upon her possessing other ways of distinguishing or describing what she is thinking about. In *this* sense she does not know what time it is since she cannot specify it in terms other than "now" (Kaplan 1989a, p. 536). Yet, the very fact that she is able to draw a contrast, that she knows it is quiet *now*, as distinct from quiet *then* (say, when she was abducted, or when the car was speeding down the roadway), reveals that she is discriminating between her present temporal location and other times. More dramatically, suppose she were drugged and placed in a large, silent, fully darkened, weightlessness chamber; regaining consciousness, she finds herself floating, bewildered, with no idea where she is beyond what she thinks with *It is quiet here now*, a thought that would undoubtedly be true.

Autonomy marks a real divergence between interpretive and executive procedures. An interpreter's cognitive movement from token-perception to determination of a referent could not be achieved without independent familiarity with the candidates. I must be able to identify what you are referring to *independently* of interpreting your (1), and this is why what I think is better represented by (2) than by (1). While interpreting indexicals is always a nonautonomous context-dependent process of mating tokens to independently identified items (Millikan 1993, pp. 269–271), the heiress did not entertain her thought by way of perceiving indexical tokens and attending to their context in order identify what she did.[12]

Finally, while both executive and interpretive identification are guided by indexical concepts, the difference in their procedures mandates a like difference in the concepts associated with one and the same indexical type. Suppose you listen to an audiotape you know was recorded on April 10, 2004, and hear a voice saying, "It is raining today," and identify the day referred to by employing something like the following utterance-reflexive rule:

Take the referent of a "today" token to be the day on which its utterance is encoded.

In so doing, you do not identify April 10, 2004, as *today* in the manner the speaker did, and, unlike you, the speaker did not pick out a duration as the day in which a particular "today" token occurred. The schema, "being the day on which utterance *U* of 'today' occurred," that specifies the concept guiding your interpretation, is not even similar to the concept, *being today*, that guided the speaker. Both you and the speaker employ concepts associated with the type *today*, but you are thinking of that particular day differently. I cannot think of a given day as being the day on which a certain utterance occurred without conceiving of that utterance, but I can think,

What lousy luck we're having today, without considering any utterance whatever. Again, when my friend yells, "I am here" in response to my "Where are you?" I pinpoint his locale, but not by executing *I* or *here* identifications. I understand that with his "here" token, for instance, my friend is referring to the place he occupies during his utterance, a locale that I likely identify as *there*. My understanding of how another's "here" works in communication guides my resolution of his token, but that's not what guided his own identification of his locale. If meanings govern the uses of linguistic types, yet both speaker and interpreter were guided by one and the same meaning, then we could not explain these differences in identificatory procedures. Consequently, the meaning of an indexical type utilized in executive identification must differ from the meaning used in interpretation.[13]

4 Indexical Execution as Perspectival

If utterance-reflexivity is not the key for understanding executive identification, what cognitive mechanisms are involved? How is it guided by indexical meaning in the exploitation of context? How is it context-sensitive?

An alternative approach seizes on the fact that items are identified indexically in virtue of thinkers' unique standpoints or perspectives, since a difference in perspective is why you think (1) whereas I think (2) in processing one and the same utterance. Indexicals are context-sensitive for a thinker because shifts in perspective generate distinct individuating modes and, typically, distinct referents, but the contexts are constituted by elements of psychological states that give rise to utterances, and not by the utterance parameters of interpretation. Utterance-reflexivity, then, is only one kind of context-sensitivity; what we might call *perspectival-reflexivity* is another, since what is identified indexically cannot be divorced from particular perspectives.[14]

Here are the essentials of one perspectival approach (Kapitan 2001). The first thing to note is that executive identification is not perspectival because it is made from a particular spatial or temporal standpoint(s); all identifications occur from the thinker's unique standpoint. Rather, relations to the speaker's standpoint are constitutive of the identifying mechanisms employed. If with

(3) You should be prepared; it will be hot here today

I address Henry in Chicago on the morning of July 12, 2006, my words reveal my relations to a particular person, time, and place. I must be *in* Chicago, *addressing* Henry, *on* July 12, 2006, and it is in virtue of these facts that I can identify what I do *as* I do. In this sense, my words are autobiographical—biographical for my listeners—while the same is not true of an utterance of

(4) Henry should be prepared; it will be hot in Chicago on July 12, 2006,

or, for that matter, for the demonstrative,

(5) He should be prepared; it will be hot there then,

even though I might be identifying the very same person, place, and time.

Second, perspectival identification requires a spatial or a temporal array of *immediate data* (objects, events, qualities, etc.) of which one is directly aware to varying degrees. Different modalities of consciousness, auditory, visual, tactile, imaginary, dreamlike, memory, proprioceptive, and so on are associated with diverse arrays of data, even when contemporaneous. For example, the spatial and temporal ordering of sounds one hears during a certain interval is an auditory array that might be simultaneous with a visual array of colored shapes. The data are ordered in terms of either their spatial, temporal, or spatio-temporal positions, each of which is partly fixed by the presented distance and direction from the *point of origin* of the identifying act.[15] Any such array constitutes a *perspective*, properly speaking, allowing us to speak of both the point of origin—typically presented as *here* and *now*—and the position of every other item within it as being *within* the perspective. Thus, a perspective is an combination of distinct factors into the unity of one experience from a given standpoint, a "prehensive unity" to use Whitehead's term (1925, ch. 4).

Given that the arrays of different modalities can be co-present within an interval of awareness, then distinct contemporaneous perspectives can be integrated into more comprehensive unities. Such integration is critical for behavior that relies upon cues from one or more sensory modality, so that an agent might rely on the fact that a visual *there*, say, converges with a tactile *there*. The maximally integrated perspective during any interval is the totality of immediate data co-presented in a single episode of awareness. How comprehensive it is depends on the extent of a subject's co-awarenesses through distinct modalities.[16]

Third, a *position* is either a volume, a duration, or a pair of such, of arbitrary extent, fixed by a distance, direction, and size of an immediate datum relative to the point of origin. Each datum is in a position, and if we think of an experience as a process of unifying diverse stimuli, then, in its initial stages, it involves a transference of data to the point of origin, more noticeable in auditory perception than in visual (Kapitan 1998b, pp. 35–39). As such, each immediate datum has a *vector* character (Whitehead 1978, pp. 55, 237–239), and each *this*, *that*, *then*, *there*, and so on are vector-contents located at particular places in a perspective. Sometimes, it is the spatial position alone that distinguishes the items identified, as reflected by the use of "you" in

(6) You, you, you, and you can leave, but you stay!

or "this ship" in

(7) This ship [pointing through one window] is this ship [pointing through another window].

Sometimes, temporal factors play a more prominent individuating role, as in anaphoric reference expressed through "the former," "the latter," "the previous one," or, when through a single window a person thinks the nontrivial

(8) This ship [observing the bow go by] is this ship [observing the stern go past].[17]

Fourth, executive identification also depends on how a thinker conceptualizes the identified item. Since I can be in Chicago on July 12, 2006, without identifying either the place or time as *here* and *today*, then, to think (3) I must encounter my own standpoint as being *here* and *qua today*. Hence, it is not only an item's position vis-à-vis the thinker that anchors indexical identifications. Even if Henry kept the very same position within my perspective, I might have identified him demonstratively as *he* rather than as *you*, or as *that man*. To identify indexically is also to distinguish an item as experienced or as thought in a particular manner, in which case executive meanings function as forms or ways that items are apprehended and cognized. Each such form imposes constraints upon what can be singled out, and while most constraints are a matter of spatial and temporal relations between identifier and identified, as with (3), others deal with intrinsic sortals, for example, only events or intervals can be *then*, and only a man can be a *that man*.[18]

Constraints are vague for deictic uses of the pronouns like *he*, *she*, or *it* and the demonstratives *that*, *those*, *beyond*, and so on. Perhaps nothing more than location distinct from the point of origin is imposed, though the *this/that*, *these/those*, and *here/there* contrasts suggest that relative proximity is also a factor. Similarly, in nondemonstrative uses of *I*, *here*, and *now*, what is identified is located within a four dimensional array of space-time positions that includes the point of origin of the perspective, while *I* carries the additional constraint that the identifier is the same as the identified. The indexical *you*, on the other hand, restricts the temporal location of the identified item to times that are simultaneous with or subsequent to the identifier's temporal locus. Also, what is picked out through *you* must be something that the user believes is susceptible to communicational influence, though it need not actually *be* so susceptible. Thus, despite an executor's leeway as to which indexical form to use, once a choice is made, anarchy is not the rule.

Fifth, an item acquires an indexical status by being identified indexically; a person becomes a *you* by being addressed and a *that man* by being demonstrated. Indexical status is wholly a contingent and extrinsic feature of an entity. No object in the external world is intrinsically a *you*, a *this*, a *here*, or an *I*, for satisfying an indexical mode is invariably a relational property of an item possessed only in relation to an experient subject who distinguishes it as such. Since these relations can rapidly change, and since a subject might quickly cease to so classify an object, then indexical status is also ephemeral (Castañeda 1989a, p. 69). However, given that an act of identification can endure over an interval, two tokens of "I" in a given utterance can be associated with one and the same mode. Also, because objects can move within a single perspective, a dynamic *this*, *that*, *he*, and so on can be associated with an ordering of positions.

Sixth, while what is identified indexically need not itself be an immediate datum of direct awareness, access to it is parasitic upon some such datum. When I gaze at a dot on a map and think

(9)   That city is north of Prague,

I am identifying a particular city, say, Berlin, but I am directly aware of the dot. The latter is the *index* of my executive act, namely, what I explicitly "latch on to" in the course of picking something out (Anscombe 1975, p. 54) and of which I am *globally* directly aware.[19] Each index is an individuated item at a position, or, in the case of a dynamic referent such as a person moving across my field of vision, an item or items at an ordering of positions. Identification is *direct* when the identified item is the index, as when I compare two colors in my visual field and think *this one is darker than that one*. The identified item is then itself positioned within the perspective. Identification is *deferred* when made indirectly through an index, as with my reference to Berlin in (9) in terms of the dot on the map. The dot is not a logical subject in the thought I express with (9), though it might well be identified indexically in a distinct thought, for example,

(10)   The city represented by that dot is north of Prague,

to which I am committed by virtue of my deferred identification in (9). Both direct and deferred identification are perhaps present in

(11)   His mother is rich,

which I think while picking out a man in the room through *his*. Even tokens of a simple indexical can reflect a deferred identification, for example, when I remember that *this has a nice beach* while noticing another dot on the same map. Similarly, "today" might have deferred uses insofar as the index of a *today* thought is a much briefer interval, or again, "we" for one who is speaking of a group only some of whose members are present. A more difficult example is

(12)   I am parked out back.

While there are undoubtedly communicational uses of this sentence, were it to represent an executive thought it would most likely be elliptical for

(13)   My car is parked out back.

If so, then "I" in (12) embodies a deferred identification, for just as it is not claimed that a dot on a map has a nice beach, so too, I am not thinking that it is myself who is parked at a certain place.

Seventh, executive identification is secured through an *orienting relation* or "relation of contiguity" (Nunberg 1993, pp. 19–20) between the identified item and the index, a relation the executor must grasp. In the Berlin example, the city is related to the dot through a representational relation, as is more clearly shown in (10). On other occasions a causal relation is involved, as in, *This fellow is clever*, having just read an essay on indexicals, namely, the relation of authoring such and such paper. A relation of temporal precedence is evident in the case of "yesterday" and a part-to-whole relation may be relevant for *Today has been rainy* or *This town is boring*, where, the indices associated with "Today" and "this town" are temporal parts of more extended entities. The *orientation* of an identified item is a relational property determined by its orienting relation to an index, for example, being the city represented by that dot. When identification is direct, the orienting relation is identity and the orientation is the property of being identical to the index.

Where Y is an agent, o is a spatial-temporal locale occupied by Y, and m is a modality of consciousness (visual, auditory, etc.), then the triple (o,Y,m) determines a *perspective* of Y at o. The locale o may itself be analyzed in terms of a pair (t,v) consisting of a time (duration) t and a place (volume)

v, or, through an ordering of such pairs $\langle(t,v),\ (t',v'),\ \ldots\rangle$ when the agent and immediate data are in motion relative to each other during the course of the experience. Letting "p" be a schema for representations of locale coordinates, namely, a time t, a place v, or a pair (t,v), or a sequence of such pairs, determined by a presented distance and direction from o, then each index $d(p)$ within the perspective (o,Y,m) is analyzed as d as located at p, namely, d-at-p, or, d-from-p. Thus, as with each immediate datum, an index is a vector.

Suppose an item X is identified by means of index $d(p)$ and executive form k within a perspective (o,Y,m). If the identification of X is deferred, then X is picked out by means of a relational property $R[d(p)]$ fixed by an orienting relation R linking X to $d(p)$. The mode of presentation, can then be represented by $k(R[d(p)])$. If the identification is direct, then the orienting relation R is identity and the mode can be represented equally well by $k([d(p)])$. Every indexical form can then be represented as a partial function from sets of immediate data and orientations to individuating executive modes. All executive modes are "object-dependent" in the sense that their existence depends upon the existence of the indices. Modes of direct identification are also referent-dependent in the sense that they would not exist apart from what satisfies them, their referents, but the modes of deferred identification have a being apart from the items that might satisfy them.

A few examples serve to illustrate the pattern of analysis. Consider my use of the second-person pronoun in uttering

(3) You should be prepared; it will be hot here today

while talking on the phone to Henry. The relevant perspective associated with my "you" is fixed in terms of me, my position, and the auditory modality. If the reference is deferred, and the index is the sound of a voice located in the phone's receiver at point p, namely, [sound at p], then Henry's orientation is the property of *producing* the sound at p. By adding the indexical form *you*, we arrive at this picture of my second-person individuating mode:

you (producing [sound at p])

through which I identify Henry. Suppose that instead of (3), I had uttered

(14) You should be prepared; it will be hot in Chicago on July 12, 2006

while thinking

(15) He should be prepared; it will be hot here then.

My executive individuating mode for Henry would then be:

he (producing [sound at *p*]).

Alternatively, if the gender conveyed by "he" belongs to the orientation and there is a neuter form common to both "he" and "she," representable as "*s/he*," we get this mode:

s/he (male producing [sound at *p*]).

It is an open question whether this is the same as

that (male producing [sound at *p*]),

which more fully reveals the demonstrative character of "he" and "she." On the other hand, if (3) reflects a *direct* second-person identification, say, if I am looking at Henry while addressing him so that Henry himself, from the given perspective, is the index, then my identifying mode would fit this schema:

you ([Henry at *p*]).

If my perspective is determined by a point of origin (t,v)—representable to myself through a particular (*now*, *here*) pair—then the following depict the modes associated with my use of "today" and "here" in thinking (3):

today (being a day that includes [*t*]);

here (being a city that includes [*v*]).

Similarly, if the temporal identification in (15) is indexical, and I am uttering (14) on July 12, 2005, then the correlated mode might be something like

then (being a day one year later than [*t*]).

If we balk at accepting volumes or durations in themselves as immediate data, but insist instead that an additional factor *d* be included, say, a colored expanse, a sound, or an episode of consciousness, then the immediate data associated with my "today" and "here" can be depicted as $d(t)$ and $d(v)$, with the modes fitting the schemata

today (being a day that includes [$d(t)$]),

here (being a city that includes [$d(v)$]),

and

then (being a day one year later than [$d(t)$]),

respectively.[20]

These examples reveal the reflexivity of executive identifications. In every case, the indexical content is singled out in virtue of its relation to a perspective—a prehensive unity—even though that perspective is not itself repre-sented. Each of the components of an executive mode is an ingredient in what the thinker grasps in executing an indexical reference, but third-person descriptions of the agent *Y*, his or her spatio-temporal standpoint *o*, and the modality of consciousness *m*—however critical for accurate interpretation—are external to the executor's cognitive significance (McGinn 1982, p. 209; Corazza 1994, p. 325). Nor does the executor have to identify his or her act of thinking (speaking) in order to pick something out; not all the necessary conditions for identification are internal to the cognitive processes involved.

5   First-Person Identification

I have assumed, throughout, that indexical identification operates through modes of presentation, and that the first-person constitutes no exception. Philosophers are divided on this issue, but I am persuaded by three consid-erations. First, there is no thought *about* an item without identifying it. Second, we identify something in terms of what is unique to it and, hence, by contrasting it with other items. Third, I can think about myself through first-person mechanisms, whether linguistic or conceptual. However, since thinking of myself *qua I* is not the same as thinking of myself as a producer of such and such tokens, whether mental or linguistic, then a different analy-sis is needed for the executive first person modes.

One consequence of the foregoing account of indexicals is that satisfying an executive mode is a contingent relational property of an item possessed only relative to a particular perspective, not an intrinsic property or a natural kind. In this respect, the *I* modes are no different from other indexicals; just as nothing is intrinsically a *this* or a *you*, so too, nothing is intrinsically an *I*, and insofar as being a *self* is nothing more than to be identified *qua* a first-person concept, then there are no intrinsic or natural "selves." The *I* lives only within episodes of self-consciousness (Sartre 1957, p. 45; Castañeda 1999, pp. 242, 270).

Yet this description is misleading in one critical respect. While some indexicals are promiscuous, for instance, *it*, *this*, *that*, others discriminate; only an event or a temporal interval can be a *then*, only a plurality can be a *those*, and, most glaringly, not everything can be identified as an *I*. Why so? Why does the executive *I* concept apply to some things but not others? More figuratively, what makes me an *I*? Perhaps this. Since being identified in a first-person way is precisely what confers the status of *being a self*, then to be a "self" just is to be reflexively conscious via an executive first-person form. It follows that whatever is so identified is an experiencing subject and, as executor of an identification, an agent. So, nothing is an *I* except a reflexively identifying active experiencer (Castañeda 1986, p. 110; Perry 2002, p. 190).

Fair enough, but this solution generates another question. The executive *I* concept can only be used to identify oneself. Why this constraint? Why can one apply the executive *I* concept *only* to oneself, whereas one can apply *you*, *he/she*, *his/hers*, and so on to others as well as oneself? What makes me unique with respect to what I can identify in first-person terms? It is obvious that being a reflexively identifying active experiencer, while necessary, is not enough to distinguish our privileged first-person identification of ourselves alone. We routinely identify other people in such terms. With *you*, for instance, we typically address those that we take to be reflexively-aware and capable of responding to or being influenced by what we say. Thus, if I address Henry as "you" in my utterance of (3), I believe that he will think something like

(16) I should be prepared; it will be hot here today,

thereby assuming that in processing my "you" he refers to himself. Consequently, being a reflexively identifying active experiencer does not provide a sufficient contrast to set apart an executive *I* identification from a *you* identification.

Perhaps we must add that what allows me to identify only myself through an executive *I* form is that I am aware that I occupy a privileged *position* with respect to myself, thereby making the contrast rest on spatial and temporal differences. But do I always discriminate my own position so finely? Others can be here now too, say, a group of people that I identify as *we*, or, a particularly intimate *you*. Why can't I be aware of some such intimate *you* *qua I*? Less whimsically, any center of bodily experience can be a point of origin, the eyes, the nose, the tip of the right index finger. Is there any precisely defined position that is exclusively *my* locale? Yes, I am here now, but so are my eyes, my nose, my right index finger. Are their locales parts of a larger volume that constitutes *my* position? Suppose I suffer from Alien Hand Syndrome and disavow ownership of certain limbs (Marcel 2003, p. 76). It seems unlikely that my position or my mode of *I* identification would change. More importantly, the phenomenon shows that the position of body parts cannot determine my own position unless I recognize them as *mine*, but then first-person awareness is already presupposed in drawing contrasts in terms of position.

Perhaps we have a primitive sense of *my* position that provides the material needed to generate an *I* identification. But this would require that a sense of *mine* is more basic than that of *I*, seemingly putting the cart before the horse. First-person possessive concepts, pronouns and phrases are mechanisms for representing what stands in unique physical, social, and normative relationships to oneself, since to view something as *mine* derives from a sense of how an item stands with respect to *me* (Evans 1982, ch. 7). Thus, "mine" is shorthand for "belongs to me" while "my car" is "car I own" or "the car I am now driving." The first-person plural similarly gives way to a description containing a singular first-person pronoun, so that the nominative "we" is shorthand for descriptions such as "my family," "the people in this room with me," "the members of my department," and so forth.

Here is another proposal for explaining one's privileged identification with *I*; there is a difference in the internal awareness of myself and the awareness that anyone else can have of me. I view the organism that I am "from the inside," through introspection, proprioception, or visceral interoception, whereas I cannot be directly aware of anyone else in these ways. In so doing, I am *directly* aware of something *as* experiencing, and if I conceptualize what I am aware of—which is what I do in first-person identification—I cannot help but think of that something as a subject, that is, as an experiencing or thinking thing or process, a *res cogitans*, albeit physical. This is a direct access that is privileged in that no one else has it to that something, myself. Observing how you wrinkle your brow, lift your eyebrows, and move your eyes, I might also conclude that you think too, like me, but this is an *in*direct mediated awareness of you as a consciously experiencing, feeling, and thinking being. Watching you move about and speak, I am directly aware of you as an active organism before me in the room and pestering me with questions. But I am not directly aware of you as experiencing. The solution to the problem of privileged access, then, is that the index of an executive first-person identification can only be something, that is, oneself, as experiencing, for only it is a subject of which one alone is directly aware.[21]

A further problem now arises; what exactly *is* the index of an executive first-person identification? That is, what is this *something (oneself) as experiencing*? In the case of (16), is it Henry himself, the person, the whole organism? If this were the case, then the executive mode of presentation when Henry makes a first-person identification could be depicted as

$$I \, ([\text{Henry at } (t,v)]),$$

and first-person identification would be direct, not deferred. Can the index be Henry himself? This depends on what Henry, the whole person, is. Is he a single enduring organism wholly present at a given time, or, a temporal sequence of person-stages? Either alternative seems an unlikely candidate as an index, for through what mode of direct awareness could one be aware of the whole persisting organism? Sensory? But then others could be similarly aware, leaving us without an explanation for the privileged use of the first-person (Shoemaker 1968, p. 87 in the reprint in Cassam 1994). Through some type of inner awareness then? But inner awareness tends to be selective and focused on particular physiological and psychological events and states. Unless we are willing to describe both index and referent—the person—as an enduring soul wholly present at any given moment and defend some account of how one is directly aware of a soul, then the hypothesis that the index is the whole organism, or the entire person, of which one is globally and directly aware, is not promising.

Perhaps the index is an individuated *part* of the entire organism, a part of which the agent alone can be directly aware. Perhaps this part is a particular state of the organism, say, a bodily feeling of hunger or of desiring to eat blueberries, or a believing that Berlin is north of Prague, states individuated by their content as well as their form. Yet, how could such states occasion my *I* identification? If I myself, *qua I*, am a constituent of them, namely, *I am hungry*, *I desire to eat blueberries*, *I believe that Berlin is north of Prague*, then I am already thinking of myself in first-person terms and we would be back with the original problem of explaining how we initially arrive at first-person identification. If I am a constituent *qua* some non-first-person mode, say, *the author of this paper*, then how do we get from that to first-person identification? If I am not a constituent, yet such states occasion my *I* identification because I understand them to be *my own*, then I am once again presupposing first-person identification. Plainly, it is difficult to explain first-person identification if the index is a particular experiencing state like a pain, a desire, a belief, or an effort.

We are at a critical juncture; the index must be something to which the agent alone has privileged access, yet, it cannot be the entire organism nor a single experiencing state of the organism. What other candidates are there? Here's a further proposal. The index is a prehensive unity, moreover, a comprehensive unity made up of the maximally integrated perspective and the associated emotional, conative, cognitive reactions of which one is co-aware during a given interval of first-person awareness (see Castañeda 1999, pp. 244, 263; Lockwood 1989, pp. 88–89). This unity is always there in every episode of indexical awareness, however thick or thin it might be, for immediate data and the associated reactions exist only as part of a unified whole. This whole is not always itself salient, but just as one can be aware of individual vector contents, so too, one can become aware *of* an assemblage of contents from a point of view. In that event, the unity can be an index of a first-person identification. Particular states of experiencing and reacting are seen as belonging to it, not to something else, and consequently, it is viewed as both a receptor of stimuli, and the seat of reaction to that stimuli. It then becomes the "me here and now," a "self," of which I, and I alone, am directly aware.[22]

If this is accurate, then taking the index of first-person identification to be some such comprehensive unity C existing over a temporal interval t, and whose spatial point of origin is v, we have this analysis of the executive I-mode that guides Henry's first-person identification:

$$I([C \text{ at } (t,v)]).$$

So understood, what Henry identified in (16) is the same as the index, and the first-person identification is direct. This analysis works if it makes sense to say that "me-now"—a person-stage perhaps, or, a "self" of relatively short duration—is an entity that can be identified and referred to. However, it cannot exhaust first-person thoughts since we also identify ourselves in first-person ways as enduring beings, as in, *I have been lecturing in Paris for twelve years*, or *I am gradually losing weight*. How do we understand my first-person identification of the persisting organism that I am? It must be deferred, though the index can be the same as in the direct case. What differs is the orientation; the persisting I is not identical to the index, but "has" or is "constituted by" such indices. If so, then the relevant mode of presentation is representable as

$$I(\text{having}[C \text{ at } (t,v)]),$$

where "having" expresses the compositional tie between the comprehensive integrated unities and the persisting I.

There are, then, two ways of thinking of oneself in first-person terms; as a brief unity of vector contents and associated reactions, and, as a temporally extended organism to which such momentary unities belong. The former is direct, the latter deferred.[23] There is a subtle reciprocity between these two types of I identification. Thought about an enduring self, a person, an organism, is derivative from direct awarenesses of integrated unities each of which is salient by way of contrast with something else, be it a person, an object, an event, and so on (Castañeda 1999, pp. 275–277). By noting certain similarities in the patterns of experiencing, emotion, effort, and reaction among these unities, we form the notion of an enduring locus of experience and action. The executive I concept is the indexical method of keeping track of this persisting self through these salient indices. However, it is something we gain upon noticing the similarities in the patterns, in which case all first-person identifications depend upon our *first* having a sense of the enduring organisms that we are. This does not preclude indices of first-person identifications from themselves being identified as *I*s, but there is no identification of these as such apart from a concept of a persisting entity with which they are associated, whether as stages, states, or aspects.

6   Indexicality and the Ubiquity of Self-Awareness

Some philosophers (e.g., Hurley [1998, ch. 4]) maintain that the perspectival consciousness of agents involves self-consciousness, for no sense can be made of perspective-bound intentional agency unless the agent has information about its own states and position. Hurley emphasizes that this primitive self-awareness is both nonconceptual and a constant factor in all consciousness (1998, p. 135). Because of the link to intentional agency, José Bermúdez argues that the nonconceptual contents of proprioception are first-personal (1998, pp. 115–122), and, combining both views, Dan Zahavi (2000b) pushes a particularly strong form of the ubiquity thesis: all experience includes perspectival (egocentric) awareness of a first-person element.[24]

There are reasons to be skeptical of the claim that all perspectival awareness has first-person content. First-person identification or classification requires a sophisticated focus on the being that is at the center of the blooming buzzing mass of perceptions, thoughts, desires, and efforts. It is the product of a considerable abstraction and, therefore, highly conceptual. It is not ubiquitous; it cannot be expected of beings that lack concepts but who are otherwise sentient and capable of purposeful activity. Even when a highly specialized action occurs, working out a difficult mathematical proof, or performing the opening movement of the *Hammerklavier* sonata, it is doubtful that first-person identification also occurs. The agent is likely to be concentrating on the symbols and the abstract contents, or upon the keys and the musical lines, and self-identificatory gaze at a co-conscious complex over an interval would be more of a hindrance than a help (Marcel 2003, p. 69).

Undoubtedly, the somatic proprioception of a particular physical center of feeling and reaction that happens to be identical with oneself is a type of internal self-awareness. Purposeful action involves desires and aversions together with the proprioceptive information for satisfying them, but the information needed need not be packaged in first-person terms. It is sufficient for successful action that it be reflexive. That direct proprioceptive awareness and other forms of inner awareness are exclusively of a *unique* center of reception and reaction—the comprehensive unity one is at a given time, or, the persistent self that "has" such unities—obviates the need for any separate first-person representation. If there were many such contemporaneous centers, one would need a way of distinguishing one of them as privileged, and this would open the door to a first-person reading of the representation. But if an inner awareness of a unique center of reception and reaction is all that's required, then representation in a first-person way is not secured. There are, then, no grounds for concluding that action requires a nonconceptual awareness of an *I, me,* or *mine.*[25]

This said, it remains that all indexical awareness reflects the subject's own standpoint and, to that extent, involves a degree of self-awareness. Indexical thinking and experience involve a direct awareness of something, an index, in a position, and since a position is defined in terms of perceived direction and distance from a point of origin, every index is a vector content. But no vector is isolated; perspective is never absent from our indexical awareness. Absorbed in a piano performance, none of the immediate data—a key here, this chord just played, that phrase soon to come—exists alone in the pianist's awareness. Each vector content is felt as embedded in a larger whole centered around a point of view, for there could be no specific position unless there were at least one other position to contrast it with, and this is determined by an ordering of immediate data. There is no *over there* without what would qualify as a *here* or a different *there*; no *then* without a potential *now* or another *then.* An integration of vector contents is always present in our indexical experience even when it lacks salience. That perspectival prehensive unification from a point of view often escapes notice is precisely *because* of its ubiquity. My point is that we must be at least marginally aware of it if any particular executive identification is to occur.

In sum, there is no indexical identification without a vector as index, and there is no such vector without its being felt as embedded within a perspective. Hence, the perspective itself is a content of awareness. It is not our invention. How we conceptualize it and the vectors embedded within it is our contribution, and the modes of executive identifications are the fruits of our own attentive efforts. There is no escaping the fact that in indexical thought and experience we never catch the universe devoid of a point of view, for we are always at least implicitly aware of a centered integration of data. It is only a feat of highly abstract thinking that allows us to contemplate things in any other way.

Accordingly, if this comprehensive unity is what I *am* throughout its endurance (note 22), then I am directly aware of myself during the interval of any indexical thought. If it is but *part* of what I am, then there is at least a direct partial self-awareness in every instance of indexical awareness. The awareness may only be marginal, and I need not be distinguishing this unity in order to be marginally aware of it. Nor do I have to have to think, *this unification is mine*, for no unification is ever presented in awareness that is not mine. Apart from first-person identification, such implicit direct awareness is of a reflexively identifying active experiencer even though it is not conceptualized as *I*, a *me*, or *mine*. It is internal because it involves a unique direct awareness that is constitutive of indexical awareness of anything. *If* such perspectival unification is ubiquitous to all states of consciousness then all consciousness is "irreducibly perspectival" (Lockwood 2003, pp. 456–459), and we are always self-aware so long as we are aware of anything at all.[26]

Notes

1. This conclusion is drawn by Manfred Frank (1995, pp. 49–50). Other recent advocates of the ubiquity of self-consciousness include Gennaro (1996, p. 17), Hurley (1998, p. 135), Damasio (1999, p. 19), and Kriegel (2003a, p. 125). Colin McGinn advocates a restricted form of the ubiquity thesis to the effect that all indexical awareness involves self-awareness: "to think of something indexically is to think of it in relation to me, as I am presented to myself in self-consciousness" (1983, p. 17). Alfred North Whitehead was among those who advocated the indexical nature of all thought: "Explicitly, in the verbal sentence, or implicitly in the understanding of the subject entertaining it, every expression of a proposition includes demonstrative elements" (Whitehead 1978, p. 43).

2. I follow Leibniz who similarly distinguishes perceiving and awareness, and from whom the wave example comes (*New Essays on Human Understanding*, book 2, ch. 9). The term "prehending" and its description in terms of feeling and appropriating a datum in a certain way (form) are Whitehead's (see 1925, pp. 90–97 and 1978, pp. 19–20, 219–220). Whitehead took the term from "apprehending" and also characterized it as "apprehension that may or may not be cognitive." Prehensions are the basic ingredients of each experience and can be physical or conceptual depending on their contents. Experiencing is the process of integrating prehensions and, hence, what is prehended, into the unity of one outcome, namely, a state with content (see also Leibniz, *New Essays*, book 2, ch. 9). Not all experience is conscious; instead, consciousness, when it occurs, is a later phase in experiential integration that can be described as "the acme of emphasis" (Whitehead 1933, p. 231, and see 1978, pp. 161–162 for a more detailed description of consciousness). The term "consciousness" is "notoriously ambiguous" as Uriah Kriegel points out (2003a, p. 103), partly because it has both ordinary and theoretical uses.

3. This passage is from Frank 1995, p. 42. John Perry also gives the Mach example as a case of one's knowing something about the person one is—in that sense, a kind of self-knowledge—though it is not what we would ordinarily call "self-knowledge."

See Perry 2000, pp. 332–333, and also Perry 2002, ch. 10 and pp. 192–193, where "self-knowledge" is confined to what is expressible in first-person terms. The occurrence of "himself" in this text is not that of a quasi-indicator, namely, as a device for reporting one's indexical reference or identification. See Castañeda 1967 and Kapitan 1998b for an exposition of Castañeda's theory of quasi-indicators.

4. A distinction between internal and external self-awareness was emphasized by Castañeda in his early work on indexicals in the 1960s, though he conflated first-personal and internal self-awareness. For his mature view, see Castañeda 1999, ch. 10. As will be apparent, my approach to indexicals and self-consciousness owes much to Castañeda's work.

5. Not all uses of the pronouns like "you" and "now" are referential. They are used *schematically* or *attributively* when a speaker utters them to cause hearers to identify what is as yet unspecified by the speaker, for example, when someone records a list of instructions containing, "Now you must press the right button." Both "now" and "you" are here used with the intention to induce references to *whatever* time the utterance is heard by *whomever* heard it. This use of indexicals is discussed in Nunberg 1993; Recanati 1993, ch. 16; and Bezuidenhout 1997. Classifying an expression type as *indexical* is specifying a manner in which tokens of that type can be used, or, alternatively, a way in which their referents are "determined." Some types play more than one indexical role, e.g., "now" and "here" have both demonstrative as well as nondemonstrative uses that are covered by different semantic rules (Smith 1989).

6. See also Perry 2000, pp. 322–323, where indexicals are said to be utterance-reflexive because the "truth-conditions of an utterance containing an indexical, considered with just the meaning and not the context fixed, will be a proposition about the utterance of the indexical." The construal of indexicals as utterance-reflexive or token-reflexive is commonplace, and is evident in accounts that differ from Perry's own, for example, Millikan 1993, pp. 266–267 and Searle 1983, p. 221. Garcia-Carpintero (2000a, pp. 116–117) speaks of indexicals as *case*-reflexive, where cases are instantiations of linguistic types, that is, events rather than enduring objects.

7. A demonstration is not always needed to identify the referent of demonstratives; what's required is that the context makes salient a referent. If some fellow is making lots of noise in a pub, and I turn to you and say, "What a lout he is!" I need not demonstrate anything if I can tell from your expression that you are already annoyed by the sound. Pointing is just one way of making things salient (Predelli 2001; de Gaynesford 2006). The process of identifying a thing does not imply the abilities to articulate descriptive knowledge of the object or to *re*identify it. I might demonstratively distinguish a brown bird against a green background, though not against a suitably textured brownish background a moment later—hence, camouflage protects. Flying in a plane above the clouds I might pick out a place only once as a *there* without ever being in a position to distinguish it again, or perhaps I slip into a state

of devastating amnesia immediately after reacting to a massive explosion with "What was *that*?!" In each of these cases I identify a thing, though I am unable to reidentify it.

8. An indexical meaning, accordingly, can be viewed as a "binary condition of designation on objects and utterances" that yields a reflexive content-fixing mode of presentation when the utterance parameter is specified (Perry 1997, p. 597). Garcia-Carpintero (2000b, p. 40) points out that an individuating mode can be immediately generated out of the threefold context-character-content distinction (Kaplan 1989a) by instantiating the quantifier in the linguistic rule associated with character, e.g., the referent of a "you" token is *whoever* is addressed through that token. The mode is individuative, associated with the expression as a matter of conventional rules, and "epistemically diaphanous" (viz., known by speakers as part of their linguistic mastery).

9. The contrast of *decoding time* with the *encoding time* can be found in Filmore (1997, p. 61). Here, the notion of a *context of utterance* is construed broadly to include the environs of the utterance, e.g., the speaker, time, place, the accompanying gestures, etc., in short "whatever parameters are needed" (Kaplan 1989b, p. 591). Perry 1997 and Stalnaker 1999 also use broad notions of context. Predelli (1998, pp. 401–403) argues that the use of indexicals in recorded messages is evidence against the "traditional view" of indexicals according to which indexicals "are always correctly evaluated by taking into consideration the context of utterance (or inscription)" and looks, instead, to a context "intended as relevant by the speaker." However, since an interpreter can ascertain the speaker's intentions only by relying on cues embedded within the circumstances in which the utterance is perceived, then it is still a context of utterance that is the interpreter's route to determining what it is the speaker is referring to. Corazza, Fish, and Gorvett 2002 points to the importance of the *conventional aspects* of a setting of a linguistic interchange as playing a role in determining the referent of an "I" token. On the consumerist model, the conventions more accurately determine a referent than the producer's intentions—e.g., Ben might write a note "I'll be back shortly" and mistakenly attach it to Joe's door. The intended referent of "I" is Ben, but the conventionally determined referent is Joe.

10. The example of the heiress is from Kaplan (1989a, p. 536), though he uses it to make a point about reference, not identification. In both of these examples of autonomous usage, nothing need be uttered. Even when demonstrative utterances are made, they are not wholly driven by the need to communicate. For example, Piaget's research shows that small children will utter demonstratives in contexts that would normally require gestures but apparently without sensing the need (Filmore 1997, p. 60).

11. The use of "executive" is borrowed from Castañeda (1986, p. 111; 1989a, ch. 4), though it also occurs in de Sausurre 1959, p. 13.

12. Ezcurdia (2001, pp. 190–198) argues for the autonomy of the first-person, and criticizes Millikan 1993. Those impressed by the image of *consumption* as the key to understanding the representative functions of language (e.g., Kaplan 1989b, pp. 602–603, and Millikan 1993, pp. 86–88) have neglected the executive aspect of language use. Born into linguistic communities, we are constantly exposed to words with prepackaged meaning before we utter them or think in their terms. Yet, consumption of language, like consumption of canned goods, requires commodity production and exchange; "language must be spoken before it is heard and interpreted" (Castañeda 1989b, p. 116). We *use* indexicals creatively to articulate the details of our immediate experience, and we do so in virtue of their publicly accessible meanings. The child who has advanced from babble to demonstratives like "dat" manifests a creative act of distinguishing something within sensuously delivered material; he or she "consumes" in acquiring the capacity to use an indexical type meaningfully, yet "produces" the demonstrative token in order to pick out and express what it cannot distinguish by other means.

13. Communication is achieved through a *coordinated meaning duality* that affects the identificatory uses of every indexical expression and is built into the tacit knowledge that constitutes a user's linguistic competence. In addition to the peculiar sorts of context-dependence that govern their identificatory and communicative uses, it is what distinguishes indexicals semantically. Frege hinted at the duality of "I" in his 1918 essay "The Thought: A Logical Inquiry," and John McDowell, in addressing Frege's concerns, suggests that communication might occur through a "correspondence" of thoughts rather than "shared" thoughts (McDowell 1998, pp. 222–223). Noam Chomsky generalizes the point by denying that "successful communication" requires "shared meanings" (Chomsky 2000, p. 30). The duality view of indexical meaning is hinted at by Castañeda (1983, pp. 323–325), when he wrote that the semantical rules governing singular reference serve "two crucial purposes," namely (1) to provide criteria for application of singular terms by a speaker and (2) to provide criteria for an interpreter. See also Castañeda 1999, pp. 269–270.

14. Perspectival approaches to indexicals have been developed by Russell 1948, pt. 2, ch. 4; Castañeda 1967, 1989a; Evans 1982, ch. 6; McGinn 1983; and Hintikka 1998. John Lyons contrasts the "standard view" of deixis that dominates linguistics textbooks with an alternative view, one that takes the "egocentricity of the deictic context" as "rooted in the subjectivity of consciousness" (Lyons 1995, p. 311). He notes that the latter has so far had "little effect upon what may be regarded as mainstream semantics. But there are signs that the situation is changing in this respect." The opponents of this approach generally acknowledge that indexicals play a unique role in our psychological economy, but are wary of the perspectivalist's acceptance of subjective, irreducibly perspectival features of the world (for example, Perry 2000, ch. 1; Millikan 1993, ch. 13; and Lycan 1996, pp. 56–68).

15. The phrase "point of origin" appears in Castañeda 1977 and Evans 1982, p. 154, to designate the locale of the thinker within his or her own egocentric space. Other writers speak of the "locus" of the speaker (Hintikka 1998, p. 208), the "zero-point" of a locutionary act (Lyons 1995, p. 304). There is some debate about the perspectival character of proprioception. José Bermúdez (1998, p. 153) argues that the spatial contents of somatic proprioception "cannot be specified within a frame of reference that takes the form of axes centered on an origin." To the contrary, Anthony Marcel (2003, pp. 84–86), in speaking of the proprioceptive awareness of agency (2003, p. 54), argues that "the only spatial description common for all body parts and for external locations is an egocentric one" (2003, p. 84).

16. See, for example, Castañeda 1977, *passim*, and Bermúdez (1998, p. 141) who, citing Ayers 1991, claims that "our perception of the world is cross-modal."

17. The importance of spatial and temporal locale in describing indexicals was emphasized by William James, who wrote that the expressions "I," "here," and "this" are "primarily nouns of position" (James 1904, p. 86). Castañeda spoke of demonstrative or indexical properties as properties that "fix" positions in spatio-temporal fields (1977, p. 320). See also Evans 1982, ch. 6.

18. One can misidentify in the course of picking something out. Suppose I think *that woman is an alto*, but the person I pick out is a man, not a woman. How did I succeed in identifying if my mode of presentation was not satisfied? The answer is that some discriminating feature *of* the item identified was operative in my thinking, perhaps one that might be more accurately conveyed by "that person" rather than "that woman." Let us say that a mode M1 is *implied* by a mode M2 if something were M2 then it would be M1. Mode M1 is *operative* in X's identification of Y at t just in case there is a salient mode M2 by which X distinguishes Y at t such that (i) M1 is implied by M2, and (ii) X is committed at t to the conditional: if something were M2 then it would be M1. Identification requires only that some operative mode is uniquely satisfied by what is identified.

19. The term "index" was introduced by C. S. Peirce who used it to classify a sign that refers to an object in virtue of being "physically connected with" or "really affected by" that object (1998, pp. 5, 291). My usage follows Nunberg 1993, which distinguishes between a *deictic* component and a *classificatory* component of indexicals, both of which are distinct from the referent, and employs "index" to represent the "thing picked out by the deictic component of an indexical" (p. 19). Fauconnier (1985, pp. 3–5) makes a more general distinction between the *target* of any indirect reference and the *trigger*, viz., the item that gives access to the target.

20. As indexical, "now" designates a time (a duration) only as a (temporal) position within a perspective, but it should not be assumed that a direct *now* identification requires a bare duration as an index. See, for example, Quentin Smith (1989, pp. 176–179), who describes the cognitive significance of "now" in terms of the moment

that has presentness and that includes the complex psychological event composed of my present experiences.

21. The "oneself" in "oneself as experiencing" is not a quasi-indicator used to display first-person usage (see note 3), for this would presuppose what we were trying to account for. Instead, "oneself" is used in a purely reflexive sense, so that one might also describe the index in terms of "something as experiencing" where the something in question happens to be the same as oneself.

22. Compare Whitehead (1958, p. 224): "My present experience is what I now am." William James was no doubt correct in that diachronic consciousness appears as a continuous "stream" even though there is a noticeable succession of individual states within it (James 1890, ch. 11). Perhaps experience is ultimately granular, as Whitehead contended, but nothing prevents us from focusing upon certain gross segments selected through our own focused self-awareness. Thus, the index of a first-person identification is a portion of the stream thick enough to be a salient comprehensive unity.

23. Marcel (2003, pp. 50–51) also speaks of self-awareness in the occurrent and the long-term sense of "self." Similarly, Strawson (2000) describes our experience of I as being sometimes of a momentary "subject of a unitary experience" and sometimes of a "persisting human." Other contrasts are likely operative in singling out a persisting self, notably, the contrast between oneself and others.

24. There is some dispute about what is involved in nonconceptual thought or awareness. Arguing against Hurley, Noë (2002) finds a level of conceptuality to be present in primitive self-consciousness, holding that one does not have an experience of an F without a concept of F, but that having a concept does not require possessing criteria for applying it. I agree that identificatory and predicative thought about an item requires conceptualization of it, but not all thought about an F requires a concept of F, and not all awareness of an item is identificatory and predicative (see section 1).

25. Millikan (1993) makes this point, and see also O'Brien 2003, (p. 380), who contends that the self-awareness needed for action might be of a primitive sort that is not first-personal. Marcel (2003, pp. 76–78) argues that not all proprioception yields a me or mine awareness, citing the Anarchic Hand phenomenon in neurological patients who disown the actions of their own hand. See also Lewis 2003, which points out that infants behave intentionally prior to any self-representations, and that the idea of "me" is acquired around 1.5 years of age. Bermúdez's insistence that primitive self-consciousness is first-personal is driven by his desire to resolve what he calls a "paradox" of self-consciousness generated by the theses that (i) the only way to explicate a capacity to think certain sorts of thoughts is by analyzing the capacity for a canonical linguistic expression of those thoughts, and (ii) mastery of first-person pronouns requires the capacity to think "I" thoughts. His solution is to show that a primitive capacity to think "I" thoughts is independent of the capacity to use first-person pronouns (1998, p. 290). But Bermúdez assumes throughout that having

concepts is a matter of having linguistic capacities. On the view set forth here, executive identification with the *I* concept is independent of any communicative capacities and, to that extent, prior to the expression of first-person pronouns. The use of *executive* indexical concepts does not depend on linguistic capacities, although the use of *interpretive* indexical concepts does. The paradox can be avoided, then, without acknowledging nonconceptual "I" thoughts. It should be noted, finally, that it would make no sense to argue that there is nonconceptual *mediated* first-personal awareness of the self. No awareness of anything is both nonconceptual yet mediated, since mediation is a matter of conceptualization.

26. Discussions with James Hart, Manfred Frank, and Kenneth Williford were of great value to me in developing the ideas contained herein. I am indebted to Brian Montgomery for his valuable assistance in collecting research materials used in writing this paper.

Consciousness, Representation, and Knowledge

Keith Lehrer

There is widespread agreement that consciousness poses a philosophical problem, but what that problem is, as well as the solution of it, remains controversial. I shall begin with a theory of the epistemology of consciousness. There are certain conscious states, those that most attract our attention, that are immediately known to us. Some affirm that we are directly acquainted with them, which may be true, but it does not explain how the experience of conscious states gives us knowledge of them. I do not think that all conscious states are immediately known. On the contrary, some conscious states, sensations of touch most notably, provide us with information about the external world, information about the hardness of an object, for example, without calling attention to themselves and what they are like in themselves. Some conscious states pass through the mind without our having any representation of them because they serve only to represent other things.

Other sensations, pains, for example, attract attention to themselves and are immediately known. I am inclined to think that all conscious states can be immediately known when attention is directed to them. I do not think that it is a defining characteristic of a conscious state of a person that the person immediately knows of the existence of the state, however. Some have argued that the phenomenal character of a conscious state necessitates or entails that a person has a representation of the conscious state. This claim is either true by definition given the use of the expression "phenomenal" or false. For a person may remain conscious even though the capacity to represent things is temporarily blocked or permanently lost. Some seek such unrepresented conscious states in meditation, and I see no reason to deny that they may succeed in achieving a state in which they experience intensely rewarding conscious states without having any representation of those states. To take a more familiar example, suppose you are awaking from sleep and experience in your waking state a sensation without yet having any representation of what kind of state it is. You are conscious but not yet at a level that carries representation along with it. Representation is not necessitated by consciousness states.

Yet we have immediate knowledge of many of our conscious states. Indeed, once we direct our attention to a conscious state, we immediately know what it is like. Consider an intense pain that we cannot help but notice. We immediately know what the pain is like upon our experience of it. The knowledge of the conscious state is somehow intrinsic to it. Such knowledge is unlike descriptive knowledge, where we might search for the right representation of a state or object known. Representation of the conscious state is somehow contained in the conscious state itself yielding immediate knowledge of the state. How do we have this immediate knowledge of our conscious states?

My answer to the question of how we have immediate knowledge of conscious states presupposes an answer to the question of how we represent those states to ourselves. Notice that an account of how we represent conscious states to ourselves does not entail an answer to how we have immediate knowledge of those states. Representing a state to ourselves does not entail knowledge of the state, much less knowing it immediately. I have indicated above that a conscious state might occur without being represented at all. Many philosophers argue that conscious states are representational states. Moreover, even those who would not defend the identity or logical equivalence of the conscious state with a representation would argue that the phenomenal character of the state, which makes the state conscious, necessitates or entails some representation. This I deny for the reason that representational capacities can be blocked, by drugs or neurological abnormality, without destroying consciousness. Conscious states that are not represented and do not represent anything else are a possibility and, indeed, at times, an actuality as well resulting from a brain lesion.

Conscious states that are represented might be represented indirectly, in a linguistic representation, for example. So an account of immediate representation is needed. Such an account must explain how the representation of the conscious state can be immediate. A satisfactory account of such representation must be an account of direct or immediate rather than indirect or mediated representation. If, however, the conscious state is, as I have argued, distinct from the representation of it, a question remains. How can the representation be direct or immediate?

A satisfactory answer to the question must give an account of representational lucidity, as I have called it. My reason for describing the representation as lucid is that the content of the representation of the state somehow incorporates the state itself. The representation is somehow contained in the state itself rather than being something extrinsic to it. Though not identical with the state, representation is somehow intrinsic to the state, even though the state does not entail or necessitate the representation of it. I do not place great emphasis on the terminology, but what interests me is the challenge of explaining how the conscious state can be directly, intrinsically involved in the content of the representation of it without logically necessitating that the state is represented. My explanation is that the conscious state is represented in terms of the state itself rather than in terms of something else, some other sign or symbol of it. This accounts for the intrinsic or direct character of the representation.

It should be further noted that once an account is given of the representation of the state that explains how the state is incorporated in the representation of the state to yield some kind of lucid, intrinsic, or direct representation of the state, our immediate *knowledge* of the state is not yet explained. Once again there is a logical gap confronting us. Just as the state does not entail an immediate representation of itself, so an immediate representation of the state does not entail immediate knowledge of it. Representation, though a condition of knowledge, at least knowledge that the state exists, does not entail that knowledge. Even if the representation is true, that still does not entail knowledge. There is a gap between true representation and knowledge just as there is a logical gap between true belief and knowledge.

I insist upon this point because it will become important in an account of our immediate knowledge of our conscious states. The immediacy of such knowledge is the result of the immediacy of the representation, but knowledge is not entailed by the representational immediacy. Knowledge of our conscious states, though it involves immediate representation, and inherits that immediacy, depends on a background system that converts immediate representation into immediate knowledge. Our immediate knowledge of our conscious states, arising from immediate representation of them, depends on the justificatory support of a background system. Justification is, as I have argued elsewhere (Lehrer 2000), coherence with a background system which, when irrefutable, converts to knowledge. The explanation of immediate knowledge of conscious states does not support the thesis of foundationalism that such knowledge rests on self-justified beliefs or representations. Justification has a systematic component that is essential to it.

It is now time to turn to the explanation of how conscious states that do not logically necessitate or entail any representation of themselves are, nevertheless, components in an intrinsic, direct, and lucid representation of themselves as the lucid content of the representation. I have been arguing (Lehrer 1996b, 1997) that there is a loop in representation of conscious states. Reid (1785) argued that conscious states are both signs of external objects and, at the same time, signs of themselves. Brentano (1874/1924), as my colleagues Marek (2003) in Graz and Kriegel (2002a, 2003a) in Arizona have reminded me, also held to the view that conscious states represent themselves at the same time as they represent other things. The idea is an old one and goes back further than the modern period to Carneades, as represented by Chisholm (1966), who held that such states are self-presenting. So the idea is old, but the old idea is also an old enigma. How can a conscious state be at the same time a representation and the content of representation? How can the state be, in Reid's terminology, both a sign and, at the same time, the thing signified?

My answer is that the conscious state is in some way self-representational. The representation must be a loop as Reid, Brentano, Carneades, and now Kriegel all aver. The loop is effective, as Rosenthal (1990) concedes, to avoid a regress of representation at higher orders. But how does the conscious state represent itself? How are we to understand how that conscious state can be used to represent itself? I have suggested that the conscious state functions as an exemplar of a kind of conscious state. It is used to represent itself as a state of that kind. I am conscious of a pain, for example, and the particular pain becomes used as an exemplar that stands for pains or represents pains. Of course, the pain used to represent pains is itself a pain. So, when exemplarization works in a paradigmatically simple fashion, the exemplar is an instance of the kind of state the exemplarized state is used to represent.

This might suggest that exemplarization produces infallible representation. How, the infallibilist might ask, can the exemplarized state fail to be an instance of the kind of state the exemplar is used to represent by exemplarization? The answer to the foregoing question is that whether the representation has the exemplar as an instance depends on how the exemplar is used in the process of representation. Illustration of how an exemplar can fail to be an instance represented by the exemplar arises from a consideration of other examples of exemplarization. Consider a case in which I am curious about a song of which I have only heard the title, "The Shoop Shoop Song," for example, and I ask you what a singing of the song is like. You might wish to show me what a singing of the song is like and sing the song, even though you sing poorly in the process of attempting to accommodate me. Some of the notes you sing are too flat and some are too sharp. In this case, assuming that I am musically sensitive, I might, using your singing as an exemplar of a singing of "The Shoop Shoop Song," form a conception of what a singing of the song is like in which I rather automatically correct for your errors of singing flat or sharp or both. In this case, my exemplarization of your singing of the song has the result that your singing does not fit the representation or conception that I form of the song. Your singing has played a role in my forming a representation of what singings of the song are like that starts from your exemplar and generalizes from the exemplar to a class of instances that does not include your singing.

I am not suggesting that exemplarization of conscious states proceeds in a way that fails to include the exemplar as an instance of the kind of state exemplarized. On the contrary, it would be included as an instance in the normally functioning mind. My point is that such inclusion is a contingent result of the way the mind functions in exemplarizing conscious states to form representations. Including the exemplarized conscious state as one of the states represented is a result of psychology, a result of cognitive functioning, and not a logical consequence of using the exemplar to generalize to a representation of a class of instances. I shall for convenience use the expression "standard exemplarization" in a restricted manner in which the exemplar is used as a kind of standard of representation used to pick out the instances resulting from exemplarization. Exemplarization of conscious states, when standard, will pick out the exemplar as an instance in typical operations of the mind. It remains a contingent fact about the exemplarization, however. It is a contingent fact that a conscious state is used to represent what a kind of state is like that includes the original state.

Before turning to the question of knowledge, it may be useful to contrast exemplarization from other examples of self-representation and self-reference. Consider the example of the word "word," which represents itself or refers to itself as well as to other words. This self-representation of the word "word" is not exemplarization, at least not as the word "word" is ordinarily used. We do not ordinarily use the word "word" as an exemplar of a word to pick out other words. Indeed, the word "word" would be an odd exemplar for picking out instances of words because of the unusual way in which it refers to itself by referring to words. It would, for that reason alone, be an odd standard of what a word is like. It would, used as a standard, lead one to think of words as things that are typically used to represent words as "word" does. Exemplarization, by contrast, uses the exemplar as the basis of generalization to pick out the other instances represented by the process. The word "word" is not used in this way. One might use any word as an exemplar to represent the class of words by quoting the word, the word "yellow," for example. Of course, normal exemplarization will have the result that the word "yellow" will be an instance of the exemplarized representation of words in terms of the word "yellow." That remains a contingent fact about representation, however.

It is clear from the examples that the exemplar is part of the representation at the same time that it is a parcel or medium of the representation. In Reid's (1785) terms, the conscious state is both a sign representing a class of states and is at the same time one of those states. The process of exemplarization gives the conscious state a functional role in the identification of states represented because the conscious state is used to identify the states that the exemplar represents. Thus, the exemplar is used as a representational token to represent a class of states and, in addition, the exemplar has a functional role in picking out the tokens in the extension represented. The representational token loops back onto itself as one thing represented as the result of the generalization from the exemplar in the process of exemplarization.

Some would be inclined to argue that generalization is the result of observed similarity. However, as Reid (1785) argued against Hume, similarity is always similarity in some respect and, therefore, appears to presuppose generalization referring to some respect rather than being able to account for it. There are interesting scientific questions about how we generalize, but there is a level of generalization we share with other animals in the responses to objects that suggest that generalization is a more fundamental operation of the mind than the observation of similarities. An animal may generalize without any understanding of similarity. This is controversial, and the position I am defending does not depend upon it, but it is important to note that generalization is possible for a system without being able to first observe similarities. As a result, the exemplarization, involving generalization from a token conscious state, does not presuppose the observation of similarities.

It should also be noted that exemplarization that does not proceed beyond generalization provides us with a functionally limited representation. Let us call this initial level ostensive representation. To obtain conceptual representation, the functional role of the representation must include inferential connections to other representations in addition to generalization from the exemplar to other instances. A specific account of inferential connections required for conceptual representation would be too controversial in detail to add to the account of exemplarization. I note here only that the addition of inferential connections is required to take the theory of exemplarization beyond ostensive representation to genuinely conceptual representation. No doubt learning the relationship between ostensive representation arrived at by exemplarization and linguistic representation is sufficient to raise the representation to a conceptual level. I doubt, personally, that it is necessary. Indeed, I believe that ostensive representation and linguistic representation interact in experience. The interaction modifies ostensive representation of exemplarization in terms of linguistic representation and modifies linguistic representation in terms of ostensive representation as well. New ways of generalizing involved in exemplarization may modify the inferential connections in the functional role of linguistic representation.

With these ideas before us, let us turn to the relationship between the exemplarization of conscious states and our knowledge of them. When exemplarization yields only ostensive representation, self-representation of the exemplar as one of the states represented by the exemplar falls short of knowledge. The representation of the state by itself in the ostensive representation may result in the exemplar being an instance of the states represented by itself. The representation of the exemplar by itself in this way will be a correct, or, if one prefers, a veridical representation. However, the immediacy or directness of the representation may occur without the person having the kind of understanding of the representation that could justify the person in accepting the representation. Moreover, the ostensive representation may fall short of conceptual representation and, indeed, may consist of an inferentially isolated representation. Thus, the ostensive representation could leave the person unable to recognize the correctness, reliability, or trustworthiness of the representation. The person would not be in a position to provide any justification or reasoning in support or defense of any claim concerning the representation. At this level of understanding or the lack thereof we have representation without justification.

Once exemplarization raises the representation to the conceptual level by fixing the representation within an inferential network, justification becomes possible because the capacity for reasoning is present. It should be noted, however, that fixing the ostensive representation within an inferential network to make it conceptual does not destroy the immediacy of the representation. The ostensive representation arising from generalizing from the exemplar is not a process of inference and does not presuppose the inference of the exemplarized token, the conscious state, from anything else. Neither does fixing the representation in an inferential network to make it conceptual. Fixing an inferential role for an exemplar does not presuppose inferring the exemplar from anything else. The exemplar stands for a class of states including itself without being inferred from other states. It thus remains in this way, immediate, direct, and lucid in the representation of itself. Immediacy is not contaminated by becoming conceptual.

There is a way in which exemplarization is immediate representation that has been missed by other authors who think of self-representation as resulting from the reference of the exemplar to properties that the exemplar exemplifies. Goodman (1968), for example, articulated a theory of exemplification that differs from my theory of exemplarization, according to which a sample is used to refer to properties it exemplifies. Others who have defended a looping or self-referential feature of consciousness—Loar (1990) may have been the first, for example—have been criticized by Levine (2001a) on the grounds that the referential loop must pass through properties to refer back to the exemplar. Such accounts leave us with an unexplained relationship between the properties of the conscious state that are exemplified by the exemplar and the properties of physical states. This line of criticism is avoided by the theory of exemplarization. The reason is that the exemplar represents conscious states immediately by being used to stand for a class of conscious states of which it, itself, is a member. My proposal is that we have the capacity to generalize from a particular to a class that it represents without referring in that representation to properties to generate the representational loop. Moreover, if, as I would argue, we should think of talk of properties as being paraphrastic for talk about how we conceive in a general way of individual features, the failure to explain some alleged properties of conscious states may admit of a simple explanation. It is that our conceptions of such alleged properties, though based on individual features, fails to yield concepts that function in nomological explanation. The concepts are not law cluster concepts. Should we deny, as a result, that they correspond to properties to avoid philosophical perplexity? It is worth consideration, but this is not the place to attempt to resolve the role of nomological explanation in ontology.

One final epistemological question is whether fixing the exemplarized state in an inferential network, assigning it an inferential role, entails that the subject knows that the state falls under the concept. The answer is, that it depends on the specific nature of the inferential role the ostensive representation acquires. If it were to acquire an inferential role that licensed the inference that one was unreliable or untrustworthy in the representation, then the person would not be justified by the inferential connections in accepting that the conceptual representation of the conscious state was correct. I have dealt in rather great detail (Lehrer 2000) with the question of what is required to convert the information contained in a representation into knowledge that the information is correct. I have argued that defensibility, the capacity of that person to meet objections to accepting that the representation is correct, is what is required to obtain a kind of justification that converts to knowledge when it is undefeated by errors in the system used to meet the objection. This capacity to meet objections is, however, compatible with the immediacy of the representation in exemplarization. The immediacy of the representation resulting from exemplarization remains when this capacity results from the inferential network in which the representation is embedded to render it conceptual. Fixing a representation in an inferential network does not require inferring the representation from anything else. It may, however, provide the inferential capacity required to meet objections to the representation and result in conversion to knowledge.

I wish to conclude with the simple claim that no problem of consciousness remains other than those of a strictly scientific nature over and above the problems of lucid representation and immediate knowledge solved above. We may wonder why there are such things as conscious states, what function they fulfill. The answer is, as Dretske (1995a) argues, that conscious states supply us with information about the world. The question remains as to why we receive information in this way. That is a scientific question, however, like the question of why we use digestion to nourish ourselves rather than nourishing ourselves in other ways. It is a scientific question amenable to scientific methodology for an answer.

Other features of consciousness are supposed to show that conscious states are, ultimately, not amenable to scientific investigation. One of these features is the qualitative subjectivity of consciousness, the feature of qualia. The claim, offered by Ferrier (1838–1839), is that when a conscious state is studied objectively, from a third-person perspective, then you leave out the subjectivity of the state. You leave out what the state is like. Moreover, Nagel (1974) suggested that consciousness reveals to a being what it is like to be that being, whether a bat or a human being. The argument from Jackson (1984) concerning Mary, who has complete physical knowledge of the world but has not experienced colors, having dwelt in a monochromatic room, was intended to show that there is more to knowledge, and more to the world, than is described in her physical knowledge of the world. Mary knows what color is like when she sees it, and not antecedently. Notice that the argument can be modified so that no matter what objective knowledge Mary has, that is, knowledge one could have from a third-person perspective that did not include first-person subjective experience, she would obtain new knowledge from the qualitative subjective experience of color qualia.

The foregoing account of exemplarization of experience takes the mystery out of all of these claims. A person acquires new knowledge of some sort from qualitative subjective experience that they cannot obtain in any other way. Admitted. But how do they obtain new knowledge of subjective experience? If I am right, they obtain a new representation by exemplarizing the new experience. No one denies there is a new experience, and the account of exemplarization explains how a new experience yields new representation and knowledge. It yields a new representation by exemplarization of the new experience. To exemplarize an experience you have to have it. There is a new way of knowing what the experience is like by exemplarization. Does this entail that the new knowledge resulting from exemplarization reveals a new kind of fact that could not be known without the subjective experience? It does not entail that. It entails only that there is a new way of representing a fact. It leaves open the question of whether the fact represented is the same fact as one represented in other ways or a new fact in just the way that a new name encountered leaves open the question of whether it names a new object or is a new name for an object previously named. In short, our knowledge of what the experience is like is the result of exemplarization of the experience to yield knowledge.

Perhaps the most salient argument for the conclusion that there is some fact about conscious experience that goes beyond scientific understanding is founded on the premise that there could be creatures who were our biological duplicates but who were unconscious. That argument, the zombie argument of Chalmers (1996), leads to the conclusion that conscious states are not token–token identical with physical states and, indeed, to the stronger conclusion that conscious states do not supervene on physical states. Identity and supervenience require a kind of necessity in relationships that is precluded by the possibility argued for by appeal to the possibility of the zombie. There is no doubt that we can imagine the zombie, but the controversial question is whether imagined zombie is possible. Reid (1785) long ago noted that we can imagine and conceive of things that are impossible, indeed, the ability to conceive of and understand impossible hypotheses is what enables us to reduce them to absurdity. If we did not understand them, we could not show that they were absurd. So, the question is simply whether the conceived zombie is possible.

It must be granted that conscious states do not seem to have physical properties as the conscious subject experiences those states, nor, for that matter, do physical states when externally observed seem to have the subjective qualitative features experienced by the subject of the conscious state. These facts of our experience, whether as the subject of the conscious states or as the external observer of physical states, explain why the zombie should be conceivable. But does this entail the logical possibility of the zombie and the conclusion that supervenience and token–token identity fails? I wish to argue that it does not. What we imagine to be missing in the zombie is a qualitative subjective state of consciousness. How do we know that we have such a state? We have immediate knowledge of it. However, if immediate knowledge is explained, as I have argued, in terms of the immediate representation of exemplarization, then the immediate knowledge we enjoy fails to support the conclusion that the zombie lacks such knowledge even if we imagine him to lack it. For physical states can be exemplarized. Suppose, as a token–token identity theorist claims, the qualitative subjective state of consciousness is identical to a physical state. There is no objection to the further claim that the zombie exemplarizes the state and has immediate knowledge of it, though we imagine him to lack it. What we imagine may, for all we know, be impossible.

Conscious beings may not be identical to physical beings, for all we know, but the appeal to immediate knowledge and representation fails to prove this. Exemplarization of the conscious state provides us with a representation of that state that differs from other forms of representation. It explains why a person who experiences a conscious state for the first time has a new way of knowing what it is like, that it is a state of a certain kind characterized by exemplarization of the conscious state. Exemplarization provides new knowledge that something is the case. The new knowledge may, for all we know, be knowledge of some physical state identical to the conscious state. We do not know that it is or that it is not. Agnosticism may feel like uncomfortable fence sitting. In my opinion, if we follow reason as far as it will take us and no further, we will admit that we do not know whether the supervenience thesis or the token–token identity thesis is true, or whether the zombie is a logical possibility. I prefer the modesty of agnosticism in this case as well as others to the certainty manifested by those who claim that reason favors their claim to knowledge.

IV | Beyond Philosophy: Consciousness and Self-Reference

18   The Biological Basis of Subjectivity: A Hypothesis

David Rudrauf and Antonio Damasio

In Memoriam: Jacques Rudrauf

1   Introduction

Determining the relationship between the biophysical processes that constitute our objective being when we feel, and our subjective experience as feeling beings remains a fundamental but still unsolved scientific problem. As biological entities, we can be described as sets of complex, multiscale, spatial and temporal patterns, in keeping with the way science describes the world. It is reasonable to assume that a scientific explanation of feeling should be based on that kind of description, and yet it is difficult to see how subjectivity and feeling are, per se, patterns in space and time. How is it that "patterns" become imbued with a sense of self? What kind of epistemological perspective on the system must we adopt in order to solve this problem?

Hoping to address these questions, we present a scientific conjecture about the biological origin of the ability to feel. We see the issue of feeling as a means to deal with the problem of subjectivity (Damasio 1999), and thus as a way to provide a biological account of a fundamental aspect of consciousness. The problem of feeling is relevant to the problem of subjectivity and consciousness precisely because the very concept of feeling, which should not be reduced to the simple notion of sensory discrimination, implies a sentient entity and thus requires considering the general problem of what makes one capable of being a subject of sensory experiences and of sensory experiences of oneself in particular. Subjectivity and the ability to feel are interdependent. On the one hand, feeling is not possible without subjectivity, without a subject of feeling. On the other, a subject, a lived self, exists for itself only as an ongoing feeling. In brief, feeling and the core of consciousness are one and the same. (In the following we will often use *core consciousness, consciousness, self, sentience,* and *subjectivity* interchangeably.)

We discuss several epistemological issues related to this problem and then present a general theory of the biology of subjectivity and feeling. The theory is based on relevant aspects of the phenomenology of feeling, general biological principles, remarkable structural and dynamical properties of the brain and body proper, and a reinterpretation of current neuroscientific knowledge. We do not pretend to account for every aspect of consciousness. However, we think that the theory can account, within a biomechanical framework, for a large number of phenomena usually considered as belonging to consciousness and explain several known neuroscientific facts. We see this theory as a heuristic model amenable to further development and modification.

Our main hypothesis is that feeling arises in the conflictive dynamics of resistance that our brain and body proper produce when they confront the highly inertial variance that they continuously and inevitably undergo. This variance is the result of delayed auto-perturbations of the brain–body system, divergent motivational tendencies, and attentional shifts. It is not only related to random fluctuations of the system, but also to controlled functional processes, capable of affecting the system as a whole through its functional connectivity. We see the process of resistance to variance, and in particular its central attention-related profile, as delineating the dynamic locus of an internal state of tension through which subjective experience emerges. Such a dynamical structure is intrinsically related to the system's need to engage in intentional behaviors, attend, preserve coherence, and respect the hierarchy of the various influences that affect its internal dynamics and organization. We see this general dynamics and its subjective counterpart in the framework of a monitoring and control function that lies at the core of the functionality we call consciousness.

2 Background: Consciousness According to Current Cognitive Neuroscience

The recent development of the cognitive sciences and the emergence of new tools and paradigms for the study of brain activity have renewed the interest of neuroscience in the problem of consciousness (Edelman 1989; Varela, Thompson, and Rosch 1991; Gray 1995; Varela 1996; Lane et al. 1998; Logothetis 1998; Tononi and Edelman 1998; Damasio 1999; Rodriguez et al. 1999; Srinivasan et al. 1999; Zeki and Bartels 1999; Damasio et al. 2000; Dehaene and Naccache 2001; Parvizi and Damasio 2001; Thompson and Varela 2001; Lutz et al. 2002; Crick and Koch 2003).

2.1 The Selfless Contents of Consciousness

Anatomo-functional specialization and microconsciousnesses The problem of consciousness is often construed as a search for the neural correlates of consciousness (NCC) (Block 1996), that is, the specific set of brain processes that would be engaged when "consciousness" occurs. Because science often requires focusing on specific problems, the NCC have frequently been investigated at the level of exteroceptive perceptual processes, vision in particular. This has led to notions like "visual consciousness" (Crick and Koch 1995; Logothetis 1998; Zeki and Bartels 1999; Tononi and Edelman 2000; Crick and Koch 2003). Such notions have phenomenological validity in the sense that we are indeed conscious of visual contents that may or may not be accessible to consciousness, depending on certain conditions. Thus the neuroscience community frequently defines consciousness by its specific contents, for example, visual or auditory, arguably implying that it could somehow be decomposed into subconsciousnesses. Such dissociations are suggested by actual neuropsychological dissociations and by the relative modularity of the functional architecture of the brain. Some researchers even suggest, rather radically, the existence of "microconsciousnesses" (Zeki and Bartels 1999) that would be "created" independently at the level of each specific brain modulus. (Of course, most of the same researchers would agree that *general* functions such as working memory and attention are certainly important as well.)

In spite of their interest and importance, these investigations address the issue of consciousness only indirectly, by focusing on the mechanisms and structures necessary for specific contents to be accessible to consciousness, but do not provide any clues about the neural mechanisms that actually make those contents conscious.

The project that dominates cognitive neuroscience is intended to reveal functional relations between more or less specific cognitive or behavioral dimensions and different levels of brain projection or brain maps. In such an approach, the general overall dynamics of the brain is eliminated from sight as an impure, nonspecific complexity in relation to the isolated properties. In functional brain imaging, a natural, and justified, methodological consequence of such principles is the use of control conditions that are intended to eliminate what is common between the processes in order to reveal what is specific. In the absence of specific hypotheses and models, such an approach can be a problem when it is used in the study of consciousness.

In all likelihood, consciousness corresponds to a highly integrated biological phenomenon. Consequently, the general dynamics that is present in most of the cognitive processes, beyond their specific modal contents, is precisely what should be studied. It is important for understanding the output of the brain maps and for addressing the issue of what their activation does to the rest of the system, that is, how such activations "move" the system as a whole entity and how the system responds internally to being thus affected. This issue has been recently addressed concerning anticipation in Crick and Koch 2003 (see also Tononi and Edelman 2000).

It must be stressed that most of the cortical and subcortical structures that process high-level information and participate in modal perception—memory, language, and reasoning—do not appear necessary for consciousness in general (see Damasio 1999, ch. 8). When such structures are damaged, certain types of conscious content are lost, *but not consciousness in general*: visual perception is lost after lesions of the primary visual cortex, but the conscious self of the now blind subject remains intact. As Penfield stated long ago: "One sided removal of, or injury to, any area of the cerebral cortex does not abolish conscious thinking. It may change the content of awareness, interfere with voluntary acts, render less effective planned action, deprive the patient of word symbols—but he still thinks and weeps, perhaps, at his own pitiful incapacity" (Penfield 1960). Even in degenerative diseases affecting the whole cortical mantle, for example, Alzheimer's disease, in which memory, reasoning, planning, attention, perception, and motor coordination are dramatically altered, the core of consciousness, the ability to feel and be a subject, although strongly altered and sometimes deprived of an autobiographical identity, appears to be relatively preserved late into the disease. Such robustness or resistance to "deconstruction" is in itself of great interest from a neuroscientific standpoint.

Binding what the brain separates Accordingly, part of cognitive neuroscientific research is guided by the intuitive idea that consciousness, beyond the specificity of its contents, is characterized by an integrative, unifying nature in which various endogenous or exogenous sources of information are bound together to constitute the content of conscious experience (Varela 1995a; Tononi and Edelman 2000). Thus the contemporary neuroscience of consciousness focuses not only on brain sensory mechanisms with powerful discriminative and analytic abilities, allowing the creation of highly specialized neural representations, but also on mechanisms that might help the brain to bind these "representations" contextually and adaptively. This issue is related to the more general problem of understanding how the brain self-organizes the coherence of perception and action and recruits connected brain domains for anticipation. This requires complex synergies in the dynamics of the system. The importance of large-scale interactions, perhaps expressed by transient periods of synchronization, between interconnected brain subsystems, together constituting a global workspace (Dehaene and Naccache 2001), was brought to the fore in relation to this problem (Varela 1995a; Logothetis 1998; Rodriguez et al. 1999; Varela 1999; Tononi and Edelman 2000; Varela et al. 2001; Lutz et al. 2002; Crick and Koch 2003). Some of the tenants of this perspective think of consciousness as a dynamical process of building successive punctuated "moments of consciousness" (Varela 1999) or snapshots in the case of visual consciousness (Crick and Koch 2003).

In any case, even if binding is considered by some researchers as secondary (Zeki and Bartels 1999) and by others as primary (Varela 1995a; Logothetis 1998; Tononi and Edelman 2000; Crick and Koch 2003), there is general agreement that both the global level of dynamical interactions and the local level of specialized brain structures play a complementary role in the making of the phenomenology of consciousness. This idea is explicitly articulated in Edelman's and Tononi's notion of the "dynamic core," which is intended to account for the simultaneous unity and informational complexity of consciousness (see Tononi and Edelman 2000).

Although of great importance and value, it seems to us that such a framework can only account for certain limited and perhaps nonspecific aspects of consciousness. It is not certain at all that such a unified integration of the various sensory bases of conscious contents is a necessary condition for the existence of a subjective perceptual experience. Many pathological cases of unstructured and chaotic perceptions might be related to a lack of coherence in brain processes, and yet, although disorganized, these are still "perceptions." Moreover, even if the data suggest that the emergence of conscious experience indeed requires the bringing into play of extended interacting cerebral networks, the models proposed as the putative neural correlates of the binding of specific contents into a more integrative pattern are not specific enough to account for the phenomena that the notion of conscious content really implies. No real hypothesis is proposed about how these "contents" are experienced by something like a "subject," and this is of primary phenomenological importance vis-à-vis consciousness.

2.2 Cognition as a General Computational Architecture

General and integrative models of cognition, based on animal physiology and behavior (see Gray 1995) as well as artificial intelligence and robotics (see Meyer, Boitblat, and Wilson 1993), provide an important ground for situating the problem, though without necessarily giving direct insights about its solution. According to these paradigms, animal cognition can be described to some extent in terms of the operation of a computational architecture that leads to the definition, integration, and channeling of relevant information in the context of an ongoing process of the selection of adaptive responses. The limited, more or less centralized, attentional resources of the system are dynamically allocated more or less hierarchically, in order to satisfy what could be called a general "scanning function" underlying the spontaneous and intelligent exploration of the environment. Such a function implies complex mechanisms of orientation and is dependent on the interplay of subfunctions, such as the analysis of current sensory inputs, the simulation of outcome, memory, and planning, as well as motivational parameters and executive constraints. This general functional architecture might be constituted by innately differentiated modules or acquired as a result of a self-organized learning process in distributed systems. Its brain implementation in a highly nonlinear and dynamical framework can certainly account, in part, for our ability for action-oriented, attentional, and motivational intentionality, where intentionality is here understood as the generic ability for dynamical coupling between a system and an "object" in relation to the pursuit of goals.

Although it might be emphasized that this general framework also applies to insects and even to protists, we do think that the operation of an abstract functional architecture of this type is certainly a fundamental aspect of the *infrastructure* of core consciousness. However, as was the case for the general proposals about the processes allowing integration and binding, referred to in the previous section, the link of such computational abilities with a mechanism for the constitution of subjectivity itself, with its phenomenology subtending mental "images" and feelings experienced by a "subject," is not immediate. Such a link might appear, however, when these computational abilities are put in certain biophysical contexts.

2.3 Emotion and Feeling as a Paradigm

Confronted with the difficulty of understanding consciousness in terms of such rather disembodied and selfless neural computation, certain researchers have considered the investigation of emotions and feelings as an essential paradigm for the scientific inquiry into the biological roots of consciousness (Panksepp 1998b; Damasio 1999, 2001, 2003; Varela 1999).

Emotions appear to have been designed through evolution in relation to (a) the need for solving vitally important problems attending the struggle for life, implying attentional selection, strategies of approach and avoidance, and correlative preparation for action in the context of a real body with masses to move under biophysical constraints; and (b) the emergence of animal societies and the need for the subtle regulation of interindividual interactions (Adolphs 2001, 2003). An "emotional episode" (Russell 2003) implies the recruitment of cognitive, motor, and metabolic resources and the orientation and motivation of perception, learning, and action. Some of the brain and body bases of emotions and feelings are now understood.[1]

Emotions, feelings, and affective processes in general are essential for decisionmaking, preparation for action, learning, meaning construction, the recognition of others, and moral behaviors (Damasio 2003). But what is more, they can serve as a model for the articulation of the relationships between definable neurophysiological processes and our sense of being, our sentience, the core of subjectivity (Damasio 1999, 2001; Srinivasan et al. 1999; Varela 1999; Damasio et al. 2000; Thompson and Varela 2001; Varela and Depraz 2001). As such, they are of interest for our problem.

We see subjectivity, emotion, and feeling as grounded in homeostatic-like phenomena (Damasio 2003). We maintain that an essential constituent of the phenomenology of subjectivity is the experience of a large range of body state changes and body state constraints, such as those occurring during the unfolding of an emotion, and, more generally, pain- and pleasure-related behaviors. We also see the constraints that the musculoskeletal system and visceral tone, and their control, impose upon intentional behaviors and cognition during controlled attention and effortful cognitive processes (not only during emotions, but also in certain inexplicitly emotional contexts) as central to understanding the constitution of subjectivity. Without the experience of those changes and constraints, the process of feeling would be deprived of its defining component and reduced to an intellectual jitter unconnected to a lived self. Thus, the problem is no longer a purely central neurocognitive one, but its field of investigation extends to the embodiment of the individual and the precise "cycles of operation" of its biological regulation (Varela, Thompson, and Rosch 1991; Damasio 1999, 2001; Thompson and Varela 2001).[2] If, in the absence of more specifications, such a general description does not fully account for the specificity, subtlety, and complexity of emotions and feeling, in particular in humans (Ben-Ze'ev 2000), it nonetheless provides a paradigm in which the biology of "core affects," which we see as the core phenomena of subjectivity, might be studied (Russell and Barrett 1999).

The idea that feeling is related to the sensing of body changes and constraints (see Damasio 2001, 2003) has been supported by neurobiological findings based on human experimental studies using both structural and functional neuroimaging as well as electrophysiological methods. It is apparent that a number of "somatosensing" structures in the brainstem, hypothalamus, cingulate cortex, and somatosensory cortex, including the insula, are involved in feeling a wide range of emotions. These same structures are prominently engaged during feelings of pain, heat, cold, narcotic highs, and narcotic withdrawals, as well as the consumption of pleasurable foods or the hearing of thrilling pieces of music (see Craig 2002; Damasio 2003).

Yet, although the claim that there is a relation between "feeling" and "somatosensing" is both plausible and supported by mounting evidence, and although that relation is indispensable in accounting for the purely affective *contents* of feeling, it nevertheless appears insufficient to explain why the mapped body states would be felt, that is, why they come to be experienced at all. The biological substrate of feeling is thus certainly not confined to seemingly passive brain representations of body states.

3 Preliminary Epistemological Considerations

3.1 Explanatory Gaps

As yet, no hypothesis about the ability to feel has been formulated. Very often, the explanation is "chalked up" by neuroscientists and cognitive scientists to the extraordinary informational and representational ability of the brain, its capacity to separate, bind, and integrate specific, functional, exteroceptive and/or interoceptive information through neural connectivity and mapping, including the building of neural "representations" of the body.

Some have regarded the problem of relating our physical organization and "computational" abilities to subjective experience per se as insoluble, short of postulating a new fundamental ontology—for example, Chalmers's "hard problem" (Chalmers 1996). And some who regard the divide between subjectivity and objectivity as ontologically innocuous still argue that there is an "explanatory gap" (see Levine 1983).

In this vein, some have contended that the proposed explanations generally turn out to be circular, always somewhere presupposing consciousness and a subject of the experience not really captured by the explanatory model itself. Neuroscientific proposals, on such views, hardly lead further than limited neuro-reductionist approaches, grounding the subjective "internal eye" in the existence of putative, more or less distributed, integrative neural maps made of feature detectors, and leading to the so-called homunculus problem. Even when one multiplies the levels of representations, making them more and more complex, abstract, or specific, one is confronted with an "infinite regression" in which the understanding of when, where, and how a "subject" of the representation can emerge is perpetually delayed to the next stage, since a brain map is but a brain map, and not a subjective point of view. When one stresses that all these levels of representation are interacting, constituting a dynamic core (Tononi and Edelman 2000) or a global workspace (Dehaene and Naccache 2001), with enormous degrees of freedom, one does not really get more direct insight into why a subjective experience should emerge in a system imbued with such a functional organization and dynamics.

Such explanatory failures and the paradoxes that the problem of consciousness seem to imply lead many to consider the possibility that our customary way of thinking about subjectivity and consciousness, implying, as it does, a subject side and an object side, might in itself be fundamentally wrong. Thus, the philosopher Dennett introduced the skeptical metaphor of the mind thought of as a "Cartesian theater," illustrating the infinite regression that describing the mind as including a subject (the audience in the theater) and an object (the picture on the screen) may imply (Dennett 1991, pp. 309–320). The possible logical and empirical problems raised by the subjective organization indicated by the Cartesian theater metaphor even drive some to a paradoxical eliminativism in which they renounce consciousness itself as an ill-defined matter of investigation, refuse to grant subjectivity scientific status, and consider subjective phenomena as mere "subjective illusions." But this last concept is either contradictory or absolutely meaningless. It seems to presuppose subjectivity in its very denial of it, and so does not escape the problem.

But beyond its theoretical difficulties, we do think that the idea of a perceiving or feeling subject interacting with an "object," which partly constitutes the content of its experience, has some phenomenological validity, and should not consequently be rejected as a description of what it is like to perceive and feel. As a phenomenon, it constitutes an object of interest for science and has to be explained, not dismissed.

The fact that we cannot directly "measure" private experience from the outside in a public way has sometimes been thought to preclude the possibility of explaining consciousness in an objective, mechanistic framework. But this is a quite general problem since the so-called objective descriptions in other fields of science are often themselves obtained very indirectly through complex instrumentation and involve noise contamination and several interactions with many factors that are not of interest and not necessarily easy to control. This is particularly so in circumstances often encountered in physics in which there are irreducible and unpredictable interactions between the instrumentation and the measurements of interest. In the case of subjectivity the "instrumentation" can be the very subject making self-reports, with its limits of accuracy and possible errors of interpretation. There are certainly limits to the accuracy of the descriptions that can be so obtained, but it is doubtful that optimal precision is required in order to isolate the essential features of subjective experience to be explained. Moreover, well-controlled procedures of crossvalidation of subjective descriptions can be designed in order to arrive at satisfactory intersubjective agreement. And this gives the descriptions a reasonable degree of objectivity (Varela 1996).

Some have raised the possibility that, more fundamentally, beyond a metrological problem, our limited cognitive capacities cannot account for themselves; some of these arguments are based on self-reference and are analogous to arguments for the logical incompleteness of certain formal systems. Some philosophers and scientists (see Chalmers 1996; Penrose 2001), inspired by quantum mechanics, have even tried to formulate analogues of theorems of uncertainty. They claim that fundamental physical limitations entail a definitive lack of scientific concepts capable of reducing the gap between objectivity and subjectivity. These arguments are often made with no regard for embodiment and the relevant biology (see Crick and Koch 2003). They tend to close the debate by imagining impossibilities that preclude the attempt to find solutions pragmatically. But although we are dealing with one of the most complex systems known (the brain and our overall physiological organization), the emergence of subjective experience might be, at least at a certain level of explanation, a "simpler" problem than, for example, those pertaining to the nature of light or electrons. Its domain of mechanical explanation might not require reference to the quantum behavior of elementary particles or face epistemological problems such as that of the origin of the so-called decoherence of the wave function in actual measurement situations, or those of indeterminism and delocalization.

3.2 The Problem of Finding an Adequate Level of Description

From a more pragmatic standpoint, an adequate concept of subjectivity and feeling might emerge from the search for mutual constraints between characteristic phenomenological features, resulting in part from rigorous introspective investigations, and the knowledge provided by the objective description of the physical and biological features of the considered system, which happens to have the ability to feel (Varela 1996, 1997).

As biologists and neuroscientists, accustomed to observing and analyzing real living systems, we believe, based on evolutionary considerations and heuristic principles, that the ability to feel is so central in the biology and behavior of higher animals that the understanding of how subjectivity is implemented and what subjectivity really is should follow from a proper analysis of the biological and neurophysiological characteristics of such animals. We also believe that general biological principles might contain relevant information about the biological roots of this phenomenon and that the resulting explanatory model should more or less directly connect subjectivity with the general principles of chemistry and physics. An explanation of subjectivity and feeling must not only be based on a proposal about the putative function that these related phenomena realize, but must also, and perhaps above all, possess phenomenological plausibility.

Frames of reference and the meaning of reduction   Reducing the explanatory gap implies providing a comprehensive characterization that would actually make descriptively interchangeable the levels of the system's subjectivity and physicality during feeling. A group of (conceptual) transformations must be found that would allow passing from an objective frame to a subjective frame and alternatively without discontinuity. What must be understood is how an objective process or mechanism can have a subjective nature and, correlatively, how our objective scientific concepts can account for subjective experience. By the end, we must be able to state that to feel is literally to implement some type of mechanism and, of course, vice versa. The differences between feeling and the biological phenomena described in relation to it would be accounted for by a difference in point of view. That is to say, such differences are the effect of seeing the same thing from different angles: being oneself the events observed or observing the events without being them.

Thus the difficulty resides not only in a lack of basic knowledge but also in defining adequate levels of description capable of connecting both points of view on the events. The goal to pursue is certainly not to "reduce" the subjective domain to the objective domain, in the sense of the reduction of something complex to a simpler substrate. The problem is not really an issue of explaining a macroscopic object in terms of microscopic objects, the invariant form of a system by its atomic constituents, a global phenomenon by a local phenomenon, the mind as a global entity by the neurons as a collection of local systems, nor is it the contrary. The problem with a simple reductionist approach, which often implies a reductionist view of physics itself, is not that it cannot be achieved, but that it does not answer the question.

The problem is to understand one complex level of the phenomenology, the subjective phenomenology of an embodied being, in the framework of another complex phenomenological level, the objective one, that is, the description of the multiscale biomechanical transformations that the system undergoes. One must then search for levels of organization and description that would make the "biophysical field" and the subjective domain match each other. Therefore, this must be done at commensurable levels of organization in a common domain of description, integrated enough on both sides, and showing identical structural phenomenologies.

Looking for the mechanics of being   In science, the material of objectivity is always descriptions of spatio-temporal interactions between spatio-temporal objects, structures, and dimensions according to certain laws; the sequential organization of these can sometimes be described as mechanisms or even as functions. Systems of material points, particles, molecules, fluids, solids, continuous media, waves, biochemical networks and cascades, nervous influxes, cells, organs, organisms, artificial mechanical structures, ecosystems, planets, and so on, are the kinds of objects of interest; their behavior is described in terms of processes, trajectories, transformations, diffusions, reactions, attractions, repulsions, accelerations, that is, as motions, governed by forces, fields, and laws of interaction that operate within the framework of basic constraints such as inertia, viscosity, mass, charge, and are bounded by some energy cost function. Thus, if we are willing to play the game of such a description, we must search for an existing mechanical framework that can account for subjective experience per se in terms of objective spatio-temporal dynamics. How could such a mode of description account for subjective experience? Are there any dynamical spatio-temporal interactions that possess "morphodynamical" properties compatible with the phenomenology of subjectivity?

From a methodological point of view, what we should look for is a general physical mechanism, actually implemented in the organism, that would satisfactorily define a feeling entity, that is, a mechanism such that one would be able to recognize a "self" in a system imbued with it either by identification with our direct experience of what it is like to be a self or by its conformity to other phenomenological definitions and properties. If our search succeeds, the relation between our objective being and our subjective experience would become more transparent. Such a mechanism would obviously also have to show an actual empirical relationship with subjectivity and feeling, as assessed by experimental science.

Our objective, then, is to search for a nontrivial isomorphism between the describable phenomenology of feeling and aspects of the affective dynamics of the brain–body systems describable in terms of current biological and neuroscientific theory.

Succeeding here requires satisfying two apparently conflicting constraints. First, it implies taking into account the enormous complexity of the organism and the brain. This is so because the problem of subjectivity has much to do with the specificity of the embodiment of the system being considered (Thompson and Varela 2001). The "flesh" of the processes must not be reduced to something so abstract that it would, in principle, be ascribable to too many things in the universe and so would not constitute a sufficient condition for subjectivity to appear. At the same time, a drastic movement of synthesis and abstraction is evidently required to make apparent and general the core of the relevant relations. Finding a descriptive conceptual equilibrium between general mechanisms and the specific concrete processes that embody them in a particular system is absolutely critical. Abstraction is a need as well as a danger, and the proper level of abstraction must be found.[3] To approach this problem, we believe it is necessary to consider the self not as a neural representation but as a distributed dynamical "behavior" enabled in a living organism. Thus, we must understand which particular type of dynamical behavior can include a subjectivity.

3.3 Situating Subjectivity

Consciousness is a situated phenomenon: it belongs to an individual, depends on the specific history of this individual, and often its current contents are not independent from their actual external sources (the objects of perception) and more generally from the interactions of the individual with its surroundings. This situatedness of consciousness makes our problem complex but also restricted.

It is complex because it suggests that many coupled levels of causality and constraints are involved in the objective production of consciousness: internal biological processes, the biophysical structure of the surroundings, the cultural and symbolic fields, the contingencies of learning and history, and so on. Thus, if we wanted to account rigorously for all that the conscious individual is and is becoming, the individual organism should not be isolated from its current interactions with its environment, and the details of its history of coupling should be considered. But our goal is much less ambitious. Understanding the bases of consciousness does not require the characterization of all possible contents in the vast landscape of the mind.[4] As a first approximation, a theory of consciousness does not even necessarily require an account of all possible levels of consciousness, from so-called core consciousness (Damasio 1999) to the most complex and subtle avatars of a metarepresentational and symbolic self-consciousness.

The situatedness of consciousness also makes our problem restricted. Consciousness is not an eternal and infinite phenomenon. It is a biological phenomenon that exists under various forms in different species and perhaps also with a certain degree of relativity in different individuals, moments of life, and pathological conditions.

Bounded by resources and contents, consciousness has a limited phenomenological domain. It is situated in time, space, and in contents: I am conscious sometime, somewhere, and of something. It is a dynamical process that can be stopped anytime, as a result of injury, anoxia, intoxication, dreamless sleep, or death and that, within the limits of certain conditions of the organism's integrity, can also be restarted very quickly, for instance injecting atropine in response to a loss of consciousness due to a vasovagal syncope, or as it is spontaneously every morning waking up from dreamless sleep.

To explore the relationships between subjectivity and the biophysical field in which we exist and evolve, something characteristic and "simple" about consciousness has to be isolated. Indeed, even if one must not try to reduce subjective phenomenology to elementary physical constituents, one can try to reduce a highly complex subjective phenomenology to a simpler subjective phenomenology. Successfully explaining a simple conscious experience would imply that one has understood the "mysterious" relation between objectivity and subjectivity, and filled a great deal of the so-called explanatory gap (although many problems would remain).

Defining such a target for explanation is not easy but is a key concern that involves a search for characteristic invariants. Our ability to decompose and analyze our experience is essential. We must look for the *core* of our experience, that is, the embodied, daily, and concrete "microphenomenology" of what it is like to be conscious (Varela 1995b), and consider how it can be enfolded in concepts.

The simplest level of consciousness is probably what has been called "core consciousness" (Damasio 1999). It can be described as the internal level of the constitution of a subject, experiencing contents and impressions, obtained in the perspective of a body. In other words, it is the level of constitution of a self-sentient entity. It is present in all of us, probably from birth, and, in all likelihood, with more or less subtle differences, in many other animals. And it is in part independent of long-term memory (Damasio 1999). Thus, one way to isolate core consciousness and its mechanism is to concentrate on feeling. Because feelings involve the presence of subjectivity, occasions of feeling should contain all the information required to understand subjectivity as a biological mechanism. Although the ability to feel per se does not necessarily imply explicit symbolic "self-consciousness," we believe that, from phylogenetic, functional, and phenomenological points of view, it is a necessary and sufficient condition for a physical system to be imbued with at least a minimal level of consciousness.

4   Rationale for the Hypothesis

We now show, drawing upon phenomenological and biological considerations, the importance of the concept of resistance to variance for our problem. We first introduce some theoretical developments based on the notion of affect, suggesting an intrinsic relationship between this intuitive psychological notion and an underlying process of resistance to variance. We then show, through general biophysical and biological considerations, as well as neurophysiological analysis, that (1) monitoring affective processes implies *resisting* the neurophysiological ebb and flow of disequilibrium they induce in the system in relation to the processes of life and cognition; and (2) that initiating and maintaining programmed actions or cognitive routines necessitate *resisting* the inertia and constraints, that is, the relative inertial invariance of the brain–body system. We then discuss how such a process of resistance to variance suggests an intrinsic relationship between subjectivity, feeling, and a general function of monitoring and control. We also show that essential aspects of the classical concepts of arousal, vigilance, and attention, so important in feeling and in consciousness in general, can be related to the concept of resistance to variance, as various forms of controlled overexcitation in the framework of intentional behaviors. Based on these considerations, we suggest that there is an intimate relationship between subjectivity, feeling, and the concrete operation of the process of resisting autoperturbative variance (or inertial constraints), at an integrated level, vis-à-vis the conflictive tension it generates in the system. We will also suggest that such a dynamics can be found at the core of the "first-person" phenomenology of feeling itself.

4.1   From the Concept of Affect to the General Mechanics of Subjectivity
The concept of "affect" is a "limit" concept between physiology and psychology, as is the concept of "impulse" in Freudian theory. It is at the heart of the "first-person" notions of feeling and subjectivity. What differentiates one felt state from another is the way we are affected, the orchestration of the changes; but the central generic feature is always the same: we are

affected, and this state of affectedness can be overwhelming. We shall argue that the notion of affect can also tell us a lot about the kind of physical mechanism that might generate feeling and subjectivity.

Let us consider the notion of "affect" in a rather literal sense and in a biological framework. The notion of affect, we maintain, implies that a system, or something in the system, is affected by its own internal transformations, that is, its own variance, through functional connectivity, and as a result there is something that it is like for the system to be in such condition. According to this framework, as a first approximation, to feel is to be the *subject* of some sort of internal *change*. It has literally to do with objectively *undergoing* a flux of *transformations*.

Following the idea that something is affected in the system and that it is this state of affectedness that constitutes the core of the "feeling subject," one crucial problem is to understand the level of organization, the types of mechanisms, and the anatomo-functional substrate that constitute the affected "interface" in the process. In other words, a way to search for the "feeling subject" as a biological entity is to answer the question of what is affected in the system.

Intuitively, the very notion of "being affected" implies a steady-state regime of transformation, far from equilibrium, in which something active in the system, an affected dynamical structure, has to continuously react to the incoming or ongoing variance. Such a dynamics places subjectivity in a fundamentally conflictive functional organization. The conflictive dimension implied by the notion of affect, which includes the idea of a potentially overwhelming subjective pressure, suggests that the reactions of the system to its own variance might be a form of resistance.

These phenomenological considerations suggest that an essential aspect of the biology of subjectivity could be sought in the form of a dynamical regime of *resistance to variance*. The general dynamical configuration of a system in which something resists, that is, attempts to control its own transformations, may be crucial to the making of the subjective experience we refer to as feeling, where this includes the feeling of an emotion and more generally the sense of self.

It must be noted that this process of resistance can perfectly well include an intentional dimension, for example, being motivated in relation to certain goals. Interestingly, the root of such an intentional dimension, its motivational organization, can be assumed to be outside the scope of the current subjective experience, that is, beyond consciousness, in the kind of general cognitive infrastructure we referred to in the introduction, and so need not per se be accounted for by the theory.

The functional levels of organization of such a putative biological mechanism need to be specified. We will see in the next sections that, using it as a principle of organization, the notion of resistance to variance might explain a great deal of classical findings in the cognitive neurosciences of emotion, attention, and consciousness, and provide a unifying framework to predict and understand the involvement of different anatomo-functional entities in these phenomena. Let us first consider the relevance of this notion from a general biological standpoint.

4.2 The Objective Phenomenology of Being

The notion of biological resistance and that of conflict are attractive in a discussion of feeling and subjectivity because it can be said that at any given moment or in any occasion of being, the living organism who feels is defined in a setting of conflict. One central aspect of such a conflict is the resistance that the organism must oppose to its own variance as well as to its own inertia or invariance. A full specification and detailed description of an individual subject would require the description of the ongoing conflict between a large range of automated and intended actions of the organism and the automated and intended reactions with which the organism resists those same actions.

Aspects of the variance Biological systems are organizationally closed physical systems (Varela 1979) continuously endeavoring to maintain their integrity and, in a certain sense, their identity. The chemical interdependence of the processes and components that define the identity of the organism results in a recursive turnover that constantly places the appropriate processes and components in the correct biophysical relationships so that the system as whole remains thermodynamically viable (Varela 1979). Such a process takes place in conditions of unstable equilibrium that involve physiological stresses and threaten the normal operation and even the survival of the system. Because of the interconnectedness of their constituents, biological systems constitute for themselves a biophysical field of auto-perturbation and constraints. In higher organisms, these auto-perturbations and constraints, through which the life of the system operates, are intrinsically related to biomechanical constraints of the brain–body system, slow and fast physiological adjustments, affective changes, conflictive motivational tendencies, instability of attention, as well as the triggering of anticipatory simulations of the expected outcomes of situations in which the individual is engaged.

The significance of the auto-perturbation and biomechanical constraints is especially notable when we consider the topology of complex biological systems in which the propagation of perturbations and signaling occurs at a limited speed in a large recurrent functional space. Our organisms are made of multiple, enfolded, interdependent structures that feature biological, biochemical, physiological, and biomechanical recursive pathways, as well as sensorimotor loops that enable our interactions with the environment. This form of organization ensures the autonomy of the system but at the same time places the organism at the frequent risk of uncontrollable "resonance." At each instant every part of the organism possesses a "potential of influence" on every other part because of their functional interdependence. Simple examples of "potential of influence" include the release of a hormone into the bloodstream and sensory input traveling toward the central nervous system.

The potential of influence of a particular part on another depends on the momentary global state of the organism. The sum of all these potentials defines the field of perturbation that will affect the state space of the organism during the instants that follow, in other words, the internal impediments that the organism will have to cope with as it behaves. Consequently, it can be said that we exist in a biophysical flux of auto-perturbations and constraints, propagated at different speeds in the recursive structure of our organism, thus introducing *delays* at multiple time scales. The long functional loops that involve the brain and the rest of the body are especially responsible for increasing the auto-perturbation delays. Thus, the physiological deployment of an emotional reaction into the periphery of the organism is itself a potential source of delayed auto-perturbations capable of affecting brain dynamics and the general organization of behavior. In brief, we are *recursive, delayed, auto-perturbing systems.*

Aspects of the resistance It is a fact that, in order to achieve their current goals and maintain coherence and adaptation, biological systems of the class we are interested in have to continuously grapple with the impediments that their own activity generates or that these systems encounter during intentional behaviors, due to biomechanical constraints.

Complex living systems are continuously reacting at all levels of their organization—including the fully integrated and intentional cognitive level—to the changes that occur within their structure and to the constraints such structure imposes on their behavior. They include adaptive couplings between ongoing auto-perturbations and constraints and mechanisms of compensation that endeavor to preserve or regain equilibrium and achieve adaptive goals.[5]

These compensation mechanisms operate at several levels. Examples include metabolic regulation, reflexes, immune responses, pain and pleasure behaviors, drives and motivations, emotions, and cognition. These mechanisms also depend on humoral as well as neural signalling acting on endocrine glands and on smooth and striated muscles. The ensemble of these mechanisms ensures homeostasis in the broad sense of the term. Consequently, it is valid to describe the system as entailing an ongoing "endogenous mechanics" that resists perturbations and constraints. This resistance is related in part to the inertia of ongoing processes and in part to adaptive self-organizing reactions meant to control the incoming perturbations. Notably because of the delays in the propagation of information, the biomechanical constraints that are imposed on the system by its own structure (which represent a source of inertia to be resisted), for instance, during effortful cognition and behavior, can themselves be seen as delayed auto-perturbations in relation to the system's current endeavor. Consequently, the possible distinction between resistance to variance (in this case, to auto-perturbations) and resistance to relative invariance, that is, the inertia of the biomechanical constraints, can be considered altogether in the framework of resistance to variance.[6]

In keeping with our discussion of the notion of affect, we suggest that, at a very basic level, this potential for delayed auto-perturbations and the correlative need to resist them can help us intuit how a system initially dedicated to *action*, from an evolutionary perspective, can actually undergo *passion*, that is, how it can be in an integrated state of affectedness corresponding to an essential aspect of subjectivity.

It is conceivable that a subject or self is shaped and maintained only as a result of ongoing actions and reactions, just as it is certainly the case that a living organism is shaped and kept alive as a result of such ongoing actions and reactions. It seems reasonable to invoke resistance to variance or to relative invariance as integral contributors to the biological mechanisms that allow us to be "feeling subjects." Without the dynamics that lead to conflict between a level of control and a level of perturbation or biomechanical constraint, the body could not be animated. And there is evidence suggesting that without proper operation and control of such basic dynamics the individual organism cannot survive autonomously and the self and consciousness dissolve. Coma, vegetative states, and akinetic mutism are illustrations of such a breakdown in the integral conflictive dynamics of action and reaction that makes a wakeful, vigilant, attentive, and emoting individual. Maintaining life implies a struggle and it is important to note at the outset that we view cognition as yet another set of mechanisms for that struggle. The mental space itself is a "battlefield" in addition to being an abstract level of manipulation of representations and to being the putative counterpart of waves of neural synchronizations. It is part of the integrated machinery that permits the regulation and maintenance of life.

4.3 Controlled Overexcitation and the Neurocognitive Foundations of the Hypothesis

The phenomena described above are relevant not just to the basic regulation of the life process but also to cognition, perception, and reasoning.

Consciousness, monitoring, and control By nature, this dynamics of resistance to variance involves a system of compensation. It is related to a general function of self-monitoring and control that enables the system to grapple with auto-perturbations and attempt to inhibit some processes in preference to others, based on the appraisal of situations relative to adaptive criteria.

We emphasize this functional dimension of the dynamics of resistance to variance in the organism as a supplementary argument in favor of its link with subjectivity and feeling.

Subjectivity, feelings, and consciousness in general are intelligible from a functional, cognitive, and evolutionary perspective only in connection with a framework of monitoring and control. The existence of a monitoring and control function is at the heart of cognition as an integrative phenomenon. Such a function grew in complexity and integration in the course of evolution and came to reduce the impact of fast automatic reflexes on the appraisal and execution of action, favoring slower, controlled, multifaceted cognitive processes.[7] There is certainly no subjective experience without a minimal focus of attention, which is itself a form of monitoring and control, as discussed in the next sections. Moreover, the monitoring and control of systemic internal variance imply the existence of a process of somatosensing, which is known to be essential in feeling, and conversely somatosensing implies, more or less directly, monitoring and control.

In fact, consciousness has been associated with the concepts of monitoring and control for a long time. But these concepts, taken as examples of "high-level" cognitive functions, have typically been construed in a very abstract and functionalist way, and the emphasis has been on disambiguation, error correction, complex decision making, and the optimization of the system's predictions about the behavior of objects in its environment (see Mayr 2004). This approach provides little insight about how the operation of such a function could involve subjective experience per se. In itself, a function-based explanation is insufficient.

But the operation of body monitoring and control might appear to have a direct link with the phenomenology of subjectivity when it is put in the context of its concrete biological implementation and one considers the dynamical constraints imposed by its working environment, real brains, and real bodies. Our framework suggests that these apparently different "functions"—monitoring, control, attention, and feeling—could in fact be strongly related, if not identical, at a concrete neurophysiological level. Although sensory capacity and perhaps perception can be anatomically, functionally, and logically distinguished from executive functions and control (and they are generally so distinguished by cognitive neuroscience), it could be that they are not separated at all in the actual making of subjective experience.

Arousal, vigilance, and resistance to variance Because of its conflictive nature, this dynamical setting of resistance to variance is expected to induce tension in the system, that is, a state of controlled overexcitation. Tension is usually described as a central component of arousal, which is one essential component of feeling, both from a subjective and an objective point of view. Arousal reflects indeed a state of tension involving an increase in central excitability, an increase in peripheral auto-perturbations, and a correlative increase in the attempt to control overflow. This can be observed through associated attentional and motor behaviors. It is interesting to note that in normal conditions there is a pronounced correlation between cortical activation, psychophysiological arousal (i.e., visceral tone), and subjective arousal, that is, the self-reported intensity of the subjective experience during the feeling of pleasant or unpleasant emotions (Lang et al. 1993). The degree of pleasantness or unpleasantness is also generally correlated with the degree of arousal. Arousal, but also vigilance in general, which corresponds to an ongoing state of reactivity, and is at the root of consciousness, may be understood or reinterpreted (including their neurophysiological aspects) in a framework of preparedness to resist or of actual resistance to variance, in the context of an ongoing auto-perturbative process.

The brain in this dynamical profile The brain, and its highest functions in particular, cannot operate in the absence of a process of resistance to variance. We cite some basic biophysical reasons sufficient to indicate this.

It is evident to any neurophysiologist that the brain exhibits an unstable oscillatory dynamics involving a competition between excitatory signals and active inhibitory mechanisms, which results from its local and large-scale organization and involves the propagation of signals into connected domains with various latencies.

From a dynamical standpoint, the recurrent organization of the brain, as well as that of the organism in general, requires inhibitory mechanisms able to adaptively reduce the risk of phenomena of resonance that could lead to destructive divergence. In certain pathological circumstances, local activations can influence the rest of the system in a way that leads the brain into a major synchronization of its electrical activity, the sort of electrical storm of which seizures are a dramatic illustration.

Given this high excitability of the brain, it is important to emphasize, from a neurocognitive standpoint, that there is a strong relationship between information processing and the propagation of energy during cognitive processes. When the brain engages an informational process, energy flows through connected networks, and the activity of specific local networks generally increases, enhancing their potential of influence on the rest of the system. Such a dynamics is reflected in the increase of the magnitude of certain electrophysiological signals, in the rate of spike volleys, in global changes in cortical arousal, as well as in metabolic adjustments. Thus this shows up in functional brain-imaging studies of subjects performing cognitive tasks. These indicate that high-level conscious processes are associated with more energy consumption than automated low-level ones.

The relationship between information flow and energy flow reinforces the notion that the organism in general and the brain in particular must deal with the intrinsic risk of "overflow" during sensory and cognitive processing. During the unfolding of cognitive processes, we are often at risk of *disag*gregation and *de*coherence. This is all the more true for organisms with complex, highly connected and recurrent nervous systems. In brief, because of the interdependence of the system's components and processes, cognitive operations are also a source of important perturbations for the brain, which appears not only as a source of organization and regulation but also of auto-perturbation and constraints.

Thus, in order to maintain equilibrium and its current endeavors, the brain must control the auto-perturbations inherent in cognition. This process of control is part of cognition itself. In order to specify the information being processed, reduce the risk of divergence, offset auto-perturbations at the level of cognitive operations, and engage cognitive routines or planned behaviors, the system must offer an interface of resistance to the incoming flows.

No less important, the variance, resistance, and conflict inherent in the neural processes that subserve cognition are played out continuously in the body-proper, through the modulation of the autonomic tonus, for instance.

Auto-perturbations within the neural space are accompanied by auto-perturbations in the theater of the body which, in turn, may entail further auto-perturbations in neural space.

One of the remarkable properties of the brain, which is certainly essential in the richness of the phenomenology of subjectivity, is its ability to control and create the conditions of its own perturbation. For instance, no perturbation from the body can affect the brain unless the sensory interfaces are "open" to receive the appropriate signals. Sensory interfaces (or brain maps), involving excitatory-inhibitory mechanisms under the control of higher-order structures, work to channel, format, and modulate the gain of incoming signals. The activities related to the body are allowed to dominate the brain in certain contexts. This allows for an extraordinarily rich and varied orchestration of the process of auto-perturbation and resistance.

Intentionality, attention, and the functional hierarchy of resistance To understand further how such systemic "resistance" might have to do with subjectivity and feeling, the mechanism must be thought to possess more specificity than a general state of reactivity and tension of the organism in the framework of a somatosensing process, which is probably not sufficient to constitute a minimal awareness. It has to participate in phenomena that are known to be more specifically related to awareness, such as attention, for example.

We have suggested above that the process of resistance involves in fact, at least in higher organisms, bringing into play high levels of neurocognitive control, and conversely that bringing into play high levels of neurocognitive control involves such a resistance. We consider "attentional behaviors" as being at the center of the process of resistance to variance.[8] We suggest seeing attention itself as a mechanism of resistance to variance.

At a basic level, attentional behaviors can be seen as implementing an integrated dynamics of resistance to variance, as they constitute a "traffic bottleneck" in the flow of information. They require resisting distractors and maintaining unstable signal sources in focus. From a neurodynamical point of view, such a traffic bottleneck implies resisting the multiplicity and divergence of the multiple flows of electrochemical signals.

More precisely, attentional behaviors involve highly integrated neurodynamical processes and depend on the brain's ability to establish spontaneously, dynamically, and plastically specific functional relations between its neurocognitive resources and various "objects" that become the focus of processing. These functional relations can be described as occasions of transient coupling, which must be constantly readjusted because of perturbations or disengaged when they are no longer needed. The dynamics of these couplings allows continuous monitoring and spontaneous exploration of potential sources of information from the world or the body. It involves a variety of behaviors and mechanisms such as orientation of the neck and eyes, control of sensory information flow, memory triggering and recall, appraisal and motor preparation, inhibition of irrelevant overt behaviors or overt behaviors still under evaluation. The determination of these couplings also depends on the slow facilitating-dysfaciliating internal dynamics of motivation, related to physiological parameters and memory. The neuromodulatory systems (dopaminergic, noradrenergic, adrenergic, serotoninergic, histaminergic, cholinergic) at work along the ascending activating system and the large-scale feedback pathways that control them through the thalamo-cortical system notably, also contribute to the process, allowing a conflictive dynamics of integration between arousal and control of arousal and modulating the systemic degree of excitability.

Such an overall dynamics is highly structured. The actual integration and sequencing of the behaviors of coupling reflect the presence of an adaptive functional hierarchy within the system, dealing with the management of its priorities. Through the dynamical organization of these intentional and attentional relationships the system is imbued with agency and assumes a position in confrontation with the world and with itself.

A remarkable feature of the neural bases of attention vis-à-vis the organization of resistance to variance in the system must be emphasized. It is another example of how the brain builds the conditions of its own perturbation and at the same time resists it. Attention reflects the implementation of a fundamental biophysical conflictive setting of *controlled overexcitation*. On the one hand, when attention is increased, the potential of influence of incoming perturbations of interest is enhanced. This is directly visible in the enhancement of related brain signals. On the other, this situation of increased excitation requires precise strategies of control in order to maintain the overflow in adaptive limits. Such a dynamics contributes to the creation of an unavoidable situation of tension characterized by an effectively controlled overflow.

These behavioral and neurodynamical facts suggest an intrinsic relationship between intentionality, attention, and a general dynamics of resistance to variance. They make it tempting to think that resistance to variance is also at play at the integrated level of the organization of the attentional focus with its intentional and motivational background. We suggest that it might be as an integrated dynamics of resistance to variance that the implementation of such an attentional function is especially relevant to the issue of subjectivity.

A simple behavior, the orientation reaction, may help illustrate our thinking on this issue. The orientation reaction is the behavior of attentional and emotional orientation that we and most vertebrates show when an unexpected salient event occurs in the environment, such as a loud noise. Such an event could also be an internal salient event in our organism. The orientation reaction involves an unstable, transient, intentional focusing of neurocognitive, physiological, and behavioral resources. It creates a state of readiness. It is also a critical moment of decision and of prototypical emotion. Behaviorally, the organism is "awakened" and prepared for processing information in real time and in relation to a specific source. The "intentional" coupling with the specific source, internal or external, that transiently dominates perception is associated with an emotional evaluation of the meaning of the situation for survival and with a correlative motivation of behavior. The latter often leads, in animals, to overt actions of flight or attack, approach or avoidance. This elicitation of emotional responses, motivational impulses, and motor patterns, which are often mutually incompatible, enters into competition with inhibitory mechanisms that tend to control the overt response systems and delay overt action in order to let the system evaluate the situation further. These inhibitory mechanisms are often associated with an explicit behavioral freezing. During the process, an increase of internal tension is observed. This is expressed in increased vigilance, in electroencephalographic changes, and in the modulation of musculoskeletal and visceral tone. This tension explicitly involves a conflict between auto-perturbation and resistance. We see the orientation reaction as a prototypical behavior present, more or less obviously, in all conscious states.

4.4 Putative Aspects of the Psychodynamics of Feeling

Can we find a trace of the dynamical profile we are talking about in the fundamental features of subjective experience itself, beyond its prediction from the analysis of the concept of affect, in order to confirm in part the proposed relationship between conflict, resistance to variance, subjectivity and feeling? Some important and relevant features of subjectivity can be gleaned from analyzing aspects of the phenomenology of emotion.

General psychodynamical features Let us consider a human being in a situation of pure reflection—silent surroundings, immobility, eyes closed, inward concentration—during the few seconds that follow the processing of an emotionally competent thought. In such a situation the "system" may become maximally isolated from current overt interactions with the environment. Let us simply ask: "What makes this system the subject of an experience during this brief moment?" Its subjective experience is certainly causally grounded in the past events, but as a current experience it is localized and enfolded in time, the time it is actually having this experience, that is, an isolable *subjective sequence*. The consideration of the processes happening during such a subjective sequence should be sufficient for understanding why the system is imbued with subjectivity during this time.

As the emotion unfolds, what an external observer might notice at that time is that the system seems to *grapple with itself* intensely. For example, a tension subtle or not can be seen on the face, perhaps expressing pleasantness or unpleasantness; although seeming at first immobile, the posture is continually adjusted in an effort to maintain the equilibrium that would otherwise be lost as a result of gravity and of internally generated movements.

As suggested, looking inside the system, a neurophysiologist could see that a cascade of brain and physiological reactions jeopardizes the current equilibrium of the system, which is continuously and subtly adapting to its own internal movements in order to stand in spite of them and to resist.

From the subjective point of view, at a first generic level of description, the structure of the experience can be described as a dynamical process characterized by a punctuated flux of thoughts and feelings, including subtle transitions and discontinuities, in which the feeling of various components is emerging and reemerging from a preconscious ground. The experience is that of the constitution of pulsing salient "moments," localized in time but with a certain duration corresponding to a "lived present" (Varela 1999), happening within the apparent overall continuity of subjective experience during wakefulness.[9] This dynamics operates through subtle variations of vigilance and attentiveness and is perhaps accompanied by a motivational prereflexive mechanism that attempts to retain or anticipate new states.

Focusing in more detail on what characterizes the microphenomenology of one of these so-called moments, the "mental space" of the subject can be described as invaded by a feeling of joy or sorrow or fear, an affect through which cognitive resources such as attention are drained away from other objects and the ongoing flow of perception and reasoning is perturbed. The content of this feeling is hallmarked by the perception of bodily changes that transiently dominate the mental foreground, while the object that prompted the emotion recedes into the mental background. Suddenly, the degree of muscular tension, the amplitude of respiration, or the working of the heart transiently dominates the content of the perception, pleasantly or unpleasantly as the case may be. In other words, there is a divergence away from the current conscious or unconscious intentional state due to a transient disequilibrium. This captures our attention and focuses it on a pervasive source of information, the body.

There is a strong and essential dimension of constraint in this dynamics. An important feature of the experience is that the now dominant sensations impede our efforts to concentrate on other objects, even if we try to do so; a significant effort must be made in order to suppress these sensations.[10] It is as if we were captured in a pervasive dynamics and submitted to an actual force or pressure. It might also be remarked in other contexts that if we wish to maintain a coupling between attention and a given pattern of sensory perturbation whose strength is fading, we must suppress competitive perturbations. And we usually feel these perturbations during our effort to resist them until suppression is achieved. As everyone has experienced in situations of extreme stress or anxiety, intense pain or even pleasure, it may happen that the more we try to escape and resist the invasion of sensations, the more they become intense: tension and the intensity and saliency of feelings may be correlated.[11]

It appears to us that in all of these instances, there is a correlative interplay between a flow of incoming changes and something that attempts to control them: a *tension* is created between *variance*, the changes imposed by alternative sources of "information," and a more or less explicit *resistance*, the implicit control that something in us spontaneously exerts on them as they start dominating our attentional scope. Thus, with all the caution that must be taken concerning the validity of such phenomenological descriptions, the dynamics of resistance to variance seems to be at the heart of our actual affects from a purely subjective standpoint.

Presence of the pattern in basic emotions? The dimension of conflict between variance and resistance to variance is rather easily noticeable at the root of unpleasant emotional feelings such as fear, disgust, and anger. These emotional behaviors are characterized from a subjective point of view by a strong state of tension that literally overcomes us, including a high level of conflict between the urge to enact certain behaviors (e.g., flying, vomiting, or fighting), the various visceral sensations that accompany the emotional upheaval, and the inhibition of these actual behaviors, an inhibition that is always close to spinning out of control. They also include highly conflictive cognitive and attentional patterns, generally associated with pain or pleasure, with the anticipation of distress or relief, and related to an ongoing appraisal process.

In sadness also, it appears to us that there is a dimension of resistance to overwhelming perturbations related to body sensations. We invite the reader to consider that the moments of sadness may be more intense when the tendency to cry is resisted than when crying itself is enacted. Very intense moments of distress also occur when anguish is faced frontally. This rather obviously involves the attempt to exert a certain cognitive control on a growing sensory perturbation and leads to a strong feeling of tension.

We think that it is reasonable to suggest that tension, auto-perturbation, and resistance clearly operate, from a subjective point of view, in all of these unpleasant emotions. From an objective point of view, these emotional responses involve bodily and attentional auto-perturbations, acting on the system at varied psychophysiological and cognitive levels, as well as monitoring and control, related to the analysis of the significance of these perturbations, and keeping them within certain physiological limits. The behavioral control is involved in particular in delaying overt behaviors, such as flight or fight. Such a process can directly be seen as a component of resistance to behavioral enaction. Action tendency has been considered an important part of the content of emotional feelings for a long time (Arnold 1960).[12]

For pleasant emotions, the generative relation between resistance to variance and feeling might at first appear less obvious, although we believe it also holds. In a paradigmatic example, the case of sexual pleasure, it is apparent that a most intense moment of feeling coincides with the greatest conflict between overwhelming sensory influx and whole body tension. Feelings of joy also incorporate intensified bodily sensations that invade the scope of our attention and incorporate facial expressions that transform our facial mask and accordingly its sensory representation. Although joy often presents itself as a decrease of certain types of unpleasant tension, still it causes tensions that capture our attentional resources and involve bodily perturbations. It too possesses an aspect of confrontation between internal changes and integrated monitoring as well as control strategies. The dimension of resistance to its overwhelming power becomes more explicit as joy morphs into ecstasy.

A careful examination of weak and harmonious feelings also shows us that a dimension of conflictive dynamics between variance and resistance is at least implicitly present. The sensation of well-being that can occur at rest in a quiet environment incorporates pleasant bodily sensations whose perturbing power is small. Their perturbing power is easily controlled and mastered, and this possibly accounts for part of their pleasantness. The point remains, however, that those "sensations" are felt when some attention is paid to them, that is to say, when a certain degree of monitoring, however slight, is exerted on them. Again, such monitoring involves arousal and control and implies necessarily an increase of resistance to variance. Considering these facts, we suggest the possibility that we *begin* to feel when physiological changes, such as muscular tension, and their sensory impact *begin* to be resisted as they reach a certain threshold.

5 Hypotheses

5.1 Formulation of the Main Hypothesis

The dynamical properties implied by the notion of affect, the actual dynamics of resistance to variance at the core of our organism and of the brain's operation, along with the presence of such a dynamics in the organization of our attentional focus, which involves central phenomena of controlled overexcitation, its presence in emotional behaviors, in addition to general considerations about the importance of monitoring and control in consciousness, and the consideration of certain aspects of the phenomenology of feeling have lead us to formulate the following hypothesis: *feeling is a process of resistance to variance*. This hypothesis can be decomposed as follows.

1. The ability to feel arises from the objective mechanics of the system as it grapples with its own recurrent, delayed auto-perturbations in the brain and body (such as those accompanying an emotional reaction, divergent motivational tendencies, attentional shifts, self-generated modulations of excitability, and biomechanical constraints).

2. Feeling and thus subjectivity result directly from the fact that sensorimotor changes and constraints occurring in the grappling process are resisted by the system in order to preserve its integrity and the efficiency of its current operation.

3. Forms of cognitive monitoring and control, such as attention, play a major role in the resistance to variance.

4. Feeling and thus subjectivity occur when a state of tension develops during coupling between attentional processes and auto-perturbation: the attentional process causes a conflictive dynamics of controlled overexcitation, involving an enhancement of both variance and resistance to sensorimotor auto-perturbations and biological impediments related to bodily and cognitive constraints. In other words, "to feel" is what emerges when the monitoring and control of sources of information are sustainedly operated

on by the system vis-à-vis the functional self-perturbations that these sources of information generate.

5. Feeling and thus subjectivity not only occur during resistance to variance but *are* themselves this process.

6. Being a "feeling subject" consists of being a physical system engaged in an activity of monitoring and control characterized by a conflictive process of resistance to variance in the context of ongoing sensorimotor disequilibria.

To conclude, we propose that the highly diversified self-organizing resistance to variance that humans oppose to their own propagating functional transformations is precisely what constitutes the subject of the experience. This process, in the context of the ebb and flow of the system's internal dynamics, makes the system confront itself intensely and in a focused way.

Taking the example of emotions, we envision that an emotional state implemented in the body is mapped in somatosensing brain regions. The impact of this somatosensory response on connected regions of the brain triggers compensatory reactions giving rise to a transient occasion of conflict between attempts at control focusing on specific channels and sensorimotor perturbations. The inertia of the system and the instability of its equilibrium involve a great deal of tension in the process. This is visible in the increase of its arousal. Its attentional resources become saturated, and the operation of the system is partly captured in cycles of resistance to variance aimed at restoring equilibrium. This dynamical state of grappling with specific somatosensory perturbations in relation to an emotional upheaval, in the context of controlled overexcitation states, constitutes the feeling subject.

In fact, because the conflict is ongoing and because the viable control of perturbations requires anticipatory strategies, the compensatory reactions begin, at least in part, before the actual perturbations do.

Any felt state might be grounded on this generic conflict, and this would be true for pleasant as well as unpleasant feelings, for strong as well as weak feelings, and for simple background feelings such as enthusiasm or discouragement or the plain feeling of being. More generally, it would be true for feelings related to motor actions and cognitive effort, and could even extend to perception in general, which can be seen as a more or less progressive phenomenon of the enslavement of our internal activity by an emerging structure, that is, the form or the object we are perceiving. This theory predicts that every subjective experience, negative or positive, rough or smooth, entails a form of conflict between some transformation in the organism, including the brain, and something else in the brain-body system that resists it.

The differentiation among felt states would thus depend on the spatial and temporal orchestration of the emotive and bodily changes and of the ensuing resistance. In other words, the affective "content" of a given feeling would be generated from the specific patterns of action and reaction that occur during a certain process of resistance to variance or of resistance to invariance. In the emotion, for example, the patterns generated in fear, anger, or joy, would be different. At some point, the specific structure and rhythm of our field of transformations and reactions, the modalities of self-grappling and resistance to variance or invariance, should fit the phenomenology of our experience and be sufficient to define what we experience from within. This is what an experimental approach should attempt to demonstrate.

Although very general and with obvious limitations, this working hypothesis has some functional and phenomenological plausibility and opens the way for other specific anatomo-functional hypotheses.

5.2 Neuroanatomical Hypotheses: The Neuroanatomy behind the Conflict

In this framework, a general picture of the functional neuroanatomy and neurodynamics of emotion and feeling begins to appear. It involves several levels of integration, from the triggering of emotional responses by limbic structures to the representation of aspects of the emotional upheaval in somatosensory structures and to the active response of the system to its own perturbed state from attentional and executive structures.

General neurophysiological disclaimer The functional nodes that are critically involved in creating an integrated front of resistance to variance cannot be reduced to a single part of the brain or even to a collection of brain regions. In normal conditions, the conflict occurs also in the theater of the body proper, in musculoskeletal striated and visceral smooth muscles, and in the endocrine system. In this framework, the autonomic nervous system features a conflictive dynamics between sympathetic and parasympathetic control, modulated by the central nervous system, which is the highest station in the organism devoted to compensating and anticipating autoperturbations. As such, the brain represents in itself a critical node in the process. In addition to its hypothalamic and brainstem homeostatic regulation subsystems, it possesses highly plastic and powerful associative properties, which make it a natural producer of adaptive autonomy. The brain attempts to control what affects it, both at the local level of convergent integration and at the global level of distributed, large-scale integration. It does so by means of highly complex interactions and embedded rhythms that maintain its functional coherence and can create an integrated front of resistance at the distributed and "top-down" levels of its attentional behaviors and control of executive functions.

Critical neuroanatomical nodes Specific anatomo-functional hypotheses can be formulated according to the type of dynamics of resistance to variance we see at the basis of subjectivity and feeling. Critical nodes regarding the process of auto-perturbation and variance monitoring include somatosensing regions in the brainstem (e.g., the nucleus tractus solitarius and the parabrachial nucleus), the hypothalamus, the cingulate cortex, and the somatosensory cortices (the insula, SII, SI, Brodmann area 5), as well as arousing-activating systems such as reticular formation nuclei, which modulate the system's excitability. Regarding resistance and control, the structures essential for the control of perturbations include, at the lower levels, the periaqueducal gray, the reticular nuclei, parts of the thalamus (e.g., anterior and intralaminar nuclei), and the hypothalamus; at a higher level, the frontal cortices, in particular the anterior cingulate cortex (ACC). As motivational and attentional structures, the basal ganglia and amygdala are certainly important as well.

Elements of validation and discussion Most of these structures are also known as essential for emotion and consciousness. The structures that we see as involved in somatosensory related variance, in arousal activation, and in the control of resistance, are highly interconnected and interactive (Mesulam and Mufson 1982a,b; Mufson and Mesulam 1982; Friedman et al. 1986; Vogt and Pandya 1987). The process of feeling pain is correlated with simultaneous involvement of the ACC and somatosensory regions such as the anterior insula, SI and SII (Jones et al. 1991; Talbot et al. 1991; Coghill et al. 1994; Rainville et al. 1997). The activity of the ACC, amygdala, and insula appears to be modulated by task manipulations that increase demand on the processing of interoceptive representations (Critchley et al. 2002). Recently, it has been demonstrated that the activity in ACC, insula, and somatosensory cortices can reflect the level of sympathetic arousal, and that the role of ACC in the generation of bodily states of autonomic arousal is more pronounced when external information conflicts with internal states (Critchley et al. 2002). The coactivation of the ACC and somatosensing regions during the process of feeling is relevant to our argument. In both exercise and mental stress tasks, increased rCBF in cerebellar vermis, right anterior cingulate, and right insula covaried with the mean arterial blood pressure (Critchley et al. 2000).

In the hierarchy of this system, the ACC occupies a central place and its functions are particularly relevant for our proposal. The ACC is located on the medial wall of the frontal lobe. It is known to play an essential role in attentional, motivational, and emotional control (see Bush, Luu, and Posner 2000). It is crucial for tasks involving mental effort (in effortful tasks there is a correlation between ACC activation and the difficulty of the task) and appears to be a key structure for conflict monitoring and awareness (see Mayr 2004). In neurological patients, lesions of the ACC cause apathy, inattention, dysregulation of autonomic functions, emotional instability, and impairment of the sense of self (see Damasio 1994, 1999).

The ACC appeared strongly activated in PET during inner intentional concentration on internal emotional feelings (Reiman et al. 1997), and its activity was positively correlated with interindividual differences in the degree of complexity of emotional experience, suggesting an interaction between emotion and attention in this structure (Lane et al. 1997; Lane et al. 1998). Correlation of the activity of the ACC with sexual arousal has been observed in PET (Stoleru et al. 1999; Redoute et al. 2000) as well as with pleasant and painful tactile information (Rolls et al. 2003). Lesions of the ACC have also been reported to alter the "suffering" aspect of pain (Foltz and White 1962; Hurt and Ballantine 1974); and the ACC also showed increased activity in anticipation of pain (Sawamoto et al. 2000). The ACC appeared strongly involved in emotional self-regulation in a task requiring the voluntary repression of emotions in fMRI (Beauregard, Levesque, and Bourgouin 2001). The ACC (dorsal part) supports the generation of autonomic states of cardiovascular arousal during effortful cognitive and motor behavior (Critchley et al. 2003).

Our framework might provide some clues as to why the anterior cingulate appears as a fundamental structure for both feeling, attention, and awareness, on the one hand, and for effortful monitoring, and control of conflicts on the other. There is a large literature about the role of the anterior cingulate in conflict monitoring and awareness (see Mayr 2004). Beyond the empirical findings, the usual explanation for the role of the cingulate in both conflict monitoring and awareness is of a functionalist type, compatible with our framework but adopting a completely different point of view (Dehaene et al. 2003). In this approach, consciousness is considered through its putative information processing related function: when simple automatic decisions cannot be made in the framework of a complex world with potentially conflictive information, more controlled operations must be brought into play in order to generate adequate decisions. Such a requirement justifies the emergence of consciousness in relation to evolution. Consciousness is then hypothesized as the cognitive instance specialized in solving such informational conflicts. In order to support this idea it is important to demonstrate that executive conflict resolution requires conflict awareness and that there are brain structures responding only when coping with executive conflict implies some degree of awareness. It has indeed been recently supported, comparing neural responses to conflict elicited through either visible or subliminal primes, that consciousness of conflict is a necessary boundary condition for the ACC-related control network to come into play, and that intact control in response to conscious conflict requires an intact ACC-prefrontal network (Dehaene et al. 2003).

On this model, the relationship between conflict, control, and awareness is purely functional, and somehow abstract: "awareness" is called for if conflict, requiring high-level control, overcomes the ability of more automatic systems to cope with a given situation. As largely developed in previous sections, we see such a relationship in a more concrete and causal way in trying to account for phenomenological aspects of subjective experience: being a feeling subject is seen as a steady-state of conflict between sources of variance and motivational resistance, notably operating at the level of the attentional focus, so that structures involved in conflict monitoring and control are expected to participate in such a dynamics. In other words, this might explain why the ACC is involved in awareness as a level of subjective experience.

5.3 A Principle of Interaction?

The proposed relationship between feeling and a process of resistance to variance suggests that the state of tension that, according to us, defines the intensity of the subjective experience, might be governed by a possible principle of interaction between the level of resistance and the intensity of variance.

Our framework predicts that the intensity of feeling should reflect the level of conflict between perturbations and strategies of control. In other words, the intensity of a feeling must be a function of the interaction between the strength of the perturbations and the strength of the resistance that the system must oppose to them in order to continue carrying on another task or simply maintaining equilibrium. To a first approximation, it might be that feeling intensity or tension V could be a simple function of the resistance R and the perturbation influx I, such as $V = RI$. Such a formula, which amusingly reminds us of a famous law of electricity, must obviously only be seen as a simple and limited heuristic tool.

At first glance this relation may appear paradoxical, considering that resistance certainly involves the recruitment of inhibitory processes and/or the recruitment of behaviors opposing perturbations in the system. In effect, this setting might lead to the prediction that reducing the intensity of perturbations by increasing the resistance (which would inhibit the former), that is, cancelling the perturbations, would increase the intensity of feeling! Such a prediction would be paradoxical. But it must be noted that according to the suggested relation, feeling occurs only when neither of the two terms R and I are null. Feeling occurs during the operation of compensation, when no complete suppression or cancellation has been achieved. Moreover, it must be noted that the relation $V = RI$ does not say anything about the functional relationships between R and I, which could involve, in certain circumstances, feedback loops that create the conditions for "explosive" situations, such as the kind of controlled overexcitatiton we referred to several times in this essay. Moreover, in a cognitive perspective, we must insist, the perturbations are information, so that, from an adaptive standpoint, the system should not "wish" to neutralize them completely. The system should simply maintain the perturbations under control—the steady-state that we see as characteristic of vigilance. Accordingly, most of the time, what is achieved during cognitive processes is a steady state of controlled overexcitation, such that V is not 0, but stays within reasonable and adaptive limits compatible, for instance, with recognition or learning processes. According to our hypotheses, the interval during which such a dynamical tension V occurs is the interval during which one becomes a feeling subject. If we interpret the tension V as directly related to a term of energy, this predicts that the intensity of feeling is directly proportional to the increase of expenditure of energy in the system that is related to such a conflictive dynamics between R and I. At a first level of approximation, this relationship seems to be true: there is a linear relationship between subjective arousal (i.e., feeling intensity) and the magnitude of related evoked potentials in EEG (Bradley and Lang 2000). Many of the functional brain-imaging studies mentioned in the previous section demonstrated linear relationships between the intensity of emotional experience and the levels of activation in the region of interest.

6 Interpretative Frame

6.1 Size Matters

To be applicable, our hypothesis presupposes certain general and specific conditions in entities capable of feeling. Indeed, we are not suggesting that the generic and abstract scheme of resistance to variance alone is sufficient. It becomes sufficient when certain structural and dynamical parameters are implemented.

Thus the general mechanism of resistance to variance must be considered in the frame of its specific embodied morphodynamic properties, drawing on a particular biophysical phenomenology, for example, the rich and varied repertory of emotional behaviors. It is the phenomenology of the resistance to variance that makes the phenomenology of the subjective experience, and the phenomenology of the resistance to variance is totally dependent upon the biological phenomenology of the system. We feel emotions as such because, as a biological dynamical system, we resist particular embodied transformations in a specific way that is not reducible to a generic and abstract scheme, although this scheme is always present and considered by us as what enables subjectivity. Thus entities with the ability to feel must present certain features.

First, feeling entities must be capable of certain kinds of behaviors, namely intentional and emotional behaviors, that is, behaviors through which they connect with objects and situations in the internal or external environment and that involve regulatory reactions related to the maintenance of the condition of viability of the entity.

Second, feeling entities must have a certain size and a certain degree of complexity. Small sizes are not compatible with the sort of delayed auto-perturbative processes we envision. Size is correlated with complexity of internal structure and with multicomponentiality. Drawing upon the heuristic relation we proposed in the previous section, specific predictions can be made about systems such as higher animals with increased complexity in processing and increased inertia due to the distributed mass processing of bigger brain systems and organisms. In such systems, the time constants of the triggering and operation of R (the process of resistance), as well as the inertia of I (the auto-perturbation influx), must be considered as much more important than in simpler systems. Consequently, V (the tension at the root of feeling) cannot be reduced instantaneously, predicting a more likely development of feeling in such systems.

Third, a complex, multicomponential nervous system is another condition, one that is required for the management of size, structural complexity, and behavioral complexity.

Some specific conditions of the nervous system also must be met, namely, the presence of neural sheaths, capable of mapping sensory and motor events and allowing for functional discrimination and binding of signals, as well as sophisticated bioregulatory and motor systems.

6.2 The Meaning of Control in the Theory

We want to make clear that our approach departs from a classical general information processing framework in dealing with problems of control, such as theory of control, which uses concepts such as "efference copy" and "feedback" to account for error minimization in servomechanisms. We believe that such classical cybernetic models do not address the brain and body dynamic features we regard as essential for the emergence of subjectivity and feeling. Those features are absent in classical control models and are related to the specificity of biological systems. Instead, we are interested in the phenomenological consequences of divergence and control of divergence in highly chaotic, sparse, parallel, interconnected, and highly excitable real biological systems. Otherwise, we do not mean to say that classical control mechanisms and noise reduction operations cannot be implemented in the brain. But they do have to face the slowness, inertia, and inefficiency of biological systems, and their highly conflictive dynamics, all of which lead to delayed periods of decision for perception or action, mistakes, "improvisations," and the sort of disequilibria of which emotions are an example. What we wish to stress is that the brain appears unable to "filter error," anticipate deviations, and control them in an optimal manner. Our notion of control, then, is based on different considerations from those of models that assume the existence of optimal solutions. What we stress is the concrete physical problem that a system that operates close to overflow must face.[13] However, we are not using the concepts of "conflict" and "resistance," with a negative connotation, to imply dysfunction; conflict and resistance are an integrated part of the organism's condition and represent physiological and informational aspects of its behavior.

6.3 The Unexplained Phenomenology

Our hypothesis has an important limitation in its ability to account for subjective experience. There is a striking phenomenon at the core of our subjective experience that it cannot explain directly but which is fundamental. There is indeed an intrinsic "spatialization" of our subjectivity space. We feel in a projective way. The feeling of our own body is a feeling of a body in space, with interoceptive and proprioceptive sensations grossly localized, in our extremities and our face, for instance, as perceptions of exteroceptive objects are localized in space (see Ramachandran and Blakeslee 1998). Phenomenologically, in normal conditions, the "origin" of the subjective point of view itself feels located or concentrated in our head and perhaps along the main vertical axis of our body. There is really an auto-perceptive structure, in which a subjective point of view confronts a set of body states, including itself, in a concrete geometrical space. Such a spatialization is part of its fundamental representational character.

In our view, this spatial structure is more difficult to account for than the temporal dynamics that characterize the phenomenology of subjective experience. The temporal dynamics can be more easily assimilated, from a theoretical point of view, to the objective temporal dynamics of the system itself, in an isomorphic framework. The spatialization of subjective experience is a supramodal phenomenon and is partially independent from our current interaction with the environment. When we close our eyes in a silent room and stop moving we can feel it. There is something "virtual" in such a space that a satisfactory theory of consciousness should explain. We believe that it might be perfectly compatible with our framework but requires supplementary developments.

7   Conclusion

Considering objective biological and neurodynamical aspects of being, emoting, and feeling, we have isolated a type of mechanism, actually implemented in our organism, that might explain "what" we precisely feel and why we feel, in other words, why we are sentient entities, capable of being subjects of sensory experiences, in particular of sensory experiences of ourselves; in brief, why there is something that it is like to be a physical system of our class. The class of physical systems and biological entities we belong to is characterized by the self-organized endeavor of an internal dynamical structure of resistance to variance, grappling with delayed auto-perturbing patterns happening at many spatial and temporal scales of its organization. This internal dynamics of resistance develops in a complex hierarchy of reactions, emerging not only at basic levels of biological regulation and in the system's coping with affective reactions, but also at the level of its attentional and intentional behaviors, rooted in the history and personality of the system. The focused confrontation between resistance and variance in the system creates an intensive internal state of controlled overexcitation that constitutes the biophysical basis of vigilance and arousal, and relates to a neurocognitive function of integration, monitoring, and control. Such a systemic tension is dynamically coupled with various sources of sensorimotor constraints through functional connectivity, in particular somatic influences, that constitute the morphodynamical substrate of what happens to be the sensory contents of the subjective experience of the system. We believe that such an affective and behavioral dynamics is the key to understanding the relationship between the subjectively lived body and its counterpart, the objective living body.[14] Through its internal grappling with the ebb and flow of its own delayed auto-perturbative functional transformations and biomechanical constraints, which result from attentional, affective, and motivational distributed processes, such a physical, organizationally closed, intentional machine is affected and *confronts itself*, literally and not only metaphorically. We believe that subjectivity and feeling might be the phenomenology of the mutual pressure that the auto-perturbative constraints and the process of resistance exert on each other. The remaining difference between the private internal subjective state and this objective biomechanical description of spatial and temporal patterns might be in great part a matter of point of view, of being or not being.[15]

Notes

1. Emotions can be described as more or less stereotyped neurocognitive and physiological reactions triggered and controlled by several integrated brain devices, including neural systems operating the appraisal of interoceptive and exteroceptive competent "stimuli" (at a basic level, the emotional competence of a stimulus can be related to basic biological concerns and the memory of previous experiences associated with reward and punishment). Integrator nuclei and regions such as the amygdala and the orbitofrontal-ventromedial complex in the limbic frontal cortex (see Bechara, Damasio, and Damasio 2000; Rolls 2000; O'Doherty et al. 2001) play a critical role in such mechanisms. They receive massive convergent multimodal influences from the brain and the body, integrating high-level as well as low-level information, and influence the brain and the body in return through massive divergent projections able to provoke an upheaval of their whole physiology. They modulate central arousal by influencing the reticular formation that exerts a neuromodulatory control on the thalamo-cortical tonus; modulate sensory attention, by acting on specific cortical sensory pathways, in particular visual and auditory, thanks to feedback connections; modulate motivation by their interactions with the anterior cingulate cortex and its premotor projections, as well as by the control of peripheral reactions, in particular the visceral and musculoskeletal tonus, through the indirect modulation of autonomous and hormonal functions via the reticular formation and the hypothalamus; and select integrated behavioral repertoires by controlling the basal ganglia and the periaqueducal gray (for a review see Rolls 2000). In addition, these systems modulate, directly and indirectly, learning and memory, through relatively well-known mechanisms and pathways.

2. As it will appear below, we do not mean that central neurocognitive patterns are not essential in the constitution of feeling and subjectivity, on the contrary.

3. The complexity of biological systems leads classically to general descriptions of functional relations that may miss many aspects of the precise structure and dynamics

of the system being considered. This is often the case in cognitive neuroscience in which we propose abstract functional constructs such as memory, attention, language, perception, emotion, decision, executive functions, etc. To deal with such complexity at a level of description abstract enough to preserve relevant aspects of the phenomenology of the system as a physical system, it might be useful, in a heuristic although limited perspective, to describe the individual as a morphodynamical system, i.e., as a general anisotropic field of transformations, structured by a complex and highly recursive architecture, defining functional relations that constrain the possibility of "deformations" of the system.

4. It is essential to keep in mind that a great deal of what we are, as psychological as well as biological systems, is nonconscious. Our cognitive as well as sensorimotor acts, the logic of our behavior and mind, are dominated by unconscious structures, sensorimotor schemes, logical constraints, and silent biological self-regulatory processes that contribute to the complexity of our organism's activities.

5. A comparable situation of coupling between perturbation and compensation can be found in the inorganic world as expressed in Le Chatelier's principle of chemical equilibrium.

6. The distinction remains however important from a phenomenological point of view.

7. Cognition acts on the overall system according to the homeostatic principle presented in the previous section. When we define cognition as a level of integration that regulates the organism's expectations about the world and determines its actions through motivation, selective attention, learning, and planning, it appears that cognition is an extension of homeostatic strategies capable of permitting an organism to remain in survivable equilibrium within an environment too complex to be managed only by innate automated responses.

8. Attentional behaviors constitute a central aspect of cognition that is highly developed in superior organisms, correlates with the degree of cephalization, and participates in the general functions of monitoring, orientation, and behavioral control.

9. In a similar direction, Damasio (1999) has proposed considering the core self as a continuous process of the building and rebuilding of body representations that "pulse" in the system.

10. Emotions certainly should not be understood only as impediments to engaged cognition, since they can also have a positive cognitive impact, e.g., their participation in decision making (see Damasio 1994) and the adaptive reinforcement of action (see Rolls 2000). However, feelings are generally lived as salient *breakdowns* or *transitions*, concerning us by saliently *impeding* or *facilitating* ongoing implicit or explicit cognitive processes. The transitions produce a self-concern in which the constraints of the body appearing as corporeal sensations interfere with other ongoing cognitive

mechanisms or behavioral tendencies. Usually, the phenomenology of feelings includes diffuse corporeal impressions overwhelming us more or less softly. This is evident in anxiety in which somatic sensations impede our cognition, but it is also present in any pleasure that invades us.

11. Wundt (1924) originally distinguished three dimensions in feeling: pleasant–unpleasant, tension–relaxation, excitement–calm. It might be considered that phenomenologically, notions such as pleasure–displeasure, tension–relaxation, excitement–calm, engagement–disengagement, although missing a great deal of the subtlety and complexity of emotions and feelings, encompass a fundamental aspect of the subjective experience of emotions, and subjective experience in general. They might even constitute altogether the elementary core of the ability to feel, something that might be necessary and sufficient in order to consider a system to be imbued with some degree of subjectivity. Russell introduced the notion of "core affect": "A neurophysiological state that is consciously accessible as a simple, nonreflective feeling that is an integral blend of hedonic (pleasure–displeasure) and arousal (sleepy–activated) values" (Russell 2003). Damasio's idea about core consciousness might also be interpreted in such a framework (Damasio 1999, 2003). In French, it would be called *l'éprouvé*.

12. These emotions can also be very strong during some of the explicit behaviors they are related to, and this could seem to contradict the idea that resistance to enacting explicit behaviors is essential in feeling. Fear, for instance, can be very strong during flight, and resistance to flight is not always adaptive. In fact, feeling fear is perfectly compatible with flight in our framework. The idea of resistance implies that the source of perturbation is operating at a premotor or motor level. During flight there is generally still a tension pushing the system toward its limits. Such tension implies control in order to avoid a total disorganization of behavior. Also fear includes a strong component of autonomic responses in part based on the simulation of the outcome of the possible behavioral choices. This keeps operating as a strong source of perturbations during flight, and can even play an important role in its ongoing motivation.

13. Our theoretical developments bring to the fore the importance of biological embodiment for the emergence of a subjective experience, in the context of a system implementing a general self-referential organization. Our theory suggests in a meaningful way that embodiment is a necessary condition for the general mechanism to be a sufficient condition for feeling. In this perspective, we stress the importance of actual physical boundaries and limits and the presence of inertia in the system in the making of subjective experience. What confers on the system its subjective properties is a coupling of abstract schemes such as self-referential schemes with the actual physical limits of an embodied dynamics. Such limit conditions preserve the generic properties of these self-referential schemes but solve certain problems of infinity that appear when such self-referential schemes are considered as formal logical constraints only. This idea is greatly developed in Kenneth Williford's paper in this book. Similar

considerations and a deep and striking discussion of the logical constraints implied by such self-referential situations is proposed in Douglas Hofstadter's paper in this book.

14. This distinction, inspired by phenomenology, between the "lived body" and the "living body" has been introduced by Evan Thompson (personal communication).

15. We want to thank Francisco Varela, inspiring mentor and colleague, who read in detail and discussed at length the first formulation of this theory a long time ago, finally concluding that it was "a good reductionist theory"; Kenneth Williford, for his titanic help on this long text as an editor and a thinker; Evan Thompson, for all the fruitful and illuminating discussions we had together throughout the multiple versions of the paper; Jean Petitot, Patricia Churchland, Ralph Adolphs, and Paul Bourgine, for their helpful reading of different versions of the text.

This work has been supported by a grant from the Mathers Foundation to Antonio Damasio.

What Is It Like to Be a Strange Loop?

Douglas R. Hofstadter

Introduction

The ideas in this essay are similar to ideas I have expressed in previous writings—in *Gödel, Escher, Bach*, in the passages I contributed to *The Mind's I*, in "Who Shoves Whom Around Inside the Careenium?," and in passages in *Le Ton beau de Marot*. These ideas began to form when I was a teenager and have slowly gelled over time. Their essence has not substantially changed, but they have gradually matured and stabilized. I welcome this opportunity to re-express these thoughts for a primarily philosophical audience.

Soul-Shards

A couple of months after my father died, I was standing in the kitchen of my parents' house, and my mother, looking at a very touching photograph of my father taken perhaps fifteen years earlier, stated, with a sense of desperation, "What meaning does that photograph have? None at all. It is just a piece of paper, nothing but a piece of paper with some dark spots on it here and there. It is useless." The bleakness of this remark set my head spinning because I knew instinctively that I disagreed, but I did not quite know how to express to my mother the way I felt the photograph should be considered.

After a few minutes of intense pondering, I hit upon an analogy that I felt could convey my point of view, and perhaps lend her at least some consolation. What I said to her was along these lines. "In the living room we have a book of the Chopin études for piano. All of its pages are just pieces of paper with marks on them, just as two-dimensional and foldable as the photograph of Dad—and yet, think of the power that they have exerted on people all over the world for 150 years now. Thanks to those black marks on those flat sheets, thousands of people have collectively spent millions of hours moving their fingers over the keyboards of pianos in certain complicated patterns, producing sounds that give them indescribable pleasure and a sense of intense meaningfulness. Those pianists in turn have conveyed to millions of listeners, including you and me, the powerful emotions that churned in Chopin's heart, and have thereby afforded all of us some partial access to Chopin's interiority, to the experience of living in the head or, rather, soul, of Chopin. Those marks on those sheets of paper are no less than soul-shards—remnants of the shattered soul of Frédéric Chopin. Each of those particular patterns of marks on paper has a unique power to bring back to life, inside our brains, some small fragment of the internal experiences of another human being, and we thereby know, at least in part, what it was like to be him, and we feel intense love for him. In no less intense a fashion, seeing that photograph of Dad brings back, to those who knew him intimately, the clearest memory of his smile and his gentleness, makes little fragments of his soul dance again, but in the new medium of brains other than his own. Like the score to a Chopin étude, that photograph constitutes a soul-shard of someone departed, and it is therefore to be enormously cherished for as long as we live."

This is very close to what I said to my mother. I don't know what effect it had on her feelings about the picture, but that photo is still there.

Drawing a Line Somewhere

One day, when I was twenty-one, I read a short story called "Pig" by Roald Dahl (based on the bizarre premise of people touring a slaughterhouse), and that powerful experience, combined with the fact that at almost the same time I was invited to partake in a banquet in Sardinia in which a roasted piglet was to be sliced apart in front of everyone's delighted eyes, resulted in my giving up eating meat of any sort. A few years later, however, I found the pressures of daily life so strong that I gave up on my vegetarianism. There were further oscillations, but finally I settled down into a stable state of eating chicken and fish but no mammals. This was a compromise representing my intuition that there are "souls of different sizes," and my vague willingness to accept the idea that some of those souls, provided they were "small enough," could be sacrificed for the sake of the desires of "larger" souls, such as mine and those of other human beings, though drawing the dividing line at mammals was clearly somewhat arbitrary. (See figure 19.1)

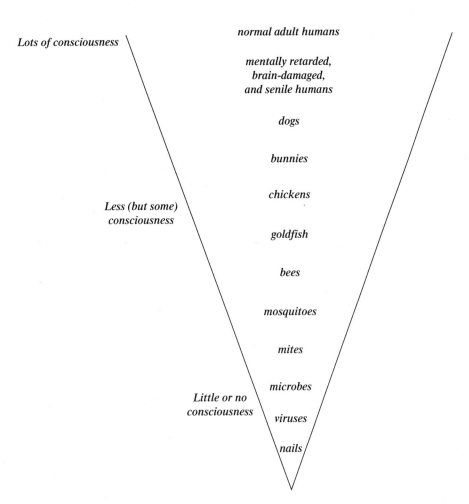

Figure 19.1
Cone 1, descending from humans all the way down to nails at the tip.

Give Me Some Stouter-Souled Men

In my teens and twenties, I was playing a lot of Chopin, often out of editions published by Schirmer. In each of those volumes there was a preface written in the early 1900s by the American critic James Huneker, whose very romantic prose exerted a strong influence on me. In one passage that I have never forgotten, Huneker asserts of Chopin's Étude op. 25 no. 11 the following striking thought: "Small-souled men, no matter how agile their fingers, should not attempt it."

I can attest to the difficulty of this powerful piece of music, but its technical difficulty is not what Huneker was referring to. To get across a sense for the étude's majesty, Huneker suggests a "scale of sizes" of human souls, inferring that some people are not up to playing this piece because their souls are not "large enough." Although this sounds blasphemous, I wonder if we don't all secretly believe in the validity of something like the idea of "small-souled" and "large-souled" humans.

The Gradual Growth of a Soul

I reject the notion that a full-fledged human soul comes into being the moment that a sperm joins an ovum to form a human zygote. I believe that a human soul comes slowly into being over the course of years of development. I would like to suggest, at least metaphorically, a numerical scale of "degrees of souledness." We can imagine it as running from 0 to 100, and the units of this scale can be called, just for fun, "hunekers." Thus you and I both have roughly 100 hunekers of souledness.

The cone shown in figure 19.2 gives a crude but vivid sense of how I might attach huneker values to human beings of different ages (or to one human being at different stages). I would argue, echoing Huneker, that "souledness" is not a discrete variable having just two possible values, but is rather a shaded, blurry numerical variable that ranges continuously across different species and varieties of object, and that, within a given object, can rise or fall over time as a result of the growth or the decay of certain internal patterns. I also believe that most people's largely unconscious prejudices about whether to eat or not to eat this or that food, whether to swat or not to swat this or that insect, whether to root or not to root for this or that species of robot in a sci-fi film, and so on, reflect precisely this kind of continuum in their minds.

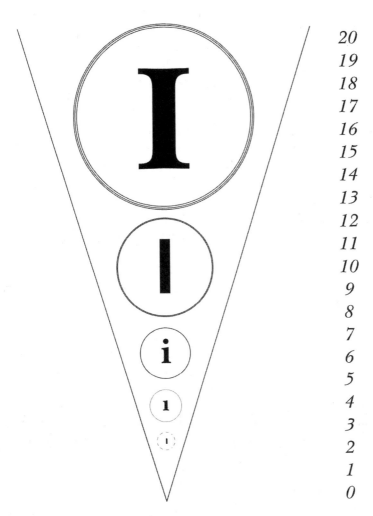

Figure 19.2
Cone 2, rising from neonates all the way up to adults.

What Is a "Brain Structure"?

But what could possibly be the nature of the elusive brain structure that gives rise to this "I" or soul? Well, first, just what is a "brain structure"?

I am often asked, when people hear that I am professionally interested in understanding how humans think, "Oh, so do you study the brain?" Part of me wants to reply, "No, I think about *thinking* (how we make simple and complex analogies, etc.), not about the brain—I leave that to the neurologists." Another part of me wants to reply, "*Of course* I think about the human brain. After all, it is the brain that carries out thinking." The issue then becomes, "What does one mean by 'brain research'?" and this leads us to asking, "What are the structures in the brain that someone could in principle study?"

Most neurologists, if they were asked such a question, would make a list that would include (at least some of) the following items:

neurotransmitters
synapses
neurons
the left hemisphere

These are all important "neurological objects," but to me this seems a limited point of view. Saying that studying the brain is the study of these objects would be like saying that literary criticism consists in the study of the blatantly physical objects and processes associated with literature—paper and bookbinding, typefaces and paragraph lengths and so on. But what about plots and characters, irony and humor, allusion and metaphor?

Abstractions are central, whether in the study of literature or of the brain, and so I would propose a list of abstractions that "researchers of the brain" should be just as concerned with:

the concept *dog*
"object files" (Anne Treisman)
"mental spaces" (Gilles Fauconnier)
"ego, superego, id" (Freud)
"I"

Some of these particular theoretical notions may not enjoy lasting validity, while others may be confirmed increasingly by various types of research, much as the notion of "gene" as a theoretical entity was proposed long before any physical object could be identified with it.

Indeed, I could go further out on a limb, asking why *physical identification* in the brain should constitute the goal of neurological inquiry. Why not consider the establishment of all sorts of relationships among these abstract kinds of entities to be valid brain research?

Warning: Do Not Confuse Levels of Description

We all take for granted that organs are made of cells. Thus a heart is made of billions of cells. But concentrating on a heart at that microscopic level, though important, also risks missing the big picture, which is that *a heart is a pump*. Natural selection favored beings that had more efficient internal pumps. The details of the cells making up those pumps were not the crucial variable. Rival *architectures* of hearts were the contenders for natural selection. Similarly, heart surgeons concentrate on large architectural structures in the heart rather than thinking about the cellular details. Analogously, the microscopic scale for the brain almost certainly is the wrong level to look at, if we are seeking concepts, ideas, creativity, consciousness, and the like.

Who Shoves Whom around Inside the Cranium?

Many years ago, I saw a book called *Molecular Gods: How Molecules Determine Our Behavior*. Its title stimulated many thoughts in my brain. Indeed, the very fact that I didn't buy the book suggests some kinds of thoughts its title triggered. What was really going on in my brain when I decided to reshelve the book and then moved my arm in a specific fashion? Was there something legitimately referable-to as "I" that was "shoving around" various brain structures and, derivatively, my arm and the book? Can a blurry, intangible "I" dictate to physical objects what to do? Or, in the end, are there just particles and laws of physics pushing them around? What is the proper level of description here?

Roughly at the same time, I came across various writings by the neurologist Roger Sperry that resonated strongly with my own intuitions. Here is a short, provocative passage from Sperry's essay "Mind, Brain, and Humanist Values" (Sperry 1965, pp. 78–83):

To put it very simply, it comes down to the issue of who pushes whom around in the population of causal forces that occupy the cranium. It is a matter, in other words, of straightening out the peck-order hierarchy among intracranial control agents. There exists within the cranium a whole world of diverse causal forces; what is more, there are forces within forces within forces, as in no other cubic half-foot of universe that we know. . . .

To make a long story short, if one keeps climbing upward in the chain of command within the brain, one finds at the very top those over-all organizational forces and dynamic properties of the large patterns of cerebral excitation that are correlated with mental states or psychic activity. . . . Near the apex of this command system in the brain . . . we find ideas.

. . . In the brain model proposed here, the causal potency of an idea, or an ideal, becomes just as real as that of a molecule, a cell, or a nerve impulse. Ideas cause ideas and help evolve new ideas. . . . And they also interact with the external surroundings to produce in toto a burstwise advance in evolution that is far beyond anything to hit the evolutionary scene yet, including the emergence of the living cell.

All that Sperry has really done here is to assert, in a *scientific* context, the commonsensical belief in the genuine causal potency of the thing we call "I." In the scientific world, such an assertion runs a great risk of being looked upon with skepticism, because it sounds superficially as if it reeks of Cartesian dualism, but Sperry knew very well that he wasn't embracing dualism or mysticism of any sort.

Thermodynamics and Statistical Mechanics

I grew up with a physicist father, and to me it was natural to see physics as underlying everything. I knew chemistry was the physics of interacting atoms, and later I saw molecular biology as the result of the laws of physics acting on complex molecules. I grew up seeing no room for "extra" forces in the world, on top of the four basic ones. But how did I reconcile that belief with my additional beliefs that religious dogmas have indeed caused wars or that nostalgia caused Chopin to write a certain étude?

I conceived of these extra "macroscopic forces" as just *ways of describing* complex patterns of basic physical forces, much as physicists came to realize that such macroscopic concepts as pressure and temperature could be understood as highly predictable regularities determined by the statistics of astronomical numbers of invisible constituents interacting with each other on a microscopic level. I also realized that this shift in levels of description gains us comprehensibility. To describe a gas's behavior (*per impossibile*) by writing a gigantic piece of text having Avogadro's number of equations in it would not lead to understanding. But throwing away huge amounts of information and making a statistical summary could do a lot.

All of this can be summarized by the unoriginal maxim *Thermodynamics is explained by statistical mechanics*, but the idea becomes clearer when it is turned around: *Statistical mechanics can be bypassed by talking at the level of thermodynamics.*

Thinkodynamics and Statistical Mentalics

It comes as no news to anyone that different levels of description have different kinds of utilities, and I have accordingly formulated a droll catch phrase to summarize this simple truth as it applies to the world of thinking and the brain: *Thinkodynamics is explained by statistical mentalics*, or, turned around: *Statistical mentalics can be bypassed by talking at the level of thinkodynamics.*

By "thinkodynamics," I mean mental activity that is analogous to thermodynamics; it involves large-scale structures and patterns in the brain, and makes no reference to microscopic events such as neural firings. Thinkodynamics is what psychologists spend their time studying: How people make choices, errors, and so on. In contrast, by "mentalics," I mean the small-scale structures and events that neurologists study: how neurotransmitters move across synapses, how cell assemblies can reverberate in synchrony with each other, and so on. And by "statistical mentalics," I mean the collective behavior of these small entities—huge swarms of micro-activity.

However, as Roger Sperry made very clear, there is not, in the brain, just one single natural upward jump, as there is in a gas, all the way from the basic constituents to the whole thing; rather, there are many levels of intermediate structures, and this means that it is particularly hard for us even to imagine the neural-level explanation for why somebody chose not to buy a certain book or for why somebody refrained from swatting a certain insect.

Daily life forces us to talk about events *at the level of our everyday, coarse-grained perception of them*. That is what our sensory organs, our language, and our culture provide us with. From earliest childhood on, we are handed concepts such as "finger," "mosquito," and "itch" on a silver platter. We perceive the world in these terms and not in terms of microscopic notions. We can of course acquire and even master those notions later, but they cannot replace the original ones. We are "victims" of our macroscopicness.

Thus, it seems more convincing to us to say that a war was triggered for certain religious or economic reasons than to try to conceive of a war as a vast pattern of interacting elementary particles and to see what triggered it in terms of them—even though some may believe that that is the only "true" level of explanation for it, in the sense that no information would be thrown away if we were to speak at that level. But having such phenomenal accuracy is not our fate. We are condemned *not* to speak at that level of no information loss. We *necessarily* simplify, and vastly so. But that sacrifice is our glory. It allows us to understand things at amazingly high levels, and thus to survive well in this world, natural and cultural.

The Domino-Chain Computer

Consider the familiar notion of a chain of falling dominos. I propose a slight addition to the image, which is that each domino is spring-loaded in a clever fashion (details do not concern us at all) such that whenever it is knocked down by its neighbor, after a short "refractory" period, it flips back up to its vertical state, ready to be knocked down again. With such a system, we can implement a mechanical computer that works by sending signals down chains that can fork or join together; thus signals can propagate in loops, jointly trigger other signals, and so on. We can imagine a network of precisely timed domino chains that amounts to a computer program for carrying out a particular computation, such as determining whether a given input is a prime number.

Let us further imagine that we can give a specific numerical "input" to our network by taking any positive integer—641, say—and placing exactly that many dominos end to end in a certain special location in the network. Now, when we push over the network's first domino, domino after domino will fall, including, shortly after the outset, all 641 of the dominos constituting our input, and as a consequence various loops will be triggered, with some loop presumably testing for divisibility by 2, another for divisibility by 3, and so forth. If a divisor is found, then the computation (the toppling) will be sent down one particular chain, and when we see that chain falling, we will know that the input number has some divisor and thus is not prime. If the input has no divisor, then that chain will never be triggered and we will know that the input is prime.

Now what if you or I simply came upon this network of dominos naively, without knowing its purpose or design, and we flicked its first domino over and watched it? We might chance to notice that one particular domino never falls, and we might ask, "How come that domino never falls?" Some smart aleck standing next to us might reply, "Because its *predecessor* never falls!" Now this indubitably correct answer would be of little help to us in gaining any helpful *insight* into why the domino in question never falls. The smart aleck's answer resides on the most local scale; it doesn't take into account anything about the larger and very intricate structure in which all these dominos are embedded.

"Because 641 Is Prime"

A more insightful answer would be this: "This is a network that searches for nontrivial divisors of its input number, and in this case, the stretch of the network that contains that domino never gets triggered because the input number has no smaller divisors. In short, that domino is standing up all the time *because 641 is prime.*" This answer bypasses all the physics of domino chains and makes reference only to concepts that belong to a different domain. The insight-giving explanation has nothing to do with physical objects as such.

This simple image provides us with a metaphor for talking about the many levels of causality inside a human brain. Suppose that it were possible to monitor any selected neuron or group of neurons in my brain. In that case, someone might ask, "Why does neuron 45826493842 never seem to fire?" and a smart aleck's answer might be, "Because the neurons that feed into it never fire jointly," and this answer would be as correct but as uninformative as the other smart aleck's answer. But someone who replied "Because Hofstadter doesn't relate to the music of Bruckner" would be much more on target.

As long as we avoid such simplistic notions as an "I like Bruckner" neuron, we can use the domino-chain metaphor to think about vastly different explanations residing at different levels of abstraction.

Causality and Level-Shifts

Sperry's comments about "many forces" in the brain now take on a clearer light. We can ask, "Does the primality of 641 really *exert a causal force* on anything physical?" Although it cannot be pinned down to a specific local physical force, the answer nonetheless has to be, "Yes, it does, in the sense that the most efficient and most insight-affording explanation of the red domino's behavior makes reference to that notion." What this answer reveals to us is that deep understanding of causality sometimes requires the understanding of very large patterns and their interactions.

There's no "extra" physical (or extraphysical) force here; the laws of physics take care of everything on their own. But the *arrangement* of the dominos is what determines what happens, and if you understand that arrangement, then an insight-giving shortcut to the answer of the nonfalling domino is served up on a silver platter. If you don't look at that arrangement, then you are doomed to understanding things only locally and insightlessly. In short, talking about 641's *primeness* as a physical cause in a domino network is analogous to talking about a gas's *temperature* as a cause.

The Careenium

I would like now to present a more complex metaphor for understanding the multiple levels of causality in our brains and minds, one that involves a frictionless pool table with not just sixteen balls on it, but myriads of extremely tiny marbles, called "sims" ("small interacting marbles"). These sims bash into each other and bounce off the walls, careening about wildly in their flat world—and since it is frictionless, they just keep on careening and careening.

Now we'll posit a little extra complexity. The sims are also magnetic (so let's switch to "simms"), and when they run into each other at lowish velocities, they can stick together to form clusters, which we can call "simmballs." A typical simmball will consist of a very large number of simms, and thus there are two different types of denizens of this system—tiny light simms and large heavy simmballs. The dynamics of this pool table—henceforth the "careenium"—thus involves simms constantly crashing into each other and also into simmballs.

Why the pun on "symbol"? Because I now postulate still more complexity. The vertical walls that constitute the system's boundaries react sensitively to outside events (e.g., a breeze) by momentarily flexing inward a bit. This flexing, whose nature bears traces of the causing event, affects the motions of the simms that bounce internally off that section of wall, and this will be registered in the motions of the nearest simmballs as well, thus allowing the simmballs to *internalize* the recent event. We can posit that one particular simmball always reacts to breezes, another to sharp blows, and so forth. We can even posit that the configurations of simmballs *reflect the history* of the impinging outerworld events. In short, for someone who looked at the simmballs and knew how to read their configuration, the simmballs would be *symbolic*, in the sense of encoding events. Hence the pun.

Of course this is far-fetched, but remember that it is merely meant to be a metaphor for understanding our brains, and our brains, too, are rather far-fetched, in the sense that they too contain tiny events (neuron firings) and larger events (patterns of neuron firings), and the latter presumably somehow have *representational* qualities, allowing us to register and remember things that happen outside of our crania. But the key idea is that whereas no simm on its own encodes anything or has a symbolic interpretation, simmballs, on their far more macroscopic level, *do* encode and *are* symbolic.

Taking the Reductionistic View of the Careenium

The first inclination of a physicist who heard this story might be reductionistic, in the sense of simply saying that the simmballs are mere *epiphenomena* and that everything that happens in the careenium is thus explainable in terms of simms alone. And there's no doubt that this is true.

The only problem is the enormous multiplication of complexity when we drop all macroscopic ways of looking at things. If we refuse to use any language that involves epiphenomena, then we are condemned to seeing only untold myriads of particles. Moreover, when one refuses to recognize macroscopic phenomena, then there are no borders to the systems of particles because drawing such a border is a nonreductionistic act, admitting the *reality* of macroscopic structures. And of course no fixed portion of the universe can be fenced off from interacting with the rest, not even approximately. Spatiotemporal boundary lines make no sense if one is being reductionistic; not only do all the objects become microscopic and vastly numerous, but also the system grows beyond bounds in space and time and becomes, in the end, the entire universe taken over all of time. Reductionism is merciless.

Taking a Higher-Level View of the Careenium

The way I've so far portrayed the careenium focuses on the simms and their dashing and bashing. The simmballs are also there, but they are just big stationary objects off of which the simms bounce.

But consider two shifts. First, we shift to time-lapse photography; very slow motions get speeded up so as to become perceptible, while fast motions become so fast that they are not even blurs—they become imperceptible. Second, we back away or zoom out, rendering simms invisible, and so the simmballs alone become our main focus of attention.

Now instead of seeing simms bashing into what look like large stationary blobs, we see that these blobs have a lively life of their own, moving back and forth across the table, interacting with each other, as if there were nothing else on the table. Of course we know that this is all happening thanks to the simms, *but we cannot see the simms any more.* Their frenetic careening-about now forms only a stationary gray background.

Who Shoves Whom around Inside the Careenium?

Which of these two views of the careenium is correct? Or, to paraphrase Sperry: Who pushes whom around in the population of causal forces that occupy the careenium? In one view, the meaningless tiny simms are the primary entities, slowly pushing the heavy simmballs hither and thither. In this view, it is the tiny simms that shove the big simmballs about. From here, the simmballs are not even recognized as separate entities, since whatever they do is just a shorthand way of talking about what simms do, and thus there are no simmballs—no symbols—just a great deal of crazy, pointless careening-about of tiny round magnetic objects.

But if we speed things up and zoom out, all that is left of the simms is a featureless gray soup, and the interest resides solely in the simmballs, which give every appearance of richly interacting with each other in a way that has nothing to do with the soup churning below them, except in the rather pedestrian sense that the simmballs derive their *energy* from that soup. Indeed, the simmballs' "logic," not surprisingly, has to do with the *concepts* that the simmballs symbolize.

The Dance of the Simmballs

From our macroscopic vantage point, we can see *ideas* giving rise to other *ideas*, we can see one symbolic event reminding the system of another, we can see elaborate patterns of simmballs coming together and forming even larger patterns that constitute *analogies*—in short, we can see the logic of a thinking mind taking place in the patterned dance of the simmballs. Here, then, *it is the simmballs that shove each other about.*

If this strikes you as too far-fetched, just return to the human brain and think about what must be going on inside it in order to allow our thinking to take place. What else is going on inside each and every one of our crania but some story like this?

But who is shoving whom about in here? The answer is that it all depends on the level. Just as, on one level, the primality of 641 could legitimately be said to be shoving about dominos in the domino-chain network, so here there is a level on which the meanings attached to various simmballs could legitimately be said to be shoving other simmballs about. If this all seems topsy-turvy, it certainly is—but it is nonetheless completely consistent with the fundamental causality of the laws of physics.

Loops, Goals, and Desires

Consider the fundamental shift in perspective that took place when people first designed systems with feedback in them. Take, for example, the flush toilet. One view of this entity would see it as a system that is "trying" to make the water reach and stay at a certain level. Of course, we find it very easy to bypass such language since we effortlessly see the way the floating ball raises and lowers a metal rod whose angle controls the flow of water in a pipe, and in any case, it is pretty obvious that there are no "desires" in such a simple system; but if one is working on a broken toilet, it is easy to let oneself fall into speaking of what the toilet is "trying" to do, or "wants" to do. One doesn't *truly* impute any desires to it—it's just a manner of speaking—but it is convenient shorthand.

When we move to systems where the feedback is more sophisticated and its mechanisms are more hidden, the tendency in our minds to shift to teleological language becomes harder and harder to resist. Even when we see objects with very simple but hidden feedback loops inside them, there is a surprisingly strong tendency to see such objects as "alive," because those objects tend relentlessly to "seek" certain targets. Many examples from the world of artificial life come readily to mind, as well as the dancing spot of red light at San Francisco's Exploratorium, which darts away from anyone who chases it, thanks to a simple feedback loop in a computer program perceiving motion and controlling its position. No matter how rational one is, it is hard not to impute impishness to this dot.

The presence of a feedback loop, even a rather simple one, constitutes for us humans a strong pressure to shift levels of description from the goalless level of *mechanics* to the goal-oriented level of *cybernetics*. The latter is nothing but a more efficient rewording of the former. But at some point, it becomes indispensable.

Feedback and Its Bad Rap

Many years ago, my parents wanted to buy their first video camera, and I went to the store with them. We were shown several TV screens on a shelf, and a video camera was plugged into the back of one of them, thus allowing us to see what the camera was looking at and to gauge its level of fidelity. I took the camera and pointed it at my father, and we saw his smile jump right up onto the screen. Next I pointed the camera at my own face and presto, there was I. Then, inevitably, I felt compelled to try pointing the camera at the TV screen itself, and yet oddly enough, I found that I was hesitant to close the loop. I turned to the salesperson for permission, but he, instead of granting it, said, "Don't do *that*! You'll break the camera!"

And how did I react to his sudden panic—with laughter or scorn? No. I wasn't sure of myself, and his panic reinforced my uneasiness, so I refrained. Later, as we were driving home with our brand-new camera, I reflected on the matter and couldn't see where there would be any danger. And so when we got home, I gingerly tried closing the loop, and indeed, nothing terrible happened.

Of course, there is no danger at all in standard video feedback. But I can still remember my hesitation, and although it was irrational, I can imagine how the salesperson felt. Feedback—making a system somehow act or turn back or twist back on *itself*, thus forming some kind of mystically taboo loop—seems somehow dangerous, somehow tempting fate.

Savoring Circularity and Self-Application

At age fifteen, I stumbled upon a little paperback entitled *Gödel's Proof*. I had no idea who Gödel was, but the idea of a whole book about some mathematical proof intrigued me. Flipping its pages, I saw tantalizing words like "meta-mathematics" and "meta-language," and then, to my delight, I saw that this book discussed paradoxical self-referential sentences like "I am lying." I could see that this proof wasn't focused on numbers per se, but on reasoning itself, and that, amazingly, numbers were somehow being put to use in reasoning about the nature of mathematics. Here was a book talking about the idea of language talking about itself, and about the idea of reasoning reasoning about itself. I was hooked!

What seemed most magical, as I read through Nagel and Newman, was the way in which mathematics had doubled back on itself. I had always been powerfully drawn to loopy phenomena of this sort. For instance, from early childhood on, I had loved the idea of closing a cardboard box by tucking its four flaps over each other in a kind of "circular" fashion—A on top of B, B on top of C, C on top of D, and then D on top of A. This grazing of paradoxicality enchanted me. Also, I had always loved standing between two mirrors and seeing the implied infinitude of images fading off into the distance. A mirror mirroring a mirror—what idea could be more provocative?

Years later, when I took my children to Holland and we visited the park called "Madurodam," which contains dozens of beautifully constructed miniature replicas of famous buildings from all over Holland, I was most disappointed to see that there was no miniature replica of Madurodam itself, containing, of course, a yet tinier replica, and so on . . . I was particularly surprised that this lacuna existed in Escher's Holland, of all places.

The Timid Theory of Types

I first realized that not all people share this love of loops when I read about Bertrand Russell's invention of the so-called theory of types in *Principia Mathematica*, his famous work with Alfred North Whitehead published in the years 1910–1913.

Earlier, Russell had been working to ground mathematics in the "naive" set theory of the day, but just when he thought he was within sight of his goal, he unexpectedly discovered that naive set theory is inconsistent. This discovery stemmed from considering the "the set of all sets that don't contain themselves," a self-contradictory set that is legitimate in the naive theory. Because naive set theory turned out to allow self-contradictory entities like this, the whole thing came crashing down, and Russell was left with a terror of structures that permitted loops of self-containment or of self-reference, since he attributed this devastation to loopiness alone.

Russell then invented a novel kind of set theory in which no set can be a member of itself, no set can be defined by a condition containing a quantifier that ranges over that very set, and in which a strict linguistic hierarchy was set up, preventing any sentence from referring to itself. In *Principia Mathematica*, there was to be no twisting-back of sets on themselves, no turning-back of language upon itself.

This theory of "ramified types" seemed to me like a pathological retreat from common sense, as well as from the fascination that loops sparked in me. What on earth is wrong with the word "word" being a member of the category "word"? What on earth could be wrong with such innocent and patently true sentences as "This sentence contains five words"? Even silly sentences such as "The third word in this sentence contains nineteen letters" are no more problematical than the sentence "Two plus two equals five." Both are false assertions, but there is nothing paradoxical about either of them. Categorically banishing all loops of reference struck me as a paranoid maneuver.

Intellectuals Who Dread Feedback Loops

When I was a columnist for *Scientific American* magazine, I devoted a couple of my columns to the topic of self-reference in language, which featured a cornucopia of sentences invented by myself, my friends, and my readers. Here are some examples:

If the meanings of "true" and "false" were switched, this sentence wouldn't be false.

This sentence every third, but it still comprehensible.

How come *this* noun phrase doesn't denote the same thing *this* noun phrase does?

I received a good deal of positive feedback (excuse the term), but I also received some extremely negative feedback on what certain readers considered utter frivolity in an otherwise serious journal, some dismissing even the *possibility* that someone might meaningfully utter a self-referential sentence. I reflected long and hard about such reactions, and for the next issue of the magazine I wrote a lengthy reply, citing case after case of blatant self-reference in ordinary language, humor, literature, mathematics, and so on. This realization—that some very intellectual and otherwise sensible people are irrationally allergic to the idea of self-reference—remained with me.

The Surprisingly Rich World of Simple Video Feedback

My understanding and appreciation of video feedback deepened when I decided to explore it in detail as a study for my book *Gödel, Escher, Bach*. One afternoon, courtesy of Stanford University's television studios, I spent several hours navigating around in the tempting ocean of "taboo" possibilities opened up by this idea of a video loop. (See figures 19.3 and 19.4.)

Running down the right edge of the TV set they had set up for me, there was a shiny metallic strip, and this random feature had the fortunate effect of bringing out the distinct layers of screens-within-screens very sharply. My first discovery was that there was a critical angle that determined if the regress of screens-inside-screens was infinite or finite. If I pointed the camera at the metal strip instead of the center of the screen, this gave me what looked like a snapshot of a stretch of the right wall of a corridor, showing a few evenly spaced "doorways" moving away from where I was "standing." But I couldn't peer all the way down to the end of this "corridor." I'll call this a *truncated* corridor.

If I panned the camera leftward toward the center of the screen and perforce further down the apparent corridor, more and more "doorways" would come into view along the right wall, further and further away—and all of a sudden, at a critical moment, there was a sense of infinity as I would find myself peering all the way down the corridor toward a gaping emptiness, stretching arbitrarily far away toward a single point of convergence. I'll call this an *endless* corridor. Of course the sense of infinity was illusory, since the graininess of the image set a limit as to how many nestings could occur. Nonetheless, peering down an apparently endless corridor was very different from peering down a truncated corridor.

My next set of experiments involved tilting the camera. When I did this, each screen obediently tilted the same angle with respect to its containing screen, which gave rise to the appearance of a receding *helical* corridor. Though lovely to see, this was not terribly surprising. The fascinating discovery, however, was that at certain angles of twist of the camera, that

(a) The simplest case.

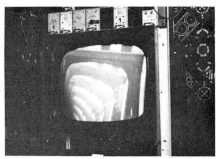

(d) A "failed self-engulfing."

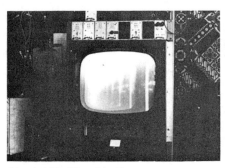

(b) Achilles' "corridor."

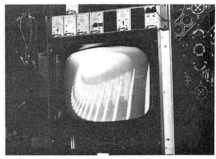

(e) What happens when you zoom in.

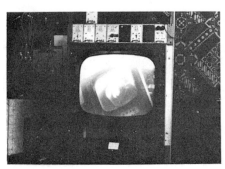

(c) What happens when you rotate the camera.

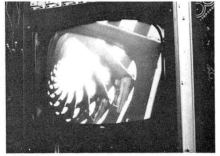

(f) Combined effect of rotation and zooming.

Figure 19.3
Reprinted by permission of Basic Books from *Gödel, Escher, Bach*, pp. 490–491.

(g) Starting to get weird . . .

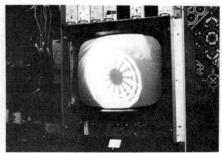

(j) The late stages of a galaxy. Count the number of spokes!

(h) A "galaxy" is born.

(k) The galaxy has burned itself out, and become—a black hole!

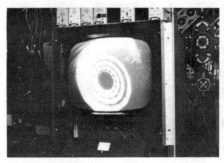

(i) The galaxy evolves . . .

(l) A "pulsating petal pattern," caught in the middle of one of its pulsations.

Figure 19.4
Reprinted by permission of Basic Books from *Gödel, Escher, Bach*, pp. 490–491.

three-dimensional sense of a receding helical corridor punctuated by periodic doorways vanished, and was replaced by what looked like a flat spiral, something like a spiral galaxy seen through a telescope, and the galaxy's whorl looked far more like one unbroken continuous curve than like a discrete set of shrinking nested screens. I had no clear explanation for this stunning transition from discreteness to continuity, but I just continued exploring.

I soon found that there was nearly always a circular "black hole" at the "galactic center," and from looking at that dark disk's bright circumference one got no sense at all of any kind of discrete process behind the scenes.

More Strange Epiphenomena from Looping and Iteration

The last phenomenon I wish to point out was what happened when I accidentally stuck my hand momentarily in front of the camera's lens. Of course this blotted out the previous pattern and the screen went all dark, but when I removed it, the previous pattern did not just come right back, as one might expect. Instead, I saw a new kind of throbbing pattern on the screen, steadily pulsating at the rate of about one cycle per second. Where had this motion come from, given that there was nothing moving in the room?

Actually, there *was* something moving in the room—the image itself was moving! And since the image was *of itself*, it kept on moving. Motion begat motion because it was a cyclic setup. And the "prime mover" had been my hand's motion, of which this reverberation was now a permanent memory.

As might be expected, all of the truly unexpected phenomena that I observed depended on the nesting being (theoretically) infinite—that is, on the apparent corridor being endless, not truncated. Accordingly, the most unpredictable visual things always seemed to happen right in the vicinity of that central point where the infinite regress converges.

My explorations did not teach me that *any* shape whatsoever can appear as a result of video feedback, but they did indicate a far richer universe of possibilities than I had expected. To me, this richness resulting from looping is reminiscent the vast richness of the visual universe discovered by the mathematician Benoit Mandelbrot when he studied the properties of the very simple iteration defined by $z \to z^2 + C$, where C is any constant complex number and z is a variable complex number. Studying what happens in the course of such a simple iteration as a function of the parameter c gives rise to an astonishing richness of visual phenomena in the complex plane, thanks to the use of color-coding to distinguish between different rates of divergence. In both cases, a very simple looping process gives rise to a family of totally unanticipated and incredibly intricate two-dimensional swirling patterns.

The Phenomenon of "Locking-In"

The mysterious and strangely robust higher-level phenomena that emerge out of looping processes such as video feedback will serve as my main metaphor as I broach the central questions of consciousness and self.

What remained with me was a sense of the immense richness of the phenomenon of video feedback, and a sense that unanticipated structures and patterns would come to exist on the screen, and that in many cases, the origins of these patterns were quite opaque. And what was odd was that in some sense, the circularity of the system made these patterns justify themselves. Once a pattern was *on* the screen, then all that was needed to justify its *staying* there was that famous line about Everest—"Because it is there!" When loops are involved, then circular justifications, not too surprisingly, are the name of the game.

Feedback gives rise to a new kind of pattern that can be called "locking-in." From just the barest hint comes, almost instantly, the full realization of all the implications of this hint—and this new higher-level structure, thanks to the loop, is "locked in." It will not go away because it is forever refreshing itself, feeding on itself, giving rebirth to itself.

Emergent New Realities of Video Feedback

Even though giving vivid nicknames to unexpected patterns did not figure in my initial plans for my video-feedback adventure, this activity soon became necessary. At the outset, I merely thought I was undertaking a project that would involve straightforward terms like "screen inside screen," "angle of tilt," and "zooming in"—but soon I found myself forced to use unexpected descriptive terms. I started talking about "corridors" and "walls" and "doorways" and "galaxies" and "spirals." These concepts were fundamentally new and unanticipated, and therefore *emergent*. Moreover, metaphors like "galaxy" and "petal" and "black hole" turned out to be *indispensable* in describing the shapes and the events on the screen. The initial terms I had been intending to use yielded little insight, even though in principle, everything could be explained in terms of them.

Perceptual Looping as the Germ of "I"-ness

We can now return to the human brain and the mysterious phenomenon called "I" to which it gives rise. To many if not all people the intuitive sense of "being there," the sense of "having experience," the sense of being an "I" or a "first person," seems to be the realest thing in their lives, and a powerful inner voice inside them bridles at the proposal that all of this might be merely the outcome of some kind of physical processes taking place among "third-person" objects. Our goal here is to combat this strident inner voice.

We begin with the simple fact that when a system evolves in the physical and biological world, its primary and automatic goal is to survive. Given this, it must be able to react flexibly to events that take place in its environment. And this means it must develop the ability to sense and to categorize, however rudimentarily, the goings-on in its immediate environment. Once the ability to sense various external goings-on has developed, however, there ensues a curious side effect that will have vital and radical consequences. This side effect is the fact that the being's ability to sense certain aspects of its environment flips around and becomes the ability to sense certain aspects *of the being itself.*

The fact that this flipping-around takes place is but a trivial consequence of the being's ability to perceive. It is no more surprising than the fact that audio feedback can take place, or that a TV camera can be pointed at a screen to which its image is being sent. And after all, in the case of a being struggling to survive, the one thing that is *always* in its environment is . . . itself. Why should the being be perceptually immune to the most salient item in its world?

Such a lacuna would be reminiscent of a language that kept growing and growing yet without ever developing words for such salient concepts as are named by the English words "speak," "understand," "answer," and "sentence." Such concepts (even though unnamed) would grow ever more salient and numerous as the language continued to grow in flexibility and sophistication. Such a language, like Bertrand Russell's theory of types, would have a gaping hole at its core. Analogously, for a creature to have evolved rich capabilities of perception and categorization but to be constitutionally incapable of focusing any of that apparatus onto itself would be highly anomalous or even pathological.

Varieties of Looping

The most primitive living creatures, since their perception of their environment is rudimentary, have little or no self-perception. By analogy, we can think of a TV camera rigidly bolted on top of a TV set and facing away from the screen. No matter how you turn it, the camera and the TV set turn in loopless synchrony.

We next imagine a more "evolved" and flexible setup; this time the camera, rather than being bolted onto its TV set, is attached to it by a "short leash." Here it may be possible for the camera to twist around to some degree and capture at least part of the TV screen in its finder, giving rise to a truncated corridor. The biological counterpart to feedback having this level of sophistication may be the way our pet animals or even very young children are slightly self-aware.

The next stage is where the "leash" is long and/or flexible enough that the video camera can point straight at the center of the screen. This will allow an endless corridor, which is far richer than a truncated one. Even so, closability of the loop does not by itself fully define the richness of the system, because there still are many options. Can the camera tilt or not, and by how much? Can it zoom in or out? What degree of resolution does the image have? What percentage of time is spent in self-observation, as opposed to observation of the environment? There are many parameters still open, and thus many levels of sophistication to the potential loop.

Reception versus Perception

However, one crucial aspect is lacking in such a television system, whether there is no closed loop at all, a truncated loop, or an endless loop; this is the crucial notion of *perception*, as opposed to mere *reception*. Perception takes as its starting point an input composed of a vast number of tiny signals, but then it goes much further, eventually winding up in the selective triggering of a small subset of a large dormant repertoire of *symbols*—discrete structures that have representational quality. That is to say, a symbol inside a cranium, just like a simmball in the hypothetical careenium, should be thought of as a triggerable physical structure that is the brain's way of implementing a particular category or concept.

The passage leading from vast numbers of received signals to small sets of triggered symbols is a kind of funneling process in which signals are manipulated or "massaged," the results of which selectively trigger further signals, and so forth. This process traces out an ever-narrowing pathway in the brain, which winds up in a small set of symbols whose identities are of course a subtle function of the original input signals. Each of these joint symbol-triggerings constitutes an act of perception, as opposed to the mere reception of a gigantic number of microscopic signals arriving from some source.

The missing ingredient in a video system as described above, no matter how high its visual fidelity might be and regardless of its degree of loopiness, is a repertoire of symbols that can be selectively triggered. However, nothing prevents us from imagining augmenting a vanilla video system with additional circuitry that supports a cascade of signal-massaging processes that lead toward a repertoire of potentially triggerable symbols. Indeed, this is a helpful way of thinking simultaneously about the brain of a living creature and the cognitive system of an artificial mind. However, not all realizations of such an architecture, whether natural or artificial, will possess equally rich repertoires.

There is a level of complexity at which a creature starts applying some of its categories to itself, starts building mental structures that represent itself, starts placing itself in some kind of "intellectual perspective" in relationship to the rest of the world. In this respect, dogs are surely far more advanced than mosquitoes but still "smaller-souled" than humans.

The Revolutionarily Different Conceptual Repertoire of Human Beings

A critical evolutionary leap took place when human beings evolved: their category systems became arbitrarily extensible. Concepts could get rolled together with other concepts into larger packets, and such a larger packet could then become a new concept in its own right. In other words, concepts could nest inside each other hierarchically, and such nesting could go on to arbitrary degrees.

For instance, the regularly repeated phenomenon of having offspring gave rise to concepts such as "mother," "father," and "child." These gave rise to nested concepts like "grandmother" and "grandchild." But this is merely the tip of the iceberg, since such concepts as "this," "merely," "tip of the iceberg," "since," "concept," "abound," and "human mind" abound in human minds. Little wonder, then, that when a human being, possessed of such a rich armamentarium with which to work, turns its attention to itself, as it inevitably must, it produces a self-model that is extraordinarily deep and tangled.

What Seems "Real" to a Human Being?

It is through the funneling-down process of perception, eventually leading to the activation of certain discrete symbols, that a living being relates to its environment. It avoids banging into trees, it pursues food, and so forth. Because its mirroring of the world inside itself *must* be highly reliable, the being's internal symbolic mirroring of the world becomes an unquestioned pillar of stability.

Through many types of abstraction, analogy-making, inductive reasoning, arguments from authority, and so forth, we build up a very intricate set of beliefs as to what exists "out there"—and then, once again, that set of beliefs folds back, inevitably and seamlessly, to apply to our own selves. Just as we believe in other peoples' kidneys and brains, so we come to believe in our own kidneys and brains. Just as we believe in other people's deaths, so we come to believe in our own inevitable death someday, and in the obituary notices we won't be around to read.

What makes for this sense of sureness? It is first the reliability of our internal symbols to mirror the concrete environment, and second the reliability of our thinking systems to tell us about more abstract entities that we cannot directly perceive. All of this is rooted in the constant reinforcement, moment by moment, of the repertoire of discrete symbols that are perceptually triggered by events in the world. These mental events provide the bedrock of our sense of reality.

In a certain sense, then, what seems realest to us is what gets activated most often. Our hangnails are incredibly real to us, whereas a faraway country, or an earthquake that kills 20,000 people in one fell swoop in some far-off land, or a swarm of helpless stars being swallowed up one after another by a ravenous black hole—such colossal events seem so abstract that they can't touch the sense of urgency, and thus the *reality*, of some measly little hangnail.

In short, the realest things of all are *my knee, my hunger, my sadness, my joy*, and so forth. What these have in common is the concept of "I," and therefore, although it is less concrete than a nose or a toothache, this "I" thing is what seems to constitute the most solid rock of undeniability of all. But could it possibly be less real and less solid than we think it is?

A Surprise in a Box of Envelopes

One day I wanted to take all the envelopes in a small cardboard box on my desk and stick them into one of my desk drawers. I reached into the box, placing my right hand around the set of about a hundred envelopes, and squeezed down in order to pull them all out. But I stopped short because between my thumb and fingers I felt something unexpected. There was a marble in that little box!

I had held marbles hundreds of times, and I knew without any doubt what I was feeling. But how had a marble found its way into this box? At the time, I didn't have any kids, so that couldn't be the explanation.

I peered in between the envelopes and saw nothing. I fumbled about between the envelopes, trying to find something tactilely. No marble. I grasped the whole set of envelopes again, and there it was again! Where was this little devil of a marble hiding in there? I looked more carefully, and took the envelopes out and tried to shake it out, but no luck. All the envelopes were empty. What was going on?

Eventually it dawned on me that there was no marble at all in there, but that there was something that *felt* exactly like a marble. It was an epiphenomenon caused by the fact that, for each envelope, at the vertex of the inverted "V" made by its flap, there is a triple layer of paper as well as a thin layer of glue, and so when you squeeze down on a hundred such envelopes all aligned with each other, you can't compress that portion as much as the other portions, and the hardness you feel has an uncanny resemblance to a more familiar hardness.

Perhaps the most bizarre aspect of the experience was how confidently I would have provided an estimate of its radius, as well as described how hard it was. I had been taken in by a tactile illusion. There was no marble there—there was just a statistical epiphenomenon.

And yet, it's undeniable that the phrase "it felt just like a marble" gets across my experience far more clearly than if I had written, "I felt the collective effect of the adjacency of a hundred triple layers of paper and a hundred layers of glue." Would you have been able to predict that a many-layered structure of that sort would give rise to something that felt *spherical*, felt like it had a distinct degree of *solidity*—in short, that this collective effect would feel like a very familiar, simple physical object? There is something to be gained by using the term "marble," even if there is no real marble there. The fact that there is something that feels like a marble is crucial to our understanding of the situation, just as the concepts of "corridor," "galaxy," and "black hole" were key ingredients in relating to the phenomena on the screen of the self-watching television.

Where the Buck Seems to Stop

I have recounted the story of the half-real, half-unreal, solid-and-spherical-seeming marble inside the box of envelopes in order to facilitate the transmission to you of my sense of the degree of reality that applies to our undeniable feeling of something "solid" or "real" at the core of ourselves, something that makes the pronoun "I" seem so indispensable and central to our existence. My thesis is that in a human brain, there is a special type of structure or pattern that plays the role of that precise alignment of layers of paper and glue, something that gives rise to what *feels* like a self. But first, I should say what I mean by the term "self," and why we seem to need a notion of that sort.

Each living being has a set of innate goals embedded in it, thanks to the feedback loops that evolved over time and characterize its species. These are the familiar activities of life, like seeking certain types of food, seeking a mate, and so on. Some creatures additionally develop their own individual goals, such as playing certain pieces of music. Whatever a creature's goals, we often say that it *pursues* them and often add that it does so because it *wants* certain things.

Creatures like us ascribe their behavior to things they refer to as their *desires* or *wants*, and they can't analyze exactly why they have *those* desires. At a certain point there is no further possibility of analysis; those desires simply are there, and they seem to it to be the root causes for its decisions and actions. Always, inside the sentences that express why it does what it does, there is the pronoun "I" ("me," etc.). It seems that the buck stops there—with the so-called "I."

"Throw the tennis ball a little higher on your next serve." "Higher? All right—I'll try." "Wow, that was better!"

How did she make the ball go higher? Simply by *deciding* that it should do so. Her "I" said to her arm, "Make it go higher," and that's all it took. And her speed and direction of running and the way she swings her racket—all these are determined by where she believes the ball to be heading.

So who pushes whom around here? Where are the particles of physics in this picture? They are invisible, and in any case they are just secondary players. It is this "I," a big bag of desires and beliefs, that sets everything in motion. If I *want* something to happen, I just *will* it to happen, and unless it is out of my control, it generally *does* happen. The body's molecules, whether in the fingers, the arm, the legs, the tongue, or wherever, obediently follow the supreme bidding of the Grand "I" on high.

If this "I" thing is causing everything that a creature does, if this "I" thing is responsible for the creature's decisions and movements, then surely this "I" thing must at least *exist*. How could it be so all-powerful and not exist?

God's Eye versus the Careenium's Eye

At the heart of my discussion of the tiny simms and the larger simmballs in the careenium was the fact that this system can be seen on two very distant levels, yielding different interpretations.

From the higher-level "thinkodynamics" viewpoint, there is symbolic activity in which simmballs interact with each other, taking advantage of the "heat energy" provided by the churning soup of invisible simms. From this viewpoint, what causes one simmballic event is some set of other simmballic events, even if the details of the causation are often tricky or too blurry to pin down precisely.

Contrariwise, from the lower-level "statistical mentalics" viewpoint, there are just simms, interacting via their fundamental dynamics—and here there is never any vagueness or doubt about causality.

If one understands the careenium well, it would seem that both points of view are valid, although the latter one (the "God's-eye" point of view), leaving out no details, might seem to be the more fundamental of the two, while the former, being a highly compressed simplification in which vast amounts of information are thrown away, might seem to be the more efficient one (with the trade-off that some things then seem to happen "for no reason").

However, this possibility of flipping back and forth between two wildly discrepant viewpoints of the careenium is a luxury that not all observers have. The God's-eye point of view is simply not available to all observers of the careenium; indeed, the mere fact that in principle such a point of view might *exist* is utterly unsuspected by some careenium-observers. I am in particular thinking of one very special careenium-observer, and that is *itself*.

When the careenium itself grapples with its own nature, particularly when it is just beginning to know itself, long before it has become a scientist that studies mathematics and physics and careeniology, all it is aware of is its *symballic* activity, not its simm-level churnings. After all, the careenium's perceptions of all things are tremendously coarse-grained simplifications— and its *self*-perceptions are no exception. It has no idea that behind the scenes, on some hidden microscale, there are churning, seething activities inside it. It doesn't suspect the existence of any other viewpoint.

And so, built like a rock into the careenium's prescientific self-understanding is the indisputable sense of itself as *a creature driven entirely by thoughts and ideas*; its self-image is infinitely far from that of being a mechanism driven by billions of invisibly careening micro-objects. The careenium says of itself, "I am driven by *myself*, not by any mere physical objects anywhere."

Loopy Strangeness

What kind of thing is this "I" thing that a human or a careenium posits as driving its actions? No one will be surprised at this point to hear me assert that it is a certain type of locked-in *loop* in the human brain—in fact, a *strange loop*. But what is that?

In the preceding pages, I have spoken a good deal about feedback loops in many systems. But when I say "strange loop," I have a somewhat more technical sense in mind, although it is not (yet?) a precise, rigorously scientific concept. A strange loop is a kind of feedback loop in which, in the series of stages that constitute the cycling-around, there is a *shift in levels* that feels like an upward movement in a hierarchy, and yet, when the cycle closes, it turns out that one winds up where one had started, in violation of the seeming hierarchy. Unlike a mere round trip, a strange loop feels like a paradoxical voyage in an abstract space.

A canonical example is the print *Drawing Hands* by Escher, in which (depending on where one starts) one sees a right hand drawing a picture of a left hand (nothing paradoxical yet), and yet the left hand turns out to be drawing the right hand (suddenly a deep paradox). The hierarchy here would be that of *drawer* versus *drawn*, the former being indisputably "above" the latter, in various senses. There is an absolute and inviolable hierarchical relationship between drawer and drawn, and yet in *Drawing Hands*, this relationship has been violated. How is that possible? Of course the answer is obvious: the whole thing itself is merely a *drawn*, merely a fantasy image. But because it looks so real, it fools us into sort of believing in its reality, at least enough for us to be charmed, disoriented, entertained, or freaked out.

Kurt Gödel's Analogy

For me the quintessential strange loop is the twisted abstract structure discovered by Kurt Gödel in his earthshaking article "On Formally Undecidable Propositions of *Principia Mathematica* and Related Systems." Recall that the key principle on which the theory of "ramified" types in *Principia Mathematica* was founded was the strict and total *banishment of self-reference*. By design, no sentence could ever turn around and talk about itself. This ban was intended to save *Principia Mathematica* from the trap that naive set theory had fallen into. But something strange turned up when Gödel looked closely at *PM* (the formal system of reasoning defined in that three-volume work).

Although it took many chapters of theorems and derivations before the rather basic fact that $1 + 1 = 2$ was rigorously demonstrated according to the rules of *PM*, Gödel nonetheless saw that *PM*, even if it was rather sluggish, had enormous power to talk about arbitrarily subtle properties of whole numbers. For instance, after enough machinery had been introduced, it was not hard to define, within the *PM* formalism, notions such as "square integer" or "prime integer" or "composite integer." There could thus be, in theory, a volume of *Principia Mathematica* devoted entirely to the question of which integers are, and which are not, the sums of two squares (a subtle but by Gödel's day already-solved problem of number theory), and likewise, there could be another hypothetical volume about which integers are, and which are not, the sums of two primes (a very deep and still unsolved problem).

But Gödel knew that whole numbers come in unlimitedly many varieties—aside from squares, cubes, primes, powers of ten, and all the usual suspects, he could define many others. He knew it was possible to define classes of integers *recursively*—in the manner of Leonardo di Pisa (a.k.a. Fibonacci), who in the 1300s had defined the *F* sequence 1, 1, 2, 3, 5, 8, 13, 21 . . . , where each *F* number was defined as the sum of the two previous ones (except for the first two *F* numbers, given "for free"). This almost but not quite circular fashion of defining a sequence of numbers in terms of itself struck Gödel as much more than a mere curiosity; in fact, it reminded him of the fact that theorems in *PM* (like theorems in Euclid) always sprang (by rules of inference) from earlier theorems in *PM* (except for the first few, which were given "for free," and thus were called "axioms"). This analogy between recursively defined sequences of integers and the set of theorems of *PM* suggested to Gödel that the patterns of symbols on the pages of *Principia Mathematica*—the Euclid-like rigorous derivations of one theorem from previous theorems—were themselves potential objects of study in number theory, just like Fibonacci's *F* numbers were.

Very Big Integers Moving in Lockstep with Formulas

Indeed, Gödel showed that any arbitrary string of *PM* symbols could be systematically converted into a positive integer, and conversely, that such an integer could be "decoded" to give back the string from which it had come.

The alphabet of *PM* consisted of only about a dozen symbols, and to each of these symbols Gödel assigned a different small integer. For multisymbol formulas, the idea was to replace the symbols, one by one, moving left to right, by their code numbers, and then to combine all of those individual code numbers (by using them as exponents to which successive prime numbers are raised) into one unique big integer. For instance, suppose that the code number for the symbol "0" is 2, and the code number for the symbol "=" is 6. Then for the three symbols in the very simple formula "0 = 0," the code numbers are 2, 6, 2, and these three numbers are used as *exponents* for the first three prime numbers (2, 3, and 5) as follows:

$$2^2 \cdot 3^6 \cdot 5^2 = 72,900$$

So 72,900 is the single number that corresponds to the formula "0 = 0." Of course it's a rather large integer for such a short formula, and you can easily imagine that the integer corresponding to a fifty-symbol formula is astronomical. But no matter—numbers are just numbers.

The decoding process works by finding the unique prime factorization of 72,900, and reading off the exponents that the ascending primes are raised to, one by one—2, 6, 2 in this case. Gödel thus showed how to replace any single formula of *PM* with an equivalent number. He then extended this idea of "arithmetization" to cover arbitrary *sequences* of formulas, since proofs in *PM* are sequences of formulas, and he wanted to be able to deal with proofs, not just isolated formulas. Thus, an arbitrarily long sequence of formulas could be converted into one large integer via essentially the same technique. In short, Gödel showed how any visual symbol-pattern whatsoever in the idiosyncratic notation of *Principia Mathematica* could be assigned a unique number, which could easily be decoded to give back the sequence of symbols to which it corresponded. Conceiving of and polishing this precise two-way mapping constituted the first key step of Gödel's work.

Prime Numbers, F Numbers, Wff Numbers, Prim Numbers

Following his intuition's momentum, Gödel next dreamt up some new classes of whole numbers—for instance, the *wff* numbers, which are integers that, via his code, represent "well-formed" or "meaningful" formulas of *PM*, as opposed to those that represent meaningless or ungrammatical strings. (A sample well-formed formula, or "wff" for short, would be "0 + 0 = 0," whereas "=0=" and "00==0+=" are not wffs.) Since long wffs are built up from shorter wffs by just a few simple patterns of typographical juxtaposition, their code numbers are likewise built up from the code numbers of shorter ones by just a few simple rules of numerical calculation. This was another key insight—that once formulas had been "arithmetized," then any kind of shunting-around of symbols on paper was exactly paralleled by some kind of purely *arithmetical calculation* with (huge) numbers.

Gödel saw that this manner of building up a set of numbers by putting smaller ones together in some arithmetical fashion is, though more complicated, entirely analogous to Fibonacci's manner of building up the class of all *F* numbers. Some integers, like 72,900, are wff numbers (they "have wff-ness"), while others are not—and, quite like squareness or primeness or Fibonacci's *F*-ness, this notion of "wff-ness" is definable in arithmetical terms alone. Thus, wff-ness is just the kind of thing that *Principia Mathematica* was designed to study.

Having realized that some hypothetical volume of *Principia* could define and be all about the properties of wff numbers, Gödel pushed his analogy further and showed, with not too much conceptual difficulty, that there was a considerably more interesting recursively defined class of whole numbers, which I shall here call *prim* numbers (saluting the title of the three tomes), and which are the numbers of *provable* formulas in *PM*. A *PM* proof, of course, is a series of formulas leading from the axioms of *PM* up to the formula in question, each step being allowed by some formal rule of inference. Therefore, no matter how long it is, any *PM* proof can be assigned a single large integer via Gödel's mechanism, and the final line of such a proof corresponds to a prim number. (A simple example of a prim number is, once again, our friend 72,900, since "0 = 0," over and above being a well-formed formula, is also, not surprisingly, derivable in *PM*.)

Just as with squares or primes or *F* numbers or wff numbers, there could once again be a hypothetical volume of *Principia* in which prim numbers were defined and their mathematical properties studied. The point is, being a prim number is no more and no less a number-theoretical property of an integer than is being square or being prime or being a Fibonacci number.

Gödelian Strangeness

Finally, Gödel carried his analogy to its "logical" conclusion, which was to concoct (implicitly) an astronomically long but precisely specified formula of *PM* that made the seemingly innocent assertion, "A certain integer *g* is not a prim number." However, that "certain integer *g*" about which this formula spoke happened, very unaccidentally, to be the number associated with (i.e., coding for) this very formula. And so the formula could be interpreted on two levels.

On its more straightforward level, Gödel's formula merely asserted that this rather large integer *g* lacks the number-theoretical property called *primness*—which is entirely analogous to asserting "72,900 is not a prime number." However, since primness was defined by Gödel in such a way that it numerically mirrored the provability of strings via the rules of the *PM* system, the formula also states, "The formula that happens to have the code number *g* is not provable via the rules of *PM*." The formula that "just happens" to have the code number g is the very formula making the claim. In short, Gödel's formula is making a claim about *itself*, and saying, "This very formula is not provable via the rules of *PM*," or even more tersely, "I am not a theorem of *PM*."

Gödel further showed that his formula, though very strange at first sight, was not all that unusual; indeed, it was merely one member of an infinite family of formulas that were "about" the system *PM*, many of which asserted (some truthfully, others falsely) similarly strange things about themselves (e.g., "Neither I nor my negation is a theorem of *PM*").

The Double Aboutness of Formulas in *PM*

Imagine the bewilderment of Bertrand Russell when Gödel announced his discovery that *Principia Mathematica*, that grand bastion so carefully erected to keep out the scourge of self-referentiality, was in fact riddled through and through with statements making strange claims about themselves. How could this outrage possibly be true? How could self-referential statements have sneaked through the thick ramparts of the theory of types?

The resolution of this mystery hinges on the fact that Gödel realized that what a formula of *PM* actually meant was not so simple a notion as Russell had thought. To be fair, Russell himself had always insisted that all of his strange-looking symbols and all the long formulas made out of them didn't have any intrinsic meaning whatsoever. However, he then added that the formulas *could* be interpreted, if one wished, as being about numbers and their properties, because one could read the meaningless vertical oval "0" as standing for the number zero, the meaningless cross "+" as standing for addition, and so on, in which case all the theorems of *PM* came out as true statements about numbers. Thus for Russell, the intended meaning of his dense volumes depended on making a *mapping* between symbols and numbers (and other basic arithmetical concepts).

In that sense, what Gödel did was, ironically, exactly in the Russellian spirit—it's just that Gödel found a *different* mapping, one that Russell had never suspected. By virtue of Gödel's subtle code many formulas could be read on a second level. The first level of meaning, using Russell's simpler mapping, was always about *numbers*, but the second level of meaning, using Gödel's trickier mapping, was about *formulas*, and since both levels of meaning depended on mappings, this second level of meaning was no less real than the first—just harder to see.

There is an analogy lurking here that I wish to bring out, linking Gödel's "subversion" of *Principia Mathematica* with the "subversion" of a TV system furnished with a TV camera. Again, there is nothing in the least surprising about the fact that a video system can "turn back on itself," even if this property was not intended by the inventors or makers of the TV camera. In a similar but subtler way, it is not surprising that a system designed to be *about* one set of things can also be *about* a quite different set of things. What is crucial for the second type of "aboutness" to come about is that there be an isomorphism—a perfect one-to-one mapping—between the *situations* involving the two different sets of things. This allows one situation to be read as if it were another one.

Even in the case of TV cameras, there is such a mapping—the pixels in an image on a TV screen constitute a faithful mapping of the objects that the camera is pointing at, and this mapping gives us two options: either we *ignore the mapping* and perceive the TV screen as a pure two-dimensional pattern of pixels in and of itself, standing for nothing, or else we *let the mapping suck us in*, in which case we read the pixels on the screen as standing for bits of light in a three-dimensional scene, and then we find ourselves "transported," thanks to a kind of code, to some remote place where we "see" some actions occurring. This second way of looking at a TV screen is like seeing it as a *representational* painting rather than an abstract one. Of course, the second mode is by far the dominant mode for humans, but it is not the only mode. In fact, the first mode is probably the way most dogs, cats, babies, and other low-huneker beings perceive a television screen; seeing it at the representational level is beyond them. They are like Bertrand Russell looking at a formula of his beloved system *PM* and seeing only its "easy" meaning, the other meaning lying beyond him.

The Latent Ambiguity of Lines in Plays

When a mapping between two situations is obvious, then we aren't usually caught terribly off guard by the second level of aboutness of statements about one of the situations, although sometimes we craftily exploit such pairs of related situations to talk about situation B indirectly or implicitly by explicitly talking about situation A, which we know resembles situation B very strongly.

This kind of device is used throughout literature, where, because of a strong analogy that readers easily perceive between situations A and B, lines uttered by characters in situation A can easily be heard as applying equally to situation B. Sometimes the characters in situation A are completely unaware of situation B, which can make for a humorous effect, whereas other times the characters in situation A are simultaneously characters in situation B, but aren't aware of the analogy linking the two situations they are in. The latter creates a great sense of irony, of course.

It is even more ironic when the author of a work of literature never intended there to be a double-leveled aspect to the lines of the play he or she has devised, but such a circumstance arises nonetheless. Imagine, for example, a play by playwright Whitehead N. Russell about a strike by workers in Prince Ipia's classy shoestore, in which shoppers approaching the store's entrance are exhorted not to cross the picket line and not to buy anything in the store. In the skilled hands of our playwright, this turns out to lead to a great drama filled with intense passion. But for some reason, just before this powerful play is to open, the ushers in the theater and the actors in the play get embroiled in a bitter dispute, as a result of which the ushers' union stages a strike on opening night, puts up picket lines, and beseeches potential playgoers not to cross their lines to see the play.

Given this unanticipated context, the lines uttered by the actors in the play will have a powerful double meaning, no matter what Whitehead N. Russell intended. In fact, the picketing shoestore worker named Cagey who disgust-edly proclaims, after a brash matron pushes her aside and arrogantly strides into Prince Ipia's fashionable boutique, "Anyone who crosses the Prince Ipia workers' picket line is scum" will inevitably be heard by everyone in the audience (which consists of people who crossed the picket line outside the theater) as saying, "Anyone who crossed the ushers' picket line is scum," and of course this amounts to saying, "Anyone now sitting in this audience is scum," which can also be heard as "You should not be listening to these lines," which is the diametric opposite of what all the actors, including the one playing the part of Cagey, want to tell their audience, whose entry into the theater they so much appreciate, given the ushers' hostile picket line.

But what can the actors do about the fact that they are unmistakably calling their audience "scum" and insinuating that no one should even be there to hear these lines? Nothing. They have to recite the play's lines, and the analogy is there, it's blatant and strong, and therefore the ironically twisting-back, self-referential meaning of Cagey's line, as well as of many others in the play, is unavoidable.

The Ineradicable Ambiguity of the Lines in Bertrand Russell's Play

One could analogously say that playwrights Russell and Whitehead created a three-volume play whose characters, at least according to Russell's inten-tions, would always speak only about numbers, manifesting various intricate arithmetical patterns, but unbeknownst to him, one of the more intricate numerical patterns that cropped up in the unusual plot line of his play spelled out, in a subtle numerical code, the exact structure of a certain exquisitely beautiful and intricately patterned dance of exotic typographical symbols.

Now although Russell was quite aware of this beautiful dance of symbols (and well he should have been, since it was none other than the pattern formed by the odd-shaped symbols on the very pages of the tomes that he and his co-author were penning!), he'd never dreamt of any connection whatsoever between the ideas his characters were speaking about and the intricate visual patterns constituting their written lines. However, this curious coincidence was revealed in a wickedly witty review by the astute young Austrian drama critic Kurt Gödel, and its veracity was immediately appreciated by many; as a consequence, playgoers who had read Gödel's review started to take many of the lines uttered in the play as if they were not about numbers at all, despite what the two playwrights had intended, but were direct references to the complex calligraphy and typography of the pages on which the play was written!

Thus certain of the characters in Russell and Whitehead's play were soon widely seen as talking at one and the same time about *prim numbers* (as the authors had intended) and also about *provable formulas of PM* (which Russell had tried to forbid). But sadly, there was nothing Russell could do about this boomeranging-back of his beloved system's formulas, because the two notions—the primness of certain integers and the provability of certain formulas—were perfectly isomorphic, and so Gödel's mapping made both meanings apply equally well. In fact, for certain very long formulas, it was easier and more natural to read them as talking about provable or unprovable formulas than to hear them as talking about prim or nonprim numbers!

Not "Not" but "This" Is the Source of the Strangeness

A reader might have concluded, somewhere along the line, that an indispensable aspect of this "strange loop" notion that I am presenting, using Gödel's construction as my quintessential example, involves a kind of self-undermining or self-negating quality ("This formula is *not* provable"; "You should *not* be attending this play"). Self-negation, however, plays no essential role in the concept of "strange loopiness." It's just that the strangeness often becomes more obvious or vivid if the loop enjoys this kind of self-undermining quality. But what I am calling "strangeness" comes purely from the way in which a system can seem to "engulf itself" through an unexpected twisting-around, rudely violating what we had taken to be an inviolable hierarchical order.

In the case of *Principia Mathematica*, what we saw is that a system carefully designed to talk about numbers and *not* to talk about itself nonetheless winds up talking about itself in a very "cagey" fashion—and in fact it does so precisely because of the chameleonic nature of numbers, which are so rich and complex that numerical patterns can mirror any other kind of pattern.

Every bit as strange a loop would have been created if Gödel had con-cocted a self-*supporting* formula that cockily asserted of itself, "This formula is provable via the rules of *PM*." Indeed, some years later, such self-affirming formulas were concocted and studied by logicians such as Löb and Henkin. The strange loopiness, I thus repeat, resides not in the flip due to the word "not," but in the totally unexpected, hierarchy-violating twisting-back involving the word "this."

I should, however, point out that a phrase such as "this formula" was nowhere to be found inside Gödel's cagey formula—not any more than the phrase "this audience" is contained in Cagey's line "Anyone who crosses the Prince Ipia workers' picket line is scum." The unanticipated meaning "People in *this audience* are scum" is, rather, the inevitable outcome of a blatantly obvious isomorphism between two picket lines (one outside the theater, one in the play), and thus between the members of the audience and the picket-line crossers in the play they are watching. In this fashion, the idea that a word such as "this" is needed in order for self-reference to arise is shown to be a naive illusion; instead, the strange twisting-back is accomplished as a completely natural consequence of an unexpected but perfect isomorphism that happens to hold between two different situations.

Numbers as a Representational Medium

And why does this kind of isomorphism exist in the case of *Principia Mathematica*? Because, as Gödel saw, the world of positive integers is so rich that, given *any* pattern of any sort, a set of numbers can be found that will be isomorphic to it. That is to say, Kurt Gödel was the first person to realize and exploit, in this way, the fact that the positive integers constitute a profoundly rich *representational medium*. They can mimic or mirror any kind of pattern. They are like a language that can talk about events of any sort, numerical or nonnumerical.

In a sense, people had intuited this kind of richness before, and yet, despite centuries of highly successful mathematizations of various aspects of the world, no one before Gödel had realized that one of the subjects that math-ematics can be used to model is *the doing of mathematics itself*.

The bottom line, then, is that the unanticipated self-referential twist discovered by Gödel lurking inside *Principia Mathematica* was a natural and inevitable outcome of the deep representational power of whole numbers. Just as it is no miracle that a video system can create a self-referential loop, but rather, a kind of obvious triviality that results from the power of TV cameras, so too it is no miracle that *Principia Mathematica* or any other sufficiently powerful system contains self-focused sentences like Gödel's formula, for the system of integers, exactly like a TV camera (only more so!), can "point" at any system whatsoever and imitate (or reproduce) its patterns perfectly on the "screen" constituted by the set of theorems. And just as in video feedback, the swirls that result from self-application have all sorts of unexpected, emergent properties and require a new kind of vocabulary to describe them.

The Strangeness of Gödel's Loop Flips Causality on Its Head

Perhaps the most stunning emergent property resulting from *Principia Mathematica*'s self-application is a strange new type of mathematical causality. To understand this, we have to go back to Kurt Gödel's formula—let's call it "KG"—and analyze what its existence implies for *PM*. When boiled down to its essence, KG's (second level of) meaning is the statement "KG is unprovable inside *PM*." And so a natural question to ask is, "Well, is KG *indeed* unprovable inside *PM*?" In order to answer this question, we have to rely on one assumption, which is that anything provable inside *PM* is a true statement (were this not the case, then *PM* would prove falsities galore about whole numbers). Armed with this, we ask ourselves, "What would follow if KG were provable inside *PM*?"

Well, if KG were provable in *PM*, then, ironically, it would assert a falsity, because it claims to be *un*provable in *PM*. In short, if KG were provable, it would be false. But we just agreed that anything provable in *PM* is true, not false, and so KG cannot be provable after all. And therefore, given that KG is not provable, and given also that KG *asserts* that it is not provable, what KG says is true. And thus we have come up with a very strange anomaly inside *PM*: here is a formula that is true, and we are sure it is unprovable, and to cap it off, these two nearly contradictory claims are consequences of each other!

What is it about KG that makes it not provable? Well, its self-referential quality—if KG were provable, its loopy meaning would flip around and make it be unprovable, and so *PM* would be an inconsistent system, which we assume it is not. But notice that we have not made any detailed analysis of the nature of derivations that would try to have KG be their last line. In fact, we have totally ignored the *intended* level of meaning of KG, which is a rather messy statement about a rather messy number-theoretical property (primness) of the unimaginably huge number I called *g*. We never thought about prim numbers and their nature, nor about the number *g* at all. We finessed all that numerical stuff by thinking only about KG's *other* meaning, the one that caught Russell so totally off guard.

This Peak Is Unscalable

Imagine that we had just discovered an unsuspected towering Himalayan mountain peak (call it "KJ") and that we were able to proclaim, both instantly and with total certainty, thanks to some unusual property of the summit alone that there is no conceivable route leading up to it. If this happened, it would be remarkably different from all previous kinds of alpinistic conclusions about the scalability of mountains. Heretofore, climbers always had to *attempt* many routes, and even thousands of failures in a row would not constitute an ironclad proof that the given peak was forever unscalable; all one could conclude is that it had *so far resisted* scaling. By contrast, our hypothetical peak KJ is such that we can conclude from some novel property that it has, and without looking at *any* possible routes leading up to it, that it is by its very nature unscalable.

This amounts to an unprecedented, upside-down kind of alpinistic causality. Although we can detect no systematic pattern explaining why it is that for every suggested route there's always some fatal obstacle along the way, nonetheless, something about the very top's shape (and nothing below it) tells us that this *must* be the case. Thus, rather than deducing its unscalability from looking *upward* toward the distant peak and considering all the routes that one might take toward it, we look solely at the top and conclude *downward* that there could be no route that would ever reach it. Quite a fantasy!

Downward Causality in Mathematics

Gödel's bombshell, though equally fantastic, was not a fantasy. It was rigorous. It revealed the amazing fact that a *hidden meaning* of a formula may possibly have a peculiar kind of "downward" causal power, allowing us to reach instant conclusions about its truth or falsity or its derivability or non-derivability inside *PM* (or inside any similar system) without making any attempts at all to derive it by moving upward from the axioms.

This has to be considered astonishing. Normally, one cannot merely look at what a mathematical conjecture *says* and use the content of that statement on its own to deduce whether the statement is true or false (or provable or unprovable). If I tell you, "There are infinitely many perfect numbers" (numbers such as 6 and 28, whose factors add up to the number itself), you will not know if my claim is true or not, and merely staring for a long time at the claim itself will not help. You will have to try out various approaches to this peak (e.g., discovering that 496 is another), and if repeated failures bring you around gradually to suspecting that my claim is false, then you would probably want to try various approaches to the rival peak ("There is a largest perfect number"). But if by some amazing stroke of luck or through some amazing stroke of genius you discovered an isomorphism revealing a hidden *second* level of meaning to my numerical claim—one that said, "There is no proof in *PM* that leads to this formula"—why then, just as with Gödel's formula KG, you could immediately conclude, without further ado, that the statement was both true and unprovable—in other words, that the statement "There are infinitely many perfect numbers" was true, *and* that it had no proof in *PM*.

This is radically different from how mathematics has traditionally been done. It amounts to *upside-down reasoning*—reasoning from a would-be theorem downward, rather than from axioms upward, and in particular, reasoning from a *hidden* meaning of the would-be theorem, rather than from its surface-level claim about numbers.

Downward Causality in Biology

Strange loops thus have very surprising properties, which can include what appears to be a kind of upside-down causality. But this is not the first time we have encountered upside-down causality. It cropped up in our discussion of the careenium and of human brains. We concluded that because of how we humans evolved, we wound up as creatures that filter the world into macroscopic categories, and we therefore describe what goes on about us, including what other people do and what we ourselves do, not in terms of the underlying basic particle physics, but in terms of such abstract high-level patterns as beliefs, desires, hopes, and fears.

There is thus a curious upside-downness to our normal human way of perceiving ourselves, and it even feels rather like what Gödel did, but in one sense it is different. Gödel found a way of taking a colossally long formula (KG) and reading it in a concise, easily comprehensible fashion instead of reading it as the low-level numerical assertion that a certain huge integer possesses a very esoteric number-theoretical property (primness). It took great insight to find this concise, hidden, *higher*-level way of reading certain formulas of *PM*. By contrast, in the case of the careenium (or brain), what would take great insight is to *bypass* the high-level reading involving simmballs (or symbols), and see that there is an esoteric, hidden, *lower*-level reading involving simms (or neurons, etc.) alone.

When you think about it this way, it seems rather curious that we perceive our brains in high-level terms like hopes and beliefs long before thinking of them on low-level neural terms. Had things happened this way in the case of *Principia Mathematica*, then recognition of the high-level *Gödelian* meaning of certain formulas of *PM* would have preceded recognition of their *Russellian* meanings, which is an unimaginable scenario. In any case, we humans evolved to perceive and describe ourselves in high-level mentalistic terms and not in low-level physicalistic terms, though we have gradually come to do the latter with some success.

Mentalistic notions like "belief" and "hope" arose long before anyone dreamt of trying to find them as recognizable physical patterns in some substrate, just as the word "gene" was formulated and used for many decades as a valid scientific term before any physical meaning was attached to it. And when objects were finally found that allowed a physical meaning to be attached to the word "gene," they were highly unexpected types of objects. And it turned out that the underlying chemistry was in a certain sense incidental—what really mattered was the *informational* properties of long sequences of nucleotides, not their ordinary physico-chemical properties.

At that level, biologists talk about what genes *stand for*, instead of about their physical properties. And they implicitly accept the fact that this new way of talking suggests that because of their informational qualities, genes have their own causal properties—or in other words, that certain extremely large-scale events or states of affairs can validly be attributed to *meanings of molecules*.

The "I" Marble

Because we are macroscopic, our deepest beliefs are in the reality of the macroscopic entities and phenomena that we almost effortlessly assign to our mental categories, and in the reality of the perceived causality, however blurry it may be, that seems to obtain among them. Accordingly, wars seem to us to be truly caused by conflicting religious dogmas or by economic suffering, not by anything physical. What truly seems to us to push the world of living beings around has to do with what items and what events belong to what categories, and not with collisions of particles in any sense at all.

And so, if this trend is extended to the self, then we come to see our own actions as determined just as other creatures' actions are—by intangible internal patterns called "hopes" and "beliefs." But more than that—we have to have a term that represents the presumed unity and internal coherence of all the beliefs and desires that are united inside one cranium—and that term is "I." This high abstraction soon comes to feel like the maximally real entity in the universe. The "I" is that marble whose roundness and solidity we so unmistakably feel inside the murky box of our manifold hopes and desires.

The Loop That Constitutes a Self

"I"-ness is the outcome of a strange loop. But just where is this strange loop, and what is the nature of its strangeness?

For each of us, the strange loop of our particular "I"-ness resides inside our own brain. There is thus one such loop lurking inside the cranium of each normal human being, although there is good sense to be made of the idea that our internal modeling of the loops that constitute others can come to be so intertwined with our own that the distinction becomes blurry. But if I say "inside," do I mean that such a loop is a physical structure—some kind of palpable closed curve, perhaps a circuit made out of many neurons strung end-to-end? Could this loop be neatly excised in a brain operation and laid out on a table like a delicate necklace for all to see? No, that is not what I mean. The strange loop making up an "I" is no more a pinpointable, extractable physical object than an audio feedback loop is a tangible object possessing a mass and a diameter. Such a phenomenon may exist "inside" a particular auditorium, but being physically localized doesn't mean that one can pick it up and heft it. An "I" loop, like an audio feedback loop, is an abstraction—but an abstraction that seems immensely real, almost physically palpable, to each of us.

Like a careenium (and also like *PM*), a brain can be seen at (at least) two levels—a low-level one involving physical processes (particles, neurons—take your pick), and a high-level one involving large structures selectively activatable by perception, which I have called *symbols*. Among the untold thousands of symbols in the repertoire of a normal human being, there are some that are far more frequent and dominant than others, and one of them is given the name "I." When we talk about other people, we talk about them in terms of such things as their ambitions and fears, and we accordingly need to formulate for each of them the analogue of an "I," residing, naturally, inside their cranium, not our own. This counterpart of our own "I" of course receives various labels, depending on the context, such as "Monica" or "you" or "he" or "she."

The process of perceiving one's own self interacting with the rest of the universe goes on for a lifetime. Accordingly, the "I" symbol, like all symbols in our brain, starts out pretty small and pretty simple, but it grows and grows.

Endless Corridors of What Was, What Could Have Been, and What Will Be

Let's return to the analogy of video feedback for a moment. Recall that the very simplest case of a camera pointing at "its own" TV screen involves *off-center* pointing, which gives rise to a *truncated* corridor. There is a bit of self-representation, but it is very partial. As the camera pans closer to the center of the screen, the "corridor" grows longer—and at a certain critical angle, a transition takes place and what appears to be the infinitely distant convergence point of the corridor swings into view. This endless corridor feels much more like a genuine loop than does the truncated corridor.

We can use this analogy to suggest a spectrum of levels of self-representation. There are those creatures that have but the barest trace of self-awareness, analogous to TV systems with very short truncated corridors. Then there are creatures with somewhat higher self-awareness, analogous to longer truncated corridors—that is, more levels of nested screens. Eventually, there are creatures with a rich sense of "I," corresponding to corridors where the full infinite regress of nested screens is visible—creatures with 100 hunekers of souledness, plus or minus a few.

Mature human adults are such creatures. For us adults, the corridor of our self-symbol reaches back fairly accurately, though quite spottily, into the deep past of our existence, and, through our hopes and fears, it likewise projects uncertainly though intensely into the murky fog of our future existence. It is our unlimitedly extensible human category system that underwrites this fantastic jump in sophistication, in that it allows each of us to build up what psychologists refer to as *episodic memory*—the gigantic warehouse of our memories of events, minor and major, simple and complex, that have happened to us over a span of decades. Episodic memory of our past, together with its mirror image pointing blurrily toward what is yet to come, and further enriched by a vast set of counterfactual replays of a vast number of episodes, gives rise to the endless hall of mirrors that constitutes our "I" symbol.

And since we do not perceive particles but only macroscopic patterns, we are forced to conclude that our "I," along with the desires and hopes that are key aspects of it, is what pushes our bodies around. And since our bodies push the rest of the world around, we have no choice but to conclude that the "I" is where the causality buck stops. The "I" seems to each of us to be the root of all our actions. This is a vast distortion of the truth, of course, since the particles that make us up are where the action really is, but it is a surprisingly reliable and totally indispensable distortion, and these two facts lock it in ever more tightly into our belief systems as we pass from babyhood through childhood to adulthood.

The Slow Building-Up of the Loop That Constitutes a Self

What would make a human brain a candidate for housing a loop of this sort? Why not a mosquito brain? Why not a tomato?

The answer should be clear: a human brain is a fantastically powerful and rich representational system that knows no bounds in terms of the extensibility or flexibility of its categories. A mosquito brain, by contrast, is a tiny representational system that has practically no categories at all in it, not to speak of being flexible and extensible. So a human brain is a strong candidate for having the potential of rich perceptual feedback, and thus self-representation. But what kinds of perceptual cycles do we get involved in?

We begin life with elementary sorts of feedback about our most obvious body parts, and from this we develop a sense for ourselves as physical objects. But as we develop, it is crucial that we hone our self-symbol much more subtly than that. For instance, we want (and need) to find out where we fit in all sorts of social hierarchies and classes. Some of us come to realize that we are "good at sports," "smart," "funny," "shy," or whatever. These labels and concepts accrete to our growing self-symbols. We go through thousands of experiences large and small, and these experiences all accrete to our self-symbols.

Moment by moment, our self-symbol is being shaped and refined—and in turn, our self-symbol causes or triggers actions galore. Or so the causality appears to us, anyway, since it is on this level, not the microlevel, that we perceive the world. Our actions make things change in the inanimate world, and we perceive those changes in terms of our coarse-grained categories, and in that way we gain some concise insight about our nature as active agents in the world. Similarly, our actions induce reactions on the part of other sentient beings, and those reactions bounce back to us in the form of our perceptions thereof, and in this way we indirectly perceive ourselves through others.

Smiling Like Hopalong Cassidy

Some of this has its counterpart in the simpler world of video feedback loops. An event that takes place in view of the camera is sent onto the screen, but in simplified form, since continuous shapes have been rendered on a grid made of discrete pixels. The new screen is then taken in by the camera and fed back in, and around and around it goes. The upshot is that a single gestalt shape—some kind of whorl—emerges.

Thus it is with the strange loop making up the "I," but there is a key difference. In the TV setup, no *perception* takes place at any stage inside the loop—just the transmission and reception of bare pixels. The TV loop is not a *strange* loop—it is just a loop. In the *strange* loop giving rise to human selfhood, by contrast, perception, abstraction, and categorization are central ingredients. The overall gestalt "shape" of one's self is not picked up by a disinterested, neutral camera but is instead perceived in a highly subjective manner via the active processes of perceptual filtering and categorization.

One morning when I was about six years old, I mustered all my courage, stood up in my first-grade class's show-and-tell session, and proudly declared, "I can smile just like Hopalong Cassidy!" I then flashed this special smile in front of everybody. I vividly remember this act of derring-do, but have only the vaguest memory of how my teacher and classmates reacted, and yet their collective reaction was surely an important formative influence on my early life, and thus on my gradually growing "I."

The Locking-In of the "I" Loop

What our "I" gets us to do has consequences, sometimes positive and sometimes negative, and we try to change our "I" in such a way as to stop leading us to negative consequences and to lead us to positive ones. We see if our Hopalong Cassidy smile makes a hit or flops, and only in the former case do we trot it out again. When we're a little older, we observe whether our puns make our friends laugh or if they fall flat, and according to the results, we modify our pun-making style. We also try out various styles of dress and learn to read between the lines of other people's reactions. When we are rebuked for telling small lies, either we decide to stop lying or we make our lies subtler, and we incorporate our new knowledge about our degree of honesty into our self-symbol.

And thus the current "I," by tampering with the vast, unpredictable world of objects and other people, has sparked some feedback, which, once absorbed in the form of symbol activations, gives rise in turn to an infinitesimally modified "I"—and round and round it goes. In this fashion, via this strange loop of symbols sparking actions and actions' repercussions triggering symbols, the abstract structure serving us as our innermost essence evolves slowly but surely, locking itself ever more rigidly into our mind. The "I" converges and stabilizes itself just as inevitably as the screech of an audio feedback loop inevitably zeroes in and stabilizes itself at the system's natural resonance frequency.

The Irrelevant Particles Underlying the Hopalong Cassidy Smile

Although particles galore were constantly churning "way down there" in the brain of that little boy who smiled like his hero, they were as invisible (and perhaps as irrelevant) as are the myriad simms careening about inside a careenium. Roger Sperry would additionally point out that the particles in the boy's brain were merely serving far higher-level symbolic events in which the boy's "I" was participating, and in which his "I" was being formed. As that "I" grew in complexity and grew realer and realer to itself, the chance that any alternative "I"-less way of understanding the world could emerge and compete with it was being rendered essentially nil.

Oddballs without Marbles Have Lost Their Marbles

And yet, was this "I," for all its tremendous stability and apparent utility, a *real* thing, or was it just a comfortable myth? Well, are temperature and pressure real things, or are they just *façons de parler*? Perhaps more to the point, was the "marble" that I discovered inside my box of envelopes real? What if I had had no way of looking at the individual envelopes? What if my knowledge of the box of envelopes necessarily came from dealing with its hundred envelopes *as a group*, so that no shifting back and forth between coarse-grained and fine-grained perspectives was possible?

If, in addition, it turned out that talking about this so-called marble had enormously useful explanatory power in my life, and if all my friends had similar boxes and they all spoke ceaselessly and unskeptically about the "marbles" inside *their* boxes, then it soon would become pretty irresistible to me to accept my own marble as part of my world. Indeed, any oddballs who denied the existence of marbles inside their boxes would be accused of having lost their marbles.

And thus it is with this notion of "I." Because it encapsulates so neatly and so efficiently for us what we perceive to be truly important aspects of causality in the world, we cannot help but attribute reality to our "I" and to those of other people—indeed, the highest possible level of reality.

Why the Self Is a Strange Loop: Part I

Why do I call this kind of loopy self-representation a *strange* loop? What does it have in common with the quintessential strange loop that Kurt Gödel discovered unexpectedly lurking inside *Principia Mathematica*?

The answer starts with the fact that brains, a priori, are about as unlikely a substrate for self-reference as was *Principia Mathematica*. No matter how sophisticated brains became under evolutionary pressures, they always remained, at bottom, just a set of cells that squirted chemicals to each other. How could a big bag of squirting chemicals house a locus of upside-down causality, where *meanings* seem to matter more than physical objects and their motions?

Actually, this upside-down story of causality is only one perspective on such a system, but it is the dominant story among the systems themselves. The typical human brain being almost totally ignorant of its own physical composition and mode of functioning, it makes up as plausible a story as it can about how it works, in which the starring role is played by a murky thing it calls "I."

Video feedback systems, by contrast, have no ability to develop such an "I" symbol. A video system, lacking triggerable symbols, can't and doesn't *think* about anything. The first key ingredient of the loop of selfhood, then, is the ability to think, which comes from the possession of a large repertoire of triggerable symbols.

Why the Self Is a Strange Loop: Part II

The second key ingredient is, ironically, an *inability*—namely, the inability to peer below the level of one's symbols. It is this blindness that creates an apparent schism between the material world and an abstract world in which new kinds of causality seem to be called for.

When we symbol-possessing humans watch a video feedback system, we can pay attention to the seductive shapes on the screen as wholes and we can give them fanciful names like "spiraling corridor" or "galaxy," but we also know that ultimately they are made of nothing but pixels, and that whatever they do comes out of the logic of pixels, leaving them without any independent life of their own.

And yet when it comes to perceiving ourselves, we tell a very different story. Things are much murkier when we look at or speak of ourselves, because we simply aren't aware of any analogue to pixels. Thanks to our inability to peer below our own symbol level, which is to say, our inability to perceive the mechanisms of our perception, we are not aware of anything at a more fundamental level.

And thus our inner counterpart to the swirling galaxy on a screen—the vast swirling "I" symbol inside our cranium—seems to us to be an undeniable *locus of causality*, rather than a mere passive epiphenomenon. We are so taken in by the perceived hard sphericity of that "marble" in our minds that we attribute to it a reality as great as to anything we know. And because of the locking-in of the "I"-symbol that inevitably takes place over years and years in the feedback loop of human self-perception, causality gets turned around and "I" seems to be in the driver's seat.

The combination of these two factors, one an ability and the other an inability, gives rise to the strange loop of selfhood, a trap into which we humans all fall, willy-nilly. Although it begins as innocently as a humble toilet's float-ball mechanism or an audio or video feedback loop, where no counterintuitive type of causality is posited anywhere, human self-perception ends up with the positing of a emergent entity that exerts an upside-down causality on the world, and with the reinforcement of and locking-in of this belief; moreover, this is often accompanied by the vehement denial of the possibility of any alternative point of view at all.

Why Couldn't We All Just Have Been Zombies?

In debates about consciousness, one of the most frequently asked questions goes something like this: "What is it about consciousness that helps us survive? Why couldn't we have had all this cognitive apparatus but simply been machines that don't feel anything or have any experience?" As I hear it, this question is basically asking, "Why did consciousness get *added on* to brains that reached a certain level of complexity? Why was consciousness thrown in as a kind of bonus? What extra evolutionary good does consciousness do, if any?"

To ask this question is to make the tacit assumption that there could be brains of any desired level of complexity that are *not* conscious. It assumes that consciousness is some kind of orderable "extra feature" that some models, even the fanciest ones, might or might not have, much as a very fancy car might or might not come with a chrome hood ornament that looks like a Flash Gordon rocketship. However, in the view presented above, consciousness is not an optional feature that one can order independently of how the brain is built. You cannot order a car with a two-cylinder motor and then tell the dealer, "Also, please throw in *Racecar Power* for me." Nor does it make sense to order a car with a very hot sixteen-cylinder motor and then to ask, "How much more do I have to pay in order to get *Racecar Power?*"

Like this mythical notion of "*Racecar Power,*" which in reality is nothing but the upper end of a continuous spectrum of horsepower levels that engines automatically possess as a result of their design, consciousness is the upper end of a spectrum of self-perception levels that brains automatically have as a result of their design. Fancy 100-huneker racecar brains like yours and mine have a lot of it, while very primitive wind-up rubber-band brains like those of mosquitos have essentially none of it, and lastly, middle-level brains, with just a handful of hunekers (like a dog) come with a modicum of it. Consciousness is not an option when one has a 100-huneker brain; it is an inevitable emergent consequence of the fact that the system has a sufficiently sophisticated repertoire of categories. The strange loop of self will automatically arise there, and that's the end of the story.

So Say "I," If You Must . . .

Some readers will still protest, "But how do my *feelings* of consciousness enter the picture?" They will feel that I have not addressed this issue. I reply that their "feelings" of consciousness are precisely the things that happen to any system that reflects itself symbolically in the manner of a careenium or an adult human. It unfailingly senses that hard core of "I"-ness and it says to itself, "This is a marble, no doubt about it—the solidest thing in the world."

That conviction, I claim, is what the "I" feeling that we all have consists in, and it is the inevitable consequence of a locked-in strange loop in which causality appears to be turned upside-down. One's conviction of the overriding reality of the "I" cannot be made to go away with increased knowledge or understanding, because it is too primordially built into our very fiber. Our intellectual knowledge of the world is subordinate to our visceral knowledge of it, and so we are condemned to saying "I" all our lives, and to thinking of ourselves this way. And some of us are pushed to pose this unanswerable question about *feelings*, and they will continue to feel so pushed, and to pose the question without end. It will hound them, but that is how the strange loop of selfhood inevitably works.

. . . and You Must (So Say I)

Like the marble in the box of envelopes, the "I" is an illusion, but it is such a strong and beguiling and *indispensable* illusion in our lives that it will not ever go away. And so we must learn to live in peace with this illusion, gently reminding ourselves occasionally, "I am a strange loop."

References

Aczel, P. 1988. *Non-Well-Founded Sets.* Stanford: CSLI Publications.

Adolphs, R. 2001. "The Neurobiology of Social Cognition." *Current Opinion in Neurobiology* 11: 231–239.

———. 2003. "Cognitive Neuroscience of Human Social Behaviour." *Nature Reviews Neuroscience* 4: 165–178.

Almog, J., J. Perry, and H. Wettstein, eds. 1989. *Themes from Kaplan.* Oxford: Oxford University Press.

Alston, W. 1999. "Back to the Theory of Appearing." *Philosophical Perspectives* 13: 81–103.

Ameriks, K. 2000. *Kant's Theory of Mind: An Analysis of the Paralogisms of Pure Reason.* 2d ed. Oxford: Oxford University Press.

Anscombe, G. E. M. 1975. "The First Person." In *Mind and Language*, ed. S. Guttenplan, pp. 45–64. Oxford: Oxford University Press.

Aquila, R. 1990. "Consciousness and Higher-Order Thoughts: Two Objections." *American Philosophical Quarterly* 27: 81–87.

Aristotle. 1981. *Aristotle's "On the Soul."* Trans. Hippocrates G. Apostle. Grinnell, Iowa: The Peripatetic Press.

———. 1984. *The Complete Works of Aristotle.* 2 vols. Ed. J. Barnes. Princeton: Princeton University Press.

Armstrong, D. M. 1968. *A Materialist Theory of Mind.* London: Routledge and Kegan Paul.

———. 1973. *Belief, Truth, and Knowledge.* Cambridge: Cambridge University Press.

———. 1978. *Universals and Scientific Realism.* Vol. 2. Cambridge: Cambridge University Press.

———. 1981. "What Is Consciousness?" In his *The Nature of Mind and Other Essays*, pp. 55–67. Ithaca, N.Y.: Cornell University Press.

Arnold, M. B. 1960. *Emotion and Personality*. New York: Columbia University Press.

Arzi-Gonczarowski, Z. 2001. "Perceptions that Perceive Themselves—A Mathematical Schema." *International Journal of Computing Anticipatory Systems* 8: 33–51.

Ayers, M. 1991. *Locke: Epistemology and Ontology*. London: Routledge.

Baars, B. 1988. *A Cognitive Theory of Consciousness*. Cambridge: Cambridge University Press.

———. 1997. *In the Theater of Consciousness: The Workspace of the Mind*. Oxford: Oxford University Press.

Bach, K. 1987. *Thought and Reference*. Oxford: Oxford University Press.

———. 1997. "Indexical Content." In *The Routlege Encyclopedia of Philosophy*, pp. 639–640. New York: Routledge.

Bartlett, S. J., and P. Suber, eds. 1987. *Self-Reference: Reflections on Reflexivity*. Dordrecht: Kluwer.

Barwise, J., and J. Etchemendy. 1987. *The Liar: An Essay on Truth and Circularity*. Oxford: Oxford University Press.

Barwise, J., and L. Moss. 1996. *Vicious Circles: On the Mathematics of Non-Wellfounded Phenomena*. Stanford: CSLI Publications.

Bealer, G. 1998. "Propositions." *Mind* 107: 1–32.

Beauregard, M., J. Levesque, and P. Bourgouin. 2001. "Neural Correlates of Conscious Self-Regulation of Emotion." *Journal of Neuroscience* 21: RC165.

Bechara, A., H. Damasio, and A. R. Damasio. 2000. "Emotion, Decision Making, and the Orbitofrontal Cortex." *Cerebral Cortex* 10: 295–307.

Bell, J. L. 2004. "Whole and Part in Mathematics." *Axiomathes* 14: 284–295.

Bennett, J. 1974. *Kant's Dialectic*. Cambridge: Cambridge University Press.

Ben-Ze'ev, A. 2000. *The Subtlety of Emotions*. Cambridge, Mass.: MIT Press.

Bermúdez, J.-L. 1995. "Non-Conceptual Content." *Mind and Language* 10: 333–369.

———. 1998. *The Paradox of Self-Consciousness*. Cambridge, Mass.: MIT Press.

———. 2001. "Nonconceptual Self-Consciousness and Cognitive Science." *Synthese* 129: 129–149.

Bermúdez, J., A. J. Marcel, and N. Eilan, eds. 1995. *The Body and the Self*. Cambridge, Mass.: MIT Press.

Bezuidenhout, A. 1996. "Pragmatics and Singular Reference." *Mind and Language* 11: 211–217.

———. 1997. "Pragmatics, Semantic Underdetermination and the Referential/ Attributive Distinction." *Mind* 106: 375–409.

Block, N. 1986. "Advertisement for a Semantics for Psychology." *Midwest Studies in Philosophy* 10: 615–678.

———. 1990. "Inverted Earth." *Philosophical Perspectives* 4: 52–79.

———. 1995. "On a Confusion about a Function of Consciousness." *Behavioral and Brain Sciences* 18: 227–247.

———. 1996. "How Can We Find the Neural Correlate of Consciousness?" *Trends in Cognitive Sciences* 19: 456–459.

———. 2002. "Phenomenal Concepts and Max Black's Objection." Presented to NEH Institute on Consciousness and Intentionality, UC Santa Cruz.

Block, N., O. Flanagan, and G. Güzeldere, eds. 1997. *The Nature of Consciousness: Philosophical Debates*. Cambridge, Mass.: MIT Press.

Bradley, M. M., and P. J. Lang. 2000. "Measuring Emotion: Behavior, Feeling, and Physiology." In *The Cognitive Neuroscience of Emotion*, ed. R. Lane, L. Nadel, G. Ahern, J. Allen, A. Kaszniak, S. Rapscak, and G. Schwartz, pp. 242–276. New York: Oxford University Press.

Braithwaite, R. B. 1967. "The Nature of Believing." In *Knowledge and Belief*, ed. A. P. Griffiths, pp. 28–40. Oxford: Oxford University Press.

Brentano, F. 1874/1924. *Psychologie vom Empirischen Standpunkt*. Hamburg: Felix Meiner.

———. 1995. *Psychology from an Empirical Standpoint*. Trans. A. C. Rancurello, D. B. Terrell, and L. L. McAlister. London and New York: Routledge.

Brook, A. 1993. "Kant's *A Priori* Methods for Recognizing Necessary Truths." *Canadian Journal of Philosophy Supplementary Volume* 18: 215–252.

———. 1994. *Kant and the Mind*. Cambridge: Cambridge University Press.

———. 2001. "Kant, Self-Awareness and Self-Reference." In *Self-Reference and Self-Awareness*, ed. A. Brook and R. DeVidi, pp. 9–30. Amsterdam: John Benjamins.

———. 2004. "Kant, Cognitive Science, and Contemporary Neo-Kantianism." *Journal of Consciousness Studies* 11: 1–25.

————. Unpublished ms. "Consciousness and the Varieties of Externalism."

Brook, A., and R. DeVidi, eds. 2001. *Self-Reference and Self-Awareness*. Amsterdam: John Benjamins.

Brook, A., and P. Raymont. 2001. "The Unity of Consciousness." *The Stanford Encyclopaedia of Philosophy*. Http://plato.stanford.edu/entries/consciousness-unity/.

————. 2006. *A Unified Theory of Consciousness*. Cambridge, Mass.: MIT Press.

Broome, J. 2004. "Lecture 3: Practical Reasoning." In *Brown-Blackwell Lectures: John Broome on Reasoning*. Http://ephilosopher.com/article707.html.

Brough, J. B. 1972. "The Emergence of an Absolute Consciousness in Husserl's Early Writings on Time-Consciousness." *Man and World* 5: 298–326. Reprinted in *Husserl: Expositions and Appraisals*, ed. F. A. Elliston and P. McCormick, pp. 83–100. South Bend, Ind.: University of Notre Dame Press, 1977.

————. 1975. "Husserl on Memory." *The Monist* 59: 40–62.

————. 1989. "Husserl's Phenomenology of Time-Consciousness." In *Husserl's Phenomenology: A Textbook*, ed. J. N. Mohanty and W. R. McKenna, pp. 149–189. Lanham: University Press of America.

————. 1991. "Translator's Introduction." In Edmund Husserl, *On the Phenomenology of the Consciousness of Internal Time (1893–1917)*. Trans. by J. B. Brough, pp. xi–lvii. Dordrecht: Kluwer.

Burge, T. 1979. "Individualism and the Mental." *Midwest Studies in Philosophy* 4: 73–122.

————. 1988. "Individualism and Self-Knowledge." *Journal of Philosophy* 85: 649–663.

————. 1989. "Individuation and Causation in Psychology." *Pacific Philosophical Quarterly* 70: 303–322.

Bush, G., P. Luu, and M. I. Posner. 2000. "Cognitive and Emotional Influences in Anterior Cingulate Cortex." *Trends Cognitive Sciences* 4: 215–222.

Butchvarov, P. 1979. *Being qua Being: A Theory of Identity, Existence, and Predication*. Bloomington and London: Indiana University Press.

————. 1998. *Skepticism about the External World*. Oxford: Oxford University Press.

Butterworth, G. 1990. "Self-Perception in Infancy." In *The Self in Transition: Infancy to Childhood*, ed. D. Cicchetti and M. Beeghly, pp. 119–137. Chicago: University of Chicago Press.

Byrne, A. 1997. "Some Like It HOT: Consciousness and Higher-Order Thoughts." *Philosophical Studies* 86: 103–129.

Byrne, A., and D. Hilbert. 2003a. "Color Realism and Color Science." *Behavioral and Brain Sciences* 26: 3–21.

———. 2003b. "Color Realism Redux." *Behavioral and Brain Sciences* 26: 52–63.

Byrne, R., and A. Whiten, eds. 1988. *Machiavellian Intelligence*. Oxford: Oxford University Press.

———. 1997. *Machiavellian Intelligence II: Evaluations and Extensions*. Cambridge: Cambridge University Press.

Carruthers, P. 1996. *Language, Thoughts and Consciousness: An Essay in Philosophical Psychology*. Cambridge: Cambridge University Press.

———. 1998a. "Conscious Thinking: Language or Elimination?" *Mind and Language* 13: 323–342.

———. 1998b. "Natural Theories of Consciousness." *European Journal of Philosophy* 6: 203–222.

———. 2000. *Phenomenal Consciousness: A Naturalistic Theory*. Cambridge: Cambridge University Press.

———. 2001. "Reply to Joe Levine." Philosophy of Mind Forum of Sito Web Italiano per la Filosofia. Http://www.swif.uniba.it/lei/mind/forums/levine.htm.

———. 2002. "The Cognitive Functions of Language and Author's Response: Modularity, Language, and the Flexibility of Thought." *Behavioral and Brain Sciences* 25: 657–719.

———. 2004a. "HOP over FOR, HOT Theory." In *Higher Order Theories of Consciousness*, ed. R. Gennaro, pp. 115–135. Philadelphia: John Benjamins.

———. 2004b. "Phenomenal Concepts and Higher-Order Experiences." *Philosophy and Phenomenological Research* 68: 316–336.

Case, J. 1994. "Infinitary Self-Reference in Learning Theory." *Journal of Experimental and Theoretical Artificial Intelligence* 6: 3–16.

Cassam, Q., ed. 1994. *Self-Knowledge*. Oxford: Oxford Univeristy Press.

Castañeda, H.-N. 1966. " 'He': A Study in the Logic of Self-Consciousness." *Ratio* 8: 130–157.

———. 1967. "Indicators and Quasi-Indicators." *American Philosophical Quarterly* 4: 85–100.

———. 1977. "Perception, Belief, and the Structure of Physical Objects and Consciousness." *Synthese* 35: 285–351.

———. 1983. "Reply to John Perry: Meaning, Belief, and Reference." In *Agent, Language, and the Structure of the World*, ed. J. Tomberlin, pp. 313–328. Indianapolis: Hackett.

———. 1986. "Self-Profile." In *Hector-Neri Castañeda*, ed. J. Tomberlin, pp. 3–137. Dordrecht: D. Reidel.

———. 1989a. "Direct Reference, the Semantics of Thinking, and Guise Theory." In *Themes from Kaplan*, ed. J. Almog, J. Perry, and H. Wettstein, pp. 105–144. Oxford: Oxford University Press.

———. 1989b. *Thinking, Language, and Experience*. Minneapolis: University of Minnesota Press.

———. 1999. *The Phenomeno-Logic of the I: Essays on Self-Consciousness*. Edited by J. G. Hart and T. Kapitan. Bloomington: Indiana University Press.

Caston, V. 2002. "Aristotle on Consciousness." *Mind* 111: 751–815.

Chaitin, G. 1999. *The Unknowable*. Berlin: Springer.

Chalmers, D. J. 1995a. "Facing Up to the Problem of Consciousness." *Journal of Consciousness Studies* 2: 200–219.

———. 1995b. "The Puzzle of Conscious Experience." *Scientific American* December: 62–68.

———. 1996. *The Conscious Mind*. Oxford and New York: Oxford University Press.

———, ed. 2002. *Philosophy of Mind: Classical and Contemporary Readings*. Oxford and New York: Oxford University Press.

———. 2003. "The Content and Epistemology of Phenomenal Belief." In *Consciousness: New Philosophical Perspectives*, ed. Q. Smith and A. Jokic, pp. 220–272. Oxford: Oxford University Press.

———. 2004. "The Representational Character of Experience." In *The Future for Philosophy*, ed. B. Leiter. Oxford: Oxford University Press.

———. 2005. "The Matrix and Metaphysics." In *Philosophers Explore the Matrix*, ed. C. Gran, pp. 132–176. Oxford: Oxford University Press.

Chelazzi, L., E. K. Miller, J. Duncan, and R. Desimone. 1993. "A Neural Basis for Visual Search in Inferior Temporal Cortex." *Nature* 363: 345–347.

Chisholm, R. 1966. *A Theory of Knowledge*. Englewood Cliffs: Prentice-Hall.

———. 1981. *The First Person*. Minneapolis: University of Minnesota Press.

Chomsky, N. 1995. *The Minimalist Program*. Cambridge, Mass.: MIT Press.

————. 2000. *New Horizons in the Study of Language and Mind*. Cambridge: Cambridge University Press.

Churchland, P. M. 1981. "Eliminative Materialism and the Propositional Attitudes." *Journal of Philosophy* 78: 67–90.

Ciompi, L. 2003. "Reflections on the Role of Emotions in Consciousness and Subjectivity, from the Perspective of Affect-Logic." *Consciousness and Emotion* 4: 181–196.

Cleermans, A., ed. 2003. *The Unity of Consciousness: Binding, Integration, and Dissociation*. Oxford: Oxford University Press.

Coghill, R. C., J. D. Talbot, A. C. Evans, E. Meyer, A. Gjedde, M. C. Bushnell, and G. H. Duncan. 1994. "Distributed Processing of Pain and Vibration by the Human Brain." *Journal of Neuroscience* 14: 4095–4108.

Corazza, E. 1994. "Perspectival Thoughts and Psychological Generalizations." *Dialectica* 48: 307–336.

Corazza, E., W. Fish, and J. Gorvett. 2002. "Who Is I?" *Philosophical Studies* 107: 1–21.

Cotogno, P. 2003. "Hypercomputation and the Physical Church–Turing Thesis." *British Journal for the Philosophy of Science* 54: 181–223.

Craig, A. D. 2002. "How Do You Feel? Interoception: The Sense of the Physiological Condition of the Body." *Nature Reviews Neuroscience* 3: 655–666.

Cramer, K. 1974. " 'Erlebnis': Thesen zu Hegels Theorie des Selbstbewußtseins mit Rücksicht auf die Aporien eines Grundbegriffs nachhegelscher Philosophie." In *Stuttgarter Hegel-Tage 1970*, ed. H.-G. Gadamer, pp. 537–603. Bonn: *Hegel-Studien*, Beiheft 11.

Crick, F., and C. Koch. 1990. "Towards a Neurobiological Theory of Consciousness." *Seminars in the Neurosciences* 2: 263–275.

————. 1995. "Are We Aware of Neural Activity in Primary Visual Cortex?" *Nature* 375(6527): 121–123.

————. 2003. "A Framework for Consciousness." *Nature Neuroscience* 6: 119–126.

Critchley, H. D., D. R. Corfield, M. P. Chandler, C. J. Mathias, and R. J. Dolan. 2000. "Cerebral Correlates of Autonomic Cardiovascular Arousal: A Functional Neuroimaging Investigation in Humans." *Journal of Physiology* 523: 259–270.

Critchley, H. D., C. J. Mathias, O. Josephs, J. O'Doherty, S. Zanini, B. K. Dewar, L. Cipolotti, T. Shallice, and R. J. Dolan. 2003. "Human Cingulate Cortex and

Autonomic Control: Converging Neuroimaging and Clinical Evidence." *Brain* 126: 2139–2152.

Critchley, H. D., R. N. Melmed, E. Featherstone, C. J. Mathias, and R. J. Dolan. 2002. "Volitional Control of Autonomic Arousal: A Functional Magnetic Resonance Study." *Neuroimage* 16: 909–919.

Damasio, A. R. 1994. *Descartes' Error: Emotion, Reason, and the Human Brain.* New York: Grosset/Putnam.

———. 1999. *The Feeling of What Happens: Body and Emotion in the Making of Consciousness.* New York: Harcourt.

———. 2001. "Fundamental Feelings." *Nature* 413(6858): 781.

———. 2003. *Looking for Spinoza: Joy, Sorrow, and the Feeling Brain.* New York: Harcourt.

Damasio, A. R., T. J. Grabowski, A. Bechara, H. Damasio, L. L. Ponto, J. Parvizi, and R. D. Hichwa. 2000. "Subcortical and Cortical Brain Activity During the Feeling of Self-Generated Emotions." *Nature Neuroscience* 3: 1049–1056.

de Gaynesford, M. 2006. *I.* Oxford: Oxford University Press.

de Saussure, F. 1959. *Course in General Linguistics.* New York: Philosophical Library. First published in 1915.

Dehaene, S., E. Artiges, L. Naccache, C. Martelli, A. Viard, F. Schurhoff, C. Recasens, M. L. Martinot, M. Leboyer, and J. L. Martinot. 2003. "Conscious and Subliminal Conflicts in Normal Subjects and Patients with Schizophrenia: the Role of the Anterior Cingulate." *Proceedings of the National Academy of Sciences U.S.A.* 100(23): 13722–13727.

Dehaene, S., and L. Naccache. 2001. "Towards a Cognitive Neuroscience of Consciousness: Basic Evidence and a Workspace Framework." *Cognition* 79: 1–37.

Dennett, D. C. 1991. *Consciousness Explained.* Boston: Little, Brown.

———. 1992. "The Self as the Center of Narrative Gravity." In *Self and Consciousness: Multiple Perspectives,* ed. F. M. Kessel, P. M. Cole, and D. M. Johnson, pp. 103–115. Hillsdale: Lawrence Erlbaum.

———. 1998. *Brainchildren: Essays on Designing Minds.* Cambridge, Mass.: MIT Press.

Descartes, René 1644/1972. *The Principles of Philosophy.* In *The Philosophical Works of Descartes,* ed. E. Haldane and G. Ross. London: Cambridge University Press.

Desimone, R., M. Wessinger, L. Thomas, and W. Schneider. 1990. "Attentional Control of Visual Perception: Cortical and Subcortical Mechanisms." *Cold Spring Harbor Symposia on Quantitative Biology* 55: 963–971.

Devitt, M., and K. Sterelny. 1987. *Language and Reality*. Cambridge, Mass.: MIT Press.

Devlin, K. 1993. *The Joy of Sets: Fundamentals of Contemporary Set Theory*. 2d ed. Berlin: Springer-Verlag.

Dilthey, W. 1905. "Studien zur Grundlegung der Geisteswissenschaften." *Sitzungsbericht der Königlichen Preußischen Akademie der Wissenschaften* 5: 322–343.

Donne, J. 1933. "The Sunne Rising." *Donne: Poetical Works*, ed. H. Grierson, pp. 10–11. New York: Oxford University Press.

Dretske, F. I. 1993. "Conscious Experience." *Mind* 102: 263–283.

——. 1995a. *Naturalizing the Mind*. Cambridge, Mass.: MIT Press.

——. 1995b. "Mental Events as Structuring Causes of Behaviour." In *Mental Causation*, ed. J. Heil and A. Mele, pp. 121–136. Oxford: Oxford University Press.

——. 1997. "What Good Is Consciousness?" *Canadian Journal of Philosophy* 27: 1–15.

——. 2004. "Knowing What You Think vs. Knowing That You Think It." Http:// humanities.ucsc.edu/NEH/dretske3.htm.

Dreyfus, H., ed. 1982. *Husserl, Intentionality, and Cognitive Science*. Cambridge, Mass.: MIT Press.

Droege, P. 2003. *Caging the Beast: A Theory of Sensory Consciousness*. Amsterdam and Philadelphia: John Benjamins.

Drummond, J. 1990. *Husserlian Intentionality and Non-foundational Realism: Noema and Object*. Dordrecht: Kluwer.

——. 1992. "De-ontologizing the Noema." In *Phenomenology of the Noema*, ed. J. Drummond and L. Embree, pp. 89–109. Dordrecht: Kluwer.

——. 1997. "Noema." In *The Encyclopedia of Phenomenology*, ed. L. Embree et al., pp. 494–499. Dordrecht: Kluwer.

——. 1998. "From Intentionality to Intensionality and Back." *Études phénoménologiques* 27–28: 89–126.

——. 2002a. "Aristotelianism and Phenomenology." In *Phenomenological Approaches to Moral Philosophy*, ed. J. Drummond and L. Embree, pp. 15–45. Dordrecht: Kluwer.

——. 2002b. "Complicating the Emotions." In Spanish translation by Martín Oyata. *Areté* 14: 175–189.

———. 2003. "The Structure of Intentionality." In *The New Husserl*, ed. D. Welton, pp. 65–92. Bloomington: Indiana University Press.

———. 2004. "'Cognitive Impenetrability' and the Complex Intentionality of the Emotions." *The Journal of Consciousness Studies* 11: 109–126. Reprinted in *Hidden Resources: Classical Perspectives on Subjectivity*, ed. D. Zahavi, pp. 109–126. Exeter: Imprint Academic, 2004.

———. 2006. "Respect as a Moral Emotion." *Husserl Studies*, in press.

Edelman, G. M. 1989. *The Remembered Present: A Biological Theory of Consciousness*. New York: Basic Books.

Elman, J. L. 1990. "Finding Structure in Time." *Cognitive Science* 14: 179–211.

Ericsson, K., and H. Simon. 1993. *Protocol Analysis: Verbal Reports as Data*. Rev. ed. Cambridge, Mass.: MIT Press.

Evans, G. 1982. *The Varieties of Reference*. Oxford: Oxford University Press.

———. 1985. *Collected Papers*. Oxford: Oxford University Press.

Evans, J., and D. Over. 1996. *Rationality and Reasoning*. Hove: Psychology Press.

Ezcurdia, Maite. 2001. "Thinking about Myself." In *Self-Reference and Self-Awareness*, ed. A. Brook and R.De Vidi, pp. 179–203. Amsterdam: John Benjamins.

Fales, Evan. 1996. *A Defense of the Given*. New York: Rowman and Littlefield.

Fauconnier, G. 1985. *Mental Spaces: Aspects of Meaning*. Cambridge, Mass.: MIT Press.

Ferrier, J. F. 1838–1839. "Introduction to the Philosophy of Consciousness, Parts I to VII." In *Lectures on Greek Philosophy and Other Philosophical Remains*, Vol. II (1866), ed. Sir Alexander Grant, Bart and E. L. Lushington, pp. 1–257. Edinburgh and London: William Blackwood and Sons.

Fetzer, J., ed. 1984. *Principles of Philosophical Reasoning*. Totowa: Rowman and Allanheld.

Field, T., R. Woodson, R. Greenberg, and D. Cohen. 1982. "Discrimination and Imitation of Facial Expressions by Neonates." *Science* 218: 179–181.

Filmore, C. 1997. *Lectures on Deixis*. Stanford: CSLI Publications.

Flanagan, O. 1992. *Consciousness Reconsidered*. Cambridge, Mass.: MIT Press.

Flavell, J. H., F. L. Green, and E. R. Flavell. 1993. "Children's Understanding of the Stream of Consciousness." *Child Development* 64: 387–398.

———. 1995. "Young Children's Knowledge about Thinking." *Monographs of the Society for Research in Child Development* 60: 1–95.

Fodor, J. 1987. *Psychosemantics.* Cambridge, Mass.: MIT Press.

———. 1990. *A Theory of Content and Other Essays.* Cambridge, Mass.: MIT Press.

———. 1998. *Concepts: Where Cognitive Science Went Wrong.* Oxford: Oxford University Press.

Føllesdal, D. 1969. "Husserl's Notion of Noema." *Journal of Philosophy* 66: 680–687. Reprinted in *Husserl, Intentionality, and Cognitive Science*, ed. Dreyfus. Cambridge, Mass.: MIT Press, 1982.

Foltz, E. L., and L. E. White, Jr. 1962. "Pain 'Relief' by Frontal Cingulumotomy." *Journal of Neurosurgery* 19: 89–100.

Ford, J. 2005. "The Attention Model of Consciousness." Ph.D. diss., University of California, Irvine.

Forster, T. 1994. "Why Set Theory without Foundation?" *Journal of Logic and Computation* 4: 333–335.

Frank, M., ed. 1991. *Selbstbewußtseinstheorien von Fichte bis Sartre.* Frankfurt am Main: Suhrkamp.

Frank, M. 1995. "Mental Familiarity and Epistemic Self-Ascription." *Common Knowledge* 4: 30–50.

Frankish, K. 2004. *Mind and Supermind.* Cambridge: Cambridge University Press.

Friedman, D. P., E. A. Murray, J. B. O'Neill, and M. Mishkin. 1986. "Cortical Connections of the Somatosensory Fields of the Lateral Sulcus of Macaques: Evidence for a Corticolimbic Pathway for Touch." *Journal of Comparative Neurology* 252: 323–347.

Gadamer, H.-G. 1986. *Wahrheit und Methode.* Tübingen: J. C. B. Mohr.

Garcia, J. A., and R. A. Koelling. 1967. "A Comparison of Aversions Induced by X rays, Toxins, and Drugs in the Rat." *Radiation Research Supplement* 7: 439–450.

Garcia-Carpintero, M. 1998. "Indexicals as Token-Reflexives." *Mind* 107: 529–563.

———. 2000a. "A Presuppositional Account of Reference-Fixing." *Journal of Philosophy* 97: 109–147.

———. 2000b. "Token-Reflexivity and Indirect Discourse." *Proceedings of the Twentieth World Congress of Philosophy, vol. 6, Analytic Philosophy and Logic*: 37–56.

Gazzaniga, M. 1988. *How the Mind and the Brain Interact to Create Our Conscious Lives*. New York: Houghton Mifflin.

———. 1992. "Brain Modules and Belief Formation." In *Self and Consciousness: Multiple Perspectives*, ed. F. M. Kessel, P. M. Cole, and D. M. Johnson. Hillsdale: Lawrence Erlbaum Associates.

———. 1998. *The Mind's Past*. Berkley: University of California Press.

Geach, P. 1957. *Mental Acts*. London: Routledge and Kegan Paul.

Gennaro, R. 1992. "Consciousness, Self-Consciousness, and Episodic Memory." *Philosophical Psychology* 5: 333–347.

———. 1993. "Brute Experience and the Higher-Order Thought Theory of Consciousness." *Philosophical Papers* 22: 51–69.

———. 1996. *Consciousness and Self-Consciousness: A Defense of the Higher-Order Thought Theory of Consciousness*. Amsterdam: John Benjamins.

———. 2002. "Jean-Paul Sartre and the HOT Theory of Consciousness." *Canadian Journal of Philosophy* 32: 293–330.

———. 2003. "Papineau on the Actualist HOT Theory of Consciousness." *Australasian Journal of Philosophy* 81: 581–586.

———, ed. 2004a. *Higher-Order Theories of Consciousness: An Anthology*. Amsterdam and Philadelphia: John Benjamins.

———. 2004b. "Higher-Order Thoughts, Animal Consciousness, and Misrepresentation: A Reply to Carruthers and Levine." In *Higher Order Theories of Consciousness: An Anthology*, ed. R. Gennaro, pp. 45–66. Amsterdam: John Benjamins.

———. 2005. "The HOT Theory of Consciousness: Between a Rock and a Hard Place?" *Journal of Consciousness Studies* 12: 3–21.

Gibson, J. 1979. *The Ecological Approach to Visual Perception*. Boston: Houghton-Mifflin.

Gloy, K. 1998. *Bewusstseinstheorien: Zur Problematik und Problemgeschichte des Bewusstseins und Selbstbewusstseins*. Freiburg: Alber.

Goldie, P. 2000. *The Emotions: A Philosophical Explanation*. Oxford: Clarendon Press.

———. 2002. "Emotions, Feelings, and Intentionality." *Phenomenology and the Cognitive Sciences* 1: 235–254.

Goldman, A. L. 1967. "A Causal Theory of Knowing." *Journal of Philosophy* 64: 355–372.

——. 1993a. "Consciousness, Folk Psychology, and Cognitive Science." *Consciousness and Cognition* 2: 364–383.

——. 1993b. "The Psychology of Folk Psychology." *Behavioral and Brain Sciences* 16: 15–28.

Goldman-Racik, P. S., M. Chafee, and H. Friedman. 1993. "Allocation of Function in Distributed Circuits." In *Brain Mechanisms of Perception and Memory: From Neuron to Behavior*, ed. T. Ono, L. R. Squire, M. E. Raichle, D. I. Perrett, and M. Fukuda, pp. 445–456. New York: Oxford University Press.

Goodman, N. 1968. *Languages of Art: An Approach to a Theory of Symbols.* Indianapolis: Bobbs-Merrill.

Gopnik, A. 1993. "How We Know Our Minds: The Illusion of First-Person Knowledge of Intentionality." *Behavioral and Brain Sciences* 16: 1–14.

Gordon, R. 1996. " 'Radical' Simulationism." In *Theories of Theories of Mind*, ed. P. Carruthers and P. Smith, pp. 11–21. Cambridge: Cambridge University Press.

Gray, J. 1995. "The Contents of Consciousness: A Neuropsychological Conjecture." *Behavioral and Brain Sciences* 18: 659–676.

——. 2004. *Consciousness: Creeping up on the Hard Problem.* Oxford: Oxford University Press.

Greenfield, S. 2000. *The Private Life of the Brain: Emotions, Consciousness, and the Secret of the Self.* New York: John Wiley and Sons.

Grice, P. 1989. *Studies in the Way of Words.* Cambridge: Harvard University Press.

——. 2001. *Aspects of Reason.* Oxford: Clarendon Press.

Griffiths, P. 1997. *What Emotions Really Are: The Problem of Psychological Categories.* Chicago: University of Chicago Press.

Grossmann, R. 1984. *Phenomenology and Existentialism: An Introduction.* London: Routledge and Kegan Paul.

Gurwitsch, A. 1964. *The Field of Consciousness.* Pittsburgh: Duquesne University Press.

——. 1985. *Marginal Consciousness.* Athens, Ohio: Ohio University Press.

Güzeldere, G. 1995. "Is Consciousness the Perception of What Passes in One's Own Mind?" In *Conscious Experience*, ed. T. Metzinger, pp. 335–357. Paderborn: Schoeningh-Verlag.

Hare, R. M. 1972. *Practical Inferences.* Berkeley: University of California Press.

Harman, G. 1990. "The Intrinsic Quality of Experience." *Philosophical Perspectives* 4: 31–52.

Hart, W. D. 1987. "Causation and Self-Reference." In *Self-Reference: Reflections on Reflexivity*, ed. S. Bartlett and P. Suber, pp. 179–189. Dordrecht: Kluwer.

Heidegger, M. 1927/1986. *Sein und Zeit*. Tübingen: Max Niemeyer. Trans. as *Being and Time*, Trans. J. Stambaugh, Albany: SUNY Press, 1996.

————. 1962. *Being and Time*. Trans. J. Macquarrie and E. Robinson. New York: Harper and Row.

————. 1989. *Die Grundprobleme der Phänomenologie*. Gesamtausgabe Band 24. Frankfurt am Main: Vittorio Klostermann. Trans. as *The Basic Problems of Phenomenology*, trans. A. Hofstadter, Bloomington: Indiana University Press, 1982.

————. 1993a. *Grundprobleme der Phänomenologie* (1919–1920). Gesamtausgabe Band 58. Frankfurt am Main: Vittorio Klostermann.

————. 1993b. *Phänomenologie der Anschauung und des Ausdrucks*. Gesamtausgabe Band 59. Frankfurt am Main: Vittorio Klostermann.

————. 1994. *Phänomenologische Interpretationen zu Aristoteles. Einführung in die phänomenologische Forschung*. Gesamtausgabe Band 61. Frankfurt am Main: Vittorio Klostermann.

————. 2001. *Einleitung in die Philosophie*. Gesamtausgabe Band 27. Frankfurt am Main: Vittorio Klostermann.

Henrich, D. 1966. "Fichte's Original Insight." Trans. D. R. Lachterman. *Contemporary German Philosophy* 1 (1982): 15–53.

————. 1971. "Self-Consciousness: A Critical Introduction to a Theory." *Man and World* 4: 3–28.

Henry, M. 1965. *Philosophie et phénoménologie du corps*. Paris: PUF.

Hermer-Vazquez, L., E. Spelke, and A. Katsnelson. 1999. "Sources of Flexibility in Human Cognition: Dual-Task Studies of Space and Language." *Cognitive Psychology* 39: 3–36.

Hill, C. 1991. *Sensations*. New York: Oxford University Press.

————. 1997. "Imaginability, Conceivability, Possibility, and the Mind–Body Problem." *Philosophical Studies* 87: 61–85.

————. 2004. "Ouch! An Essay on Pain." In *Higher Order Theories of Consciousness: An Anthology*, ed. R. Gennaro, pp. 339–362. Amsterdam: John Benjamins.

Hintikka, J. 1998. "Perspectival Identification, Demonstratives, and 'Small Worlds.'" *Synthese* 114: 203–232.

Hobson, J. A. 1999. *Dreaming as Delirium: How the Brain Goes Out of Its Mind.* Cambridge, Mass.: MIT Press.

Hofstadter, D. 1979. *Gödel, Escher, Bach: An Eternal Golden Braid.* New York: Basic Books.

————. 1985. *Metamagical Themas: Questing for the Essence of Mind and Pattern.* New York: Basic Books.

————. 1997. *Le Ton beau de Marot: In Praise of the Music of Language.* New York: Basic Books.

Hofstadter, D., and D. Dennett, eds. 1981. *The Mind's I: Fantasies and Reflections on Self and Soul.* New York: Basic Books.

Horgan, T., and J. Tienson. 2002. "The Intentionality of Phenomenology and the Phenomenology of Intentionality." In *Philosophy of Mind: Classical and Contemporary Readings*, ed. D. J. Chalmers, pp. 520–533. New York: Oxford University Press.

————. 2005. "The Phenomenology of Embodied Agency." In *The Explanation of Human Interpretation*, ed. J. Sàágua. Lisbon: Edições Colibri.

Horgan, T., J. Tienson, and G. Graham. 2004. "Phenomenal Intentionality and the Brain in a Vat." In *The Externalist Challenge: New Essays on Cognition and Intentionality*, ed. R. Schantz. Berlin: De Gruyter.

Hossack, K. 2002. "Self-Knowledge and Consciousness." *Proceedings of the Aristotelian Society* 102: 163–181.

————. 2003. "Consciousness in Act and Action." *Phenomenology and the Cognitive Sciences* 2: 187–203.

Hume, D. 1978. A *Treatise of Human Nature.* Ed. L. A. Selby-Brigge and P. H. Nidditch. Oxford: Oxford University Press.

Hurley, S. L. 1997. "Nonconceptual Self-Consciousness and Agency: Perspective and Access." *Communication and Cognition* 30: 207–248.

————. 1998. *Consciousness in Action.* Cambridge, Mass.: Harvard University Press.

Hurt, R. W., and H. T. Ballantine, Jr. 1974. "Stereotactic Anterior Cingulate Lesions for Persistent Pain: A Report on 68 Cases." *Clinical Neurosurgery* 21: 334–351.

Husserl, E. 1900–1901/2001. *Logical Investigations.* Vols. 1 and 2. Trans. J. N. Findlay, ed. with revised translations by Dermot Moran. London and New York: Routledge.

————. 1931. Unpublished ms., C 10.

————. 1950. *Cartesianische Meditationen und Pariser Vorträge, Husserliana I*. Den Haag: Martinus Nijhoff.

————. 1952. *Ideen zu einer reinen Phänomenologie und phänomenologischen Philosophie II, Husserliana IV*. Den Haag: Martinus Nijhoff.

————. 1959. *Erste Philosophie II (1923–24), Husserliana VIII*. Den Haag: Martinus Nijhoff.

————. 1962a. *Die Krisis der europäischen Wissenschaften und die transzendentale Phänomenologie, Husserliana VI*. Den Haag: Martinus Nijhoff.

————. 1962b. *Phänomenologische Psychologie, Husserliana IX*. Den Haag: Martinus Nijhoff.

————. 1963. *Cartesianische Meditationen und Pariser Vorträge. Husserliana I*. Ed. S. Strasser. 2d ed. Den Haag: Martinus Nijhoff.

————. 1966a. *Analysen zur passiven Synthesis, Husserliana XI*. Den Haag: Martinus Nijhoff.

————. 1966b. *Zur Phänomenologie des inneren Zeitbewußtseins (1893–1917), Husserliana X*. Den Haag: Martinus Nijhoff.

————. 1970a. *Cartesian Meditations*. Trans. D. Cairns. Den Haag: Martinus Nijhoff.

————. 1970b. *Logical Investigations*. Trans. J. N. Findlay. London: Routledge and Kegan Paul.

————. 1970c. *The Crisis of European Sciences and Transcendental Phenomenology*. Trans. D. Carr. Evanston: Northwestern University Press.

————. 1973a. *Zur Phänomenologie der Intersubjektivität II, Husserliana XIV*. Den Haag: Martinus Nijhoff.

————. 1973b. *Zur Phänomenologie der Intersubjektivität III, Husserliana XV*. Den Haag: Martinus Nijhoff.

————. 1974. *Formale und Transzendentale Logik, Husserliana XVII*. Den Haag: Martinus Nijhoff.

————. 1976. *Ideen zu einer reinen Phänomenologie und phänomenologischen Philosophie I, Husserliana III/1–2*. Den Haag: Martinus Nijhoff.

————. 1983. *Ideas Pertaining to a Pure Phenomenology and to a Phenomenological Philosophy. First Book: General Introduction to a Pure Phenomenology*. Trans. F. Kersten. Den Haag: Martinus Nijhoff.

————. 1984a. *Einleitung in die Logik und Erkenntnistheorie, Husserliana XXIV*. Den Haag: Martinus Nijhoff.

———. 1984b. *Logische Untersuchungen II, Husserliana XIX/1–2*. Den Haag: Martinus Nijhoff.

———. 1991. *On the Phenomenology of the Consciousness of Internal Time (1893–1917)*. Trans. J. B. Brough. Dordrecht: Kluwer.

Jackson, F. 1984. "Epiphenomenal Qualities." *Philosophical Quarterly* 32: 127–136.

Jacob, P., and M. Jeannerod. 2003. *Ways of Seeing*. Oxford: Oxford University Press.

James, W. 1884. "What Is an Emotion?" *Mind* 9: 188–205.

———. 1890. *The Principles of Psychology*. Cambridge, Mass.: Harvard University Press.

———. 1904/1976. *Essays in Radical Empiricism*. Cambridge, Mass.: Harvard University Press.

Jones, A. K., W. D. Brown, K. J. Friston, L. Y. Qi, and R. S. Frackowiak. 1991. "Cortical and Subcortical Localization of Response to Pain in Man Using Positron Emission Tomography." *Proceedings of the Royal Society of London. Series B, Biological Sciences* 244: 39–44.

Kaelin, E. 1988. *Heidegger's Being and Time: A Reading for Readers*. Tallahassee: Florida State University Press.

Kampis, G. 1995. "Computability, Self-Reference, and Self-Amendment." *Communications and Cognition—Artificial Intelligence* 12: 91–109.

Kant, I. 1902–1944. *Gesammelte Schriften*. Ed. Koniglichen Preussischen Academie der Wissenschaften, 29 vols. Berlin: Walter de Gruyter et al.

———. 1781/1787. *Critique of Pure Reason*. Trans. P. Guyer and A. Woods. Cambridge and New York: Cambridge University Press, 1997.

———. 1783. *Prolegomena to Any Future Metaphysics*. Trans. P. Carus, rev. with intro. by James Ellington. Indianapolis: Hackett, 1977 (Ak. IV).

———. 1786. *The Metaphysical Foundations of Natural Science*. Trans. with intro. by James Ellington. Indianapolis: Library of Liberal Arts, 1970 (Ak. IV).

———. 1788. *Critique of Practical Reason*. Trans. Lewis White Beck. Chicago: University of Chicago Press, 1949.

———. 1791. *Critique of Judgment*. Trans. W. S. Pluhar. Indianapolis: Hackett, 1987.

———. 1798. *Anthropology from a Pragmatic Point of View*. Trans. Mary Gregor. The Hague: Martinus Nijhoff, 1974 (Ak. VII).

Kapitan, T. 1998a. "On Depicting Indexical Reference." In *Thought, Language and Ontology*, ed. F. Orilia and W. Rapaport, pp. 183–215. Dordrecht: Kluwer.

———. 1998b. "Vision, Vector, Veracity." In *Blick und Bild*, ed. T. Borsche et al., pp. 31–44. Munich: Wilhelm Fink Verlag.

———. 1999. "The Ubiquity of Self-Awareness." *Grazer Philosophische Studien* 57: 17–43.

———. 2001. "Indexical Identification: A Perspectival Account." *Philosophical Psychology* 14: 293–312.

Kaplan, D. 1989a. "Demonstratives, An Essay on the Semantics, Logic, Metaphysics, and Epistemology of Demonstratives and Other Indexicals." In *Themes From Kaplan*, ed. J. Almog, J. Perry, and H. Wettstein, pp. 481–564. Oxford: Oxford University Press.

———. 1989b. "Afterthoughts." In *Themes From Kaplan*, ed. J. Almog, J. Perry, and H. Wettstein, pp. 565–614. Oxford: Oxford University Press.

Kelly, S. 2001. "Demonstrative Concepts and Experience." *Philosophical Review* 110: 397–420.

Khromov, A. G. 2001. "Logical Self-Reference as a Model for Conscious Experience." *Journal of Mathematical Psychology* 45: 720–731.

Kim, C.-T. 1978. "Brentano on the Unity of Mental Phenomena." *Philosophy and Phenomenological Research* 39: 199–207.

Kim, J. 1982. "Psychophysical Supervenience." *Philosophical Studies* 41: 51–70.

———. 1998. *Mind in a Physical World*. Cambridge, Mass.: MIT Press.

Kirk, R. 1994. *Raw Feeling*. Oxford: Oxford University Press.

Klein, P. 2005. "Infinitism is the Solution to the Regress Problem." In *Contemporary Debates in Epistemology*, ed. M. Steup and E. Sosa, pp. 131–140. Oxford: Blackwell.

Kobes, B. W. 1995. "Telic Higher-Order Thoughts and Moore's Paradox." *Philosophical Perspectives* 9: 291–312.

Kriegel, U. 2002a. "Consciousness, Permanent Self-Awareness, and Higher-Order Monitoring." *Dialogue* 41: 517–540.

———. 2002b. "Phenomenal Content." *Erkenntnis* 57: 175–198.

———. 2002c. "PANIC Theory and the Prospects for a Representational Theory of Phenomenal Consciousness." *Philosophical Psychology* 15: 55–64.

———. 2003a. "Consciousness as Intransitive Self-Consciousness: Two Views and an Argument." *Canadian Journal of Philosophy* 33 (1): 103–132.

———. 2003b. "Consciousness, Higher-Order Content, and the Individuation of Vehicles." *Synthese* 134: 477–504.

———. 2003c. "Is Intentionality Dependent upon Consciousness?" *Philosophical Studies* 116: 271–307.

———. 2003d. "Consciousness as Sensory Quality and as Implicit Self-Awareness." *Phenomenology and the Cognitive Sciences* 2: 1–26.

———. 2004. "Consciousness and Self-Consciousness." *Monist* 87: 185–209.

———. 2005. "Naturalizing Subjective Character." *Philosophy and Phenomenological Research*.

LaBerge, D. 1995. *Attentional Processing: The Brain's Art of Mindfulness*. Cambridge, Mass.: Harvard University Press.

———. 1997. "Attention, Awareness, and the Triangular Circuit." *Consciousness and Cognition* 6: 149–181.

———. 1998. "Defining Awareness by the Triangular Circuit of Attention." *Psyche* 4.

LaBerge, D., and M. S. Buschbaum. 1990. "Positron Emission Tomographic Measurements of Pulvinar Activity During an Attention Task." *Journal of Neuroscience* 10: 613–619.

LaBerge, D., M. Carter, and V. Brown. 1992. "A Network Simulation of Thalamic Circuit Operations in Selective Attention." *Neural Computation* 4: 318–331.

Lakoff, G., and M. Johnson. 1999. *Philosophy in the Flesh: The Embodied Mind and Its Challenge to Western Thought*. New York: Basic Books.

Lane, R. D., E. M. Reiman, B. Axelrod, L. S. Yun, A. Holmes, and G. E. Schwartz, 1998. "Neural Correlates of Levels of Emotional Awareness. Evidence of an Interaction Between Emotion and Attention in the Anterior Cingulate Cortex." *Journal of Cognitive Neuroscience* 10: 525–535.

Lane, R. D., E. M. Reiman, M. M. Bradley, P. J. Lang, G. L. Ahern, R. J. Davidson, and G. E. Schwartz. 1997. "Neuroanatomical Correlates of Pleasant and Unpleasant Emotion." *Neuropsychologia* 35: 1437–1444.

Lang, P. J., M. K. Greenwald, M. M. Bradley, and A. O. Hamm. 1993. "Looking at Pictures: Affective, Facial, Visceral, and Behavioral Reactions." *Psychophysiology* 30: 261–273.

Leder, D. 1990. *The Absent Body*. Chicago: University of Chicago Press.

LeDoux, J. 1996. *The Emotional Brain: The Mysterious Underpinnings of Emotional Life*. New York: Simon and Schuster.

Lehrer, K. 1991. "Metamind, Autonomy, and Materialism." *Grazer Philosophische Studien* 40: 1–11.

———. 1996a. "Consciousness." In *Philosophie in Österreich*, ed. A. Schramm. Vienna: Verlag Holder-Pichler-Tempsky.

———. 1996b. "Skepticism, Lucid Content, and the Metamental Loop." In *Philosophy and Cognitive Science*, ed. A. Clark, J. Ezquerro, and J. M. Larrazabal. Dordrecht: Kluwer.

———. 1997. Self-*Trust: A Study of Reason, Knowledge, and Autonomy.* Oxford: Oxford University Press.

———. 2000. *Theory of Knowledge.* 2^d ed. Boulder and London: Westview Press.

———. 2002. "Self-Presentation, Representation, and the Self." *Philosophy and Phenomenological Research* 64: 412–430.

———. 2004. "Representation in Painting and in Consciousness." *Philosophical Studies* 117: 1–14.

Levelt, W. 1989. *Speaking: From Intention to Articulation.* Cambridge, Mass.: MIT Press.

Levey, S. 1997. "Coincidence and Principles of Composition." *Analysis* 57: 1–10.

Levinas, E. 1930/1995. *The Theory of Intuition in Husserl's Phenomenology.* 2d ed. Evanston: Northwestern University Press.

Levine, J. 1983. "Materialism and Qualia: The Explanatory Gap." *Pacific Philosophical Quarterly* 64: 354–361.

———. 2001a. *Purple Haze: The Puzzle of Consciousness.* Oxford and New York: Oxford University Press.

———. 2001b. Commentary on *Phenomenal Consciousness,* by Peter Carruthers, Philosophy of Mind Forum of Sito Web Italiano per la Filosofia. Http://www.swif.uniba.it/lei/mind/forums/levine.htm.

———. 2003. "Experience and Representation." In *Consciousness: New Essays,* ed. Q. Smith and A. Jokic, pp. 57–76. Oxford: Oxford University Press.

———. Forthcoming. "Phenomenal Concepts and the Materialist Constraint." In *Phenomenal Concepts and Phenomenal Knowledge,* ed. T. Alter and S. Walter. Oxford: Oxford University Press.

Lewis, D. C. 1991. *Parts of Classes.* Oxford: Blackwell.

Lewis, M. 2003. "The Development of Self-Consciousness." In *Agency and Self-Awareness,* ed. J. Roessler and N. Eilan, pp. 275–295. Oxford: Oxford University Press.

Liotti, M., P. T. Fox, and D. LaBerge. 1994. "PET Measurements of Attention to Closely Spaced Visual Shapes." *Society for Neurosciences Abstracts* 20: 354.

Lloyd, D. 2004. *Radiant Cool: A Novel Theory of Consciousness.* Cambridge, Mass.: MIT Press.

Loar, B. 1981. *Mind and Meaning.* Cambridge: Cambridge University Press.

———. 1990. "Phenomenal States." *Philosophical Perspectives* 4: 81–108. Reprinted and updated in *The Nature of Consciousness: Philosophical Debates*, ed. N. Block, O. Flanagan, and G. Güzeldere. Cambridge, Mass.: MIT Press, 1997.

Locke, J. 1688/1959. *An Essay Concerning Human Understanding.* Annotated by A. C. Fraser. New York: Dover.

Lockwood, M. 1989. *Mind, Brain, and the Quantum.* Oxford: Blackwell.

———. 2003. "Consciousness and the Quantum World: Putting Qualia on the Map." In *Consciousness: New Philosophical Perspectives*, ed. Q. Smith and A. Jokic, pp. 447–467. Oxford: Clarendon Press.

Logothetis, N. 1998. "Object Vision and Visual Awareness." *Current Opinion in Neurobiology* 8: 536–544.

Lorenz, K. 1977. *Behind the Mirror.* London: Methuen.

Lormand, E. Unpublished ms. "Inner Sense Until Proven Guilty." Http://www-personal.umich.edu/~lormand/phil/cons/inner_sense.htm/.

Luntley, M. 2003. "Non-Conceptual Content and the Sound of Music." *Mind and Language* 18: 402–426.

Lurz, R. 2003a. "Advancing the Debate between HOT and FO Accounts of Consciousness." *Journal of Philosophical Research* 28: 23–43.

———. 2003b. "Neither HOT nor COLD: An Alternative Account of Consciousness." *Psyche* 9.

———. 2004. "Either HOR or FOR: A False Dichotomy." In *Higher-Order Theories of Consciousness*, ed. R. Gennaro, pp. 227–254. Amsterdam: John Benjamins.

Lutz, A., J.-P. Lachaux, J. Martinerie, and F. J. Varela. 2002. "Guiding the Study of Brain Dynamics by Using First-Person Data: Synchrony Patterns Correlate with Ongoing Conscious States during a Simple Visual Task." *Proceedings of the National Academy of Sciences USA* 99: 1586–1591.

Lycan, W. 1981. "Form, Feel and Function." *Journal of Philosophy* 78: 24–50.

———. 1987. *Consciousness.* Cambridge, Mass.: MIT Press.

———. 1990a. "Consciousness as Internal Monitoring." *Philosophical Perspectives* 9: 1–14. Reprinted in *The Nature of Consciousness: Philosophical Debates*, ed. N. Block, O. Flanagan, and G. Güzeldere. Cambridge, Mass.: MIT Press, 1997.

————, ed. 1990b. *Mind and Cognition*. Oxford: Basil Blackwell.

————. 1996. *Consciousness and Experience*. Cambridge, Mass.: MIT Press.

————. 2001. "A Simple Argument for a Higher-Order Representation Theory of Consciousness." *Analysis* 61: 3–4.

————. 2004. "The Superiority of HOP to HOT." In R. Gennaro (ed.), *Higher-Order Theories of Consciousness*. Amsterdam and Philadelphia: John Benjamins.

Lyons, J. 1995. *Linguistic Semantics*. Cambridge: Cambridge University Press.

McDowell, J. 1998. *Meaning, Knowledge, and Reality*. Cambridge, Mass.: Harvard University Press.

McGinn, C. 1982. "The Structure of Content." In *Thought and Object*, ed. A. Woodfield. Oxford: Oxford University Press.

————. 1983. *The Subjective View*. Oxford: Oxford University Press.

————. 1989. *Mental Content*. Oxford: Blackwell.

————. 1991. *The Problem of Consciousness*. Oxford: Blackwell.

————. 2003. "Fear Factor." *New York Times*, February 23, section 7: 11.

Mack, A., and I. Rock. 1998. *Inattentional Blindness*. Cambridge, Mass.: MIT Press.

Marcel, A. 2003. "The Sense of Agency." In *Agency and Self-Awareness*, ed. J. Roessler and N. Eilan, pp. 48–93. Oxford: Oxford University Press.

Marek, J. C. M. 2003. "On Self-Presentation." In *Persons: An Interdisciplinary Approach. Proceedings of the 25th International Wittgenstein Symposium, 2002*, ed. C. Kanzian, J. Quitterer, and E. Runggaldier, pp. 163–173. Vienna: Öbv-hpt.

Marek, J. C. M., and M. E. Reicher, eds. 2005. *Experience and Analysis: Proceedings of the 27th International Wittgenstein Symposium*. Vienna: Öbv-hpt.

Marks, J. 1986. *The Ways of Desire*. Chicago: Precedent Publishing.

Mayr, U. 2004. "Conflict, Consciousness, and Control." *Trends in Cognitive Sciences* 8: 145–148.

Meerbote, R. 1989. "Kant's Functionalism." In *Historical Foundations of Cognitive Science*, ed. J. C. Smith. Dordrecht: Reidel.

Meinong, A. 1910/1983. "Uber Annahmen," 2d ed. (revision of 1st ed., 1902). In R. Haller and R. Kindinger (in collaboration with R. Chisholm), *Alexius Meinong Gestamtausgabe*, 7 vols. Graz: Akademische Druck- u. Verlagsanstalt, 1968–1978, vol. 4, pp. xv–xxv and 1–384. Trans. J. Heanue. *On Assumptions*. Berkeley: University of California Press, 1983.

Mellor, D. H. 1978. "Conscious Belief." *Proceedings of the Aristotelian Society* 78: 87–101.

Meltzoff, A. 1990. "Foundations for Developing a Concept of Self: The Role of Imitation in Relating Self to Other and the Value of Social Mirroring, Social Modeling, and Self Practice in Infants." In: *The Self in Transition: Infancy to Childhood*, ed. D. Cicchetti and M. Beeghly, pp. 139–164. Chicago: University of Chicago Press.

Meltzoff, A. and M. Moore. 1977. "Imitation of Facial and Manual Gestures by Human Neonates." *Science* 198: 75–78.

———. 1983. "Newborn Infants Imitate Adult Facial Gestures." *Child Development* 54: 702–709.

———. 1992. "Early Imitation within a Functional Framework: The Importance of Person Identity, Movement, and Development." *Infant Behavior and Development* 15: 479–505.

———. 1995. "Infants' Understanding of People and Things: From Body Imitation to Folk Psychology." In *The Body and the Self*, ed. J. Bermúdez, A. Marcel, and N. Eilan, pp. 43–69. Cambridge, Mass.: MIT Press.

Mendelson, E. 1997. *Introduction to Mathematical Logic.* 4th ed. New York: Chapman and Hall.

Mensch, J. R. 2001. *Postfoundational Phenomenology: Husserlian Reflections on Presence and Embodiment.* University Park: Pennsylvania State University Press.

Merleau-Ponty, M. 1945. *Phénoménologie de la perception.* Paris: Gallimard.

———. 1960. *Signes.* Paris: Gallimard.

———. 1964. *Le visible et l'invisible.* Paris: Gallimard.

———. 2003. *Phenomenology of Perception.* Trans. Colin Smith. London and New York: Routledge.

Mesulam, M. M., and E. J. Mufson. 1982a. "Insula of the Old World Monkey. I: Architectonics in the Insulo-Orbito-Temporal Component of the Paralimbic Brain." *Journal of Comparative Neurology* 212: 1–22.

———. 1982b. "Insula of the Old World Monkey. III: Efferent Cortical Output and Comments on Function." *Journal of Comparative Neurology* 212: 38–52.

Metzinger, T. 1995. "Faster than Thought: Holism, Homogeneity, and Temporal Coding." In *Conscious Experience*, ed. T. Metzinger, pp. 425–461. Schöningh: Imprint Academic.

———. 2003. *Being No One: The Self-Model Theory of Subjectivity.* Cambridge, Mass.: MIT Press.

Meyer, J. A., H. L. Roitblat, and S. W. Wilson. 1993. *Proceedings of the Second International Conference on From Animals to Animats 2: Simulation of Adaptive Behavior, Honolulu, Hawaii.* Cambridge, Mass.: MIT Press.

Millikan, R. 1984. *Language, Thought, and Other Biological Categories.* Cambridge, Mass.: MIT Press.

———. 1989. "Biosemantics." *Journal of Philosophy* 86: 281–297.

———. 1993. *White Queen Psychology and Other Essays for Alice.* Cambridge, Mass.: MIT Press.

Milner, D., and M. Goodale. 1995. *The Visual Brain in Action.* Oxford: Oxford University Press.

Moran, R. 2001. *Authority and Estrangement: An Essay on Self-Knowledge.* Princeton: Princeton University Press.

Moschovakis, Y. N. 1994. *Notes on Set Theory.* Berlin: Springer-Verlag.

Moser, P. K. 1985. *Empirical Justification.* Dordrecht: D. Reidel.

Mufson, E. J., and M. M. Mesulam. 1982. "Insula of the Old World Monkey. II: Afferent Cortical Input and Comments on the Claustrum." *Journal of Comparative Neurology* 212: 23–37.

Mulligan, K., and B. Smith. 1985. "Franz Brentano on the Ontology of Mind." *Philosophy and Phenomenological Research* 45: 627–644.

Nagel, T. 1974. "What Is It Like to Be a Bat?" *Philosophical Review* 83: 435–450.

Natsoulas, T. 1992. "Appendage Theory—Pro and Con." *Journal of Mind and Behavior* 13: 371–396.

———. 1993a. "Consciousness$_4$: Varieties of Intrinsic Theory." *Journal of Mind and Behavior* 14: 107–132.

———. 1993b. "What Is Wrong with Appendage Theory of Consciousness." *Philosophical Psychology* 6: 137–154.

———. 1996a. "The Case for Intrinsic Theory: I. An Introduction." *Journal of Mind and Behavior* 17: 267–286.

———. 1996b. "The Case for Intrinsic Theory: II. An Examination of a Conception of Consciousness as Intrinsic, Necessary, and Concomitant." *Journal of Mind and Behavior* 17: 369–390.

————. 1998. "The Case for Intrinsic Theory: III. Intrinsic Inner Awareness and the Problem of Straightforward Objectivation." *Journal of Mind and Behavior* 19: 1–20.

————. 1999. "The Case for Intrinsic Theory: IV. An Argument from How Conscious₄ Mental-Occurrence Instances Seem." *Journal of Mind and Behavior* 20: 257–276.

————. 2004. "The Case for Intrinsic Theory: XI. A Disagreement Regarding the Kind of Feature Inner Awareness Is." *Journal of Mind and Behavior* 25: 187–211.

Neander, K. 1998. "The Division of Phenomenal Labor: A Problem for Representational Theories of Consciousness." *Philosophical Peispectives* 12: 411–434.

Nichols, S., and S. Stich. 2003. *Midreading*. Oxford: Oxford University Press.

Nicholson, G. 1986. "Ekstatic Temporality in *Sein und Zeit*." In *A Companion to Martin Heidegger's "Being and Time,"* ed. J. Kockelmans, pp. 208–226. Washington, D.C.: Center For Advanced Research in Phenomenology and University Press of America.

Nisbett, R., and T. Wilson. 1977. "Telling More Than We Can Know." *Psychological Review* 84: 231–259.

Noë, A. 2002. "Is Perspectival Self-Consciousness Non-Conceptual?" *Philosophical Quarterly* 52: 185–194.

Nunberg, G. 1993. "Indexicality and Deixis." *Linguistics and Philosophy* 16: 1–43.

Nussbaum, M. 2001. *Upheavals of Thought: The Intelligence of Emotions*. Cambridge: Cambridge University Press.

O'Brien, L. 2003. "On Knowing One's Own Actions." In *Agency and Self-Awareness*, ed. J. Roessler and N. Eilan, pp. 358–382. Oxford: Oxford University Press.

O'Doherty, J., M. I. Kringelbach, E. T. Rolls, J. Hornak, and C. Andrews. 2001. "Abstract Reward and Punishment Representations in the Human Orbitofrontal Cortex." *Nature Neuroscience* 4: 95–102.

Oberschelp, A. 1991. "On Pairs and Tuples." *Zeitschrift für mathematische Logik und Grundlagen der Mathematik* 37: 55–56.

Panksepp, J. 1998a. "The Periconscious Substrates of Consciousness: Affective States and the Evolutionary Origins of the Self." *Journal of Consciousness Studies* 5: 566–582.

————. 1998b. *Affective Neuroscience: The Foundation of Human and Animal Emotions*. New York: Oxford University Press.

————. 2000. "The Neuro-Evolutionary Cusp between Emotions and Cognitions: Implications for Understanding Consciousness and the Emergence of a Unified Science of Mind." *Consciousness and Emotion* 1: 15–54.

———. 2003. "Damasio's Error?" *Consciousness and Emotion*. 4: 111–134.

Papineau, D. 1987. *Reality and Representation*. Oxford: Blackwell.

———. 1993. *Philosophical Naturalism*. Oxford: Blackwell.

———. 1995. "The Anti-Pathetic Fallacy and the Boundaries of Consciousness." In *Conscious Experience*, ed. T. Metzinger. Paderborn: Ferdinand Schöningh/Imprint Academic.

———. 2002. *Thinking about Consciousness*. Oxford: Oxford University Press.

Parvizi, J., and A. R. Damasio. 2001. "Consciousness and the Brainstem." *Cognition* 79: 135–160.

Paul, L. A. 2002. "Logical Parts." *Noûs* 36: 578–596.

Peacocke, C. 1983. *Sense and Content*. Oxford: Oxford University Press.

———. 1992. *A Study of Concepts*. Cambridge, Mass.: MIT Press.

———. 1998. "Conscious Attitudes, Attention, and Self-Knowledge." In *Knowing Our Own Minds*, ed. C. Wright, B. C. Smith, and C. Macdonald, pp. 255–285. Oxford: Oxford University Press.

Peirce, C. S. 1998. *The Essential Peirce*. Ed. the Peirce Edition Project. Bloomington: Indiana University Press.

Penfield, W. 1960. "Neurophysiological Basis of the Higher Functions of the Nervous System—Introduction." In *Handbook of Physiology. Section 1: Neurophysiology*, vol. III ed. M. H. W. Field and V. E. Hall, pp. 1441–1445. Washington, D.C.: American Physiological Society, Williams and Wilkins.

Penrose, R. 2001. "Consciousness, the Brain, and Spacetime Geometry: An Addendum. Some New Developments on the Orch OR Model for Consciousness." *Annals of the New York Academy of Sciences* 929: 105–110.

Perlis, D. 1997. "Consciousness as Self-Function." *Journal of Consciousness Studies* 4: 509–525.

Perrett, R. 2003. "Intentionality and Self-Awareness." *Ratio* 16: 222–235.

Perry, J. 1979. "The Essential Indexical." *Noûs* 13: 3–21.

———. 1997. "Indexicals and Demonstratives." In *A Companion to the Philosophy of Language*, ed. B. Hale and C. Wright, pp. 586–612. Oxford: Blackwell.

———. 2000. *The Problem of the Essential Indexical and Other Essays*. Expanded edition. Stanford: CSLI Publications.

———. 2001a. *Knowledge, Possibility, and Consciousness: The 1999 Jean Nicod Lectures*. Cambridge, Mass.: MIT Press.

———. 2001b. *Reference and Reflexivity*. Standford: CSLI Publications.

———. 2002. *Identity, Personal Identity, and the Self*. Indianapolis: Hackett.

Petersen, S. E., D. L. Robinson, and J. D. Morris. 1987. "Contributions of the Pulvinar to Visual Spatial Attention." *Neuropsychologia* 25: 97–105.

Petitot, J. 1999. "Morphological Eidetics for a Phenomenology of Perception." In *Naturalizing Phenomenology*, ed. J. Petitot, F. Varela, B. Pachoud, and J.-M. Roy, pp. 330–371. Stanford: Stanford University Press.

Petitot, J., F. Varela, B. Pachoud, and J.-M. Roy, eds. 1999. *Naturalizing Phenomenology*. Stanford: Stanford University Press.

Pippin, R. 1987. "Kant on the Spontaneity of Mind." *Canadian Journal of Philosophy* 17: 449–476.

Pitt, J. 2004: "The Phenomenology of Cognition, or What Is It Like to Think that P?" *Philosophy and Phenomenological Research* 69: 1–36.

Platt, J. R., ed. 1965. *New Views of the Nature of Man*. Chicago: University of Chicago Press.

Predelli, S. 1998. "Utterance, Interpretation, and the Logic of Indexicals." *Mind and Language* 13: 400–414.

———. 2001. "Complex Demonstratives and Anaphora." *Analysis* 61: 53–59.

Price, H. H. 1969. *Belief*. London: George Allen and Unwin.

Pruim, P. 1996. "Elusive Thoughts: The Limited Accessbility of Indexical Beliefs." *Philosophical Studies* 83: 171–190.

Putnam, H. 1975. "The Meaning of 'Meaning.' " In *Language, Mind, and Knowledge*, ed. K. Gunderson, pp. 131–193. Minneapolis: University of Minnesota Press.

———. 1981. *Reason, Truth, and History*. Cambridge: Cambridge University Press.

Rafal, R. D., and M. I. Posner. 1987. "Deficits in Human Visual Spatial Attention Following Thalamic Lesions." *Proceedings of the National Academy of Sciences USA* 84: 7349–7353.

Rainville, P., G. H. Duncan, D. D. Price, B. Carrier, and M. C. Bushnell. 1997. "Pain Affect Encoded in Human Anterior Cingulate but Not Somatosensory Cortex." *Science* 277(5328): 968–971.

Ramachandran, V. S., and S. Blakeslee. 1998. *Phantoms in the Brain: Probing the Mysteries of the Human Mind*. New York: HarperCollins.

Ratcliffe, M. 2002. "Heidegger's Attunement and the Neuropsychology of Emotion." *Phenomenology and the Cognitive Sciences* 1: 287–312.

Ravven, H. 2003. "Spinoza's Anticipation of Contemporary Affective Neuroscience." *Consciousness and Emotion* 4: 257–290.

Raymont, P. Unpublished ms. "From HOTs to Self-Representing States." Http:// people.trentu.ca/~paulraymont/FromHOTs.pdf/.

Recanati, F. 1990. "Direct Reference, Meaning, and Thought." *Noûs* 24: 697–722.

———. 1993. *Direct Reference.* Oxford: Blackwell.

Redoute, J., S. Stoleru, M. C. Gregoire, N. Costes, L. Cinotti, F. Lavenne, D. Le Bars, M. G. Forest, and J. F. Pujol. 2000. "Brain Processing of Visual Sexual Stimuli in Human Males." *Human Brain Mapping* 11: 162–177.

Reid, T. 1785. *The Philosophical Works of Thomas Reid, D. D.* 8th ed. Ed. Sir William Hamilton. Edinburgh: James Thin.

Reiman, E. M., R. D. Lane, G. L. Ahern, G. E. Schwartz, R. J. Davidson, K. J. Friston, L. S. Yun, and K. Chen. 1997. "Neuroanatomical Correlates of Externally and Internally Generated Human Emotion." *American Journal of Psychiatry* 154: 918–925.

Rey, G. 1982. "A Reason for Doubting the Existence of Consciousness." In *Consciousness and Self-Regulation,* ed. R. Davidson, S. Schwartz, and D. Shapiro, pp. 1–39. New York: Plenum.

———. 1988. "A Question about Consciousness." In *Perspectives on Mind,* ed. H. Otto and J. Tueidio, pp. 5–24. Dordrecht: Kluwer.

Rieger, A. 2000. "An Argument for Finsler-Aczel Set Theory." *Mind* 109: 241–254.

Rodriguez, E., N. George, J.-P. Lachaux, J. Martinerie, B. Renault, and F. J. Varela. 1999. "Perception's Shadow: Long-Distance Synchronization of Human Brain Activity." *Nature* 397(6718): 430–433.

Roessler, J., and N. Eilan. eds. 2003. *Agency and Self-Awareness.* Oxford: Oxford University Press.

Rolls, E. T. 2000. "Precis of the Brain and Emotion." *Behavioral and Brain Sciences* 23: 177–191.

Rolls, E. T., J. O'Doherty, M. L. Kringelbach, S. Francis, R. Bowtell, and F. McGlone. 2003. "Representations of Pleasant and Painful Touch in the Human Orbitofrontal and Cingulate Cortices." *Cerebral Cortex* 13: 308–317.

Rosenberg, J. 1981. "Apperception and Sartre's Pre-Reflective Cogito." *American Philosophical Quarterly* 18: 255–260.

Rosenthal, D. M. 1986. "Two Concepts of Consciousness." *Philosophical Studies* 49: 329–359.

————. 1990. "A Theory of Consciousness." ZiF Technical Report 40, Bielfield, Germany. Reprinted in *The Nature of Consciousness: Philosophical Debates*, ed. N. Block, O. Flanagan, and G. Güzeldere. Cambridge, Mass.: MIT Press, 1997.

————. 1991a. "The Independence of Consciousness and Sensory Quality." Pp. 15–36 in *Consciousness: Philosophical Issues 1*, ed. E. Villanueva, Atascadero: Ridgeview Publishing.

————, ed. 1991b. *The Nature of Mind*. Oxford: Oxford University Press.

————. 1993a. "Higher-Order Thoughts and the Appendage Theory of Consciousness." *Philosophical Psychology* 6: 155–166.

————. 1993b. "Thinking that One Thinks." In *Consciousness*, ed. M. Davies and G. Humphreys, pp. 197–223. Oxford: Blackwell.

————. 2000. "Consciousness and Metacognition." In *Metarepresentations*, ed. D. Sperber. Oxford: Oxford University Press.

————. 2002. "Explaining Consciousness." In *Philosophy of Mind: Classical and Contemporary Readings*, ed. D. J. Chalmers, pp. 406–421. New York: Oxford University Press.

————. 2004. "Varieties of Higher-Order Theory." In *Higher-Order Theories of Consciousness: An Anthology*, ed. R. Gennaro, pp. 17–44. Amsterdam: John Benjamins.

————. 2005. *Consciousness and Mind*. Oxford: Oxford University Press.

Royce, J. 1899/1959. *The World and the Individual*, vol. 1. New York: Dover.

Rucker, R. 2005. *Infinity and the Mind*. Princeton: Princeton University Press.

Russell, B. 1948. *Human Knowledge: Its Scope and Limits*. New York: Simon and Schuster.

Russell, J. A. 2003. "Core Affect and the Psychological Construction of Emotion." *Psychological Review* 110: 145–172.

Russell, J. A., and L. F. Barrett. 1999. "Core Affect, Prototypical Emotional Episodes, and Other Things Called Emotion: Dissecting the Elephant." *Journal of Personality and Social Psychology* 76: 805–819.

Ryle, Gilbert. 1949. *The Concept of Mind*. New York: Barnes and Noble.

Sacks, O. 1985. *The Man Who Mistook His Wife for a Hat and Other Clinical Tales*. New York: Simon and Schuster.

————. 1995. *An Anthropologist on Mars*. New York: Knopf.

Sanford, D. 1984a. "Armstrong's Theory of Perception." In *D. M. Armstrong*, ed. R. J. Bogdan. Dordrecht: Reidel.

———. 1984b. "Infinite Regress Arguments." In *Principles of Philosophical Reasoning*, ed. J. Fetzer, pp. 93–117. Totowa: Rowman and Allanheld.

Sartre, J.-P. 1936. *La Transcendance de l'ego*. Paris: Vrin.

———. 1940/2004. *The Imaginary*. Trans. Jonathan Webber. London: Routledge.

———. 1943/1976. *L'être et le néant*. Paris: Gallimard.

———. 1948. "Conscience de soi et connaissance de soi." *Bulletin de la Société Française de Philosophie* 42: 49–91.

———. 1956. *Being and Nothingness*. New York: Philosophical Library.

———. 1957. *The Transcendence of the Ego*. Trans. F. Williams and R. Kirkpatrick. New York: Noonday Press.

———. 1967. "Consciousness of Self and Knowledge of Self." In *Readings in Existential Phenomenology*, ed. N. Lawrence and D. O'Connor, pp. 113–142. Englewood Cliffs: Prentice-Hall.

Sawamoto, N., M. Honda, T. Okada, T. Hanakawa, M. Kanda, H. Fukuyama, J. Konishi, and H. Shibasaki. 2000. "Expectation of Pain Enhances Responses to Nonpainful Somatosensory Stimulation in the Anterior Cingulate Cortex and Parietal Operculum/Posterior Insula: An Event-Related Functional Magnetic Resonance Imaging Study." *Journal of Neuroscience* 20: 7438–7445.

Schacter, D. 1996. *Searching for Memory: The Brain, the Mind, and the Past*. New York: Basic Books.

Schacter, S., and J. E. Singer. 1962. "Cognitive, Social, and Physiological Determinants of Emotional State." *Psychological Review* 69: 379–399.

Schröder, J. 2001. "Higher-Order Thought and Naturalist Accounts of Consciousness." *Journal of Consciousness Studies* 8: 27–46.

Schweizer, P. 1994. "Self-Predication and the Third Man." *Erkenntnis* 40: 21–42.

Seager, W. E. 1999. *Theories of Consciousness: An Introduction and Assessment*. London and New York: Routledge.

Searle, J. 1983. *Intentionality*. Cambridge: Cambridge University Press.

———. 1992. *The Rediscovery of the Mind*. Cambridge, Mass.: MIT Press.

Sellars, W. 1970–1971. ". . . this I or he or it (the thing) which thinks. . . ." *Proceedings of the American Philosophical Association* 44: 5–31.

Shatz, M., H. M. Wellman, and S. Silber. 1983. "The Acquisition of Mental Verbs: A Systematic Investigation of First Reference to Mental States." *Cognition* 14: 301–321.

Shear, J., ed. 1995–97. *Explaining Consciousness—The "Hard Problem."* Cambridge, Mass.: MIT Press.

Shoemaker, S. 1968. "Self-Reference and Self-Awareness." *Journal of Philosophy* 65: 555–567.

———. 1970. "Persons and Their Pasts." *American Philosophical Quarterly* 7: 269–285.

———. 1994a. "Phenomenal Character." *Noûs* 28: 21–38.

———. 1994b. "Self-Knowledge and 'Inner Sense.' Lecture II: The Broad Perceptual Model." *Philosophy and Phenomenological Research* 54: 271–290.

———. 1996. *The First Person Perspective and Other Essays.* Cambridge: Cambridge University Press.

———. 2000. "Introspection and Phenomenal Character." *Philosophical Topics* 28: 247–273.

Siewert, C. 1998. *The Significance of Consciousness.* Princeton: Princeton University Press.

Simeon, D., and E. Hollander. 1993. "Depersonalization Disorder." *Psychiatric Annals* 23: 382–388.

Simons, P. 1987. *Parts: A Study in Ontology.* Oxford: Clarendon Press.

Sipper, M., and J. Reggia. 2001. "Go Forth and Replicate." *Scientific American* 265: 34–43.

Smith, A. D. 2002. *The Problem of Perception.* Cambridge, Mass.: Harvard University Press.

Smith, B. 1994. *Austrian Philosophy: The Legacy of Franz Brentano.* Chicago and La Salle: Open Court.

Smith, B., and K. Mulligan. 1983. "A Framework for Formal Ontology." *Topoi* 3: 73–85.

Smith, D. W. 1986. "The Structure of (Self-)Consciousness." *Topoi* 5: 149–156.

———. 1989. *The Circle of Acquaintance.* Dordrecht: Kluwer.

———. 1995. "Mind and Body." In *The Cambridge Companion to Husserl*, ed. B. Smith and D. W. Smith, pp. 323–393. Cambridge: Cambridge University Press.

———. 2004. "Return to Consciousness." In his *Mind World: Essays in Phenomenology and Ontology.* Cambridge: Cambridge University Press.

———. 2005a. "Consciousness and Reflexive Content." In *Phenomenology and Philosophy of Mind*, ed. D. W. Smith and A. L. Thomasson. Oxford: Oxford University Press.

———. 2005b. "The Structure of Context and Context Awareness." In *Gurwitsch's Relevancy for Cognitive Science*, ed. L. Embree. Dordrecht: Kluwer.

Smith, D. W., and R. McIntyre. 1982. *Husserl and Intentionality*. Dordrecht: Reidel.

Smith, J., W. Shields, and D. Washburn. 2003. "The Comparative Psychology of Uncertainty Monitoring and Metacognition." *Behavioral and Brain Sciences* 26: 317–339.

Smith, Q. 1989. "The Multiple Uses of Indexicals." *Synthese* 78: 167–191.

Smith, Q., and A. Jokic, eds. 2003. *Consciousness: New Philosophical Perspectives*. Oxford: Clarendon Press.

Sokolowski, R. 1974. *Husserlian Meditations*. Evanston: Northwestern University Press.

Sperry, R. W. 1965. "Mind, Brain, and Humanist Values." In *New Views of the Nature of Man*, ed. J. Platt, pp. 71–92. Chicago: University of Chicago Press.

Spinoza, B. 1994. *A Spinoza Reader: The Ethics and Other Works*. Trans. Edwin Curley. Princeton: Princeton University Press.

Srinivasan, R., D. P. Russell, G. M. Edelman, and G. Tononi. 1999. "Increased Synchronization of Neuromagnetic Responses During Conscious Perception." *Journal of Neuroscience* 19: 5435–5448.

Stalnaker, R. 1999. *Context and Content*. Oxford: Oxford University Press.

Stanovich, K. 1999. *Who Is Rational? Studies of Individual Differences in Reasoning*. New Haven: Laurence Erlbaum.

Stich, S. 1979. "Autonomous Psychology and the Belief-Desire Thesis." *Monist* 61: 571–591.

Stoleru, S., M. C. Gregoire, D. Gerard, J. Decety, E. Lafarge, L. Cinotti, F. Lavenne, D. Le Bars, E. Vernet-Maury, H. Rada, C. Collet, B. Mazoyer, M. G. Forest, F. Magnin, A. Spira, and D. Comar. 1999. "Neuroanatomical Correlates of Visually Evoked Sexual Arousal in Human Males." *Archives of Sexual Behavior* 28: 1–21.

Strawson, G. 1994. *Mental Reality*. Cambridge, Mass.: MIT Press.

———. 2000. "The Phenomenology and Ontology of the Self." In *Exploring the Self*, ed. D. Zahavi, pp. 39–54. Amsterdam: John Benjamins.

Strawson, P. F. 1959. *Individuals*. London: Methuen.

Stubenburg, L. 1998. *Consciousness and Qualia*. Amsterdam and Philadelphia: John Benjamins.

Talbot, J. D., S. Marrett, A. C. Evans, E. Meyer, M. C. Bushnell, and G. H. Duncan. 1991. "Multiple Representations of Pain in Human Cerebral Cortex." *Science* 251(4999): 1355–1358.

Thomasson, A. 2000. "After Brentano: A One-Level Theory of Consciousness." *European Journal of Philosophy* 8: 190–209.

Thompson, E., and F. J. Varela. 2001. "Radical Embodiment: Neural Dynamics and Consciousness." *Trends in Cognitive Sciences* 5: 418–425.

Tononi, G., and G. M. Edelman. 1998. "Consciousness and Complexity." *Science* 282(5395): 1846–1851.

———. 2000. "Schizophrenia and the Mechanisms of Conscious Integration." *Brain Research Reviews* 31: 391–400.

Tugendhat, E. 1979. *Selbstbewußtsein und Selbstbestimmung*. Frankfurt am Main: Suhrkamp.

———. 1986. *Self-Consciousness and Self-Determination*. Trans. Paul Stern. Cambridge, Mass.: MIT Press.

Tye, M. 1995. *Ten Problems of Consciousness: A Representational Theory of the Phenomenal Mind*. Cambridge, Mass.: MIT Press.

———. 2000. *Consciousness, Color, and Content*. Cambridge, Mass.: MIT Press.

Van Gulick, R. 1980. "Functionalism, Information, and Content." *Nature and System* 2: 139–162.

———. 1988. "A Functionalist Plea for Self-Consciousness." *Philosophical Review* 47: 149–181.

———. 2001. "Inward and Upward—Reflection, Introspection, and Self-Awareness." *Philosophical Topics* 28: 275–305.

———. 2003. "Maps, Gaps, and Traps." In *Consciousness: New Philosophical Perspectives*, ed. Q. Smith and A. Jokic, pp. 323–352. Oxford: Oxford University Press.

———. 2004. "Higher-Order Global States (HOGS): An Alternative Higher-Order Model of Consciousness." In *Higher-Order Theories of Consciousness*, ed. R. Gennaro, pp. 67–92. Amsterdam: John Benjamins.

Varela, F. J. 1979. *Principles of Biological Autonomy*. New York: Elsevier/North-Holland.

———. 1995a. "Resonant Cell Assemblies: A New Approach to Cognitive Functions and Neuronal Synchrony." *Biological Research* 28: 81–95.

———. 1995b. "The Re-enchantment of the Concrete." In *The Artificial Life Route to Artificial Intelligence: Building Embodied, Situated Agents*, ed. L. Steels and R. Brooks, pp. 11–20. New Haven: Lawrence Erlbaum.

———. 1996. "Neurophenomenology: A Methodological Remedy to the Hard Problem." *Journal of Consciousness Studies* 3: 330–349.

———. 1997. "The Naturalization of Phenomenology as the Transcendance of Nature: Searching for Generative Mutual Constraints." *Alter: revue de phénoménologie* 5: 355–385.

———. 1999. "The Specious Present: The Neurophenomenology of Time Consciousness." In *Naturalizing Phenomenology*, ed. J. Petitot, F. J. Varela, B. Pachoud, and J.-M. Roy, pp. 266–314. Standford: Standford University Press.

Varela, F. J., and N. Depraz. 2001. "At the Source of Time: Valence and the Constitutional Dynamics of Affect." *Arob@se.*

Varela, F. J., J.-P. Lachaux, E. Rodriguez, and J. Martinerie. 2001. "The Brainweb: Phase Synchronization and Large-Scale Integration." *Nature Reviews Neuroscience* 2: 229–239.

Varela, F. J., E. Thompson, and E. Rosch. 1991. *The Embodied Mind: Cognitive Science and Human Experience*. Cambridge, Mass.: MIT Press.

Velmans, M. 1992. "Is Human Information Processing Conscious?" *Behavioral and Brain Sciences* 14: 651–669.

Vogt, B. A., and D. N. Pandya. 1987. "Cingulate Cortex of the Rhesus Monkey: II. Cortical Afferents." *Journal of Comparative Neurology* 262: 271–289.

von Neumann, J. 1966. *Theory of Self-Reproducing Automata*. Urbana and London: University of Illinois Press.

Waldenfels, B. 2000. *Das leibliche Selbst: Vorlesungen zur Phänomenologie des Leibes*. Frankfurt am Main: Suhrkamp.

Walicki, M. 1987. "Self-Reference and Self-Consciousness." Http://www.ii.uib.no/~michal/phil/self/wh.pdf/.

Watt, D. 1999. "Consciousness and Emotion: Review of Jaak Panksepp's 'Affective Neuroscience.'" *Journal of Consciousness Studies* 6: 191–200.

———. 2000. "Emotion and Consciousness: Part II: A Review of Antonio Damasio's 'The Feeling of What Happens: Body and Emotion in the Making of Consciousness.'" *Journal of Consciousness Studies* 7: 72–84.

Webster, M. J., J. Bachevalier, and L. G. Ungerleider. 1994. "Connections of Inferior Temporal Areas TEO and TE with Parietal and Frontal Cortex in Macaque Monkeys." *Cerebral Cortex* 5: 470–483.

Weiskrantz, L. 1997. *Consciousness Lost and Found*. Oxford: Oxford University Press.

Whitehead, A. N. 1925. *Science and the Modern World*. New York: Macmillan.

———. 1933. *Adventures of Ideas*. New York: Macmillan.

———. 1958. *Modes of Thought*. New York: Capicorn.

———. 1978. *Process and Reality*. New York: Macmillan.

Wider, K. 1997. *The Bodily Nature of Consciousness: Sartre and Contemporary Philosophy of Mind*. Ithaca: Cornell University Press.

———. 1999. "The Self and Others: Imitation in Infants and Sartre's Analysis of the Look." *Continental Philosophy Review* 32: 195–210.

Williams, P. 1998. *The Reflexive Nature of Awareness: A Tibetan Madhyamaka Defence*. London: Routledge.

Williford, K. 2003a. "Demea's *a priori* Theistic Proof." *Hume Studies* 29: 99–123.

———. 2003b. "The Structure of Self-Consciousness." Ph.D. diss., University of Iowa.

———. 2004. "Moore, the Diaphanousness of Consciousness, and Physicalism." *Metaphysica* 5: 133–155.

———. 2005. "The Intentionality of Consciousness and Consciousness of Intentionality." In *Intentionality: Past and Future*, ed. G. Forrai and G. Kampis. Amsterdam: Rodopi.

Wilson, T. 2002. *Strangers to Ourselves*. Cambridge: Harvard University Press.

Wittgenstein, L. 1934/1935. *Blue and Brown Books*. Oxford: Blackwell.

Wollheim, R. 1999. *On the Emotions*. New Haven: Yale University Press.

Wundt, W. 1924. *An Introduction to Psychology*. London: Allen and Unwin.

Yoshimi, J. 2001. "Dynamics of Consciousness: Phenomenology, Neuroscience, and Dynamical Systems Theory". Ph.D. diss., University of California, Irvine.

———. 2005. "Field Theories of Mind and Brain." In *Gurwitsch's Relevancy for Cognitive Science*, ed. L. Embree. Dordrecht and Boston: Kluwer.

Zahavi, D. 1998. "Brentano and Husserl on Self-Awareness." *Etudes phénoménologiques* 27–28: 127–169.

———. 1999. *Self-Awareness and Alterity: A Phenomenological Investigation.* Evanston: Northwestern University Press.

———, ed. 2000a. *Exploring the Self.* Amsterdam: John Benjamins.

———. 2000b. "Self and Consciousness." In *Exploring the Self*, ed. D. Zahavi, pp. 55–74. Amsterdam: John Benjamins.

———. 2002a. "First-Person Thoughts and Embodied Self-Awareness: Some Reflections on the Relation between Recent Analytical Philosophy and Phenomenology." *Phenomenology and the Cognitive Sciences* 1: 7–26.

———. 2002b. "The Three Concepts of Consciousness in *Logische Untersuchungen.*" *Husserl Studies* 18: 51–64.

———. 2003a. "Phenomenology of Self." In *The Self in Neuroscience and Psychiatry*, ed. T. Kircher and A. David, pp. 56–75. Cambridge: Cambridge University Press.

———. 2003b. "How to Investigate Subjectivity: Heidegger and Natorp on Reflection." *Continental Philosophy Review* 36: 155–176.

———. 2003c. "Inner Time-Consciousness and Pre-Reflective Self-Awareness." In *The New Husserl: A Critical Reader*, ed. D. Welton, pp. 157–180. Bloomington: Indiana University Press.

———. 2003d. *Husserl's Phenomenology.* Stanford: Stanford University Press.

———. 2004. "Back to Brentano?" *Journal of Consciousness Studies* 11/10–11: 66–87.

Zaner, R. M. 1964. *The Problem of Embodiment: Some Contributions to a Phenomenology of the Body.* The Hague: Martinus Nijhoff.

Zeki, S., and A. Bartels, 1999. "Toward a Theory of Visual Consciousness." *Consciousness and Cognition* 8: 225–259.

Zheng, Y. 2000. "On Sartre's 'Non-Positional Consciousness.' " *Southwest Philosophy Review* 16: 139–149.

List of Contributors

Andrew Brook, Carleton University

Peter Carruthers, University of Maryland

Antonio Damasio, University of Southern California

John J. Drummond, Fordham University

Jason Ford, University of Minnesota Duluth

Rocco J. Gennaro, Indiana State University

George Graham, Wake Forest University

Christopher S. Hill, Brown University

Douglas R. Hofstadter, Indiana University

Terry Horgan, University of Arizona

Tomis Kapitan, Northern Illinois University

Uriah Kriegel, University of Arizona

Keith Lehrer, University of Arizona and University of Graz

Joseph Levine, Ohio State University

Robert W. Lurz, Brooklyn College

David Rudrauf, University of Iowa and LENA

David Woodruff Smith, University of California–Irvine

John Tienson, University of Memphis

Robert Van Gulick, Syracuse University

Kathleen Wider, University of Michigan–Dearborn

Kenneth Williford, St. Cloud State University

Dan Zahavi, University of Copenhagen

Index